Current Debates in International Relations

Eric B. Shiraev

George Mason University

Vladislav M. Zubok

London School of Economics

New York Oxford
OXFORD UNIVERSITY PRESS

Oxford University Press
Oxford University Press is a department of the University of Oxford.
It furthers the University's objective of excellence in research,
scholarship, and education by publishing worldwide.

Oxford New York
Auckland Cape Town Dar es Salaam Hong Kong Karachi
Kuala Lumpur Madrid Melbourne Mexico City Nairobi
New Delhi Shanghai Taipei Toronto

With offices in
Argentina Austria Brazil Chile Czech Republic France Greece
Guatemala Hungary Italy Japan Poland Portugal Singapore
South Korea Switzerland Thailand Turkey Ukraine Vietnam

Published in the United States of America by
Oxford University Press
198 Madison Avenue, New York, NY 10016

Library of Congress Cataloging-in-Publication Data
Current debates in international relations / edited by
Eric B. Shiraev, Vladislav M. Zubok.
pages cm
ISBN 978-0-19-934851-0
1. International relations. 2. World politics—21st century. I. Shiraev, Eric, 1960- editor of compilation. II. Zubok, V. M. (Vladislav Martinovich) editor of compilation.
JZ1242.C87 2016
327--dc23

2014047430

Printed in the United States of America
on acid-free paper

Contents

Preface

This reader is a supplementary source for courses in the fields of international relations, global affairs, foreign policy, and international politics. It introduces the best examples of scholarship and provides pedagogical tools to assist instructors and students in teaching and learning about international relations.

As editors, we pursued several goals. First, we intended to give the reader a concise yet comprehensive overview of the studies and debates in international relations today. The research and discussions in this field have become far more complex and dynamic after the end of the Cold War. The field of international relations has embraced new interdisciplinary approaches and novel methodological tools, including the methods and models adopted from economics, history, political psychology, anthropology, and comparative cultural studies. New international developments constantly bring new intellectual challenges.

Second, we wanted to revisit several classical works in this field. We hoped to examine these works' ability to address and explain not only several key issues in international relations of the past century or even a more distant past, but also to look at their more contemporary applications. Indeed, some of these works' assumptions appear quite relevant today.

Third, we intended to remind students of the fundamental concepts of international relations such as states, sovereignty, power, and international structure. We also brought and discuss the new ones, those that have been the focus of growing attention over the past two decades: international terrorism, environmental issues and policies, humanitarian issues and policies, and human rights, as well as culture and identity in international politics. New threats and new concerns constantly emerge, and we hoped to forecast and reflect on them in the current reader.

Finally, while describing problems, challenges, and threats, we also sought success stories in the field of international relations. We wanted to pay attention to those "teachable moments" involving good examples of conflict resolution, peaceful growth, democratic governance, and international cooperation.

In a general sense, this book can also be used as a key source of educational knowledge for the current generation of students, who have unprecedented access to global information yet often lack the background to fully understand and evaluate it. We want to guide students through this information while paying special attention to critical evaluation of studies, facts, and theories.

With that in mind, we present a consistent framework, to keep students focused and facilitate their learning. This reader will assist students in steering through major international issues, offer contending approaches, and consider real-world applications of theory.

We hold the view that the complexities of the global world are not likely to fit a single approach or theory. The reader includes educational tools to equip students not only with facts and concepts for a solid background but also with the skills for critical thinking. We encourage students, with the help of case studies and questions, to cross the boundaries of research traditions in search of new answers.

As we stated earlier, we welcome a wide range of explanatory approaches borrowed from various fields, the ideas and concepts that have most relevance to the problems of today's world. These approaches are complementary rather than antagonistic: they all add something unique, useful, and critical to the study of international relations. The students will be welcome to "multitask" by studying and discussing data, opinions, and their applications obtained from different fields.

THREE PARTS: AN OVERVIEW

The reader has three major parts divided into eleven sections. Based on our teaching experience, each section may be studied in one week during a standard one-semester course. Some sections may require more attention and time, while others may be studied more expeditiously—all depending on the instructors' preferences and the structure of their course.

Part I, *Studying International Relations* (Sections 1–4), introduces the field and emphasizes different, often contrasting ways of thinking and reasoning about international relations. The first section of Part I discusses sovereignty as a concept and key political issue in today's world. This section also discusses the contrasting processes of "globalization" and "tribalization" of international relations and looks at the ways the events on the ground complement and challenge most established theories. The following three sections present the debates in historical contexts associated with major perspectives on international relations—realism, liberalism—as well as several other approaches, including constructivism, conflict theories, feminism, and political psychology.

Part II, *Three Facets of the Global World* (Sections 5–7), discusses three major, most essential facets of international relations: war and security; international law and international community; and international political economy. The section on war and security discusses both the traditional issues related to armed conflicts, as well as new developments involving asymmetrical threats and cyber security. The next section focuses on international law and its development, and it also addresses debates about international community and extraterritoriality. The section about

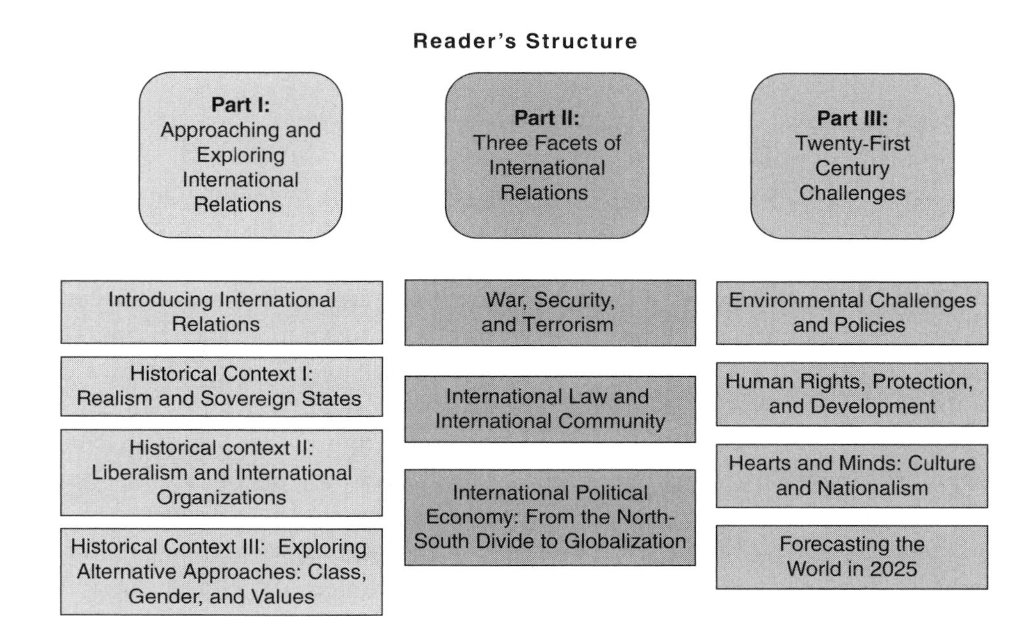

international political economy deals with the application of key economic theories to recent developments, such as emerging new economies and the blurring of the traditional North-South gap.

Part III, *Twenty-First Century Challenges* (Sections 8–11), explores significant and complex challenges of today's world, the challenges that are likely to impact international relations of tomorrow. One section addresses environmental problems and environmental policies. The next one directs attention to human rights and humanitarian policies. The discussion focuses on concepts such as "the responsibility to protect" and universal jurisdiction among others. The next section emphasizes the identity issue in international politics and focuses on culture, nationalism, and the meaning of "hearts and minds" in today's global world. The concluding section of the book provides critical evaluations of various theoretical predictions about the future of international relations.

THREE TYPES OF ARTICLES: AN OVERVIEW

Each section contains original research articles, essays, commentaries, or sizable excerpts from such articles, published by outstanding scholars. Three types of articles have been selected for this book.

The first type includes key theoretical and other fundamental works that describe the structure and dynamics of international relations, key actors and institutions, major international events, and key approaches to their understanding. We can call these works "classical" because of their known impact on the past and current debates in the discipline. These classical articles or book chapters are presented in full or shortened.

The second type is contemporary research articles, social commentaries, and essays that focus on specific theoretical and applied issues of contemporary studies of international relations.

The third type is mostly illustrative. The articles are selected from academic and nonacademic sources. These entries provide factual materials and opinions as practical applications of theory to contemporary international relations.

In addition, a selection of articles, essays, or critical commentaries—relevant to each section of the book—appears on the companion website (http://oup.com/us/shiraev). Some of these materials refer to key historic documents, such as treaties and international agreements. Other materials serve as illustrations to most contemporary international events. We hope that the accompanying site will be an important supplementary and illustrative source for this reader.

An overview and critical thinking questions for class use or homework assignments accompany each section. These overviews comment on the debates in specific fields in the discipline of international relations as well as refer to contemporary developments relevant to the section's articles.

The majority of works selected for this volume were published in the United States or the United Kingdom. Do these choices reveal a deliberate bias in our selection of the articles? We do not think so. For several decades, the United States has been the world's leader in the studies of international relations. The openness and innovativeness of the American research and educational system rooted in the university, both public and private, have strengthened the academic community involved in the study of international relations. American and British professional, peer-reviewed journals invite contributions from any authors, with different perspectives from many countries and regions. Many talented scholars writing and publishing in English are from Latin America, Africa, China, India, Pakistan, Russia, and several other countries and regions. These scholars contribute to the scientific discussion by bringing their fresh perspectives, multidisciplinary methods, and, of course, critical thinking.

THINKING CRITICALLY WITH THE READER

Critical thinking is not simply passing skeptical judgments. It is a set of skills that we all can master. It is a process of inquiry, based on the important virtues of *curiosity*, *doubt*, and *intellectual honesty*. Curiosity helps us dig below the surface to distinguish facts from opinions. Doubt keeps us from being satisfied with overly simple explanations. And intellectual honesty helps in recognizing and addressing discrepancy or even bias in our own opinions.

Distinguishing Facts From Opinions

The study of international relations is not basic science like physics or biology. The behavior of states, nongovernment organizations, and international organizations is often difficult to describe in mathematical formulas and test in controlled experiments. A single event can be judged from many different angles. We still, however, should learn to separate facts from opinions. Facts are verifiable events and developments. Opinions are speculations or intuitions about how and why such developments have taken place.

Distinguishing facts and opinions is not so easy. Some facts are deliberately hidden or distorted by government authorities or interest groups. Other facts remain in dispute. In 1945 the British novelist and journalist Georges Orwell wrote about the uncertainty of information about the events of World War II:

> There can often be a genuine doubt about the most enormous events. [. . .] The calamities that are constantly being reported—battles, massacres, famines, revolutions—tend to inspire in the average person a feeling of unreality. [. . .] One has no way of verifying the facts, one is not even fully certain that they have happened, and one is always presented with totally different interpretations from different sources.

Orwell's warnings are even more valid today. The Internet has lowered the information barriers and we are now flooded with news, reports, and opinions. Yet anyone seeking information on the Internet must be especially cautious: many seemingly reliable reports can be full of speculations often presented as "facts." In reality, they are just opinions. Even more often, facts are presented in a selective, one-sided way. Take, for example, any ongoing conflict and see how different the accounts of this conflict are in the eyes of the opposing sides. We, as viewers and listeners, tend to embrace the facts we like but ignore or criticize information that contradicts our views. As an example, passionate supporters of democracy may happily read an article describing how democracy is associated with stability and peace. However, this person could easily overlook facts showing that a transition to democracy, especially in the countries with a history of ethnic and religious hostility, could contribute to even greater violence. Could you suggest a few specific examples on your own?

Our desire to be objective is often constrained by the limits of language. Because people use language to communicate, they frequently "frame" facts, or put them into a convenient arrangement. Reports about international politics are often framed so that contradictory and confusing information becomes simple: "bad" countries are supposed to act badly; "good" countries are supposed to conduct virtuous policies. Uncertainties and gray areas are often omitted. Framing by the mass media works with remarkable effectiveness, camouflaging incomplete or even biased selection of facts and opinions.

Separating facts from opinions should help you navigate the sea of information related to world events. It can start with you looking for new and more reliable sources of facts. Whenever appropriate, try to establish as many facts as possible related to the issue you are studying. Do not limit yourself only to the facts that are easily available. Check your sources: how reliable are they? If there is a disagreement about the facts in two different reports, discuss why these differences occur. Pay attention to how the articles "frame" the facts and opinions in a certain direction. What are the motivations that have contributed to a certain point of view? The more often you ask yourself these questions, the more accurate your analysis of the received information will be.

Looking for Multiple Causes

Why do countries go to war? You often hear simple and categorical explanations and statements like "this war took place because of this country's oil-driven interests" or "that war happened because of that country's imperial ambitions," and so on. In fact, every war is a result of someone's interests and ambitions but also of many interconnected developments. Moreover, virtually any international event—not only war—has many underlying reasons or causes. As critical thinkers studying international relations, we need to consider a wide range of possible influences and factors, all of which could be involved to varying degrees in the shaping of international events and global developments. For example, some tend to explain the collapse of Communism in Eastern Europe and the Soviet Union in the late 1980s by President Ronald Reagan's unrelenting military and economic pressure on these countries. Although this pressure was real, the Soviet Union's demise was caused not only by one policy but rather by several intertwining factors, including people's disillusionment with Communist ideology, a growing economic and financial crisis, and the destabilizing domestic policies of Soviet leadership.

Being Aware of Bias

We have to keep in mind that our opinions, as well as the opinions of people around us, may be inaccurate. Every interpretation of the facts is made from someone's point of view. And people tend to avoid information that challenges their assumptions and gravitate to information that supports their views. When it comes to international relations, it is easy to support leaders we like and to oppose the policies of those we dislike. Our personal attachments, interests, preferences, and values have a tremendous impact on the facts we gather and judgments we make about international events. Ask your professor which online or printed periodical she or he read first, with their morning tea or coffee. Opinion polls show that people's political affiliation is correlated with their choice of news sources.

Bias is often caused by different experiences and life circumstances. Personal emotions can deepen misunderstandings and disagreements, by causing us to refuse to learn new facts and accept new information. Parochialism, a worldview limited to the small piece of land on which we live, necessarily narrows the experiences we can have. It is a powerful roadblock in the study and practice of international relations.

An emphasis on critical thinking will help all of us, as students of international relations. You will learn to retrieve verifiable knowledge from apparently endless fountains of information, from media reports to statistical databanks. You will also learn to be an informed skeptic and a decision maker.

KEY PEDAGOGICAL TOOLS: AN OVERVIEW

- In addition to this introduction, each of the three parts of the book starts with critical introductory remarks, which contain a preview of the topics and the selected articles.
- These introductory remarks also provide critical-thinking questions for class discussions or reading assignments.
- Each section (there are eleven sections in the book) contains a visual review.
- Critical-thinking questions related to the articles appear at the end of each part of the book.
- Practice test questions accompany every section of the book and appear on the companion website (http://oup.com/us/shiraev).
- The companion website (http://oup.com/us/shiraev) contains additional sources relevant to the articles in the book and current media reports to better illustrate or critically discuss the contents of the articles. Power Point slides posted on the site summarize the articles in the book.
- There are other Web-based interactive tools relevant to successful teaching and learning.

CONTENTS

The reader contains three parts, which are further divided into eleven sections. Again, the first part introduces the major approaches to the field of international relations. The second part examines three major facets of international relations. The third part refers to three of the most important domestic, regional, and global challenges and emphasizes the importance of knowledge and global understanding in the practice of international relations.

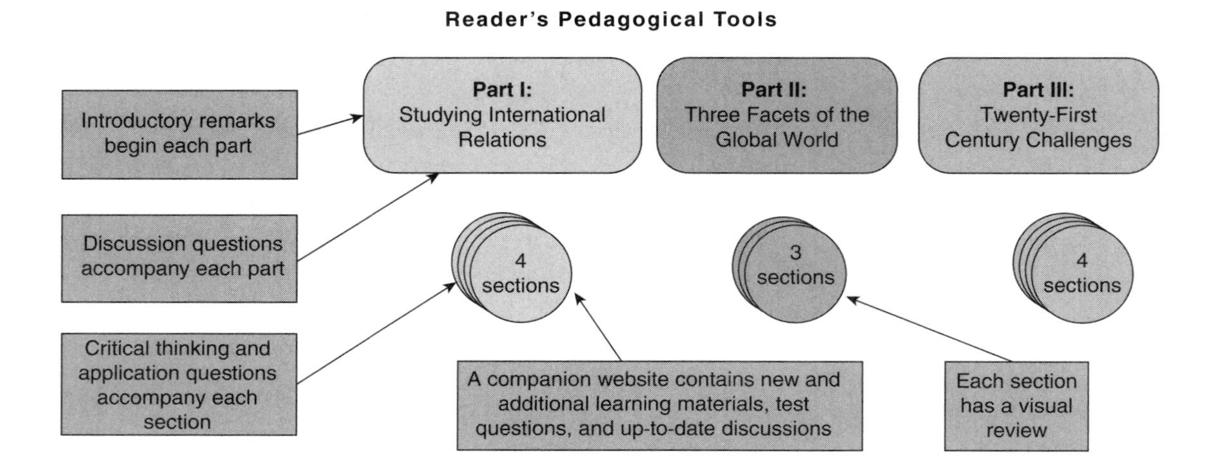

In sum, we hope that the current reader addresses at least two main challenges to teaching the introductory International Relations course or similar courses.

First, we believe that our students should learn to appreciate the latest professional achievements in the field and, in their understanding of international relations, take a variety of factors into account. We also believe it is crucial to show the relevance of these approaches to real-world problems. On the other hand, we do not want to overwhelm undergraduates with a deluge of theoretical nuances.

Second, students need to become informed skeptics and to develop a critical view toward discussions of world events. Statistics, video clips, tweets, maps, eyewitness reports, theoretical articles, and biographies—all are just a click away. We try to bank on this opportunity while also paying special attention to critical evaluation of facts and theories. We seek to focus on development of basic skills of critical fact-analysis and theoretical thinking—a major task in understanding and teaching international relations today.

TO THE STUDENT

We always ask students who take our classes to imagine that they have obtained the power to travel in time and space. Could you do the same? How far back and where would you go? Would you pick a seat in an inaugural session of the United Nations? Or would you choose to be a fly on the wall in the White House, listening to a president's top-secret discussion of a new global strategy? Or would you prefer to climb atop the Berlin Wall on November 9, 1989, to chip off a chunk of this monstrous barrier, the symbol of the Cold War? Or would you rather listen to the discussion in the White House about the decision to kill Bin Laden? Would you rather be among the few physicians contemplating Doctors Without Borders in 1971? Or maybe you would like to attend the NATO meeting when a decision to bomb Libya was reached in 2011. How about a chance to listen to U.S. and Cuban leaders in 2015 negotiating a new type of relationships between these two countries?

Too many choices, too many people. . . . But even if you saw everything you wanted and met everybody you planned, what exactly could you learn from that experience? And what lessons could you draw when everything in the world is so rapidly changing? Do you feel that there are too many opinions, judgments, and suggestions made every minute on television and on the Web about the evolving world?

We believe that this book not only will help you in your study of international relations. It should provide you with at least three crucial opportunities that give you an advantage over many commentators in the media and cyberspace.

First, we believe that you will adopt the right language to speak about and explain international relations, beginning with simple but crucial terms such as "anarchy," "states," "balance of power, "interests," "cooperation," "security," and several others.

Second, you will be able to gain and strengthen your knowledge about how governments and international organizations respond to crises and wars, and why they make such choices. Third, you will better understand why the world of today remains unstable, unpredictable, and even "messy."

Finally, we hope that in our studies of international relations, in our analyses of great decisions and significant mistakes, we also will build your confidence in your ability to contribute to a better, peaceful, and prosperous world of the future. It is up to you to accept the challenge.

PART I

STUDYING INTERNATIONAL RELATIONS

Main Perspectives: Their Evolution and Relevance Today (Editorial Introduction)

Everywhere we taught international relations over the past twenty years—in Washington, D.C. and Philadelphia, Rome and Warsaw, London and Moscow—we often heard these similar questions from our students early in the course: *Why do we have to study these theories and perspectives? Could we just skip them and turn to the issues of the day?* The obvious impatience of a young person who is dreaming about a career in diplomacy, international politics, or international law is understandable. Besides, today's global world is evolving faster than ever. Following and understanding its rapid developments become increasingly challenging and even at times frustrating. And now comes the theory. *Who needs it?*

Eventually, most of our skeptical students change their minds. After a semester of lectures and class discussions, they realize that studying these approaches and theories makes sense. Not only do these approaches and theories help them understand the dramatic events of 1914, 1941, and 2001, but this conceptual thinking also helps them critically evaluate international challenges, tragedies, and triumphs that unfold before our eyes. The students see that their knowledge of international relations theory serves as a much-needed "navigator" in understanding today's world.

As a discipline, international relations is still relatively young. It took its early steady steps only in the previous century. Several dramatic developments and collective experiences impacted the growth of this discipline. The world's periods of peace and prosperity took turns with economic breakdowns and two world wars. The Cold War—a major confrontation between the Soviet bloc and Western states—threatened humankind with a nuclear Armageddon. Yet the Soviet Union has fallen and the United States has remained the only superpower standing. About the same time, China began its economic and political ascendance. The world is evolving, and so is the discipline of international relations. This means that theories and approaches that we study today are not immutable, timeless "laws," but rather conceptual summaries of the rich and evolving experiences. Every new generation, every new cohort of scholars revisits and reevaluates these principal approaches, compares them to the current developments, and updates them accordingly.

The two approaches that dominated the study of international relations at the universities of the United States and Great Britain during the past half a century are realism and liberalism (sometimes called international liberalism). Realism focuses on the power of states (sovereign countries), their interests, and their search for security. According to this theoretical approach, the very nature of international relations is anarchic. This means that states (sovereign countries) can act on the world stage as they want, without any authority above them. They defend their core interests, protect their resources, create alliances with other states, respond to outside threats, and, if necessary, impose their will on others. States, according to the followers of realism, are constantly preoccupied with *balance of power* and look for the best position within the international order. They also balance one another by trying to prevent other states from gaining a significant advantage over others. Among common instruments of this balancing are strategic alliances, armament increases, threats of using military force, and, ultimately, war.

Liberalism is a different approach. It claims that international anarchy does not necessarily lead to conflicts and wars. It may result in cooperation among states. Liberalism emphasizes international collaboration, economic ties, international law, and shared values. It also sees international organizations and nonstate actors as influencing state choices and policies.

Modern realism and liberalism may differ substantially from their original formulations. Back in 1948, Hans Morgenthau, a refugee from Germany who had found a new life in the United States, formulated his famous "six principles of realism." To propose these principles, Morgenthau first synthesized his broad knowledge of European and ancient Greco-Roman history as well as the tragic experiences of the two world wars of the twentieth century. He taught that leaders of sovereign states should conduct foreign policy in terms of their state's interests defined through power. Ethical principles that guide the behavior of individuals should not necessarily be tied to states' actions. Moral values still may play an important role in foreign policy, but in most cases, states should pursue these two interconnected goals: maximize their benefits and reduce their losses. Morgenthau's ideas gained significant support. Many American and British textbooks on international relations discussed and endorsed his ideas, which seemed timely and very much appropriate.

Yet just thirty years after Morgenthau introduced his principles, the world was very different. A new international system had emerged that was shaped by the Cold War. The world's affairs were dominated by the United States and the Soviet Union, which were commonly called "superpowers." Reflecting on and critically rethinking that global change, the American political scientist Kenneth Waltz redesigned the concept of realism. Analyzing the Cold War, Waltz concluded that the most important single factor that shaped international relations was the distribution of power, which

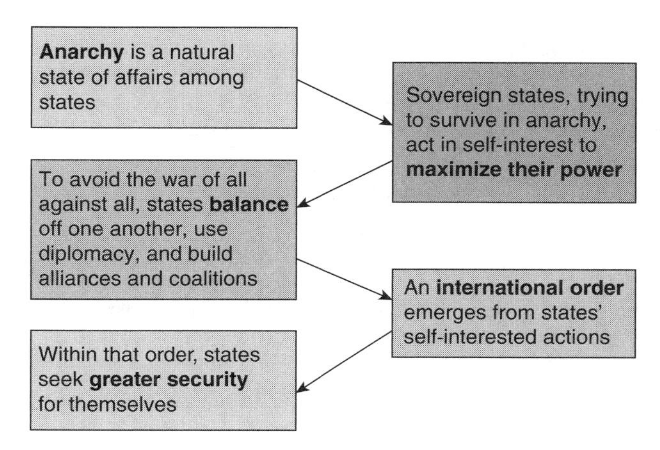

Figure 1. The Logic of Realism

was resulting in a certain *structure* of international relations. He then argued that states respond to the condition of international anarchy according to an existing structure for an international system. Because during the Cold War this structure was bipolar, shaped by the global rivalry between the United States and the Soviet Union, all other states had to adapt to this structure. The followers of Waltz were labeled "structural realists" or "neorealists." See Figure 1.

Liberalism, like realism, was rooted in the European history and the early twentieth-century experience. It stemmed from the principles of liberal idealism (related to humanism and Enlightenment), and political liberalism. Liberal thinkers believed that human reason could bring about an international system of peaceful and prosperous sovereign states. Political liberals formed a powerful social and political movement that originated in the nineteenth century; it challenged inherited privileges of the nobility and called for universal political rights.

Although the problems of security and the challenges of the arms race dominated the foreign policy agenda of many countries during the Cold War, liberal views became increasingly influential. A certain belief was gaining strength in Western Europe and the United States: if mutual interests and common values were to drive countries' foreign policy, this could reduce international tensions and bring substantial benefits to all countries. In the 1950s and 1960s, Western democracies enjoyed tremendous economic growth, in part because of international trade and technological exchanges. War, power balancing, and arms races were increasingly seen as outdated phenomena from the past. The international organizations, led by the United States, and the European economic integration began to influence and even challenge the old realist agenda of power balance, deterrence, and containment.

Supporters of liberalism, while continuing their criticism of realism, now focused on states' cooperation. Liberal scholars followed several conceptual paths. Some scholars such as Robert Keohane showed that the growth of economic dependence among sovereign countries was becoming increasingly complex and multilayered. Others, like Hedley Bull, focused on the increasing influence of intergovernmental and non-governmental organizations, as well as the emergence of a so-called international

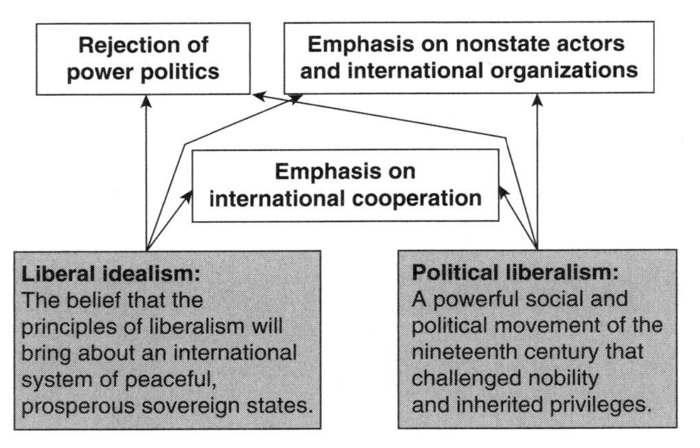

Figure 2. The Logic of Liberalism

society where sovereign states voluntarily followed common norms of behavior, to enhance their security and prosperity. See Figure 2.

Other liberal scholars turned to human rights, environmental challenges, and international law. Individual actions of sovereign states, in view of these scholars, should become history. These were the areas, they argued, that should alter the nature of international relations and lead to some new international settings called "global governance." Another important debate emerged among supporters of liberalism who argued whether or not the global spread of democracy would diminish the danger of major wars. Scholars like Michael Doyle argued that developed democracies do not go to war against each other. To put it simply, the more democratic countries emerge, the more stable the world's peace becomes. Critics argued that countries that can be characterized as "young" or "unstable" democracies in fact go to war more frequently than nondemocracies. The debates on this subject continue.

The concepts of realism and liberalism have always been based on several broad assumptions and key concepts such as states (or sovereign countries), state interests, international anarchy, and balance of power. Most scholars of these two approaches rarely probed into such assumptions. In contrast, a number of alternative approaches and theories did so: they looked at international relations quite differently than liberalism and realism.

From the nineteenth century, Marxism has remained the strongest conceptual framework or inspiration for some alternative approaches. Marxist ideas, developed by thinkers such as Vladimir Lenin in Russia, Antonio Gramsci in Italy, and others, rejected the assumptions that states were independent actors in world politics. Instead, they argued, states reflected the interests of dominant social groups (or *ruling classes* in Marxist's terminology), including industrial and financial elites, international corporations, banks, and even big influential international organizations. Several neo-Marxist scholars, particularly economists from Latin America, argued that the structure of international relations—and trade in particular—makes it impossible for poor countries to quickly move out of poverty by following Western models of development and modernization. The free market keeps poor states excessively dependent on rich states, while supplying the latter with cheap labor and raw materials. Such dependency can be reduced if states build their own industries and substitute their products for foreign goods. These views became the foundation of *dependency theory* by the Argentine economist Raul Prebisch. Advancing similar arguments, several sociologists created *world-systems theory*, according to which the world is divided into a core, consisting of the developed states that exercise their hegemonic power and the periphery, including former colonies and underdeveloped and chronically poor states. Using the neo-Marxist concept of hegemony in international relations, Immanuel Wallerstein claimed that a small group of wealthy Western states have for many decades maintained their decisive supremacy over the rest of the world. Supporters of these views also maintained that actually the "real" conflict in international relations has not been between the West and the Soviet bloc (the East), but rather between the wealthy "North" and the poor "South." Sovereign states, as the British political scientist Susan Strange contended, could not be viewed as main actors in international relations: instead, they sacrificed their sovereignty in the economic and financial sphere to international financial organizations.

Since the 1970s, feminist scholars have produced a wealth of innovative work linking gender and gender inequality to international relations. Feminist authors like Ann Tickner, Carol Cohn, and others asserted that defense and security policies reflect a masculine culture that accepts confrontation, war, and violence, rather than consensus and peace. For centuries, ruling elites did not take into consideration women's values and priorities. Feminist authors also argued that domestic gender inequality and violence against women are highly correlated with states' choices between violence and cooperation, and peace and war in international affairs.

Most of these concepts described earlier emerged in the shadow of the Cold War between the Soviet bloc and the alliance of Western states. The end of the Cold War and the collapse of the Soviet Union produced new challenges and uncertainties in international relations. Structural realists were poorly prepared to explain the sudden end of the Cold War and the disappearance of the Soviet Union. As a result, facing a surprising end of the twentieth century's global rivalry, some supporters of realism began to question its assumptions. To add to the list of challenges for realists, the terrorist attacks on September 11, 2001, demonstrated that the new threats to the international system could come not only from sovereign countries but also from nonstate networks that remain clandestine while empowered by radical ideologies, such as al-Qaida. The events of 2014 and later showed that radical nonstate groups such as ISIS—a jihadist network operating in Iraq and Syria—could significantly affect international stability in entire regions. Experts in history and theory of realism constantly search for and test new hypotheses to explain international terrorism. Meanwhile, the Russian-Ukrainian conflict, in 2014 and 2015, demonstrated that some state leaders, like Vladimir Putin, are still guided by principles of power, power balancing, and territorial control.

The wars in Iraq and Afghanistan led to a discussion about how the international unipolar structure—where the United States remains the only great power—affects international relations. Critics maintained that the United States, despite its overwhelming military superiority, would eventually fail to dominate in the increasingly turbulent world. America should, therefore, continue to play a leading role in international affairs but restrain its involvement in international conflicts. Washington, critics argued, should act cautiously, pay greater respect to other states' interests, and better use the strengths of its allies. At the same time, some structural realists for years forecasted the emergence of another center of power, an alternative to the United States. They argued that America's unipolarity of the 1990s should have been only a brief moment in history. Yet there is no clear indication that any of the rising economic powers, including China, are prepared to replace American global leadership and form a new multipolar system. Russia, despite its assertive actions that often generate media headlines, remains a regional oil-rich power wrestling with economic decline and conflicting with its neighbors.

Kenneth Waltz, the founder of structural realism, died in 2013. It remains to be seen if his elegant, parsimonious theory retains its appeal for younger scholars of international relations. In any case, it is premature to treat realism as an outdated approach. The world is changing rapidly, and the conflicts in the Middle East, between Russia and Ukraine, and the tensions between Japan and China tell us that international peace and cooperation are not firmly established in many parts of the world.

The end of the Cold War brought numerous challenges to thinkers of liberalism, too. Some of them were probably overwhelmed by their optimism when the Soviet bloc and the Soviet Union collapsed: it seemed that most significant sources for international tensions had been eliminated. Some, like Francis Fukuyama, claimed the coming of "the end of history." The democratic West, as he had anticipated, governed by principles of liberal freedoms, would no longer face a serious ideological challenge from other countries. These scholars assumed that the traditional priorities of the Cold War international relations, such as political and military security, nuclear deterrence, proxy wars, the arms race, and arms control should be replaced by a new agenda emphasizing economic and social development, trade, education, human rights, and environmental security. The rapid and seemingly successful integration of a large group of countries into the European Union produced a new flow of optimistic arguments about the end of the international system based on sovereign states and balance of power.

When a chain of ethnic wars erupted in the Balkans, Africa, and other regions in the 1990s, liberal scholars argued that it was now the responsibility of the "international community" (meaning the United Nations, but also NATO and the European Union) to stop ethnic violence and tribal genocide. They further maintained that sovereignty as a key concept of international relations might be disregarded if there are legitimate grounds for an international intervention to stop massive violence and save lives threatened by governments or nongovernmental groups. Scores of experts and journalists began to use a new language, where *promotion of democracy*, *humanitarian intervention*, and the *responsibility to protect* replaced the traditional *containment*, *nuclear deterrence*, and *balance of power* from the Cold War days. Liberal authors preferred using concepts such as *common rules*, *values*, and *networks* instead of *power*. They spoke about *intergovernmental organizations* and deemphasized the importance of sovereign states and governments.

However, the realities on the ground and especially the ongoing regional conflicts revealed serious limitations of liberal concepts and approaches to international relations. The intergovernmental organizations and nongovernmental organizations, as it turned out, could not effectively replace states and alliances of states. The United

States and its NATO allies, such as the United Kingdom and France, carried out almost all significant interventions involving the use of force or requiring massive and urgent assistance of the last two decades. The United Nations' involvement was, unfortunately, underwhelming. The general expectation about the inevitable erosion of national sovereignty, as Stephen Krasner underlined, proved to be premature. International anarchy seems hard to avoid. Because of continuing disagreements among Russia, China, and the United States, it is difficult to set common rules of global governance. The conflict in the former Yugoslavia in the 1990s, the failure of the Arab Spring in 2011–2013, the near-collapse of the Iraqi government in 2014, and the Russian-Ukrainian conflict started in the same year have made democratic peace supporters acknowledge that the emergence of new, unstable democracies could lead to more, not fewer, international conflicts.

Above all, the economic rise of China, India, and Brazil, and the anti-Western behavior of Russia produced a tough intellectual challenge to some American, British, and other liberal scholars. They argued that an eagerly proclaimed new international system based on liberal principles of peace and cooperation was declining along with the decline of Western countries' power. Responding to this argument, the American scholar G. John Ikenberry contended that the emerging international society requires its own "liberal Leviathan," or more specifically, the United States as a global leader. This strong country would guarantee that the rest of the world, and above all other economically powerful states, would continue to abide by rules of international cooperation developed predominantly in the West.

The collapse of communist states back in the late 1980s also meant the rapid decline in popularity of neo-Marxist concepts and their derivatives, such as dependency theory and the world system theory. The number of studies and journal articles based on alternative approaches has plummeted. At the same time, a new and increasingly popular approach emerged in the 1990s, called constructivism. One of its founders, Alexander Wendt, postulated that states' actions and policies are based on how leaders, bureaucracies, and societies interpret or construct the information available to them. This does not mean that politicians could easily manipulate realities and images of realities. Constructivism posits that power, anarchy, and security are socially created, within a cultural process where people's interests and identities are formed. For that reason, these key notions of international relations should have different meanings for different states. One state (country) may see a serious foreign threat where others see only a positive development. Like individuals, states can exaggerate external threats, undervalue them, or completely overlook them. During the past twenty years, constructivism became a third major theoretical approach to international relations, and some scholars believe it has even become a serious rival to both realism and liberalism. See Figure 3.

New theories have also appeared that emphasized cultural factors, such as identity, and differences between ethnic and cultural groups. Samuel Huntington and his followers argued that the major conflicts in world politics are not between states, but rather between "civilizations" unified by cultural or spiritual values. Iran and Saudi Arabia, in this view, struggle not just over oil or influence in the region, but rather because of a deep-seated animosity between Persian and Arab civilizations. Similarly, some countries of Europe have for centuries treated Russia with great suspicion not just because of its policies, but because they viewed it as an alien, unpredictable, and dangerous culture.

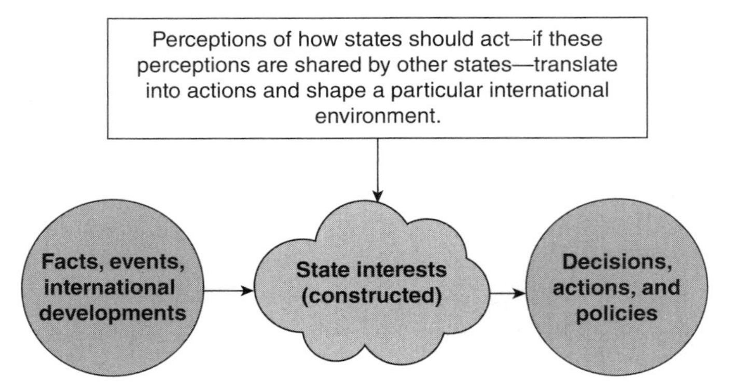

Figure 3. The Logic of Constructivism

Almost every recent international development reveals other problems and issues that affect international relations as a discipline and its applications. Other developments reflect the discipline itself, such as the choice of research methods or the gap between university-based theoretical studies, on the one hand, and foreign policy agenda, on the other. A significant proportion of contemporary studies rely mostly on sophisticated quantitative approaches incorporating advanced statistics. The process of quantification of knowledge is a positive development, as it helps in establishing trends and verifying research hypotheses. At the same time, we should not forget that formulas and regressions are just a tool in advancing scientific knowledge. Statistical correlations cannot replace an expert's historical erudition and his or her ability for critical thinking, analysis, generalizations, and creativity. The trend toward mathematization of international relations should not lead to the advancement of "science for science's sake" if it remains detached from specific policies and, most essentially, the interests of human beings. There are strong voices among scholars warning that the gap between international relations as a field and international realities has grown.

So what do we have to do to bring research closer to the needs of the young generation that is exploring and entering the field of international relations? A good start will be to learn the skills of our predecessors in this discipline: their capacity for bold innovative thinking and generalizations, their reliance on the knowledge in modern and contemporary history, and their ability to conduct interdisciplinary research and apply it to the challenging realities of the evolving world.

GENERAL DISCUSSION QUESTIONS RELATED TO THE READINGS ON MAIN PERSPECTIVES, THEIR EVOLUTION, AND RELEVANCE

These general questions are for class discussions as well as individual assignments. The discussion of these questions should help students think more critically and better understand the materials in this section. Other, more specific critical-thinking and practice questions related to the reading materials appear at the end of Part I.

- Why is it important that the international relations discipline is drawing from a variety of fields such as sociology, economics, history, and political psychology?
- Consider several international events or developments of the past three or five years. Which approach—realist or liberal—is more suitable, from your perspective, for interpreting these developments?
  - Iran's nuclear program and the debates around it
  - An international military operation in Libya in 2011
  - Territorial claims of several counties in the Arctic region
  - Events in and around Ukraine in 2014–2015, and later
  - Events in Egypt, Syria, and Iraq in 2013–2015, and later
- The disagreement between realists and liberal internationalists is about when and how force should be used in international relations. Discuss two or three (a) realist and (b) liberal arguments that should justify, in your view, the use of military force of one country against other countries. In other words, when can war be justified?
- Liberalism argues that cooperation, not confrontation such as military threats or annexation of territory, should foster international stability. Find and discuss facts from recent history or today's developments to (a) support and (b) challenge this assertion.
- What are the shortcomings of realism and liberalism in understanding international relations?
- Propose your own theory that will creatively "blend" the key principles of realism and liberalism. Use your theory to explain any international development of this year.
- Compose a list of major international military conflicts from 1990 (the end of the Cold War) until today. Which countries have been directly involved? List these countries and divide them in three categories: "established democracies," "developing democracies," and "nondemocracies." Use the *Democracy Index* (available online) to judge the selected countries. Based on this list, discuss the liberal thesis that "democracies do not go to war against one another."
- Kenneth Waltz argued that sovereign states respond to the condition of international anarchy according to an existing structure for an international system. During the Cold War, the system was bipolar. Consider the following:
  - What system do you envision in 10 years and why?
  - Will it be bipolar, unipolar, tripolar, or multipolar?
  - Which countries will be in these poles?
- Dependency and Marxist theories seem to have regained their popularity in recent years. Why is this happening from your standpoint? Which international and domestic developments in various countries could you explain using these theories?
- How many male and female secretaries of state have been there since 1992? Find this on the Web, including http://www.state.gov. Do your findings suggest that feminist criticisms of contemporary politics are no longer valid when applied to U.S. foreign policy? Explain your opinion.
- Americans often criticize their presidents for their foreign-policy actions or inaction. Would you criticize the current president? If so, for which foreign policies?

Section 1

Introducing the Field

Russian President Vladimir Putin traveled to Crimea, a Black Sea peninsula that Russia seized from Ukraine in March 2014. People in the Crimea region, a majority of whom are ethnic Russians, supported seceding from Ukraine, voted in a referendum, and sought annexation by Russia in 2014. How well does this case illustrate the *kin-country syndrome* described by Samuel Huntington?
Source: Alexei Nikolsky/Associated Press

The Clash of Civilizations?

SAMUEL P. HUNTINGTON

THE NEXT PATTERN OF CONFLICT

World politics is entering a new phase, and intellectuals have not hesitated to proliferate visions of what it will be—the end of history, the return of traditional rivalries between nation states, and the decline of the nation state from the conflicting pulls of tribalism and globalism, among others. Each of these visions catches aspects of the emerging reality. Yet they all miss a crucial, indeed a central, aspect of what global politics is likely to be in the coming years.

It is my hypothesis that the fundamental source of conflict in this new world will not be primarily ideological or primarily economic. The great divisions among humankind and the dominating source of conflict will be cultural. Nation states will remain the most powerful actors in world affairs, but the principal conflicts of global politics will occur between nations and groups of different civilizations. The clash of civilizations will dominate global politics. The fault lines between civilizations will be the battle lines of the future.

Conflict between civilizations will be the latest phase in the evolution of conflict in the modern world. For a century and a half after the emergence of the modern international system with the Peace of Westphalia, the conflicts of the Western world were largely among princes—emperors, absolute monarchs and constitutional monarchs attempting to expand their bureaucracies, their armies, their mercantilist economic strength and, most important, the territory they ruled. In the process they created nation states, and beginning with the French Revolution the principal lines of conflict were between nations rather than princes. In 1793, as R. R. Palmer put it, "The wars of kings were over; the wars of peoples had begun." This nineteenth-century pattern lasted until the end of World War I. Then, as a result of the Russian Revolution and the reaction against it, the conflict of nations yielded to the conflict of ideologies, first among communism, fascism-Nazism and liberal democracy, and then between communism and liberal democracy. During the Cold War, this latter conflict became embodied in the struggle between the two superpowers, neither of which was a nation state in the classical European sense and each of which defined its identity in terms of its ideology.

These conflicts between princes, nation states and ideologies were primarily conflicts within Western civilization, "Western civil wars," as William Lind has labeled them. This was as true of the Cold War as it was of the world wars and the earlier wars of the seventeenth, eighteenth and nineteenth centuries. With the end of the Cold War, international politics moves out of its Western phase, and its centerpiece becomes the interaction between the West and non-Western civilizations and among non-Western civilizations. In the politics of civilizations, the peoples and governments of non-Western civilizations no longer remain the objects of history as targets of Western colonialism but join the West as movers and shapers of history.

THE NATURE OF CIVILIZATIONS

During the Cold War the world was divided into the First, Second and Third Worlds. Those divisions are no longer relevant. It is far more meaningful now to group countries not in terms of their political or economic systems or in terms of their level of economic development but rather in terms of their culture and civilization.

What do we mean when we talk of a civilization? A civilization is a cultural entity. Villages, regions, ethnic groups, nationalities, religious groups, all have distinct cultures at different levels of cultural heterogeneity. The culture of a village in southern Italy may be different from that of a village in northern Italy, but both will share in a common Italian culture that distinguishes them from German villages. European communities, in turn, will share cultural features that distinguish them from Arab or Chinese communities. Arabs, Chinese and Westerners, however, are not part of any broader cultural entity. They constitute civilizations. A civilization is thus the highest cultural grouping of people and the broadest level of cultural identity people have short of that which distinguishes humans from other species. It is defined both by common objective elements, such as language, history, religion, customs, institutions, and by the subjective self-identification of people. People have levels of identity: a resident of Rome may define himself with varying degrees of intensity as a Roman, an Italian, a Catholic, a Christian, a European, a Westerner. The civilization to which he belongs is the broadest level of identification with which he intensely identifies. People can and do redefine their identities and, as a result, the composition and boundaries of civilizations change.

Civilizations may involve a large number of people, as with China ("a civilization pretending to be a state," as Lucian Pye put it), or a very small number of people, such as the Anglophone Caribbean. A civilization may include several nation states, as is the case with Western, Latin American and Arab civilizations, or only one, as is the case with Japanese civilization. Civilizations obviously blend and overlap, and may include subcivilizations. Western civilization has two major variants, European and North American, and Islam has its Arab, Turkic and Malay subdivisions. Civilizations are nonetheless meaningful entities, and while the lines between them are seldom sharp, they are real. Civilizations are dynamic; they rise and fall; they divide and merge. And, as any student of history knows, civilizations disappear and are buried in the sands of time.

Westerners tend to think of nation states as the principal actors in global affairs. They have been that, however, for only a few centuries. The broader reaches of human history have been the history of civilizations. In *A Study of History,* Arnold Toynbee identified 21 major civilizations; only six of them exist in the contemporary world.

WHY CIVILIZATIONS WILL CLASH

Civilization identity will be increasingly important in the future, and the world will be shaped in large measure by the interactions among seven or eight major civilizations. These include Western, Confucian, Japanese, Islamic, Hindu, Slavic-Orthodox, Latin American and possibly African civilization. The most important conflicts of the future will occur along the cultural fault lines separating these civilizations from one another.

Why will this be the case?

First, differences among civilizations are not only real; they are basic. Civilizations are differentiated from each other by history, language, culture, tradition and, most important, religion. The people of different civilizations have different views on the relations between God and man, the individual and the group, the citizen and the state, parents and children, husband and wife, as well as differing views of the relative importance of rights and responsibilities, liberty and authority, equality and hierarchy. These differences are the product of centuries. They will not soon disappear. They are far more fundamental than differences among political ideologies and political regimes. Differences do not necessarily mean conflict, and conflict does not necessarily mean violence. Over the centuries, however, differences among civilizations have generated the most prolonged and the most violent conflicts.

The conflicts of the future will occur along the cultural fault lines separating civilizations.

Second, the world is becoming a smaller place. The interactions between peoples of different civilizations are increasing; these increasing interactions intensify civilization consciousness and awareness of differences between civilizations and commonalities within civilizations. North African immigration to France generates hostility among Frenchmen and at the same time increased receptivity to immigration by "good" European

Catholic Poles. Americans react far more negatively to Japanese investment than to larger investments from Canada and European countries. Similarly, as Donald Horowitz has pointed out, "An Ibo may be . . . an Owerri Ibo or an Onitsha Ibo in what was the Eastern region of Nigeria. In Lagos, he is simply an Ibo. In London, he is a Nigerian. In New York, he is an African." The interactions among peoples of different civilizations enhance the civilization-consciousness of people that, in turn, invigorates differences and animosities stretching or thought to stretch back deep into history.

Third, the processes of economic modernization and social change throughout the world are separating people from longstanding local identities. They also weaken the nation state as a source of identity. In much of the world religion has moved in to fill this gap, often in the form of movements that are labeled "fundamentalist." Such movements are found in Western Christianity, Judaism, Buddhism and Hinduism, as well as in Islam. In most countries and most religions the people active in fundamentalist movements are young, college-educated, middle-class technicians, professionals and business persons. The "unsecularization of the world," George Weigel has remarked, "is one of the dominant social facts of life in the late twentieth century." The revival of religion, "la revanche de Dieu," as Gilles Kepel labeled it, provides a basis for identity and commitment that transcends national boundaries and unites civilizations.

Fourth, the growth of civilization-consciousness is enhanced by the dual role of the West. On the one hand, the West is at a peak of power. At the same time, however, and perhaps as a result, a return to the roots phenomenon is occurring among non-Western civilizations. Increasingly one hears references to trends toward a turning inward and "Asianization" in Japan, the end of the Nehru legacy and the "Hinduization" of India, the failure of Western ideas of socialism and nationalism and hence "re-Islamization" of the Middle East, and now a debate over Westernization versus Russianization in Boris Yeltsin's country. A West at the peak of its power confronts non-Wests that increasingly have the desire, the will and the resources to shape the world in non-Western ways.

In the past, the elites of non-Western societies were usually the people who were most involved with the West, had been educated at Oxford, the Sorbonne or Sandhurst, and had absorbed Western attitudes and values. At the same time, the populace in non-Western countries often remained deeply imbued with the indigenous culture. Now, however, these relationships are being reversed. A de-Westernization and indigenization of elites is occurring in many non-Western countries at the same time that Western, usually American, cultures, styles and habits become more popular among the mass of the people.

Fifth, cultural characteristics and differences are less mutable and hence less easily compromised and resolved than political and economic ones. In the former Soviet Union, communists can become democrats, the rich can become poor and the poor rich, but Russians cannot become Estonians and Azeris cannot become Armenians. In class and ideological conflicts, the key question was "Which side are you on?" and people could and did choose sides and change sides. In conflicts between civilizations, the question is "What are you?" That is a given that cannot be changed. And as we know, from Bosnia to the Caucasus to the Sudan, the wrong answer to that question can mean a bullet in the head. Even more than ethnicity, religion discriminates sharply and exclusively among people. A person can be half-French and half-Arab and simultaneously even a citizen of two countries. It is more difficult to be half-Catholic and half-Muslim.

Finally, economic regionalism is increasing. The proportions of total trade that were intraregional rose between 1980 and 1989 from 51 percent to 59 percent in Europe, 33 percent to 37 percent in East Asia, and 32 percent to 36 percent in North America. The importance of regional economic blocs is likely to continue to increase in the future. On the one hand, successful economic regionalism will reinforce civilization-consciousness. On the other hand, economic regionalism may succeed only when it is rooted in a common civilization. The European Community rests on the shared foundation of European culture and Western Christianity. The success of the North American Free Trade Area depends on the convergence now underway of Mexican, Canadian and American cultures. Japan, in contrast, faces difficulties in creating a comparable economic entity in East Asia because Japan is a society and civilization unique to itself. However strong the trade and investment links Japan may develop with other East Asian countries, its cultural differences with those countries inhibit and perhaps preclude its promoting regional economic integration like that in Europe and North America.

Common culture, in contrast, is clearly facilitating the rapid expansion of the economic relations between the People's Republic of China and Hong Kong, Taiwan, Singapore and the overseas Chinese communities in other Asian countries. With the Cold War over, cultural commonalities increasingly overcome ideological differences, and mainland China and Taiwan move closer together. If cultural commonality is a prerequisite for economic integration, the principal East Asian economic bloc of the future is likely to be centered on China. This bloc is, in fact, already coming into existence. As Murray Weidenbaum has observed,

> Despite the current Japanese dominance of the region, the Chinese-based economy of Asia is rapidly emerging as a new epicenter for industry, commerce and finance. This strategic area contains substantial amounts of technology and manufacturing capability (Taiwan), outstanding entrepreneurial, marketing and services acumen (Hong Kong), a fine communications network (Singapore), a tremendous pool of financial capital (all three), and very large endowments of land, resources and labor (mainland China). . . . From Guangzhou to Singapore, from Kuala Lumpur to Manila, this influential network—often based on extensions of the traditional clans—has been described as the backbone of the East Asian economy.[1]

Culture and religion also form the basis of the Economic Cooperation Organization, which brings together ten non-Arab Muslim countries: Iran, Pakistan, Turkey, Azerbaijan, Kazakhstan, Kyrgyzstan, Turkmenistan, Tadjikistan, Uzbekistan and Afghanistan. One impetus to the revival and expansion of this organization, founded originally in the 1960s by Turkey, Pakistan and Iran, is the realization by the leaders of several of these countries that they had no chance of admission to the European Community. Similarly, Caricom, the Central American Common Market and Mercosur rest on common cultural foundations. Efforts to build a broader Caribbean-Central American economic entity bridging the Anglo-Latin divide, however, have to date failed.

As people define their identity in ethnic and religious terms, they are likely to see an "us" versus "them" relation existing between themselves and people of different ethnicity or religion. The end of ideologically defined states in Eastern Europe and the former Soviet Union permits traditional ethnic identities and animosities to come to the fore. Differences in culture and religion create differences over policy issues, ranging from human rights to immigration to trade and commerce to the environment. Geographical propinquity gives rise to conflicting territorial claims from Bosnia to Mindanao. Most important, the efforts of the West to promote its values of democracy and liberalism as universal values, to maintain its military predominance and to advance its economic interests engender countering responses from other civilizations. Decreasingly able to mobilize support and form coalitions on the basis of ideology, governments and groups will increasingly attempt to mobilize support by appealing to common religion and civilization identity.

The clash of civilizations thus occurs at two levels. At the micro-level, adjacent groups along the fault lines between civilizations struggle, often violently, over the control of territory and each other. At the macro-level, states from different civilizations compete for relative military and economic power, struggle over the control of international institutions and third parties, and competitively promote their particular political and religious values.

THE FAULT LINES BETWEEN CIVILIZATIONS

The fault lines between civilizations are replacing the political and ideological boundaries of the Cold War as the flash points for crisis and bloodshed. The Cold War began when the Iron Curtain divided Europe politically and ideologically. The Cold War ended with the end of the Iron Curtain. As the ideological division of Europe has disappeared, the cultural division of Europe between Western Christianity, on the one hand, and Orthodox Christianity and Islam, on the other, has reemerged. The most significant dividing line in Europe, as William Wallace has suggested, may well be the eastern boundary of Western Christianity in the year 1500. This line runs along what are now the boundaries between Finland and Russia and between the Baltic states and Russia, cuts through Belarus and Ukraine separating the more Catholic western Ukraine from Orthodox eastern Ukraine, swings westward separating Transylvania from the rest of Romania, and then goes through Yugoslavia almost exactly along the line now separating Croatia and Slovenia from the rest of Yugoslavia. In the Balkans this line, of course, coincides with the historic boundary between the Hapsburg and Ottoman empires. The peoples to the north and west of this line are Protestant or Catholic; they shared the common experiences of European history—feudalism, the Renaissance, the Reformation, the Enlightenment, the French Revolution, the Industrial Revolution; they are generally economically better off than the peoples to the east; and they may now look forward to increasing involvement in a common European economy and to the consolidation of democratic political systems. The peoples to the east and south of this line are Orthodox or Muslim; they historically belonged to the Ottoman or Tsarist empires and were only lightly touched by the shaping events in the rest of Europe; they are generally less advanced economically; they seem much less likely to develop stable democratic political systems. The Velvet Curtain of culture has replaced the Iron Curtain of ideology as the most significant dividing line in Europe. As the events in Yugoslavia show, it is not only a line of difference; it is also at times a line of bloody conflict.

Conflict along the fault line between Western and Islamic civilizations has been going on for 1,300 years. After the founding of Islam, the Arab and Moorish surge west and north only ended at Tours in 732. From the eleventh to the thirteenth century the Crusaders attempted with temporary success to bring Christianity and Christian rule to the Holy Land. From the fourteenth to the seventeenth century, the Ottoman Turks reversed the balance, extended their sway over the Middle East and the Balkans, captured Constantinople, and twice laid siege to Vienna. In the nineteenth and early twentieth centuries as Ottoman power declined Britain, France, and Italy established Western control over most of North Africa and the Middle East.

After World War II, the West, in turn, began to retreat; the colonial empires disappeared; first Arab nationalism and then Islamic fundamentalism manifested themselves; the West became heavily dependent on the Persian Gulf countries for its energy; the oil-rich Muslim countries became money-rich and, when they wished to, weapons-rich. Several wars occurred between Arabs and Israel (created by the West). France fought a bloody and ruthless war in Algeria for most of the 1950s; British and French forces invaded Egypt in 1956; American forces went into Lebanon in 1958; subsequently American forces returned to Lebanon, attacked Libya, and engaged in various military encounters with Iran; Arab and Islamic terrorists, supported by at least three Middle Eastern governments, employed the weapon of the weak and bombed Western planes and installations and seized Western hostages. This warfare between Arabs and the West culminated in 1990, when the United States sent a massive army to the Persian Gulf to defend some Arab countries against aggression by another. In its aftermath NATO planning is increasingly directed to potential threats and instability along its "southern tier."

This centuries-old military interaction between the West and Islam is unlikely to decline. It could become more virulent. The Gulf War left some Arabs feeling proud that Saddam Hussein had attacked Israel and stood up to the West. It also left many feeling humiliated and resentful of the West's military presence in the Persian Gulf, the West's overwhelming military dominance, and their apparent inability to shape their own destiny.

Many Arab countries, in addition to the oil exporters, are reaching levels of economic and social development where autocratic forms of government become inappropriate and efforts to introduce democracy become stronger. Some openings in Arab political systems have already occurred. The principal beneficiaries of these openings have been Islamist movements. In the Arab world, in short, Western democracy strengthens anti-Western political forces. This may be a passing phenomenon, but it surely complicates relations between Islamic countries and the West.

Those relations are also complicated by demography. The spectacular population growth in Arab countries, particularly in North Africa, has led to increased migration to Western Europe. The movement within Western Europe toward minimizing internal boundaries has sharpened political sensitivities with respect to this development. In Italy, France and Germany, racism is increasingly open, and political reactions and violence against Arab and Turkish migrants have become more intense and more widespread since 1990.

On both sides the interaction between Islam and the West is seen as a clash of civilizations. The West's "next confrontation," observes M. J. Akbar, an Indian Muslim author, "is definitely going to come from the Muslim world. It is in the sweep of the Islamic nations from the Maghreb to Pakistan that the struggle for a new world order will begin." Bernard Lewis comes to a similar conclusion:

> We are facing a mood and a movement far transcending the level of issues and policies and the governments that pursue them. This is no less than a clash of civilizations—the perhaps irrational but surely historic reaction of an ancient rival against our Judeo-Christian heritage, our secular present, and the worldwide expansion of both.[2]

Historically, the other great antagonistic interaction of Arab Islamic civilization has been with the pagan, animist, and now increasingly Christian black peoples to the south. In the past, this antagonism was epitomized in the image of Arab slave dealers and black slaves. It has been reflected in the on-going civil war in the Sudan between Arabs and blacks, the fighting in Chad between Libyan-supported insurgents and the government, the tensions between Orthodox Christians and Muslims in the Horn of Africa, and the political conflicts, recurring riots and communal violence between Muslims and Christians in Nigeria. The modernization of Africa and the spread of Christianity are likely to enhance the probability of violence along this fault line. Symptomatic of the intensification of this conflict was the Pope John Paul II's speech in Khartoum in February 1993 attacking the actions of the Sudan's Islamist government against the Christian minority there.

On the northern border of Islam, conflict has increasingly erupted between Orthodox and Muslim peoples, including the carnage of Bosnia and Sarajevo, the simmering violence between Serb and Albanian, the tenuous relations between Bulgarians and their Turkish minority, the violence between Ossetians and Ingush, the unremitting slaughter of each other by Armenians and Azeris, the tense relations between Russians and Muslims in Central Asia, and the deployment of Russian troops to protect Russian interests in the Caucasus and Central Asia. Religion reinforces the revival of ethnic identities and restimulates Russian fears about the security of their southern borders. This concern is well captured by Archie Roosevelt:

> Much of Russian history concerns the struggle between the Slavs and the Turkic peoples on their borders, which dates back to the foundation of the Russian state more than a thousand years ago. In the Slavs' millennium-long confrontation with their eastern neighbors lies the key to an understanding not only of Russian history, but Russian character. To understand Russian realities today one has to have a concept of the great Turkic ethnic group that has preoccupied Russians through the centuries.[3]

The conflict of civilizations is deeply rooted elsewhere in Asia. The historic clash between Muslim and Hindu in the subcontinent manifests itself now not only in the rivalry between Pakistan and India but also in intensifying religious strife within India between increasingly militant Hindu groups and India's substantial Muslim minority. The destruction of the Ayodhya mosque in December 1992 brought to the fore the issue of whether India will remain a secular democratic state or become a Hindu one. In East Asia, China has outstanding territorial disputes with most of its neighbors. It has pursued a ruthless policy toward the Buddhist people of Tibet, and it is pursuing an increasingly ruthless policy toward its Turkic-Muslim minority. With the Cold War over, the underlying differences between China and the United States have reasserted themselves in areas such as human rights, trade and weapons proliferation. These differences are unlikely to moderate. A "new cold war," Deng Xaioping reportedly asserted in 1991, is under way between China and America.

The crescent-shaped Islamic bloc, from the bulge of Africa to central Asia, has bloody borders.

The same phrase has been applied to the increasingly difficult relations between Japan and the United States. Here cultural difference exacerbates economic conflict. People on each side allege racism on the other, but at least on the American side the antipathies are not racial but cultural. The basic values, attitudes, behavioral patterns of the two societies could hardly be more different. The economic issues between the United States and Europe are no less serious than those between the United States and Japan, but they do not have the same political salience and emotional intensity because the differences between American culture and European culture are so much less than those between American civilization and Japanese civilization.

The interactions between civilizations vary greatly in the extent to which they are likely to be characterized by violence. Economic competition clearly predominates between the American and European subcivilizations of the West and between both of them and Japan. On the Eurasian continent, however, the proliferation of ethnic conflict, epitomized at the extreme in "ethnic cleansing," has not been totally random. It has been most frequent and most violent between groups belonging to different civilizations. In Eurasia the great historic fault lines between civilizations are once more aflame. This is particularly true along the boundaries of the crescent-shaped Islamic bloc of nations from the bulge of Africa to central Asia. Violence also occurs between Muslims, on the one hand, and Orthodox Serbs in the Balkans, Jews in Israel, Hindus in India, Buddhists in Burma and Catholics in the Philippines. Islam has bloody borders.

CIVILIZATION RALLYING: THE KIN-COUNTRY SYNDROME

Groups or states belonging to one civilization that become involved in war with people from a different civilization naturally try to rally support from other members of their own civilization. As the post-Cold War world evolves, civilization commonality, what H. D. S. Greenway has termed the "kin-country" syndrome, is replacing political ideology and traditional balance of power considerations as the principal basis for cooperation and coalitions. It can be seen gradually emerging in the post-Cold War conflicts in the Persian Gulf, the Caucasus and Bosnia. None of these was a full-scale war between civilizations, but each involved some elements of civilizational rallying, which seemed to become more important as the conflict continued and which may provide a foretaste of the future.

First, in the Gulf War one Arab state invaded another and then fought a coalition of Arab, Western and other states. While only a few Muslim governments overtly supported Saddam Hussein, many Arab elites privately cheered him on, and he was highly popular among large sections of the Arab publics. Islamic fundamentalist movements universally supported Iraq rather than the Western-backed governments of Kuwait and Saudi Arabia. Forswearing Arab nationalism, Saddam Hussein explicitly invoked an Islamic appeal. He and his supporters attempted to define the war as a war between civilizations. "It is not the world against Iraq," as Safar Al-Hawali, dean of Islamic Studies at the Umm Al-Qura University in Mecca, put it in a widely circulated tape. "It is the West against Islam." Ignoring the rivalry between Iran and Iraq, the chief Iranian religious leader, Ayatollah Ali Khamenei, called for a holy war against the West: "The struggle against American aggression, greed, plans and policies will be counted as a jihad, and anybody who is killed on that path is a martyr." "This is a war," King Hussein of Jordan argued, "against all Arabs and all Muslims and not against Iraq alone."

The rallying of substantial sections of Arab elites and publics behind Saddam Hussein caused those Arab governments in the anti-Iraq coalition to moderate their activities and temper their public statements. Arab governments opposed or distanced themselves from subsequent Western efforts to apply pressure on Iraq, including enforcement of a no-fly zone in the summer of 1992 and the bombing of Iraq in January 1993. The Western-Soviet-Turkish-Arab anti-Iraq coalition of 1990 had by 1993 become a coalition of almost only the West and Kuwait against Iraq.

Muslims contrasted Western actions against Iraq with the West's failure to protect Bosnians against Serbs and to impose sanctions on Israel for violating U.N. resolutions. The West, they alleged, was using a double standard. A world of clashing civilizations, however, is inevitably a world of double standards: people apply one standard to their kin-countries and a different standard to others.

Second, the kin-country syndrome also appeared in conflicts in the former Soviet Union. Armenian military successes in 1992 and 1993 stimulated Turkey to become increasingly supportive of its religious, ethnic and linguistic brethren in Azerbaijan. "We have a Turkish nation feeling the same sentiments as the Azerbaijanis," said one Turkish official in 1992. "We are under pressure. Our newspapers are full of the photos of atrocities and are asking us if we are still serious about pursuing our neutral policy. Maybe we should show Armenia that there's a big Turkey in the region." President Turgut Özal agreed, remarking that Turkey should at least "scare the Armenians a little bit." Turkey, Özal threatened again in 1993, would "show its fangs." Turkish Air Force jets flew reconnaissance flights along the Armenian border; Turkey suspended food shipments and air flights to Armenia; and Turkey and Iran announced they would not accept dismemberment of Azerbaijan. In the last years of its existence, the Soviet government supported Azerbaijan because its government was dominated by former communists. With the end of the Soviet Union, however, political considerations gave way to religious ones. Russian troops fought on the side of the Armenians, and Azerbaijan accused the "Russian government of turning 180 degrees" toward support for Christian Armenia.

Third, with respect to the fighting in the former Yugoslavia, Western publics manifested sympathy and support for the Bosnian Muslims and the horrors they suffered at the hands of the Serbs. Relatively little concern was expressed, however, over Croatian attacks on Muslims and participation in the dismemberment of Bosnia-Herzegovina. In the early stages of the Yugoslav breakup, Germany, in an unusual display of diplomatic initiative and muscle, induced the other 11 members of the European Community to follow its lead in recognizing Slovenia and Croatia. As a result of the pope's determination to provide strong backing to the two Catholic countries, the Vatican extended recognition even before the Community did. The United States followed the European lead. Thus the leading actors in Western civilization rallied behind their coreligionists. Subsequently Croatia was reported to be receiving substantial quantities of arms from Central European and other Western countries. Boris Yeltsin's government, on the other hand, attempted to pursue a middle course that would be sympathetic to the Orthodox Serbs but not alienate Russia from the West. Russian conservative and nationalist groups, however, including many legislators, attacked the government for not being more forthcoming in its support for the Serbs. By early 1993 several hundred Russians apparently were serving with the Serbian forces, and reports circulated of Russian arms being supplied to Serbia.

Islamic governments and groups, on the other hand, castigated the West for not coming to the defense of the Bosnians. Iranian leaders urged Muslims from all countries to provide help to Bosnia; in violation of the U.N. arms embargo,

Iran supplied weapons and men for the Bosnians; Iranian-supported Lebanese groups sent guerrillas to train and organize the Bosnian forces. In 1993 up to 4,000 Muslims from over two dozen Islamic countries were reported to be fighting in Bosnia. The governments of Saudi Arabia and other countries felt under increasing pressure from fundamentalist groups in their own societies to provide more vigorous support for the Bosnians. By the end of 1992, Saudi Arabia had reportedly supplied substantial funding for weapons and supplies for the Bosnians, which significantly increased their military capabilities vis-à-vis the Serbs.

In the 1930s the Spanish Civil War provoked intervention from countries that politically were fascist, communist and democratic. In the 1990s the Yugoslav conflict is provoking intervention from countries that are Muslim, Orthodox and Western Christian. The parallel has not gone unnoticed. "The war in Bosnia-Herzegovina has become the emotional equivalent of the fight against fascism in the Spanish Civil War," one Saudi editor observed. "Those who died there are regarded as martyrs who tried to save their fellow Muslims."

Conflicts and violence will also occur between states and groups within the same civilization. Such conflicts, however, are likely to be less intense and less likely to expand than conflicts between civilizations. Common membership in a civilization reduces the probability of violence in situations where it might otherwise occur. In 1991 and 1992 many people were alarmed by the possibility of violent conflict between Russia and Ukraine over territory, particularly Crimea, the Black Sea fleet, nuclear weapons and economic issues. If civilization is what counts, however, the likelihood of violence between Ukrainians and Russians should be low. They are two Slavic, primarily Orthodox peoples who have had close relationships with each other for centuries. As of early 1993, despite all the reasons for conflict, the leaders of the two countries were effectively negotiating and defusing the issues between the two countries. While there has been serious fighting between Muslims and Christians elsewhere in the former Soviet Union and much tension and some fighting between Western and Orthodox Christians in the Baltic states, there has been virtually no violence between Russians and Ukrainians.

Civilization rallying to date has been limited, but it has been growing, and it clearly has the potential to spread much further. As the conflicts in the Persian Gulf, the Caucasus and Bosnia continued, the positions of nations and the cleavages between them increasingly were along civilizational lines. Populist politicians, religious leaders and the media have found it a potent means of arousing mass support and of pressuring hesitant governments. In the coming years, the local conflicts most likely to escalate into major wars will be those, as in Bosnia and the Caucasus, along the fault lines between civilizations. The next world war, if there is one, will be a war between civilizations.

THE WEST VERSUS THE REST

The West is now at an extraordinary peak of power in relation to other civilizations. Its superpower opponent has disappeared from the map. Military conflict among Western states is unthinkable, and Western military power is unrivaled. Apart from Japan, the West faces no economic challenge. It dominates international political and security institutions and with Japan international economic institutions. Global political and security issues are effectively settled by a directorate of the United States, Britain and France, world economic issues by a directorate of the United States, Germany and Japan, all of which maintain extraordinarily close relations with each other to the exclusion of lesser and largely non-Western countries. Decisions made at the U.N. Security Council or in the International Monetary Fund that reflect the interests of the West are presented to the world as reflecting the desires of the world community. The very phrase "the world community" has become the euphemistic collective noun (replacing "the Free World") to give global legitimacy to actions reflecting the interests of the United States and other Western powers.[4] Through the IMF and other international economic institutions, the West promotes its economic interests and imposes on other nations the economic policies it thinks appropriate. In any poll of non-Western peoples, the IMF undoubtedly would win the support of finance ministers and a few others, but get an overwhelmingly unfavorable rating from just about everyone else, who would agree with Georgy Arbatov's characterization of IMF officials as "neo-Bolsheviks who love expropriating other people's money, imposing undemocratic and alien rules of economic and political conduct and stifling economic freedom."

Western domination of the U.N. Security Council and its decisions, tempered only by occasional abstention by China, produced U.N. legitimation of the West's use of force to drive Iraq out of Kuwait and its elimination of Iraq's sophisticated weapons and capacity to produce such weapons. It also produced the quite unprecedented action by the United States, Britain and France in getting the Security Council to demand that Libya hand over the Pan Am 103 bombing suspects and then to impose sanctions when Libya refused. After defeating the largest Arab army, the West did not hesitate to throw its weight around in the Arab world. The West in effect is using international institutions, military power and economic resources to run the world in ways that will maintain Western predominance, protect Western interests and promote Western political and economic values.

The very phrase "world community" has become a euphemism to give legitimacy to the actions of the West.

That at least is the way in which non-Westerners see the new world, and there is a significant element of truth in their view. Differences in power and struggles for military, economic and institutional power are thus one source of conflict between the West and other civilizations. Differences in culture, that is basic values and beliefs, are a second source of conflict. V. S. Naipaul has argued that Western civilization is the "universal civilization" that "fits all men." At a superficial level much of Western culture has indeed permeated the rest of the world. At a more basic level, however, Western concepts differ fundamentally from those prevalent in other civilizations. Western ideas of individualism, liberalism, constitutionalism, human rights, equality, liberty, the rule of law, democracy, free markets, the separation of church and state, often have little resonance in Islamic, Confucian, Japanese, Hindu, Buddhist or Orthodox cultures. Western efforts to propagate such ideas produce instead a reaction against "human rights imperialism" and a reaffirmation of indigenous values, as can be seen in the support for religious fundamentalism by the younger generation in non-Western cultures. The very notion that there could be a "universal civilization" is a Western idea, directly at odds with the particularism of most Asian societies and their emphasis on what distinguishes one people from another. Indeed, the author of a review of 100 comparative studies of values in different societies concluded that "the values that are most important in the West are least important worldwide."[5] In the political realm, of course, these differences are most manifest in the efforts of the United States and other Western powers to induce other peoples to adopt Western ideas concerning democracy and human rights. Modern democratic government originated in the West. When it has developed in non-Western societies it has usually been the product of Western colonialism or imposition.

The central axis of world politics in the future is likely to be, in Kishore Mahbubani's phrase, the conflict between "the West and the Rest" and the responses of non-Western civilizations to Western power and values.[6] Those responses generally take one or a combination of three forms. At one extreme, non-Western states can, like Burma and North Korea, attempt to pursue a course of isolation, to insulate their societies from penetration or "corruption" by the West, and, in effect, to opt out of participation in the Western-dominated global community. The costs of this course, however, are high, and few states have pursued it exclusively. A second alternative, the equivalent of "bandwagoning" in international relations theory, is to attempt to join the West and accept its values and institutions. The third alternative is to attempt to "balance" the West by developing economic and military power and cooperating with other non-Western societies against the West, while preserving indigenous values and institutions; in short, to modernize but not to Westernize.

THE TORN COUNTRIES

In the future, as people differentiate themselves by civilization, countries with large numbers of peoples of different civilizations, such as the Soviet Union and Yugoslavia, are candidates for dismemberment. Some other countries have a fair degree of cultural homogeneity but are divided over whether their society belongs to one civilization or another. These are torn countries. Their leaders typically wish to pursue a bandwagoning strategy and to make their countries members of the West, but the history, culture and traditions of their countries are non-Western. The most obvious and prototypical torn country is Turkey. The late twentieth-century leaders of Turkey have followed in the Attatürk tradition and defined Turkey as a modern, secular, Western nation state. They allied Turkey with the West in NATO and in the Gulf War; they applied for membership in the European Community. At the same time, however, elements in Turkish society have supported an Islamic revival and have argued that Turkey is basically a Middle Eastern Muslim society. In addition, while the elite of Turkey has defined Turkey as a Western society, the elite of the West refuses to accept Turkey as such. Turkey will not become a member of the European Community, and the real reason, as President Özal said, "is that we are Muslim and they are Christian and they don't say that." Having rejected Mecca, and then being rejected by Brussels, where does Turkey look? Tashkent may be the answer. The end of the Soviet Union gives Turkey the opportunity to become the leader of a revived Turkic civilization involving seven countries from the borders of Greece to those of China. Encouraged by the West, Turkey is making strenuous efforts to carve out this new identity for itself.

During the past decade Mexico has assumed a position somewhat similar to that of Turkey. Just as Turkey abandoned its historic opposition to Europe and attempted to join Europe, Mexico has stopped defining itself by its opposition to the United States and is instead attempting to imitate the United States and to join it in the North American Free Trade Area. Mexican leaders are engaged in the great task of redefining Mexican identity and have introduced fundamental economic reforms that eventually will lead to fundamental political change. In 1991 a top adviser to President Carlos Salinas de Gortari described at length to me all the changes the Salinas government was making. When he finished, I remarked: "That's most impressive. It seems to me that basically you want to change Mexico from a Latin American country into a North American country." He looked at me with surprise and exclaimed: "Exactly! That's precisely what we are trying to do, but of course we could never say so publicly." As his remark indicates, in Mexico as in Turkey, significant elements in society resist the redefinition of their country's identity. In Turkey, European-oriented leaders have to make gestures to Islam (Özal's pilgrimage to Mecca); so also Mexico's North American-oriented leaders have to make gestures to those who hold Mexico to be a Latin American country (Salinas' Ibero-American Guadalajara summit).

Historically Turkey has been the most profoundly torn country. For the United States, Mexico is the most immediate torn country. Globally the most important torn country is Russia. The question of whether Russia is part of the West or the leader of a distinct Slavic-Orthodox civilization has been a recurring one in Russian history. That issue was obscured by the communist victory in Russia, which imported a Western ideology, adapted it to Russian conditions and then challenged the West in the name of that ideology. The dominance of communism shut off the historic debate over Westernization versus Russification. With communism discredited Russians once again face that question.

President Yeltsin is adopting Western principles and goals and seeking to make Russia a "normal" country and a part of the West. Yet both the Russian elite and the Russian public are divided on this issue. Among the more moderate dissenters, Sergei Stankevich argues that Russia should reject the "Atlanticist" course, which would lead it "to become European, to become a part of the world economy in rapid and organized fashion, to become the eighth member of the Seven, and to put particular emphasis on Germany and the United States as the two dominant members of the Atlantic alliance." While also rejecting an exclusively Eurasian policy, Stankevich nonetheless argues that Russia should give priority to the protection of Russians in other countries, emphasize its Turkic and Muslim connections, and promote "an appreciable redistribution of our resources, our options, our ties, and our interests in favor of Asia, of the eastern direction." People of this persuasion criticize Yeltsin for subordinating Russia's interests to those of the West, for reducing Russian military strength, for failing to support traditional friends such as Serbia, and for pushing economic and political reform in ways injurious to the Russian people. Indicative of this trend is the new popularity of the ideas of Petr Savitsky, who in the 1920s argued that Russia was a unique Eurasian civilization.[7] More extreme dissidents voice much more blatantly nationalist, anti-Western and anti-Semitic views, and urge Russia to redevelop its military strength and to establish closer ties with China and Muslim countries. The people of Russia are as divided as the elite. An opinion survey in European Russia in the spring of 1992 revealed that 40 percent of the public had positive attitudes toward the West and 36 percent had negative attitudes. As it has been for much of its history, Russia in the early 1990s is truly a torn country.

To redefine its civilization identity, a torn country must meet three requirements. First, its political and economic elite has to be generally supportive of and enthusiastic about this move. Second, its public has to be willing to acquiesce in the redefinition. Third, the dominant groups in the recipient civilization have to be willing to embrace the convert. All three requirements in large part exist with respect to Mexico. The first two in large part exist with respect to Turkey. It is not clear that any of them exist with respect to Russia's joining the West. The conflict between liberal democracy and Marxism-Leninism was between ideologies which, despite their major differences, ostensibly shared ultimate goals of freedom, equality and prosperity. A traditional, authoritarian, nationalist Russia could have quite different goals. A Western democrat could carry on an intellectual debate with a Soviet Marxist. It would be virtually impossible for him to do that with a Russian traditionalist. If, as the Russians stop behaving like Marxists, they reject liberal democracy and begin behaving like Russians but not like Westerners, the relations between Russia and the West could again become distant and conflictual.[8]

THE CONFUCIAN-ISLAMIC CONNECTION

The obstacles to non-Western countries joining the West vary considerably. They are least for Latin American and East European countries. They are greater for the Orthodox countries of the former Soviet Union. They are still greater for Muslim, Confucian, Hindu and Buddhist societies. Japan has established a unique position for itself as an associate member of the West: it is in the West in some respects but clearly not of the West in important dimensions. Those countries that for reason of culture and power do not wish to, or cannot, join the West compete with the West by developing their own economic, military and political power. They do this by promoting their internal development and by cooperating with other non-Western countries. The most prominent form of this cooperation is the Confucian-Islamic connection that has emerged to challenge Western interests, values and power.

Almost without exception, Western countries are reducing their military power; under Yeltsin's leadership so also is Russia. China, North Korea and several Middle Eastern states, however, are significantly expanding their military capabilities. They are doing this by the import of arms from Western and non-Western sources and by the development of indigenous arms industries. One result is the emergence of what Charles Krauthammer has called "Weapon States," and the Weapon States are not Western states. Another result is the redefinition of arms control, which is a Western concept and a Western goal. During the Cold War the primary purpose of arms control was to establish a stable military balance between the United States and its allies and the Soviet Union and its allies. In the post-Cold War world the primary objective of arms control is to prevent the development by non-Western societies of military capabilities that could threaten Western interests. The West attempts to do this through international agreements, economic pressure and controls on the transfer of arms and weapons technologies.

The conflict between the West and the Confucian-Islamic states focuses largely, although not exclusively, on nuclear, chemical and biological weapons, ballistic missiles and other sophisticated means for delivering them, and the guidance, intelligence and other electronic capabilities for achieving that goal. The West promotes non-proliferation as a universal norm and nonproliferation treaties and inspections as means of realizing that norm. It also threatens a variety of sanctions against those who promote the spread of sophisticated weapons and proposes some benefits for those who do not. The attention of the West focuses, naturally, on nations that are actually or potentially hostile to the West.

A Confucian-Islamic connection has emerged to challenge Western interests, values and power.

The non-Western nations, on the other hand, assert their right to acquire and to deploy whatever weapons they think necessary for their security. They also have absorbed, to the full, the truth of the response of the Indian defense minister when asked what lesson he learned from the Gulf War: "Don't fight the United States unless you have nuclear weapons." Nuclear weapons, chemical weapons and missiles are viewed, probably erroneously, as the potential equalizer of superior Western conventional power. China, of course, already has nuclear weapons; Pakistan and India have the capability to deploy them. North Korea, Iran, Iraq, Libya and Algeria appear to be attempting to acquire them. A top Iranian official has declared that all Muslim states should acquire nuclear weapons, and in 1988 the president of Iran reportedly issued a directive calling for development of "offensive and defensive chemical, biological and radiological weapons."

Centrally important to the development of counter-West military capabilities is the sustained expansion of China's military power and its means to create military power. Buoyed by spectacular economic development, China is rapidly increasing its military spending and vigorously moving forward with the modernization of its armed forces. It is purchasing weapons from the former Soviet states; it is developing long-range missiles; in 1992 it tested a one-megaton nuclear device. It is developing power-projection capabilities, acquiring aerial refueling technology, and trying to purchase an aircraft carrier. Its military buildup and assertion of sovereignty over the South China Sea are provoking a multilateral regional arms race in East Asia. China is also a major exporter of arms and weapons technology. It has exported materials to Libya and Iraq that could be used to manufacture nuclear weapons and nerve gas. It has helped Algeria build a reactor suitable for nuclear weapons research and production. China has sold to Iran nuclear technology that American officials believe could only be used to create weapons and apparently has shipped components of 300-mile-range missiles to Pakistan. North Korea has had a nuclear weapons program under way for some while and has sold advanced missiles and missile technology to Syria and Iran. The flow of weapons and weapons technology is generally from East Asia to the Middle East. There is, however, some movement in the reverse direction; China has received Stinger missiles from Pakistan.

A Confucian-Islamic military connection has thus come into being, designed to promote acquisition by its members of the weapons and weapons technologies needed to counter the military power of the West. It may or may not last. At present, however, it is, as Dave McCurdy has said, "a renegades' mutual support pact, run by the proliferators and their backers." A new form of arms competition is thus occurring between Islamic-Confucian states and the West. In an old-fashioned arms race, each side developed its own arms to balance or to achieve superiority against the other side. In this new form of arms competition, one side is developing its arms and the other side is attempting not to balance but to limit and prevent that arms build-up while at the same time reducing its own military capabilities.

IMPLICATIONS FOR THE WEST

This article does not argue that civilization identities will replace all other identities, that nation states will disappear, that each civilization will become a single coherent political entity, that groups within a civilization will not conflict with and even fight each other. This paper does set forth the hypotheses that differences between civilizations are real and important; civilization-consciousness is increasing; conflict between civilizations will supplant ideological and other forms of conflict as the dominant global form of conflict; international relations, historically a game played out within Western civilization, will increasingly be de-Westernized and become a game in which non-Western civilizations are actors and not simply objects; successful political, security and economic international institutions are more likely to develop within civilizations than across civilizations; conflicts between groups in different civilizations will be more frequent, more sustained and more violent than conflicts between groups in the same civilization; violent conflicts between groups in different civilizations are the most likely and most dangerous source of escalation that could lead to global wars; the paramount axis of world politics will be the relations between "the West and the Rest"; the elites in some torn non-Western countries will try to make their countries part of the West, but in most cases face major obstacles to accomplishing this; a central focus of conflict for the immediate future will be between the West and several Islamic-Confucian states.

This is not to advocate the desirability of conflicts between civilizations. It is to set forth descriptive hypotheses as to what the future may be like. If these are plausible hypotheses, however, it is necessary to consider their implications for Western policy. These implications should be divided between short-term advantage and long-term accommodation. In the short term it is clearly in the interest of the West to promote greater cooperation and unity within its own civilization, particularly between its European and North American components; to incorporate into the West societies in Eastern Europe and Latin America whose cultures are close to those of the West; to promote and maintain cooperative relations with Russia and Japan; to prevent escalation of local inter-civilization conflicts into major inter-civilization wars; to limit the expansion of the military strength of Confucian and Islamic states; to moderate the reduction of Western military capabilities and maintain military superiority in East and Southwest Asia; to exploit differences and conflicts among Confucian and Islamic states; to support in other civilizations groups sympathetic to Western values and interests; to strengthen international institutions that reflect and legitimate Western interests and values and to promote the involvement of non-Western states in those institutions.

In the longer term other measures would be called for. Western civilization is both Western and modern. Non-Western civilizations have attempted to become modern without becoming Western. To date only Japan has fully succeeded in this quest. Non-Western civilizations will continue to attempt to acquire the wealth, technology, skills, machines and weapons that are part of being modern. They will also attempt to reconcile this modernity with their traditional culture and values. Their economic and military strength relative to the West will increase. Hence the West will increasingly have to accommodate these non-Western modern civilizations whose power approaches that of the West but whose values and interests differ significantly from those of the West. This will require the West to maintain the economic and military power necessary to protect its interests in relation to these civilizations. It will also, however, require the West to develop a more profound understanding of the basic religious and philosophical assumptions underlying other civilizations and the ways in which people in those civilizations see their interests. It will require an effort to identify elements of commonality between Western and other civilizations. For the relevant future, there will be no universal civilization, but instead a world of different civilizations, each of which will have to learn to coexist with the others.

Notes

[1]Murray Weidenbaum, *Greater China: The Next Economic Superpower?*, St. Louis: Washington University Center for the Study of American Business, Contemporary Issues, Series 57, February 1993, pp. 2–3.
[2]Bernard Lewis, "The Roots of Muslim Rage," *The Atlantic Monthly*, vol. 266, September 1990, p. 60; *Time*, June 15, 1992, pp. 24–28.
[3]Archie Roosevelt, *For Lust of Knowing*, Boston: Little, Brown, 1988, pp. 332–333.
[4]Almost invariably Western leaders claim they are acting on behalf of "the world community." One minor lapse occurred during the run-up to the Gulf War. In an interview on "Good Morning America," Dec. 21, 1990, British Prime Minister John Major referred to the actions "the West" was taking against Saddam Hussein. He quickly corrected himself and subsequently referred to "the world community." He was, however, right when he erred.
[5]Harry C. Triandis, *The New York Times*, Dec. 25, 1990, p. 41, and "Cross-Cultural Studies of Individualism and Collectivism," Nebraska Symposium on Motivation, vol. 37, 1989, pp. 41–133.
[6]Kishore Mahbubani, "The West and the Rest," *The National Interest*, Summer 1992, pp. 3–13.
[7]Sergei Stankevich, "Russia in Search of Itself," *The National Interest*, Summer 1992, pp. 47–51; Daniel Schneider, "A Russian Movement Rejects Western Tilt," *Christian Science Monitor*, Feb. 5, 1993, pp. 5–7.
[8]Owen Harries has pointed out that Australia is trying (unwisely in his view) to become a torn country in reverse. Although it has been a full member not only of the West but also of the ABCA military and intelligence core of the West, its current leaders are in effect proposing that it defect from the West, redefine itself as an Asian country and cultivate close ties with its neighbors. Australia's future, they argue, is with the dynamic economies of East Asia. But, as I have suggested, close economic cooperation normally requires a common cultural base. In addition, none of the three conditions necessary for a torn country to join another civilization is likely to exist in Australia's case.

"Walls" Between "Those People"? Contrasting Perspectives on World Politics

PETER J. KATZENSTEIN

CIVILIZATIONS—PLURALIST IN A GLOBAL ECUMENE OR UNITARY IN AN INTERNATIONAL SYSTEM?

Civilizations are based on urban forms of life and a division of labor by which urban elites extract resources from peasants. There are two basic views on civilization. I argue here for a pluralist view of civilizations that are embedded in a global ecumene. This ecumene describes a universal system of knowledge and practices that differs from a competitive international state system reinforcing civilizational unity. At the center of civilizational complexes we typically find religious traditions, which at times intermingle with literary ones. People can escape the taxing and conscription powers of civilizing states, as James Scott has shown. The movement of peoples back and forth between hills and valleys and across continents and oceans, as well as the tensions within and between religious and literary traditions, account for the pluralism of civilizations.

An alternative view of civilizations holds that they are unitary cultural programs, organized hierarchically around uncontested core values that

Peter Katzenstein, "Walls" between "Those People"? Contrasting Perspectives on World Politics, Perspectives on Politics, volume 8, issue 1, pp. 11–25, reproduced with permission.

yield unambiguous criteria for judging good conduct. This view was a European invention of the eighteenth century. In the nineteenth century it was enshrined in one standard of civilization. That standard was grounded in race, ethnic affiliation, religion, and a firm belief in the superiority of European civilization over all others. The distinction between civilized and uncivilized peoples is not specific to the European past. It enjoys broad support today among many conservative supporters of Huntington's thesis of the clash of civilizations—a book that was translated into 39 languages. It is also held by many liberals who are committed to improving the rule of law and global standards of good governance. Furthermore, the unitary argument is widely used by non-Europeans in their analysis of civilizational politics. Everywhere and at all times barbarians have knocked on the doors of civilizations.

Pluralist or Unitary

Civilizations, I argue here, are pluralist. Islam and China, for example, do not cohere around religious fundamentalism or Asian values. Instead, just like America, Islam and China experience conflicts over contested truths reflecting their internal pluralism and external context. Since this is a vast subject, let me offer here only a few illustrations from these two cases (leaving aside similar evidence easily adduced for Europe, India, Japan, Africa, and Russia). The two cases, China and Islam, are instructive because they illustrate territorially more and less compact civilizational complexes, and because they differ more than any other in their political organization: China is a vast state that looks exceptionally centralized compared to Islam's stateless polity. Furthermore, China and Islam are often thought to be most antagonistic to America. My illustrative examples are informed by my own reading and the work of several colleagues with whom I collaborated in a book project.

Chinese civilization is pluralist. The different strands of Sinic civilization have emerged from numerous reinventions of Confucianism in China and the various forms through which they grafted themselves onto the socio-cultural systems of China's neighbors. Although they never fully abandoned their indigenous and Buddhist traditions, Korea, Vietnam, and Japan in different ways and for different reasons adopted or emulated characteristic Chinese state practices.

The same is true of Islam. According to Marshall Hodgson, Islam belongs to neither East nor West. A truly global civilization, Islam is a bridge between both. In the past, the Indian Ocean was for this global civilization the center for the blending of different Islamic traditions, including Persian, Southeast Asian, Arabian, Ottoman, and South Asian. Today this rich legacy continues undiminished. Hyphenated-Islam, as in the existence of a richly polyglot Afro-Islam, a vigorous debate over Euro-Islam, and a pragmatic Islam in Southeast and Central Asia, contrasts with an internally deeply divided Islam in the Middle East and North Africa.

Unitary conceptions assume that civilizations are culturally cohesive and that their collective identities are unchanging. Because of both the recent and the distant history of the "West," this is implausible for both questions of security and political economy. Recently, after World War II, Germany—the most determined enemy of the West—was firmly integrated into a coalition of Western civilized democracies that were seeking to stem the tide of Eastern uncivilized autocracies. Furthermore, in the second half of the twentieth century, despite the importance of the Anglo-American model, varieties of capitalist democracies have remained a distinctive feature of the West. In the distant past, Medieval Europe, according to Karl Deutsch, featured six separate civilizational strands: monastic Christianity around the Mediterranean; Latin Christendom in Western and Central Europe; and Byzantium in Southeastern Europe. These three major civilizations were connected by the Afro-Eurasian trade networks of Islam, which for centuries took hold on the Iberian peninsula, as well as elements of two other trading civilizations, Jews and Vikings. Like the Islamic and Sinic civilizations, the West is pluralist.

In contrast to this pluralist view, Samuel Huntington's *Clash of Civilizations* restates the old, unitary thesis for our times. His became arguably the most influential book published on international relations since the end of the Cold War. For Huntington, civilizations are coherent, consensual, invariant, and equipped with a state-like capacity to act. Huntington succeeded brilliantly in his objective of providing a new paradigm for looking at world politics after the end of the Cold War. His correct anticipation of 9/11 gave the book a claim to validity that helps account for its continued relevance. Less noticed in public than in academic discourse is the fact that Huntington greatly overstates his case. Numerous analyses have established beyond any reasonable doubt that clashes occur primarily within rather than between civilizations. Furthermore, the book's appeal has not been undermined by the failure of the second of its two main claims. Since the end of the Cold War, the relations between Sinic and American civilizations are summarized best by terms such as encounter or engagement rather than clash.

In rethinking civilizational analysis, however, it would be a big mistake to focus only on Huntington's writings. Huntington insisted on a unitary conception of civilizations but accepted multiple standards of proper conduct in a world of numerous civilizations. Liberals follow an inverse logic. Unlike Huntington, they are often more willing to acknowledge the existence of diverse cultural programs in a given civilization. And unlike Huntington, they have a difficult time letting go of the notion of a single standard of good international and intercivilizational conduct. This is illustrated by vigorous and extended debates over failing states, standards of good governance, property rights, and transparent markets. On all of these issues, and many others, liberal arguments often proceed from the unquestioned assumption of the existence of a single standard of good conduct. In liberal American and European public discourse, the West thus is widely referred to in the singular: a universal, substantive form of perfectability that is integrating all parts of the world based on the growth of Western reason. A very similar, anti-Western counter-discourse, also steeped in Western reasoning, exists in Asia. The voices proclaiming the dawn of Asia's civilizational primacy may shift from yesterday's Japan to today's China and tomorrow's India. But these voices are growing louder. Like "Orientalism," "Occidentalism" characterizes East and West in the singular.

Ecumene and Balance of Practice or Anarchy and Balance of Power

I argue here that the internal pluralism of civilizations is reinforced by a larger context in which they are embedded. That context is not the international system or global markets, frequently deployed concepts that suffer from excessive sparseness and abstraction. It is instead a global ecumene that expresses not a common standard but a loose sense of shared values entailing often contradictory notions of diversity in a common humanity. This loose sense of shared values centers on the material and psychological well-being of all humans. "Well-being" and the rights of all "humans" are no longer the prerogative or product of any one civilization or constellation of civilizations or political structures. Instead, technology serving human well-being and norms of human rights are deterritorialized processes that have taken on a life of their own and provide the script for all civilizations and polities. This ecumene does not specify the political route toward implementation. It does offer a script, often not adhered to, that provides everywhere today the basis for political authority and legitimacy. All polities claim to serve the well-being of individuals. And all individuals are acknowledged to have inherent rights. The existence of these processes enhances the pluralism that inheres in civilizations. It undercuts both the imperialism of imposing single standards and the relativism of accepting all political practices.

Recognition of the importance of this global ecumene is central to the trenchant self-critique that William McNeil wrote of his own brilliant book, *The Rise of the West,* more than a quarter of a century after he had completed it and six years before the publication of Huntington's book. For McNeill, civilizations are internally variegated, loosely coupled, elite-centered social systems that are integrated in a commonly shared global context. He argues that his earlier path-breaking book was wrongheaded. It was based on the faulty assumption of the existence of civilizations conceived as separate groupings whose interaction was the main engine of world history. Instead, McNeill insists now that an adequate account must give proper consideration to the broader context in which all civilizations are embedded. Since civilizations are internally differentiated, they transplant selectively. And since they are loosely integrated, they generate debates and contestations that tend to make them salient to others. What historically was true for South Asia and the Islamic world is even more true for all contemporary civilizations under the impact of modern communications technologies. A global ecumene pluralizes civilizations within a loose sense of shared values.

Such a pluralist conceptualization of civilization is attuned to the emergence of new forces, cultural and political, that reflects on the richness of the politically available repertoires of different civilizations. Analysis of pluralist civilizations stresses the balance of human practices. Shifting balances are producing and reproducing behavioral and symbolic boundaries within and between civilizations that are more or less closely tied to political power. Islamicization and Sinicization offer two ready examples.

Viewed globally and historically, Islamicization centered on Indonesia, an important way station between Canton, South Asia, and the Arab peninsula. Indonesia's Islamicization was peaceful, the work of Sufi missionaries from Gujarat and Bengal whose outlook was quite compatible with Hinduism. This focus on Indonesia, furthermore, serves as a useful reminder that today Arabs make up only 15 percent of the world's total Muslim population, with South and Southeast Asia accounting for more than half of the world's total. Indonesia has the world's largest Muslim population, and Islam acts as a strong unifying force for a fragmented archipelago. Although almost 90 percent of Indonesians are Muslim, Indonesia is not an Islamic state, and Islam is not the national faith.

Contemporary media coverage suggests that Islamicization centers on the violence perpetrated by tiny sects of radicals of the world's 1.2 billion Muslims. Many academics and members of the general public appreciate, however, that Islamicization encompasses also other practices such as the annual hajj and long-term migration, a fully developed consumption culture (including food, dress, and pop culture), and transnational communication channels—radio in the era of Pan-Arabism in the 1950s and 1960s, Al-Jazeera satellite TV and websites such as Islam online today. Islamicization is dynamic and open-ended and defies easy summary under simplified labels.

Historically, writes Wang Gungwu, Sinicization "was not associated with coercion and the need to dominate." Rather, it was a matter of China's neighbors emulating Chinese practices that they found to be effective in exercising domestic control and in managing their foreign affairs, especially with China. For example, the calendar, education systems, and civil service exams all required knowledge of Confucianism and Chinese culture. Although Korea was most directly exposed to China, it was not China but Korean Neo-Confucians who imposed Chinese standards and practices. Vietnam underwent a process of self-Confucianization to avoid Chinese occupation. And even though Japan was less exposed to Chinese influences than were these two countries, it, too, imported Tang dynasty norms and practices.

Today, Sinicization is a highly differentiated set of social processes. During the last two to three decades, East and Southeast Asia have developed a regional consumer society in which the Chinese diaspora plays an important role as both producer and consumer. The upper strata of the overseas Chinese are making different choices about their preferred use among the three major Chinese dialects and English. And they have to decide where to send their children for education—Hong Kong, Singapore, Britain, or the United States. Southeast Asia is being remade by the emergence of a new group of Anglo-Chinese who are fluent in English and comfortable with Anglo-American liberal norms.

AMERICA—SINGLE OR MULTIPLE TRADITIONS?

Let us then turn to thinking about America as an exemplar of an imperial civilization. I do not view the United States and America as a conventional nation-state. The conventional nomenclature is not wrong, but incomplete. Compared to others the United States is a state on steroids, inhabiting the border that separates state from empire. And compared to others America is an assertive nation that is also a civilization, endowed with a syncretist amalgam of identities. Should we think about America in unitary or pluralist terms?

The Good, the Bad and the Ugly is the title of Sergio Leone's spaghetti Western from the 1960s—and an apt summary of single tradition arguments. In conventional accounts the United States is good, in revisionist ones it is bad, and in realist ones it is ugly. I argue that single-tradition arguments (as developed, for example, by Louis Hartz and Samuel Huntington) yield a less comprehensive and compelling understanding of the United States than do multiple-tradition arguments (as developed, for example, by Rogers Smith and Stephen Skowronek).

Single-Tradition Arguments

More than half a century ago, Louis Hartz's *Liberal Tradition in America* developed an argument that has remained foundational for how we understand America today. Hartz proposed a consensus view of American culture and identity. Without a reactionary, feudal past, America lacks a revolutionary socialist future. Lockean liberalism has snuffed out all alternative political traditions and imaginations. And American liberalism is a frozen fragment of bourgeois liberalism, transplanted from the Old World to the New. The American South, to be sure, resembled Europe in several ways. But after the Civil War it was relegated to a position of political marginality. America thus remained in the iron grip of a tyrannical liberal tradition.

This single-tradition theory yields many interesting insights. Hartz argues, for example, that American law is so important because America's political philosophy is so impoverished. Pragmatism as America's only genuine philosophical innovation is deeply shaped by Lockean liberalism. Only a country that takes its ethics for granted can convert all problems into matters of technique. Furthermore, because liberalism is hegemonic, it needs no party as its advocate. David Vogel has shown how the hegemony of Lockean liberalism has emasculated the self-confidence of American business. As the main pillar and beneficiary of hegemonic liberalism, it has never been tested in serious political battle with other actors. Liberal unanimity can easily tip over from a lack of tolerance into tyrannical conformity. And foreign policy feeds a messianic impulse to impose Lockean liberalism on a global scale. Making America safe for the world, as Theodore Lowi famously argued, remains today as pressing a task as making the world safe for democracy.

Although his views have shifted over time, Samuel Huntington initially proposed a single-tradition theory of America. In his book *American Politics: The Promise of Disharmony*, Huntington followed Hartz in defining the American Creed first and foremost in terms of political ideals of rights, democracy, and the rule of law. Twenty-five years later, in his last book, *Who Are We?*, Huntington rejects this view as too one-sided and insists that the American Creed has been rooted primarily in a culture shaped by dissenting Protestantism and English political traditions that are now at risk. This more recent view of the American Creed is broader in the sense of incorporating both cultural and political components, and narrower in the sense of including fewer types of people. His original conception, inspired by Hartz, Huntington now argues is inadequate for building or rebuilding America's walls. The thrust of Huntington's civilizational argument is division and clash; the focus of his Creedal argument is assimilation or exclusion.

Huntington views the American Constitution as the source of liberal political ideals and a secular, constitutional patriotism that simply lacks sufficient Creedal power. Multiculturalism and multiracialism have become mainstream values. Business and the professions embrace economic globalization. And an unprecedented wave of legal and illegal immigration is threatening to make America Hispanic. The result is a surging of subgroup identities that are both eroding and fracturing the American Creed. Huntington's argument overlooks that the Constitution crystallized one of the civilizational identities of the New World.

The constitution has become an inexhaustible source of contestation over a civil religion that intertwines America's biblical and republican traditions.

For Huntington, the glue that holds America together is not the Constitution but a culture of seventeenth and eighteenth century dissenting Anglo-Protestant sects expressing Christian religious commitments, adherence to a common language, and English concepts of the rule of law, the responsibility of rulers, and the rights of individuals. That culture empowers individualism, supports a strong work ethic, and creates a duty for individuals to create heaven on earth. The empirical evidence, both historical and contemporary, puts into question some of Huntington's most important claims.

Contra Huntington, Alan Wolfe argues that America was not shaped by dissenting Anglo-Protestant sects. In the seventeenth century two of the American churches were established rather than dissenting. Puritans, to be sure, were a dissenting sect in England. But once they arrived in America, they became an established church in Massachusetts. New York and New Jersey were settled largely by Dutch immigrants. Catholics came to play a prominent role in Maryland. Baptists founded Rhode Island. And in Pennsylvania, German and British Quakers played a prominent role. Historians point out that Protestants have disagreed vehemently about the content of their culture. Dissenting Protestants were at the forefront of the Second Great Awakening of the 1820s and 1830s, a rebellion against the orthodoxies of the more established Calvinist Churches. To them, individuals had some influence over their own salvation rather than leaving matters to a distant God. Protestantism is too lumpy a category to engage the historical evidence. While it is true that congregationalism eventually conquered all American churches, an unending stream of immigrants continues to shape church culture while assimilating into it. The American Creed emerged thus not from dissenting Anglo-Protestant sects but from multiple religious traditions that date back to the very origins of the American Republic. Wolfe's critique offers a form of multiple-tradition theory in the religious sphere.

Similarly, students of contemporary immigration take exception to Huntington's argument about Mexican immigration compared to prior waves of immigrants. In this view, discriminatory practices and power differences between those subscribing to the American Creed and those trying to join it—not the choices and plans of Mexican or Latino immigrants—are slowing the process of integration and assimilation. Worries about immigration predate the origin of the United States. Most specialists agree that there is precious little evidence suggesting that the adaptability of the most recent wave of immigrants is very different from that of earlier ones.

"THOSE PEOPLE"

Let me conclude. The analysis of global and American politics offer different analytical perspectives to articulate, more or less explicitly, contrasting political visions about building up and tearing down walls. I have argued that pluralist conceptions of civilizations and multiple-tradition theories of American politics capture global and American politics more accurately than do unitary conceptions and single-tradition theories. They provide for our analysis of world politics and American foreign policy an analytically less confining and empirically better-grounded view than does the assumption of international anarchy. Furthermore, they capture better the core of American politics. The divisions over its multiple traditions, not its unity, show America as the deeply flawed political community it is, and the enormous promise it holds. Debates and disagreements make America more engaging to and engaged with other civilizations than single-tradition theories and unitary conceptions can convey.

A few years ago I listened to a lecture by Gregory Ward, a linguist teaching at Northwestern. Ward spoke about generic demonstratives. Genericity, he argued, is a widespread linguistic category that forms the basis of knowledge acquisition, distinctively realized in each language. Demonstratives are noun phrases headed by a demonstrative article such as in "those Canadians," "those Americans," and "those people." Generic demonstratives tend to create distance between self and other, imposing uniformity on both rather than emphasizing plurality. They are based on shared beliefs or common knowledge as an essential precondition to, and integral part of, the collective identities we hold.

Unitary conceptions of civilizations and single-tradition theories of American politics are rich in the implicit and unacknowledged common knowledge about self and other that generic demonstratives activate. The success that Huntington's thesis of civilizational clash enjoyed with a broad reading public in the United States and abroad had much to do with the fact that his new paradigm did not differ very much from the old—in two senses of the word. It built on the nineteenth-century tradition of civilizational analysis. And it replaced the political and economic clash between Communist authoritarianism in the East and capitalist democracy in the West with the civilizational clash between a cultural West and an Islamic and Sinic East. Far from replacing our intellectual map of the world, Huntington's book offered no more than a modest updating, based on unacknowledged, common knowledge.

The argument I have developed here has implications for some of the central issues widely debated in political science. Common knowledge is often enormously important for understanding the success of our arguments. Success often hinges on implicitly shared assumptions between author and audience. What is and what is not common knowledge? How does that knowledge emerge and change? Is it tacit or explicit? And what are its implications for politics? Besides the development of arguments based on strong evidence, inquiring into the common-knowledge assumptions of widely shared theories strikes me as an important task of contemporary political analysis. Beholden to a specific cultural context, common knowledge assumptions are too often taken for granted rather than questioned. Political science benefits from both analyses that simplify and analyses that problematize. Those rationalists or model builders must simplify and express themselves with numerical symbols requiring mathematical and statistical training. And those theorists—normative, critical, comparative, constructivist, and otherwise—must problematize foundational philosophical issues and express themselves in prose requiring the mastery of foreign languages. "Those people," it seems, dot our walled political science landscape. We encounter them at every occasion—in the lecture hall, in seminar, and at conferences.

Many of our most important theories of international relations and foreign policy share in unacknowledged common knowledge. The distinction between enemy and friend, for example, surely improves the analytical power of realist theory. But it risks entrapping us in what Susanne Hoeber Rudolph has called the "imperialism of categories," which forces a complicated reality into rigid preconceptions. The conceptual apparatus that such simplifications rely upon typically offers us a definition of political problems and solutions that makes us take for granted what should be questioned—the politics of primordiality. Our understanding is enhanced less by the labeling of self and other, and more by the analysis of the political processes by which real and fabricated enemies and threats are made and unmade—an explosive subject, as Americans have learned once again in recent years. In teaching our students, writing our books, speaking up as citizens, and advising our governments, it is one of our most urgent tasks as scholars to acknowledge, through the analytical lenses we deploy, the pluralism, multiplicity, and contradictions that define both American and world politics. If we fail to do so, we risk rebuilding a world of walls separating us unnecessarily from "those people."

Champions of a parsimonious social science embrace the "imperialism of categories." They seek to free us, mistakenly in my opinion, from context as they build a social science grounded in universal standards. In doing so, they overlook that universal assumptions and arguments are always deeply embedded in unacknowledged common knowledge and the unexamined parochialism it reflects. International and comparative perspectives can counteract what we tend to take for granted and thus protect us from a myopic view of American politics. A rigorous political science needs to be built on the foundation of contextual and comparative historical studies, which helps us to uncover tacit knowledge. Within particular parameters, we can arrive at historically bounded generalizations that identify material and ideational structures and the agents that move within and between them to create, over time, both choice and change. Such contextual knowledge is also indispensable for informed political judgments about the trade-offs between universalistic and particularistic standards by which we evaluate different political practices.

Let me then end this lecture with a reading of an excerpt from Constantine Cavafy's poem "Waiting for the Barbarians," written in 1898 and first published in 1904:

Why all of a sudden this unrest
and confusion? (How solemn the faces have become).
Why are the streets and squares clearing quickly,
and all return to their homes, so deep in thought?
Because night is here but the barbarians have not come.
And some people arrived from the borders,
and said that there are no longer any barbarians.
And now what shall become of us without any barbarians?
Those people were some kind of solution.

The Sovereign State Is Just About Dead

FROM, "SOVEREIGNTY" BY STEPHEN D. KRASNER

Very wrong. Sovereignty was never quite as vibrant as many contemporary observers suggest. The conventional norms of sovereignty have always been challenged. A few states, most notably the United States, have had autonomy, control, and recognition for most of their existence, but most others have not. The polities of many weaker states have been persistently penetrated, and stronger nations have not been immune to external influence. China was occupied. The constitutional arrangements of Japan and Germany were directed by the United States after World War II. The United Kingdom, despite its rejection of the euro, is part of the European Union.

Even for weaker states—whose domestic structures have been influenced by outside actors, and whose leaders have very little control over transborder movements or even activities within their own country—sovereignty remains attractive. Although sovereignty might provide little more than international recognition, that recognition guarantees access to international organizations and sometimes to international finance. It offers status to individual leaders. While the great powers of Europe have eschewed many elements of sovereignty, the United States, China, and Japan have neither the interest nor the inclination to abandon their usually effective claims to domestic autonomy.

In various parts of the world, national borders still represent the fault lines of conflict, whether it is Israelis and Palestinians fighting over the status of Jerusalem, Indians and Pakistanis threatening to go nuclear over Kashmir, or Ethiopia and Eritrea clashing over disputed territories. Yet commentators nowadays are mostly concerned about the erosion of national borders as a consequence of globalization. Governments and activists alike complain that multilateral institutions such as the United Nations, the World Trade Organization, and the International Monetary Fund overstep their authority by promoting universal standards for everything from human rights and the environment to monetary policy and immigration. However, the most important impact of economic globalization and transnational norms will be to alter the scope of state authority rather than to generate some fundamentally new way to organize political life.

SOVEREIGNTY MEANS FINAL AUTHORITY

Not anymore, if ever. When philosophers Jean Bodin and Thomas Hobbes first elaborated the notion of sovereignty in the 16th and 17th centuries, they were concerned with establishing the legitimacy of a single hierarchy of domestic authority. Although Bodin and Hobbes accepted the existence of divine and natural law, they both (especially Hobbes) believed the word of the sovereign was law. Subjects had no right to revolt. Bodin and Hobbes realized that imbuing the sovereign with such overweening power invited tyranny, but they were predominately concerned with maintaining domestic order, without which they believed there could be no justice. Both were writing in a world riven by sectarian strife. Bodin was almost killed in religious riots in France in 1572. Hobbes published his seminal work, *Leviathan,* only a few years after parliament (composed of Britain's emerging wealthy middle class) had executed Charles I in a civil war that had sought to wrest state control from the monarchy.

This idea of supreme power was compelling, but irrelevant in practice. By the end of the 17th century, political authority in Britain was divided between king and parliament. In the United States, the Founding Fathers established a constitutional structure of checks and balances and multiple sovereignties distributed among local and national interests that were inconsistent with hierarchy and supremacy. The principles of justice, and especially order, so valued by Bodin and Hobbes, have best been provided by modern democratic states whose organizing principles are antithetical to the idea that sovereignty means uncontrolled domestic power.

If sovereignty does not mean a domestic order with a single hierarchy of authority, what does it mean? In the contemporary world, sovereignty primarily has been linked with the idea that states are autonomous and independent from each other. Within their own boundaries, the members of a polity are free to choose their own form of government. A necessary corollary of this claim is the principle of nonintervention: One state does not have a right to intervene in the internal affairs of another.

More recently, sovereignty has come to be associated with the idea of control over transborder movements. When contemporary observers assert that the sovereign state is just about dead, they do not mean that constitutional structures are about to disappear. Instead, they mean that technological change has made it very difficult, or perhaps impossible, for states to control movements across their borders of all kinds of material things (from coffee to cocaine) and not-so-material things (from Hollywood movies to capital flows).

Finally, sovereignty has meant that political authorities can enter into international agreements. They are free to endorse any contract they find attractive. Any treaty among states is legitimate provided that it has not been coerced.

THE PEACE OF WESTPHALIA PRODUCED THE MODERN SOVEREIGN STATE

No, it came later. Contemporary pundits often cite the 1648 Peace of Westphalia (actually two separate treaties, Münster and Osnabrück) as the political big bang that created the modern system of autonomous states. Westphalia—which ended the Thirty Years' War against the hegemonic power of the Holy Roman Empire—delegitimized the already waning transnational role of the Catholic Church and validated the idea that international relations should be driven by balance-of-power considerations rather than the ideals of Christendom. But Westphalia was first and foremost a new constitution for the Holy Roman Empire. The preexisting right of the principalities in the empire to make treaties was affirmed, but the Treaty of Münster stated that "such Alliances be not against the Emperor, and the Empire, nor against the Publick Peace, and this Treaty, and without prejudice to the Oath by which every one is bound to the Emperor and the Empire." The domestic political structures of the principalities remained embedded in the Holy Roman Empire. The Duke of Saxony, the Margrave of Brandenburg, the Count of Palatine, and the Duke of Bavaria were affirmed as electors who (along with the archbishops of Mainz,

Trier, and Cologne) chose the emperor. They did not become or claim to be kings in their own right.

Perhaps most important, Westphalia established rules for religious tolerance in Germany. The treaties gave lip service to the principle (*cuius regio, eius religio*) that the prince could set the religion of his territory—and then went on to violate this very principle through many specific provisions. The signatories agreed that the religious rules already in effect would stay in place. Catholics and Protestants in German cities with mixed populations would share offices. Religious issues had to be settled by a majority of both Catholics and Protestants in the diet and courts of the empire. None of the major political leaders in Europe endorsed religious toleration in principle, but they recognized that religious conflicts were so volatile that it was essential to contain rather than repress sectarian differences. All in all, Westphalia is a pretty medieval document, and its biggest explicit innovation—provisions that undermined the power of princes to control religious affairs within their territories—was antithetical to the ideas of national sovereignty that later became associated with the so-called Westphalian system.

UNIVERSAL HUMAN RIGHTS ARE AN UNPRECEDENTED CHALLENGE TO SOVEREIGNTY

Wrong. The struggle to establish international rules that compel leaders to treat their subjects in a certain way has been going on for a long time. Over the centuries the emphasis has shifted from religious toleration, to minority rights (often focusing on specific ethnic groups in specific countries), to human rights (emphasizing rights enjoyed by all or broad classes of individuals). In a few instances states have voluntarily embraced international supervision, but generally the weak have acceded to the preferences of the strong: The Vienna settlement following the Napoleonic wars guaranteed religious toleration for Catholics in the Netherlands. All of the successor states of the Ottoman Empire, beginning with Greece in 1832 and ending with Albania in 1913, had to accept provisions for civic and political equality for religious minorities as a condition for international recognition. The peace settlements following World War I included extensive provisions for the protection of minorities. Poland, for instance, agreed to refrain from holding elections on Saturday because such balloting would have violated the Jewish Sabbath. Individuals could bring complaints against governments through a minority rights bureau established within the League of Nations.

But as the Holocaust tragically demonstrated, interwar efforts at international constraints on domestic practices failed dismally. After World War II, human, rather than minority, rights became the focus of attention. The United Nations Charter endorsed both human rights and the classic sovereignty principle of nonintervention. The 20-plus human rights accords that have been signed during the last half century cover a wide range of issues including genocide, torture, slavery, refugees, stateless persons, women's rights, racial discrimination, children's rights, and forced labor. These U.N. agreements, however, have few enforcement mechanisms, and even their provisions for reporting violations are often ineffective.

The tragic and bloody disintegration of Yugoslavia in the 1990s revived earlier concerns with ethnic rights. International recognition of the Yugoslav successor states was conditional upon their acceptance of constitutional provisions guaranteeing minority rights. The Dayton accords established externally controlled authority structures in Bosnia, including a Human Rights Commission (a majority of whose members were appointed by the Western European states). NATO created a de facto protectorate in Kosovo.

The motivations for such interventions—humanitarianism and security—have hardly changed. Indeed, the considerations that brought the great powers into the Balkans following the wars of the 1870s were hardly different from those that engaged NATO and Russia in the 1990s.

GLOBALIZATION UNDERMINES STATE CONTROL

No. State control could never be taken for granted. Technological changes over the last 200 years have increased the flow of people, goods, capital, and ideas—but the problems posed by such movements are not new. In many ways, states are better able to respond now than they were in the past.

The impact of the global media on political authority (the so-called CNN effect) pales in comparison to the havoc that followed the invention of the printing press. Within a decade after Martin Luther purportedly nailed his 95 theses to the Wittenberg church door, his ideas had circulated throughout Europe. Some political leaders seized upon the principles of the Protestant Reformation as a way to legitimize secular political authority. No sovereign monarch could contain the spread of these concepts, and some lost not only their lands but also their heads. The sectarian controversies of the 16th and 17th centuries were perhaps more politically consequential than any subsequent transnational flow of ideas.

In some ways, international capital movements were more significant in earlier periods than they are now. During the 19th century, Latin American states (and to a lesser extent Canada, the United States, and Europe) were beset by boom-and-bust cycles associated with global financial crises. The Great Depression, which had a powerful effect on the domestic politics of all major states, was precipitated by an international collapse of credit. The Asian financial crisis of the late 1990s was not nearly as devastating. Indeed, the speed with which countries recovered from the Asian flu reflects how a better working knowledge of economic theories and more effective central banks have made it easier for states to secure the advantages (while at the same time minimizing the risks) of being enmeshed in global financial markets.

In addition to attempting to control the flows of capital and ideas, states have long struggled to manage the impact of international trade. The opening of long-distance trade for bulk commodities in the 19th century created fundamental cleavages in all of the major states. Depression and plummeting grain prices made it possible for German Chancellor Otto von Bismarck to prod the landholding aristocracy into a protectionist alliance with urban heavy industry (this coalition of "iron and rye" dominated German politics for decades). The tariff question was a basic divide in U.S. politics for much of the last half of the 19th and first half of the 20th centuries. But, despite growing levels of imports and exports since 1950, the political salience of trade has receded because national governments have developed social welfare strategies that cushion the impact of international competition, and workers with higher skill levels are better able to adjust to changing international conditions. It has become easier, not harder, for states to manage the flow of goods and services.

GLOBALIZATION IS CHANGING THE SCOPE OF STATE CONTROL

Yes. The reach of the state has increased in some areas but contracted in others. Rulers have recognized that their effective control can be enhanced by walking away from issues they cannot resolve. For instance, beginning with the Peace of Westphalia, leaders chose to surrender their control over religion because it proved too volatile. Keeping religion within the scope of state authority undermined, rather than strengthened, political stability.

Monetary policy is an area where state control expanded and then ultimately contracted. Before the 20th century, states had neither the administrative competence nor the inclination to conduct independent monetary policies. The mid-20th century effort to control monetary affairs, which was associated with Keynesian economics, has now been reversed due to the magnitude of short-term capital flows and the inability of some states to control inflation. With the exception of Great Britain, the major European states have established a single monetary authority. Confronting recurrent hyperinflation, Ecuador adopted the U.S. dollar as its currency in 2000.

Along with the erosion of national currencies, we now see the erosion of national citizenship—the notion that an individual should be a citizen of one and only one country, and that the state has exclusive claims to that person's loyalty. For many states, there is no longer a sharp distinction between citizens and noncitizens. Permanent residents, guest workers, refugees, and undocumented immigrants are entitled to some bundle of rights even if they cannot vote. The ease of travel and the desire of many countries to attract either capital or skilled workers have increased incentives to make citizenship a more flexible category.

Although government involvement in religion, monetary affairs, and claims to loyalty has declined, overall government activity, as reflected in taxation and government expenditures, has increased as a percentage of national income since the 1950s among the most economically advanced states. The extent of a country's social welfare programs tends to go hand in hand with its level of integration within the global economy. Crises of authority and control have been most pronounced in the states that have been the most isolated, with sub-Saharan Africa offering the largest number of unhappy examples.

NGOs ARE NIBBLING AT NATIONAL SOVEREIGNTY

To some extent. Transnational nongovernmental organizations (NGOs) have been around for quite awhile, especially if you include corporations. In the 18th century, the East India Company possessed political power (and even an expeditionary military force) that rivaled many national governments. Throughout the 19th century, there were transnational movements to abolish slavery, promote the rights of women, and improve conditions for workers.

The number of transnational NGOs, however, has grown tremendously, from around 200 in 1909 to over 17,000 today. The availability of inexpensive and very fast communications technology has made it easier for such groups to organize and make an impact on public policy and international law—the international agreement banning land mines being a recent case in point. Such groups prompt questions about sovereignty because they appear to threaten the integrity of domestic decision making. Activists who lose on their home territory can pressure foreign governments, which may in turn influence decision makers in the activists' own nation.

But for all of the talk of growing NGO influence, their power to affect a country's domestic affairs has been limited when compared to governments, international organizations, and multinational corporations. The United Fruit Company had more influence in Central America in the early part of the 20th century than any NGO could hope to have anywhere in the contemporary world. The International Monetary Fund and other multilateral financial institutions now routinely negotiate conditionality agreements that involve not only specific economic targets but also domestic institutional changes, such as pledges to crack down on corruption and break up cartels.

Smaller, weaker states are the most frequent targets of external efforts to alter domestic institutions, but more powerful states are not immune. The openness of the U.S. political system means that not only NGOs, but also foreign governments, can play some role in political decisions. (The Mexican government, for instance, lobbied heavily for the passage of the North American Free Trade Agreement.) In fact, the permeability of the American polity makes the United States a less threatening partner; nations are more willing to sign on to U.S.-sponsored international arrangements because they have some confidence that they can play a role in U.S. decision making.

SOVEREIGNTY BLOCKS CONFLICT RESOLUTION

Yes, sometimes. Rulers as well as their constituents have some reasonably clear notion of what sovereignty means—exclusive control within a given territory—even if this norm has been challenged frequently by inconsistent principles (such as universal human rights) and violated in practice (the U.S.- and British-enforced no-fly zones over Iraq). In fact, the political importance of conventional sovereignty rules has made it harder to solve some problems. There is, for instance, no conventional sovereignty solution for Jerusalem, but it doesn't require much imagination to think of alternatives: Divide the city into small pieces; divide the Temple Mount vertically with the Palestinians controlling the top and the Israelis the bottom; establish some kind of international authority; divide control over different issues (religious practices versus taxation, for instance) among different authorities. Any one of these solutions would be better for most Israelis and Palestinians than an ongoing stalemate, but political leaders on both sides have had trouble delivering a settlement because they are subject to attacks by counterelites who can wave the sovereignty flag.

Conventional rules have also been problematic for Tibet. Both the Chinese and the Tibetans might be better off if Tibet could regain some of the autonomy it had as a tributary state within the traditional Chinese empire. Tibet had extensive local control, but symbolically (and sometimes through tribute payments) recognized the supremacy of the emperor. Today, few on either side would even know what a tributary state is, and even if the leaders of Tibet worked out some kind of settlement that would give their country more self-government, there would be no guarantee that they could gain the support of their own constituents.

If, however, leaders can reach mutual agreements, bring along their constituents, or are willing to use coercion, sovereignty rules can be violated in inventive ways. The Chinese, for instance, made Hong Kong a special administrative region after the transfer from British rule, allowed a foreign judge to sit on the Court of Final Appeal, and secured acceptance by other states not only for Hong Kong's participation in a number of international organizations but also for separate visa agreements and recognition of a distinct Hong Kong passport. All of these measures violate conventional sovereignty rules since Hong Kong does not have juridical independence. Only by inventing a unique status for Hong Kong, which involved the acquiescence of other states, could China claim sovereignty while simultaneously preserving the confidence of the business community.

THE EUROPEAN UNION IS A NEW MODEL FOR SUPRANATIONAL GOVERNANCE

Yes, but only for the Europeans. The European Union (EU) really is a new thing, far more interesting in terms of sovereignty than Hong Kong. It is not a conventional international organization because its member states are now so intimately linked with one another that withdrawal is not a viable option. It is not likely to become a "United States of Europe"—a large federal state that might look something like the United States of America—because the interests, cultures, economies, and domestic institutional arrangements of its members are too diverse. Widening the EU to include the former communist states of Central Europe would further complicate any efforts to move toward a political organization that looks like a conventional sovereign state.

The EU is inconsistent with conventional sovereignty rules. Its member states have created supranational institutions (the European Court of Justice, the European Commission, and the Council of Ministers) that can make decisions opposed by some member states. The rulings of the court have direct effect and supremacy within national judicial systems, even though these doctrines were never explicitly endorsed in any treaty. The European Monetary Union created a central bank that now controls monetary affairs for three of the union's four largest states. The Single European Act and the Maastricht Treaty provide for majority or qualified majority, but not unanimous, voting in some issue areas. In one sense, the European Union is a product of state sovereignty because it has been created through voluntary agreements among its member states. But, in another sense, it fundamentally contradicts conventional understandings of sovereignty because these same agreements have undermined the juridical autonomy of its individual members.

The European Union, however, is not a model that other parts of the world can imitate. The initial moves toward integration could not have taken place without the political and economic support of the United States, which was, in the early years of the Cold War, much more interested in creating a strong alliance that could effectively oppose the Soviet Union than it was in any potential European challenge to U.S. leadership. Germany, one of the largest states in the European Union, has been the most consistent supporter of an institutional structure that would limit Berlin's own freedom of action, a reflection of the lessons of two devastating wars and the attractiveness of a European identity for a country still grappling with the sins of the Nazi era. It is hard to imagine that other regional powers such as China, Japan, or Brazil, much less the United States, would have any interest in tying their own hands in similar ways. (Regional trading agreements such as Mercosur and NAFTA have very limited supranational provisions and show few signs of evolving into broader monetary or political unions.) The EU is a new and unique institutional structure, but it will coexist with, not displace, the sovereign-state model.

The Future of American Power

JOSEPH S. NYE JR.

The twenty-first century began with a very unequal distribution of power resources. With five percent of the world's population, the United States accounted for about a quarter of the world's economic output, was responsible for nearly half of global military expenditures, and had the most extensive cultural and educational soft-power resources. All this is still true, but the future of U.S. power is hotly debated. Many observers have interpreted the 2008 global financial crisis as the beginning of American decline. The National Intelligence Council, for example, has projected that in 2025, "the U.S. will remain the preeminent power, but that American dominance will be much diminished."

Power is the ability to attain the outcomes one wants, and the resources that produce it vary in different contexts. Spain in the sixteenth century took advantage of its control of colonies and gold bullion, the Netherlands in the seventeenth century profited from trade and finance, France in the eighteenth century benefited from its large population and armies, and the United Kingdom in the nineteenth century derived power from its primacy in the Industrial Revolution and its navy. This century is marked by a burgeoning revolution in information technology and globalization, and to understand this revolution, certain pitfalls need to be avoided.

First, one must beware of misleading metaphors of organic decline. Nations are not like humans, with predictable life spans. Rome remained dominant for more than three centuries after the peak of its power, and even then it did not succumb to the rise of another state. For all the fashionable predictions of China, India, or Brazil surpassing the United States in the next decades, the greater threat may come from modern barbarians and nonstate actors. In an information-based world, power diffusion may pose a bigger danger than power transition. Conventional wisdom holds that the state with the largest army prevails, but in the information age, the state (or the nonstate actor) with the best story may sometimes win.

Power today is distributed in a pattern that resembles a complex three-dimensional chess game. On the top chessboard, military power is largely unipolar, and the United States is likely to retain primacy for quite some time. On the middle chessboard, economic power has been multipolar for more than a decade, with the United States, Europe, Japan, and China as the major players and others gaining in importance. The bottom chessboard is the realm of transnational relations. It includes nonstate actors as diverse as bankers who electronically transfer funds, terrorists who traffic weapons, hackers who threaten cybersecurity, and challenges such as pandemics and climate change. On this

Foreign Affairs, November/December, pg. 2–12

bottom board, power is widely diffused, and it makes no sense to speak of unipolarity, multipolarity, or hegemony.

In interstate politics, the most important factor will be the continuing return of Asia to the world stage. In 1750, Asia had more than half the world's population and economic output. By 1900, after the Industrial Revolution in Europe and the United States, Asia's share shrank to one-fifth of global economic output. By 2050, Asia will be well on its way back to its historical share. The rise of China and India may create instability, but this is a problem with precedents, and history suggests how policies can affect the outcome.

HEGEMONIC DECLINE?

It is currently fashionable to compare the United States' power to that of the United Kingdom a century ago and to predict a similar hegemonic decline. Some Americans react emotionally to the idea of decline, but it would be counterintuitive and ahistorical to believe that the United States will have a preponderant share of power resources forever. The word "decline" mixes up two different dimensions: absolute decline, in the sense of decay, and relative decline, in which the power resources of other states grow or are used more effectively.

The analogy with British decline is misleading. The United Kingdom had naval supremacy and an empire on which the sun never set, but by World War I, the country ranked only fourth among the great powers in its share of military personnel, fourth in GDP, and third in military spending. With the rise of nationalism, protecting the empire became more of a burden than an asset. For all the talk of an American empire, the United States has more freedom of action than the United Kingdom did. And whereas the United Kingdom faced rising neighbors, Germany and Russia, the United States benefits from being surrounded by two oceans and weaker neighbors.

Despite such differences, Americans are prone to cycles of belief in their own decline. The Founding Fathers worried about comparisons to the Roman republic. Charles Dickens observed a century and a half ago, "If its individual citizens, to a man, are to be believed, [the United States] always is depressed, and always is stagnated, and always is at an alarming crisis, and never was otherwise." In the last half century, belief in American decline rose after the Soviet Union launched Sputnik in 1957, after President Richard Nixon's economic adjustments and the oil shocks in the 1970s, and after the closing of rust-belt industries and the budget deficits in the Reagan era. Ten years later, Americans believed that the United States was the sole superpower, and now polls show that many believe in decline again.

Pundits lament the inability of Washington to control states such as Afghanistan or Iran, but they allow the golden glow of the past to color their appraisals. The United States' power is not what it used to be, but it also never really was as great as assumed. After World War II, the United States had nuclear weapons and an overwhelming preponderance of economic power but nonetheless was unable to prevent the "loss" of China, to roll back communism in Eastern Europe, to overcome stalemate in the Korean War, to stop the "loss" of North Vietnam, or to dislodge the Castro regime in Cuba. Power measured in resources rarely equals power measured in preferred outcomes, and cycles of belief in decline reveal more about psychology than they do about real shifts in power resources. Unfortunately, mistaken beliefs in decline—at home and abroad—can lead to dangerous mistakes in policy.

DEBATING DECLINE

Any net assessment of American power in the coming decades will remain uncertain, but analysis is not helped by misleading metaphors of decline. Declinists should be chastened by remembering how wildly exaggerated U.S. estimates of Soviet power in the 1970s and of Japanese power in the 1980s were. Equally misguided were those prophets of unipolarity who argued a decade ago that the United States was so powerful that it could do as it wished and others had no choice but to follow. Today, some confidently predict that the twenty-first century will see China replace the United States as the world's leading state, whereas others argue with equal confidence that the twenty-first century will be the American century. But unforeseen events often confound such projections. There is always a range of possible futures, not one.

As for the United States' power relative to China's, much will depend on the uncertainties of future political change in China. Barring any political upheaval, China's size and high rate of economic growth will almost certainly increase its relative strength vis-à-vis the United States. This will bring China closer to the United States in power resources, but it does not necessarily mean that China will surpass the United States as the most powerful country—even if China suffers no major domestic political setbacks. Projections based on GDP growth alone are one-dimensional. They ignore U.S. advantages in military and soft power, as well as China's geopolitical disadvantages in the Asian balance of power.

Among the range of possible futures, the more likely are those in which China gives the United States a run for its money but does not surpass it in overall power in the first half of this century. Looking back at history, the British strategist Lawrence Freedman has noted that the United States has "two features which distinguish it from the dominant great powers of the past: American power is based on alliances rather than colonies and is associated with an ideology that is flexible. . . . Together they provide a core of relationships and values to which America can return even after it has overextended itself." And looking to the future, the scholar Anne-Marie Slaughter has argued that the United States' culture of openness and innovation will keep it central in a world where networks supplement, if not fully replace, hierarchical power.

The United States is well placed to benefit from such networks and alliances, if it follows smart strategies. Given Japanese concerns about the rise of Chinese power, Japan is more likely to seek U.S. support to preserve its independence than ally with China. This enhances the United States' position. Unless Americans act foolishly with regard to Japan, an allied East Asia is not a plausible candidate to displace the United States. It matters that the two entities in the world with per capita incomes and sophisticated economies similar to those of the United States—the European Union and Japan—both are U.S. allies. In traditional realist terms of balances of power resources, that makes a large difference for the net position of U.S. power. And in a more positive-sum view of power—that of holding power with, rather than over, other countries—Europe and Japan provide the largest pools of resources for dealing with common transnational problems. Although their interests are not identical to those of the United States, they share overlapping social and governmental networks with it that provide opportunities for cooperation.

On the question of absolute, rather than relative, American decline, the United States faces serious problems in areas such as debt, secondary education, and political gridlock. But they are only part of the picture. Of the multiple possible futures, stronger cases can be made for the positive ones than the negative ones. But among the negative futures, the most plausible is one in which the United States overreacts to terrorist attacks by turning inward and thus cuts itself off from the strength it obtains from openness. Barring such mistaken strategies, however, there are solutions to the major American problems of today. (Long-term debt, for example, could be solved by putting in place, after the economy recovers, spending cuts and consumption taxes that could pay for entitlements.) Of course, such solutions may forever remain out of reach. But it is important to distinguish hopeless situations for which there are no solutions from those that could in principle be solved. After all, the bipartisan reforms of the Progressive era a century ago rejuvenated a badly troubled country.

A NEW NARRATIVE

It is time for a new narrative about the future of U.S. power. Describing power transition in the twenty-first century as a traditional case of hegemonic decline is inaccurate, and it can lead to dangerous policy implications if it encourages China to engage in adventurous policies or the United States to overreact out of fear. The United States is not in absolute decline, and in relative terms, there is a reasonable probability that it will remain more powerful than any single state in the coming decades.

At the same time, the country will certainly face a rise in the power resources of many others—both states and nonstate actors. Because globalization will spread technological capabilities and information technology will allow more people to communicate, U.S. culture and the U.S. economy will become less globally dominant than they were at the start of this century. Yet it is unlikely that the United States will decay like ancient Rome, or even that it will be surpassed by another state, including China.

The problem of American power in the twenty-first century, then, is not one of decline but what to do in light of the realization that even the largest country cannot achieve the outcomes it wants without the help of others. An increasing number of challenges will require the United States to exercise power with others as much as power over others. This, in turn, will require a deeper understanding of power, how it is changing, and how to construct "smart power" strategies that combine hard- and soft-power resources in an information age. The country's capacity to maintain alliances and create networks will be an important dimension of its hard and soft power.

Power is not good or bad per se. It is like calories in a diet: more is not always better. If a country has too few power resources, it is less likely to obtain its preferred outcomes. But too much power (in terms of resources) has often proved to be a curse when it leads to overconfidence and inappropriate strategies. David slew Goliath because Goliath's superior power resources led him to pursue an inferior strategy, which in turn led to his defeat and death. A smart-power narrative for the twenty-first century is not about maximizing power or preserving hegemony. It is about finding ways to combine resources in successful strategies in the new context of power diffusion and "the rise of the rest."

As the largest power, the United States will remain important in global affairs, but the twentieth century narrative about an American century and American primacy—as well as narratives of American decline—is misleading when it is used as a guide to the type of strategy that will be necessary in the twenty-first century. The coming decades are not likely to see a post-American world, but the United States will need a smart strategy that combines hard- and soft-power resources—and that emphasizes alliances and networks that are responsive to the new context of a global information age.

VISUAL REVIEW

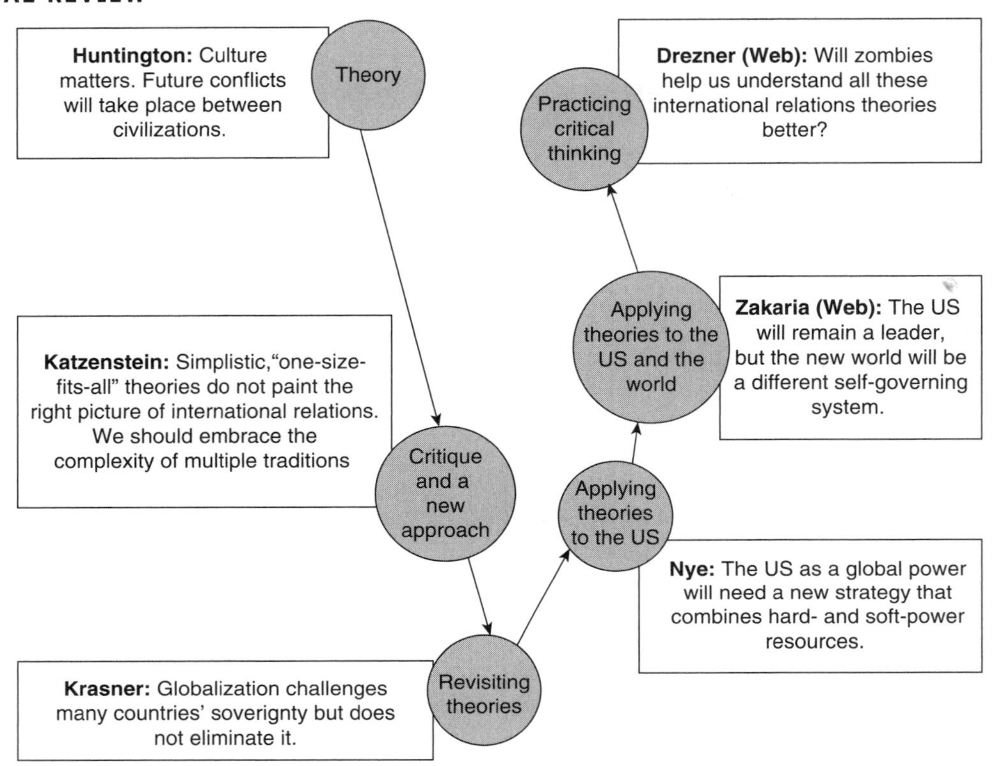

Section 2

Historical Context I: Realism and Sovereign States

China's moves to assert its territorial claims in the South China Sea are adding to the growing tensions in the region. Several Asian countries such as Japan and South Korea are quickly modernizing their forces. Did Stephen Walt's claim of "distribution of burdens" within an alliance mean that the United States, as a traditional guarantor of Japan's and South Korean's security, may be under threat of being dragged in a conflict in South China Sea?
Source: Chinatopix/Associated Press

Thomas Hobbes: Man in a State of Nature Is in a State of War

FROM, *LEVIATHAN* BY THOMAS HOBBES (1588–1679)

Nature hath made men so equal in the faculties of body and mind as that, though there be found one man sometimes manifestly stronger in body or of quicker mind than another, yet when all is reckoned together the difference between man and man is not so considerable as that one man can thereupon claim to himself any benefit to which another may not pretend as well as he. For as to the strength of body, the weakest has strength enough to kill the strongest, either by secret machination or by confederacy with others that are in the same danger with himself.

For such is the nature of men that howsoever they may acknowledge many others to be more witty, or more eloquent or more learned, yet they will hardly believe there be many so wise as themselves; for they see their own wit at hand, and other men's at a distance. But this proveth rather that men are in that point equal, than unequal. For there is not ordinarily a greater sign of the equal distribution of anything than that every man is contented with his share.

From this equality of ability ariseth equality of hope in the attaining of our ends. And therefore if any two men desire the same thing, which nevertheless they cannot both enjoy, they become enemies; and in the way to their end (which is principally their own conservation, and sometimes their delectation only) endeavour to destroy or subdue one another. And from hence it comes to pass that where an invader hath no more to fear than another man's single power, if one plant, sow, build, or possess a convenient seat, others may probably be expected to come prepared with forces united to dispossess and deprive him, not only of the fruit of his labour, but also of his life or liberty. And the invader again is in the like danger of another.

So that in the nature of man, we find three principal causes of quarrel. First, competition; secondly, diffidence; thirdly, glory.

The first maketh men invade for gain; the second, for safety; and the third, for reputation. The first use violence, to make themselves masters of other men's persons, wives, children, and cattle; the second, to defend them; the third, for trifles, as a word, a smile, a different opinion, and any other sign of undervalue, either direct in their persons or by reflection in their kindred, their friends, their nation, their profession, or their name.

Hereby it is manifest that during the time men live without a common power to keep them all in awe, they are in that condition which is called war; and such a war as is of every man against every man. For war consisteth not in battle only, or the act of fighting, but in a tract of time, wherein the will to contend by battle is sufficiently known: and therefore the notion of time is to be considered in the nature of war, as it is in the nature of weather. For as the nature of foul weather lieth not in a shower or two of rain, but in an inclination thereto of many days together: so the nature of war consisteth not in actual fighting, but in the known disposition thereto during all the time there is no assurance to the contrary. All other time is peace.

In such condition there is no place for industry, because the fruit thereof is uncertain: and consequently no culture of the earth; no navigation, nor use of the commodities that may be imported by sea; no commodious building; no instruments of moving and removing such things as require much force; no knowledge of the face of the earth; no account of time; no arts; no letters; no society; and which is worst of all, continual fear, and danger of violent death; and the life of man, solitary, poor, nasty, brutish, and short.

It may peradventure be thought there was never such a time nor condition of war as this; and I believe it was never generally so, over all the world: but there are many places where they live so now. For the savage people in many places of America,

Leviathan (1660)

except the government of small families, the concord whereof dependeth on natural lust, have no government at all, and live at this day in that brutish manner, as I said before. Howsoever, it may be perceived what manner of life there would be, where there were no common power to fear, by the manner of life which men that have formerly lived under a peaceful government use to degenerate into a civil war.

To this war of every man against every man, this also is consequent; that nothing can be unjust. The notions of right and wrong, justice and injustice, have there no place. Where there is no common power, there is no law; where no law, no injustice. Force and fraud are in war the two cardinal virtues. Justice and injustice are none of the faculties neither of the body nor mind. If they were, they might be in a man that were alone in the world, as well as his senses and passions. They are qualities that relate to men in society, not in solitude. It is consequent also to the same condition that there be no propriety, no dominion, no mine and thine distinct; but only that to be every man's that he can get, and for so long as he can keep it. And thus much for the ill condition which man by mere nature is actually placed in; though with a possibility to come out of it, consisting partly in the passions, partly in his reason.

The Twenty Years' Crisis, 1919–1939

EDWARD CARR

The three essential tenets implicit in Machiavelli's doctrine are the foundation-stones of the realist philosophy. In the first place, history is a sequence of cause and effect, whose course can be analyzed and understood by intellectual effort, but not (as the utopians believe) directed by "imagination." Secondly, theory does not (as the utopians assume) create practice, but practice theory. In Machiavelli's words, "good counsels, whencesoever they come, are born of the wisdom of the prince, and not the wisdom of the prince from good counsels." Thirdly, politics are not (as the utopians pretend) a function of ethics, but ethics of politics. Men "are kept honest by constraint." Machiavelli recognized the importance of morality, but thought that there could be no effective morality where there was no effective authority. Morality is the product of power.

The extraordinary vigor and vitality of Machiavelli's challenge to orthodoxy may be attested by the fact that, more than four centuries after he wrote, the most conclusive way of discrediting a political opponent is still to describe him as a disciple of Machiavelli. Bacon was one of the first to praise him for "saying openly and without hypocrisy what men are in the habit of doing, not what they ought to do." Henceforth no political thinker could ignore him. ... "Before the names of just and Unjust can have place," said Hobbes, "there must be some coercive power." Spinoza believed that practical statesmen had contributed more to the understanding of politics than men of theory "and, above all, theologians"; for "they have put themselves to the school of experience, and have therefore taught nothing which does not bear upon our practical needs." In anticipation of Hegel, Spinoza declares that "every man does what he does according to the laws of his nature and to the highest right of nature." The way is thus opened for determinism; and ethics become, in the last analysis, the study of reality.

Modern realism differs, however, in one important respect from that of the sixteenth and seventeenth centuries. Both utopianism and realism accepted and incorporated in their philosophies the eighteenth-century belief in progress, with the

New York: Perrenial, 2001

curious and somewhat paradoxical result that realism became in appearance more "progressive" than utopianism. Utopianism grafted its belief in progress on to its belief in an absolute ethical standard, which remained ex hypothesi static. Realism, having no such sheet-anchor, became more and more dynamic and relativist. Progress became part of the inner essence of the historical process; and mankind was moving forward towards a goal which was left undefined, or was differently defined by different philosophers. The "historical school" of realists had its home in Germany, and its development is traced through the great names of Hegel and Marx.

There can be no reality outside the historical process. It is recorded that Venizelos, on reading in Fisher's *History of Europe* that the Greek invasion of Asia Minor in 1919… was a mistake, smiled ironically and said: "Every enterprise that does not succeed is a mistake." If Wat Tyler's rebellion had succeeded, he would be an English national hero. If the American War of Independence had ended in disaster, the Founding Fathers of the United States would be briefly recorded in history as a gang of turbulent and unscrupulous fanatics. Nothing succeeds like success. "World history," in the famous phrase which Hegel borrowed from Schiller, "is the world court." The popular paraphrase "Might is Right" is misleading only if we attach too restricted a meaning to the word "Might." History creates rights, and therefore right. The doctrine of the survival of the fittest proves that the survivor was, in fact, the fittest to survive. Marx does not seem to have maintained that the victory of the proletariat was just in any other sense than that it was historically inevitable. Hitler believed in the historical mission of the German people.

THE RELATIVITY OF THOUGHT

. . . The realist has thus been enabled to demonstrate that the intellectual theories and ethical standards of utopianism, far from being the expression of absolute and a priori principles, are historically conditioned, being both products of circumstances and interests and weapons framed for the furtherance of interests. "Ethical notions," as Mr. Bertrand Russell has remarked, "are very seldom a cause, but almost always an effect, a means of claiming universal legislative authority for our own preferences, not, as we fondly imagine, the actual ground of those preferences." This is by far the most formidable attack which utopianism has to face; for here the very foundations of its belief are undermined by the realist critique.

"When I was young," writes Mr. Bertrand Russell, "the French ate frogs and were called 'froggies,' but they apparently abandoned this practice when we concluded our *entente* with them in 1904—at any rate, I have never heard it mentioned since that date." Some years later, "the gallant little Jap" of 1905 underwent a converse metamorphosis into "the Prussian of the East." In the nineteenth century, it was a commonplace of British opinion that Germans were efficient and enlightened, and Russians backward and barbarous. About 1910, it was ascertained that Germans (who turned out to be mostly Prussians) were coarse, brutal and narrow-minded, and that Russians had a Slav soul. The vogue of Russian literature in Great Britain, which set in about the same time, was a direct outcome of the political *rapprochement* with Russia. The vogue of Marxism in Great Britain and France, which began on a modest scale after the success of the Bolshevik revolution in Russia, rapidly gathered momentum, particularly among intellectuals, after 1934, when :it was discovered that Soviet Russia was a potential military ally against Germany. It is symptomatic that most people, when challenged, will indignantly deny that they form their opinions in this way; for as Acton long ago observed, "few discoveries are more irritating than those which expose the pedigree of ideas." The conditioning of thought is necessarily a subconscious process.

THE ADJUSTMENT OF THOUGHT TO PURPOSE

. . . For the realist, as a witty writer has put it, truth is "no more than the perception of discordant experience pragmatically adjusted for a particular purpose and for the time being." The purposeful character of thought has been discussed in a previous chapter; and a few examples will suffice here to illustrate the importance of this phenomenon in international politics.

Theories designed to discredit an enemy or potential enemy are one of the commonest forms of purposeful thinking. To depict one's enemies or one's prospective victims as inferior beings in the sight of God has been a familiar technique at any rate since the days of the Old Testament. . . .

More recently, Mr. Churchill told the House of Commons that "there must be a moral basis for British rearmament and foreign policy." It is rare, however, for modern statesmen to express themselves with this frankness; and in contemporary British and American politics, the most powerful influence has been wielded by those more utopian statesmen who are sincerely convinced that policy is deduced from ethical principles, not ethical principles from policy. The realist is nevertheless obliged to uncover the hollowness of this conviction. "The right," said Woodrow Wilson to the United States Congress in 1917, "is more precious than peace,"

The double process of morally discrediting the policy of a potential enemy and morally justifying one's own may be abundantly illustrated from the discussions of disarmament between the two wars. The experience of the Anglo-Saxon Powers, whose naval predominance had been threatened by the submarine, provided an ample opportunity of denouncing the immorality of this new weapon. "Civilization demands," wrote the naval adviser to the American Delegation at the Peace Conference, "that naval warfare be placed on a higher plane" by the abolition of the submarine. Unfortunately the submarine was regarded as a convenient weapon by the weaker French, Italian and Japanese navies; and this particular demand of civilization could not therefore be complied with.

NATIONAL INTEREST AND THE UNIVERSAL GOOD

. . . In 1891, the most popular and brilliant journalist of the day, W. T. Stead, founded the *Review of Reviews*. "We believe in God, in England and in Humanity," ran the editorial manifesto in its opening number. "The English-speaking race is one of the chief of God's chosen agents for executing coming improvements in the lot of mankind." An Oxford professor was convinced in 1912 that the secret of Britain's history was that "in fighting for her own independence she has been fighting for the freedom of Europe, and that the service thus rendered to Europe and to mankind has carried with it the possibility of that larger service to which we give the name Empire."

The first world war carried this conviction to a pitch of emotional frenzy. . . . In 1917, Balfour told the New York Chamber of Commerce that "since August, 1914, the fight has been for the highest spiritual advantages of mankind, without a petty thought or ambition."

In recent times, the same phenomenon has become endemic in the United States. The story how McKinley prayed for divine guidance and decided to annex the Philippines is a classic of modern American history; and this annexation was the occasion of a popular outburst of moral self-approval hitherto more familiar in the foreign policy of Great Britain, than of the United States. Theodore Roosevelt, who believed more firmly than any previous American President in the doctrine *L'etat, c'est moi,* carried the process a step further. The following curious dialogue occurred in his cross-examination during a libel action brought against him in 1915 by a Tammany leader:

> QUERY: How did you know that substantial justice was done?
>
> ROOSEVELT: Because I did it, because . . . I was doing my best.
>
> QUERY: You mean to say that, when you do a thing, thereby substantial justice is done.
>
> ROOSEVELT: I do. When I do a thing, I do it so as to do substantial justice. I mean just that.

Woodrow Wilson was less naively egotistical, but more profoundly confident of the identity of American policy and universal justice. After the bombardment of Vera Cruz in 1914, he assured the world that "the United States bad gone down to Mexico to serve mankind." During the first world war, he advised American naval cadets "not only always to think first of America, but Always, also, to think, first of humanity"—a feat rendered slightly less difficult by his explanation that the United States had been "founded for the benefit of humanity." . . .

It will be observed that utterances of this character proceed almost exclusively from Anglo-Saxon statesmen and writers. . . . —the first explanation, which is popular in English-speaking countries, is that the policies of the English-speaking nations are in fact more virtuous and disinterested than those of Continental states, so that Wilson and Professor Toynbee and Lord Cecil are, broadly speaking, right when they identify the American and British national interests with the interest of mankind. The second explanation, which is popular in Continental countries, is that the English-speaking peoples are past masters in the art of concealing their selfish national interests in the guise of the general good, and that this kind of hypocrisy is a special and characteristic peculiarity of the Anglo-Saxon mind.

It seems unnecessary to accept either of these heroic attempts to cut the knot. The solution is a simple one. Theories of social morality are always the product of a dominant group which identifies itself with the community as a whole, and which possesses facilities denied to subordinate groups or individuals for imposing its view of life on the community. Theories of international morality are, for the same reason and in virtue of the same process, the product of dominant nations or groups of nations. For the past hundred years, and more especially since 1918, the English-speaking peoples have formed the dominant group in the world; and current theories of international morality have been designed to perpetuate their supremacy and expressed in the idiom peculiar to them. . . .

THE REALIST CRITIQUE OF THE HARMONY OF INTERESTS

. . . It is the natural assumption of a prosperous and privileged class, whose members have a dominant voice in the community and are therefore naturally prone to identify its interest with their own. In virtue of this identification, any assailant of the interests of the dominant group is made to incur the odium of assailing the alleged common interest of the whole community, and is told that in making this assault he is attacking his own higher interests. The doctrine of the harmony of interests thus serves as an ingenious moral device invoked, in perfect sincerity, by privileged groups in order to justify and maintain their dominant position. . . . In so far, therefore, as the alleged natural harmony of interests has any reality, it is created by the overwhelming power of the privileged group, and is an excellent illustration of the Machiavellian maxim that morality is the product of Power.

The same analysis may be applied in international relations. British nineteenth-century statesmen, having discovered that free trade promoted British prosperity, were sincerely convinced that, in doing so, it also promoted the prosperity of the world as a whole. British predominance in world trade was at that time so overwhelming that there was a certain undeniable harmony between British interests and the interests of the world. British prosperity flowed over into other countries, and a British economic collapse would have meant world-wide ruin. . . . Nevertheless, this alleged international harmony of interests seemed a mockery to those under-privileged nations whose inferior status and insignificant stake in international trade were consecrated by it. The revolt against it destroyed that overwhelming British preponderance which had provided: a plausible basis for the theory. Economically, Great Britain in the nineteenth century was dominant enough to make a bold bid to impose on the world her own conception of international economic morality. When competition of all against all replaced the domination of the world market by a single Power, conceptions of international economic morality necessarily became chaotic.

THE REALIST CRITIQUE OF INTERNATIONALISM

The concept of internationalism is a special form of the doctrine of the harmony of interests. It yields to the same analysis; and there are the same difficulties about regarding it as an absolute standard independent of the interests and policies of those who promulgate it. . . . It was symptomatic of the growing international predominance of the United States when widespread popularity was enjoyed in the late nineteen-thirties by the book of an American journalist advocating a world union of democracies, in which the United States would play the predominant role.

The exposure of the real basis of the professedly abstract principles commonly invoked in international politics is the most damning and most convincing part of the realist indictment of utopianism. The nature of the charge is frequently misunderstood by those who seek to refute it. The charge is not that human beings fail to live up to their principles. It matters little that Wilson, who thought that the right was more precious than peace, and Briand, who thought that peace came even before justice, and Mr. Eden, who believed in collective security, failed themselves, or failed to induce their countrymen, to apply these principles consistently. What matters is that these supposedly absolute and universal principles were not principles at all, but the unconscious reflections of national policy based on a particular interpretation of national interest at a particular time. There is a sense in which peace and cooperation between nations or classes or individuals is a common and universal end irrespective of conflicting interests and politics. There is a sense in which a common interest exists in the maintenance of order, whether it be international order or "law and order" within the nation. But as soon as the attempt is made to apply these supposedly abstract principles to a concrete political situation, they are revealed as the transparent disguises of selfish vested interests. The bankruptcy of utopianism resides not in its failure to live up to its principles, but in the exposure of its inability to provide any absolute and disinterested standard for the conduct of international affairs. The utopian, faced by the collapse of standards whose interested character he has failed to penetrate, takes refuge in condemnation of a reality which refuses to conform to these standards. . . .

Politics Among Nations: The Struggle for Power and Peace

HANS J. MORGENTHAU

SIX PRINCIPLES OF POLITICAL REALISM

1. Political realism believes that politics, like society in general, is governed by objective laws that have their roots in human nature. In order to improve society it is first necessary to understand the laws by which society lives. The operation of these laws being impervious to our preferences, men will challenge them only at the risk of failure.

Realism, believing as it does in the objectivity of the laws of politics, must also believe in the possibility of developing a rational theory that reflects, however imperfectly and one-sidedly, these objective laws. It believes also, then, in the possibility of distinguishing in politics between truth and opinion-between what is true objectively and rationally, supported by evidence and illuminated by reason, and what is only a subjective judgment, divorced from the facts as they are and informed by prejudice and wishful thinking.

. . . To give meaning to the factual raw material of foreign policy, we must approach political reality with a kind of rational outline, a map that suggests to us the possible meanings of foreign policy. In other words, we put ourselves in the position of a statesman who must meet a certain problem of foreign policy under certain circumstances, and we ask ourselves what the rational alternatives are from which a statesman may choose who must

New York: Alfred A. Knopf, 1978 pp. 4–15

meet this problem under these circumstances (presuming always that he acts in a rational manner), and which of these rational alternatives this particular statesman, acting under these circumstances, is likely to choose. It is the testing of this rational hypothesis against the actual facts and their consequences that gives theoretical meaning to the facts of international politics.

2. The main signpost that helps political realism to find its way through the landscape of international politics is the concept of interest defined in terms of power. This concept provides the link between reason trying to understand international politics and the facts to be understood. It sets politics as an autonomous sphere of action and understanding apart from other spheres, such as economics (understood in terms of interest defined as wealth), ethics, aesthetics, or religion. Without such a concept a theory of politics, international or domestic, would be altogether impossible, for without it we could not distinguish between political and nonpolitical facts, nor could we bring at least a measure of systematic order to the political sphere.

. . . A realist theory of international politics, then, will guard against two popular fallacies: the concern with motives and the concern with ideological preferences.

To search for the clue to foreign policy exclusively in the motives of statesmen is both futile and deceptive. It is futile because motives are the most illusive of psychological data, distorted as they are, frequently beyond recognition, by the interests and emotions of actor and observer alike. Do we really know what our own motives are? And what do we know of the motives of others?

We cannot conclude from the good intentions of a statesman that his foreign policies will be either morally praiseworthy or politically successful. Judging his motives, we can say that he will not intentionally pursue policies that are morally wrong, but we can say nothing about the probability of their success. If we want to know the moral and political qualities of his actions, we must know them, not his motives. How often have statesmen been motivated by the desire to improve the world, and ended by making it worse? And how often have they sought one goal, and ended by achieving something they neither expected nor desired?

Neville Chamberlain's politics of appeasement were, as far as we can judge, inspired by good motives; he was probably less motivated by considerations of personal power than were many other British prime ministers, and he sought to preserve peace and to assure the happiness of all concerned. Yet his policies helped to make the Second World War inevitable, and to bring untold miseries to millions of men. Sir Winston Churchill's motives, on the other hand, were much less universal in scope and much more narrowly directed toward personal and national power, yet the foreign policies that sprang from these inferior motives were certainly superior in moral and political quality to those pursued by his predecessor. . . .

A realist theory of international politics will also avoid the other popular fallacy of equating the foreign policies of a statesman with his philosophic or political sympathies, and of deducing the former from the latter. Statesmen, especially under contemporary conditions, may well make a habit of presenting their foreign policies in terms of their philosophic and political sympathies in order to gain popular support for them. . . .

Especially where foreign policy is conducted under the conditions of democratic control, the need to marshal popular emotions to the support of foreign policy cannot fail to impair the rationality of foreign policy itself. Yet a theory of foreign policy which aims at rationality must for the time being, as it were, abstract from these irrational elements and seek to paint a picture of foreign policy which presents the rational essence to be found in experience, without the contingent deviations from rationality which are also found in experience.

The difference between international politics as it actually is and a rational theory derived from it is like the difference between a photograph and a painted portrait. The photograph shows everything that can be seen by the naked eye; the painted portrait does not show everything that can be seen by the naked eye, but it shows, or at least seeks to show, one thing that the naked eye cannot see: the human essence of the person portrayed.

Political realism contains not only a theoretical but also a normative element. It knows that political reality is replete with contingencies and systemic irrationalities and points to the typical influences they exert upon foreign policy. Yet it shares with all social theory the need, for the sake of theoretical understanding, to stress the rational elements of political reality; for it is these rational elements that make reality intelligible for theory. Political realism presents the theoretical construct of a rational foreign policy which experience can never completely achieve.

At the same time political realism considers a rational foreign policy to be good foreign policy; for only a rational foreign policy minimizes risks and maximizes benefits and, hence, complies both with the moral precept of prudence and the political requirement of success. Political realism wants the photographic picture of the political world to resemble as much as possible its painted portrait. . . .

3. Realism assumes that its key concept of interest defined as power is an objective category which is universally valid, but it does not endow that concept with a meaning that is fixed once and for all. The idea of interest is indeed of the essence of politics and is unaffected by the circumstances of time and place . . .

A small knowledge of human nature will convince us, that, with far the greatest part of mankind, interest is the governing principle; and that almost every man is more or less, under its influence. Motives of public virtue may for a time, or in particular instances, actuate men to the observance of a conduct purely disinterested; but they are not of themselves sufficient to produce persevering conformity to the refined dictates and obligations of social duty. Few men are capable of making a continual sacrifice of all views of private interest, or advantage, to the common good.

. . . The same observations apply to the concept of power. Its content and the manner of its use are determined by the political and cultural environment. Power may comprise anything that establishes and maintains the control of man over man. Thus power covers all social relationships which serve that end, from physical violence to the most subtle psychological ties by which one mind controls another. Power covers the domination of man by man, both when it is disciplined by moral ends and controlled by constitutional safeguards, as in Western democracies, and when it is that untamed and barbaric force which finds its laws in nothing but its own strength and its sole justification in its aggrandizement.

Political realism does not assume that the contemporary conditions under which foreign policy operates, with their extreme instability and the ever present threat of large-scale violence, cannot be changed. The balance of power, for instance, is indeed a perennial element of all pluralistic societies, as the authors of *The Federalist* papers well knew; yet it is capable of operating, as it does in the United States, under the conditions of relative stability and peaceful conflict. If the factors that have given rise to these conditions can be duplicated on the international scene, similar conditions of stability and peace will then prevail there, as they have over long stretches of history among certain nations.

What is true of the general character of international relations is also true of the nation state as the ultimate point of reference of contemporary foreign policy. While the realist indeed believes that interest is the perennial standard by which political action must be judged and directed, the contemporary connection between interest and the nation state is a product of history, and is therefore bound to disappear in the course of history. Nothing in the realist position militates against the assumption that the present division of the political world into nation states will be replaced by larger units of a quite different character, more in keeping with the technical potentialities and the moral requirements of the contemporary world. . . .

4. Political realism is aware of the moral significance of political action. It is also aware of the ineluctable tension between the moral command and the requirements of successful political action

The individual may say for himself: "*Fiat justitia, pereat mundus* (Let justice be done, even if the world perish)," but the state has no right to say so in the name of those who are in its care. Both individual and state must judge political action by universal moral principles, such as that of liberty. Yet while the individual has a moral right to sacrifice himself in defense of such a moral principle, the state has no right to let its moral disapprobation of the infringement of liberty get in the way of successful political action, itself inspired by the moral principle of national survival.

Ethics in the abstract judges action by its conformity with the moral law; political ethics judges action by its political consequences. Classical and medieval philosophy knew this, and so did Lincoln when he said:

I do the very best I know how, the very best I can, and I mean to keep doing so until the end. If the end brings me out all right, what is said against me won't amount to anything. If the end brings me out wrong, ten angels swearing I was right would make no difference.

5. Political realism refuses to identify the moral aspirations of a particular nation with the moral laws that govern the universe.

The lighthearted equation between a particular nationalism and the counsels of Providence is morally indefensible, for it is that very sin of pride against which the Greek tragedians and the Biblical prophets have warned rulers and ruled. That equation is also politically pernicious, for it is liable to engender the distortion in judgment which, in the blindness of crusading frenzy, destroys nations and civilizations-in the name of moral principle, ideal, or God himself.

On the other hand, it is exactly the concept of interest defined in terms of power that saves us from both that moral excess and that political folly. For if we look at all nations, our own included, as political entities pursuing their respective interests defined in terms of power, we are able to do justice to all of them. . . .

6. The difference, then, between political realism and other schools of thought is real, and it is profound. . . .

Intellectually, the political realist maintains the autonomy of the political sphere, as the economist, the lawyer, the moralist maintain theirs. He thinks in terms of interest defined as power, as the economist thinks in terms of interest defined as wealth; the lawyer, of the conformity of action with legal rules; the moralist, of the conformity of action with moral principles. The economist asks: "How does this policy affect the wealth of society, or a segment of it?" The lawyer asks: "Is this policy in accord with the rules of law?" The moralist asks: "Is this policy in accord with moral principles?" And the political realist asks: "How does this policy affect the power of the nation?" (Or of the federal government, of Congress, of the party, of agriculture, as the case may be.)

In 1939 the Soviet Union attacked Finland. This action confronted France and Great Britain with two issues, one legal, the other political. Did that action violate the Covenant of the League of Nations and, if it did, what countermeasures should France and Great Britain take? The legal question could easily be answered in the affirmative, for obviously the Soviet Union had done what was prohibited by the Covenant. The answer to the political question depends, first, upon the manner in which the Russian action affected the interests of France and Great Britain; second, upon the existing distribution of power between France and Great Britain, on the one hand, and the Soviet Union and other potentially hostile nations, especially Germany, on the other; and, third, upon the influence that the countermeasures were likely to have upon the interests of France and Great Britain and the future distribution of power. France and Great Britain, as the leading members of the League of Nations, saw to it that the Soviet Union was expelled from the League, and they were prevented from joining Finland in the war against the Soviet Union only by Sweden's refusal to allow their troops to pass through Swedish territory on their way to Finland. If this refusal by Sweden had not saved them, France and Great Britain would shortly have found themselves at war with the Soviet Union and Germany at the same time.

The policy of France and Great Britain was a classic example of legalism in that they allowed the answer to the legal question, legitimate within its sphere, to determine their political actions. Instead of asking both questions, that of law and that of power, they asked only the question of law; and the answer they received could have no bearing on the issue that their very existence might have depended upon.

This realist defense of the autonomy of the political sphere against its subversion by other modes of thought does not imply disregard for the existence and importance of these other modes of thought. It rather implies that each should be assigned its proper sphere and function. Political realism is based upon a pluralistic conception of human nature. Real man is a composite of "economic man," "political man," "moral man," "religious man," etc. A man who was nothing but "political man" would be a beast, for he would be completely lacking in moral restraints. A man who was nothing but "moral man" would be a fool, for he would be completely lacking in prudence. A man who was nothing but "religious man" would be a saint, for he would be completely lacking in worldly desires.

Recognizing that these different facets of human nature exist, political realism also recognizes that in order to understand one of them one has to deal with it on its own terms. . . .

It is in the nature of things that a theory of politics which is based upon such principles will not meet with unanimous approval—nor does, for that matter, such a foreign policy. For theory and policy alike run counter to two trends in our culture which are not able to reconcile themselves to the assumptions and results of a rational, objective theory of politics. One of these trends disparages the role of power in society on grounds that stem from the experience and philosophy of the nineteenth century; we shall address ourselves to this tendency later in greater detail. The other trend, opposed to the realist theory and practice of politics, stems from the very relationship that exists, and must exist, between the human mind and the political sphere . . . the human mind in its day-by-day operations cannot bear to look the truth of politics straight in the face. It must disguise, distort, belittle, and embellish the truth-the more so, the more the individual is actively involved in the processes of politics, and particularly in those of international politics. For only by deceiving himself about the nature of politics and the role he plays on the political scene is man able to live contentedly as a political animal with himself and his fellow men.

An Interview on a Theory of International Relations and the Role of Structure

KENNETH WALTZ

THE IMPORTANCE OF STRUCTURE IN IR

Always, until World War II in modern history, there were five or so great powers contending. World War II eventuated in a world in which there were only two: the United States and the Soviet Union. States acting in those two different worlds face different kinds of problems. . . . That is, the difficulty, for example, that previous great powers—countries like Great Britain and France—had coming to terms with the fact that they were no longer great powers, that they were reduced to the level of major powers. . . . It explains how Europe could develop as a somewhat distinct political realm. France no longer had to worry about a possible war with Germany, or, as it had in previous times, a possible war against Britain. We worried about that, and the Soviet Union worried about that . . .

Whole new kinds of behavior become possible for the previous great powers, because they're no longer great powers, just for that simple reason. And the United States assumed new responsibilities that it never dreamed of assuming. In the 1930s, to tell an American that America would begin to take the responsibility for the security of major parts of the world would have been laughable. Nobody could even imagine such a condition. But when the structure of international politics dramatically changed, we accommodated ourselves to that new condition.

It takes an act of the mind to conceive of how the conditions under which these actions and interactions occur influence the actions and interactions themselves. That's not something that you open your eyes and look at and see, or read about in *The New York Times* every morning. It takes an act of thought to do that.

. . . Looking back, the article on stability of a bipolar world was published in 1964. It was strangely controversial. It made people mad. I first gave the paper as a talk to the Harvard/MIT Arms Control Seminar. There was a lively and heated discussion following the presentation of the simple idea that this has become a world of two powers, in other words, a bipolar world. People were saying, "No, wait a minute. Europe still counts." Well, of course, Europe still counted, but not nearly as much, obviously, as it once did, and not merely as much as the United States and the Soviet Union. Ultimately, the world's fate depended on the United States, the Soviet Union, and the interaction between them.

In economic terms, it was not a world of interdependence at all: the United States and the Soviet Union scarcely traded with one another. Militarily, the interdependence was close, because each could do grievous damage to the other. And in international politics, again, a realm of self-help; ultimately, that's what counts.

Within, I'd say, certainly within ten years, probably less than ten years, it became accepted: "Yes, of course, the world is bipolar." And that makes the really deep controversy by which this article was greeted all the more striking.

. . . One of the striking things about nuclear deterrence is that it has worked, no matter what country we're talking about, no matter what kind of government the country has, no matter what kind of ruler the country has had. The most striking case, of course, is Mao Zedong and the Cultural Revolution. It lasted from 1966 to 1976 in China, where China was in seemingly unheard-of chaos. And yet China, a country with a fair number of nuclear weapons at the time, managed to take care of those weapons very well indeed! The government separated foreign policy to a certain extent, and nuclear policy completely, from the Cultural Revolution.

AFTER THE SOVIET UNION DISAPPEARED

. . . If you recall, the 1980s was when Reagan and those who agreed with him were saying that the Soviet Union was catching up with us, they were going to pass us. "The Soviet Union has become the most powerful military country in the world"—Reagan, you know. "They passed us on all fronts—strategic and conventional alike."

Well, the opposite was the truth, and one could see it. I mean, you can look at data. You could look at the demographic composition of the Soviet Union, with the Russian component sinking and the non-Russian component of the population rising. You could look at the extent to which the Soviet Union was falling behind in military technology—indeed, in technology across the board, and therefore in military technology as well. It looked to me as though the Soviet Union was on a losing course.

. . . I remember, especially, being in China for the first time in 1982, and presenting this analysis to one of the institutes, which I've now talked at over the years about four or five times. The last time was in 1996, and I reminded them of 1982. What they were saying was, "Hey, the Soviet Union is getting ahead." In fact, that's why China was moving toward the United States, because it felt that the United States was getting weaker, and in order to form a block of sufficient strength against the Soviet Union, they had to edge over toward our side. Again, perceptions of what the structure of international politics is at a given time strongly influence the policy that one follows. So I was saying, "No, the Soviet Union is getting weaker. The United State is getting relatively stronger." And the people at this institute who were charged with thinking about this—this was the purpose of their institute, to think about things like this—had reached the opposite conclusion. They . . . well, they were wrong.

UNIPOLAR WORLD: THE US AS THE ONLY SUPERPOWER

Checks and balances are supposed to work in the United States; it's ingrained in our thinking. But, in fact, they don't work very well, or at least in my view they are not working very well. They do not place effective constraints on what the government can do abroad. They do not place effective constraints on how much we spend on our military forces. In 1998, for example, we outspent the next eight big spenders. We're now spending about as much as the next fourteen or fifteen. And, according to *The New York Times,* projecting the spending until next year, we will be spending as much as all the other countries in the world combined on our military forces. Now, what do we want all that military force for? Other countries are bound to ask that question. They do ask that question. And they worry about it, because power can be so easily abused.

. . . No combination of other countries and no other country singly in the foreseeable future is going to be able to balance the power of the United States. Now, in the end, power will balance power, and there isn't any doubt that the Chinese are smarting, very uncomfortable with the extent to which the United States dominates the world militarily. I'm not implying that it doesn't bother other countries as well. But China, if it maintains its political coherence, its political capabilities, will have in due course the economic and the technological means of competing. But how far away is that? Certainly, twenty years. Probably more than twenty years.

China's Unpeaceful Rise

JOHN J. MEARSHEIMER

Can China rise peacefully? My answer is no. If China continues its impressive economic growth over the next few decades, the United States and China are likely to engage in an intense security competition with considerable potential for war. Most of China's neighbors—including India, Japan, Singapore, South Korea, Russia, and Vietnam—will join with the United States to contain China's power.

To predict the future in Asia, one needs a theory of international politics that explains how rising great powers are likely to act and how other states in the system will react to them. That theory must be logically sound and it must account for the past behavior of rising great powers.

My theory of international politics says that the mightiest states attempt to establish hegemony in their region of the world while making sure that no rival great power dominates another region. This theory, which helps explain US foreign policy since the country's founding, also has implications for future relations between China and the United States.

THE CONTEST FOR POWER

According to my understanding of international politics, survival is a state's most important goal, because a state cannot pursue any other goals if it does not survive. The basic structure of the international system forces states concerned about their security to compete with each other for power. The ultimate goal of every great power is to maximize its share of world power and eventually dominate the system.

The international system has three defining characteristics. First, the main actors are states that operate in anarchy, which simply means that there is no higher authority above them. Second, all great powers have some offensive military capability, which means that they have the wherewithal to hurt each other. Third, no state can know the intentions of other states with certainty, especially their future intentions. It is simply impossible, for example, to know what Germany or Japan's intentions will be toward their neighbors in 2025.

Current History, Volume 105, No. 690 (April), pg. 160–162

In a world where other states might have malign intentions as well as significant offensive capabilities, states tend to fear each other. That fear is compounded by the fact that in an anarchic system there is no night watchman for states to call if trouble comes knocking at their door. Therefore, states recognize that the best way to survive in such a system is to be as powerful as possible relative to potential rivals. The mightier a state is, the less likely it is that another state will attack it. No Americans, for example, worry that Canada or Mexico will attack the United States, because neither of those countries is powerful enough to contemplate a fight with Washington. But great powers do not merely strive to be the strongest great power, although that is a welcome outcome. Their ultimate aim is to be the hegemon—that is, the only great power in the system.

What exactly does it mean to be a hegemon in the modern world? It is almost impossible for any state to achieve global hegemony, because it is too hard to project and sustain power around the globe and onto the territory of distant great powers. The best outcome that a state can hope for is to be a regional hegemon, and thus dominate one's own geographical area. The United States has been a regional hegemon in the Western Hemisphere since the late 1800s. Although the United States is clearly the most powerful state on the planet today, it is not a global hegemon.

States that gain regional hegemony have a further aim: they seek to prevent great powers in other regions from duplicating their feat. Regional hegemons do not want peers. Instead, they want to keep other regions divided among several great powers, so that these states will compete with each other and be unable to focus on them. In sum, my theory says that the ideal situation for any great power is to be the only regional hegemon in the world.

THE AMERICAN HEGEMON

A brief look at the history of American foreign policy illustrates the explanatory power of this theory. When the United States won its independence from Britain in 1783, it was a small and weak country comprised of 13 states strung along the Atlantic seaboard. The new country was surrounded by the British and Spanish empires and much of the territory between the Appalachian Mountains and the Mississippi River was controlled by hostile Native American tribes. It was a dangerous, threat-filled environment.

Over the course of the next 115 years, American policy makers of all stripes worked assiduously to turn the United States into a regional hegemon. They expanded America's boundaries from the Atlantic to the Pacific oceans as part of a policy commonly referred to as "Manifest Destiny." The United States fought wars against Mexico and various Native American tribes and took huge chunks of land from them. The nation became an expansionist power of the first order. As Senator Henry Cabot Lodge put it, the United States had a "record of conquest, colonization, and territorial expansion unequalled by any people in the nineteenth century."

American policy makers in that century were not just concerned with turning the United States into a powerful territorial state. They were also determined to push the European great powers out of the Western Hemisphere and make it clear to them that they were not welcome back. This policy, known as the Monroe Doctrine, was laid out for the first time in 1823 by President James Monroe in his annual message to Congress. By 1898, the last European empire in the Americas had collapsed and the United States had become the first regional hegemon in modern history.

However, a great power's work is not done once it achieves regional hegemony. It then must make sure that no other great power follows suit and dominates its area of the world. During the twentieth century, there were four great powers that had the capability to make a run at regional hegemony: Imperial Germany (1900–1918), Imperial Japan (1931–1945), Nazi Germany (1933–1945), and the Soviet Union during the cold war (1945–1989). Not surprisingly, each tried to match what the United States had achieved in the Western Hemisphere in the nineteenth century.

America is likely to behave toward China much the way it behaved toward the Soviet Union during the cold war.

How did the United States react? In each case, it played a key role in defeating and dismantling those aspiring hegemons. The United States entered World War I in April 1917 when Imperial Germany looked like it would win the war and rule Europe. American troops played a critical role in tipping the balance against the Kaiserreich, which collapsed in November 1918. In the early 1940s, President Franklin Delano Roosevelt went to great lengths to maneuver the United States into World War II to thwart Japan's ambitions in Asia and especially Germany's ambitions in Europe. During the war, the United States helped destroy both Axis powers. And after 1945, American policy makers made certain that Germany and Japan remained militarily weak. Finally, during the cold war, the United States steadfastly worked to prevent the Soviet Union from dominating Eurasia, and in the late 1980s helped relegate its empire to the scrap heap of history.

Shortly after the cold war ended, the first Bush administration's "Defense Guidance" of 1992, which was leaked to the press, boldly stated that the United States was now the most powerful state in the world by far and it planned to remain in that exalted position. In other words, the United States would not tolerate a peer competitor.

That same message was repeated in the famous "National Security Strategy" issued by the second Bush administration in October 2002. There was much criticism of this document, especially its claims about "preemptive war." But hardly a word of protest was raised about the assertion that the United States should check rising powers and maintain its commanding position in the global balance of power.

The bottom line is that the United States—for sound strategic reasons—worked hard for more than a century to gain hegemony in the Western Hemisphere. After achieving regional dominance, it has gone to great lengths to prevent other great powers from controlling either Asia or Europe.

What are the implications of America's past behavior for the rise of China? In short, how is China likely to behave as it grows more powerful? And how are the United States and the other states in Asia likely to react to a mighty China?

PREDICTING CHINA'S FUTURE

China is likely to try to dominate Asia the way the United States dominates the Western Hemisphere. Specifically, China will seek to maximize the power gap between itself and its neighbors, especially Japan and Russia. China will want to make sure that it is so powerful that no state in Asia has the wherewithal to threaten it. It is unlikely that China will pursue military superiority so that it can go on a rampage and conquer other Asian countries, although that is always possible. Instead, it is more likely that China will want to dictate the boundaries of acceptable behavior to neighboring countries, much the way the United States makes it clear to other states in the Americas that it is the boss. Gaining regional hegemony, I might add, is probably the only way that China will get Taiwan back.

An increasingly powerful China is also likely to try to push the United States out of Asia, much the way the United States pushed the European great powers out of the Western Hemisphere. We should expect China to come up with its own version of the Monroe Doctrine, as Japan did in the 1930s.

These policy goals make good strategic sense for China. Beijing should want a militarily weak Japan and Russia as its neighbors, just as the United States prefers a militarily weak Canada and Mexico on its borders. What state in its right mind would want other powerful states located in its region? Most Chinese surely remember what happened in the past century when Japan was powerful and China was weak. In the anarchic world of international politics, it is better to be Godzilla than Bambi.

Furthermore, why would a powerful China accept US military forces operating in its backyard? American policy makers, after all, become apoplectic when other great powers send military forces into the Western Hemisphere. Those foreign forces are invariably seen as a potential threat to American security. The same logic should apply to China. Why would China feel safe with US forces deployed on its doorstep? Following the logic of the Monroe Doctrine, would not China's security be better served by pushing the American military out of Asia?

Why should we expect China to act any differently from how the United States did? Is Beijing more principled than Washington? More ethical? Less nationalistic? Less concerned about survival? China is none of these things, of course, which is why it is likely to imitate the United States and attempt to become a regional hegemon.

TROUBLE AHEAD

It is clear from the historical record how American policy makers will react if China attempts to dominate Asia. The United States does not tolerate peer competitors. As it demonstrated in the twentieth century, it is determined to remain the world's only regional hegemon. Therefore, the United States can be expected to go to great lengths to contain China and ultimately weaken it to the point where it is no longer capable of ruling the roost in Asia. In essence, America is likely to behave toward China much the way it behaved toward the Soviet Union during the cold war.

China's neighbors are certain to fear its rise as well, and they too will do whatever they can to prevent the Chinese from achieving regional hegemony. Indeed, there is already substantial evidence that countries like India, Japan, and Russia, as well as smaller powers like Singapore, South Korea, and Vietnam, are worried about China's ascendancy and are looking for ways to contain it. In the end, they will join an American-led balancing coalition to check China's rise, much the way Britain, France, Germany, Italy, Japan, and even China joined forces with the United States to contain the Soviet Union during the cold war.

Finally, given Taiwan's strategic importance for controlling the sea lanes in East Asia, it is hard to imagine the United States, as well as Japan, allowing China to control that large island. In fact, Taiwan is likely to be an important player in the anti-China balancing coalition, which is certain to infuriate China and fuel the security competition between Beijing and Washington.

The picture I have painted of what is likely to happen if China continues its rise is not a pretty one. I actually find it categorically depressing and wish that I could tell a more optimistic story about the future. But the fact is that international politics is a nasty and dangerous business, and no amount of goodwill can ameliorate the intense security competition that sets in when an aspiring hegemon appears in Eurasia. That is the tragedy of great power politics.

Inflating the China Threat

STEPHEN WALT

If you were focusing on Hurricane Isaac or the continued violence in Syria, you might have missed the latest round of threat inflation about China. Last week, the *New York Times* reported that China was "increasing its existing ability to deliver nuclear warheads to the United States and to overwhelm missile defense systems." The online journal *Salon* offered an even more breathless appraisal: the headline announced a "big story"—that "China's missiles could thwart U.S."—the text offered the alarming forecast that "the United States may be falling behind China when it comes to weapon technology."

What is really going on here? Not much. China presently has a modest strategic nuclear force. It is believed to have only about 240 nuclear warheads, and only a handful of its ballistic missiles can presently reach the United States. By way of comparison, the United States has over 2000 operational nuclear warheads deployed on ICBMs, SLBMs, and cruise missiles, all of them capable of reaching China. And if that were not enough, the U.S. has nearly 3000 nuclear warheads in reserve.

Three further points should be kept in mind. First, hawks are likely to use developments such as these to portray China as a rising revisionist threat, but such claims do not follow logically from the evidence presented. To repeat: what China is doing is a sensible defensive move, motivated by the same concerns for deterrent stability that led the United States to create a "strategic triad" back in the 1950s.

Second, if you wanted to cap or slow Chinese nuclear modernization, the smart way to do it would be to abandon the futile pursuit of strategic missile defenses and bring China into the same negotiating framework that capped and eventually reduced the U.S. and Russian arsenals. And remember: once nuclear-armed states have secure second-strike capabilities, the relative size of their respective arsenals is irrelevant. If neither side can prevent the other from retaliating and destroying its major population centers, it simply doesn't matter if one side has twice as many warheads before the war. Or ten times as many. Or a hundred times. . . .

Third, this episode reminds us that trying to protect the country by building missile defenses is a fool's errand. It is always going to be cheaper for opponents to come up with ways to override a missile defense. Why? Because given how destructive nuclear weapons are, a missile defense system has to work almost perfectly in order to prevent massive damage. If you fired a hundred warheads and 95% were intercepted—an astonishingly high level of performance—that would still let five warheads through and that means losing five cities. And if an opponent were convinced that your defenses would work perfectly—a highly unlikely proposition—there are plenty of other ways to deliver a nuclear weapon. Ballistic missile defense never made much sense either strategically or economically, except as a make-work program for the aerospace industry and an enduring component of right-wing nuclear theology.

VISUAL REVIEW

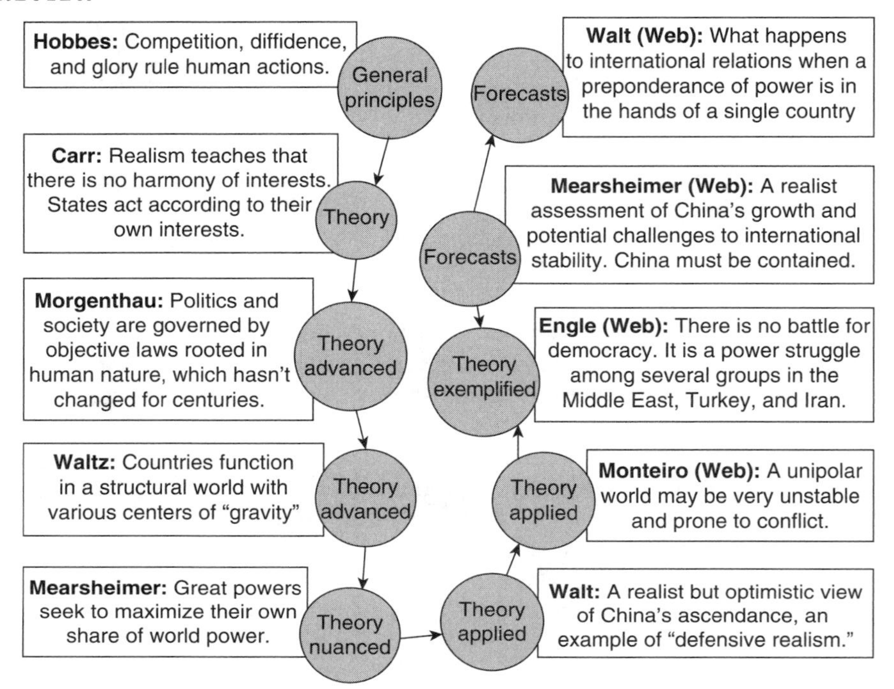

Section 3

Historical Context II: Liberalism and International Organizations

Uganda President Yoweri Museveni (center) arrives to a discussion with other presidents of the East African Community at the U.S. Chamber of Commerce in Washington, 2014. In 2000, Tanzania, Uganda, Burundi, Kenya, and Rwanda formed this economic and political union, with the goal of a common economic market, a single currency, and one unified state. Although a similar plan collapsed back in the 1970s, steps thus far suggest that these countries can achieve their goal. Most important, the East African Community example, if it is a success, will show that sovereign countries can put aside religious, tribal, and political differences, accept binding legal rules, and move toward an international community. It was planned to have a union soon. Check if this plan has been achieved.
Source: Molly Riley/Associated Press

Perpetual Peace: A Philosophical Sketch

IMMANUEL KANT

Perpetual Peace

Whether this satirical inscription on a Dutch innkeeper's sign upon which a burial ground was painted had for its object mankind in general, or the rulers of states in particular, who are insatiable of war, or merely the philosophers who dream this sweet dream, it is not for us to decide. But one condition the author of this essay wishes to lay down. The practical politician assumes the attitude of looking down with great self-satisfaction on the political theorist as a pedant whose empty ideas in no way threaten the security of the state, inasmuch as the state must proceed on empirical principles; so the theorist is allowed to play his game without interference from the worldly-wise statesman. Such being his attitude, the practical politician—and this is the condition I make—should at least act consistently in the case of a conflict and not suspect some danger to the state in the political theorist's opinions which are ventured and publicly expressed without any ulterior purpose. By this *clausula salvatoria* the author desires formally and emphatically to deprecate herewith any malevolent interpretation which might be placed on his words.

SECTION I

Containing the Preliminary Articles for Perpetual Peace Among States

1. "No Treaty of Peace Shall Be Held Valid in Which There Is Tacitly Reserved Matter for a Future War"
2. "No Independent States, Large or Small, Shall Come under the Dominion of Another State by Inheritance, Exchange, Purchase, or Donation"
3. "Standing Armies (*miles perpetuus*) Shall in Time Be Totally Abolished"
4. "National Debts Shall Not Be Contracted with a View to the External Friction of States"
5. "No State Shall by Force Interfere with the Constitution or Government of Another State"
6. "No State Shall, during War, Permit Such Acts of Hostility Which Would Make Mutual Confidence in the Subsequent Peace Impossible: Such Are the Employment of Assassins (*percussores*), Poisoners (*venefici*), Breach of Capitulation, and Incitement to Treason (*perduellio*) in the Opposing State"

SECTION II

Containing the Definitive Articles for Perpetual Peace Among States First Definitive Article for Perpetual Peace

The Civil Constitution of Every State Should Be Republican

The only constitution which derives from the idea of the original compact, and on which all juridical legislation of a people must be based, is the republican. This constitution is established, firstly, by principles of the freedom of the members of a society (as men); secondly, by principles of dependence of all upon a single common legislation (as subjects); and, thirdly, by the law of their equality (as citizens). The republican constitution, therefore, is, with respect to law, the one which is the original basis of every form of civil constitution. The only question now is: Is it also the one which can lead to perpetual peace?

The republican constitution, besides the purity of its origin (having sprung from the pure source of the concept of law), also gives a favorable prospect for the desired consequence, i.e., perpetual peace. The reason is this: if the consent of the citizens is required in order to decide that war should be declared (and in this constitution it cannot but be the case), nothing is more natural than that they would be very cautious in commencing such a poor game, decreeing for themselves all the calamities of war. Among the latter would be: having to fight, having to pay the costs of war from their own resources, having painfully to repair the devastation war leaves behind, and, to fill up the measure of evils, load themselves with a heavy national debt that would embitter peace itself and that can never be liquidated on account of constant wars in the future. But, on the other hand, in a constitution which is not republican, and under which the subjects are not citizens, a declaration of war is the easiest thing in the world to decide upon, because war does not require of the ruler, who is the proprietor and not a member of the state, the least sacrifice of the pleasures of his table, the chase, his country houses, his court functions, and the like. He may, therefore, resolve on war as on a pleasure party for the most trivial reasons, and with perfect indifference leave the justification which decency requires to the diplomatic corps who are ever ready to provide it.

In order not to confuse the republican constitution with the democratic (as is commonly done), the following should be noted. The forms of a state *(civitas)* can be divided either according to the persons who possess the sovereign power or according to the mode of administration exercised over the people by the chief, whoever he may be. The first is properly called the form of sovereignty (*forma imperii*), and there are only three possible forms of it: autocracy, in which one, aristocracy, in which some associated together, or democracy, in which all those who constitute society, possess sovereign power. They may be characterized, respectively, as the power of a monarch, of the nobility, or of the people. The second division is that by the form of government (*forma regiminis*) and is based on the way in which the state makes use of its power; this way is based on the constitution, which is the act of the general will through which the many persons become one nation. In this respect government is either republican or despotic. Republicanism is the political principle of the separation of the executive power (the administration) from the legislative; despotism is that of the autonomous execution by the state of laws which it has itself decreed. Thus in a despotism the public will is administered by the ruler as his own will. Of the three forms of the state, that of democracy is, properly speaking, necessarily a despotism, because it establishes an executive power in which "all" decide for or even against one who does not agree; that is, "all," who are not quite all, decide, and this is a contradiction of the general will with itself and with freedom.

Every form of government which is not representative is, properly speaking, without form. The legislator can unite in one and the same person his function as legislative and as executor of his will just as little as the universal of the major premise in a syllogism can also be the subsumption of the particular under the universal in the minor. And even though the other two constitutions are always defective to the extent that they do leave room for this mode of administration, it is at least possible for them to assume a mode of government conforming to the spirit of a representative system (as when Frederick II at least *said* he was merely the first servant of the state). On the other hand, the democratic mode of government makes this impossible, since everyone wishes to be master. Therefore, we can say: the smaller the personnel of the government (the smaller the number of rulers), the greater is their representation and the more nearly the constitution approaches to the possibility of republicanism; thus the constitution may be expected by gradual reform finally to raise itself to republicanism. For these reasons it is more difficult for an aristocracy than for a monarchy to achieve the one completely juridical constitution, and it is impossible for a democracy to do so except by violent revolution.

The mode of governments, however, is incomparably more important to the people than the form of sovereignty, although much depends on the greater or lesser suitability of the latter to the end of [good] government. To conform to the concept of law, however, government must have a representative form, and in this system only a republican mode of government is possible; without it, government is despotic and arbitrary, whatever the constitution may be. None of the ancient so-called "republics" knew this system, and they all finally and inevitably degenerated into despotism under the sovereignty of one, which is the most bearable of all forms of despotism.

Second Definitive Article for a Perpetual Peace

The Law of Nations Shall be Founded on a Federation of Free States

Peoples, as states, like individuals, may be judged to injure one another merely by their coexistence in the state of nature (i.e., while independent of external laws). Each of them may and should for the sake of its own security demand that the others enter with it into a constitution similar to the civil constitution, for under such a constitution each can be secure in his right. This would be a league of nations, but it would not have to be a state consisting of nations. That would be contradictory, since a state implies the relation of a superior (legislating) to an inferior (obeying), i.e., the people, and many nations in one state would then constitute only one nation. This contradicts the presupposition, for here we have to weigh the rights of nations against each other so far as they are distinct states and not amalgamated into one.

When we see the attachment of savages to their lawless freedom, preferring ceaseless combat to subjection to a lawful constraint which they might establish, and thus preferring senseless freedom to rational freedom, we regard it with deep contempt as barbarity, rudeness, and a brutish degradation of humanity. Accordingly, one would think that civilized people (each united in a state) would hasten all the more to escape, the sooner the better, from such a depraved condition. But, instead, each state places its majesty (for it is absurd to speak of the majesty of the people) in being subject to no external juridical restraint, and the splendor of its sovereign consists in the fact that many thousands stand at his command to sacrifice themselves for something that does not concern them and without his needing to place himself in the least danger. The chief difference between European and American savages lies in the fact that many tribes of the latter have been eaten by their enemies, while the former know how to make better use of their conquered enemies than to dine off them; they know better how to use them to increase the number of their subjects and thus the quantity of instruments for even more extensive wars.

When we consider the perverseness of human nature which is nakedly revealed in the uncontrolled relations between nations (this perverseness being veiled in the state of civil law by the constraint exercised by government), we may well be astonished that the word "law" has not yet been banished from war politics as pedantic, and that no state has yet been bold enough to advocate this point of view. Up to the present, Hugo Grotius, Pufendorf, Vattel, and many other irritating comforters have been cited in justification of war, though their code, philosophically or diplomatically formulated, has not and cannot have the least legal force, because states as such do not stand under a common external power. There is no instance on record that a state has ever been moved to desist from its purpose because of arguments backed up by the testimony of such great men. But the homage which each state pays (at least in words) to the concept of law proves that there is slumbering in man an even greater moral disposition to become master of the evil principle in himself (which he cannot disclaim) and to hope for the same from others. Otherwise the word "law" would never be pronounced by states which wish to war upon one another; it would be used only ironically, as a Gallic prince interpreted it when he said, "It is the prerogative which nature has given the stronger that the weaker should obey him."

States do not plead their cause before a tribunal; war alone is their way of bringing suit. But by war and its favorable issue, in victory, right is not decided, and though by a treaty of peace this particular war is brought to an end, the state of war, of always finding a new pretext to hostilities, is not terminated. Nor can this be declared wrong, considering the fact that in this state each is the judge of his own case. Notwithstanding, the obligation which men in a lawless condition have under the natural law, and which requires them to abandon the state of nature, does not quite apply to states under the law of nations, for as states they already have an internal juridical constitution and have thus outgrown compulsion from others to submit to a more extended lawful constitution according to their ideas of right. This is true in spite of the fact that reason, from its throne of supreme moral legislating authority, absolutely condemns war as a legal recourse and makes a state of peace a direct duty, even though peace cannot be established or secured except by a compact among nations.

For these reasons there must be a league of a particular kind, which can be called a league of peace (*foedus pacificum*), and which would be distinguished from a treaty of peace (*pactum pacis*) by the fact that the latter terminates only one war, while the former seeks to make an end of all wars forever. This league does not tend to any dominion over the power of the state but only to the maintenance and security of the freedom of the state itself and of other states in league with it, without there being any need for them to submit to civil laws and their compulsion, as men in a state of nature must submit.

The Great Illusion

NORMAN ANGELL

What are the fundamental motives that explain the present rivalry of armaments in Europe, notably the Anglo-German? Each nation pleads the need for defense; but this implies that someone is likely to attack, and has therefore a presumed interest in so doing. What are the motives, which each State thus fears its neighbors may obey?

They are based on the universal assumption that a nation, in order to find outlets for expanding population and increasing industry, or simply to ensure the best conditions possible for its people, is necessarily pushed to territorial expansion and the exercise of political force against others (German naval competition is assumed to be the expression of the growing need of an expanding population for a larger place in the world, a need which will find a realization in the conquest of English Colonies or trade, unless these are defended); it is assumed, therefore, that a nation's relative prosperity is broadly determined by its political power; that nations being competing units, advantage, in the last resort, goes to the possessor of preponderant military force, the weaker going to the wall, as in the other forms of the struggle for life.

The author challenges this whole doctrine. He attempts to show that it belongs to a stage of development out of which we have passed; that the commerce and industry of a people no longer depend upon the expansion of its political frontiers; that a nation's political and economic frontiers do not now necessarily coincide; that military power is socially and economically futile, and can have no relation to the prosperity of the people exercising it; that it is impossible for one nation to seize by force the wealth or trade of another—to enrich itself by subjugating, or imposing its will by force on another; that, in short, war, even when victorious, can no longer achieve those aims for which peoples strive. He establishes this apparent paradox, in so far as the economic problem is concerned, by showing that wealth in the economically civilized world is founded upon credit and commercial contract (these being the outgrowth of an economic interdependence due to the increasing division of labor and greatly developed communication). If credit and commercial contract are tampered with in an attempt at confiscation, the credit-dependent wealth is undermined, and its collapse involves that of the conqueror; so that if conquest is not to be self-injurious it must respect the enemy's property, in which case it becomes economically futile. Thus the wealth of conquered territory remains in the hands of the population of such territory. When Germany annexed Alsatia, no individual German secured a single mark's worth of Alsatian property as the spoils of war. Conquest in the modem world is a process of multiplying by Synopsis xi X, and then obtaining the original figure by dividing by X. For a modern nation to add to its territory no more adds to the wealth of the people of such nation than it would add to the wealth of Londoners if the City of London were to annex the county of Hertford. The author also shows that international finance has become so interdependent and so interwoven with trade and industry that the intangibility of an enemy's property extends to his trade. It results that political and military power can in reality do nothing for trade; the individual merchants and manufacturers of small nations, exercising no such power, compete successfully with those of the great. Swiss and Belgian merchants drive English from the British Colonial market; Norway has, relatively to population, a greater mercantile, marine than Great Britain; the public credit (as a rough-and-ready indication, among others, of security and wealth) of small States possessing no political power often stands higher than that of the Great Powers of Europe, Belgian Three per Cents, standing at 96, and German at 82; Norwegian Three and a Half per Cents, at 102, and Russian Three and a Half per Cents, at 81. The forces which have brought about the economic futility of military power have also rendered it futile as a means of enforcing a nation's moral ideals or imposing social institutions upon a conquered people. Germany could not turn Canada or Australia into German colonies—i.e., stamp out their language, law, literature, traditions, etc.—by "capturing" them. The necessary security in their material possessions enjoyed by the inhabitants of such conquered provinces, quick intercommunication by a cheap press, widely-read literature, enable even small communities to become articulate and effectively to defend their special social or moral possessions, even when military conquest has been complete. The fight for ideals can no longer take the form of fight between nations, because the lines of division on moral questions are within the nations themselves and intersect the political frontiers. There is no modem State which is completely Catholic or Protestant, or liberal or autocratic, or aristocratic or democratic, or socialist or individualist; the moral and spiritual struggles of the modem world go on between citizens of the same State in unconscious intellectual co-operation with corresponding groups in other States, not between the public powers of rival States. This classification by strata involves necessarily a redirection of human pugnacity, based rather on the rivalry of classes and interests than on State divisions. War has no longer the justification that it makes for the survival of the fittest; it involves the survival of the less fit. The idea that the struggle between nations is a part of the evolutionary law of man's advance involves a profound misreading of the biological analogy. The warlike nations do not inherit the earth; they represent the decaying human element. The diminishing of physical force in all spheres of human activity carries with it profound psychological modifications. These tendencies, mainly the outcome of purely modem conditions (e.g. rapidity of communication), have rendered the problems of modern international politics profoundly and essentially different from the ancient; yet our ideas are still dominated by the principles and axioms, images and terminology of the bygone days.

The author urges that these little-recognized facts may be utilized for the solution of the armament difficulty on at present untried lines—by such modification of opinion in Europe that much of the present motive to aggression will cease to be operative, and by thus diminishing the risk of attack, diminishing to the same extent the need for defense. He shows how such a political reformation is within the scope of practical politics, and the methods which should be employed to bring it about.

Liberalism and World Politics

MICHAEL W. DOYLE

LIBERAL PACIFISM

There is no canonical description of liberalism. What we tend to call *liberal* resembles a family portrait of principles and institutions, recognizable by certain characteristics—for example, individual freedom, political participation, private property, and equality of opportunity—that most liberal states share, although none has perfected them all. Joseph Schumpeter clearly fits within this family when he considers the international effects of capitalism and democracy.

Schumpeter's "Sociology of Imperialisms," published in 1919, made a coherent and sustained argument concerning the pacifying (in the sense of nonaggressive) effects of liberal institutions and principles. Unlike some of the earlier liberal theorists who focused on a single feature such as trade or failed to examine critically the arguments they were advancing, Schumpeter saw the interaction of capitalism and democracy as the foundation of liberal pacifism, and he tested his arguments in a sociology of historical imperialisms.

He defines *imperialism* as "an objectless disposition on the part of a state to unlimited forcible expansion". Excluding imperialisms that were mere "catchwords" and those that were "objectful" (e.g., defensive imperialism), he traces the roots of objectless imperialism to three sources, each an atavism. Modern imperialism, according to Schumpeter, resulted from the combined impact of a "war machine," warlike instincts, and export monopolism.

Once necessary, the war machine later developed a life of its own and took control of a state's foreign policy: "Created by the wars that required it, the machine now created the wars it required". Thus, Schumpeter tells us that the army of ancient Egypt, created to drive the Hyksos out of Egypt, took over the state and pursued militaristic imperialism. Like the later armies of the courts of absolutist Europe, it fought wars for the sake of glory and booty, for the sake of warriors and monarchs—wars *gratia* warriors.

A warlike disposition, elsewhere called "instinctual elements of bloody primitivism," is the natural ideology of a war machine. It also exists independently; the Persians, says Schumpeter, were a warrior nation from the outset.

Under modern capitalism, export monopolists, the third source of modern imperialism, push for imperialist expansion as a way to expand their closed markets. The absolute monarchies were the last clear-cut imperialisms. Nineteenth century imperialisms merely represent the vestiges of the imperialisms created by Louis XIV and Catherine the Great. Thus, the export monopolists are an atavism of the absolute monarchies, for they depend completely on the tariffs imposed by the monarchs and their militaristic successors for revenue. Without tariffs, monopolies would be eliminated by foreign competition.

Modern (nineteenth century) imperialism, therefore, rests on an atavistic war machine, militaristic attitudes left over from the days of monarchical wars, and export monopolism, which is nothing more than the economic residue of monarchical finance. In the modern era, imperialists gratify their private interests. From the national perspective, their imperialistic wars are objectless.

Schumpeter's theme now emerges. Capitalism and democracy are forces for peace. Indeed, they are antithetical to imperialism. For Schumpeter, the further development of capitalism and democracy means that imperialism will inevitably disappear.

Schumpeter's explanation for liberal pacifism is quite simple: Only war profiteers and military aristocrats gain from wars. No democracy would pursue a minority interest and tolerate the high costs of imperialism. When free trade prevails, "no class" gains from forcible expansion because

> foreign raw materials and food stuffs are as accessible to each nation as though they were in its own territory. Where the cultural backwardness of a region makes normal economic intercourse dependent on colonization it does not matter, assuming free trade, which of the "civilized" nations undertakes the task of colonization.

Schumpeter's arguments are difficult to evaluate. In partial tests of quasi-Schumpeterian propositions, Michael Haas discovered a cluster that associates democracy, development, and sustained modernization with peaceful conditions. However, M. Small and J. D. Singer have discovered that there is no clearly negative correlation between democracy and war in the period 1816–1965—the period that would be central to Schumpeter's argument.

Later in his career, in *Capitalism, Socialism, and Democracy,* Schumpeter acknowledged that "almost purely bourgeois commonwealths were often aggressive when it seemed to pay—like the Athenian or the Venetian commonwealths." Yet he stuck to his pacifistic guns, restating the view that capitalist democracy "steadily tells . . . against the use of military force and for peaceful arrangements, even when the balance of pecuniary advantage is clearly on the side of war which, under modern circumstances, is not in general very likely". A recent study by R. J. Rummel of "libertarianism" and international violence is the closest test Schumpeterian pacifism has received. "Free" states (those enjoying political and economic freedom) were shown to have considerably less conflict at or above the level of economic sanctions than "nonfree" states. The free states, the partly free states (including the democratic socialist countries such as Sweden), and the nonfree states accounted for 24%, 26%, and 61%, respectively, of the international violence during the period examined.

LIBERAL IMPERIALISM

Machiavelli argues, not only that republics are not pacifistic, but that they are the best form of state for imperial expansion. Establishing a republic fit for imperial expansion is, moreover, the best way to guarantee the survival of a state.

Machiavelli's republic is a classical mixed republic. It is not a democracy—which he thought would quickly degenerate into a tyranny—but is characterized by social equality, popular liberty, and political participation.

Liberty results from "disunion"—the competition and necessity for compromise required by the division of powers among senate, consuls, and tribunes (the last representing the common people). Liberty also results from the popular veto. The powerful few threaten the rest with tyranny, Machiavelli says, because they seek to dominate.

Strength, and then imperial expansion, results from the way liberty encourages increased population and property, which grow when the citizens know their lives and goods are secure from arbitrary seizure. Free citizens equip large armies and provide soldiers who fight for public glory and the common good because these are, in fact, their own. If you seek the honor of having your state expand, Machiavelli advises, you should organize it as a free and popular republic like Rome, rather than as an aristocratic republic like Sparta or Venice. Expansion thus calls for a free republic.

"Necessity"—political survival—calls for expansion. If a stable aristocratic republic is forced by foreign conflict "to extend her territory, in such a case we shall see her foundations give way and herself quickly brought to ruin"; if, on the other hand, domestic security prevails, "the continued tranquility would enervate her, or provoke internal disensions, which together, or either of them seperately, will apt to prove her ruin". Machiavelli therefore believes it is necessary to take the constitution of Rome, rather than that of Sparta or Venice, as our model.

Hence, this belief leads to liberal imperialism. We are lovers of glory, Machiavelli announces. We seek to rule or, at least, to avoid being oppressed. In either case, we want more for ourselves and our states than just material welfare (materialistic monism). Because other states with similar aims thereby threaten us, we prepare ourselves for expansion. Because our fellow citizens threaten us if we do not allow them either to satisfy their ambition or to release their political energies through imperial expansion, we expand.

LIBERAL INTERNATIONALISM

Modern liberalism carries with it two legacies. They do not affect liberal states separately, according to whether they are pacifistic or imperialistic, but simultaneously.

The first of these legacies is the pacification of foreign relations among liberal states. During the nineteenth century, the United States and Great Britain engaged in nearly continual strife; however, after the Reform Act of 1832 defined actual representation as the formal source of the sovereignty of the British parliament, Britain and the United States negotiated their disputes. They negotiated despite, for example, British grievances during the Civil War against the North's blockade of the South, with which Britain had close economic ties. Despite severe Anglo-French colonial rivalry, liberal France and liberal Britain formed an entente against illiberal Germany before World War I. And from 1914 to 1915, Italy, the liberal member of the Triple Alliance with Germany and Austria, chose not to fulfill its obligations under that treaty to support its allies. Instead, Italy joined in an alliance with Britain and France, which prevented it from having to fight other liberal states and then declared war on Germany and Austria. Despite generations of Anglo-American tension and Britain's wartime restrictions on American trade with Germany, the United States leaned toward Britain and France from 1914 to 1917 before entering World War I on their side.

Beginning in the eighteenth century and slowly growing since then, a zone of peace, which Kant called the "pacific federation" or "pacific union," has begun to be established among liberal societies. More than 40 liberal states currently make up the union. Most are in Europe and North America, but they can be found on every continent.

Here the predictions of liberal pacifists (and President Reagan) are borne out: liberal states do exercise peaceful restraint, and a separate peace exists among them. This separate peace provides a solid foundation for the United States' crucial alliances with the liberal powers, e.g., the North Atlantic Treaty Organization and our Japanese alliance. This foundation appears to be impervious to the quarrels with our allies that bedeviled the Carter and Reagan administrations. It also offers the promise of a continuing peace among liberal states, and as the number of liberal states increases, it announces the possibility of global peace this side of the grave or world conquest.

Of course, the probability of the outbreak of war in any given year between any two given states is low. The occurrence of a war between any two adjacent states, considered over a long period of time, would be more probable. The apparent absence of war between liberal states, whether adjacent or not, for almost 200 years thus may have significance. Similar claims cannot be made for feudal, fascist, communist, authoritarian, or totalitarian forms of rule, nor for pluralistic or merely similar societies. More significant perhaps is that when states are forced to decide on which side of an impending world war they will fight, liberal states all wind up on the same side despite the complexity of the paths that take them there. These characteristics do not prove that the peace among liberals is statistically significant nor that liberalism is the sole valid explanation for the peace. They do suggest that we consider the possibility that liberals have indeed established a separate peace—but only among themselves.

Liberalism also carries with it a second legacy: international "imprudence". Peaceful restraint only seems to work in liberals' relations with other liberals. Liberal states have fought numerous wars with nonliberal states.

Many of these wars have been defensive and thus prudent by necessity. Liberal states have been attacked and threatened by nonliberal states that do not exercise any special restraint in their dealings with the liberal states. Authoritarian rulers both stimulate and respond to an international political environment in which conflicts of prestige, interest, and pure fear of what other states might do all lead states toward war. War and conquest have thus characterized the careers of many authoritarian rulers and ruling parties, from Louis XIV and Napoleon to Mussolini's fascists, Hitler's Nazis, and Stalin's communists.

Yet we cannot simply blame warfare on the authoritarians or totalitarians, as many of our more enthusiastic politicians would have us do. Most wars arise out of calculations and miscalculations of interest, misunderstandings, and mutual suspicions, such as those that characterized the origins of World War I. However, aggression by the liberal state has also characterized a large number of wars. Both France and Britain fought expansionist colonial wars throughout the nineteenth century. The United States fought a similar war with Mexico from 1846 to 1848, waged a war of annihilation against the American Indians, and intervened militarily against sovereign states many times before and after World War II. Liberal states invade weak nonliberal states and display striking distrust in dealings with powerful nonliberal states.

Kant's theory of liberal internationalism helps us understand these two legacies. The importance of Immanuel Kant as a theorist of international ethics has been well appreciated, but Kant also has an important analytical theory of international politics. *Perpetual Peace,* written in 1795, helps us understand the interactive nature of international relations. Kant tries to teach us methodologically that we can study neither the systemic relations of states nor the varieties of state behavior in isolation from each other. Substantively, he anticipates for us the ever-widening pacification of a liberal pacific union, explains this pacification, and at the same time suggests why liberal states are not pacific in their relations with nonliberal states. Kant argues that perpetual peace will be guaranteed by the ever-widening acceptance of three "definitive articles" of peace. When all nations have accepted the definitive articles in a metaphorical "treaty" of perpetual peace he asks them to sign, perpetual peace will have been established.

Kant shows how republics, once established, lead to peaceful relations. He argues that once the aggressive interests of absolutist monarchies are tamed and the habit of respect for individual rights engrained by republican government, wars would appear as the disaster to the people's welfare that he and the other liberals thought them to be. The fundamental reason is this:

> If, as is inevitability the case under this constitution, the consent of the citizens is required to decide whether or not war should be declared, it is very natural that they will have a great hesitation in embarking on so dangerous an enterprise. For this would mean calling down on themselves all the miseries of war, such as doing the fighting themselves, supplying the costs of the war from their own resources, painfully making good the ensuing devastation, and, as the crowning evil, having to take upon themselves a burden of debts which will embitter peace itself and which can never be paid off on account of the constant threat of new wars. But under a constitution where the subject is not a citizen, and which is therefore not republican, it is the simplest thing in the world to go to war. For the head of state is not a fellow citizen, but the owner of the state, and war will not force him to make the slightest sacrifice so far as his banquets, hunts, pleasure palaces and court festivals are concerned. He can thus decide on war, without any significant reason, as a kind of amusement, and unconcernedly leave it to the diplomatic corps (who are always ready for such purposes) to justify the war for the sake of propriety.

Yet these domestic republican restraints do not end war. If they did, liberal states would not be warlike, which is far from the case. They do introduce republican caution—Kant's "hesitation"—in place of monarchical caprice. Liberal wars are only fought for popular, liberal purposes. The historical liberal legacy is laden with popular wars fought to promote freedom, to protect private property, or to support liberal allies against nonliberal enemies. Kant's position is ambiguous. He regards these wars as unjust and warns liberals of their susceptibility to them. At the same time, Kant argues that each nation "can and ought to" demand that its neighboring nations enter into the pacific union of liberal states. Thus to see how the pacific union removes the occasion of wars among liberal states and not wars between liberal and nonliberal states, we need to shift our attention from constitutional law to international law, Kant's second source.

Complementing the constitutional guarantee of caution, international law adds a second source for the definitive articles: a guarantee of respect.

The separation of nations that asocial sociability encourages is reinforced by the development of separate languages and religions. These further guarantee a world of separate states—an essential condition needed to avoid a "global, soul-less despotism." Yet, at the same time, they also morally integrate liberal states: "as culture grows and men gradually move towards greater agreement over their principles, they lead to mutual understanding and peace". As republics emerge (the first source) and as culture progresses, an understanding of the legitimate rights of all citizens and of all republics comes into play; and this, now that caution characterizes policy, sets up the moral foundations for the liberal peace. Correspondingly, international law highlights the importance of Kantian publicity. Domestically, publicity helps ensure that the officials of republics act according to the principles they profess to hold just and according to the interests of the electors they claim to represent. Internationally, free speech and the effective communication of accurate conceptions of the political life of foreign peoples is essential to establishing and preserving the understanding on which the guarantee of respect depends. Domestically just republics, which rest on consent, then presume foreign republics also to be consensual, just, and therefore deserving of accommodation. The experience of cooperation helps engender further cooperative behavior when the consequences of state policy are unclear but (potentially) mutually beneficial. At the same time, liberal states assume that nonliberal states, which do not rest on free consent, are not just. Because nonliberal governments are in a state of aggression with their own people, their foreign relations become for liberal governments deeply suspect. In short, fellow liberals benefit from a presumption of amity; nonliberals suffer from a presumption of enmity. Both presumptions may be accurate; each, however, may also be self-confirming.

Lastly, cosmopolitan law adds material incentives to moral commitments. The cosmopolitan right to hospitality permits the "spirit of commerce" sooner or later to take hold of every nation, thus impelling states to promote peace and to try to avert war. Liberal economic theory holds that these cosmopolitan ties derive from a cooperative international division of labor and free trade according to comparative advantage. Each economy is said to be better off than it would have been under autarky; each thus acquires an incentive to avoid policies that would lead the other to break these economic ties. Because keeping open markets rests upon the assumption that the next set of transactions will also be determined by prices rather than coercion, a sense of mutual security is vital to avoid security-motivated searches for economic autarky. Thus, avoiding a challenge to another liberal state's security or even enhancing each other's security by means of alliance naturally follows economic interdependence.

A further cosmopolitan source of liberal peace is the international market's removal of difficult decisions of production and distribution from the direct sphere of state policy. A foreign state thus does not appear directly responsible for these outcomes, and states can stand aside from, and to some degree above, these contentious market rivalries and be ready to step in to resolve crises. The interdependence of commerce and the international contacts of state officials help create crosscutting transnational ties that serve as lobbies for mutual accommodation. According to modern liberal scholars, international financiers and transnational and transgovernmental organizations create interests in favor of accommodation. Moreover, their variety has ensured that no single conflict sours an entire relationship by setting off a spiral of reciprocated retaliation. Conversely, a sense of suspicion, such as that characterizing relations between liberal and nonliberal governments, can lead to restrictions on the range of contacts between societies, and this can increase the prospect that a single conflict will determine an entire relationship.

No single constitutional, international, or cosmopolitan source is alone sufficient, but together (and only together) they plausibly connect the characteristics of liberal polities and economies with sustained liberal peace. Alliances founded on mutual strategic interest among liberal and nonliberal states have been broken; economic ties between liberal and non-liberal states have proven fragile; but the political bonds of liberal rights and interests have proven a remarkably firm foundation for mutual nonaggression. A separate peace exists among liberal states.

In their relations with nonliberal states, however, liberal states have not escaped from the insecurity caused by anarchy in the world political system considered as a whole. Moreover, the very constitutional restraint, international respect for individual rights, and shared commercial interests that establish grounds for peace among liberal states establish grounds for additional conflict in relations between liberal and nonliberal societies.

CONCLUSION

Kant's liberal internationalism, Machiavelli's liberal imperialism, and Schumpeter's liberal pacifism rest on fundamentally different views of the nature of the human being, the state, and international relations. Schumpeter's humans are rationalized, individualized, and democratized. They are also homogenized, pursuing material interests "monistically." Because their material interests lie in peaceful trade, they and the democratic state that these fellow citizens control are pacifistic. Machiavelli's citizens are splendidly diverse in their goals but fundamentally unequal in them as well, seeking to rule or fearing being dominated. Extending the rule of the dominant elite or avoiding the political collapse of their state, each calls for imperial expansion.

Kant's citizens, too, are diverse in their goals and individualized and rationalized, but most importantly, they are capable of appreciating the moral equality of all individuals and of treating other individuals as ends rather than as means. The Kantian state thus is governed publicly according to law, as a republic. Kant's is the state that solves the problem of governing individualized equals, whether they are the "rational devils" he says we often find ourselves to be or the ethical agents we can and should become. Republics tell us that

> in order to organize a group of rational beings who together require universal laws for their survival, but of whom each separate individual is secretly inclined to exempt himself from them, the constitution must be so designed so that, although the citizens are opposed to one another in their private attitudes, these opposing views may inhibit one another in such a way that the public conduct of the citizens will be the same as if they did not have such evil attitudes.

Unlike Machiavelli's republics, Kant's republics are capable of achieving peace among themselves because they exercise democratic caution and are capable of appreciating the international rights of foreign republics. These international rights of republics derive from the representation of foreign individuals, who are our moral equals. Unlike Schumpeter's capitalist democracies, Kant's republics—including our own—remain in a state of war with nonrepublics. Liberal republics see themselves as threatened by aggression from nonrepublics that are not constrained by representation. Even though wars often cost more than the economic return they generate, liberal republics also are prepared to protect and promote—sometimes forcibly—democracy, private property, and the rights of individuals overseas against nonrepublics, which, because they do not authentically represent the rights of individuals, have no rights to noninterference. These wars may liberate oppressed individuals overseas; they also can generate enormous suffering.

Preserving the legacy of the liberal peace without succumbing to the legacy of liberal imprudence is both a moral and a strategic challenge. The bipolar stability of the international system, and the near certainty of mutual devastation resulting from a nuclear war between the superpowers, have created a "crystal ball effect" that has helped to constrain the tendency toward miscalculation present at the outbreak of so many wars in the past. However, this "nuclear peace" appears to be limited to the superpowers. It has not curbed military interventions in the Third World. Moreover, it is subject to a desperate technological race designed to overcome its constraints and to crises that have pushed even the superpowers to the brink of war. We must still reckon with the war fevers and moods of appeasement that have almost alternately swept liberal democracies.

Yet restraining liberal imprudence, whether aggressive or passive, may not be possible without threatening liberal pacification. Improving the strategic acumen of our foreign policy calls for introducing steadier strategic calculations of the national interest in the long run and more flexible responses to changes in the international political environment. Constraining the indiscriminate meddling of our foreign interventions calls for a deeper appreciation of the "particularism of history, culture, and membership", but both the improvement in strategy and the constraint on intervention seem, in turn, to require an executive freed from the restraints of a representative legislature in the management of foreign policy and a political culture indifferent to the universal rights of individuals. These conditions, in their turn, could break the chain of constitutional guarantees, the respect for representative government, and the web of transnational contact that have sustained the pacific union of liberal states.

Perpetual peace, Kant says, is the end point of the hard journey his republics will take. The promise of perpetual peace, the violent lessons of war, and the experience of a partial peace are proof of the need for and the possibility of world peace. They are also the grounds for moral citizens and statesmen to assume the duty of striving for peace.

Twenty Years of Institutional Liberalism

ROBERT O. KEOHANE

The social purpose of Institutional Liberalism is to promote beneficial effects on human security, human welfare and human liberty as a result of a more peaceful, prosperous and free world. Institutional Liberalism justifies the use of power in constructing institutions on the basis of this conception of social purpose.

Institutional Liberalism is very different from what E. H. Carr, in *The Twenty Years' Crisis*, described as "liberalism." Carr had in mind nineteenth century liberalism, which was based on abstract rational principles taken out of context and therefore believed, in Carr's words, that "public opinion can be relied on to judge rightly on any question rationally presented to it." This form of liberalism, according to Carr, believed in a harmony of interests based on a "synthesis of morality and reason." And it separated power from economics. Carr's critique of this harmony-of-interest form of liberalism was convincing. Contemporary Institutional Liberals, such as myself, have learned from Carr and appropriated his insights.

The roots of Institutional Liberalism lay less in specific views of capitalism and the state than in pluralist conceptions of power and interests that are well expressed in the works of James Madison. Madison was a republican: the people should govern. He did not believe that people are good and easily ruled, but rather that power needs to be checked for fear of the consequences of unchecked power. So domestically, the people should govern, but they need to establish institutions to control themselves, guarding against bad leaders and moments of passion. My views on democracy represent an ethnically, racially and gender-egalitarian adaptation of Madison's arguments. The people, broadly conceived, should rule, but they have to rule through institutions. At some moments, when publics are attuned to political events and leadership is responsive, government "by the people" is very progressive and effective. An American naturally thinks in this respect of the first years of the Civil War in the North, when attitudes toward both slavery and racism changed dramatically along with policy; and the New Deal. But when the people are not engaged, or when they are misled by demagoguery, democracy may merely be, as Churchill is said to have commented, the worst form of government except for all the others.

One of the most important contemporary liberal theorists of international relations, Michael W. Doyle, sees liberalism as resembling "a family portrait of principles and institutions," focused on the essential principle of freedom of the individual and associated with negative freedom (freedom from arbitrary authority), positive freedom (social rights essential for promoting the capacity for freedom), and democratic participation or representation. Institutions are essential for exercising these rights.

Internationally, Institutional Liberals believe that power should be used in the interests of liberal values but with caution and restraint. Institutions serve a crucial social purpose because they are essential for sustained cooperation that enhances the interests of most, if not of all, people. In world politics, a sophisticated liberalism is, as I have written, "an antidote to fatalism and a source of hope." Unlike Realism, it strives for, and believes in, improvement of the human condition and provides a rationale for building cooperative institutions that can facilitate better lives for human beings.

QUESTIONING INSTITUTIONAL LIBERALISM

But I write not to celebrate Institutional Liberalism but to question it. Invoking the ideas and spirit of E. H. Carr, but focusing on a different form of liberalism, I seek to evaluate the last 20 years of liberal dominance in world politics. Only since the collapse of the Soviet Union has it been possible to evaluate the impact of liberal institutionalism on world politics.

Before 1991, institution-building by the United States and its allies had a significant security justification: to create economic prosperity and patterns of cooperation that would reinforce the position of the West in the struggle with the Soviet Union. Furthermore, American hegemony was crucial: the international institutions created after World War II "were constructed on the basis of principles espoused by the United States, and American power was essential for their construction and maintenance." Cooperation persisted longer than most Realists would have expected, but as long as the Soviet Union remained a rival and a threat, a Realist emphasis on relative gains was consistent with continued cooperation between the United States and other advanced industrialized countries. The relative gains that mattered were between the West and the Soviet bloc. In other words, an interpretation that explains institutions on the basis of the functions that they serve and a Realist one could both explain the patterns of cooperation that emerged and persisted.

The international institutions that operated during this period facilitated mutually beneficial cooperation on issues ranging from security to monetary cooperation to trade. Most of these institutions were not highly legalized. Sovereignty was not taken away from states, but became a *bargaining resource* that states could negotiate away, to some extent, in order to obtain other benefits, such as influence over other states' regulatory policies. Cooperation occurred on the basis of mutual self-interest and reciprocity, without much legalization.

Yet these patterns of cooperation led to remarkably robust international regimes: sets of principles, norms and rules governing the relations among well-defined sets of actors. Under the international monetary regime that prevailed between 1958 and 1971, for instance, membership in fixed exchange rate regimes was well defined and the rules were followed, with some relatively minor exceptions. Until the early 1970s the international oil regime was also quite clear, although the rules were largely set by major international oil companies, not by states. Finally, the trade regime built around the General Agreements on Tariffs and Trade (GATT) became progressively stronger as well, at least until the mid-1980s. In the early 1980s both Ruggie and I, despite our different perspectives, anticipated a continuation and gradual strengthening of international institutions grounded in domestic politics and achieving substantial cooperation on the basis largely of specific reciprocity, as in the GATT trade system.

Since the early 1990s we can observe three developments of note: an increase in legalization; increasing legalism and moralism expressed by people leading civil society efforts to create and modify international institutions; and a decline in the coherence of some international regimes along with a failure to increase the coherence of others. Increasing legalism and moralism might have been expected 20 years ago by those of us who studied liberalism; but in different ways the increases in legalization and the recent apparent decline in the coherence of international regimes seem anomalous.

In what follows I reassess Institutional Liberalism in the light of the experience of the last 20 years. Does Institutional Liberalism contain a formerly hidden logic linking legalization, the upsurge of legalism and moralism, and decreased regime coherence? That is, do these apparently contradictory developments all represent manifestations of liberalism, which only became fully evident when it became dominant in world politics? Or do some or all of these tendencies not reflect liberalism as such, but the impact of changes in power structures in tension with liberalism, or of domestic politics? In this latter view, the changes that we see are not direct effects of liberalism but only of the inability of liberal values to be realized in a world of fragmented power and pluralist domestic politics.

Before developing my argument, it is essential that I define what I mean by "legalization," "international regimes," "legalism," and "moralism."

Legalization is a property of *institutions*. The rules of legalized institutions are precise and obligatory, and they provide arrangements for third-party adjudication. Legalization has facilitated the progressive extension of rights, and legal protection, to oppressed persons and peoples. Even in situations when formal legalization is not feasible, an orientation toward legalization can promote the rise of "soft law," which helps reduce uncertainty and facilitate rule-implementation.

Coherence is also a property of institutions, but refers more to the relationship among institutions than to the properties of any single institution. Coherent institutions or clusters of institutions have clear lines of authority linking them, so that for any given situation it is clear which rules apply, or at least which adjudicatory institutions are authorized to determine which rules apply.

Finally, there seems to have been a rise in legalism and moralism in the discourse of international relations. Legalism and moralism are not properties of institutions but rather of the *human mind.* Legalism is the belief that moral and political progress can be made through the extension of law. Moralism is the belief that moral principles provide valuable, if not necessarily sufficient, guides to how political actors should behave, and that actions by those in power can properly be judged on the basis of their conformity to general moral principles developed chiefly to govern the actions of individuals.

Although many authors, particularly international legal scholars, have celebrated both legalism and legalization without distinguishing them, I wish to distinguish them from one another in this essay, since I am particularly ambivalent about legalism. I believe with E. H. Carr that law, and its efficacy, always rests on structures of power. So legalism, when taken as the description of a causal process, seems misleading to me in an ideological sense: that is, it can serve as a veil, hiding the exercise of power. In practice, the application of law can become quite uneven under situations of unequal power, leading to a form of what Stephen Krasner calls "organized hypocrisy."

E. H. Carr was critical of utopian thinking, which is often moralistic; and he was also critical of legalism. As he said, "Law is a function of political society, is dependent for its development on the development of that society, and is conditioned by the political presuppositions which that society shares in common." So an appropriate entry-point into our inquiry is to start with Carr's own thinking about morality in world politics and the role of law. What would Carr, observing the revival of legalism and moralism in world politics, make of their revival? We cannot really answer this question, but in this essay I take up some of E. H. Carr's themes to see what insights, and cautions, they may raise about contemporary international liberalism, and the moralistic and legalistic tone that it seems increasingly to be taking.

I begin with the revival of moralism, since it is fundamental—often providing a justification for legalization and legalism—and it seems to me relatively easy to explain. I will then turn to legalization and legalism, seeking to account for their growth as well. Finally, I reflect on what appears to be a counter-trend: the growing incoherence of major international regimes and the failure of coherent regimes to emerge in other areas, where functional arguments might expect them to develop.

IDEALISM AND INTERESTS: THE REVIVAL OF MORALISM IN WORLD POLITICS

The collapse of the Soviet Union in 1991 made the US and liberal democratic states elsewhere believe that they could construct "a new world order" more consistent with the values and practices of liberal domestic politics. The language of moralism, which had previously been used in conjunction with efforts to stop the spread of Communism during the Cold War, was now detached from great power struggles. Four examples of morally justified activities are as follows:

- The conclusion of a number of major human rights treaties in the decades of the 1960s, 1970s and 1980s, and the continual push for their implementation by nongovernmental organizations committed to human rights and by some governments. These efforts included efforts to protect the rights of women and children in societies with well-entrenched practices adverse to the protection of these rights.
- Efforts by democratic governments and civil society to promote democracy in Eastern Europe after the Cold War and around the world. These efforts were institutionalized in what Sarah Bush has called "The Democracy Establishment"—a network of individuals in governments and NGOs working to institute democratic practices in countries that were not stable democracies. The institution of extensive international election monitoring provides one notable aspect of the work of the Democracy Establishment.
- The Responsibility to Protect Doctrine, agreed by the Millennium Summit of the United Nations in 2005, which calls on states to protect their populations and provides for UN Security Council action to protect populations if the state with formal jurisdiction fails to do so. R2P, as it is called, has become a strong norm affecting UN action, although it is not a legal rule. R2P is a good example of moralism as I have defined it: the belief that moral principles provide a valuable guide to political action.
- NATO's use of military force to prevent the domination of neighboring peoples by Serbia, and last year to overthrow the Qaddafi regime in Libya. UN Security Council Resolution 1973 of 17 March 2011, authorizing the use of force against the government of Libya, referred to the Libyan government's responsibility to protect its citizens, and expressed the Council's determination to protect civilians, without explicitly invoking the R2P doctrine. In defending his support for military intervention, Barack Obama, on 28 March 2011, declared: "Some nations may be able to turn a blind eye to atrocities in other countries. The United States of America is different. And as President, I refused to wait for the images of slaughter and mass graves before taking action."

So we should give *two cheers for moralism* in an era lacking vital threats to the security of our societies and our democratic institutions. First, moralism provides an impetus to social movements that provide incentives for democratic politicians to promote liberal democratic values abroad. Second, as Carr pointed out, moralism, if enunciated in moderation and practiced more or less consistently, can enhance the legitimacy of hegemonic states and the orders they seek to maintain. But we withhold the third cheer: the Realists are right to point out that power corrupts, so we need to beware that moralism can also generate arrogance, facilitate the distortion of reality, and even conceal nefarious purposes.

THE REVIVAL OF LEGALISM AND ITS PENUMBRA

Since 1991, as I have noted, Institutional Liberalism has increasingly been legalized. The social movements of democratic liberalism have tried to institute what Ruti Teitel calls "humanity law": the "law of persons and peoples" rather than the law of states.

Liberals naturally turn to law as a constraint on power. For Institutional Liberals, this emphasis on law reflects neither a naïve belief in human goodness nor the automatic power of rules, but the view that human beings require institutional constraints to ensure that they behave well. Since 1991 there has been a remarkable increase in the number and significance of international legal institutions. Four prominent examples include the following:

- The International Criminal Tribunal for the Former Yugoslavia (ICTFY) was founded in May 1993 and is expected to operate for two or three more years.
- World trade law was legalized in the World Trade Organization, which came into force on 1 January 1995.
- The European Court of Human Rights (ECHR) was established on a permanent basis in 1998, with jurisdiction over 800 million people in the 47 member countries of the Council.
- The International Criminal Court (ICC) came into being on 1 July 2002, and now has over 115 member states.

CHANGES IN STRUCTURE AND THE DECREASING COHERENCE OF INTERNATIONAL ECONOMIC AND ENVIRONMENTAL REGIMES

Realists look for cycles and therefore have a tendency to expect observed changes to reverse themselves, because, as Robert G. Gilpin said 30 years ago, "the fundamental nature of international relations has not changed over the millennia. International relations continue to be a recurring struggle for wealth and power among independent actors in a state of anarchy."

Pursuing this line of thought, John J. Mearsheimer famously, and wrongly, predicted in 1990 that the collapse of the Soviet Union would take the world "back to the future"—to a world of power politics in Europe. The liberal "prediction of peace in a multipolar Europe is flawed." Waltz's theory of balancing would have led us to believe that the dominance of the United States would generate a blocking coalition against it. Neither of these scenarios occurred. But the broader claim of Realism is embedded in balance of power theory: that power generates attempts to counter it. And in this light 9/11 can be seen as supportive of the Realist worldview, which is profoundly cyclical and anti-progressive. Concentrated power does motivate efforts to oppose it. American dominance has been challenged by al-Qaeda, by North Korea and from Iran, and in a less radical but more enduring and fundamental sense there will be a continuing challenge over the next few decades from China. The point is that there is a counter-narrative to the progressive and pacific narrative of Institutional Liberalism.

Countries such as Brazil, China, and India have different interests from those of the established industrialized democracies—with respect to trade, foreign investment, monetary arrangements and governing arrangements for limiting climate change. It is therefore not surprising that the Doha Round trade talks seem permanently stalled, that China and other exporting countries keep their exchange rate undervalued and build up enormous foreign currency reserves, that rivalry rather than cooperation characterizes oil politics, or that the non-Annex I countries under the Kyoto Protocol, exempted from rules for emissions controls when they were weak and small, refused until the Durban meetings in December 2011 to agree to be governed by common emissions rules despite being the major sources of increases in emissions.

As a generalization, it seems to me that what could have been seen in the mid-1990s as a progressive extension of international regimes, with stronger rules and larger jurisdictions, has been halted if not reversed. The hopes of observers such as John Ikenberry for a revival of liberal regimes under a more capacious form of American hegemony are not, so far, being realized. And here again Realism remains relevant: to understand institutions and international law, we need to peer through the veil of rhetoric and law, to discern the power and interest structures that lie below. Those power and interest structures moved strongly toward greater coherence and uniformity with the collapse of the Soviet Union: when the WTO was formed, the West was at a historic high point of dominance. With the rise of China, India and other emerging economies, structures of power and interest have become more diverse; and as Structural Realism would have anticipated, the institutions that link major powers have been weakened, with more contention over their proper arrangements. Liberal regimes with United States leadership may be easy to join, as Ikenberry asserts; but they can also be rejected by states with sufficient independent power. As institutional theorists anticipated, many of these institutions persist despite changes in patterns of power and interests; but as Realists claimed, it has become increasingly difficult to construct strong new institutions.

CONCLUSION

At the beginning of this essay I asked whether moralism and legalism, legalization, and declines in the coherence of international regimes reflected intrinsic qualities of liberalism or the impact of changes in structures of power. My answer is mixed. I attribute increased legalization, moralism and legalism to intrinsic features of liberalism and to the dominance since 1991 of liberal states. But I attribute declines in the coherence of international regimes to the anticipated as well as actual diversification of power and interests in world politics as well as the inhibitions on learning built into domestic politics in most countries in an era of slow economic growth and increasing economic inequality. Collapse is avoided because, as Joseph Nye and I wrote in *Power and Interdependence*, "a set of networks, norms and institutions, once established, will be difficult either to eradicate or drastically rearrange." But progress toward more coherent and comprehensive regimes has also come to a halt.

So we see the persistence and in some areas the expansion of legalization, coupled with legalism and moralism, at the same time as urgent problems no longer generate the creation of multilateral regimes. Contradictory patterns continue to appear.

My own liberalism has little in common with either laissez-faire economics or with the notion that liberals are optimists about human nature. It has much more in common with Judith N. Sklar's concept of the "liberalism of fear." As I implied at the beginning of this article, I share much of James Madison's political philosophy. I am a liberal not because I think people are good and easily ruled, but because I think that unchecked power is dangerous and that power-holders therefore need to be held in check. Institutional Liberalism offers not the promise of continuous progress but a source of hope for improvement coupled with institutional checks against retrogression.

Power continues to be important but institutions can help to tame it, and states whose leaders seek both to maintain and use power must be attentive, as E. H. Carr recognized, to issues of legitimacy. At the moment, legalism and moralism thrive, but the comprehensiveness and coherence of multilateral institutions are suffering. We need at this time less to profess and preach legalism and moralism than to figure out how to form coalitions that will build and maintain coherent multilateral institutions to address the major challenges of our time. The fact that these institutions are not foolproof is less a counsel of despair than a motivation to build them on as firm foundations as we can.

VISUAL REVIEW

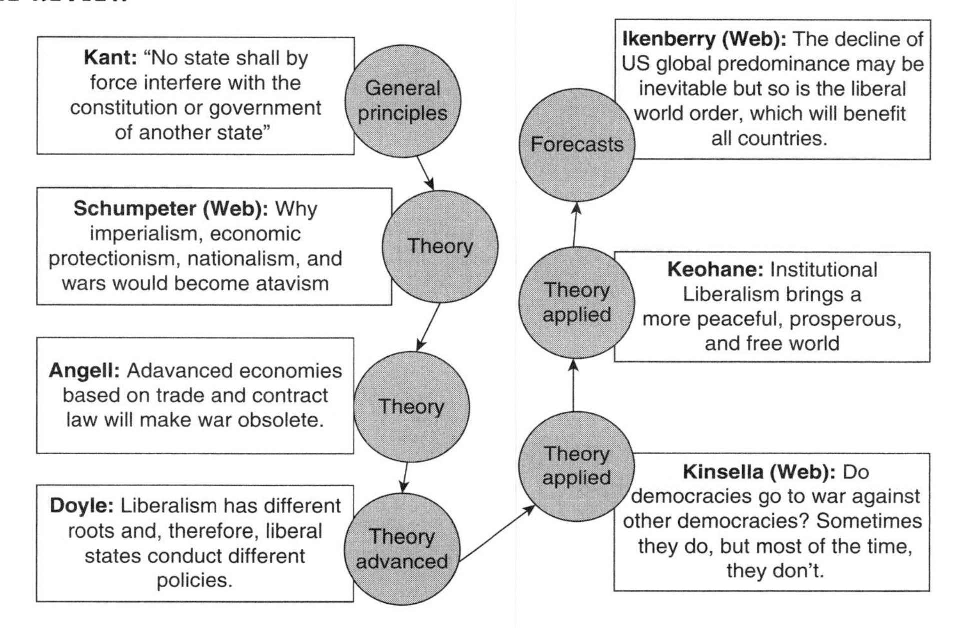

Section 4

Historical Context III: Exploring Alternatives: Class, Gender, and Values

The only female pilot in Afghanistan's air force poses for a photo in 2014. She trained for two and a half years at special facilities in western Afghanistan to become a pilot. One of the arguments of feminist theorists of international relations is that the more women participate in diplomatic, security, and military policies, the better it will be for international stability and peace. Do you agree with this argument and why? Why, for example, has the name of this pilot not been revealed?
Source: Kyodo/Associated Press

Structural Crises

IMMANUEL WALLERSTEIN

Capitalism is a system in which the endless accumulation of capital is the raison d'être. To accumulate capital, producers must obtain profits from their operations, which is possible on a significant scale only if the product can be sold for considerably more than it cost to produce. In a situation of perfect competition, it is impossible to make profits on such a scale: a monopoly, or at least a quasi-monopoly, of world-economic power is required. The seller can then demand any price, as long as he does not go beyond what the elasticity of demand permits. Whenever the world-economy is expanding significantly some "leading" products are relatively monopolized, and it is from the profits on these that large amounts of capital can be accumulated. The forward and backward linkages of such products form the basis for an overall expansion of the world-economy. We call this the A-phase of a Kondratieff cycle. The problem for capitalists is that all monopolies are self-liquidating, due to the fact that new producers can enter the world market, however politically well defended a given monopoly may be. Of course, entry takes time; but sooner or later the degree of competition rises, prices go down and therefore profits go down too. When profits for the leading products decline sufficiently, the world-economy ceases to expand, and enters into a period of stagnation—the B-phase of a Kondratieff cycle.

The second condition for capitalist profit is that there be some kind of relative global order. While world wars offer some entrepreneurs opportunities to do very well, they also occasion enormous destruction of fixed capital and considerable interference with world trade. The overall balance-sheet of world wars is not positive, a point Schumpeter repeatedly made. Ensuring the relatively stable situation required for profit-making is the task of a hegemonic power strong enough to impose it on the world-system as a whole. Hegemonic cycles have been much longer than Kondratieff cycles: in a world of multiple so-called sovereign states, it is not easy for one to establish itself as the hegemonic power. It was done first by the United Provinces in the mid-17th century, then by the United Kingdom in the mid-19th century, and finally by the United States in the mid-20th century. The rise of each hegemonic power has been the result of a long struggle with other potential hegemons. Up to now the winner has been the state that has been able to assemble the most efficient productive machinery, and then to win a "thirty years' war" with its principal rival. The hegemon is then able to set the rules by which the interstate system operates, to assure its smooth functioning and to maximize the flow of accumulated capital to its citizens and productive enterprises. One could call this a quasi-monopoly of geopolitical power.

The problem for the hegemonic power is the same as that facing a leading industry: its monopoly is self-liquidating. Firstly, the hegemon has on occasion to exercise its military power to maintain order. But wars cost money and lives, and have a negative impact on its citizens, whose initial pride in victory may evaporate as they pay the increasing costs of military action. Large-scale military operations are often less effective than expected, and this strengthens those who wish to resist in the future. Secondly, even if the hegemon's economic efficiency does not immediately falter, that of other countries begins to rise, making them less ready to accept its dictates. The hegemon enters into a process of gradual decline relative to the rising powers. The decline may be slow, but it is nonetheless essentially irreversible.

What made the moment of 1965–70 so remarkable was the conjoining of these two kinds of downturn—the end of the historically most expansive Kondratieff A-phase, and the beginning of the decline of the historically most powerful hegemon. It is no accident that the world revolution of

62, March–April, New Left Review, March/April.

An earlier version of this paper was given at the World Congress of the International Institute of Sociology in Yerevan on 13 June 2009.

1968 (actually 1966–70) took place at that turning point, as an expression of it.

DISPLACING THE OLD LEFT

The world revolution of 1968 marked a third downturn—one that has occurred only once, however, in the history of the modern world-system: the decline of the traditional anti-systemic movements, the so-called Old Left. Composed essentially of the Communists, Social-Democrats and national-liberation movements, the Old Left arose slowly and laboriously across the world-system, primarily throughout the last third of the nineteenth century and the first half of the twentieth; ascending from a position of political marginality and weakness as of, say, 1870, to one of political centrality and considerable strength around 1950. These movements reached the summit of their mobilizing power in the period from 1945 to 1968—exactly the moment of both the extraordinary Kondratieff A-phase expansion and the height of US hegemony. I do not think this was fortuitous, although it might seem counter-intuitive. The world economic boom led entrepreneurs to believe that concessions to the material demands of their workers cost them less than interruptions to the productive process. Over time, this meant rising costs of production, one of the factors behind the end of the quasi-monopolies in leading industries. But most entrepreneurs make decisions that maximize short-term profits—over the succeeding three years, say—and leave the future to the gods.

Parallel considerations influenced the policies of the hegemonic power. Maintaining relative stability in the world-system was an essential objective, but the United States had to weigh the cost of repressive activity against the cost of concessions to demands from national-liberation movements. Reluctantly at first, but later more deliberately, Washington began to favour a controlled "decolonization," which had the effect of bringing such movements to power. Hence, by the middle of the 1960s, one could say that the Old Left movements had achieved their historic goal of state power almost everywhere—at least on paper. Communist parties ruled one-third of the world, social-democratic parties were in power, or alternating power, in most of another third: the pan-European world; in addition, the principal policy of the social-democratic parties—the welfare state—was accepted and practised by their conservative opponents. National-liberation movements had come to power in most of the former colonial world, as had populist movements in Latin America. Many analysts and militants today would criticize the performance of these movements, but this is to forget the fear that pervaded the world's wealthier and more conservative strata in face of what looked to them like a juggernaut of destructive egalitarianism, equipped with state power.

The world revolution of 1968 changed all that. Three themes predominated in its multiple uprisings: the first was that US hegemonic power was overstretched and vulnerable—in Vietnam the Tet offensive was taken to be the death knell for US military operations. Revolutionaries also attacked the role of the Soviet Union, which they saw as a collusive participant in US hegemony—a feeling that had been growing everywhere since at least 1956. The second theme was that the Old Left movements had failed to deliver on their historic promises. All three varieties had been premised on the so-called two-stage strategy—first take state power, then change the world. The militants in effect said: "You have taken state power but have not changed the world. If we wish to change the world, we need new movements and new strategies." The Chinese Cultural Revolution was taken by many as the model for this possibility. The third theme was that the Old Left had ignored the forgotten peoples—those downtrodden because of their race, gender, ethnicity or sexuality. The militants insisted that demands for equal treatment could no longer be deferred—they constituted part of the urgent present. In many ways, the Black Power movement in the United States was the paradigmatic example.

The world revolution of 1968 was both an enormous political success and an enormous political failure. It rose like a phoenix, burned bright across the globe, but by the mid-1970s seemed to be extinguished almost everywhere. What had been accomplished by this wild brushfire? Centrist liberalism had been dethroned as the governing ideology of the world-system, and was reduced to being simply one alternative among others; the Old Left movements were destroyed as mobilizers of any kind of fundamental change. But the triumphalism of 1968 proved shallow and unsustainable. The world right was equally liberated from any attachment to centrist liberalism. It took advantage of the world-economic stagnation and the collapse of the Old Left to launch a counter-offensive, that of neoliberal globalization. The prime objectives were to reverse all the gains of the lower strata during the Kondratieff A-phase: to reduce the costs of production, to destroy the welfare state and to slow the decline of US power. Its onward march seemed to culminate in 1989, as the ending of Soviet control over its East-Central European satellites and the dismantling of the USSR itself led to a new triumphalism on the right.

The offensive of the world right was both a great success and a great failure. What has sustained the accumulation of capital since the 1970s has been a turn from seeking profits through productive efficiency to seeking them through financial manipulations, more correctly called speculation. The key mechanism has been the fostering of consumption via indebtedness. This has happened in every Kondratieff B-phase; the difference this time has been the scale. After the biggest A-phase expansion in history, there has followed the biggest speculative mania. Bubbles moved through the whole world-system—from the national debts of the Third World and socialist bloc in the 1970s to the junk bonds of large corporations in the 1980s, the consumer indebtedness of the 1990s and the US government indebtedness of the Bush era. The system has gone from bubble to bubble, and is currently trying to inflate yet another, with bank bailouts and the printing of dollars.

The downturn into which the world has fallen will continue now for some time, and will be quite deep. It will destroy the last remaining pillar of relative economic stability, the role of the US dollar as reserve currency for safeguarding wealth. As this happens, the main concern of every government in the world will be to avert uprisings of unemployed workers and the middle strata whose savings and pensions are disappearing. Governments are currently turning to protectionism and printing money as their first line of defence. Such measures may assuage momentarily the pain of ordinary people, but it is probable that they will make the situation even worse. We are entering systemic gridlock, from which exit will be extremely difficult. This will express itself in ever wilder fluctuations, which will make short-term predictions—both economic and political—virtually guesswork. This in turn will aggravate popular fears and the sense of alienation.

Some claim that the greatly improved relative economic position of Asia—Japan, South Korea, Taiwan, China and to a lesser extent India—will allow a resurgence of capitalist enterprise, through a simple geographical shift of location. One more illusion! The relative rise of Asia is a reality, but one that undermines further the capitalist system by over-extending the distribution of surplus-value, thus reducing overall accumulation for individual capitals rather than increasing it. China's expansion accelerates the structural profit squeeze of the capitalist world-economy.

Capitalists aim to externalize costs, that is, to not pay the full bill for handling toxic waste, renewing raw materials and building infrastructure. From the sixteenth century to the 1960s, such externalization of costs had been normal practice, more or less unquestioned by political authorities. Toxic waste was simply dumped in the public domain. But the world has been running out of vacant public space—parallel to the deruralization of the world's workforce. The health consequences and costs have become so high and so close to home as to produce demands for environmental clean-up and control. Resources have also become a major concern, the consequence of the sharp increase in world population. There is now widespread discussion about shortages of energy sources, water, forestation, fish and meat. Transport and communication costs have also gone up as these have become faster and more efficient. Entrepreneurs have historically paid only a small part of the bill for infrastructure. The consequence of all of this has been political pressure for governments to assume more of the costs of detoxification, resource renewal and infra-structural expansion. To do this, governments must increase taxes and insist on more internalization of costs by entrepreneurs, which of course cuts into profit margins.

Finally, taxation has been going up. There are multiple levels of taxation, including private taxation in the form of corruption and organized mafias. Taxation has risen as the scope of world-economic activity has extended and state bureaucracies have expanded, but the major impetus has come from the world's anti-systemic movements, which have pushed for state-guarantees of education, health and life-long revenue flows. Each of these has expanded, both geographically and in terms of the levels of services demanded. No government today is exempt from the pressure to maintain a welfare state, even if the levels of provision vary.

STRUGGLES FOR SUCCESSION

The conjunction of the three elements—the magnitude of the "normal" crash, the rise in costs of production, and the extra pressure on the system of Chinese (and Asian) growth—means that we have entered a structural crisis. The system is very far from equilibrium, and the fluctuations are enormous. From now on, we will be living amidst a bifurcation of the systemic process. The question is no longer, "how will the capitalist system mend itself, and renew its forward thrust?," but rather, "what will replace this system? What order will emerge from this chaos?"

We may think of this period of systemic crisis as an arena of struggle for the successor system. The outcome may be inherently unpredictable, but the nature of the struggle is clear. We are faced with alternative choices, which cannot be spelled out in institutional detail, but may be suggested in broad outline. We can choose collectively a new system that essentially resembles the present one: hierarchical, exploitative and polarizing. There are many forms this could take, and some could be harsher than the capitalist world-system in which we have been living. Alternatively we can choose a radically different system, one that has never previously existed—a system that is relatively democratic and relatively egalitarian.

First we must note two crucial characteristics of a structural crisis. Because the fluctuations are so wild, there is little pressure to return to equilibrium. During the long, "normal" lifetime of the system, such pressure was the reason why extensive social mobilizations—so-called "revolutions"—had always been limited in their effects. But when the system is far from equilibrium, the opposite can happen—small social mobilizations can have very great repercussions, what complexity science refers to as the "butterfly effect." We might also call it the moment when political agency prevails over structural determinism. The second crucial characteristic is that in neither of the two camps is there a small group at the top calling all the shots: a functioning "executive committee of the ruling class," or a politburo of the oppressed masses. Even among those committed to the struggle for a successor system, there are multiple players, advocating different emphases. The two groups of conscious militants on both sides are also finding it difficult to persuade the larger groups that form their potential bases of the utility and possibility of organizing the transition. In short, the chaos of the structural crisis is reflected in the relatively disordered configuration of the two camps.

What practical steps can any of us take to further this process? There is no formulaic agenda, there are only lines of emphasis. I would put at the head of the list actions that we can take, in the short run, to minimize the pain that arises from the breakdown of the existing system, and from the confusions of the transition. These might include winning an election in order to obtain more material benefits for those who have least; greater protection of judicial and political rights; measures to combat further erosion of our planetary wealth and conditions for collective survival. Nevertheless, these are not in themselves steps towards creating the new successor system that we need. Serious intellectual debate is required about the parameters of the kind of world-system we want, and the strategy for transition. This requires a willingness to hear those we deem of good will, even if they do not share our views. Open debate will surely build greater camaraderie, and will perhaps keep us from falling into the sectarianism that has always defeated anti-systemic movements. Finally, wherever possible we should construct alternative decommodified modes of production. By doing this we can discover the limits of many particular methods, and demonstrate that there are other modes of ensuring sustainable production than a reward system based on the profit motive. In addition, struggle against the fundamental inequalities of the world—gender, class and race/ethnicity/religion—must be at the forefront of our thoughts and deeds. This is the hardest task of all, since none of us are guiltless, and the world culture that we have inherited militates against us. Does it also need to be said that we must avoid any sense that history is on our side? We have at best a 50–50 chance of creating a better world-system than the one in which we now live. But 50–50 is a lot. We must try to seize Fortuna, even if it escapes us. What more useful thing can any of us do?

Constructing International Politics

ALEXANDER WENDT

Indeed, one of our main objections to neorealism is that it is not structural enough: that adopting the individualistic metaphors of micro-economics restricts the effects of structures to state behavior, ignoring how they might also constitute state identities and interests. Constructivists think that state interests are in important part constructed by systemic structures, not exogenous to them; this leads to a sociological rather than micro-economic structuralism.

Where neorealist and constructivist structuralisms really differ, however, is in their assumptions about what structure is made of. Neorealists think it is made only of a distribution of material capabilities, whereas constructivists think it is also made of social relationships. Social structures have three elements: shared knowledge, material resources, and practices.

First, social structures are defined, in part, by shared understandings, expectations, or knowledge. These constitute the actors in a situation and the nature of their relationships, whether cooperative or conflictual.

Second, social structures include material resources like gold and tanks. In contrast to neorealists' desocialized view of such capabilities, constructivists argue that material resources only acquire meaning for human action through the structure of shared knowledge in which they are embedded. For example, 500 British nuclear weapons are less threatening to the United States than 5 North Korean nuclear weapons, because the British are friends of the United States and the North Koreans are not, and amity or enmity is a function of shared understandings. As students of world politics, neorealists would probably not disagree, but as theorists the example poses a big problem, since it completely eludes their materialist definition of structure. Material capabilities as such explain nothing; their effects presuppose structures of shared knowledge, which vary and which are not reducible to capabilities. Constructivism is therefore compatible with changes in material power affecting social relations, as long as those effects can be shown to presuppose still deeper social relations.

Third, social structures exist, not in actors' heads nor in material capabilities, but in practices. Social structure exists only in process. The Cold War was a structure of shared knowledge that governed great power relations for forty years, but once they stopped acting on this basis, it was "over."

Alexander Wendt, 'Constructing International Politics', International Security, 20:1 (Summer, 1995), pp.71–81.

In sum, social structures are real and objective, not "just talk." But this objectivity depends on shared knowledge, and in that sense social life is "ideas all the way down" (until you get to biology and natural resources). Thus, to ask "when do ideas, as opposed to power and interest, matter?" is to ask the wrong question. Ideas always matter, since power and interest do not have effects apart from the shared knowledge that constitutes them as such.

EXPLAINING WAR AND PEACE

In "Anarchy is What States Make of It" I argued that such behavior is a self-fulfilling prophecy, and that this is due to both agency and social structure. Thus, on the agency side, what states do to each other affects the social structure in which they are embedded, by a logic of reciprocity. If they militarize, others will be threatened and arm themselves, creating security dilemmas in terms of which they will define egoistic identities and interests. But if they engage in policies of reassurance, as the Soviets did in the late 1980s, this will have a different effect on the structure of shared knowledge, moving it toward a security community. The depth of interdependence is a factor here, as is the role of revisionist states, whose actions are likely to be especially threatening. However, on the structural side, the ability of revisionist states to create a war of all against all depends on the structure of shared knowledge into which they enter. If past interactions have created a structure in which status quo states are divided or naive, revisionists will prosper and the system will tend toward a Hobbesian world in which power and self-interest rule. In contrast, if past interactions have created a structure in which status quo states trust and identify with each other, predators are more likely to face collective security responses like the Gulf War. *History matters.* Security dilemmas are not acts of God: they are effects of practice. This does not mean that once created they can necessarily be escaped (they are, after all, "dilemmas"), but it puts the causal locus in the right place.

Anarchy as such is not a structural cause of anything. What matters is its social structure, which varies across anarchies. An anarchy of friends differs from one of enemies, one of self-help from one of collective security, and these are all constituted by structures of shared knowledge.

In order to get from anarchy and material forces to power politics and war, therefore, neorealists have been forced to make additional, ad hoc assumptions about the social structure of the international system.

The problem becomes even more acute when neorealists try to explain the relative absence of inter-state war in today's world. If anarchy is so determining, why are there not more Bosnias? Why are weak states not getting killed off left and right? It stretches credulity to think that the peace between Norway and Sweden, or the United States and Canada, or Nigeria and Benin are all due to material balancing.

RESPONSIBILITY

To say that structures are socially constructed is no guarantee that they can be changed. Sometimes social structures so constrain action that transformative strategies are impossible. This goes back to the collective nature of social structures; structural change depends on changing a system of expectations that may be mutually reinforcing. A key issue in determining policymakers' responsibilities, therefore, is how much "slack" a social structure contains. Neorealists think there is little slack in the system, and thus states that deviate from power politics will get punished or killed by the "logic" of anarchy. Institutionalists think such dangers have been greatly reduced by institutions such as sovereignty and the democratic peace, and that there is therefore more possibility for peaceful change.

The example of Gorbachev is instructive in this respect, since the Cold War was a highly conflictual social structure. What is so important about the Gorbachev regime is that it had the courage to see how the Soviets' own practices sustained the Cold War, and to undertake a reassessment of Western intentions. This is exactly what a constructivist would do, but not a neorealist, who would eschew attention to such social factors as naive and as mere superstructure. Indeed, what is so striking about neorealism is its total neglect of the explanatory role of state practice. It does not seem to matter what states do: Brezhnev, Gorbachev, Zhirinovsky, what difference does it make? The logic of anarchy will always bring us back to square one. This is a disturbing attitude if *realpolitik* causes the very conditions to which it is a response; to the extent that realism counsels *realpolitik*, therefore, it is part of the problem.

To analyze the social construction of international politics is to analyze how processes of interaction produce and reproduce the social structures—cooperative or conflictual—that shape actors' identities and interests and the significance of their material contexts. It is opposed to two rivals: the materialist view, of which neorealism is one expression, that material forces per se determine international life, and the rational choice–theoretic view that interaction does not change identities and interests.

The Growth and Future of Feminist Theories in International Relations

J. ANN TICKNER

BROWN JOURNAL OF WORLD AFFAIRS: What has been your overall personal experience as a woman feminist theorist in the field of International Relations?

J. ANN TICKNER: I have certainly found the experience very rewarding. It has been wonderful to be part of a community of scholars who are building a new approach in the discipline of International Relations (IR). Feminist approaches got started at the end of the 1980s so we've had about 12 or 13 years and it's been a very exciting and intellectually stimulating time. In 1989, I spent some months at the London School of Economics and it was very interesting that there were scholars and graduate students there who were beginning to think along the same lines, but independently of those of us in the United States. About the same time Jindy Pettman wrote a feminist critique of IR in the *Australian Journal of International Affairs*. It was intriguing that, in three different parts of the world, similar themes were emerging at about the same time.

Since that time there's been some great work in feminist international relations that critiques the discipline from a gendered perspective and articulates some new feminist approaches. There is now a growing body of empirical work that looks at global issues from a feminist perspective and highlights research about women. There are a lot of wonderful scholars in this field and it's been a privilege to be a part of it.

JOURNAL: How has your work evolved throughout your career? How has this process been affected by the way in which your theories are viewed in the greater international community?

TICKNER: My interest in feminism began in the mid-1980s when I was teaching at Holy Cross College, a hospitable environment in which to do non-mainstream work. Each year I taught the introductory undergraduate IR course

Courtesy of Brown Journal of World Affairs. Winter/Spring, 10, 2, pg. 47–56 for our majors. This was during the Cold War so there was a heavy emphasis on security issues and nuclear strategy. I noticed that a number of my female students would come to my office and say, "I'm just not cut out for this kind of stuff." When I asked them to explain why, it would often come down to the fact that they thought the male students were somehow more qualified to talk about weapons and military strategy. Often they felt disempowered around these issues. In trying to understand why they felt this way when many of them did very well in the course, I began to look at some feminist work in other fields to find the answer to this puzzle.

The first book I read that helped me with this puzzle and really influenced my thinking about how IR is a masculine gendered discipline was Evelyn Fox Keller's *Reflections on Gender and Science.* It is a wonderfully perceptive feminist critique of the natural sciences as gendered masculine. When I read the book it made me think that a lot of what Keller had to say about the natural sciences would actually apply to IR. By this I mean the way we construct theories in IR and how we evaluate them. I then started reading more feminist theory, but feminist theory from other disciplines, because feminist IR theory did not really exist at that time. My book, *Gender in International Relations,* was the first singly authored feminist text that critiqued the discipline from a gendered perspective. While, of necessity, I constructed my critique out of feminist theory from other disciplines, I also tried to seriously engage with IR. I have always tried to acknowledge, and engage with, the things that IR can tell us, but there are many things we need to know that it doesn't tell us.

JOURNAL: What are the themes of your current project?

TICKNER: I am undertaking a writing project about feminist research practices for IR. I would like to direct it towards graduate students who, when they want to take up topics having to do with gender, race, and other similar issues, find that there are not many methodological guidelines upon which they can draw—at least not in IR. We need more texts that focus specifically on feminist methodologies for IR.

JOURNAL: Where do you see feminist theory heading in the future?

TICKNER: I am hopeful that feminist theory will continue to flourish, but I am also aware that it is hard for it to gain acceptance, particularly in what I am calling the mainstream of the discipline. As I said before, there is a lot of excellent "second generation" feminist empirical work, but there's also a lot of gate keeping in the discipline. At the moment there is an extremely tight job market in academia and I think that graduate students often feel pressured to adopt more mainstream approaches because they think it will help them find academic jobs. This is too bad because there's so much interest and demand on the part of students, not only for feminist IR, but also for other critical perspectives. The dominance of rational choice and game theory is very strong and the tolerance for critical perspectives, other than a certain form of constructivism, is not very high. It's worrisome.

JOURNAL: As feminist discourse and theories appear to be developing a greater legitimacy within the discipline of IR, how do you see feminist theory best implemented beyond academics in the current world system? Do you think feminist theory runs the risk of being able to speak only to other academics?

TICKNER: I was actually rather heartened that you thought that feminist theory had already achieved this legitimacy! It has amongst some people, but it is still rather precarious as I just mentioned. However, I do notice that a lot of introductory IR textbooks now have a section on feminist approaches. I think we are making progress. I agree with you about the problems of writing for academics. However, I would like to emphasize that I think that more conventional IR theory is also written for academics. I don't think you can talk only about feminists being guilty of this, but maybe that's not what you meant. I think much of IR theory is quite esoteric, removed from the "real world" and hard for lay people to understand. In my view, it is quite astonishing how much of our discipline has so little to tell us about what's actually going on in the real world today.

Feminist theory is a tool for those who want to write about gendered perspectives in IR. It seems unfamiliar and esoteric to some because we are not used to gender analysis and, in IR at least, we don't have the requisite training for it. Gender is a sociological category; it doesn't fit well with the methodologies, more typical of mainstream IR, that draw on microeconomics and rational choice. With its focus on social relations, feminist theory is more akin to sociological perspectives.

A lot of the empirical IR feminist work that's now coming out, is grounded in the "real world." Or maybe we should talk about multiple "real worlds" since the worlds that feminists are writing about have frequently been hidden from the agendas of international politics. Take Kathy Moon's book which talks about military prostitution in Korea, or Elizabeth Prügl's work on home-based labor. Jacqui True has just finished a book on the effects on women of the post-Communist transition in the Czech Republic. And all of Cynthia Enloe's work is grounded in the "real world" although not the same "real world"—the world of states and states*men*—that IR has studied. While some feminist theory may be esoteric, much of it has evolved out of social movements and political practice. Frequently, feminists emphasize constructing theory out of practice, particularly the practice of everyday lives of ordinary people. I think that this is a strength of feminist theory. However, many IR theorists don't think that it's a legitimate way to build knowledge.

JOURNAL: How do you think the greater IR community perceives feminist theory?

TICKNER: I don't think the greater IR community understands feminist theory very well. If you limit the question to mainstream IR, they honestly believe that feminist approaches to IR are not "scientific." I think this is one of the greatest barriers to mutual understanding, and it's why I have begun to work on methodology. IR scholars will often say that it is really interesting to bring women into the picture but that you have to do it in a "scientific" way. The methodological problems are much harder to resolve than the legitimacy of the subject matter. I think that mainstream IR theorists are quite willing to think that they might learn something from the kind of work we do, but they find the way we go about doing it problematic.

Another problem is that gender is always equated with women. We must understand that gender is also about men and masculinity—something that is central to international politics since so much of the discipline is about men and masculinity. A big problem is that many people who don't understand feminist theory very well assume that it can tell us something about women, but they don't assume that it can tell us anything about global politics more generally. This is important but it is very hard for scholars who don't work in this perspective to understand.

Another obstacle is that gender is something that is very threatening to people's identities. When you talk about feminism or gender, many people feel personally threatened. It's often very difficult to get beyond this personal worry and move on to acknowledge that gender can help us understand the world better. Questions such as, "Oh, so you don't like men?" or "Are you trying to tell me that women are more peaceful than men?" continue to crop-up. But I am hopeful that this problem is diminishing in your generation now that feminist literature is included in more IR courses.

JOURNAL: What is the relationship between marginalization and women in feminist theory?

TICKNER: Feminism *is* a perspective from the margins because so many women throughout the world have been marginalized. Not all women of course. Feminist theory emerges from what we might call a standpoint of those who are disempowered and subordinated but there are certainly other theories that come from similar standpoints—Marxist class analysis, for example. Indeed, certain strands of feminist theory draw on class analysis. Feminisms have emerged out of multiple standpoints. I do think it is useful to analyze the world from marginal perspectives because you see things that you do not see from the center. In fact, 1990s' feminism was very focused on difference—that is women's differing positionality, based on their race, class, ethnic origins, nationalities, etc.

The bigger worry for feminist theory is the danger of seeing women as victims who lack agency. Another related worry is that more empowered women speak for those who have less power and voice. For example, there has been much criticism by Third World feminists of Western feminists' inclination to speak for them. One of the positive aspects of this is the emergence of African-American and post-colonial feminist theories. This has also been a big issue around the Middle East and U.S. foreign policy—the view that women "over there" are helpless victims to whom we need to reach out and offer our enlightened ideas. That is a difficult issue for feminists and women in the Middle East more generally who do need our support but who also ask us to respect their right to liberate themselves in ways that make sense for them.

JOURNAL: How would you compare the Islamic and secular nations based on their structure and views on women?

TICKNER: In general I think that secularism is better for women although one must respect the views of those women who struggle for their rights using a sense of religious identity. There have been some very depressing reports from Iraq recently about how women feel much more insecure post-Saddam Hussein than before. I have read several stories in the *New York Times* which say that things are actually getting worse for women because, as religious fundamentalism is on the rise, women are being pushed back into the private sphere and are suffering from increased sexual violence. Based on interviews with Iraqi women, the *Times* also stated that the occupation forces have not paid much attention to these problems. Even were there to be a more democratic Iraq we cannot assume that things will be better for women. Very often when you look at what are applauded as progressive transformational moments in history you find that things did not actually improve for women.

JOURNAL: Do you perceive the U.S. occupation of Iraq as a masculine approach to managing conflict?

TICKNER: I would like to talk first about what "a masculine approach to managing conflict" might mean. Certainly no policy maker would use this term. That in itself is something we should find interesting.

Let me begin by discussing the definition of gender, which is very much encoded in our everyday lives and practices. We all know what masculine means but we are not called upon to define it very often. Gender is about a set of relational characteristics that we associate with masculinity and femininity—characteristics such as power, autonomy, rationality, and agency are seen as typically masculine. Other characteristics, such as weakness, dependency, emotion and passivity, are associated with femininity. However, these are not necessarily attributes of individual women and men. In fact, one of the exercises that I do with my undergraduates, who often have never consciously thought about gender in these terms, is to ask them to come up with lists of characteristics they would associate with masculinity and femininity. I write them on the board in two columns. When I ask them which characteristics they identify with, most of the students will identify with the masculine ones, even though the majority of them are women. But they know that these are the characteristics they should display to be successful in the public sphere. So we all know what masculinity means—the norms to which we aspire in our public lives and which come to be seen as universal.

However, I would like to point out that when you say a "masculine approach," it's not *the only* masculine approach. It's what I and others have called "hegemonic masculinity." It's this sort of masculinity that we don't have to explain. We know that it is something that we should try to live up to. But most people don't act this way, including many men who often feel quite uncomfortable with trying to "act like a man." Nevertheless, it legitimates certain ways of behaving and delegitimates others including other forms of masculinity. It is interesting to map these hegemonic masculine characteristics onto the international behavior of states. To me, this is a big problem. It's not that these ways of acting—seeking power, being autonomous—are always bad, but it does tend to delegitimate other valid ways of behaving that use more cooperative, less power-centered strategies. And often these alternative ways for states to behave are judged inferior by being associated with women and femininity.

I think that the way that we're going to get beyond this problem is by questioning these gender stereotypes. We must be able to acknowledge that, while autonomy is important, there may be times when more interdependent, less autonomous, more multilateral strategies might be more appropriate. If you pay attention to academic and media accounts of foreign policy, it's amazing how much of it is described and evaluated in these gendered terms. I ask my students to analyze newspaper articles in terms of this gender coding. They find it all over the place although often they say that they had never noticed it before. Feminism is all about questioning what we normally take for granted.

So to get back to your question, yes, I do think that the war in Iraq is a masculine approach. The emphasis on a strong military response closes off other more conciliatory options. This is not the same thing as saying that men always favor the use of force while women always favor more peaceful responses. Women supported this war, too, although there was a significant gender gap on the issue, at least until the war started. What I am saying that we are *all* socialized into regarding masculine norms as the correct way to operate—particularly in matters of foreign policy. This has the negative effect of shutting off other options. And the framing of the war on terrorism as good versus evil reflects the kind of dichotomous thinking that feminists find deeply problematic, as I have illustrated with my definition of gender. Feminists have written a great deal about the dangers of either/or categorizations and the tolerance for ambiguity, both of which could be useful here.

JOURNAL: One of your arguments in your article "Feminist Perspectives on 9/11" was that 9/11 happened in part because al-Qaeda thought the United States was becoming "feminine" and thus vulnerable. How can you incorporate a feminist perspective into current discourse about the war on terror?

TICKNER: I don't think that this was the whole reason why it happened although I don't think that al-Qaeda

> expected such a massive response from what it perceived as a country unwilling to fight, a view that was often articulated through reference to the "feminization" of the United States. And Bin Laden used gender coding to rally his supporters behind fighting against "weak, wimpy, feminized" Westerners. But he also talked about Westerners as crusaders, which isn't a feminized image. The gender messages were very strong but they were very complicated.

And we feminize Islamic nations. Our foreign policy plays on the notion of feminizing the "Other," but only certain others. We did not feminize the Soviet Union to the same extent. They were our adversaries, but they were rational people to whom we could talk sensibly about not blowing each other up. This selective feminization of other nations is quite racial—we tend to feminize nonwhite nations. There is a fascinating literature about the gendering of colonialism: for example, the British discourse of nineteenth century imperialism was highly gendered with those who were colonized frequently depicted in gendered feminine terms.

An interesting complication today is that, as I said, "they" are also feminizing "us." To quote Osama bin Laden, "Our brothers who fought in Somalia saw wonders about the weakness, feebleness, and cowardliness of the U.S. soldier." In this speech, Bin Laden goes on to berate the U.S. military for having women in it. There's a lot in the rhetoric of al-Qaeda about the West being weak and feminized. And there's a lot of talk in the Middle East about the dangers posed by liberated western women that serves to police Middle Eastern women and keep them out of public life.

But we must remember that religious fundamentalist discourses of all faiths, Christian as well as Muslim, inside as well as outside the United States, talk about the dangers of the United States becoming feminized if women get too much power. And, as I said in the article you mentioned, it gets much more pronounced in times of upheaval and insecurity as it did after 9/11.

> JOURNAL: What influence can women in power have? How can women in positions of power achieve a feminist agenda?
>
> TICKNER: Women *are* in power, though not in large numbers. They are playing all sorts of roles. There have been women presidents, prime ministers, and even ministers of defense. But how much better it will be when we no longer refer to them as "women presidents" but just as "presidents!" Women have had powerful roles just like men. I am aware that in some countries this is not possible, but in many it is. The big question is why there are *so few* women in positions of power even in countries where legal equality has been in place for a long time. The power that gender role expectations exert can tell us a lot about this.

The question of feminists in power is a different one. It is a much more difficult issue. There has been a lot of speculation about whether women would more likely pursue feminist agendas if they were in a majority of leadership positions. We have so little empirical evidence on this score that it is very hard to say whether it would make a difference. I am intrigued by the Scandinavian states which have a fairly large proportion of women in political power. Could there be a connection with these states' friendliness to social welfare policy—better day care, etc.? It is very hard to say whether these relatively women-friendly policies happened because there were so many women in power, or vice versa. But I do have the sense that it might make a difference if you had a critical mass of women in power.

And if we didn't have such hierarchical gendered societies it would certainly be easier to get things on the agenda that feminists believe in. But it's a big leap to think that people who identify themselves as feminists would be in power anywhere. In the United States, Hillary Clinton has been vilified for being a feminist but she's pretty cautious about this identification. It is very important to think *why* the term "feminist' carries so many negative connotations. This is a very political issue that has a lot to do with preserving power for those who already have it.

The Kennedy Experiment Revisited

AMITAI ETZIONI

Many of the critical issues and conflicts in international relations today bear a significant resemblance to the geopolitical circumstances that led to the development of the theorem I published in these pages forty years ago. States, grappling over nuclear proliferation and other security issues, still face off against one another, brimming with mutual hostility and mistrust that render it difficult for them to move forward with bilateral or multilateral negotiations. The emergence of nonstate actors as significant players in international relations has even further exacerbated the effects of such suspicion in hampering prospects for negotiations (e.g., Russia and Chechen separatists and Israel and Hamas). In light of these developments, my theorem, which outlines measures that can be taken in the face of such mutual hostility and suspicion in order to reduce the tensions and pave the way to productive negotiations, remains at least as relevant today as when I initially formulated it at the height of the Cold War.

THE THEOREM OUTLINED

My theorem maps out a certain pattern of action for agents to pursue where they face a situation in which mutual suspicion and hostility effectively prevent progress toward negotiations. Specifically, it points toward a course of (1) *unilateral,* (2) *reciprocal,* and (3) *symbolic* actions between mutually mistrustful agents. This pattern of actions, my theorem suggests, is the best road to travel toward the possibility of "normal" negotiations.

1. Steps down this road are unilateral—states should pursue acts that do not rely on any of the usual give and take of international relations. My theorem stands in contrast to those realists who frown upon such unilateral concessions, believing that they damage one's interest and stature.
2. Steps down the road that my theorem maps out must be reciprocal—if one side does not reciprocate after one or several gestures, the pattern is broken.
3. Finally, and most centrally, steps down the road that my theorem maps out are symbolic—states should pursue actions with predominantly "psychological" weight rather than with significant military, economic, or any other "real" value. In this regard, my theorem stands in contrast to those "grand unilateralists" who posit that, for example, if one nation were to give up its nuclear military capabilities, its adversary would be compelled to do the same. Instead, the idea here is merely to open a window to see if fresh air can be introduced, not to blow off the roof and knock down the walls.

In contrast to major theories of international relations that focus on "real" factors, such as the number of nuclear bombs a nation commands, the size of its military, the rate of its economic growth, and so on, my theorem holds that "psychology" matters a great deal. I do not, however, take the extreme version of this position as held by some social constructivists who argue, for example, that since "war begins in the minds of men," it is exactly there where efforts to end and prevent war must be waged. On my theorem, psychological factors are not taken to be all powerful in this way; I do not argue that if nations ceased to fear or threaten one another, peace would simply break out all over. Instead, psychological factors are best viewed as playing an important but limited role; they can and do have "real" consequences, including helping pave the way toward multilateral negotiations, but are not in and of themselves taken as a cure-all remedy.

In the forty years since my original article was published, the need for foreign policy makers to recognize the importance of psychological factors has become increasingly necessary. Specifically, "legitimacy"—the successful drawing of psychological connections between new international facts to people's perceptions and values—has come to matter a great deal. This is in part a result of the spread of education and means of communication ("the CNN factor") that has allowed more people to become more informed and involved in public and international affairs. Yet many policy makers continue to ignore the significance of legitimacy and other psychological factors—usually at their own peril.

For example, a clear and striking pattern has emerged in which important agreements (e.g., the Camp David Accords, the Oslo Agreements, and the proposed European Constitution) that are made without sufficient consideration or accommodation of these factors—the perceptions, sentiments, and values of the public involved—have failed or have subsequently collapsed.

As another example, look at the most common reaction to Yasser Arafat, who is frequently criticized for his rejection of what many consider a very accommodating offer made by then Israeli Prime Minister Ehud Barak but was in fact paying close attention to the psychological factors at play. He recognized (unlike most of his critics) that to sign such an agreement would be tantamount to asking that Palestinians change their perception of Israel overnight, from the evil, dreaded enemy that deserves to be demolished to a partner for peace in a two-state solution. In short, Arafat recognized that acquiring legitimacy for such an agreement would have been impossible. Similarly, Arafat recognized that there was an Israeli minority that was strongly opposed to such a deal and that was not prepared to accept it. In rejecting this deal, Arafat was keenly attuned to the psychological factors at play both among his own people and in his opponents.

These examples show that legitimacy and other psychological factors have become critical factors in evaluating policy making not only in looking to the behavior and actions of opponents but also in looking domestically at one's own people. The *unilateral-reciprocal* model that my theorem lays out can be and is profitably applicable not only to other actors but also toward the population of one's own state in order to build legitimacy.

A "NATURAL" EXPERIMENT

President Kennedy was probably unaware of the academic work being done on the unilateral-reciprocal approach to tension reduction and conflict resolution. (However, I did send memos to this effect to his staff, as I believe did Charles Osgood, a colleague who developed a similar theorem.) Hence, the events of 1963 are best viewed as a "natural experiment"—as providing an inadvertent but nevertheless valid test of my theorem. Here follows a brief overview of the pattern of unilateral steps and reciprocations undertaken that cumulatively led to a thawing of the Cold War as well as to bilateral and multilateral negotiated agreements.

On June 10, 1963, in his "Strategy for Peace" speech, Kennedy struck a reconciliatory tone toward the Union of Soviet Socialist Republics (USSR) and announced that the United States would stop all nuclear tests in the atmosphere. The USSR permitted Kennedy's speech to be published in its media outlets and broadcast without interruption—such public exposure was highly unusual for a speech by an American president. The day after this speech, the USSR withdrew its objection to Western-backed proposals to send United Nations (UN) observers to Yemen. Next, the United States withdrew its objection to granting full membership status to the Hungarian delegation to the UN. Four days later, Khrushchev delivered a speech with a reconciliatory tone similar to Kennedy's, welcoming the president's initiative and announcing that the USSR's production of strategic bombers had been halted. Soon thereafter Khrushchev agreed to a U.S.–USSR communications link first proposed by the United States in late 1962 and also announced that the USSR would not test nuclear weapons in the atmosphere (several months prior to the August 1963 treaty on this issue).

Further gestures were made in late September. Kennedy suggested each of the following: a possible exchange of observer posts at key points to reduce the danger of a surprise attack, the expansion of the test treaty to include underground testing, direct flights between Moscow and New York, and the opening of consulates in Leningrad and Chicago. Meanwhile, Soviet foreign minister Andrei Gromyko called for a NATO–Warsaw Pact nonaggression pact and pursued an agreement to foreswear the orbiting of nuclear weapons.

In October, Kennedy called for reducing the trade barriers between East and West and approved the sale of $250 million in wheat to the USSR. The president also declared an agreement in principle not to put nuclear weapons in orbit. By late October, a resolution was passed by the UN General Assembly to this effect.

November marked a slowdown in U.S. unilateral initiatives. The administration was concerned that hope for more USSR–U.S. measures was running too high and wanted to reduce some of the mounting pressure. Allies in Western Europe had begun to voice anxiety about the apparent growing willingness to compromise they observed in U.S. behavior. And perhaps most significantly, Kennedy was about to face elections against a Republican party that viewed conciliatory measures as weakening the nation's resolve and power. Prior to President Kennedy's premature death, it was widely expected that this pattern of reciprocal moves would resume after the 1964 presidential election.

Three points are particularly worth highlighting from this narration:

1. For each unilateral move the United States made, the USSR not only reciprocated but did so proportionally so that over the course of the exchange, neither side made a disproportionate gain in advantage or status.
2. None of the moves was costly in military, economic, or any other "real" terms but were, rather, symbolic or "psychological." For example, the U.S. halting of atmospheric nuclear testing came after the United States had already conducted twice as much testing as the USSR and had amassed enough data to take at least a year of analysis to digest. At the time of Khrushchev's announcement about halting production of the strategic bomber, the USSR was likely planning on phasing out those bombers anyway. In addition, his announcement contained no proposed method of verification for the United States to ensure that production was actually stopped. In terms of the initiatives made regarding East–West trade, overall trade policy was never really in question and did not change, and the total value of the wheat ultimately sold to the USSR was not $250 million but only $65 million. In short, the concessions made by both sides were for the most part highly symbolic.
3. Both sides initiated actions. The USSR offered some initiatives of its own, including the withdrawal of objections to Yemen observers, the proposal for a NATO–Warsaw Pact nonaggression agreement, and the proposal of an air treaty.

Overall, as I found in my paper forty years ago, the unilateral-reciprocal approach led to reduced tensions between the United States and the USSR and paved the way toward multilateral-simultaneous measures. When the pattern of symbolic gestures was interrupted in November 1963, the tension reduction ceased.

A RANGE OF CONCEPTUAL RESPONSES

My analysis of the "Kennedy Experiment" published on these pages more than a generation ago sparked a debate among my colleagues on the power of psychological or symbolic concessions in international relations. Not all of my colleagues were convinced of the validity of the analysis.

Some realists charged that the effects credited to the applications of the theorem were actually products of deterrence—they argued that the threat of nuclear annihilation itself produced détente.

Still others pointed out that the theorem was not fully specified. For instance, Johan Niezing (1978) wrote,

> What happens if the opposite party does not react? The various authors writing on the idea of unilateral steps do not agree. Some, like Etzioni, advocate stopping after several steps. Others propose initiating the process all the same, by taking one big step which the opposing party cannot but interpret as a cognitively dissonant element.

In toto, my theorem has received the kind of varied and relevant observations those who formulate theorems aspire to. My only regret it that there have been very few attempts to apply this theorem to subsequent international conflicts as a tension-reducing tactic; there have, in other words, been too few subsequent "natural experiments" of my theory. Little wonder that various parties find it so difficult to move from hostile confrontations to multilateral negotiations.

The Lucifer Effect: Understanding How Good People Turn Evil

PHILIP ZIMBARDO

Zimbardo creates a masterpiece of political psychology, investigating and explaining how basic underlying psychological processes are informed and defined by the political, economic, social, religious, cultural, and historical contexts and situations in which they exist. Throughout this analysis, Zimbardo reflects on the nature of good and evil, the nebulous boundaries between these realities, and the myriad ways in which individuals can be transformed from angels into devils, and, perhaps, how it may be possible for them to revert back into heroism.

This book is essentially divided into two temporal aspects. The first part, constituting the first 11 chapters, provides a detailed description of the Stanford Prison Experiment on a day-by-day basis. This discussion provides unique documentation into the process by which two dozen ordinary boys, all screened beforehand (from 75 volunteers) to assure their normal cognitive and emotional functioning, soon became transformed—many into brutal guards and neurotic prisoners. At the outset, these boys were randomly assigned to the "guard" and "prisoner" conditions, but within 24 hours, the bored guards were inventing novel ways to abuse their prisoners. While Zimbardo told the guards that they could not physically abuse the prisoners, the guards quickly invented 17 largely arbitrary rules by which the prisoners had to abide, including night drills and public humiliation. Prisoners who did not comply were subjected to a variety of punishments, including solitary confinement. Within a matter of days, individual prisoners tried to organize resistance, went on a hunger strike, and one broke down and had to be released from the experiment. Everyone became deeply involved in the situation; a former prisoner served as a parole hearing officer; a priest came to counsel; parents tried to engage lawyers to set their children free. This section of the book, much of it written in the present tense, immediately draws the reader into an involving and engaging world, allowing observers an eyewitness view on one of the most important and influential experiments in the history of social psychology.

Zimbardo freely admits his own engagement with the role of Warden; and credits Christina

Maslach, who had been his graduate student, for being the hero who saw through the situation and forced him to stop the experiment a week before its scheduled conclusion. In fact, an entire chapter is devoted to an ethical examination of the Prison experiment. Prior to this study and the infamous Milgram experiment, human subjects' boards did not exist. In many ways, these institutional review boards grew out of opposition to the perceived excess in these studies. And yet, good things clearly emerged; for instance, one of the subjects went on to become an important advocate of prison reform as a chief psychologist in the California prison system.

This study received particular attention at the time because it came out just prior to the infamous Attica prison riots in upstate New York in September 1971 in which 39 people were killed. Just as the Stanford Prison Experiment proved relevant then, it remained hauntingly relevant upon the release of the photos from Abu Ghraib prison some 30 years later. This book contains many photos from the original experiment, and they will strike any viewer as startlingly familiar in design to the more recent Abu Ghraib pictures. Some of the poses in which guards placed prisoners reemerge as identical in nature and scope.

The second half of the book focuses on these similarities and strives to explain how, like Lucifer, God's favorite angel who transformed into the devil once he defied God's authority, young American soldiers of impeccable character became torturers in the context of the Abu Ghraib prison. In so doing, Zimbardo takes the opportunity to reflect deeply, and in profound ways, on what 50 years of research in social psychology can teach us about the nature of conformity, obedience, and deindividuation, and how these realities can create environments which foster evil action. In particular, he discusses in detail the case of Sergeant Ivan "Chip" Frederick, one of eight men sentenced to military prison for participation in torture in Abu Ghraib. As an expert witness in this trial, Zimbardo draws on his exceptional access to the relevant materials to show how a neat and clean young American soldier came to engage in acts of torture through the combination of fear, filth, boredom, disorder, isolation, social pressure, lack of leadership and oversight, and uncertainty which characterized his night shift on Tier 1A in Abu Ghraib. In this discussion, Zimbardo brilliantly intertwines the nature of basic psychological needs for order and human contact, within the specific political context of a guerrilla war, to examine and explain how responsibility for evil actions goes beyond the individual to hold equally accountable those who knowingly create and sustain the environments and situations which instigate such behavior. In this regard, those who establish and maintain a system which encourages and allows situations predisposing individuals within them to commit evil acts are themselves responsible for structuring opportunities for sin to flourish.

In a final chapter on heroism, Zimbardo discusses how humility, awareness, and responsibility can encourage heroism. He uses the case of Joe Darby, the young American whistle-blower in Abu Ghraib, to illustrate the social challenges associated with calling attention to bad behavior on the part of peers.

Drawing on path-breaking experimental work conducted in the 1970s in the Stanford Prison Experiment, Zimbardo examines the current Abu Ghraib prison torture scandal. He meticulously details the situational factors which can make good people engage in evil acts in order to meet natural and normal human needs for safety, knowledge, and affection. In so doing, he demonstrates the systematic political and institutional responsibility for such horrible outcomes. The book's final instructions encouraging personal awareness, accountability, and responsibility should challenge readers to take action to change and improve the world around them by recognizing, and resisting, the subtle ways politicians and others use the environment to manipulate unsuspecting bystanders into doing their dirty work for them. Yet the ultimate message of hope encourages the possibility of redemption for those who have learned the secrets of human behavior detailed in this book.

ROSE MCDERMOTT
University of California Santa Barbara

VISUAL REVIEW

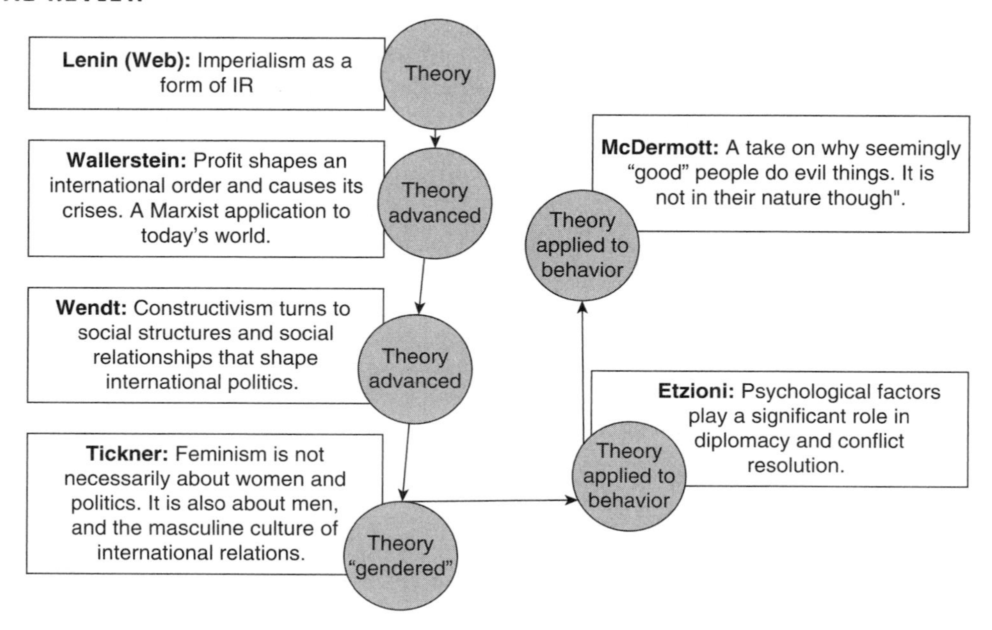

Critical Thinking and Discussion Questions for Part I

SECTION 1

1. **Huntington wrote in 1993: "The fault lines between civilizations will be the battle lines of the future." Locate on a world map at least four such fault lines.**
   - Which countries do they include?
   - Check the most recent news from these "fault lines" related to tensions or conflicts.
   - How stable today are the regions on the "fault lines" compared to other regions?

2. **Huntington offered six reasons why civilizations would clash.**
   - Which of the reasons do you consider the most plausible and why?
   - Argue against any one of these reasons.
   - What should be done globally to avoid a clash of civilizations?

3. **Explain the kin-country syndrome. From the list of countries below, select three pairs, which, if you apply Huntington's ideas, should be viewed as "kin" countries:**

   Japan Vietnam Libya Cuba France Russia Mexico Egypt
   Argentina Belgium Serbia Germany Venezuela Ukraine

Explain your choices.

4. **Give an example involving two contemporary conflicts: one that proves and the other that disproves the kin-country syndrome.**
   - Suggested cases for starters: the 2014 crisis in Crimea; the 2010 crisis in South Kyrgyzstan; the China-Taiwan relations; relations between North and South Korea; and the conflict in Syria involving ISIS.

5. **Provide several examples of today's "torn" countries. Explain your selections.**

6. **In Katzenstein's view, what are the differences between pluralist and unitary cultures? Provide examples.**

7. **How was the race factor incorporated in the U.S. foreign policy before the 1960s? How did it play out recently in your opinion?**

8. Give several examples of *generic demonstratives* (Katzenstein) in judgments about:
- other countries
- your country's foreign policy
- international relations

9. Explain why globalization, according to Krasner, does not undermine state control. How can it undermine state control in the future?

10. The European Union is an example of supranational governance. Which cluster of countries outside Europe would you like to see as another model for supranational governance? Explain your choice.

11. Looking at the United States' policies today, why is the analogy with British decline in the 1940s–1950s misleading, according to Nye?

12. What are the specific factors in U.S. domestic politics, mentioned by Nye, that are negatively affecting its foreign policy?
- Could you suggest—using your personal opinion—specific factors in U.S. domestic politics, which are positively affecting its foreign policy?

13. What is absolute and relative decline of a country's power? Give examples.

14. Nye suggests that the United States' "capacity to maintain alliances and create networks will be an important dimension of its hard and soft power." Which alliances and networks does he have in mind?

15. Explain the "flat world" metaphor in one sentence to a nonprofessional.

16. Which factors (according to Fareed Zakaria) created the flat world?

17. Explain what an "unflat" political world means. Give an example.

18. Suggest at least three arguments to claim that:
- today's world is flat
- today's world is not flat

19. Apply (1) Krasner's views of state sovereignty and (2) Huntington's clash of civilizations to suggest how the world should deal with Zombies (based on Drezner's article).

SECTION 2

1. **Explain "three principal causes of quarrel" among people according to Hobbes.**
   - Suggest three cases from history that support Hobbes's thesis.
   - Suggest three cases from contemporary international relations that support Hobbes's thesis.

2. **Hobbes wrote: "Where there is no common power, there is no law; where no law, no injustice."**
   - How would you understand and interpret "common power" today?
   - Can you identify places in the world without "common power"?

3. **Identify and discuss the three essential tenets implicit in Machiavelli's doctrine and borrowed by E. H. Carr as the foundation stones of the realist philosophy.**

4. **Suggest and discuss three examples of the adjustment of "thought to purpose" in international politics.**

5. **Explain the realist critique of the harmony of interests.**
   - Defend this point of view using history and contemporary examples.
   - Criticize this point of view using history and contemporary examples.

6. **According to Carr, sometimes pursuit of moral goals in international relations can spell disaster for security interests.**
   - Can you think of any examples of such clashes between morality and security interests today?

7. **Suggest today's examples to illustrate each of Morgenthau's "six points."**

8. **Can moral principles, according to Realism, be applied to the actions of states and why?**

9. **When in the past, according to Waltz, did the multipolar and bipolar worlds exist?**

10. **In Waltz's view, why did deterrence work during the Cold War?**

11. **Explain the two reasons suggested by Mearsheimer why world powers couldn't commit themselves to the pursuit of a peaceful world order.**

12. **Using today's examples, discuss the two factors (Mearsheimer) that inhibit cooperation among states.**

13. Walt writes about the "distribution of burdens" within an alliance: larger countries tend to bear a disproportionate share of the costs compared to smaller countries.
- Provide examples to support/prove this statement.
- Provide examples to challenge/disprove this statement.

14. Find contemporary examples of three choices prescribed by Walt for "weaker powers" in a unipolar world.

15. Unipolarity, according to Walt, implies that the single superpower, such as the United States, faces no ideological rival of equal status or influence.
- In your view, has any other country today offered an ideological alternative that may soon become a model for other states to imitate?
- Which country do you think could offer such an alternative in the near future?

16. Explain the differences between "hard balancing" and "soft balancing."

17. Unipolar systems have three defining features, according to Monteiro (on the companion website [http://oup.com/us/shiraev]). Name and describe them.

18. A unipolar power can pursue one of three grand strategies: defensive dominance, offensive dominance, or disengagement.
- Which policy did the United States pursue in your view ten years ago? Explain your opinion.
- Which policy does the United States pursue in your view now? Explain your opinion.

19. What is the difference between offensive and defensive dominance in a unipolar system? Give examples.

20. Explain why unipolarity possesses much potential for conflict.
- Provide two contemporary examples to support this argument.
- Provide an example to disprove this argument

21. In the context of the Engle's article (on the companion website [http://oup.com/us/shiraev]), discuss the state of the Iran–Syria alliance today.
- Does this alliance continue to reflect the Sunni–Shiite divide?
- Discuss which countries in this region are U.S. allies now?

22. Mearsheimer argues (on the companion website [http://oup.com/us/shiraev]) that by claiming regional hegemony, some countries

seek to prevent great powers in other regions from duplicating their feat.

- Discuss this assumption by analyzing U.S.–China relations.
- Discuss this assumption by analyzing U.S.–Russia relations.
- Discuss this assumption by analyzing China–Russia relations.

23. What could be China's own "version" of the Monroe doctrine in Asia? Suggest a possible scenario.

- Is Russia using its own "version" of the Monroe doctrine to conduct its foreign policy these days?

24. What would be the best way, according to Walt, to cap or slow Chinese nuclear modernization?

- What is your view on China's nuclear modernization? Will this modernization contribute to regional or global stability? Will it provoke instability?

SECTION 3

1. Immanuel Kant put together six preliminary articles or conditions for perpetual peace among countries. Describe them.

- Which of these conditions appear to you most important than others and why?
- Which one of these conditions does, in your view, appear most advanced (developed) in today's world?
- Do you think it would be possible today to implement most of the Kantian peace principles without the use of force, or do you think that from time to time the use of limited force would be necessary?

2. Why would free trade lead to economic prosperity, according to Schumpeter (on the companion website [http://oup.com/us/shiraev])?

- Is economic prosperity of a country possible if this country is engaged only in limited trade?

3. Why should nationalism and militarism weaken under capitalism, in Schumpeter's view?

- Find and discuss contemporary examples that prove Schumpeter's view.
- Find and discuss contemporary examples of governments "blending" nationalism and capitalism.

4. Norman Angel offered several arguments against war. Discuss them.

- Which argument do you find most applicable to today's international relations and why?
- Which argument by Angell do you consider least compelling?

5. **How did Norman Angell explain his thesis that the fight for ideals can no longer take the form of fight between countries?**
   - Search for examples in recent history and today suggestive of an opposite point that countries continue to fight for ideals. How compelling are these examples?

6. **After reading Michael Doyle's article, name the liberal reasons for aggression of one country against another.**
   - Discuss aggression and its forms. Does aggression, from your view, stand for any type of violence?
   - Provide examples from recent history or contemporary international politics showing countries using the liberal principles to use violence.

7. **Using examples from the past twenty years, find several cases of foreign policy based on the principles of (1) liberal imperialism and (2) liberal pacifism.**
   - In your view, under which conditions are these principles most effective?

8. **Describe two major legacies of liberalism according to Doyle.**
   - Discuss the legacies using the U.S.–Japanese relations.
   - Discuss the legacies using the U.S.–Russian relations.

9. **Kant's liberal internationalism, Machiavelli's liberal imperialism, and Schumpeter's liberal pacifism rest on fundamentally different views of the nature of the human being, the state, and international relations. Describe these views.**
   - Which strategy (liberal internationalism, liberal imperialism, or liberal pacifism) is closer to your view of international relations and why? (There should be no pressure to give a "politically correct" answer here.)
   - Under which international and domestic circumstances would one strategy be more effective than the two others?
   - Select an international problem or a development that has taken place this year and explain it using one of these three strategies.
   - In a few years you may advise on important foreign policy decisions. Which strategy (liberal internationalism, liberal imperialism, or liberal pacifism) would you use toward Africa? Toward Russia? Toward China?

10. **Discuss the classical liberal argument that people in democratic countries, because these people bear the costs of war (such as taxes, restrictions, etc.), have a fundamental interest in peace. Provide contemporary examples.**

11. **Discuss the classical liberal argument that mass publics in democracies, because their voices are heard through opinion polls, grassroots organizations, and elections, are a powerful force against war.**

12. **After reading David Kinsella's article (on the companion website [http://oup.com/us/shiraev]), search for several examples showing democratic countries at war with other democratic states for reasons not related with self-defense. Discuss these examples.**

13. **Put a list of military conflicts in which Canada, Japan, Germany, the United Kingdom, the United States, and Argentina were involved in the last twenty-five years. Discuss your findings in the context of the democratic peace theory.**
    - Did these conflicts involve democratic or nondemocratic countries?
    - What were the causes of these conflicts?
    - What were these conflicts' outcomes?

14. **The article by Kinsella discusses whether after losing wars, democratic leaders, not autocrats, are more likely to be removed from office. This article was published in 2005.**
    - Discuss his finding looking for historical examples from the twentieth century.
    - Look at wars and other violent international conflicts after 2005 and discuss the empirical evident to prove or challenge Kinsella's assumption.

15. **The project of constructing a liberal order, according to Ikenberry (on the companion website [http://oup.com/us/shiraev]), went through several stages. Discuss them.**

16. **What is Institutional Liberalism according to Keohane and how is it different from the traditional liberalism?**

17. **Explain Keohane's "legalization," "international regimes," "legalism," and "moralism."**

18. **Discuss morally justified activities (Keohane) and provide examples from today's international relations.**

19. **Keohane criticizes Mearsheimer for his apparently wrong prediction that the 1990 collapse of the Soviet Union would take the world "back to the future"—to a world of power politics in Europe. From today's point of view, was Mearsheimer right?**

20. **The liberal international order is not just a collection of liberal democratic states. What does it involve?**

21. **John Ikenberry (on the companion website [http://oup.com/us/shiraev]) argues about the future of the liberal world order. Discuss his main conclusions.**

- Do you think that the future of international order will be (1) very likely, (2) somewhat likely, or (3) unlikely to be shaped by countries like China or Russia, which push world politics in an authoritarian direction?
- Which countries in Asia, Africa, and Latin America, in your estimation, could be the strongest and most capable supporters of the liberal world order?

22. **Why do countries like China have to accept the established liberal international order, according to Ikenberry?**

SECTION 4

1. **Lenin's definition of imperialism (on the companion website [http://oup.com/us/shiraev]) is different from most contemporary ones. How did Lenin define imperialism?**
   - Why did Lenin call imperialism the last stage of capitalism?
   - Why did Lenin call imperialism "parasitic" and "decaying" capitalism?

2. **Lenin defines four characteristics of monopolies. Discuss them.**
   - How well or how poorly do these features describe contemporary international corporations?

3. **How did hegemonic powers emerge, according to Wallerstein?**
   - Do you see any examples of new hegemonic powers emerging in this century? If yes, what are they? If not, why there are no emerging hegemonic powers today?

4. **What were the "old Left" movements and what was their global political goal?**

5. **Which systems did Wallerstein suggest in his article to replace the capitalist system? Discuss his proposal.**

6. **Which three imponderables in the process of systemic transition from capitalism did Wallerstein suggest in his 2013 article (see the companion website [http://oup.com/us/shiraev)? How could they affect, as he put it, "the balance of political forces in the struggle"?**

7. **Social structures have three elements, according to Wendt. Name them.**
   - Explain them using the Cold War as an example.
   - Explain them using examples from the twenty-first century

8. **Explain Wendt's suggestion that the meaning of power depends on the underlying structure of shared knowledge.**
   - If you agree with this assertion, provide an example.
   - If you disagree with this assertion, provide an example.

9. It is assumed that individual decisions of political leaders change social structures and therefore international relations.

- Suggest examples from history.
- Provide examples from contemporary international politics.

10. Which international events in the past (not mentioned in the text) could, in your view, illustrate the Lucifer effect?

11. Describe the essence of the *unilateral reciprocal approach* to tension reduction.

- Choose a country with which the United States has contentious or tense relations and suggest a contemporary diplomatic strategy based on the unilateral reciprocal approach.
- Suggest several weaknesses of the unilateral reciprocal approach.
- What can be and should be done when the opposite party (country) does not behave in a reciprocal way?

12. In the context of the U.S.–China relationship, what do (1) optimistic and (2) pessimistic constructivists generally emphasize?

- What is your assessment of the optimistic and pessimistic claims today?

13. What is gender socialization? Explain using your own case as an example.

- When and how did you learn about politics and international relations?
- Did your views evolve? If so, when and in which direction?

14. How could gender socialization affect people's views of foreign countries and international politics?

15. What is the "masculine" approach to international conflicts?

- Provide a few examples of the "masculine" approach from contemporary international relations.
- Suggest alternatives to the "masculine" approach using the same examples.

PART II

THREE FACETS OF THE GLOBAL WORLD

International Security, International Law, and International Political Economy (Editorial Introduction)

In this part we will examine how sovereign countries and international organizations engage in conflicts and pursue security. Then, we will discuss international law as a basic source of rules governing international community. Finally, we will review how countries and organizations engage in economic activities in the context of international relations.

National security has traditionally been understood as the protection of a state's sovereignty, territorial integrity, and interests. *International security* refers to mutual security issues involving more than one state. Governments act to protect their countries' sovereignty and territorial integrity from domestic and foreign threats. Some act alone, relying on their economic might and armed forces. Others seek protection and cooperation from neighbors, more distant countries, and international organizations like the United Nations or NATO. To protect their strategic interests, and to reduce or eliminate domestic and international threats, individual countries and international organizations develop security policies. Such policies are constantly evolving and typically born out of continuous debates among researchers, political elites, security officials, military experts, and the media.

At least two major and competing perspectives on national and international security have been dominant for more than the past several decades. According to *realism*, the main postulates of which we have discussed in Part I, security is the vital and exclusive responsibility of sovereign countries. They always try to maximize their power, tend to act according to their interests, and use these interests in assessing external threats and their own defensive capabilities. In a security regime, a powerful country provides protection to others in exchange for their cooperation. The core element of every state's security, according to realism, is power and the ability to use it.

On the contrary, supporters of *liberalism* (also discussed in Part I) recognize the primary role of states in security policies but also point to the increasing role of international organizations and nonstate actors. Liberals believe that the power of states and security regimes is no longer the only key to lasting peace in today's world. In the liberal view, neither economic nor military power alone can bring long-term security, and military threats are seldom the best choice of action in security policies. Instead, the desire for mutually acceptable outcomes and the complexity of international problems give countries the incentive to cooperate.

Wars, conflicts, and terrorism are the main challenges to international security. A conflict is any antagonism between countries (sovereign states), international organizations, or nongovernmental organizations. Some conflicts remain nonviolent. Others become war, which is an organized violent confrontation between states or other social and political entities, such as ethnic or religious groups. Today's debates about conflict and war continue to focus on the nature of war and its types, causes and consequences of war, offensive and defensive strategies, the possibility of preventing war, and, of course, conflict resolution.

The argument that a country's military strength and its reliance on technologies alone could guarantee victory in a military conflict has a long history. For centuries, countries' leaders associated security policies with military power and its effective use to prevent war or in the time of war. Maintaining the armed forces, obtaining and modernizing weapons, keeping aircraft and battleships, training specialists, and developing mass-mobilization plans were always essential for national security. In most recent times, security experts added to this debate by turning to so-called *revolution in military affairs*, which is the most up-to-date and rapid advance of communications, information, and precision munitions technologies. Military victories during the Gulf War of 1991 and the Kosovo campaign in 1999 have persuaded some specialists that modern technologies have fundamentally changed the nature of war and, therefore, set security policies. These experts assumed that modern weapons and technologies alone—if they are used correctly—should win any modern war.

However, almost two hundred years ago, academics and practitioners were already aware of broader aspects of war. Carl von Clausewitz (1780–1831), a Prussian officer and military expert—who is widely regarded as one of the most prominent military theorists—wrote in *On the Nature of War* that wars should not be viewed exclusively in military terms. War is also a complex sociopolitical and even psychological phenomenon. Von Clausewitz furthered the idea that war is an ultimate confrontation, which states constantly use to achieve their political goals. Yet every war in his view involves individual decision making, calculations and mistakes, emotions, and a degree of risk. This idea received additional support in recent studies showing that state leaders often make fateful military decisions because they misjudge their adversaries' intentions and they also misperceive their own strengths and weaknesses. You can discuss in class which international conflicts can demonstrate the misjudgments and misinterpretations of the leaders involved in such conflicts. Today, the supporters of the *constructivist* view of international relations (which maintains, as you should remember, that countries act according to their identities, perceptions, and social norms) argue that separating modern war from its political, cultural, and psychological context and turning military campaigns to "targeting exercises" would likely lead to failure. Factors, such as cultural, tribal, and political identities, increase complexity and influence the course of events. The validity of all these arguments is being tested in modern conflicts in new contexts. One of them is international terrorism.

Twenty years ago, international terrorism was not a major topic in textbooks and in the mainstream academic publications. After the attacks of September 11, 2001, however, this subject has become a distinct field of study, next to the discussion of war and security. Definitions of *terrorism* vary. Yet most of them refer to it as violence by nonstate actors, such as individuals or groups, to achieve radical political goals. It is essentially a form of political radicalism—ideas and methods to produce rapid, dramatic change in the social or political order. Domestic and international terrorism overlap but remain different. Domestic terrorism does not necessarily present a direct and significant danger to other sovereign countries or international organizations. International terrorists, on the contrary, challenge international stability by threatening a country or a group of states.

Effective security strategies to counter terrorism cannot be designed without first understanding the strategic logic that motivates terrorist violence. Terrorist groups may pursue different goals, but most of their strategies remain consistent. There are at least five such strategies: (1) attrition, (2) intimidation, (3) provocation, (4) spoiling, and (5) outbidding. Terrorist strategies can be effective, as Kydd and Walter write in *The Strategies of Terrorism*, not simply because acts of terrorism spark fear in people, but because they cause governments, international organizations, and individuals to respond in ways that aid the terrorists' cause.

Terrorism is an evolving phenomenon, which should be studied in a historical perspective. Thus, Michel Wieviorka in *From Classical Terrorism to Global Terrorism* distinguishes between "classical" and contemporary forms of terrorism. The "classical" form in his opinion was perpetrated by radicals of the political Left and the political Right, and often took the form of anticapitalist or nationalist movements. This form of terrorism usually operated within separate states, threatened their domestic order, and sometimes, their territorial integrity. Modern terrorism has emerged in the 2000s. It spreads beyond sovereign borders, and its motives are rooted in religious fundamentalism as well as in a cultural, anti-Western sentiment. Whether this global wave will remain associated exclusively with radical Islamism remains to be seen. Other dangerous forms may also occur.

International terrorism differs from guerrilla warfare, which is political violence by identifiable, irregular combat units, usually to seize state power, win autonomy, or found new sovereign states. The discussion of contemporary terrorism and guerilla warfare has revived an old debate about the nature of threats in international relations. Realism teaches that there usually is a balance of forces and threats. This means that an attack by one country causes a symmetrical response from the other. Symmetry helps to maintain international stability, as sovereign states seek a balance between peace and war. Terrorism and guerilla warfare, however, pose an asymmetrical threat to sovereign countries. Because terrorists do not officially represent a government and guerilla fighters often hide among civilians, governments may find it difficult to identify the perpetrators and retaliate effectively. Nonstate actors can disrupt the balance of power in an international context, much like sovereign countries. In an asymmetrical conflict, governments can run two types of risks. First, they may overreact or launch ineffective responses. Second, inaction in response to terrorism may encourage terrorists to strike again. Therefore, asymmetrical warfare is often a powerful tool of international destabilization. And it is not necessarily clear what to do to effectively address terrorism and other types of asymmetrical threats. See Figure 4.

Most experts writing about terrorism underline the need to understand strategies that perpetrators of asymmetrical conflicts use. Guerrilla warfare, for example, is not a new form of military struggle. In twentieth-century conflicts, quite a few political leaders gained power in their countries by launching protracted guerilla wars. History shows that most guerilla movements hoped to push the superior, better organized, and better equipped enemy close to physical and psychological attrition. New international contexts may favor insurgents and complicate the attempts of states to deal with guerillas. As Max Boot suggests, because mass media in democratic countries report heavily on casualties and destruction caused by insurgency's actions, public opinion in such countries may fast develop a negative view of an ongoing conflict. This may exhaust the will of democratic countries to engage in protracted counterinsurgencies, especially outside their own territory, and heighten the ability of insurgents to survive even after suffering grave military setbacks.

In the past, technology was relatively unimportant in guerrilla war. Today's guerillas can use sophisticated technological devices, cyber weapons, and mobile phones to detonate bombs; they can also use drones to target governments and civilians. Can governments strike back using similar methods? For several years, the debates have persisted about the use of drones in antiterrorist operations. There is evidence that drones are effective and civilian deaths from armed drone strikes are far fewer than from traditional combat aircraft. Yet debates about legal and moral justifications of such policy intensify. The simplest question for you to discuss is: What if other countries adopt the same rationale as the United States for carrying out lethal strikes against individuals outside of declared war zones and in violation of territorial sovereignty? What if another country, for example, starts using drones to target and kill certain individuals in Australia or United Kingdom?

Effective security policies require assessments of emerging security threats. For centuries, it meant the assessment and protection of natural resources and their

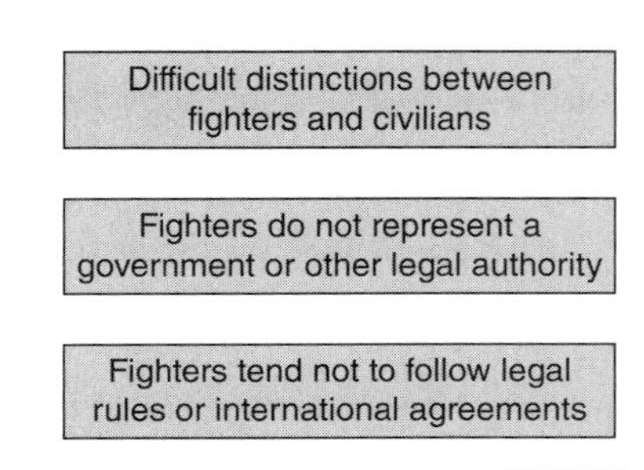

Figure 4. Key Elements of Asymmetrical Conflicts

delivery. Will future threats involve natural resources? Many specialists believe this is the case: the increasing contest for oil and other mineral resources may generate armed conflicts. The new round of struggle for markets, and especially for raw materials, can be intensified by the growth of the economy of China and other countries in Asia, Africa, and South America. What are possible consequences of these developments for global security?

Neorealists suggest that in the unfolding competition for energy resources new political alliances may emerge. Former ideological and political allies may turn away from their former partners and gravitate toward energy-rich countries, thus weakening some "traditional" strategic security regimes. New emerging energy alliances could easily be perceived as threats to other states' security. Also, as Charles Glaser in *How Oil Influences U.S. National Security* indicates, energy demands may increase the value of resources-rich territories. Such conflicts may draw the United States into a military confrontation. Further, the United States' energy independence does not necessarily guarantee security. Other countries are likely to make substantial investments in their militaries to protect energy resources. Of particular importance is, as Glaser writes, the potential danger that Chinese oil imports create for U.S. security—China's efforts to protect its sea lines of communication are fueling military competition that could strain U.S.-China relations and increase the probability of conflict between them.

Identifying several emerging security threats is just the first step of security policy. The next step is to find a strategy to deal with them. Traditionally, countries used geopolitics—the concept and practice of using geographical position and territorial gains to achieve political power or seek security. Geographical position gave some countries clear advantages in security matters, while others remained vulnerable. Today, however, as Luca Kello writes in *The Meaning of the Cyber Revolution,* the meaning of territory is changing. A few individuals located miles away may disrupt activities of sovereign states, private businesses, and nongovernmental organizations. Cyberterrorism is capable of launching paralyzing Internet attacks on political, financial, and economic centers. These threats are real and may range from significant theft of data and disruption of computer operations to more serious and even deadly attacks that destroy or paralyze entire energy grids. Cyberattacks undermine a country's military capabilities and may disturb a regional or global order. All in all, the cyber revolution brings new and significant challenges to international security.

Feminism offers a fundamentally different, alternative outlook on security. Since the mid-twentieth century, feminists have criticized the government monopoly on security issues. They were particularly wary of realism because it defined national and international security in terms of state sovereignty and domination—two key values associated with masculinity. During the 1980s and later, feminists argued that the male-dominated narrative of force and war should be replaced with other narratives, including individual safety, interdependence, agreement, and shared power. Judith Stiehm in her *Theses on the Military, Security, War and Women* offers thirty-five arguments in support of new global security policies. She calls, for instance, to reconsider and reject the whole concept of war as a "natural" way by which sovereign states protect themselves from threats. Security specialists, as she argues, must consider the value of the golden rule: do not do to others what you do not want others do to you.

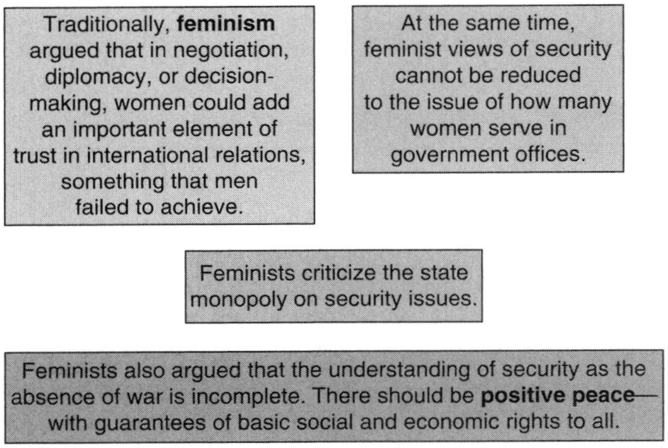

Figure 5. Feminist View of International Security

Security policies also need to be "gender mainstreamed": more women must be involved in institutional policies, and masculine "values" on conflict and war must be questioned and rejected. See Figure 5.

Overall, it is clear that organizing an international effort to deal with a variety of security threats must remain a constant effort, involving governments, nongovernmental organizations, media, and broad segments of population. Also, there could not be only one winning strategy. Instead, each different case dictates a different mix of policies. They may range from military action and surveillance to public diplomacy, economic sanctions, economic aid, law enforcement, education, training, and application of legal rulings.

The next section is dedicated to international law, which is a set of principles, rules, and agreements that regulate the behavior of states and other international actors.

Stephen Neff in *A Short History of International Law* shows that the meaning of international law has been evolving over centuries. Indeed, an early model that is reflected in international laws today can be found in the law of nations (Jus Gentium)—a codification of Roman law compiled during the rule of the Byzantine emperor Justinian I (482–565). The law of nations was based on natural law— rules that are not just common to the laws of all lands but reflect universal interests, such as the safety of sea commerce from piracy or honoring treaties. Eleven centuries later the Dutch diplomat and jurist Hugo Grotius (1583–1645) formulated the principle of freedom of the seas: a state's sovereignty ends at the edge of its territorial waters. This principle survived for centuries. In his later work, *On the Law of War and Peace*, Grotius further connected international law to natural law. He argued that wars between sovereign countries could be justifiable but only under particular circumstances. Like individuals, sovereign countries have the right to self-defense. But even in a state of war, countries should abide by certain rules. Grotius has laid an intellectual foundation for contemporary *just war theory.*

By the twentieth century, as Neff underlines, international law was increasingly understood as a corpus of rules determined by sovereign countries. At that time, formal accords between more than two countries began to play a major role in international affairs. The Hague Peace Conferences of 1899 and 1907 were inspired by the desire of a number of the world leaders to establish a set of common rules to reduce the risk of war and diminish its cruelties. However, for all the good intentions of these diplomatic initiatives, wars and atrocities did not stop. The League of Nations created after World War I did not protect against aggressive wars. The founding of the United Nations in 1945, to replace the defunct League of Nations, was a critical step in the building of a more efficient and viable system of international law, the process that continues today. The debates about the sources, functions, enforcement, and effectiveness of international law continue as well.

Not all sovereign countries and international organizations recognize and observe international law at all times. Does it mean that it is still necessary and practical to have such a law? The answer is yes. At least three reasons explain why. First, countries need a secure international environment. Sovereign states, organizations, businesses, and ordinary people need a secure environment rather than lawlessness. States and international organizations set rules and establish sanctions against violations of such rules. Take piracy, for example. It disrupts maritime communication, inhibits trade, and endangers lives. The United States appealed to international legal norms to fight piracy since the end of the eighteenth century. A significant increase of piracy near Somalia and the Horn of Africa in the twenty-first century created a collective and mostly successful international response to uphold and enforce international antipiracy laws.

Second, countries need a way to resolve conflict by peaceful means. Although international actors constantly engage in disputes, they realize that force alone is not the most efficient way to resolve them. Wars are simply too destructive and lead to further conflicts. When international political organizations are incapable or unwilling to move forward, international courts should. Despite difficulties, international law has played and continues to play a significant role in the peaceful settlement of many international disputes. As the records of diplomacy suggest, strong legal arguments play a particularly important role in settling territorial disputes between two countries. For instance, in the 1990s, Yemen and Eritrea fought over control of the Hanish Islands in the Red Sea. Violence was about to erupt. In 1998, the Permanent Court of Arbitration, one of the oldest institutions for dispute resolution, determined that the archipelago belonged to Yemen. Eritrea accepted this legal decision, and violence was avoided. In *Does International Law Promote the Peaceful Settlement of International Disputes?* Huth and his colleagues argue that, under the right conditions, international law becomes a more powerful force to bring stability, order, and peaceful change than military action.

Third, countries need to coordinate domestic laws in a globally interdependent world. Because countries have different constitutional, administrative, criminal, contract, family, and property laws, numerous practical problems and disagreements naturally emerge, especially in an era of global communication, trade, and travel. International law is therefore essential in regulating the relationships (a) among private citizens living in different countries, (b) between private citizens and foreign governments or organizations, and (c) among international organizations. Think of divorce and custody disputes, trademark violations, traffic accidents, financial obligations,

A need for a secure International Environment.
Countries, organizations, businesses, and ordinary people need a secure environment rather than lawlessness.

A need for conflict resolution.
Countries realize that force alone is not the most efficient way to resolve disagreements and disputes.

A need to coordinate domestic laws in a global world.
Because countries have different laws, numerous practical problems and disagreements naturally emerge, especially in an era of global trade and travel.

Figure 6. Why the World Needs International Law

and compensations for faulty products or services. However, there is a need for a strong enforcement mechanism built into international law. If such a mechanism is created, international law should also be more efficiently applied to fight transnational organized crime, including extortion, drug and human trafficking, kidnapping, and money laundering. See Figure 6.

The field of international political economy studies how politics and economics interact in an international context. One of the key debates in this field focuses on the question: Should there be economic policies developed by experts and state bureaucracies, or should economic development be left to market forces and international trade? Can it be a third way?

Robert Keohane in *The Old IPE and the New* writes that in the 1970s most economists were ignoring international politics, and international relations specialists were dismissing political economy. Yet later it was becoming clear that international economy affects international politics and vice versa. Today, for example, five big changes are taking place within the process of such interaction. In the past, the world was divided into "developing" and "developed" countries. Today, genuine economic development is taking place for much of the world's population. China has emerged as a big player in international manufacturing, trade, and finance. Volatility in financial and energy markets has been extreme. New global actors emerged: they are global corporations and nongovernmental organizations. And finally, new communication technologies now significantly affect commerce, finance, and investment, and, as it appears, politics.

Major concepts and debates in international political economy have been developing for many years. Mercantilism as one of the oldest economic approaches calls for the accumulation and protection of available resources in the name of the sovereign country. This economic theory was widely accepted several centuries ago, when absolute monarchies, such as France, followed mercantilist recipes to aggrandize power at the expense of their neighbors. At the heart of mercantilism is the view that maximizing net exports is the best route to national prosperity. Mercantilism is very much alive today: many countries, including China, use its core principles (such as maximizing employment and subsidizing exports) to adapt to the global market.

Another somewhat old-fashioned concept is so-called Keynesian economics. These are the principles proposed by John M. Keynes (1883–1946), a British economist, who was a founder of macroeconomics, that is, a theory of how economy worked within a single sovereign country. Keynes and his followers argued that, contrary to the assumption of the efficiency of free markets, governments should actively regulate business and especially finances. According to Keynesian economics, national governments can ease the undesirable effects of economic recessions by spending more money than their revenues allow. By putting money into the economy, government can fuel business transactions and purchases, stimulate production and consumption, lower unemployment, and create a prosperous middle class. Keynes' principles have played a key role in the understanding of the structure and performance of economics for half of the twentieth century. Today some economists argue in favor of returning to Keynesian economic policies, in view of unstable international markets and because of the decline of middle classes in some developed countries under the pressure of globalization.

Economic liberalism is an influential concept that criticizes both mercantilism and Keynesian economics. Liberal economists maintain that the free market would remain the key strategic answer to most economic challenges. The American economist Milton Friedman (1912–2006) in his classic work, *Capitalism and Freedom*, asserted that state regulations of economy are inflationary and counterproductive. He contended that people are rational actors, and that individual choices of millions of economic actors (businesses, consumers, etc.) work better for economic development than the regulations and policies developed by a few economic experts and state bureaucrats. Friedman, who taught at the University of Chicago, argued that the state does have a limited role to play: it should gradually increase the amount of money in circulation—an idea called monetarism. He was against the gold standard, the guaranteed exchange of paper money for gold in state reserves. He advocated policies under which governments abandoned the gold standard and started to manipulate the supply of money through banking interest rates—a process known as monetary policy. He supported a system of freely floating exchange rates determined by market transactions without governmental intervention.

A serious discussion continues about the direction of economic politics and the revision of the economic and political guidelines offered to developing countries in the past. One of such "recipes" has been the maximum deregulation of production and finances to "jumpstart" stagnant and inefficient economies of a wide range of countries. This approach has been called the *Washington Consensus* (because the International Monetary Fund and other financial institution that advocated this "consensus" are located in Washington, D.C.). How successful were such policies? Although liberal economists continue emphasizing the benefits of the "free market," many criticisms of the Washington Consensus deserve attention and careful analysis. Critics, for example, argue that the rigid application of the Washington Consensus may unintentionally destroy the middle class, bring instability, jeopardize democracy, and give excessive power to transnational corporations and export-oriented lobbies. In the end, a few enrich themselves at the expense of many others. Economic inequality between countries and regions has always been an important topic of discussion in international relations.

Not surprisingly, Marxist economic ideas continue to be influential today, sometimes feeding on the discontent among the supporters of the Washington Consensus. Marxism's key economic and political argument is that there is a ruling class that owns the major means of production, natural resources, and services and thus dominates the world. Throughout the twentieth century and after, this ruling class became increasingly global, as capital moved across borders and continents. Vladimir Lenin argued a century ago about the growing threat of strengthening the domination of the "parasitical" financial "oligarchy" and international monopolies trying to establish global economic and political domination. Today Marxist views inspire some activists of the antiglobalist movement who demand high taxes on the rich and rigorous social control over banks and corporations. Marxists claim that international corporations and banks, not the governments of sovereign countries, are the true holders of global power because of their financial resources. States serve the interests of the ruling class of billionaires using diplomacy, international agreements, and international law to manage international relations, which in effect should lead to higher profits.

Supporters of dependency theory maintain that developed nations with modern technologies and capital, called the *core*, have been receiving more benefits from international trade than the countries without technology and capital, called the *periphery*. The core countries invest in new technologies and make significant profits. The periphery countries, in contrast, suffer from technological backwardness and their inability to overcome it. As a result, the countries of the global periphery have to sell natural resources and provide cheap labor for the core countries. The core countries make the rules of international trade, often by direct political control of the periphery. Local elites in the periphery also are interested in this economic order, because they pocket most profits from selling natural resources of their countries to the core countries.

Supporters of these views maintain that the discriminatory structure of the world's economy and trade is the main cause of global inequality and chronic poverty. The poor, agricultural nations of the South (because most of the poorer countries are in the Southern hemisphere) are totally dependent on the developed industrial North, both economically and politically. Unlike Marxists, supporters of dependency theory accept private property and acknowledge the importance of some elements of a free-market economy. Nevertheless, they believe that the rules governing markets should change and the world's economic order should be restructured.

The demise of Western-style capitalism is probably what supporters of Marxism and world-systems theories hope will take place. Giovanni Arrighi and Li Zhan believe that the Washington Consensus did not really intend to help the emerging economies. They argue that South Korea, Taiwan, Singapore, and then China did not follow the Washington Consensus and achieved spectacular success in their economic development. In their view, liberalization of foreign trade and capital movements benefitted most of all the American economy and the interests of the West. They also believe that the core of the global capitalist system would inevitably shift from the United States to China. When Chinese manufacturing and economy surpass that of the United States, Chinese *yuan* would challenge the U.S. dollar as a world chief currency. The Washington Consensus, based on a neoliberal model of free trade, would be replaced, as the authors think, by a "Beijing consensus" based on state-run capitalism.

These assumptions echo postcolonial studies, in which former colonies were expected to demand an end to Western global domination. They would also be hoping for greater restraints on international capital markets. Susan Strange, a neo-Marxist, while acknowledging that the world is dependent on the market economy, urges us to turn attention to the disadvantaged social groups. In today's world, she wrote, some state and nonstate authorities have power to manage, restrict, exploit, or profit from branches of the world market. Others do not. In her view, the world is still driven by material interests of social classes behind the façade of government. See Figure 7.

International political economists are careful observers of the emerging trends and commonly welcome several viewpoints to critically understand the global economic developments. Nancy Birdsall and Francis Fukuyama write in *The Post-Washington Consensus* that open capital markets combined with unregulated financial sectors often lead to disastrous economic and political outcomes in some countries. The pressure on the governments today grows to become less focused on the free flow of capital and to become more concerned with social disruptions caused by global competition for well-paid jobs and by fiscal crises of social safety nets. Although the Washington Consensus did not necessarily disregard social policies, its focus on efficiency and fiscal discipline often led to cuts in social spending, which contributed to excessive pressures on middle classes and to social instability. Therefore, governments of developing countries today increasingly turn to "reindustrialization": they are supporting domestic industries through state subsidies and other incentives.

The past decade has also brought the realization that the countries of the emerging markets have begun playing a more serious role in global economic affairs on their own. Yet there is no guarantee that their economic growth and stability are sustainable for a long period. Economies of China, India, and Brazil driven by cheap labor and imported technology are likely to show signs of slowing down. In many ways, the

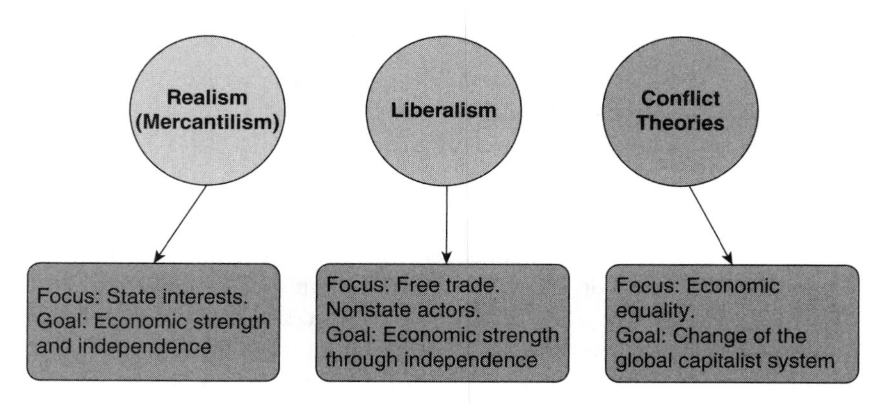

Figure 7. Major Approaches in International Political Economy

success or failure of these countries' policies will determine if an American-style liberal trade system of international economic relations would fall from its pedestal or get stronger.

Economic theories rise and fall with the tides of history. Global interdependence challenges past theories. In the past, a few wealthy states could define economic and financial policies for others as well. For decades, liberal trade and market principles worked well in Western Europe, Japan, and North America. More recently, many Asian countries found a way to benefit from an international liberal trade market, while pursuing domestically a combination of mercantilist and Keynesian policies. Apparently, "one-size-fits-all" free-market policies can damage rather than help countries. Also, world experience demonstrates that countries need to be stable financial, governmental, and social institutions to prosper in the conditions of today's global economy. For example, China has gradually liberalized some sections of its economy and trade without liberalizing its politics. China achieved a remarkable economic success. In contrast, Russia's attempts to shift rapidly and simultaneously to a liberal market economy and liberal democracy cost it dearly; its productive capacities declined dramatically and the population suffered. Today's studies suggest that each country's political, social, and cultural conditions significantly determine which economic policies will likely to succeed or fail.

GENERAL DISCUSSION QUESTIONS RELATED TO THE MATERIALS ABOUT INTERNATIONAL SECURITY, INTERNATIONAL LAW, AND INTERNATIONAL POLITICAL ECONOMY

These general questions are for class discussions as well as individual assignments. The discussion of these questions should help students think critically and better understand the materials in this part of the book. Other, more specific critical-thinking and practice questions related to the reading materials appear at the end of Part II.

- Give an example of a security policy or security-related decision you consider (a) mostly effective and one you consider (b) mostly ineffective. Explain your choices. Suggested examples:
    - U.S. border control policies
    - U.S. occupation of Afghanistan in 2001
    - Israel-Palestinian conflict today
- Select two or three international conflicts to demonstrate the misjudgments and misinterpretations of the leaders involved in such conflicts. World War I comes to mind, as do the 2003 war in Iraq and Russia's annexation of Crimea and the conflict in Eastern Ukraine in 2014. Also ask your professor which conflict she or he could recommend for this analysis.
- Suggest contemporary examples to illustrate *revolution in military affairs*. Discuss the impact that new technological innovations could have on security policies and diplomacy.

- Suggest several regions or countries in which or around which new conflicts related to energy and resources may occur ten years from now. Explain your choices.
- Geographical position gave some countries clear advantages in security matters, while others remained vulnerable. Which countries will remain more vulnerable than others from their security standpoint in the first half of the twenty-first century? Explain your opinion.
- Why are definitions of *terrorism* important? Discuss this from the position of international law and diplomacy.
- Suggest and discuss several examples of the actual or potential misuse of the term *terrorism*. Why do people and governments misuse this term?
- Explain why terrorism is an asymmetrical threat. Find and discuss a few examples to illustrate this point.
- Consider the statement: "Almost every fundamentalist or radical group supports terrorism." Could you prove or disprove this statement? Do your own research and provide examples of political radicalism and fundamentalism that reject violence.
- Why are the statements of Osama bin Laden important in the study of international relations? How do they relate to the current crisis in Iraq? Explain your view.
- Is it possible to eradicate international terrorism for the most part by 2025? Why or why not? Discuss your view.
- Hugo Grotius formulated the principle of *freedom of the seas*: A state's sovereignty ends at the edge of its territorial waters. Imagine for a moment that territorial waters are no longer recognized.
    - How would this development affect the United States? The United Kingdom?
    - How would this development affect international relations?
    - How do you think countries would react to this new legal reality?
- What are the main limitations of international law? Is it really necessary or practical to have international law? Explain your answer. Suggest one or two arguments not listed earlier in this book in support of international law.
- The Treaty on the Nonproliferation of Nuclear Weapons attempts to stop the spread of nuclear weapons. Will it be possible, in your view, to reach a more ambitious agreement and eliminate all nuclear weapons in fifteen years?
- Imagine the United Nations passes an international law to ban wars altogether.
    - Will this law be effective? Will wars stop?
    - Based on what you have read in this part of the book, suggest several conditions under which this new international law could be effective.
    - Which country or organization could be capable of creating and maintaining such conditions, and how?
- Would supporters of economic liberalism—in your view—also support international trade sanctions and under what circumstances?

- Discuss how probable will be the process of replacement of the Washington Consensus (based on deregulation of finance and the liberal model of trade) by a Beijing consensus (based on state controls over trade and finances). Which countries do you think will turn to state-run capitalism and which will not? Consider the period from today until 2025.
- China has become the main beneficiary of economic globalization early in the twenty-first century. Discuss whether a country can be economically successful and globally isolated at the same time.

Section 5

War, Security, and Terrorism

Former U.S. Defense Secretary Chuck Hagel (center) is welcomed by Saudi Deputy Defense Minister Salman bin Sultan (left) and Gen. Lloyd Austin, commander of U.S. Central command (right), upon his arrival in Jiddah, Saudi Arabia in 2014. What are the benefits for the United States to support the Kingdom of Saudi Arabia? Apply David Lake's argument that security policies depend on the balance of gains and losses to specific policies of the United States. What are the benefits for Saudi Arabia to seek U.S. support?
Source: Mandel Ngan/Associated Press

The Strategies of Terrorism

ANDREW H. KYDD AND BARBARA F. WALTER

Terrorism often works. Extremist organizations such as al-Qaida, Hamas, and the Tamil Tigers engage in terrorism because it frequently delivers the desired response. Hijacking planes, blowing up buses, and kidnapping individuals may seem irrational and incoherent to outside observers, but these tactics can be surprisingly effective in achieving a terrorist group's political aims.

Despite the salience of terrorism today, scholars and policymakers are only beginning to understand how and why it works. Much has been written on the origins of terror, the motivations of terrorists, and counterterror responses, but little has appeared on the strategies terrorist organizations employ and the conditions under which these strategies succeed or fail.

Effective counterstrategies cannot be designed without first understanding the strategic logic that drives terrorist violence. Terrorism works not simply because it instills fear in target populations, but because it causes governments and individuals to respond in ways that aid the terrorists' cause.

In this article we seek answers to four questions. First, what types of goals do terrorists seek to achieve? Second, what strategies do they pursue to achieve these goals? Third, why do these strategies work in some cases but not in others? And fourth, given these strategies, what are the targeted governments' best responses to prevent terrorism and protect their countries from future attacks?

The core of our argument is that terrorist violence is a form of costly signaling. Terrorists are too weak to impose their will directly by force of arms. They are sometimes strong enough, however, to persuade audiences to do as they wish by altering the audience's beliefs about such matters as the terrorist's ability to impose costs and their degree of commitment to their cause. Given the conflict of interest between terrorists and their targets, ordinary communication or "cheap talk" is insufficient to change minds or influence behavior. If al-Qaida had informed the United States on September 10, 2001, that it would kill 3,000 Americans unless the United States withdrew from Saudi Arabia, the threat might have sparked concern, but it would not have had the same impact as the attacks that followed. Because it is hard for weak actors to make credible threats, terrorists are forced to display publicly just how far they are willing to go to obtain their desired results.

There are five principal strategic logics of costly signaling at work in terrorist campaigns: (1) attrition, (2) intimidation, (3) provocation, (4) spoiling, and (5) outbidding. In an attrition strategy, terrorists seek to persuade the enemy that the terrorists are strong enough to impose considerable costs if the enemy continues a particular policy. Terrorists using intimidation try to convince the population that the terrorists are strong enough to punish disobedience and that the government is too weak to stop them, so that people behave as the terrorists wish. A provocation strategy is an attempt to induce the enemy to respond to terrorism with indiscriminate violence, which radicalizes the population and moves them to support the terrorists. Spoilers attack in an effort to persuade the enemy that moderates on the terrorists' side are weak and untrustworthy, thus undermining attempts to reach a peace settlement. Groups engaged in outbidding use violence to convince the public that the terrorists have greater resolve to fight the enemy than rival groups, and therefore are worthy of support. Understanding these five distinct strategic logics is crucial not only for understanding terrorism but also for designing effective antiterror policies.

Kydd, Andrew and Walter, Barbara, 'The Strategies of Terrorism', International Security, 31:1, pp.49-80.

THE GOALS OF TERRORISM

For years the press has portrayed terrorists as crazy extremists who commit indiscriminate acts of violence, without any larger goal beyond revenge or a desire to produce fear in an enemy population. By contrast, the goals driving terrorist organizations are usually political objectives, and it is these goals that determine whether and how terrorist campaigns will be launched.

We define "terrorism" as the use of violence against civilians by nonstate actors to attain political goals. These goals can be conceptualized in a variety of ways. Individuals and groups often have hierarchies of objectives, where broader goals lead to more proximate objectives, which then become specific goals in more tactical analyses. For the sake of simplicity, we adopt the common distinction between goals (or ultimate desires) and strategies (or plans of action to attain the goals).

Although the ultimate goals of terrorists have varied over time, five have had enduring importance: regime change, territorial change, policy change, social control, and status quo maintenance.

A fruitful starting point for a theory of terrorist strategies is the literature on uncertainty, conflict, and costly signaling. Uncertainty has long been understood to be a cause of conflict. Geoffrey Blainey argued that wars begin when states disagree about their relative power, and they end when states agree again. James Fearon and other theorists built upon this insight and showed that uncertainty about a state's willingness to fight can cause conflict. If states are unsure what other states will fight for, they may demand too much in negotiations and end up in conflict. This uncertainty could reflect a disagreement about power, as Blainey understood, or a disagreement over resolve, willpower, or the intensity of preferences over the issue. The United States and North Vietnam did not disagree over their relative power, but the United States fatally underestimated North Vietnamese determination to achieve victory.

Uncertainty about trustworthiness or moderation of preferences can also cause conflict. States are often uncertain about each other's ultimate ambitions, intentions, and preferences. Because of this, anything that increases one side's belief that the other is deceitful, expansionist, risk acceptant, or hostile increases incentives to fight rather than cooperate.

If uncertainty about power, resolve, and trustworthiness can lead to violence, then communication on these topics is the key to preventing (or instigating) conflict. The problem is that simple verbal statements are often not credible, because actors frequently have incentives to lie and bluff. If by saying "We're resolved," the North Vietnamese could have persuaded the United States to abandon the South in 1965, then North Vietnam would have had every incentive to say so even if it was not that resolute. In reality, they had to fight a long and costly war to prove their point. Similarly, when Mikhail Gorbachev wanted to reassure the West and end the Cold War, verbal declarations of innocent intentions were insufficient, because previous Soviet leaders had made similar statements. Instead, real arms reductions, such as the 1987 Intermediate-Range Nuclear Forces Treaty, were necessary for Western opinion to change.

Because talk is cheap, states and terrorists who wish to influence the behavior of an adversary must resort to costly signals. Costly signals are actions so costly that bluffers and liars are unwilling to take them. In international crises, mobilizing forces or drawing a very public line in the sand are examples of strategies that less resolved actors might find too costly to take. War itself, or the willingness to endure it, can serve as a forceful signal of resolve and provide believable information about power and capabilities. Costly signals separate the wheat from the chaff and allow honest communication, although sometimes at a terrible price.

To obtain their political goals, terrorists need to provide credible information to the audiences whose behavior they hope to influence. Terrorists play to two key audiences: governments whose policies they wish to influence and individuals on the terrorists' own side whose support or obedience they seek to gain. The targeted governments are central because they can grant concessions over policy or territory that the terrorists are seeking. The terrorists' domestic audience is also important, because they can provide resources to the terrorist group and must obey its edicts on social or political issues.

		Target of Persuasion	
		Enemy	Own Population
Subject of Uncertainty	Power	Attrition	Intimidation
	Resolve		Outbidding
	Trustworthiness	Spoiling	Provocation

Figure 8. Strategies of Terrorist Violence

Figure 8 shows how the three subjects of uncertainty (power, resolve, and trustworthiness) combine with the two targets of persuasion (the enemy government and the domestic population) to yield a family of five signaling strategies. These strategies form a theoretically cohesive set that we believe represents most of the commonly used strategies in important terrorist campaigns around the world today. A terrorist organization can of course pursue more than one strategy at a time. The September 11 terrorist attacks, for example, were probably part of both an attrition strategy and a provocation strategy. By targeting the heart of the United States' financial district, al-Qaida may have been attempting to increase the cost of the U.S. policy of stationing soldiers in Saudi Arabia. But by targeting prominent symbols of American economic and military power, al-Qaida may also have been trying to goad the United States into an extreme military response that would serve al-Qaida's larger goal of radicalizing the world's Muslim population. The challenge for policymakers in targeted countries is to calibrate their responses in ways that do not further any of the terrorists' goals.

Below we analyze the five terrorist strategies in greater detail, discuss the conditions under which each is likely to succeed, and relate these conditions to the appropriate counterterrorism strategies.

ATTRITION: A BATTLE OF WILLS

The most important task for any terrorist group is to persuade the enemy that the group is strong and resolute enough to inflict serious costs, so that the enemy yields to the terrorists' demands. The attrition strategy is designed to accomplish this task. In an attrition campaign, the greater the costs a terrorist organization is able to inflict, the more credible its threat to inflict future costs, and the more likely the target is to grant concessions. During the last years of the British Empire, the Greeks in Cyprus, Jews in Palestine, and Arabs in Aden used a war of attrition strategy against their colonizer. By targeting Britain with terrorist attacks, they eventually convinced the political leadership that maintaining control over these territories would not be worth the cost in British lives.

Robert Pape presents the most thorough exposition of terrorism as a war of attrition in his analysis of suicide bombing. Based on a data set of all suicide attacks from 1980 to 2003 (315 in total), Pape argues that suicide terrorism is employed by weak actors for whom peaceful tactics have failed and conventional military tactics are infeasible because of the imbalance of power. The strategy is to inflict costs on the enemy until it withdraws its occupying forces: the greater the costs inflicted, the more likely the enemy is to withdraw.

Conditions Favorable to Attrition

A war of attrition strategy is more effective against some targets than others. Three variables are likely to figure in the outcome: the state's level of interest in the issue under dispute, the constraints on its ability to retaliate, and its sensitivity to the costs of violence.

The first variable, the state's degree of interest in the disputed issue, is fundamental. States with only peripheral interests at stake often capitulate to terrorist demands; states with more important interests at stake rarely do. United States withdrew from Lebanon following the bombing of the marine barracks because it had only a marginal interest in maintaining stability and preventing Syrian domination of that country.

The second variable, constraints on retaliation, affects the costs paid by the terrorists for pursuing a war of attrition. Terrorist organizations almost always are weaker than the governments they target and, as a result, are vulnerable to government retaliation. The more constrained the government is in its use of force, the less costly an attrition strategy is, and the longer the terrorists can hold out in the hopes of achieving their goal.

The ease with which a terrorist organization can be targeted also influences a country's ability to retaliate forcefully. Terrorist organizations such as al-Qaida that are widely dispersed, difficult to identify, or otherwise hard to target are at an advantage in a war of attrition because their enemies will have difficulty delivering punishment.

The third variable is a target's cost tolerance. Governments that are able to absorb heavier costs and hold out longer are less inviting targets for an attrition strategy. Terrorist organizations are likely to gauge a target's cost tolerance based on at least two factors: the target's regime type and the target's past behavior toward other terrorists. Regime type is important because democracies may be less able to tolerate the painful effects of terrorism than nondemocracies. Citizens of democracies, their fears stoked by media reports and warnings of continued vulnerability, are more likely to demand an end to the attacks. In more authoritarian states, the government exerts more control over the media and can disregard public opinion to a greater extent.

Among democratic states, sensitivity to costs may vary with the party in power. When more dovish parties are in charge, the target may be perceived to have lower cost tolerances than if a more hawkish party were at the helm. The dove-hawk dimension may correlate with the left-right dimension in domestic politics, leading left-wing parties to be more likely to grant terrorist demands. This traditional divide between peace and security has characterized Israeli politics for years.

The number of prior concessions made to other terrorists is also likely to influence perceptions of the target's cost tolerance. Governments that have already yielded to terrorist demands are more likely to experience additional terrorist attacks. Evidence abounds that terrorists explicitly consider the prior behavior of states and are encouraged by signs of weakness. The past behavior of a targeted government, therefore, also provides important information to terrorist groups about its likely future behavior and the success of this particular strategy.

Best Responses to Attrition

There are at least five counterstrategies available to a state engaged in a war of attrition. First, the targeted government can concede inessential issues in exchange for peace, a strategy that we believe is frequently pursued though rarely admitted. In some cases, the terrorists will genuinely care more about the disputed issue and be willing to outlast the target. In such cases, concessions are likely to be the state's best response. Other potential challengers, however, may perceive this response as a sign of weakness, which could lead them to launch their own attacks. To reduce the damage to its reputation, the target can vigorously fight other wars of attrition over issues it cares more deeply about, thus signaling a willingness to bear costs if the matter is of sufficient consequence.

Second, where the issue under dispute is important enough to the targeted state that it does not want to grant any concessions, the government may engage in targeted retaliation. Retaliation can target the leadership of the terrorist group, its followers, their assets, and other objects of value. Care must be taken, however, that the retaliation is precisely targeted, because the terrorist organization could simultaneously be pursuing a strategy of provocation. A harsh, indiscriminate response might make a war of attrition more costly for the terrorists, but it would also harm innocent civilians who might then serve as willing recruits for the terrorists. The Israeli policy of assassination of terrorist leaders is shaped by this concern.

Third, a state can harden likely targets to minimize the costs the terrorist organization can inflict. If targeted governments can prevent most attacks from being executed, a war of attrition strategy will not be able to inflict the costs necessary to convince the target to concede. The wall separating Israel from the West Bank and Gaza is a large-scale example of this counterstrategy. The United States has been less successful in hardening its own valuable targets, such as nuclear and chemical plants and the container shipping system, despite the creation of the Department of Homeland Security. Protecting these types of targets is essential if one seeks to deter additional attacks and discourage the use of attrition.

Fourth, states should seek to deny terrorists access to the most destructive weapons, especially nuclear and biological ones. Any weapon that can inflict enormous costs will be particularly attractive to terrorists pursuing a war of attrition. The greater the destruction, the higher the likelihood that the target will concede increasingly consequential issues. Particular attention should be placed on securing Russian stockpiles of fissile material and on halting the spread of uranium enrichment technology to Iran and North Korea. No other country has as much material under so little government control as Russia, and Iran and North Korea are vital because of the links both countries have to terrorist organizations.

Finally, states can strive to minimize the psychological costs of terrorism and the tendency people have to overreact. John Mueller has noted that the risks associated with terrorism are actually quite small; for the average U.S. citizen, the likelihood of being a victim of a terrorist attack is about the same as that of being struck by lightning. Government public education programs should therefore be careful not to overstate the threat, for this plays into the hands of the terrorists. If Americans become convinced that terrorism, while a deadly problem, is no more of a health risk than drunk driving, smoking, or obesity, then al-Qaida's attrition strategy will be undercut. What the United States should seek to avoid are any unnecessary costs associated with wasteful and misguided counterterror programs. The more costs the United States inflicts on itself in the name of counterterrorism policies of dubious utility, the more likely a war of attrition strategy is to succeed.

INTIMIDATION: THE REIGN OF TERROR

Intimidation is akin to the strategy of deterrence, preventing some undesired behavior by means of threats and costly signals. It is most frequently used when terrorist organizations wish to overthrow a government in power or gain social control over a given population. It works by demonstrating that the terrorists have the power to punish whoever disobeys them, and that the government is powerless to stop them.

Terrorists are often in competition with the government for the support of the population. Terrorists who wish to bring down a government must somehow convince the government's defenders that continued backing of the government will be costly. One way to do this is to provide clear evidence that the terrorist organization can kill those individuals who continue to sustain the regime. By targeting the government's more visible agents and supporters, such as mayors, police, prosecutors, and pro-regime citizens, terrorist organizations demonstrate that they have the ability to hurt their opponents and that the government is too weak to punish the terrorists or protect future victims.

An intimidation strategy can encompass a range of actions—from assassinations of individuals in positions of power to car bombings of police recruits, such as those carried out by the Zarqawi group in Iraq. It can also include massacres of civilians who have cooperated with the government or rival groups, such as the 1957 massacre at Melouza by the National Liberation Front during the Algerian war for independence.

Conditions Favorable to Intimidation

When the goal is regime change, weak states and rough terrain are two factors that facilitate intimidation. James Fearon and David Laitin argue that civil wars are likely to erupt and continue where the government is weak and the territory is large and difficult to traverse. These conditions allow small insurgent groups to carve out portions of a country as a base for challenging the central government. Intimidation is likely to be used against civilians on the fault lines between rebel and government control to deter individuals from supporting the government.

When the goal is social control, weak states again facilitate intimidation. When the justice system is too feeble to effectively prosecute crimes associated with intimidation, people will either live in fear or seek protection from non-state actors such as local militias or gangs. Penetration of the justice system by sympathizers of a terrorist group also facilitates an intimidation strategy, because police and courts will be reluctant to prosecute crimes and may even be complicit in them.

Best Responses to Intimidation

When the terrorist goal is regime change, the best response to intimidation is to retake territory from the rebels in discrete chunks and in a decisive fashion. Ambiguity about who is in charge should be minimized, even if this means temporarily ceding some areas to the rebels to concentrate resources on selected sections of territory. This response is embodied in the "clear-and-hold strategy" The U.S. military developed the clear-and-hold strategy during the final years of U.S. involvement in Vietnam. A principal strategy of the Vietcong was intimidation—to prevent collaboration with the government and build up control in the countryside. In the early years of the war, the United States responded with search and destroy missions, essentially an attrition strategy. Given that the insurgents were not pursuing an attrition strategy, and were not particularly vulnerable to one, this initial counterstrategy was a mistake.

Clear-and-hold has its limitations. It is usually impossible to completely deny terrorists entry into the government-controlled zones. In 2002 Chechen terrorists were able to hold a theater audience of 912 people hostage in the heart of Moscow, and 130 were killed in the operation to retake the building. The Shining Path frequently struck in Lima, far from its mountain strongholds. In such situations, a more effective counterstrategy would be to invest in protecting the targets of attacks. In most states, most of the time, the majority of state agents do not need to worry about their physical security, because no one wants to harm them. However, certain state agents, such as prosecutors of organized crime, are more accustomed to danger, and procedures have been developed to protect them. These procedures should be applied to election workers, rural officials and police, community activists, and any individual who plays a visible role in the support and functioning of the embattled government.

When the terrorist goal is social control, the best response is strengthening law enforcement. This may require more resources to enable the government to effectively investigate and prosecute crimes. More controversial, it may mean using national agencies such as the Federal Bureau of Investigation to bypass local officials who are sympathetic to the terrorist group and investigating law enforcement agencies to purge such sympathizers if they obstruct justice.

PROVOCATION: LIGHTING THE FUSE

A provocation strategy is often used in pursuit of regime change and territorial change, the most popular goals of the FTOs listed by the State Department. It is designed to persuade the domestic audience that the target of attacks is evil and untrustworthy and must be vigorously resisted.

Terrorist organizations seeking to replace a regime face a significant challenge: they are usually much more hostile to the regime than a majority of the state's citizens. Al-Qaida may wish to topple the House of Saud, but if a majority of citizens do not support this goal, al-Qaida is unlikely to achieve it.

Provocation helps shift citizen support away from the incumbent regime. In a provocation strategy, terrorists seek to goad the target government into a military response that harms civilians within the terrorist organization's home territory. The aim is to convince them that the government is so evil that the radical goals of the terrorists are justified and support for their organization is warranted. Provocation, therefore, is a way for terrorists to force an enemy government to reveal information about itself that then helps the organization recruit additional members.

Conditions Favorable to Provocation

Constraints on retaliation and regime type are again important in determining when provocation is successful. For provocation to work, the government must be capable of middling levels of brutality. A government willing and able to commit genocide makes a bad target for provocation, as the response will destroy the constituency the terrorists represent. At the opposite pole, a government so committed to human rights and the rule of law that it is incapable of inflicting indiscriminate punishment also makes a bad target, because it cannot be provoked. Such a government might be an attractive target for an attrition strategy if it is not very good at stopping attacks, but provocation will be ineffective.

What explains why a government would choose a less discriminating counterstrategy over a more precise one? In some instances, a large-scale military response will enhance the security of a country rather than detract from it. If the target government is able to eliminate the leadership of a terrorist organization and its operatives, terrorism is likely to cease or be greatly reduced even if collateral damage radicalizes moderates to some extent. A large-scale military response may also enhance the security of a country, despite radicalizing some moderates, if it deters additional attacks from other terrorist groups that may be considering a war of attrition. Target governments may calculate that the negative consequences of a provocation strategy are acceptable under these conditions.

Domestic political considerations are also likely to influence the type of response that the leadership of a target state chooses. Democracies may be more susceptible to provocation than nondemocracies. Populations that have suffered from terrorist violence will naturally want their government to take action to stop terrorism. Unfortunately, many of the more discriminating tools of counterterrorism, such as infiltrating terrorist cells, sharing intelligence with other countries, and arresting individuals, are not visible to the publics these actions serve to protect.

Best Responses to Provocation

The best response to provocation is a discriminating strategy that inflicts as little collateral damage as possible. Countries should seek out and destroy the terrorists and their immediate backers to reduce the likelihood of future terror attacks, but they must carefully isolate these targets from the general population, which may or may not be sympathetic to the terrorists. This type of discriminating response will require superior intelligence capabilities.

SPOILING: SABOTAGING THE PEACE

The goal of a spoiling strategy is to ensure that peace overtures between moderate leaders on the terrorists' side and the target government do not succeed. It works by playing on the mistrust between these two groups and succeeds when one or both parties fail to sign or implement a settlement. It is often employed when the ultimate objective is territorial change.

Terrorists resort to a spoiling strategy when relations between two enemies are improving and a peace agreement threatens the terrorists' more far-reaching goals. Peace agreements alarm terrorists because they understand that moderate citizens are less likely to support ongoing violence once a compromise agreement between more moderate groups has been reached.

A spoiling strategy works by persuading the enemy that moderates on the terrorists' side cannot be trusted to abide by a peace deal. Whenever two sides negotiate a peace agreement, there is uncertainty about whether the deal is self-enforcing. Each side fears that even if it honors its commitments, the other side may not, catapulting it back to war on disadvantageous terms.

Terrorist acts are particularly effective during peace negotiations because opposing parties are naturally distrustful of each other's motives and have limited sources of information about each other's intentions. Thus, even if moderate leaders are willing to aggressively suppress extremists on their side, terrorists know that isolated violence might still convince the target to reject the deal. A reason for this is that the targeted group may not be able to readily observe the extent of the crackdown and must base its judgments primarily on whether terrorism occurs or not. Even a sincere effort at self-policing, therefore, will not necessarily convince the targeted group to proceed with a settlement if a terrorist attack occurs.

Conditions Favorable to Spoiling

Terrorists pursuing a spoiling strategy are likely to be more successful when the enemy perceives moderates on their side to be strong and therefore more capable of halting terrorism. When an attack occurs, the target cannot be sure whether moderates on the other side can suppress their own extremists but choose not to, or are weak and lack the ability to stop them.

Best Responses to Spoiling

When mutual trust is high, a peace settlement can be implemented despite ongoing terrorist acts and the potential vulnerabilities the agreement can create. Trust, however, is rarely high after long conflicts, which is why spoilers can strike with a reasonable chance that their attack will be successful. Strategies that build trust and reduce vulnerability are, therefore, the best response to spoiling.

Vulnerabilities emerge in peace processes in two ways. Symmetric vulnerabilities occur during the implementation of a deal because both sides must lower their guard. The Israelis, for example, have had to relax controls over the occupied territories, and the Palestinians were obligated to disarm militant groups.

Vulnerabilities can also be longer term and asymmetric. In any peace deal between Israel and the Palestinians, the ability of the Palestinians to harm Israel will inevitably grow as Palestinians build their own state and acquire greater military capabilities. This change in the balance of power can make it difficult for the side that will see an increase in its power to credibly commit not to take advantage of this increase later on. This commitment problem can cause conflicts to be prolonged even though there are possible peace agreements that both sides would prefer to war.

OUTBIDDING: ZEALOTS VERSUS SELLOUTS

Outbidding arises when two key conditions hold: two or more domestic parties are competing for leadership of their side, and the general population is uncertain about which of the groups best represents their interests. The competition between Hamas and Fatah is a classic case where two groups vie for the support of the Palestinian citizens and where the average Palestinian is uncertain about which side he or she ought to back.

If citizens had full information about the preferences of the competing groups, an outbidding strategy would be unnecessary and ineffective; citizens would simply support the group that best aligned with their own interests. In reality, however, citizens cannot be sure if the group competing for power truly represents their preferences. The group could be a strong and resolute defender of the cause (zealots) or weak and ineffective stooges of the enemy (sellouts). If citizens support zealots, they get a strong champion but with some risk that they will be dragged into a confrontation with the enemy that they end up losing. If citizens support sellouts, they get peace but at the price of accepting a worse outcome than might have been achieved with additional armed struggle. Groups competing for power have an incentive to signal that they are zealots rather than sellouts. Terrorist attacks can serve this function by signaling that a group has the will to continue the armed struggle despite its costs.

Three reasons help to explain why groups are likely to be rewarded for being more militant rather than less. First, in bargaining contexts, it is often useful to be represented by an agent who is more hard-line than oneself. Hard-line agents will reject deals that one would accept, which will force the adversary to make a better offer than one would get by representing oneself in the negotiations. Palestinians might therefore prefer Hamas as a negotiating agent with Israel because it has a reputation for resolve and will reject inferior deals.

Second, uncertainty may also exist about the type of adversary the population and its competing groups are facing. If the population believes there is some chance that their adversary is untrustworthy (unwilling to compromise under any condition), then they know that conflict may be inevitable, in which case being represented by zealots may be advantageous.

A third factor that may favor outbidding is that office-holding itself may produce incentives to sell out. Here, the problem lies with the benefits groups receive once in office (i.e., income and power). Citizens fear that their leaders, once in office, may betray important principles and decide to settle with the enemy on unfavorable terms. They know that holding office skews one's preferences toward selling out, but they remain unsure about which of their leaders is most likely to give in. Terrorist organizations exploit this uncertainty by using violence to signal their commitment to a cause. Being perceived as more extreme than the median voter works to the terrorists' benefit because it balances out the "tempering effect" of being in office.

Conditions Favorable to Outbidding

Outbidding will be favored when multiple groups are competing for the allegiance of a similar demographic base of support. In Peru, the 1970s saw the development of a number of leftist groups seeking to represent the poor and indigenous population. When the military turned over power to an elected government in 1980, the Shining Path took up an armed struggle to distinguish itself from groups that chose to pursue electoral politics. It also embarked on an assassination campaign designed to weaken rival leftist groups and intimidate their followers. When organizations encounter less competition for the support of their main constituents, outbidding will be less appealing.

Best Responses to Outbidding

One solution to the problem of outbidding would be to eliminate the struggle for power by encouraging competing groups to consolidate into a unified opposition. If competition among resistance groups is eliminated, the incentive for outbidding also disappears. The downside of this counterstrategy is that a unified opposition may be stronger than a divided one. United oppositions, however, can make peace and deliver, whereas divided ones may face greater structural disincentives to do so.

An alternative strategy for the government to pursue in the face of outbidding is to validate the strategy chosen by nonviolent groups by granting them concessions and attempting to satisfy the demands of their constituents. If outbidding can be shown to yield poor results in comparison to playing within the system, groups may be persuaded to abandon the strategy.

CONCLUSION

Terrorist violence is a form of costly signaling by which terrorists attempt to influence the beliefs of their enemy and the population they represent or wish to control. They use violence to signal their strength and resolve in an effort to produce concessions from their enemy and obedience and support from their followers. They also attack both to sow mistrust between moderates who might want to make peace and to provoke a reaction that makes the enemy appear barbarous and untrustworthy.

In this article, we have laid out the five main goals terrorist organizations seek and the five most important terrorist strategies, and we have outlined when they are likely to be tried and what the best counterstrategies might look like. What becomes clear in this brief analysis is that a deeper study of each of the five strategies is needed to reveal the nuanced ways in which terrorism works, and to refine responses to it.

Our analysis suggests that democracies are more likely to be sensitive to the costs of terrorist attacks, to grant concessions to terrorists so as to limit future attacks, to be constrained in their ability to pursue a lengthy attritional campaign against an organization, but also to be under greater pressure to "do something." This does not mean that all democracies will behave incorrectly in the face of terrorist attacks all the time. Democratic regimes may possess certain structural features, however, that make them attractive targets for terrorism.

Finally, we realize that our discussion is only a beginning and that further elaboration of each of the strategies and their corresponding counterstrategies awaits future research. We also understand that not all counterterrorism policies are predicated on the specific strategy terrorists pursue. Our analysis is at the middling level of strategic interaction. At the tactical level are all the tools of intelligence gathering and target defense that make sense no matter what the terrorist's strategy is. At the higher level are the primary sources of terrorism such as poverty, education, international conflict, and chauvinistic indoctrination that enable terrorist organizations to operate and survive in the first place. Our aim in this article has been to try to understand why these organizations choose certain forms of violence, and how this violence serves their larger purposes. The United States has the ability to reduce the likelihood of additional attacks on its territory and citizens. But it will be much more successful if it first understands the goals terrorists are seeking and the underlying strategic logic by which a plane flying into a skyscraper might deliver the desired response.

From Classical Terrorism to "Global" Terrorism

MICHEL WIEVIORKA

CLASSICAL TERRORISM

As a historical reality, terrorism is like many other social or political phenomena: it has undergone considerable transformations since the period between 1960 and 1980. To be more precise, it has moved from the classical era to the global era. Some observers challenge this image of distinct change or break. Hans Magnus Enzensberger, for example, while not minimizing the innovations brought in by radical Islamism which has, in his words, "replaced the omniscient and all powerful Central Committee by a flexible network," insists on recalling that "modern terrorism is a European invention dating from the nineteenth century... In recent years," he points out, "its main source of inspiration has been the extreme left terrorism of the 1960s and 1970s". He considers that the techniques of the Islamists, their symbols, the style of their communiqués, etc., borrow on a wide scale from the extreme left groups of the past. One might add, to go for a moment in his direction, that the practice of suicide is not a novelty in terrorism. The terrorists of the end of the nineteenth and beginning of the twentieth century took risks which verged on suicide in approaching their target with a bomb, a pistol, or a knife. Bobby Sands in 1981, other members of the (Irish) IRA, Ulrike Meinhof in 1976, Andreas Baader in 1977, and other members of the (German) Red Army Fraction all committed suicide in prison—although it is true that their gestures did not involve the deaths of anyone other than themselves.

The fact remains that Enzensberger himself, a few lines later in the book quoted above, weakens the thesis of historical continuity by noting that the Islamist terrorists "are in reality pure products of the globalized world which they are fighting" and that "in comparison to their predecessors, they have gone considerably further, not only in the techniques which they use but in their use of the media". While it would be absurd to postulate an absolute break, it nevertheless does seem to us more relevant to insist on the elements of a move from one era to another, rather than those which indicate a degree of continuity. This move can be observed in material terms by analyzing the forms and the meanings which terrorism assumed yesterday and by comparing them with present-day forms and meanings. It also involves the considerable changes in the categories which we can now use in considering this phenomenon. In the period 1960–1980 terrorism came in the main within the province of the analytical framework of the nation-state and its extension, international relations. Within the nation-state—or, at least, the sovereign state—it corresponded to three major registers. It could be on the extreme left, the extreme right, or nationalist and in favor of independence.

By far the most widespread expression of extreme left terrorism was played out in Italy, but it was also to be found in numerous other societies in varying stages of industrialization: West Germany with the Red Army Faction and the Revolutionary Cells, France with *Action Directe,* Japan with its Red Army, Belgium with the Revolutionary Communist Cells, Greece, Portugal, etc. It was the outcome of what I termed, at the time, an *inversion* in which the perpetrators of violence, in a deviation of post-68 leftism, took over the categories of Marxism-Leninism to subvert them in the name of a working-class proletariat which they in no way represented. In each instance terrorism challenged the authority of the state, even if in some cases the state had endeavored to become international and to establish itself in a space other than national, and even if it did denounce American imperialism in no uncertain terms. Extreme right terrorism, which was less widespread, was also prompted by projects to take over the state, often associated with the presence in the machinery of the states concerned of sectors which were themselves open to projects of this type. Finally, still internal to sovereign states, terrorism could be the mode of action of nationalist movements wishing to force the independence of a nation, where it might also be a question for them of awakening by means of violence. In Europe, the Basque and Irish movements were thus characterized by their resort to the armed struggle and by comparable forms of organization with, in particular, the same type of tensions between bellicose "military" rationales and "political" rationales which were more open to negotiation.

Elsewhere, international terrorism was in the main carried out by actors claiming to adhere to the Palestinian cause, whether it be at the center—for example with the killing of Israeli athletes carried out by El Fatah in 1972 in the Olympic village in Munich—or on the periphery with, in these instance, the intervention of groups possibly manipulated by state "sponsors" (Syria, Libya, Iraq) endeavoring to weaken the central rationale of the PLO and to prevent any negotiated solution to the Israeli-Palestinian conflict. In some respects, the terrorism of the ASALA (Secret Army for the Liberation of Armenia) resembled that of the Palestinian groups on which it was modeled in particular as, like them, it found in Lebanon in crisis a territory propitious to its short-lived prosperity.

The specificity of classical terrorism, that of the period between 1960 and 1980, is that it unfolded in a "Westphalian" world, as some political analysts call it today—a world which it was possible and legitimate to approach in terms of the categories of what Ulrich Beck calls "methodological nationalism." Terrorism originated within societies which are themselves established within states; it conveyed political and ideological deviations which referred to projects for taking power at state level or for the construction of a state; and it was conveyed by an avant-garde who saw themselves as being the direction of history, the working class, and the nation. In counterpart, the campaign against terrorism was an affair in which each of the states concerned became involved for itself—which did not exclude appeals to international solidarity. Classical terrorism was conceived of and described as being primarily a danger threatening states, their order, and possibly, their territorial integrity.

"GLOBAL" TERRORISM

The 9/11 attacks revealed what could in fact be glimpsed almost ten years previously: the entry into the "global" era of terrorism. This era had been inaugurated by various episodes bearing the mark of radical Islamism with, in particular, the first attempted Islamist attack in New York in 1993, even then aimed at the World Trade Center towers, or again the hijacking of an Air France plane in Algiers in December 1994 by Islamists who planned to crash the plane on Paris—a hijacking which was followed a few months later by a series of attacks in France falling within the same "global" rationale since international dimensions (the extension of the Algerian Islamist struggle outside Algerian national space) were combined with dimensions internal to French society (crisis in the *banlieues,* social exclusion, and the transformation of the experience of racism into violence).

It is even possible to go further back in time to find the first signs of "global" terrorism in the attacks using a suicide bomber in a delivery truck which destroyed the American Embassy in Beirut (April 1983) and then the barracks of the French contingent of the multinational force in Lebanon and the local headquarters of the United States Marines (October 1983): many believe that these were the first actions of the Hezbollah, a movement which described itself as planning an Islamist revolution throughout the region, which also intended to destroy the state of Israel and which, from then on, was capable of mobilizing people destined to kill themselves in their action.

Whatever the case may be, the "globalization" of terrorism was demonstrated in spectacular fashion by the 9/11 attacks. "Globalization" means that the phenomenon can no longer be thought of in the categories of "methodological nationalism" as it blurs the classical frontiers between rationales which are internal to sovereign states and the external or international rationales. The perpetrators of the 9/11 attack circulated in what had become a global space, their career paths took them from the society in which they were born, in this instance Saudi Arabia and Egypt, to other societies, Sudan, Pakistan and Afghanistan where they met, were formed and trained, creating links of solidarity which again fanned out to form networks all over the world and in which they had the advantage of total freedom of action in the state of the Taliban, which they subjugated. They were at ease in several countries in Europe—in Germany, where some of them attended university; in the England of "Londonistan" and its mosques, where the most radical opinions were expressed freely; and in the French *banlieues.* These players, contrary to popular opinion, were not the spokespersons of an actual, to some extent traditional, community from which they issued forth expressing directly the expectations of the community; on the contrary, they were the products of rootlessness and were far from a community of this type; they were the products of a *transnational neo-umma,* to use the words of Farhad Khosrokhavar, of an imaginary community which tended to be constructed in the poorer areas of the major "global" cities in the modern world rather than in traditional rural areas. There were rationales in their action which mirrored the most modern possible capitalism—Bin Laden, the leader of al Qaeda, was even said to have committed the offense of "insider dealing" by speculating on the stock exchange on the consequences of the attacks which his organization was preparing.

Actors of this type are highly flexible. Functioning in networks, they know how to connect and disconnect themselves without difficulty and, instrumental rationality being to the fore, they use the most advanced communication technologies, beginning with the Internet. Their terrorism is also "global" by definition and is not restricted to a single state in which it would be a question of taking power, or separating therefrom. Their aims are indeed global and go even further than the context of the world in which we live, to be projected into the next. Having broken with the traditional forms of community life, their Islamism, inseparable from the notion of *jihad*—the holy war—transcends national frontiers and aims—including through martyrdom and therefore through sacred death—at destroying the West which at one and the same time fascinates them and excludes and despises Islam and the Muslims.

The attacks of September 11, 2001, were not the first expression of this terrorism perpetrated by transnational actors and probably to be transcended in future, but a climactic moment, an extreme case. For thereafter, numerous attacks were made in the name of al Qaeda, or at least associated with this organization, but without presenting the same transnational purity, in other words, mixing world level dimensions with others, more classically established in the context of the state targeted. Moreover it is to these hybrid expressions, which conjugate world and supranational aspects with aspects which are internal to the states concerned that the idea of globalization of terrorism best applies. Whether it be a question of the attacks in Riyadh, Casablanca, and Istanbul in 2003, of those in Madrid (March 2004), or yet again in London (July 2005), on each occasion, and along lines which vary from one experience to another, the actors combine the two dimensions which constitute "global" terrorism. On one hand at least some of them are at one and the same time to some extent immersed in the society in which they act, and are then subjected to rationales of social exclusion and contempt and express a strong sense of not finding their place in this society, or else they express their rejection of its international policies. On the other hand they are bearers of transnational, religious rationales and if need be are connected to global networks. They are therefore simultaneously part of an imaginary community of believers with no material basis and of a real community, for example of Moroccan immigrants (in Spain) or Pakistanis (in England), or yet again of the impoverished masses living in the most deprived areas of Casablanca and Istanbul. Their action is neither solely internal and classical nor solely transnational, it is both at once. This moreover is why the answers to "global" terrorism themselves combine the two dimensions, one being military ensuring defense in relation to the outside world and the other involving policing and internal security.

But is "global" terrorism really new? In the past, terrorists could have transnational trajectories and appear to be far from having solid roots in the national society they come from. For instance, the three Japanese terrorists who killed twenty-six persons at the airport in Lod, Israel, on May 30, 1972, were acting in name of the Palestinian cause—nothing to do with Japan. And the German activists belonging to terrorist organizations that joined Palestinian extremist groups or collaborated with "sponsor states" (i.e. Iraq, Syria, Libya) during the seventies did not relate their acts to Germany. There was some transnationalism, and some networking then too. But what was at stake was international support for a national cause, and not "global" action. And networks, which many experts considered to be organized from communist countries, could exist only due to the will or tolerance of some states.

However, in some cases of "global terrorism" the transnational dimension itself is weak, even nonexistent, and terrorist action is mainly restricted to its classical dimensions. The suicide attacks by the Palestinians against targets in Israel are of this type. The practice of martyrdom is an innovation in Palestinian action and the latter only recently became Islamist. But above all, this violence proceeds directly from a specific community—the populations in the territories placed under the control of the Palestinian Authority—and the references to Islam remain subordinate to the national struggle. The transnational dimensions of the action are of little import and, while it is possible to speak of terrorism, it must be clearly understood that the latter remains classical and not global.

"Global" terrorism unfolds in a space which is therefore bounded by two poles. At one extremity, it is purely transnational—this was the case with the September 11, 2001, attacks; and at the other extremity, it is classical, at least as far as its framework of reference is concerned—this is the case with the Palestinian attacks in Israeli territory.

Is this "global" terrorism the monopoly of radical Islamism? It is true that terrorist players other than Muslim do exist today in the world and that many armed movements, be they nationalist, ethnic, or the product of another religion (Hinduism, for example), do resort thereto. But radical Islamism is the only one to combine global, metapolitical aims and a possible foothold within a sovereign state in various parts of the world. As a result, this leaves less space for violent actors other than Islamist, as was seen in spectacular fashion in Spain: the terrible attacks on March 11, 2004, in Madrid (191 persons killed) were in the first instance attributed by the government to ETA before it became clear that they were the work of North African migrants. Not only did José Maria Aznar's *Partido Popular* lose the elections which took place a few days later for having wrongly accused ETA, but the Basque separatist organization found itself in a way the victim of Islamist terrorism, forced as they also were to refute such extreme violence. Henceforth their legitimacy to resort to arms or explosives was weakened. For this reason it has been said that al Qaeda, by its intervention in Spain, could signify the beginning of the historical decline of ETA.

More generally, if we consider classical terrorism, that of the 1960s and 1970s, one may have an image of a form of fragmentation. The rationales of yesteryear were indeed political, obsessed, it was said, by taking state power or by the setting up of a new state. In the present-day world terrorist action has either become more than political, overdetermined by its dimensions of sacred world-level struggle, with no possible negotiation—radical Islamism reigns here, it is metapolitical—or else less than political, concerned in these instances with economic profit, as is the case, for example, of many of the guerrilla movements in Latin America, which become infrapolitical forces. This does not prevent nationalist, or comparable, movements from continuing to exist, still liable to resort, classically, to terrorism, but necessarily restricted and reduced to their local-level issues.

The sociology of "global" terrorism thus creates a relation between what, at first sight, may seem extremely distant: on one hand, the major transformations in the world, transnational rationales and the way in which they link up with rationales which are more restricted because they are rooted within the framework of a state; and, on the other hand, the subjectivity of the actors which borders on the most intimate, their most private personal experiences, their dreams and their despair. But the creation of this relation, which is not unlike a balancing act, is possible and necessary quite simply because the subjectivity of the actors—the way in which they mentally construct themselves, produce their personal and collective imaginary world—owes a great deal to their exposure to the most "global" modernity, to their belonging but also to their peregrinations in the universe of globalization which simultaneously fascinates and rejects them.

The Guerrilla Myth

MAX BOOT

For a student of military history, the most astonishing fact about the current international scene is that there isn't a single conflict in which two uniformed militaries are pitted against each other. The last one was a brief clash in 2008 between Russia and Georgia. In our day, the specter of conventional conflict, which has dominated the imagination of the West since the days of the Greek hoplites, has almost been lifted.

But the world is hardly at peace. Algeria fights hostage-takers at a gas plant. France fights Islamist extremists in Mali. Israel fights Hamas. The U.S. and its allies fight the Taliban in Afghanistan. Syria's Bashar al-Assad fights rebels seeking to overthrow him. Colombia fights and negotiates with the FARC. Mexico fights drug gangs. And various African countries fight the Lord's Resistance Army.

These are wars without front lines, without neatly defined starting and end points. They are messy, bloody affairs, in which attackers, typically without uniforms, engage in hit-and-run raids and often target civilians. They are, in short, guerrilla wars, and they are deadly. In Syria alone, more than 60,000 people have died since 2011, according to the United Nations. In Mexico, nearly 50,000 have died in drug violence since 2006. Hundreds of thousands more have perished in Africa's civil wars. The past decade has also seen unprecedented terrorist attacks, ranging from 9/11 to suicide bombings in Iraq. To understand today's world, you have to understand guerrillas and the terrorist movements that are their close cousins.

Unfortunately, our ignorance of guerrilla war runs deep, even as we find ourselves increasingly entangled in such conflicts. Contrary to popular lore, guerrilla warfare wasn't invented by Che Guevara or Mao Zedong, and terrorism long predates the 1972 Munich Olympics. Nor is insurgency, as some have suggested, a distinctively "Oriental" form of warfare, difficult for Westerners to grasp.

This article appears in full on CFR.org by permission of its original publisher.

Examining guerrilla warfare's long history not only brings to light many compelling, half-forgotten characters; it lays to rest numerous myths and allows us to come to grips with the most pressing national security issue of our time. What follows are lessons that we need to learn—but haven't—from the history of guerrilla war.

1. Guerrilla warfare is not new. Tribal war, pitting one guerrilla force against another, is as old as humankind. A new form of warfare, pitting guerrillas against "conventional" forces, is of only slightly more recent vintage—it arose in Mesopotamia 5,000 years ago. Calling guerrilla warfare "irregular" or "unconventional" has it backward: It is the norm of armed conflict.

Many of the world's current boundaries and forms of government were determined by battles between standing armies and insurgencies. Think of the United Kingdom, which was "united" by the success of the English in defeating centuries-old Scottish and Irish guerrilla movements. The retreat of the British Empire was partly the result of successful armed resistance, by groups ranging from the Irish Republican Army in the 1920s to the Zionists in the 1940s. Earlier still, the war waged by American colonists, some of them fighting as guerrillas, created the U.S., which reached its present borders, in turn, by waging centuries of unremitting warfare against Native American insurgents.

It is hard to think of any country in the world that has avoided the ravages of guerrilla warfare—just as it hard to think of any organized military force that hasn't spent a considerable portion of its energy fighting guerrillas.

2. Guerrilla warfare is the form of conflict universally favored by the weak, not an "Eastern" way of war. Thanks largely to the success of Chinese and Vietnamese Communists in seizing power in the 20th century, there has been a tendency to portray guerrilla tactics as the outgrowth of Sun Tzu and other Chinese philosophers who were supposedly at odds with the conventional tactics espoused by Western sages such as Carl von Clausewitz.

In reality, ancient Chinese and Indian armies were as massive and conventional in their orientation as the Roman legions. It wasn't the Chinese who had a cultural proclivity toward guerrilla warfare but rather their nomadic enemies in Inner Asia. For these tribesmen, as for others ranging from the Sioux to the Pashtuns, irregular warfare was a way of life.

But even tribal peoples such as the Turks, Arabs and Mongols, who employed guerrilla tactics in their rise to power, turned to conventional armies to safeguard their hard-won empires. Their experience suggests that few people have ever chosen guerrilla warfare voluntarily; it is the tactic of last resort for those too weak to create regular armies. Likewise, terrorism is the tactic of last resort for those too weak to create guerrilla forces.

3. Guerrilla warfare has been both underestimated and overestimated. Before 1945, the value of guerrilla campaigns was generally underestimated, leading overconfident officers such as George Armstrong Custer to disaster. Because irregulars refuse to engage in face-to-face battle, they have not gotten the respect they deserve—notwithstanding their consistent ability, ever since the barbarian assaults on Rome, to humble the world's greatest empires.

Since 1945, opinion has swung too far toward considering guerrilla movements invincible. This is largely because of the success enjoyed by a handful of rebels such as Mao Zedong, Ho Chi Minh, and Fidel Castro. But focusing on their exploits distracts from the ignominious end suffered by most insurgents, including Castro's celebrated protégé, Che Guevara, who was killed by Bolivian Rangers in 1967.

In reality, though guerrillas have often been able to fight for years and inflict great losses on their enemies, they have seldom achieved their objectives. Terrorists have been even less successful.

4. Insurgencies have been getting more successful since 1945, but they still lose most of the time. According to a database that I have compiled, out of 443 insurgencies since 1775, insurgents succeeded in 25.2% of the concluded wars while incumbents prevailed in 63.8%. The rest were draws.

This lack of historical success flies in the face of the widespread deification of guerrillas such as Guevara. Since 1945, the win rate for insurgents has indeed gone up, to 39.6%. But counter-insurgency campaigns still won 51.1% of post-1945 wars.

And those figures overstate insurgents' odds of success because many rebel groups that are still in the field, such as the Kachin separatists in Myanmar, have scant chance of success. If ongoing uprisings are judged as failures, the win rate for insurgents would go down to 23.2% in the post-1945 period, while the counter-insurgents' winning percentage would rise to 66.1%.

Like most business startups, most insurgent organizations go bust. Yet some groups such as the Provisional IRA and Palestine Liberation Organization, which fail to achieve their ultimate objectives, can still win concessions from the other side.

5. The most important recent development in guerrilla warfare has been the rise of public opinion. What accounts for the fact that guerrillas have been getting more successful since 1945? Much of the explanation can be found in the growing power of public opinion, brought about by the spread of democracy, education, communications technology, mass media and international organizations—all of which have sapped the will of states to engage in protracted counter-insurgencies, especially outside their own territory, and heightened the ability of insurgents to survive even after suffering setbacks.

The term "public opinion" first appeared in print in 1776, which is fitting, since it played a major role in persuading the British to negotiate an end to their conflict with the American colonies. Greek rebels in the 1820s benefited from public opinion in the West, where sympathizers such as Lord Byron rallied their governments to oppose Ottoman abuses. A similar strategy of relying on international support was pursued by Cubans against Spain in the 1890s and Algerians against France in the 1950s; it remains a key Palestinian strategy against Israel.

A spectacular vindication of this approach occurred during the Vietnam War, when the U.S. was defeated not because it had lost on the battlefield but because public opinion had turned against the war. The same thing almost happened in Iraq in 2007, and it may yet happen in Afghanistan.

6. Few counter-insurgency campaigns have ever succeeded by inflicting mass terror—at least in foreign lands. When faced with elusive foes, armies often have resorted to torturing suspects for information, as the U.S. did after 9/11, and inflicting bloody reprisals on civilians, as Mr. Assad's forces are now doing in Syria. Such strategies have worked on occasion (usually when rebels were cut off from outside support), but just as often they have failed.

The armies of the French Revolution provide an example of successful brutality at home: They killed indiscriminately to suppress the revolt in the Vendée region in the 1790s. As one republican general wrote, "I have not a single prisoner to reproach myself with. I exterminated them all." But the French could not match this feat in Haiti, where they used equally brutal measures but could not put down a slave revolt led by the "Black Spartacus," Toussaint L'Ouverture.

Even in the ancient world, when there were no human-rights activists or cable news channels, empires found that pacifying restive populations usually involved carrots as well as sticks. There were considerable benefits to participating in the Pax Romana, which won over subject populations by offering "bread and circuses," roads, aqueducts and (most important) security from roving guerrillas and bandits.

7. "Winning hearts and minds" is often successful as an anti-guerrilla strategy, but it isn't as touchy-feely as commonly supposed. The fact that the U.S. and other liberal democratic states cannot be as brutal as dictatorial regimes—or, more precisely, choose not to be—doesn't mean they cannot succeed in putting down insurgencies. They simply have to do it in a more humane style. In Iraq in 2007–08, Gen. David Petraeus showed how successful a "population-centric" strategy could be, at least in narrow security terms, by sending troops to live in urban areas and by wooing Sunni tribes.

The best-known term for this strategy is "winning hearts and minds"—a phrase popularized by the British Gen. Gerald Templer, who saved Malaya from a communist insurgency in the 1950s. But the term is misleading, since it suggests that a counter-insurgency campaign is trying to win a popularity contest. In reality, the populace will embrace the government only if it is less dangerous to do so than to support the insurgency. That is why successful population-centric policies aim to control the people with a 24/7 deployment of security forces, not to win their love and gratitude by handing out soccer balls, medical supplies and other goodies.

8. Most insurgencies are long-lasting; attempts to win a quick victory backfire. The average insurgency since 1775 has lasted seven years. The figure is even longer for post-1945 insurgencies—nearly 10 years. The length of low-intensity conflicts can be a source of frustration for both sides, but attempts to short-circuit the process usually backfire. The U.S. tried to do just that in the early years of the Vietnam and Iraq wars by using its conventional might to hunt down insurgents in a push for what John Paul Vann, a legendary adviser in Vietnam, decried as "fast, superficial results." It was only when the U.S. gave up hopes of a quick victory that it started to get results.

A particularly seductive version of the "quick win" strategy is to try to eliminate the insurgency's leadership, as the U.S. and Israel regularly try to do with airstrikes against groups such as al Qaeda and Hamas. Such strategies sometimes work. The Romans, for example, stamped out a revolt in Spain by inducing some of the rebels to kill their leader, Viriathus, in 139 B.C.

But there are just as many cases where leaders were eliminated but the movement went on stronger than ever—as Hezbollah did after the loss of its secretary-general in an Israeli airstrike in 1992. Targeting leadership is most effective when integrated into a broader counter- insurgency effort designed to separate the insurgents from the population. If conducted in isolation, such raids are about as effective as mowing the lawn; the organization can usually regenerate itself.

9. Technology has been relatively unimportant in guerrilla war—but that may be changing. All guerrilla and terrorist tactics, from airplane hijacking and suicide bombing to hostage-taking and roadside ambushes, are designed to negate the firepower advantage of conventional forces. In this type of war, technology counts for less than in conventional conflict. Even the possession of nuclear bombs hasn't prevented the Soviet Union and the U.S. from suffering ignominious defeat at guerrilla hands. To the extent that technology has mattered in low-intensity conflicts, it has often been the non-shooting kind. As T.E. Lawrence ("Lawrence of Arabia") said, "The printing press is the greatest weapon in the armory of the modern commander." A rebel today might substitute "the Internet" for "the printing press," but the essential insight remains.

The role of destructive technology will grow in the future, however, if insurgents get their hands on chemical, biological or nuclear weapons. A terrorist cell the size of a platoon might then have more killing capacity than the entire army of a nonnuclear state like Brazil or Egypt. Cyberweapons also have the potential to wreak havoc.

That is a sobering thought on which to end. It suggests that in the future, guerrilla warfare and terrorism could pose even greater problems for the world's leading powers than they have in the past. And those problems have been substantial, varied and long-lasting.

The Meaning of the Cyber Revolution: Perils to Theory and Statecraft

LUCAS KELLO

Security policy in the information age faces formidable challenges. Chief among these is to evaluate correctly the impact of cyberweapons on strategy: Does the new technology require a revolution in how scholars and policymakers think about force and conflict? Practitioners confront a predicament in addressing this question: the cyber revolution gives rise to novel threats and opportunities requiring immediate policy responses; yet understanding its nature and its consequences for

International Security, Vol. 38, No. 2 Fall pg. 7–40

security is a slow learning process. Interpretation of cyber phenomena involves analysis of a new body of experience that existing theories may be unable to clarify. It presupposes, moreover, a technical understanding of a transforming technology, whose implications require time to master because of its scientific complexity.

The inevitable result has been a delay in the strategic adaptation to cyber realities. If decisionmakers are right—and their views are not equivocal—the contemporary world confronts an enormous cyber threat. The U.S. intelligence community rates this threat higher than global terrorism and warns of the potential for a calamitous cyberattack. Yet as the chief of U.S. Cyber Command, Gen. Keith Alexander, has observed, there is no consensus "on how to characterize the strategic instability" of cyber interactions "or on what to do about it." The range of conceivable cyber conflict is poorly understood by scholars and decisionmakers, and it is unclear how conventional security mechanisms, such as deterrence and collective defense, apply to this phenomenon. In addition, the principles of cyber offense and cyber defense remain rudimentary. The growth of cyber arsenals, in short, is outpacing the design of doctrines to limit their risks.

Against this backdrop, there is an evident need for scholars of international relations and security to contribute to the theoretical evaluation of the cyber revolution. Removed from the pressures of having to defeat the cyber threat, yet possessing concepts necessary to analyze it, academics are in a privileged position to resolve its strategic problems. Yet there has been little systematic theoretical or empirical analysis of the cyber issue from the perspective of international security. This article provides such an analysis: it makes a case and establishes guidelines for the scholarly study of cyber conflict.

The article makes three main arguments. First, integrating cyber realities into the international security studies agenda is necessary both for developing effective policies and for enhancing the field's intellectual progress. Second, the scientific intricacies of cyber technology and methodological issues do not prohibit scholarly investigation; a nascent realm of cyber studies has already begun to emerge. Third, because cyberweapons are not overtly violent, their use is unlikely to fit the traditional criterion of interstate war; rather, the new capability is expanding the range of possible harm and outcomes between the concepts of war and peace—with important consequences for national and international security. Although the cyber revolution has not fundamentally altered the nature of war, it nevertheless has consequences for important issues in the field of security studies, including nonmilitary foreign threats and the ability of nontraditional players to inflict economic and social harm. Three factors underscore the cyber danger for international security: the potency of cyberweapons, complications relating to cyber defense, and problems of strategic instability.

This study has two important caveats: first, its scope is limited because many aspects of national and international security lie beyond the reach of cyberspace though increasingly less so; second, its conclusions are provisional because the observed phenomena are still incipient and could evolve in ways difficult to predict. Thus, although the nature of the cyber threat is open to debate, the danger cannot be ignored. If scholars accept the existence of a cyber peril, then they must begin to develop a theoretical framework for understanding both the threat and its consequences for security. Conversely, if the danger appears inflated or has been misinterpreted, then they are obliged to articulate theoretical and empirical challenges to the conventional policy wisdom.

WHY STUDY THE CYBER ISSUE?

It is superfluous to state that the field of international security studies is skeptical of the existence of a cyber danger: it has barely acknowledged the issue, as reflected in the scant relevant literature. Thus the prevailing skepticism seems more visceral.

Common Technical Concepts

The field of international security studies requires commonly accepted technical concepts that lay out the various dimensions of the cyber issue. Such a schematization can perform three important functions. The first is to frame the complex scientific properties of the cyber issue in a manageable way. The second is to identify the features of the technology and its related phenomena that are most relevant to the field while eliminating activity that does not rise to the level of national or international security. The third function of the framework is to orient theory development, allowing scholars to organize and codify data collected after a cyber event becomes known, search for causal chains linking determining factors to the event, and establish conceptual benchmarks for evaluating competing explanations of it. The schematization below fills the conceptual void. It contains the following six elements: cyberspace, cyber-security, malware, cyber crime, cyberattack, and cyber exploitation.

Cyberspace

Cyberspace is the most elemental concept in the cyber field: it establishes the technical markers within which the virtual weapon can operate. One common definition construes cyberspace as all computer systems and networks in existence, including air-gapped systems. Another excludes isolated nodes. For the purposes of this study, the first definition is appropriate. Total isolation of computer systems is rarely feasible today. The ubiquity of computing devices, ranging from removable drives to personal laptops—each a potential carrier of malware—has multiplied the access vectors through which an attacker can bridge an air gap. Moreover, the computer systems likeliest to be shielded by air (e.g., nuclear facilities) are ordinarily of high significance to national security and therefore should not be excluded from the plane of action. Cyberspace can thus be conceived as comprising three partially overlapping terrains: (1) the internet, encompassing all interconnected computers, including (2) the world wide web, consisting only of nodes accessible via a URL interface; and (3) a cyber "archipelago" comprising all other computer systems that exist in theoretical seclusion (i.e., not connected to the internet or the web). This conceptualization reflects an important consideration in security planning: not all threats propagated through the web can transmit via the internet, and those that are transmissible cannot use the internet to breach the cyber archipelago. On these terms, there are two basic kinds of targets: (1) remote-access and (2) closed-access. Each is susceptible to different methods of approach in a cyberattack.

Cybersecurity

Cybersecurity consists of measures to protect the operations of a computer system or the integrity of its data from hostile action. Cybersecurity can also be conceived of as a state of affairs: the absence of unauthorized intrusion into computer systems and their proper functioning. Crucially, the concept encompasses the safety and survivability of functions operating beyond cyberspace but still reliant on a computer host, to which they are linked at the logical or information layer. Insofar as measures of security are the purview of the military or impinge on military capabilities, they constitute cyber defense. An alternative conception of cybersecurity, often labeled "information security," involves government protection of channels of information flow in domestic society (e.g., internet censorship). Such differences of interpretation of the meaning of cybersecurity have hindered efforts to establish international regimes of rules and norms of cyber conduct.

Malware

Malware involves software designed to interfere with computer functionality or to degrade the integrity of data. It encompasses the gamut of mischievous computer code—viruses, worms, Trojans, spyware, adware, and so on. Malware can be designed to open an avenue of access to an adversary's computer system, or to attack it, or both. Thus, the use of malware is an instrument of cyber hostility and not, as is sometimes implied, a separate category of action. Almost all cyber hostilities involve the use of malware.

Cyber Crime

Cyber crime entails the use of a computer for an illicit purpose under the existing penal code of a nation. It includes credit card fraud and transmission of prohibited data such as child pornography. Because domestic criminal law is unenforceable against states, cyber crime prevention focuses on private agents prosecutable in national jurisdictions. For this reason, it is the least contentious aspect of the cyber issue at the intergovernmental level. It is also the only dimension expressly regulated by treaty (the 2008 Council of Europe Convention on Cyber Crime). In the usage proposed here, cyber crime lacks political or strategic intent; therefore, it rarely has an impact on national or international security.

Cyberattack

Cyberattack refers to the use of code to interfere with the functionality of a computer system for a political or strategic purpose. The first significant cyberattack reportedly occurred in 1982, when a so-called logic bomb caused a Soviet oil pipeline to explode. Cyberattacks are characterized by the attackers' desire and capability to disrupt computer operations or to destroy physical assets via cyberspace; thus, if the defender unnecessarily ceases computer operations as a consequence of misinformation or misinterpretation, the incident does not constitute cyberattack. Neither the goal nor the effects of a cyberattack need be contained in cyberspace. That is, the final object may be to incapacitate the computer system itself or to degrade social, economic, or government functions dependent on its proper operation. Accordingly, two main types of cyberattack "effects" can be identified: (1) direct effects, which unfold within the logical environment of the target machine complex (e.g., destruction of nuclear centrifuges by manipulating their industrial controller); and (2) indirect effects, which hinder activity or functions that lie beyond the logical habitat of the compromised computer system but which rely on that system (e.g., interruption of the chemical process of uranium isotope separation necessary for the material's weaponization).

This description of the effects of a cyberattack departs from common understanding, which situates the effects boundary at the physical frontier of logically tied machines. Take, for example, Olympic Games. The custom-built Stuxnet worm was designed to attack the logical environment of the Siemens S7-315 PLC at the Natanz nuclear facility in Iran. The attack sequence injected malicious code into the PLC to alter the behavior of IR-1 centrifuge cascades controlled by it. Commentators ordinarily describe the effects on the PLC as direct and those on centrifuges as indirect, because the latter effects were "transmitted" via the PLC. This standard definition is nonsensical from the perspective of strategic analysis because it unnecessarily discriminates between effects exerted on an industrial controller and those on its constituent machines. In contrast, the usage proposed above assumes a more general perspective: it separates effects occurring within a unitary logical environment such as the Natanz facility from those affecting, say, Iran's ability to purify uranium—a far more useful distinction for strategic analysis. Moreover, because malware manipulates the logical unison of a computer system to execute a payload, treating effects within that system as direct and those beyond it as indirect makes more sense. In short, the interesting segmentation of cyber-attack effects lies at the logical, not the physical, boundary of cyberspace.

If the effects of a cyberattack produce significant physical destruction or loss of life, the action can be labeled "cyberwar," a term that should be used sparingly given that the vast majority of cyberattacks do not meet this criterion. If the attack is perpetrated by a private actor for political or ideological purposes, it is an example of "hacktivism." Moreover, cyberattacks can be customized or generalized. In a customized attack, the payload is designed to manipulate only machines within a specific logical habitat (e.g., Olympic Games). In a generalized attack, no machine reachable via the internet is in principle spared (e.g., the DDoS attacks that paralyzed computer systems in Estonia in 2007).

Cyber Exploitation

Cyber exploitation refers to the penetration of an adversary's computer system for the purpose of exfiltrating (but not defiling) data. One of the first major acts of cyber exploitation occurred in 1986 with a foreign breach of military and government computers in the United States. Another notable incident was the seizure by Chinese agents of several terabytes of secret U.S. government data in 2003. Essentially an intelligence-gathering activity, cyber exploitation relies on stealth and undetectability; thus disruption of the host system, which can lead to discovery and closure of access, defeats the purpose of exploitation. One objective of exploitation may be to seize a nation's military or industrial secrets, an activity known as "cyber espionage." The technique can also be employed to acquire knowledge of an adversary's computer systems to plan future cyber-attacks, in which case exploitation is an element of a multistage cyberattack.

The protection of military, industrial, and commercial secrets from cyber exploitation is a key preoccupation of national security policy. Nevertheless, cyberattack poses potentially greater dangers to international security, because the threshold of proven cyberattack effects has been rising steadily in recent years—it now includes physical destruction. In addition, the new weapons pose enormous defense challenges while disturbing interstate strategic stability. Whether security scholars grasp these implications of the cyber danger for international security depends on their ability to break free from their preconceptions as to what constitutes a serious threat.

THE SHAPE OF THE CYBER DANGER

Some skeptics argue that the cyber peril is overblown, contending that cyber-weapons have no intrinsic capacity for violence and do not alter the nature or means of war. This strategy to puncture the perceived threat inflation works by conceptual fiat: because the method of harm lacks similarities with interstate armed conflict, by definition there can be no such thing as cyber "war."

In a sense, the skeptics are correct. The cyber revolution—as far as we can tell—has not fundamentally changed warfighting. At the same time, this skepticism, grounded in traditional thinking about war and peace, fails to acknowledge the broader agenda of international security studies, which encompasses issues such as protection against nonmilitary foreign threats and the ability of nonstate actors to inflict economic and social harm. The Clausewitzian philosophical framework misses the essence of the cyber danger and conceals its true significance: the virtual weapon is expanding the range of possible harm and outcomes between the concepts of war and peace, with important consequences for national and international security. Of course, the impact of cyber technology on military affairs is an important concern and, for some thinkers, will be a starting point of theory—but it is not a point of terminus. An appraisal of the cyber danger in its fuller dimensions is therefore needed. Three main factors underscore this danger: (1) the potency of cyberweapons, (2) complications relating to defense, and (3) the potential to disturb international order.

The Potency of Cyberweapons

A unique feature of a cyberattack is its virtual method. To reach its target, a weapon traditionally had to traverse a geographic medium—land, sea, air, or outer space. Upon arrival, it inflicted direct material harm. The cyber revolution has dramatically altered this situation. Malware can travel the information surface and obeys the protocols of TCP/IP, not the laws of geography. It is little constrained by space and obliterates traditional distinctions between local and distant conflict. The payload, too, is an intangible: it operates through complex coding, which means that the weapon's "charge" is not the most proximate cause of damage. Instead, the infliction of harm requires a remote object—such as an industrial controller—that can be manipulated. The use of weaponized code, nevertheless, can have potent effects on the political and social world.

Until recently, the ability of cyber artifacts to damage physical facilities remained entirely in the realm of theoretical speculation. Olympic Games changed that. The direct effects of this operation, as revealed in a report by the International Atomic Energy Agency, included the decommissioning of approximately 1,000 centrifuges at Iran's Natanz facility during a three-month period. The indirect effects of the attack are subject to dispute, but they were almost certainly greater than this figure suggests. Indeed, the most powerful effect may have been psychological. Discord and mistrust within Iran's nuclear establishment, arising from paranoia that a rogue scientist was among its ranks, and fears of intrusion elsewhere in the nation's cyber archipelago, may have slowed Iran's ability to acquire the bomb by as many as two years—significantly longer than the time required to replace the impaired centrifuges.

The use of cyberweapons, however, need not result in physical destruction to pose a serious danger to society. Even if a cyberattack lacks intrinsic violence because the execution of code is a remote as opposed to proximate cause of injury, the effects can still cause serious economic and social harm. "It may not be a bomb coming down our middle chimney of our house," Jonathan Zittrain explained, "but it could be something that greatly affects our way of life." Or as Chairman of the Joint Chiefs of Staff Gen. Martin Dempsey stated, "The uncomfortable reality of our world is that bits and bytes can be as threatening as bullets and bombs." The Estonian and Georgian cyberattacks, according to NATO's Supreme Allied Commander Europe, Adm. James Stavridis, provide a "glimpse of this future [of conflict]" by demonstrating the potent indirect effects of nonviolent and generalized cyberweapons. The DDoS attacks on Estonia in 2007 froze the country's government and financial activities for approximately three weeks. Because there was no physical wreckage or loss of life, the label of cyberwar does not apply. At the same time, the incident was far more than just a "large popular demonstration," as Thomas Rid portrays it; rather, the cyberattack in Estonia represents a wholly new type of social and economic disturbance. Three factors explain why traditional analogies of political disturbance do not apply: (1) the perpetrators resided mostly outside the affected territory; (2) the attack procedure crossed more than 100 national jurisdictions via the internet with awesome speed; and (3) identifying and punishing the perpetrators proved very difficult because of Moscow's refusal to provide forensic assistance to Estonian investigators, who possessed log files of affected machines revealing that many of the culprits had operated out of Russia.

The cyberattacks on Georgia further demonstrate the potency of nondiscriminating cyberweapons. The attacks, which were carried out by nonstate agents including Russian criminal syndicates, occurred against the backdrop of Russia's ground incursion into Georgia in the summer of 2008. A detailed study of the case concludes that the disruption of Georgia's computer systems tactically benefited the Russians in two important ways. First, it crippled the Georgian government's communications infrastructures, hindering Tbilisi's ability to coordinate domestic civil defenses. Second, it paralyzed the operations of the National Bank of Georgia, which impeded procurement of essential war material from private industry. Although these same tactical effects could have been achieved using conventional arms, it is important to note that cyber technology offered a feasible substitute that did not directly implicate Russia's military services, was cheap and readily available to nonstate agents, and proved impervious to conventional defenses.

Traditional notions of warfare confront five difficulties in conceptualizing cyberattacks, as the above cases illustrate. First, cyberattacks lack a proximate cause of injury and may not even be violent. Second, the conception of war as the use of armed force sets a high threshold in terms of scope, duration, and intensity that cyber actions may not meet. Third, the perpetrators of a cyberattack can be nonstate parties who are not typically considered subjects of international law and thus are not subject to its penalties. Fourth, an offensive cyber operation by nontraditional players, such as that conducted against Estonia, need not involve the strategic purposes of states or their militaries. Fifth, at least in the case of a generalized cyberattack, the important distinction between military and civilian targets dissolves owing to the broad diffusion of computer systems in society and their interdependencies. Two other possible analogies to cyberattacks, "sanctions" and "sabotage," are also misleading. Sanctions are an exercise in negative power: they operate through the denial of gain rather than the direct infliction of loss. Yet offensive cyberpower clearly exerts positive effects. It initiates harmful activity that otherwise would not occur and causes direct injury to the victim. The label of sabotage, which has been applied to Stuxnet, is an empty concept: there is no precise definition of the term in this or other domains of conflict. Use of the term adds nothing to the resolution of the conceptual problems of cyber phenomena.

The principle of "equivalence" that underpins U.S. and NATO cyber defense policy represents an attempt to resolve the conceptual muddles attached to the cyber issue. It maintains that the direct and indirect effects of cyberattack, not its method, should determine the manner and severity of retaliation—including conventional force—but without identifying specific thresholds of response. The deliberate declaratory vagueness of the principle is an attempt to adapt the doctrine of "calculated ambiguity" to the peculiar conditions of the cyber domain. Although it is tempting to see in this a crude treatment of cyberattacks a form of "war," the equivalence principle reflects a willingness to reinterpret and transcend, on a case-by-case basis, the limitations that traditional concepts of violence place on the retaliator. It leaves open the possibility of a forcible response even if the initial cyberattack is not construed as an act of war. As one U.S. soldier put it rather cavalierly, "If you shut down our power grid, maybe we will put a missile down one of your smokestacks." The implications for international security are potentially serious: according to this principle, a cyber event can occur that does not meet the traditional definition of war but that nevertheless elicits a reprisal of commensurate severity.

In the future, war by malware may occur if a cyberattack results in a similar number of deaths or level of physical destruction as a major kinetic strike. To make sense of such an eventuality, traditional concepts of interstate warfighting are needed. The capacity of cyber arsenals to augment military force is not, however, their main contribution. Rather, the new weapons expand the available methods of harm that do not fit established conceptions of war but that may be no less harmful to national security.

The ability of a cyberattack to inflict economic and other damage without resort to traditional violence affords this virtual weapon a special utility: it expands the choice of actions and outcomes available to the strategic offense. Again, Olympic Games underscores the point. The operation was part of a broader campaign to deprive Iran of the ability to produce weapons-grade uranium. The United States and Israel agreed on this objective but differed on how to achieve it, with Israel eventually favoring airstrikes on Iranian nuclear plants. Officials in Washington agonized over the potential consequences of such a move, fearing it could ignite a regional conflagration and only intensify Tehran's resolve to obtain the bomb. The Stuxnet worm offered the two countries at least a temporary solution to their differences: it promised to deliver some of the tactical results of a military strike while avoiding certain retaliation. Thus, the fact that the direct effects of Stuxnet were not comparable to the scale of destruction possible in an air attack was the new weapon's principal appeal. The Stuxnet worm alone could never prevent an Iranian bomb, but it could at least delay enrichment while averting a regional war.

Tehran's response to Olympic Games, as far as is known, has been muted. This demonstrates that the phenomenon of cyberattack merits strategic analysis as much for the consequences it avoids as for those it produces. Indeed, it is tempting to conclude that cyberweapons promote international security—after all, their use may avert traditional forms of war. Although this argument may have some merit in specific cases, it is too simplistic as a general observation; gains to the offense produce enormous losses in defense as well as conditions for strategic instability.

Complications of Cyber Defense

Security planners repeatedly warn that, in the cyber domain, the offense holds the advantage. Some skeptics seek to dispel this notion by emphasizing the high costs of staging a destructive cyberattack. They cite Olympic Games to make their point: the operation required years of meticulous planning, involved a preliminary intrusion into the Natanz PLC to gain knowledge of the target, manipulated no less than six vulnerabilities in the PLC (each an expensive technical feat), and required a skilled operative in situ or close by to deliver the worm across the air gap. Moreover, once the worm's coding secrets were revealed, systems operators were able to patch the programming defects that the worm exploited, rendering knowledge of these weaknesses useless to aspiring proliferants. For these reasons, skeptics assert, the defense, not the offense, has the advantage. This conclusion is only half complete: it ignores or downplays the other half of the strategic picture—the enormous costs of defense against a cyberattack. Following is a description of five such costs.

Offense Unpredictability and Undetectability

The use of code to achieve destructive direct effects requires the manipulation of vulnerabilities in the target's computer system. By definition, the defender is unaware of such "zero-day" weaknesses. The universe of unknown and manipulable weaknesses renders a cyberattack difficult to predict, complicating the design of measures to repulse it. Incomplete knowledge of weaknesses also hinders remediation of intrusion post facto, because this requires understanding the zero-day exploits in question. Furthermore, the abundance of possible access vectors that an attacker can utilize complicates the interception of malware "in transit." Olympic Games demonstrates these points. Stealth was a genial feature of this multistage operation. The method of access, which may have involved the use of infected removable drives, was unanticipated. For three years, the Stuxnet worm and its antecedents (which acted as "beacons" for the offense) resided in the logical environment of the target PLC without the plant operators noticing their presence. Remarkably, the worm was able to mask its damaging effects from the controllers even after the attack sequence had begun. Only a few months later did the Iranians determine, with outside assistance, the source of the centrifuge malfunction.

Defense Denial

The possibility that attack code will reside undiscovered in a defender's computer system is perhaps the most worrisome feature of the cyber strategic landscape. Residency within a logical habitat affords the invader means to deprive the defense of the ability to manage its own protection in at least two ways. One is peer-to-peer monitoring, which allows an attacker to adjust the attack sequence remotely and in real time; another is the use of an intelligent malware agent with self-adaptive capacities that enable it to learn and override defensive acts. The ability of malware to generate multiple versions of itself means that the threat variants during a cyberattack are theoretically limitless. Nevertheless, permanent breach of a computer system need not entail permanent insecurity if the defensive terrain can be organized in concentric zones of access so that the most prized nodes are quarantined from less secure compartments. This approach, however, runs counter to the very purpose of information technologies, namely, to ease transmission of data between machines. Therein lies the root dilemma of cybersecurity: an impregnable computer system is inaccessible to legitimate users while an accessible machine is inherently manipulable by pernicious code.

Complex Defense Surface

Computer systems are becoming more intricate at all stages of design and use. As software and hardware complexity rises, so do the costs of customizing weaponized code. This increases the work factor of the attacker, who requires greater resources of manpower and intelligence to tailor the payload. At the same time, the costs to the defender, who has more node interdependencies to map and greater vulnerabilities to patch, also increase. The result is a fundamental offense-defense imbalance. Whereas the attacker need understand only the procedures of entry and attack it decides to employ, the defender must continuously protect the entire network surface against the vast universe of conceivable attacks; the growing tendency to join critical computer systems to the internet is multiplying the available points of entry for use in a customized cyberattack. Moreover, society's increasing reliance on interconnected computer systems to support basic economic and social functions is increasing the opportunities to cause harm through a generalized cyberattack. The expanding network surface provides conditions for a shock offensive or, as John Mearsheimer puts it, "the ability to choose the main point"—indeed multiple points simultaneously—"of attack for the initial battles, to move forces there surreptitiously, and to surprise the defender."

Defense Fragmentation

The majority of critical computer infrastructures are owned and operated by private industry. Thus, the challenge of cyber security is essentially one of civil defense: how to equip the private sector to protect its computer systems in the absence of government direction. This ordinarily involves passive measures, such as resiliency and redundancy (the equivalents of underground shelters and target dispersal in nuclear defense), which thicken the defensive glacis and can absorb damage from offensive hits. Yet a passive approach will pay only limited defensive returns if it is unable to implement the highest level of protection across the entire network surface. A proactive strategy, in contrast, seeks to neutralize threats before they can be carried out—for instance, by dismantling an attacker's command and control. Proactive defenses, however, are difficult to implement, not least because the authority to execute offense-as-defense rarely belongs to the operators of systems subject to attack; instead, it resides with the government and internet service providers, which may not even be aware of an attack. Such fragmentation of defense responsibilities is a limiting factor when formulating a coherent response to a cyberattack.

Supply Chain Risks

Computer systems increasingly rely on off-the-shelf and offshore manufacturers for components, introducing vulnerabilities into the supply chain. Foreign agents or private contractors could preload software and hardware components with malware, whether for attack or exploitative purposes. In 2009 Britain's Joint Intelligence Committee warned that Chinese-stocked components of British Telecom's phone network could be preloaded with malware or zero-day weaknesses, giving Beijing the ability to interrupt the country's power and food supplies. A "sleeper" payload of this kind could be remotely executed to achieve a preferred outcome in a future diplomatic or military crisis. In 2012 the U.S. House of Representatives Intelligence Committee warned that machine parts supplied by Huawei, a Chinese company founded by a former officer of the People's Liberation Army, could be used to exfiltrate data from government computers. Protection against such supply chain risks requires government- and industrywide coordination, yet such efforts have barely commenced.

None of the above observations is axiomatic: we are only at the early stages of the cyber phenomenon. In combination, however, they underscore the immense disadvantages of defense against cyberattack. Nothing in the available historical record suggests that defensive costs are low or diminishing—certainly not Olympic Games, a case cherished by skeptics who challenge the common wisdom of offense dominance. The enormity of the defender's challenge is convincingly illustrated by the successful penetration of computer systems at Google and RSA, two companies that represent the quintessence of technological ability in the current information age.

Disturbances to Strategic Stability and International Order

A third manifestation of the cyber danger concerns the potential for global disorder. As Chairman of the Joint Chiefs of Staff Adm. Michael Mullen once remarked, "We're going to have a catastrophic [cyber] event. Some of these tools already being built"—not least by the Pentagon—"are going to leak or be sold or be given up to a group that wants to change the world order, and we're incredibly vulnerable." Admiral Stavridis voiced a similar concern. "In the world of cyber, we are at the beach at Kitty Hawk," he observed, referring to the advent of aviation in 1903. "We are just at the beginning," he went on. "We don't have 100 years [of experience] in cyber [conflict]. . . . We have to take steps today to bring order to [this] chaotic world." The argument of this section—that cyber technology is exerting a limited but observable influence on regularized patterns of interstate rivalry—elaborates on such apprehensions and draws important observations for theory.

Concerns over global chaos lead—inevitably—to a theme familiar to the theoretician: the nature and requirements of order under conditions of international anarchy—most important, the stability of strategic interactions among states. Everyone knows that international politics transpires in the absence of a constraining authority, which produces incessant rivalry and occasional violence among actors competing for security. The interesting feature of anarchy, however, is not the recurrence of conflict—that is obvious—but its regularity. Although conceptions of national interest differ, even quarrelling states recognize the need to preserve order in their security relationships. This recognition underpins states' acceptance of common elementary goals (e.g., survival) as well as rules and principles of conduct; it helps to sustain the constancy of anarchic interactions and makes the permanent "state of war" tolerable because its contests for security are in the main regularized.

The revolutionary impact of technological change upsets this basic political framework of international society, whether because the transforming technology empowers unrecognized players with subversive motives and aims or because it deprives states of clear "if-then" assumptions necessary to conduct a restrained rivalry. The first factor, the concern voiced by Admiral Mullen above, contributes to fundamental instability in security relationships: a condition where the appearance of nontraditional or dissatisfied players undermines strategic stability. The second factor, alluded to by Admiral Stavridis, can produce instrumental instability, whereby accidents and misinterpretation of the new technology destabilize the dealings even of rational state adversaries. The advent of the atom bomb, for instance, proved transformative only in the second sense: it elevated the horrors of war and disturbed the interstate strategic equation without altering the basic Hobbesian framework that defines how nuclear states compete for survival. Ongoing efforts to deprive terrorists and rogue states of the bomb, in contrast, are motivated by a desire to avert a nuclear revolution of the first order. In short, more important than the nature of a new weapon are the nature of its possessor and the purposes that instigate its use.

The cyber domain is a perfect breeding ground for political disorder and strategic instability. Six factors contribute to instrumental instability: offense dominance, attribution difficulties, technological volatility, poor strategic depth, and escalatory ambiguity. Another—the "large-N" problem—carries with it fundamental instability as well.

Offense Dominance

For the reasons enumerated in the preceding section, cyberspace is an offense-superior domain. This poses instrumentalist obstacles to the preservation of strategic stability among state rivals. Most notably, it exacerbates the security dilemma in three ways. First, the recognition of offense superiority has instigated an arms race as states seek to avert strategic upsets in the new strategic arena. Cyber arms verification, the chief prerequisite of successful arms control, confronts enormous challenges—not least the intangibility of cyberweapons, which complicates their detection. At present, no international limitations exist on the production of offensive cyber artifacts, and no such regulatory framework has yet been foreseen. Second, the perceived advantages of offensive use elevate the chances that those in possession of the new capability will actually employ it. Adversaries of the United States will have taken note of the tactical and strategic returns paid by Olympic Games; they may consider similar policy adventures in the future. Third, attempts to redress the defensive gap with "active defenses," a class of proactive measures that involves preemption or prevention of cyberattack by infiltrating or disrupting an opponent's computer systems, obscures the offense-defense boundary in weapons systems. Consequently, defensive actions may be misconstrued as overt attacks and produce pressures for an accidental exchange of blows.

Attribution Difficulties

Authentication of the source of a cyberattack is ordinarily difficult. Five characteristics of cyber conflict contribute to this problem. First, the ease of proliferation of cyberweapons means that, except in case of the most sophisticated offensive actions, the number of possible assailants is large. Second, proving the identity or location of any one of these assailants can be a huge challenge, because cyberspace affords an attacker an inordinate degree of anonymity. Third, where attribution is possible, it may not be of the right kind to organize a punitive response. Knowing the IP address of an attacking machine—the most basic form of technical attribution—does not necessarily reveal the identity of its human handler and, even if it does, this does not mean that the identity and motives of the sponsoring party will be divulged. Fourth, because malware crosses multiple jurisdictions with ease, obtaining forensic evidence in the aftermath of an attack will be difficult without effective international cooperation. Fifth, even if all of these complications are resolved, it is still possible that attribution will not be prompt enough for timely retaliation. By the time their identity is known, the perpetrators may have relocated beyond the ability of the victim to respond. The most important strategic consequence of the attribution problem is that it weakens deterrence by reducing an assailant's expectation of unacceptable penalties. Moreover, because reprisal to a cyberattack in the absence of convincing attribution incurs legitimacy costs for the retaliator, acceptable options following a failure to deter may be limited.

Technological Volatility

The technology itself is a third destabilizing factor: cyberweapons are so novel and the vulnerabilities they seek to manipulate so inscrutable as to impede interpretation of probable effects of their use. Put simply, it is difficult to know how pernicious code will behave. The very short life cycle of advanced malware strains (many of which can be updated almost instantly upon release) contributes to this problem. Another difficulty concerns collateral damage. A poorly customized cyber artifact can cause far-reaching effects beyond the intended target if it infects a large number of third-party machines. The customization of malware only partly resolves the problem of unintentional civilian harm. Although the scope of possible direct effects may be reduced, the indirect consequences can still be enormous if the affected computer systems support essential social and economic activities. These indirect effects may be difficult to model or predict. A single brief interruption of stock-trading platforms, for instance, could produce little impact, or it could exert psychological effects that undermine public confidence in the entire financial system. Another related difficulty is the potential for "blowback": the possibility that the negative effects of a cyberattack will be felt by the attacker, whether through the self-propagative tendencies of malware (causing direct effects on home computer systems) or through cascading economic damage (indirect effects on the home society).

Poor Strategic Depth

A fourth destabilizing factor is the short time a defender has between the detection and impact of a cyberattack. The speed of cyberweapons eliminates temporal limitations to the infliction of harm. The new capability pushes the upper speed of weapons systems from Mach 20 (the speed of the fastest intercontinental ballistic missiles) to the velocity of electrons. Consequently, the interaction domain of cyber conflict unfolds in milliseconds—an infinitesimally narrow response time for which existing crisis management procedures, which move at the speed of bureaucracy, may not be adequate. Traditional precedents that regulate the role of government agencies in the conduct of national defense can be difficult to interpret in a cyber emergency. And even where the necessary tactical action is known, the ability of operational and command structures to implement it may not exist. To illustrate, the U.S. National Security Agency has authority to retaliate against foreign-based cyberattacks, but it may lack access to forensic data necessary to tailor a timely response if such information resides in private computer systems or in foreign jurisdictions. The implementation of automated "tactical fires" can go far toward restoring strategic depth, but by removing the human agent from the response procedure, it introduces unknown risks of inappropriate reaction.

Escalatory Ambiguity

Traditionally, an international crisis could be averted through confidence-building measures such as established signaling procedures and diplomatic "hotlines." Failing that, common rules and norms could still provide a minimum measure of expectations and moderating behavior. These safety valves disappear when dealing with a cyberattack. Signaling becomes murky; channels of communication break down or vanish; shared norms are rudimentary or unenforceable; and the identity, motives, or location of an attacker may not be known. Moreover, the tactical and strategic ambiguities of the related technology impede attempts to design escalatory models for the full spectrum of conceivable cyber conflict. The absence of clear "conversion tables" to orient interpretation of the equivalence principle could prompt an excessive response from a victim of an attack; lack of agreed standards of proportionality may produce further unreasonable counterresponses; and all the while, the lack of confidence-building measures could hinder attempts to de-escalate or terminate the crisis. What may begin as a low-intensity cyber exchange could intensify into a major showdown, possibly of conventional proportions. Such a crisis could be set in motion by cyber exploitation if the defender misconstrues it as a step in preparation for attack and instigates a preemptive blow.

"Large-N" Problem

Low barriers to entry mean that the cyber domain features a variety of relevant players, ranging from states to private organized groups and individuals. This can upset strategic stability in three ways, the first two of which are instrumental. One problem involves cooperation difficulties among unitarily rational states. As the number of cyber-capable states rises, the transaction and information costs of cooperation among them increase; there is less heterogeneity in discount rates for future payoffs (which raises the chances of a defection spiral); and the punishment of defection itself becomes a collective-action problem. Second, the rising number of players in the domestic cyber establishment can impede the ability of states to act as coherent units. Although the United States has operated a unified cyber command since 2009, the first steps to standardize cyber operations across the combatant commands and their respective cyber outfits began only in mid-2012. In the civilian domain, it is possible, according to Secretary of Homeland Security Janet Napolitano in remarks made in 2012, that private industry will be authorized by the government to conduct its own proactive measures. Moreover, some countries—notably, Russia and China—increasingly employ cyber "militias" to prepare and execute hostilities. Such use of civilian proxies provides states plausible deniability if they chose to initiate a cyberattack, but it also risks instigating a catalytic exchange should the lines of authority and communication break down or if agents decide to act alone.

A third, deeper source of instability stems from the dispersion of power away from governments. While states remain the most powerful cyber players, they are not alone; the new technology empowers a variety of nontraditional actors such as religious extremist groups, political activists, criminal syndicates, and individuals. The cyberattacks against Estonia and Georgia demonstrate the ease with which civilian culprits can use the new weapons to exert economic and tactical effects outside their borders. Even lone agents can generate astonishing impact. A virus created in 2000 by a disaffected Filipino teenager infected one in ten machines worldwide, causing billions of dollars in economic losses and forcing the closure of computer networks at the Pentagon. Secretary of Defense Panetta warned of far worse scenarios, stating that militant groups could use cyber instruments to derail trains transporting hazardous chemicals or to contaminate the water supplies of large cities. Cyber conflict, therefore, can fit four basic agent frames: (1) state-to-state, in which one state targets another state's strategic computer assets, such as in Olympic Games (this category includes the use by government of obedient civilian proxies); (2) private-to-state, which includes cyberattacks by militant groups or "patriotic" hackers such as in the Estonian case; (3) private-to-private, involving an exchange of cyber blows between nonstate entities such as private companies (a possible contingency of Secretary Napolitano's consideration); and (4) state-to-private, in which a state attacks the private computer systems of another nation, possibly for commercial or other economic gain.

The diversity of potential cyber adversaries and the possibility of cooperation among them establish conditions for fundamental instability; rather than hew to the familiar logic of interstate rivalry, cyber phenomena are likely to strain established theoretical models of security competition. Analysts must grapple, in effect, with two distinct but interrelated "states of nature," each of which may exhibit its own peculiarities: the traditional one of states locked in familiar contests for security but featuring a largely untested weapon whose use is difficult to model and regulate even among rational contenders; and a chaotic "global" system comprising nontraditional actors who may not accept or even understand the delicate political framework of anarchic international relations.

The greatest test of international relations theory may well be its ability to assess instances of convergence and collision between these two universes. On the one hand, the wide diffusion of cyber technology enables new modes of cooperation between state and nonstate players who share certain goals and adversaries. An example of this phenomenon is the reported collusion between Iran and company insiders at Saudi Aramco to incapacitate tens of thousands of the firm's machines in 2012. There is also the danger of collision, however: a cyber event in which nonstate cyber activity encounters the high stakes of interstate competition. The cyberattacks that were conducted by nonstate actors to freeze financial activity in Estonia prompted officials in the capital, Tallinn, to consider invoking NATO's collective defense clause, a move that would have embroiled the Alliance in a major crisis with Moscow. Contamination of the preference pool with nontraditional players can impede the ability of states to maintain the restrained stability of their relations. States have demonstrated reserve in the use of cyberweapons against each other, as illustrated by the United States' decision in 2003 not to attack computer systems in Iraq for fear of causing indiscriminate effects and setting dangerous precedents for future action. Nontraditional players, however, may not be so inhibited: they may use the new technology in ways that disrupt habitualized interstate rivalries, perhaps initiating a catalytic event that instigates a military showdown.

Thus, a dangerous separation of power and diplomacy is occurring. Even if problems of instrumental instability in the cyber domain were soluble through intergovernmental agreement—a Sisyphean task thus far—private culprits could still unsettle the interstate equilibrium by defying the consensus. Overall, concerns about the possibility of global chaos voiced by practitioners may be overstated, but they contain the germ of an important truth about the contemporary cyber danger.

VISUAL REVIEW

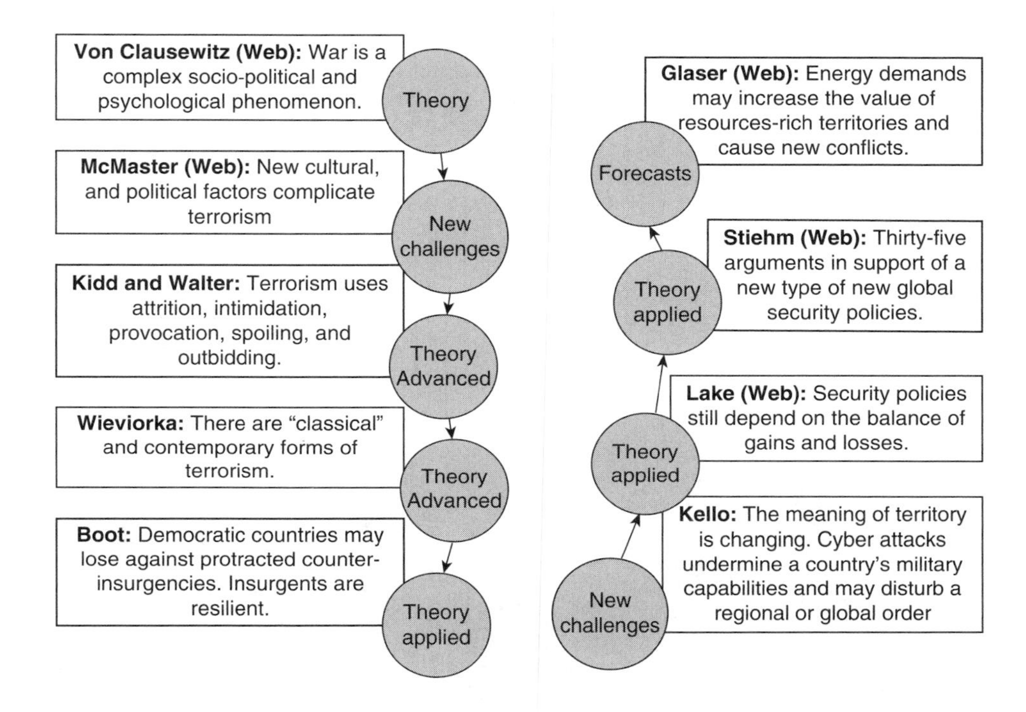

Section 6

Law and International Community

Palestinians carry a fellow protester overcome by tear gas in clashes with Israeli security forces during a demonstration in 2014 protesting against the Israeli-built West Bank separation barrier. The construction of this barrier began in 2001. In 2003, the UN International Court of Justice decided that the wall was illegal and obliged Israel to cease construction. The Israeli Supreme Court disagreed and ruled that the fence was legal. In your opinion, should governments of sovereign countries obey the decisions of international courts, and who should enforce such decisions?
Source: Nasser Ishtayeh/Associated Press

A Short History of International Law

STEPHEN C. NEFF

Indeed, the ambiguity of the term "international law" leads to various different answers to the question of when international law "began." If by "international law" is meant merely the ensemble of methods or devices which give an element of predictability to international relations (as in the silent-trading illustration), then the origin may be placed virtually as far back as recorded history itself. If by "international law" is meant a more or less comprehensive substantive code of conduct applying to nations, then the late classical period and Middle Ages was the time of its birth. If "international law" is taken to mean a set of substantive principles applying *uniquely* to States as such, then the seventeenth century would be the starting time. If "international law" is defined as the integration of the world at large into something like a single community under a rule of law, then the nineteenth century would be the earliest date (perhaps a trifle optimistically). If, finally, "international law" is understood to mean the enactments and judicial decisions of a world government, then its birth lies (if at all) somewhere in the future—and, in all likelihood, the distant future at that.

If we take the most restricted of these definitions, then we could expect to find the best evidence for a nascent international law in the three areas of ancient Eurasia that were characterized by dense networks of small, independent States sharing a more or less common religious and cultural value system: Mesopotamia (by, say, the fourth or third millennium BC), northern India (in the Vedic period after about 1600 B.C.), and classical Greece.

With the advent of the great universal religions, far more broadly-based systems of world order became possible. One outstanding example was the Islamic empire of the seventh century A.D. and afterwards. Significantly, the body of law on relations between States within the Muslim world (the *Dar al-Islam,* or "House of Islam") was much richer than that regarding relations with the outside world (the *Dar al-Harb,* or "House of war"). But even with infidel States and nationals, a number of pragmatic devices evolved to permit relations to occur in predictable ways—such as "temporary" truces (in lieu of treaties) or safe-conducts issued to individuals (sometimes on a very large scale).

In Western history, the supreme exemplar of the multinational empire was Rome. But the Roman Empire was, in its formative period, a somewhat tentative and ramshackle affair, without an over-arching ethical or religious basis comparable to the Islamic religion in the later Arab empire. That began to change, however, when certain philosophical concepts were imported from Greece (from about the second century B.C.). The most important of these was the idea of a set of universal principles of justice: the belief that, amidst the welter of varying laws of different States, certain substantive rules of conduct were present in *all* human societies. This idea first surfaced in the writings of Aristotle. But it was taken much further by the philosophers of the Stoic school, who envisaged the entire world as a single "world city-State" (or *kosmopolis*) governed by the law of nature. Cicero, writing under Stoic influence, characterized this law of nature as being "spread through the whole human community, unchanging and eternal".

This concept of a universal and eternal natural law was later adopted by two other groups, the Roman lawyers and the Christian Church, and then bequeathed by them to medieval Europe. The lawyers in particular made a distinction that would have a very long life ahead of it: between a *jus naturale* (or natural law properly speaking) and a *jus gentium* (or law of peoples). The two were distinct, but at the same time so closely interconnected that the differences between them were

Michael Evans, International Law. New York: Oxford University Press often very easily ignored. Natural law was the broader concept. It was something like what we would now call a body of scientific laws, applicable not just to human beings but to the whole animal kingdom as well. The *jus gentium* was the human component, or sub-category, of it. Just as the law of nature was universal in the natural world, so was the *jus gentium* universal in the *human* world.

The European Middle Ages became the great age of natural-law thought. During this period, natural-law conceptions developed under the umbrella of the Catholic Church. But it must be remembered that the idea was not specifically Christian in its inception, but rather was a legacy of the classical Stoic and Roman legal traditions. The dominant tradition—represented outstandingly by Thomas Aquinas—was rationalist in outlook, holding the content of the natural law to be susceptible of discovery and application by means of human reason rather than of revelation.

Natural law is one of the many parts of international law that have never received the systematic study that they merit. In the present context, only a few of its most salient features can be noted. Perhaps its single most outstanding feature was its all-embracing character. It encompassed and regulated the natural and social life of the universe in all its infinite variety—from the movements of the stars in their courses to the gurgling of the four humours through the veins and arteries of the human body, from the thoughts and deeds of all of the creatures of land, sea, and air, to those of human beings and the angels in the heavens. Its strictures applied universally to all cultures and civilizations, past, present, and future.

There continued to be, as in the ancient period, a distinction between the *jus naturale* and the *jus gentium,* though still without any very sharp line between the two. The *jus gentium* was much the lesser of the two, being seen largely as an application of the broader natural law to specifically human affairs. Sometimes it was regarded as comprising universal customs of purely human creation—and therefore as a sort of supplement to natural law properly speaking.

Beginning in about the eleventh century, European (chiefly Italian) States began to conclude bilateral treaties that spelled out various reciprocal guarantees of fair treatment. These agreements, sometimes concluded with Muslim States, granted a range of privileges to the foreign merchants based in the contracting States, such as the right to use their own law and courts when dealing with one another. The same process was at work in the sphere of maritime trading. The seafaring community made use of the laws of Oléron (which were actually a series of court decisions from the small island of that name in the Bay of Biscay), and also of a code of rules called the *Consolato del Mare,* compiled in about the thirteenth century for the maritime community of Barcelona. These codes governed the broad range of maritime activities, including the earliest rules on the rights of neutral traders in wartime.

With the European explorations of Africa and, particularly, the New World from the fourteenth century onward, questions of relations with non-European societies assumed an urgent importance—while, at the same time, posing an immense practical test for the universality of natural law. The Spanish conquest of the Indian kingdoms in the New World sparked especially vigorous legal and moral debates (even if only after the fact). The Dominican scholar, Francisco de Vitoria, in a series of lectures at the University of Salamanca, concluded that the Spanish conquest was justified, on the ground that the Indians had unlawfully attempted to exclude Spanish traders from their kingdoms, contrary to natural-law rules. But he also confessed that his blood froze in his veins at the thought of the terrible atrocities committed by the Spanish in the process. In 1550–51, there occurred one of the major legal confrontations of history, when two prominent figures—Juan Inés de Sepúlveda and Barolomé de las Casas—debated, at length, the lawfulness and legal bases of the Spanish conquest of the New World, under the judgeship of the theologian and philosopher Domingo de Soto. The result, alas, was inconclusive, as Soto declined to render a judgment.

In the seventeenth and eighteenth centuries, a new spirit entered into doctrinal thought on international law. This is sometimes put in terms of a secularization of natural-law thought. That, however, is a very misleading characterization, since natural-law itself was (and had always been) primarily secular in nature. What was new in the seventeenth century was a willingness to give a degree of formal recognition to State practice as a true source of law, rather than regarding it as merely illustrative of natural-law principles. The result was a kind of dualistic outlook, with natural law and State practice maintaining a wary, and rather uneasy, form of co-existence—a state of affairs much in evidence to the present day.

The principal harbinger of this new outlook was the Dutch writer Hugo Grotius, whose major work *On the Law of War and Peace* was published in Paris in 1625—a work so dense and rich that one could easily spend a lifetime studying it (as a number of scholars have). As a natural-law writer, he was a conservative, writing squarely in the rationalist tradition inherited from the Middle Ages. In international law specifically, he had important forerunners, most notably the Italian writer, Alberico Gentili, who produced the first truly systematic study of the law of war at the end of the sixteenth century.

Where Grotius did break important new ground—and where he fully earned the renown that still attaches to his name—was in his transformation of the old *jus gentium* into something importantly different, called the *law of nations.* The distinctive feature of this law of nations was that it was regarded as something distinct from the law of *nature,* rather than as a sub-category or means of application of natural law. Furthermore, and most significantly, this law of nations was not regarded (like the old *jus gentium*) as a body of law governing human social affairs in general. Instead, it was a set rules applying specifically to one particular and distinctive category of human beings: rulers of States. Now, for the first time in history, there was a clear conception of a systematic body of law applicable specifically to the relationship between nations. Eventually, although not until the late eighteenth century, the label "international law" would be applied to this corpus of rules—with Jeremy Bentham as the coiner of the term.

It should be appreciated that Grotius's law of nations, or "voluntary law" as it was sometimes known, was not designed to supplant or undermine traditional natural law. The law of nature and the law of nations, in short, were seen as partners rather than as rivals.

There were some, however, who contended that the partnership between the law of nature and the law of nations was anything but a happy one. Foremost amongst these dissidents was the English writer Thomas Hobbes, whose master work *Leviathan* was written in 1651, shortly after Grotius's death. In sharp contrast to Grotius, Hobbes denied that the pre-political condition of human society had been orderly and law-governed. He maintained, instead, that it was a chaotic, even violent, world, with self-preservation as the only true natural right. Security could only be attained by the radical step of having all of the persons in a state of nature surrender their natural rights to a sovereign power of their own creation—with the result that, henceforth, the *only* law which they would live under would be the law promulgated by that sovereign. Natural law was not rejected in its entirety, but it was radically stripped-down, to the point of being reduced, in essence to two fundamental tenets: a right of self-preservation, and a duty to perform contracts or promises. It was this stripped-down version of natural law which, in the opinion of Hobbes, constituted the sole body of law between independent nation-states.

On this thesis, the only possible way in which States could construct a stable international system was through the painstaking process of entering into agreements whenever this proved feasible. The natural-law duty to perform promises was the fundamental basis of this system, with the detailed substantive rules being provided by the various agreements that were actually concluded. These agreements could take either of two forms: written or unwritten. The written form, of course, comprised treaties, of the sort of that States had been concluding for many centuries. The unwritten form was customary law, which in this period was seen predominantly as simply a tacit or unwritten treaty.

Instead of setting out a grand philosophical scheme, Vattel's intention was to provide a sort of handbook for lawyers and statesmen.

The writing of Grotius and Hobbes and their followers was not done in a vacuum. Various forces were at work in this period, which served to give this new law of nations a concrete reality. One of the most important of these trends was the emergence (gradual to be sure) of strong central governments, at least in Western Europe, which increasingly gained the upper hand over the older, diffused jurisdictions of the feudal age. Particularly important for this trend was the innovation of standing armies in place of the older temporary feudal levies. In addition, these centralizing Nation-States were coming to be seen as permanently existing, corporate entities in their own right, separate from the rulers who governed them at any given time—with long-term interests and political agendas of their own.

At least some of the flavour of the medieval natural law survived, however, chiefly in the form of the idea of the existence of something that has come to be called the "community of States." The clearest symbol of this—if that is the right word for it—was the peace settlement arrived at in Westphalia in 1648, at the conclusion of the Thirty Years War in Germany. It is curious that something called the "Westphalian system" is sometimes spoken of as a synonym of anarchy or of radical views of absolute State sovereignty—conceptions which actually belong (as will be seen) to the nineteenth century and not to the seventeenth. In reality, the Westphalian settlement was an arrangement reached *within* the framework of the Holy Roman Empire, with certain prerogatives of the imperial government carefully preserved—ie, with the older medieval idea of "independent" States being subject, at the same time, to certain higher norms. The Peace of Westphalia did, however, provide a sort of template for later times in the way in which it marked out a division of labour (so to speak) between national and international spheres, placing religion carefully in the realm of domestic law.

The idea of a community of a community States—distinct from, but also analogous to, a community of individual persons—was apparent in sundry other ways in the seventeenth and eighteenth centuries. One of these was in the concept of a balance of power. This was hardly an altogether new idea, but in this period it attained a formal articulation and recognition that it had never had before (most notably in the Peace of Utrecht in 1713, at the conclusion of the War of the Spanish Succession). In conjunction with this concept, the period was one of limited—though also of frequent—warfare. At least in Western Europe, war was largely conducted with trained professional forces, and for limited ends. As a result, European diplomacy bore more resemblance to a meticulous game of chess than to a lurid Hobbesian inferno of mayhem and turmoil. Even warfare often had a ritualistic air, with its emphasis on manoeuvre and siege rather than on pitched battle.

With the definitive defeat of revolutionary and imperial France in 1815, the victorious European powers (Britain, Prussia, Russia and Austria) crafted a new kind of peace settlement, based not merely on the balance of material power between the major States but also on a set of general principles of a more substantive character. These general principles were, to be sure, of a decidedly conservative character. The goal was to craft a continent-wide set of political arrangements that would (it was hoped) keep the scourge of revolution from breaking out again.

The peace settlement was to be policed by the major powers—who were, of course, self-appointed to the task—by way of military intervention where necessary. The powers even had a grand name for their enterprise: the "public law and system of Europe." This legal order was based on faithful adherence to treaty commitments, together with respect for established laws and legitimate governments and property rights *within* the States of Europe. But it also included a duty on the part of rulers to "earn" their legitimacy by providing responsible and efficient government to their peoples and also by cooperating with movements for orderly and peaceful change.

The Concert of Europe "system" (if it could really be called that) was overtly hegemonic, in modern parlance. There was little sign of any principle of equality of States. Still, the Concert of Europe did at least provide an ideal—if not always the reality—of collective, orchestrated State action for the preservation of international peace. To that extent, it foreshadowed the post-1945 United Nations. International lawyers, however, never gave it much attention. Instead, their ambitions were directed to another end: to unshackling international law from its natural-law heritage and making it something like a science in the modern sense of that term.

On the conceptual front, the major feature of the nineteenth century was the dominant role of positivism.

In its original form, positivism envisaged the emergence of a sort of technocratic utopia, in which the world would be governed not by clerics or politicians or lawyers (as in the past benighted ages of theology and metaphysics), but rather by engineers and industrialists and financiers. This vision had first been put forward by the eccentric French nobleman, the Comte de St-Simon, in the early nineteenth century. This early vision, taken to its logical conclusion, envisaged the obsolescence of the nation-state.

One of the most central aspects of positivism was its close attention to questions of the sources of international law—and, in particular, to the proposition that international law was, fundamentally, an outgrowth or feature of the will of the States of the world. Rules of law were created by the States themselves, by consent, whether express (in written treaties) or tacit (in the form of custom). International law was therefore now seen as the sum total, or aggregation, of agreements which the States of the world happen to have arrived at, at any given time. In a phrase that became proverbial amongst positivists, international law must now be seen as a law *between* States and not as a law *above* States. International law, in other words, was now regarded as a corpus of rules arising from, as it were, the bottom up, as the conscious creation of the States themselves, rather than as a pre-existing, eternal, all-enveloping framework, in the manner of the old natural law. As a consequence, the notion of a systematic, all-encompassing body of law—so striking a feature of natural law—was now discarded. International law was now seen as, so to speak, a world of fragments, an accumulation of specific, agreed rules, rather than as a single coherent picture. In any area where agreement between States happened to be lacking, international law was, perforce, silent.

The stress on the basic rights of States also gave to positivism a strongly pluralistic cast. Each nation-State possessed its own distinctive set of national interests, which it was striving to achieve in an inherently competitive, even hostile, environment. Each State was sovereign within its territory. And each State's domestic law could reflect that country's own particular history, values, aspirations, traditions, and so forth. It was in this period that the principle of "the sovereign equality of States" became the fundamental cornerstone—or even the central dogma—of international law, along with the concomitant rule of nonintervention of States into the internal affairs of one another.

Positivists tended to view the rights and wrongs of a State's decision to resort to war (the *jus ad bellum*) as a political rather than a legal issue. Therefore, war was now seen as an inevitable and permanent feature of the inter-State system, in the way that friction was an inevitable and permanent feature of a mechanical system.

If positivism was by far the dominant trend in nineteenth century international law, it did fall short of having a complete monopoly. Two other schools of thought in particular should be noted.

At the core of the historical school's philosophy was the thesis that each culture, or cultural unit, or nation possessed a distinctive group consciousness or ethos, which marked it off from other cultures or nations. Each of these cultural units, as a consequence, could only really be understood in its own terms. The historical school therefore rejected the universalist outlook of natural law. This opposition to universal natural law was one of the most important features that the historical school shared with the positivists.

In international law, the impact of the historical school is evident in three principal areas. The first was with regard to customary law, where its distinctive contribution was the insistence that this law was not a matter merely of consistent practice, however widespread or venerable it might be. A rule of customary law required, in addition, a mental element—a kind of group consciousness, or collective decision on the part of the actors to enact that practice into a rule of law (albeit an unwritten one). In fact, this collective mental element was seen as the most important component of custom, with material practice relegated to a clear second place. Customary law was therefore seen, on this view, as a kind of informal legislation rather than as an unwritten treaty (as the positivists tended to hold). This thesis marked the origin of the modern concept of *opinio juris* as a key component of customary international law.

The second major contribution of the historical school to international law was its theory that the fundamental unit of social and historical existence was not—or not quite—the State, as it was for the positivists, but rather the *nation*-state. In this vision, the State, when properly constituted, comprised the organization of a particular culture into a political unit. It was but a short step from this thesis to the proposition that a "people" (ie, a cultural collectivity or nation or, in the German term, *Volk*) had a moral right to organize itself politically as a State. And it was no large step from there to the assertion that such a collectivity possesses a *legal* right so to organize itself. This "nationality school" (as it was sometimes called) had the most impact in Italy, where its leading spokesman was Pasquale Mancini, who was a professor at the University of Turin (as well as an office-holder in the government of unified Italy). Although the nationality thesis did not attract significant support amongst international lawyers generally at the time, it did prefigure the later law of self-determination of peoples.

The third area where the influence of the historical school was felt was regarding imperialism—a subject that has attracted strangely little attention from international lawyers. It need only be mentioned here that the historical school inherited from the eighteenth century a fascination with "stages" of history. Under the impact of nineteenth-century anthropological thought, there came to be wide agreement on a three-fold categorization of States: as civilized, barbarian, and savage.

It has been observed that positivism basically accepted the outbreak of war as an unavoidable fact of international life, and contented itself with regulating the conduct of hostilities. But that approach applied to war properly speaking. Regarding lesser measures of coercion, the legacy of just-war thought lingered on. This was the thesis that a resort to armed self-help was permissible to obtain respect for legal rights, if peaceful means proved unavailing. The most important of these forcible self-help measures were armed reprisals.

It is one of history's great ironies that the natural-law tradition, which had once been so grand an expression of idealism and world brotherhood, should come to such an ignominiously blood-spattered pass. A philosophy that had once insisted so strongly on the protection of the weak against the strong was now used as a weapon of the strong against the weak. It is, of course, unfair to condemn a whole system of justice on the basis of abuses. But the abuses were many, and the power relations too naked and too ugly for the tastes of many from the developing world. Along with imperialism, forcible self-help actions left a long-lasting stain on relations between the developed and the developing worlds.

The culmination of nineteenth-century international legislation—and the arrival of parliamentary-style diplomacy and treaty-drafting—came with the two Hague Peace Conferences of 1899 and 1907. The first Conference drafted two major conventions: one on the laws of war and one on the establishment of a Permanent Court of Arbitration (which was actually a roster of experts prepared to act as judges on an ad hoc basis, and not a standing court). The Second Hague Peace Conference, in 1907, was a much larger gathering than the earlier one (and hence less Europe-dominated). It produced 13 conventions on various topics, mostly on aspects of war and neutrality.

Yet another major achievement of the nineteenth century was in the area of the peaceful settlement of disputes. Although it was widely agreed that fundamental security issues were not justiciable, the nineteenth century marked a great step forward in the practice of inter-State arbitration. The trend began with the Jay Treaty of 1794, in which the United States and Britain agreed to set up two arbitration commissions (comprising nationals of each country) to resolve a range of neutrality and property-seizure issues that had arisen in the preceding years. These were followed by a number of ad hoc inter-State arbitrations in the nineteenth century, of which the most famous, again between Britain and the United States, took place in 1871–72, for the settlement of a host of neutrality-related issues arising from the American Civil War.

For all the impressiveness of these achievements, though, the state of the world was well short of utopian. Economic inequality grew steadily even as growth accelerated. The subjection of much of the world to the European imperial powers, together with the "gunboat diplomacy" that sometimes followed in the wake of legal claims, stored up a strong reservoir of ill-will between the developed and the developing worlds.

The carnage of the Great War of 1914–18 concentrated many minds, in addition to squandering many lives. Many persons now held that nothing short of a permanently existing organization dedicated to the maintenance of peace would suffice to prevent future ghastly wars. Their most prominent spokesman was American President Woodrow Wilson. The fruit of their labours was the establishment of the League of Nations, whose Covenant was set out in the Versailles Treaty of 1919. This new system of public order would be of an open, parliamentary, democratic character, in contrast to the discreet great-power dealings of the Concert of Europe. The League was, however, tainted from the outset by its close association with the Versailles peace settlement, an incubus which it never managed to shake off.

Although the League failed as a protector against aggressors, it would be far wrong to suppose that the inter-war period was a sterile time in international law generally. Precisely the opposite was the case. It was a time of ferment, experiment, and excitement unprecedented in the history of the discipline. A World Court (known formally, if optimistically, as the Permanent Court of International Justice) was established as a standing body, with its seat at the Hague in the Netherlands. It did not have compulsory jurisdiction over all disputes. But it decided several dozen cases, building up, for the first time, a substantial body of international judicial practice. These cases were supplemented by a large number of claims commissions and arbitrations, whose outpourings gave international lawyers a volume of case law far richer than anything that had ever existed before.

The codification of international law was one of the ambitious projects of the period. A conference was convened for that purpose by the League of Nations in 1930, but its fruits were decidedly modest (consisting mainly of clarifications of various issues relating to nationality). But there were further initiatives by the American States in a variety of fields. These included a convention on the rights and duties of States in 1933, which included what many lawyers regard as the canonical definition of a "State" for legal purposes. The American States also concluded conventions on maritime neutrality, civil wars, asylum, and extradition.

The inter-war period also witnessed the first multilateral initiatives on human rights. A number of bilateral conventions for the protection of minorities were concluded between various newly created States and the League of Nations. In the event, these proved not to be very effective; but they set the stage for later efforts to protect minority rights after 1945, as well as human rights generally. The principle of trusteeship of dependent territories was embodied in the mandates system, in which the ex-colonies of the defeated countries were to be administered by member States of the League. But this was to be a mission of stewardship—"a sacred trust of civilization"—under the oversight of the League. Finally, the League performed heroic labours for the relief of refugees, in the face of very great obstacles—in the process virtually creating what would become one of the most important components of the law of human rights.

It was a period also of innovative thinking about international law. That the doctrinaire positivism of the nineteenth century was far from dead was made apparent by the World Court in 1927, when it reaffirmed the consensual basis of international law, in the famous (or infamous) *Lotus* case. But positivism also came under attack during this period, from several quarters. One set of attackers were the enthusiasts for collective security, as embodied in the League of Nations.

In short, the inter-war period did not bring an end to war or aggression. But it was the most vibrant and exciting era in the history of the discipline up to that time (and perhaps since).

The founding of the United Nations in 1945, to replace the defunct League of Nations, was a critical step in the creation of a new world order. With the UN came a new World Court (the International Court of Justice, or ICJ), though still without compulsory jurisdiction over States. The heart of the organization was the Security Council, where (it was hoped) the victorious powers from the Second World War would continue their wartime alliance in perpetuity as a collective bulwark against future aggressors. (It may be noted that "United Nations" had been the official name for the wartime alliance.) The UN therefore marked something of a return to the old Concert of Europe approach. The special status of the five major powers (the principal victors in the Second World War, of course) was formally reflected in their possession of permanent seats on the Security Council, together with the power of veto over its decisions.

The UN Charter went further than the League Covenant in restricting violence. It did this by prohibiting not only war as such, but also "the use of force" in general—thereby encompassing measures short of war, such as armed reprisals. An express exception was made for self-defence.

Parallel to this security programme was another one for the promotion of global economic prosperity. The economic-integration effort of the nineteenth century, shattered by the Great War and by the Great Depression of the 1930s, was to be restructured and given institutional embodiments. The International Monetary Fund was founded to ensure currency stability, and the World Bank to protect and promote foreign investment and (in due course) economic development. Trade liberalization would be overseen by a body to be called the International Trade Organization (ITO).

The euphoric atmosphere proved, alas, to be very short-lived. Scarcely had the UN begun to function than it became paralysed by Cold-War rivalry between the major power blocs—with the notable exception of the action in Korea in 1950–53 (only made possible by an ill-advised Soviet boycott of the Security Council at the relevant time). Nor did the new World Court find much effective use in its early decades. The ITO never came into being (because of a loss of interest by the United States). Plans for the establishment of a permanent international criminal court were also quietly dropped. Nor did the UN Charter's general ban against force have much apparent effect, beyond a cruelly ironic one: of propelling self-defence from a comparative legal backwater into the very forefront of international legal consciousness. Since self-defence was now the only clearly lawful category of unilateral use of force, the UN era became littered with self-defence claims of varying degrees of credibility, from the obvious to the risible. In particular, actions that previously would have been unashamedly presented as reprisals now tended to be deftly re-labelled as self-defence.

Around the 1980s, a certain change of atmosphere in international law became evident, as something like the idealism of the early post-war years began, very cautiously, to return. The end of the Cold War led to tangible hopes that the original vision of the UN as an effective collective-security agency might, at last, be realized. The expulsion of Iraq from Kuwait in 1991 lent strong support to this hope. Perhaps most remarkable of all was the rebirth of plans for an international criminal court, after a half-century of dormancy. A statute for a permanent International Criminal Court was drafted in 1998, entering into force in 2002 (with the first trial commencing in 2009).

In this second round of optimism, there was less in the way of euphoria than there had been in the first one, and more of a feeling that international law might be entering an age of new—and dangerous—challenge. International lawyers were now promising, or threatening, to bring international norms to bear upon States in an increasingly intrusive manner. A striking demonstration of this occurred in 1994, when the UN Security Council authorized the use of force to overthrow an unconstitutional government in Haiti. In 1999, the UN Security Council acquiesced in (although it did not actually authorize) a humanitarian intervention in Kosovo by a coalition of Western powers. It was far from clear how the world would respond to this new-found activism—in particular, whether the world would really be content to entrust its security, in perpetuity, to a Concert-of-Europe style directorate of major powers.

International legal claims were being asserted on a wide range of other fronts as well, and frequently in controversial ways and generally with results that were unwelcome to some. For example, lawyers who pressed for self-determination rights for various minority groups and indigenous peoples were accused of encouraging secession movements. Some human-rights lawyers were loudly demanding changes in the traditional practices of non-Western peoples. And newly found (or newly rejuvenated) concerns over democracy, governance, and corruption posed, potentially, a large threat to governments all over the world. Some environmental lawyers were insisting that, in the interest of protecting a fragile planet, countries should deliberately curb economic growth. (But which countries? And by how much?) Economic globalization also became intensely controversial, as the IMF's policy of "surveillance" (a somewhat ominous term to some) became increasingly detailed and intrusive, and as "structural adjustment" was seen to have potentially far-reaching consequences in volatile societies. Fears were also increasingly voiced that the globalization process was bringing an increase in economic inequality.

Does International Law Promote the Peaceful Settlement of International Disputes? Evidence From the Study of Territorial Conflicts Since 1945

PAUL K. HUTH, SARAH E. CROCO, AND BENJAMIN J. APPEL

Is a legal advantage an important source of bargaining leverage for state leaders as they negotiate over security issues in international disputes? Does international law provide the foundation for the peaceful settlement of security-related disputes? In a system defined by anarchy, there are reasons to question whether international law can play a central role in the orderly and peaceful resolution of disputes when security issues are at stake for leaders. Indeed, many would argue that the shadow of military power is an ever-present influence over such bargaining processes and that international law is, therefore, not a viable substitute for military strength and credible threats of force to secure the peace.

In this article, we apply this approach to explain the role of international law in the resolution of territorial disputes from 1945 to 2000. In doing so, we ask three related questions. First, when leaders are unsatisfied with the territorial status quo, why do some allow it to persist, whereas others actively challenge it through either force or negotiations? Second, if both sides agree to negotiate, then under what circumstances is a settlement most likely to materialize? Finally, if the parties decide to pursue a settlement, then when do leaders prefer to have an international legal body determine the final terms as opposed to negotiating the terms themselves? Answering these questions, we believe, requires an understanding of the strength of a state's legal claim to the disputed territory relative to its adversary's. More specifically, we argue that international law will facilitate the dispute resolution process when one of the parties has a clear legal advantage.

This article offers at least four important contributions. First, we identify when international law will be most capable of helping states resolve disputes. We posit that the bargaining solution suggested by international law will only emerge as a

Huth, Paul; Croco, Sarah; Appel, Benjamin, Does International Law Promote the Peaceful Settlement of International Disputes? Evidence from the Study of Territorial Conflicts since 1945, American Political Science Review. Volume 105, No. 2, pp. 415-436, reproduced with permission.

focal point for states if two conditions are present: namely, if the legal principles relevant to the dispute are clear and if one state has an unambiguous legal advantage over its adversary. As we argue in more detail later in the article, if either or both conditions fail to hold, then international law is far less likely to contribute to the peaceful settlement of territorial disputes.

Second, this article represents one of the few attempts to measure the concept of a legal advantage. This allows us to undertake a rigorous test of theoretical claims regarding the role played by international law in settling international security-related disputes peacefully.

The context of territorial disputes is an appropriate proving ground in this regard because it provides an especially "hard test" of the potential for international law to influence state behavior. Territorial disputes are often highly salient to domestic political audiences, regardless of the strategic or economic value of the land in question. The potential backlash for a leader who would offer even limited concessions creates a strong incentive for many leaders to refrain from compromise in any form.

Third, focusing on the context of territorial disputes allows us to broaden what we mean by "international law." As the literature currently stands, much of the research centers on state compliance with formal treaties. Although this is a logical and important topic to study, treaties are far from the only source of international law. In fact, there are several others sources, such as customary international law, rulings from international judicial bodies, and the writings of legal scholars.

Fourth, as many scholars have noted, problems of selection bias create substantial inference problems for researchers interested in determining the effectiveness of international law. We avoid issues associated with selection effects by incorporating multiple sources of international law into our analysis.

Overall, we find strong support for our hypotheses regarding the pacifying effect of international law. More specifically, leaders with strong legal claims who are dissatisfied with the territorial status quo are more likely to challenge it by opening negotiations and less likely to resort to threats or the use of force. Furthermore, disputes in which one of the states enjoys a clear legal advantage relative to its opponent are more likely to be resolved through negotiations than disputes where neither side has strong claims to the territory in question. Finally, we also find support for the notion that the lack of a legal advantage will cause democratic leaders to prefer a settlement arranged by international legal bodies to one that is a product of direct, bilateral negotiations.

TERRITORIAL DISPUTES AND THE PEACEFUL PATH TO SETTLEMENT

Our analyses focus on three interrelated yet distinct stages of this "peaceful pathway" to dispute resolution. The first stage, which we term the "challenge the status quo" phase, involves three possible choices available to the challenger: he or she can challenge the present border by either calling for negotiations or threatening military force, or he or she can maintain the status quo without actively confronting the target with diplomatic or military challenges.

If a challenger pursues talks, then the dispute moves into the second stage, which we refer to as the "negotiations" phase. Theoretically, the central question we address is whether an asymmetry in the relative strength of the states' legal claims affects the probability of the dispute being resolved peacefully through *either* type of agreement. Put differently, for this particular stage, we are only interested in whether the parties can agree to end the dispute peacefully, not the venue in which they end it.

We consider the choice of settlement venue in the third stage ("mode of settlement"), which models the decision to end the dispute through either (1) direct negotiations or (2) an agreement to settle the dispute by a formal process of legal dispute resolution in which an arbitration panel or the International Court of Justice (ICJ) resolves the dispute by issuing a ruling on competing territorial claims. Theoretically, the key issue is whether the strength of a state's legal claims influences the leader's choice of settlement venue.

THEORY

Bargaining and Focal Points

We argue that when legal principles are able to act as a focal point, they can help resolve the distribution problem and break the bargaining impasse by indicating how the disputed territory should be divided between the two states. This is true for at least two reasons. First, international law can help leaders identify which legal principles are relevant to the dispute. In doing so, international law provides a way to frame the problem by focusing on evidence and arguments that establish the legal merits of each state's claims to the territory in question. Once these legal principles have been identified, states can then begin to craft an agreement based on the merits of legal claims.

Second, as Schelling argues, focal points help leaders overcome distribution problems by providing them with a way for leaders to "coordinate their expectations." The need for convergent expectations is critical because many failures to settle stem from the fact that bargaining "includes maneuver, indirect communication, jockeying for position, or speaking to be overheard, or [a confusion of] a multitude of participants and divergent interests". If parties are to reach an agreement, Schelling posits, then they must identify a single point (or a narrow range of points) within the bargaining range that neither side expects the other to reject. Recognizing this strategic element of bargaining wherein one state attempts to predict what *its adversary* expects *it* to offer, as well as how this facilitates the convergence of expectations, is crucial to understanding how focal points can help parties overcome distribution problems.

On a related point, the ability of the focal point to narrow the range of acceptable outcomes also helps make negotiations more productive by limiting the ability of a state with weak legal claims to persist in misrepresenting the strength of its bargaining position in negotiations over a possible settlement. Leaders with weak legal claims are less able to make credible bluffs about the terms they are willing to accept if those terms are inconsistent with the distribution of territory called for by the focal point. By narrowing the set of possible agreements, the focal point solves both the coordination and distribution problems by identifying which of the infinite number of potential settlements to start with. It also makes negotiations more efficient by deterring states from offering terms their adversaries would reject. Consequently, even though the existence of a distribution problem necessarily implies that parties have divergent preferences regarding the terms of the final settlement, having a focal point that identifies a particular solution can still influence leader behavior.

Focal Points and International Law

First, international law and legal principles are common knowledge among states, having been established through either formal channels (e.g., treaties, agreements, court rulings) or less formal means (e.g., customary international law, general principles, writings of legal scholars). Consequently, they are a well-known source of third-party expression for leaders to reference when they disagree.

Second, international law provides a common set of standards to assess the relative merits of competing claims. This feature is particularly important for resolving the distribution problems because it provides a means of identifying which of the many potential ways to divide the contested territory the leaders should choose. We have at least three reasons for arguing this.

First, many of the legal principles relevant to territorial disputes predate the territorial disputes we examine here. Therefore, although the great powers may have originally crafted specific legal principles to serve their interests in a particular dispute, it is possible that those same principles will work *against* the interests of the leaders of those same states in the future when new disputes arise. Second, international law is not simply a reflection of past or current great power preferences; the roster of great powers changes over time through war and other types of power shifts, and the number of new, smaller states has grown considerably in the post–World War II era. Third, the rulings from international courts and other legal bodies are seen by states as largely unbiased, or at least, not partial to a particular disputant before a decision is made.

Hypotheses Regarding the Effect of the Focal Point

The preceding logic suggests two hypotheses for leader behavior in the first and second stages. For the first stage, the existence of a focal point should encourage leaders with a legal advantage to press for negotiations. There are at least two reasons for them to choose this option over either revising the status quo by force or leaving it unchallenged. First and foremost, because the terms of settlement suggested by international law align with their preferences for how their respective disputes should be resolved, they will be bargaining from a position of strength. Because a strong legal claim on their part necessarily implies that their opponents have weak legal positions, they should enter negotiations confident that they will be able to secure favorable settlements, via either a bilateral treaty or a formal legal ruling. As a result, once negotiations begin, they will be motivated to push their opponents to either accept agreements that reflect the legal superiority of their claims or consent to a formal process of legal dispute resolution. By a similar logic, they will also resist making significant territorial concessions to their adversaries.

The second reason legally advantaged leaders should prefer negotiations to revising the status quo through violence has to do with the clear legal principle against acquiring title to territory by force. The preceding logic implies the following hypothesis:

> **H1:** Leaders of challenger states with relatively strong legal claims are more likely to challenge the status quo by pursuing talks instead of threatening force or maintaining the status quo. These leaders are also less likely to threaten force compared to the status quo.

The existence of a focal point will also inform the behavior of both leaders in the second stage, where they must decide (collectively) to either end the dispute through some type of agreement or allow the dispute to continue. To understand why both leaders will have reason to accept a settlement that is grounded in international law, it is instructive to examine the strategic choices of each leader. For the leader of the state with the legal advantage, settling the dispute is the best option. As we argued previously, any settlements that materialize will likely favor leaders in this position. In light of this, they should have a strong preference to end the disputes rather than let them continue.

Settling the dispute creates the possibility of a peaceful future and the associated benefits that come with it. Making peace with an adversary can free up resources that would otherwise be tied up in the dispute, allowing the leader to redistribute them to other domestic sectors (e.g., health care, education). Ending a dispute can also lead to a more collaborative and mutually beneficial relationship with the former adversary. In short, there are multiple reasons why a disadvantaged leader would choose to abide by the terms suggested by the focal point. The previous logic suggests the following hypothesis:

> **H2:** Rounds of talks in which one state has superior legal claims are more likely to end in settlement agreements than talks in which neither side has a clear legal advantage.

Domestic Cover

In this section, we posit that the decision to pursue formal legal dispute resolution compared to bilateral settlements can be explained by identifying which leaders face higher political costs for making territorial concessions. Because territorial disputes are typically salient for the domestic public, leaders that are more accountable at home must consider the response of domestic actors before they agree to make concessions. Given this, we argue that leaders who require more domestic cover will be more likely to pursue legal dispute resolution. More specifically, we hypothesize that legally disadvantaged leaders of democracies will more often prefer a formal process of legal dispute resolution, whereas their autocratic counterparts will be more likely to accept a settlement brokered in bilateral negotiations.

We believe that democratic leaders with weak legal claims require greater domestic cover because of two domestic political institutions that exist in modern democracies: a viable opposition and an electoral check. The combination of these two factors encourages the executive to distance him- or herself from politically unpopular decisions. Failing to do so will leave him or her open to accusations of policy incompetence that opposition elites will have every incentive to make as part of their effort to weaken the executive's hold on power. Such policy missteps will also trigger a negative reaction from domestic audiences, who prefer leaders who demonstrate political acumen, thereby decreasing the probability of reelection for the incumbent. This potential for domestic punishment is especially high for concessions made in the context of territorial disputes because nationalism is often linked to maintaining state borders, making leaders who agree to concessions vulnerable to charges of sacrificing national interests.

In light of this heightened likelihood of punishment, we expect that a democratic leader facing probable concessions as part of a territorial settlement will attempt to disassociate him- or herself from the terms of settlement as much as possible to insulate against any domestic political fallout.

First, as many scholars have argued, international legal bodies that would undertake the dispute resolution process are generally able to serve as unbiased third parties. Second, within these legal bodies, it is customary to place a primacy on the importance of following formal procedures and giving both parties an equal chance to state their case. Third, and perhaps most importantly from the executive's perspective, the fact that both parties must agree *in advance* to the arbitrator's or court's terms of settlement helps to absolve the legally disadvantaged leader of any direct responsibility for the final outcome. This advantage is apparent when one considers the more direct and obvious role the executive would play if the settlement emerged from bilateral negotiations, where the leader would have had more control over the terms of the agreement.

Taken together, these institutional characteristics imply that domestic opponents of the executive will have a difficult time questioning the agreement on grounds of fairness or neutrality, or attributing the settlement as a failure on the part of the leader. This logic suggests the following hypothesis:

> **H3:** Leaders of democracies with weak legal claims are more likely to reach agreements to settle disputes by a formal process of legal dispute resolution than by direct bilateral negotiations.

CONCLUSION

As Morgenthau claims, "the actions of states are determined not by moral principles and legal commitments but by considerations of interest and power. Moral principles and legal commitments may be invoked to justify a policy arrived at by other grounds, but they do not determine the choice among different courses of action." More recently, other scholars have argued that international law is, at most, epiphenomenal to state interests. In this article, we attempt to determine whether the critics of international law are right or, in contrast, whether international law can play a central role in peaceful dispute resolution.

Our results are unambiguous. In all three dispute stages, the relative strength of a state's legal claims (conditional on regime type in the third stage) was a strong predictor of a leader's behavior. Leaders with strong legal claims are more likely to push for negotiations and less likely to resort to force when they are dissatisfied with the status quo than are leaders who lack a clear legal advantage. Similarly, disputes that are marked by an asymmetry in the strength of the parties' legal claims are more likely to be resolved than disputes where neither side can marshal a compelling legal case for the contested territory. Furthermore, we also found support for our domestic cover argument in that democratic leaders with *weak* legal claims are significantly more likely to pursue a settlement through a process of formal dispute resolution than are other types of states. Finally, even when asymmetric legal claims did not lead to a final agreement, territorial disputes where one side had a legal advantage were less violent.

The strong and consistent performance of the international law variables, even in the presence of several important controls, such as relative military strength, poses a clear challenge to theoretical approaches that question the impact and importance of international law. That we were able to obtain such results in the context of territorial disputes—which are known for their intractability and high propensity for violence—further bolsters the importance of our findings. Our theoretical framework and findings, therefore, suggest that although the shadow of power is one important consideration for students of world politics to study, the rule of law must not be ignored. Indeed, we would argue that based on our results, a legal advantage is more beneficial to state leaders than is a decisive military advantage in securing territorial interests in the process of peacefully settling such disputes. As such, one can view our findings as suggesting that international law under the right conditions is a more powerful force for order and peaceful change than is military strength.

Our theoretical framework and research design also advance the current state of the literature on the effectiveness of international law. For instance, identifying the circumstances under which a focal point will emerge from international law to help states resolve the problem of how to allocate disputed territory (i.e., when the relevant legal principles are clear *and* unambiguously favor one side) constitutes an important theoretical contribution. Specifying these conditions allows us to move beyond the assumption that international law's effects are uniform. The coding scheme we designed, which allowed us to codify and aggregate several legal principles in a systematic way across all disputes, is complimentary in this regard because it gives us the ability to highlight cases in which a focal point is most likely to materialize with respect to the specific legal principles in question. In doing so, our article provides the means to evaluate empirically insights from bargaining theory that are underexamined in the literature, such as the importance of distribution problems and the role of focal points in the dispute resolution process.

The theory's ability to explain state behavior in response to a variety of sources of law, instead of simply focusing on treaties, is also significant. As we point out at the beginning of the article, doing so not only helps mitigate any selection issues, but also allows us to move beyond questions that are limited to compliance with only one source of international law. Instead, as the preceding analyses demonstrate, taking other forms of law under consideration (e.g., customary international law) in addition to our research design based on the three stages of dispute resolution can help us explain a leader's decisions at several points throughout the process of attaining international cooperation—not just whether states will comply with the final agreement. Consequently, our findings avoid problems of selection bias that have hampered the empirical literature on international law.

The Palestine Problem: The Search for Statehood and the Benefits of International Law

ADAM G. YOFFIE

INTRODUCTION

Palestine has had a long and checkered past in its efforts to attain statehood. Although international law failed to facilitate Palestinian statehood more than half a century ago, the legal landscape at the international level is changing. Whereas conventional wisdom assumes that international law reduces state sovereignty, this Comment argues that international political organizations and legal institutions can actually increase Palestinian chances of achieving statehood.

By the conclusion of World War II, Palestine had been ruled by Great Britain for nearly three decades. Assuming control from the Ottomans

The Yale Journal of International Law, 36, 2: 497–511

following World War I, the British never established a coherent policy for governing the disputed territory. British rule, however, did not last: on November 29, 1947—with thirty-three votes in favor, thirteen against, ten abstentions, and one absence—the U.N. General Assembly passed Resolution 181 calling for the exit of British forces and the partition of Palestine into "[i]ndependent Arab and Jewish States." The United Nations, then a nascent organization formed out of the ashes of the Second World War, recognized that "the present situation in Palestine [was] one which [was] likely to impair the general welfare and friendly relations among nations" and that the only sensible solution was "the Plan of Partition." Based on the recommendations of the U.N. Special Committee on Palestine, Resolution 181 aimed to find a peaceful solution to the problem, but instead led to regional warfare. The Arab League, which included the states neighboring Palestine, refused to accept the United Nations' creation of a Jewish State. As a result, Palestine failed to attain the statehood it so desperately craved. This failure is indicative of international law's shortcomings; international law can offer concrete steps toward statehood, but if applied too rapidly or too harshly, can also undermine stability.

Israel's road to internationally recognized statehood has been somewhat smoother. Battling its neighbors while awaiting the formal withdrawal of British forces, the State of Israel did not formally declare its independence until May 14, 1948. Yet it was not until a year after independence that Israel gained admittance to the United Nations, on May 11, 1949. As fighting continued through the first half of the year, the U.N. Security Council refrained from referring the matter to the General Assembly for a vote. After signing a series of armistice agreements with its neighbors, Israel gained majority support in the Security Council and subsequently in the General Assembly to become an official member of the United Nations. Fast-forward sixty years, and Israel—a state born out of two General Assembly resolutions with a positive recommendation from the Security Council in between—faces the prospect of bearing witness to similar action by the United Nations on behalf of the Palestinians. This time around, the Israeli government has firmly stated its opposition to what Palestinian leaders are referring to as "Plan B."

"Plan B" represents a multifaceted approach to achieving recognition of a Palestinian State from four major international bodies: the U.N. Security Council, the U.N. General Assembly, the International Court of Justice (ICJ), and the International Criminal Court (ICC). The Palestinian Authority (PA), which declared unilateral statehood more than two decades ago, is thus not restricting its push for recognition to individual nations. Following another round of collapsed peace talks brokered by the United States, Palestinian Foreign Minister Riad Malki publicly declared his intention to seek U.N. recognition of a Palestinian state in September 2011. The U.N. route, however, is not an easy process. To obtain U.N. membership, Malki would first need to gain support from the Security Council, as the General Assembly can only vote on membership based on a positive recommendation from the Security Council. But the foreign minister has made clear that in the face of an expected Security Council veto by the United States, the Palestinians will still push for a vote in the General Assembly, where they are more likely to garner majority support. Such action would not result in membership but function as a purely symbolic measure on the part of the General Assembly.

In addition to focusing on the United Nations, the PA is also likely to appeal to the ICJ and ICC. The emergence of a nascent but rapidly expanding international judicial system over the past three decades has contributed to the perceived legitimacy and actual authority of international courts. In addition to the long tenure of the ICJ and the approaching ten-year anniversary of the ICC, the international legal system now includes a number of specialized tribunals, as well as hybrid and regional courts, charged with meting out justice outside of and across traditional national boundaries. The ICJ and ICC thus offer additional forums for focusing international attention on the issue of Palestinian statehood and influencing Israeli policy in the process—powerful tools that are part of a greater judicial system that was unavailable to the Palestinians in the mid-twentieth century.

The PA's Plan B, therefore, would invert the standard relationship between international bodies and state sovereignty, as it seeks to use the former to advance the latter. In other words, the PA intends to use international bodies that generally take a state's sovereignty as an axiom to establish that sovereignty in the first place. Palestine has been an aspiring state for sixty years, and international bodies can and should play a more direct role in helping Palestinians achieve their decades-long goal.

INTERNATIONAL LAW AS A STEP LADDER, NOT A STUMBLING BLOCK, TO STATE SOVEREIGNTY FOR ASPIRING STATES

International law, enforced through international legal institutions and political organizations, is generally considered to infringe upon state sovereignty. By signing on to any form of international agreement, states necessarily surrender some form of control over their internal affairs. Palestine, for example, joined the Arab League in 1974, and in the event of a war with Israel, a majority vote within the League would subject the signatory to the League's mediation and arbitration decisions. Yet such external, extra-state influence is in keeping with the writing of political science professor Eric Leonard, who describes a modern shift beyond the "Westphalian Order" to a new form of "global civil society" in which a wide range of non-state actors are able to intervene in intrastate matters. Citing the creation of the International Criminal Tribunals for the former Yugoslavia (ICTY) and Rwanda (ICTR), Leonard writes: "These Courts were given the ability, by the U.N. Security Council, to intervene in the affairs of two sovereign states, and prosecute their citizenry at an international tribunal that is held outside of their territorial boundaries." Leonard correctly states that such a mandate violates the theoretical underpinnings of Westphalian sovereignty. But he takes a far too narrow view of the world—and of the concept of sovereignty—by failing to recognize the sovereignty-enhancing potential of such international bodies, particularly for aspiring states.

According to Stanford political scientist Stephen D. Krasner, the ever-elusive concept of "sovereignty" can be broken down into four different forms: international legal sovereignty, Westphalian sovereignty, domestic sovereignty, and interdependence sovereignty. The former two "involve issues of authority and legitimacy, but not control," whereas the latter two revolve around "control." Within the Israeli/Palestinian context, international bodies have the most potential to enhance international legal sovereignty, which Krasner defines as "practices associated with mutual recognition, usually between territorial entities that have formal juridical independence." Note that Krasner's definition speaks of "territorial entities," as opposed to states, and revolves around that entity's standing in a judicial setting. Thus, international bodies tasked with carrying out international law may infringe upon the Westphalian sovereignty of current states but actually advance the international legal sovereignty of aspiring states.

THE ROLE OF INTERNATIONAL BODIES IN SECURING STATEHOOD: GARNERING INTERNATIONAL SUPPORT UNDER "PLAN B"

The Conventional Path—The United Nations

The conventional path to statehood runs through the United Nations, and the Security Council and General Assembly have wrestled with the complicated questions of Israeli and Palestinian statehood since those bodies' founding. In an indication of the inevitable role the United Nations will play in any future agreement, former Israeli Prime Minister Ehud Olmert envisioned Palestinian statehood arising out of resolutions in the Security Council and General Assembly. Olmert, describing the two-state agreement that was nearly reached with his Palestinian counterpart Mahmoud Abbas, stated: "My idea was that, before presenting it to our own peoples, we first would go to the U.N. Security Council and get a unanimous vote for support . . . . Then we would ask the General Assembly to support us . . . ."

The "conventional path," provides a plausible scenario for advancing Palestinian sovereignty, but the PA is ultimately unwilling to rely solely on an international body that has failed to deliver over the past sixty years. Therefore, the Palestinians are adopting a broader view of international law that is not restricted to the United Nations.

The Unconventional Path—International Courts

International courts provide an unconventional path to statehood that was largely unavailable during the twentieth century. Less mired in politics, international courts are not beholden to nearly two hundred member states and thus have the capacity to "intervene" in seemingly intractable disputes. They also have the judicial independence and nonpolitical disposition to be wary of making a decision that could reignite conflict in the region. The following two Subsections explain how the two most visible international courts—the ICJ and ICC—should help advance Palestinian statehood.

The International Court of Justice

The International Court of Justice is not a newcomer to the "Palestine Problem"; the United Nations pulled the Court into the fray seven years ago. In a highly scrutinized advisory opinion—issued at the request of the General Assembly—the ICJ held that Israel's security wall in the Occupied Palestinian Territories violated international law. Addressing American and Israeli objections to the Court's jurisdiction, the ICJ even noted its "permanent responsibility" to Palestine due to the U.N. system that has granted Palestine the "special status of observer." Building upon such earlier involvement, the PA is not restricted to asking the General Assembly to recognize a Palestinian state within the 1967 borders. The PA could also ask the General Assembly to submit a request for an advisory opinion to the ICJ. The language could be similar to that presented following Kosovo's declaration of independence: are efforts by the Palestinian people to declare a state within the internationally recognized 1967 borders in accordance with international law? An ICJ advisory opinion would serve as another crucial, falling domino in the greater push toward statehood.

The controversial issue of Israeli settlements offers countless opportunities for the General Assembly to submit questions to the ICJ. In the aforementioned 2004 advisory opinion regarding Israel's security wall, the Court used the opportunity to highlight earlier U.N. resolutions condemning the illegality of Israeli settlement building in the West Bank and East Jerusalem. The ICJ also allowed Palestine to submit a written statement and participate in oral arguments in spite of the Court's statute restricting such participation to states parties or intergovernmental organizations. The Court justified the decision by "taking into account the fact that the General Assembly had granted Palestine a special status of observer and that [Palestine] was co-sponsor of the draft resolution requesting the advisory opinion." Participating in advisory opinions is a significant step toward full recognition as a state party with the power to bring a contentious dispute. Unlike blanket U.N. resolutions, such participation offers a more measured approach to the advancement of Palestinian sovereignty without the same risk of a backlash or full-scale conflict.

The International Criminal Court

Despite the relative youth of the ICC, which began operating in 2002, it is already considering engaging the Palestinian issue. The ICC has a limited jurisdiction that is still developing. Less than a decade old, the court had been criticized for undermining peace efforts in Uganda and Sudan. Yet that did not stop the ICC from considering whether it had jurisdiction to prosecute Israel for the alleged crimes it perpetrated in the Gaza Strip during its 2009 offensive. The PA has already argued its case and is awaiting chief prosecutor Luis Moreno-Ocampo's jurisdictional decision. If the ICC allows the suit to proceed, it will implicitly be recognizing Palestinian statehood. The Rome Statute states: "The Court may exercise its functions and powers, as provided in this Statute, on the territory of any State Party and, by special agreement, on the territory of any other State." Israel is not a State Party; thus Palestine would have to be a state for the court to exercise its jurisdiction. Article 12, "Preconditions to the exercise of jurisdiction," explicitly refers to "State" parties in all three paragraphs.

If the court dismisses the case, the Palestinians could petition for an investigation of ongoing Israeli "war crimes" committed in the Occupied Territories of the West Bank. By maintaining a continual presence on the court's agenda, the Palestinians would then invite the Israeli Supreme Court to respond. Less than two weeks before the ICJ handed down its decision regarding the legality of Israel's separation barrier, the Israeli Supreme Court issued its own opinion on the subject. The Court held that the separation fence's route in several areas caused disproportionate harm to Palestinian inhabitants, and ordered the government to reexamine the fence's route in those areas. If the Israeli Supreme Court responded to an anticipated ICJ decision, it will likely do the same in advance of any potential ruling by the ICC. The mere specter of a case before the ICC could thereby advance the international legal sovereignty of Palestine through the Israeli Supreme Court's judicial recognition of Palestinian grievances.

CONCLUSION—STRIKING A BALANCE

International organizations need to strike a balance between recognizing a people's grievances by openly acknowledging their statehood ambitions and contributing to interparty warfare between existing and aspiring states. Efforts by the United Nations and international courts thus need to be carefully calibrated, as the potential for sweeping declarations by the former drives the incremental steps of the latter.

The case of East Timor independence offers a cautionary tale to other aspiring states intent on advancing their international legal sovereignty through international bodies operating out of sync with one another. Four years after Portugal, the former colonizing power, levied a complaint against Australia on behalf of East Timor, the ICJ ultimately determined that it lacked jurisdiction due to Indonesia's refusal to grant consent to the Court to adjudicate the dispute. By a vote of fourteen to two, the Court decided not to rule on Portugal's claim that Australia had violated its duty to respect the former's role as the Administering Power and the Timorese people's right to self-determination, despite recognizing that such a right existed. The drawn-out legal dispute and muddled result likely contributed to the geopolitical instability that paved the way for increasing violence in East Timor during the final years of the twentieth century. The aspiring state ultimately needed a 1999 U.N.-sponsored referendum and three years under the U.N. Transitional Authority to achieve statehood.

Further research on the advancement of international legal sovereignty is therefore necessary to examine what conditions render an aspiring state most receptive to the involvement of international political organizations and courts—and the extent to which international bodies need to coordinate their efforts under alternative scenarios. What is already clear, however, is that international law holds tremendous power to help facilitate statehood ambitions. With regard to Palestine, the cumulative impact is already evident at the international level. On April 6, 2011, the International Monetary Fund declared that the Palestinian Authority has the capability to direct the economy of an independent state.

After *Chabad*: Enforcement in Cultural Property Disputes

GISELLE BARCIA

INTRODUCTION

Cultural property is a unique form of property. It may be at once personal property and real property; it is non-fungible; it carries deep historical value; it educates; it is part tangible, part transient. Cultural property is property that has

The Yale Journal of International Law, 37, 2: 463-478

acquired a special social status inextricably linked to a certain group's identity. Its value to the group is unconnected to how outsiders might assess its economic worth. If, as Hegel posited, property is an extension of personhood, then cultural property, for some, is an extension of nationhood.

Perhaps because of that unique status, specialized rules have developed, both domestically and internationally, to resolve some of the legal ambiguities inherent in "owning" cultural property. The United States, for example, has passed numerous laws protecting cultural property and has joined treaties and participated in international conventions affirming cultural property's special legal status. Those rules focus primarily on conflict *prevention* and rely upon strong protections to preempt cultural property disputes. But specialized cultural property laws, in the United States and elsewhere, pay scant attention to the issues that arise when prevention fails. Specifically, those laws neglect to provide adequate guidelines for cultural property litigation and enforcement.

That legal lacuna underlies the recent developments in the cultural property case *Agudas Chasidei Chabad v. Russian Federation,* more commonly known as *Chabad v. Russia.* This Comment addresses the problem of enforcement in international cultural property law, as manifested in *Chabad v. Russia.* The Chabad organization brought litigation against Russia in U.S. federal court to recover the Schneerson Collection, held at the Russian State Library. The Collection consists of sacred Jewish texts on Chabad Chassidic tradition amassed by successive generations of Rebbes beginning in 1772. The Collection has two components: the "Library," nationalized during the Bolshevik Revolution, and the "Archive," plundered during the Second World War. The Collection, then, is simultaneously a part of Russian heritage and integral to the historical, religious, and ethnic identity of Chabad. After a decades-long diplomatic campaign to recover ownership of the Collection, Chabad challenged the legality of those two takings in U.S. federal court in 2006. In July 2010, the Court of Appeals for the D.C. Circuit ruled in Chabad's favor.

Despite that judgment for Chabad, Russia refused to return the Collection. Russia's Foreign Ministry deemed the judgment "an unlawful decision" and stipulated that "[t]he Schneerson [Collection] has never belonged to Chabad." Most importantly, the Ministry stated, "[t]here is no agreement between Russia and the U.S. on mutual recognition and enforcement of civil judgments." Chabad, in fact, had established jurisdiction in the United States under the Foreign Sovereign Immunities Act (FSIA). Chabad's lawyers, in response to Russia's nonperformance, reportedly considered asking the court to confiscate art in the United States on loan from Russia "as a kind of legal hostage." Although U.S. law indemnifies against the loss of or damage to loaned works, the threat nevertheless spread rapidly until one of Chabad's attorneys finally intervened, stating that it would not seek to enforce the judgment through attachment of any indemnified cultural work.

Such assurance notwithstanding, Russian cultural officials warned the country's museums that artwork on loan in the United States could be confiscated. In early 2011, Russian museums canceled existing art loans to American institutions and issued a lending freeze. The National Gallery of Art in Washington, the J. Paul Getty Museum, the Los Angeles County Museum of Art, and the Metropolitan Museum of Art (the Met) were all left with costly gaps to fill for long-planned exhibitions. Despite assurances from many U.S. government officials, Russia's Minister of Culture issued a "verbal force majeure" in March 2011 to the Museum of Russian Icons in Clinton, Massachusetts. The museum had thirty-seven icons and artifacts on loan for its "Treasures From Moscow" exhibit, but Russia sent a curator immediately to supervise the objects' return. In the midst of the revocation from the Museum of Russian Icons, the Russian Special Presidential Envoy for International Cultural Cooperation, Mikhail Shvydkoy, stated that the Schneerson Collection would not be moved from Moscow, and that until the conflict with Chabad was resolved, there would be no exhibition of Russian cultural property in the United States.

A sort of cultural cold war began when American museums and institutions responded in kind to Russia's cancelations. In May 2011, the Met warned Russian museums that unless and until

Russia lifted the ban, the Met would not send costumes for a planned touring exhibition. Other major lending institutions followed the Met's lead, revealing that they, too, were considering discontinuing their own loans of cultural property to Russian museums and other cultural institutions. In response to the standoff, the parties returned to court, and Chabad chastised Russia's behavior in the suit: "Russia's conduct is an affront to this Court. It's a slap in the face of international and American law, let alone morality." Yet, after another year in court trying to enforce the judgment, Chabad has temporarily abandoned litigation and has again engaged Russia in negotiations outside the courtroom.

Chabad's struggle to enforce the U.S. decree escalated from a legal dispute to a political and cultural public relations battle between the two countries. The protracted conflict had a profound impact in the art world as well as the political world. It resulted in diplomatic tension between the United States and Russia, inefficiencies in the market for art loans, and, accordingly, decreased access to cultural property. The post-judgment conflict in *Chabad* also exposes a gap in cultural property law: an absence of clear guidelines on enforcement. It suggests that the existing options for enforcement are inappropriate for international cultural property disputes. Although cultural property law perhaps rightly focuses on dispute prevention, it must also provide an enforcement mechanism for international "conflicts of culture" litigation. Until then, parties in cultural property disputes should rely on an impartial, nonbinding recommendation before litigation.

As *Chabad* illustrates, cultural property is not above the law—it is subject to many of the same rules and regulations governing other kinds of property. But addressing international cultural property disputes like any other right of action under the FSIA will not motivate enforcement. Without a forceful international treaty addressing those issues, perhaps independent arbitration as a precursor to litigation could help curb some of these issues. Then, both parties in the dispute might exhaust fact-finding and argumentation and receive an impartial, preliminary judgment that could provide guidance on how to approach international litigation if necessary. Without enforcement mechanisms built into cultural property law, the struggles in *Chabad* will doubtless repeat themselves in future cultural property disputes involving foreign sovereigns.

ENFORCEMENT IN CULTURAL PROPERTY DISPUTES

Chabad illustrates that performance itself can sometimes carry deep cultural implications for the losing party. Those effects may be just as powerful as those on the winning side: for Chabad, repatriation of cultural property, and for Russia, the cultural heritage of the Russian Revolution and the trophies of the war campaign. Cultural property laws, both domestically and internationally, do not offer a mechanism for judicial enforcement in such conflicts.

If specific performance decrees already challenge enforcement, then cultural property specific performance decrees present an added layer of difficulty: the defining quality of cultural property—subjective valuation based on deep cultural, ethnic, or historical identification—renders enforcement even more problematic. The losing party, for example, may subjectively value keeping the cultural property (i.e., nonperformance) over returning it (i.e., complying with the specific performance decree), despite the possible legal ramifications in that calculus.

In *Chabad*, all of those obstacles to enforcement feature in the post-litigation conflict. Yet *Chabad* features other unique challenges as well. The court established jurisdiction over Russia, but Russia has refused to recognize that determination—a move that, regardless of its legal merits, further emphasizes the U.S. court's powerlessness to enforce its decisions in Russia. Russia may value nonperformance itself for reasons other than the cultural qualities of owning the Collection. Cultural property judgments amplify the difficulties already present in specific performance decrees. The uniqueness of cultural property distinguishes cultural property disputes from other kinds of litigation that also seek specific performance.

Resolution Methods for Cultural Property Disputes: Agreements, Arbitration, and Litigation

The method of resolution chosen for resolving a cultural property dispute—ranging from a bilateral agreement to arbitration and litigation—often influences the difficulty of subsequent enforcement.

Two parties who are willing to compromise can draft a bilateral agreement. One of the most successful bilateral agreements has been the import restriction on Italian archaeological material between the United States and Italy. In 2001, the two countries signed a bilateral agreement that created import restrictions on antiquities from Italy. The Department of Homeland Security, in cooperation with museums and cultural institutions, enforces those import restrictions. Throughout the last decade, the United States has returned more than 120 objects from public and private collections, most notably the Princeton University Art Museum and the Met. The agreement was renewed in 2006 and again in 2011; that most recent iteration created a new subcategory for specific coins. But the agreement allows some flexibility for rotation and lending between Italy and the institutions that lost antiquities. That model allows for a compromise with low risk of enforcement difficulties since both parties were willing to initiate a bargain in the first place.

When the two parties disagree and fail to reach an agreement, arbitration provides a seemingly ideal alternative for resolving their cultural property dispute. Given the tense nature of such disputes, arbitration offers a relatively informal route, with "the procedures of the decision-making process . . . shaped by the parties to fit their needs." Arbitration thus allows the parties to limit the amount of time and money they spend on resolving the dispute. Moreover, with the sensitive quality of cultural property disputes, arbitration offers the advantages of privacy and confidentiality, without upsetting any art markets.

Arbitration, however, is not the only way to secure a successful resolution in a cultural property dispute. Although advocates for the use of arbitration in cultural property disputes claim that litigation is "a most costly and destructive way to deal with [art-related] disputes," litigation can, in some cases, provide an effective, enforceable specific performance remedy. With public oversight of litigation, too, nonperformance can ignite media frenzy. That factor can pressure the losing party to perform. Although the challenges of specific performance will always be present, litigation of cultural property will not pose a substantially greater challenge than litigation of any other kind of property; in most circumstances, the underlying legal system will enforce the specific performance decree. Enforcing a specific performance decree in litigation becomes more challenging, however, when the suit is international—when existing conflicts of law and jurisdiction issues are more likely to complicate the cultural property dispute.

Challenges to Enforcement in *Chabad*

The circumstances of *Chabad* reveal enforcement difficulties beyond the typical challenges characteristic of specific performance suits. First, *Chabad* presents a disconnect between the actors in the lawsuit and the trend toward repatriation in cultural property disputes.

In *Chabad*, repatriation (giving the Collection to Chabad) is *also* internationalist (spreading resources beyond the borders of the source nation). Thus, the standard model of the cultural property dispute no longer applies. Usually, a foreign party from a resource-rich nation brings a suit to recover property in a resource-poor nation, where the cultural property has been bought through the black market. In the recent trend toward repatriation, the resource-poor nation applies the new, strict cultural property ownership laws of the resource-rich nation, and repatriation usually follows. That structure does not follow in *Chabad*. Instead, the foreign party (i.e., Russia, the source nation) possesses the cultural property and is forced into litigation in the resource-poor nation, which asserts ownership of the cultural property. Russia's 1919 and 1920 nationalization statutes, moreover, act as the traditional ownership statutes, but, in this case, they pose hindrances to repatriation, unlike in most cultural property cases. That odd mismatch of traditional motivations in *Chabad* led to the application of the FSIA in a cultural property dispute.

Second, *Chabad* presents unique "conflicts of culture," a fact that underscores the difficulty of enforcement. Enforcement has proved especially challenging in this case because Russia's *fulfillment* of the specific performance decree would, in a way, suggest a betrayal of its own cultural heritage. If Russia returns the Library, it undermines the legality of takings during nationalization in the Soviet Union. If Russia returns the Archive, it undermines its legal claim to all the cultural treasures it acquired during the Soviet "retrieval" of Nazi loot, jeopardizing a significant portion of its holdings in museums and cultural institutions. Meanwhile, if Russia retains the Schneerson Collection, then Chabad remains without a central piece of its cultural heritage. That tension between two cultural heritages further complicates the cultural property aspect of *Chabad*. There is no international mechanism to resolve such "conflicts of culture" that can emerge in cultural property disputes. *Chabad* represents a cultural cold war not only because of the standoff between American and Russian museums, but also because there will be a forfeiture of cultural heritage regardless of whether Russia performs.

The Foreign Sovereign Immunities Act

The FSIA became law on October 21, 1976. The purpose of the Act was to define jurisdiction in disputes involving foreign sovereigns and, especially, "[t]o define . . . the circumstances in which foreign states are immune from suit and in which execution may not be levied on their property, and for other purposes." The statute came as a reaction against complete deference to the sovereign immunity doctrine, in which U.S. courts had had to dismiss cases against foreign states when they pled sovereign immunity. The State Department's famous "Tate Letter" in 1952 first brought the problem of absolute sovereign immunity to light: with every dismissed plea also came a citizen who was denied access to litigation. As courts over the next two decades gradually moved away from absolute sovereign immunity, they granted sovereign immunity unevenly, and the FSIA sought to eliminate those inconsistent applications. Accordingly, the FSIA represents "a substantial contribution to the harmonization of international sovereign immunity law."

Given that history, the statute itself is consciously structured to favor foreign sovereigns. It assumes that foreign states are immune from the jurisdiction of U.S. courts. The law specifies that baseline assumption directly and also suggests its benefit: the assumption "serve[s] the interests of justice and would protect the rights of both foreign states and litigants in United States courts." That restrictive principle was consistent with the prevailing view on sovereign immunity in international law as well.

The statute goes on to stipulate the situations in which a foreign sovereign is *not* immune from U.S. jurisdiction. Exceptions occur when, for example, the foreign state actor (1) has waived its immunity, explicitly or implicitly; (2) has conducted commercial activity in the United States; (3) has taken property in violation of international law, and that property is connected to the commercial activity; (4) is situated in the United States; or (5) may be potentially liable for a tortious act or omission occurring in the United States.

The exception at issue in *Chabad* is the commercial activity exception to foreign immunity from U.S. jurisdiction. The Act defines "commercial activity" as "either a regular course of commercial conduct or a particular commercial transaction or act." The standard for determining commercial conduct is not by reference to its purpose, but rather "by reference to the nature of the course of conduct or particular transaction or act."

The commercial activity prong of the FSIA has a parallel in international law. However, although the Russian Federation and the United States are parties to the Hague Convention on the Service Abroad of Judicial and Extrajudicial Documents in Civil or Commercial Matters, Russia does not currently recognize this treaty relationship with the United States. In July 2003, Russia unilaterally suspended all judicial cooperation with the United States in civil and commercial matters.

Challenges to Enforcement Under the FSIA in *Chabad*

After the D.C. Circuit made its ruling in *Chabad*, Russia's Ministry of Culture released a statement on its website denying the legality of U.S. jurisdiction. "Unfortunately," the statement read, "the U.S. judge made an unlawful decision, which cannot be enforced in Russia, as a matter of fact. There is no agreement between Russia and the U.S. on mutual recognition and enforcement of civil judgments."

In April 2011, Chabad filed a motion to permit attachment and execution on the default judgment.

Chabad's lawyers threatened that the assets they planned to attach were Russian artworks on loan in the United States. Although Chabad's lawyers denied that they ever intended that attachment, in theory it logically follows from the attachment process in many FSIA judgment enforcement strategies: attaching cultural property in cultural property disputes is analogous to attaching financial assets held in the United States in commercial disputes. In this case, the Russian Federation has not returned the Schneerson Collection to Chabad. Chabad's lawyers, in turn, threatened to hold loaned Russian artworks hostage until Russia fulfills the judgment. That threat, of course, had a weak legal basis. The FSIA acknowledges that the ability to attach property is not absolute. If property is "entitled to enjoy the privileges, exemptions, and immunities provided by the International Organizations Immunities Act," then it is not available for attachment. Works of art, moreover, are independently protected; they are immune from seizure while on loan in the United States.

Although Chabad's threat to seize Russian artworks on loan in the United States was weak from a legal perspective, it nevertheless had very concrete repercussions. First, it prompted Russia to retain all the art it had planned to loan to U.S. museum exhibits, as well as to revoke artworks already loaned to one museum. Second, diplomatic relations between Russia and the United States have frayed. With the cultural feud simmering, the State Department initially only became involved in a diplomatic capacity, in hopes of quelling the tensions between the two nations. As tensions between the two sides failed to subside, in 2011 the United States became an interested party in the lawsuit.

The FSIA, then, served its purpose in *Chabad* in establishing U.S. federal jurisdiction over Russia's commercial activity with archival material in the United States. The purpose of the FSIA, however, is inconsistent with the structure of cultural property litigation. Although the FSIA was useful in *Chabad* in establishing jurisdiction, the problem of enforcement stubbornly remains.

CONCLUSION

As *Chabad* illustrates, blindly addressing international cultural property disputes under the commercial prong of the FSIA will not ensure enforcement. Cultural property law needs an international mechanism that directly addresses enforcement. Without such an enforcement mechanism built into international law, future cultural property disputes involving foreign sovereigns would stand to benefit from internationally required, nonbinding, independent arbitration. Then, perhaps, both parties to the dispute would exhaust fact-finding and argumentation and receive an impartial, preliminary judgment or recommendation for how to draft an agreement. With that recommendation, parties would be better advised on how to proceed in their dispute. It is possible that the parties would choose to limit the costs of protracted litigation and draft an agreement, according to the recommendation. If the parties choose to proceed in international litigation, then the preliminary judgment could inform future strategy. Regardless, the *Chabad* case reveals both the strength and limitation of the legal protections of cultural property: those protections require an enforcement mechanism tailored to the unique challenges of cultural property disputes.

VISUAL REVIEW

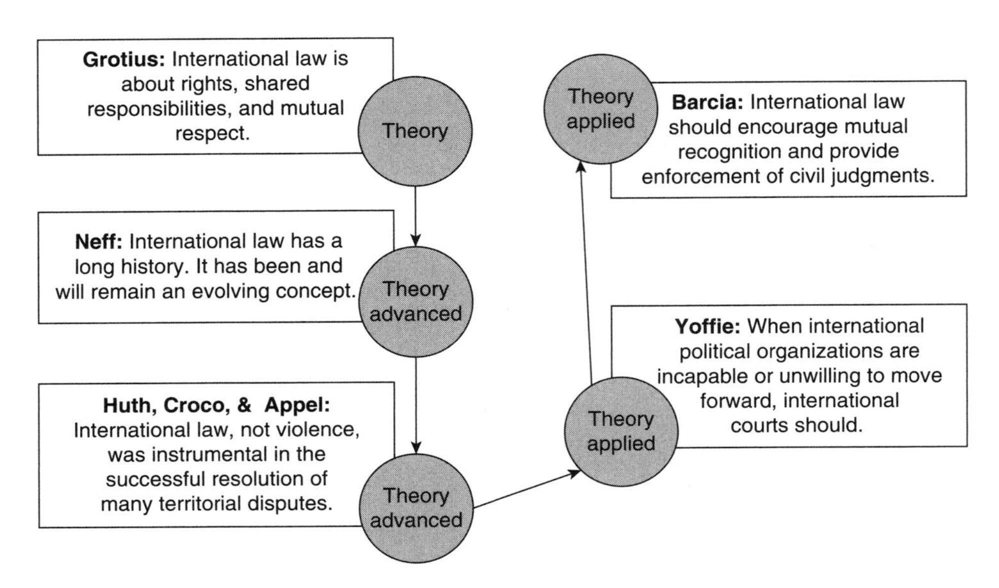

Section 7

International Political Economy: From the North-South Divide to Globalization

Jack Ma, founder of Alibaba, one of the most successful Internet companies in the world, smiles at the New York Stock Exchange. Chinese entrepreneurs have shown a remarkable ability to generate wealth. But will China's state-run capitalism demonstrate its lasting ability to generate innovation and embrace openness?
Source: Mark Lennihan/Associated Press

The Old IPE and the New

ROBERT O. KEOHANE

THE OLD IPE

When Susan Strange, Joseph Nye, Peter Katzenstein, Stephen Krasner, John Ruggie, and I started to explore IPE—Susan in the 1960s, Joe and Steve and I around 1970, Peter and John a few years later—there was no field. Very little research was being done. Most economists were ignoring politics, and international relations specialists saw political economy as "low politics," minor, boring, and incomprehensible. So our task—and opportunity—was first one of identification, then of broad interpretation. In his RIPE paper and his book, Professor Cohen provides an >account that closely corresponds to my memory of these early days. Identification of IPE as a proper subject of study was inaugurated in the United Kingdom by Strange's 1970 article in *International Affairs*, "International Economics and International Relations: A Case of Mutual Neglect", followed by her book, *Sterling and British Policy*, which traced connections between politics and economically historically. The key markers in the United States were three special issues of *International Organization* during the 1970s—on transnational relations, politics and economics, and foreign economic policies of advanced industrialized states.

It would be misleading to give the impression that these new formulations were entirely original. Indeed, we responded in part to what Richard Cooper, in *The Economics of Interdependence*, defined as the central problem of international economic cooperation: how to maintain openness while enabling states to retain sufficient autonomy to pursue legitimate objectives. In 1970 Charles Kindleberger edited a volume on the multinational corporation that contained an essay by Kenneth Waltz on the "myth" of interdependence that presented an important challenge for Nye and me, and in 1973 Kindleberger published *The World in Depression*, which made a great impact on all of us. In 1971 Raymond Vernon, who was at the Center for International Affairs at Harvard, published his book on multinational corporations, *Sovereignty at Bay*, as the culmination of years of work on this subject. Finally, Nye's work, and mine, were influenced by the contributions of Ernst B. Haas, particularly to the study of regional integration.

Nye and I contrasted what we called the "politics of interdependence" with then-dominant statist and security-oriented conceptions of international relations. We sketched out broad concepts—such as transnational relations, transgovernmental relations, and connections between asymmetrical interdependence and power. We characterized what Realists viewed as "reality" in world politics as an ideal type, and contrasted it with another ideal type, that of "complex interdependence." In situations of complex interdependence, we argued, there were multiple actors (rather than just states), multiple issues that were not necessarily hierarchically ordered, and force and the threat of force were not valuable tools of policy. In our view, neither the Realist model nor complex interdependence fully described world politics; but regional politics, and issue areas, varied in how close they were to one pole or the other.

Nye and I also elaborated a concept first brought to the IPE literature in another special issue of *International Organization* by Ruggie: that of *international regimes*. In *Power and Interdependence* we sought to describe and explain regime change, not merely theoretically but also with systematic empirical work on the politics of money and oceans, and on US relations with Australia and Canada. In his edited volume on foreign economic policies, which also appeared in 1977, Katzenstein demonstrated that our international relations analysis of what was now called "international political economy," or IPE, was too one-dimensional. Genuinely comparative analysis was required, since there was no single template of state responses to interdependence. Peter Gourevitch brilliantly pursued a related theme in his notable 1978 article on "the second image reversed", and Ruggie followed several years later with his creative concept of "embedded liberalism". During the 1970s this cluster of challenges to Realism was itself challenged most cogently by Robert Gilpin, most notably in his 1975 book on *U.S. Power and the Multinational Corporation*; and by Krasner, in a major article on "State Power and the Structure of International Trade".

We were young, exuberant, and friends with one another, neither expecting nor wanting general agreement. In her brilliant paper in this symposium, Kathleen McNamara captures well the richness—I would say, "joyous contestation"—of these debates. To us, the under-explored area of political economy offered irresistible territory for intellectual adventure and, one might say, conquest. To paraphrase the words of a famous Tammany Hall boss, "we seen our chance and we 'tuk' it." But in the context of contemporary political science, our empiricism was loose and sketchy, and we did not engage in sophisticated causal inference to support our grand theories.

FIVE BIG QUESTIONS ABOUT CHANGE

Suppose we asked, as Nye, Strange and I did in 1970: what are the big changes going on in the world political economy? Surely one could make a longer list, including such issues as outsourcing and migration, but I will mention five major changes:

1. *For the first time in human history, genuine economic development is taking place for much of the world's population.* East Asia (excluding China) led the way with four decades of high sustained growth, and growth has for over two decades been rapid in India and extremely fast in China. In more recent years, there have been indications that sustained rates of high growth may be emerging in parts of Latin America, although the situation in most of sub-Saharan Africa remains bleak. Our theories of IPE were constructed in a very different world: of "developed" and "developing" countries—the latter identified mostly by the fact that they were *not* developing. Indeed, for this reason perhaps, Gourevitch, Katzenstein, Nye, and I paid most of our attention to developed countries. Dependency theory, of course, emphasized—and it now seems, exaggerated—the structural differences between countries in the center and in the periphery. It is perhaps less obvious that the assumption of political as well as economic hierarchy between rich and poor is also deeply embedded in the theories of asymmetrical interdependence that Nye and I, and others developed, and in realist or quasi-realist theories of American hegemony and western dominance such as those of Krasner. I expect that our implicit hegemonic assumptions will continue to hamper our vision until scholars from Brazil, India and China, and other emerging great powers, become more prominent in the field.

2. *China in particular has become a huge player in international trade and finance,* as the manufacturing center of the world for a huge number of products in ordinary life. China was the largest economic power for centuries, before the industrial revolution, although in those times economic interdependence was much lower than now. China's re-entry into the world political economy since 1978 has been a huge shock to the system—it would seem to be at least comparable to the opening up of the North Atlantic grain trade in the 1870s so memorably studied by Gourevitch. An appropriate metaphor is that of an elephant jumping into a small pond. The effects are already evident in trade, and will increasingly be apparent on financial issues, since China's foreign reserves of well over $1 trillion constitute a political as well as an economic resource. In the West, scholars have been slow to take China sufficiently into account, although there are signs of change. Without China, we would be staging *Hamlet* without the Prince.

3. *Volatility in financial and energy markets has been extreme.* Kindleberger long ago emphasized the tendency of capitalism toward "manias,

panics, and crashes," and his insight was borne out again in 2008. At the same time, oil price shifts have again been driving shifts in power and asymmetrical interdependence. The sharp rise in oil prices up until mid-2008 contributed to policy changes such as the resistance of oil producers, from Venezuela to Russia and even to Saudi Arabia, to American demands; Brazil's leadership in ethanol production and technologies to use ethanol in automobiles; and China's drive for energy resources in Africa, which is undercutting "good governance" initiatives, and the influence of the international organizations like the World Bank, on that continent. In the 1970s, rising oil prices, and greater leverage for producers, had major effects on world politics, reflected in the creation and persistence of OPEC and the Arab oil embargo of 1973, which led to the creation of the International Energy Agency, associated with the OECD. But OPEC turned out to be ineffective and prices declined sharply in the mid-1980s and stayed well below late 1970s prices, in real terms, throughout the twentieth century. What will happen to them now is a great unknown. There is some discussion now of how oil affects democracy, civil conflict, and aggressive foreign policy, but the demand for analysis of the causes and consequences of oil price fluctuations surely exceeds by far the supply of serious scholarship on the subject.

4. *Truly global actors are now important in world politics.* Global corporations and NGOs such as Human Rights Watch, Oxfam, or Greenpeace are exemplary. As John Ruggie comments, "This isn't 'IPE' any more, and it certainly isn't 'CPE.' Global actors demand global rules." There is some work on this aspect of globalization, but we still have relatively little systematic knowledge about the implications of global civil society for political outcomes. Law faculties have paid attention: one of the most important research programs on this topic focuses on the new field of "global administrative law". Anne-Marie Slaughter has written about a "new world order," in which the state is disaggregated and networks of governmental sub-units, NGOs, private corporations, and a variety of regulatory and coordinating bodies become prominent participants in rule-making. John Ruggie has played an important policy role in this emerging global society and has also commented on the politics that ensues. It would be good if some IPE scholars could turn their attention, and their analytical tools, toward what might be called "GPE," or "Global Political Economy."

5. *Electronic technologies have become the basis for global communications.* We are aware of how such technologies have affected commerce, finance, and investment, but what about their effects on political power? To exercise influence, sets of individuals with common values or interests need to be able to communicate with one another, to form groups, and to act collectively. Indeed, Hannah Arendt once defined power as "the ability to act in common." Historically, such communication has been very difficult except through formal organizations, including the state, and all but impossible across state boundaries except with the aid of states. This formerly constant reality has been changing with incredible speed during the last two decades, but we have hardly begun to understand the implications of this momentous fact. One implication may be that collective action on a global scale, for good or ill, is easier than it has ever been before. In this sense, there is *more power* in the system than in the past. Since variations in power are crucial to world politics, the changes in electronic technology have to be important, but I have not seen recent work addressing these issues of communication and power.

In discussing these big questions, innovative scholars may discover rigorous and quantitative methods that can illuminate them. If so, more power to them. But we cannot afford to wait to address these questions for such methods, if they are not available now. As Finnemore and Farrell, and McNamara argue, more attention needs to be paid in graduate programs to rigorous qualitative methods, which have undergone a renaissance during the last 15 years; and as Katzenstein argues, more problem-oriented research is needed to maintain a focus on really important questions. I would urge scholars now active in the IPE field to spend more of their time pondering the big questions about change, and asking not only what the best existing research tells us about them, but what interpretive leaps may be necessary to point the way to more profound and relevant scholarship. I offer this admonition particularly to those scholars who have attained reputations for science and can therefore afford to let the wings of imagination spread.

Study major changes in world politics using a diverse portfolio of methods: this is the message of my brief essay. The best insights of the British school and contemporary American IPE are both valuable—so are contributions from historical and economic sociology, and from the "ideational turn" in much international relations scholarship. Our standards should be high; but a monoculture, as McNamara implies, depletes the soil from which it grows.

Normatively, I value the critical spirit of British IPE, and of Susan Strange and Robert Cox, because, like them, I am unwilling to accept the contemporary political-economic system as either natural or good. Injustice and inequality are endemic to IPE. But I also value the discipline of social science, as reflected in American IPE, which seeks to separate value judgments from positive analysis. I believe that in the long run, social scientists can have a more positive impact on the human condition through rigorous, persuasive analysis than through subjective criticism. But for us to help improve the human condition, we need to reflect on the big questions.

Concluding Notes on the Social Philosophy Towards Which the General Theory Might Lead

JOHN MAYNARD KEYNES

The outstanding faults of the economic society in which we live are its failure to provide for full employment and its arbitrary and inequitable distribution of wealth and incomes. The bearing of the foregoing theory on the first of these is obvious. But there are also two important respects in which it is relevant to the second.

Since the end of the nineteenth century significant progress towards the removal of very great disparities of wealth and income has been achieved through the instrument of direct taxation—income tax and surtax and death duties—especially in Great Britain. Many people would wish to see this process carried much further, but they are deterred by two considerations; partly by the fear of making skilful evasions too much worth while and also of diminishing unduly the motive towards risk-taking, but mainly, I think, by the belief that the growth of capital depends upon the strength of the motive towards individual saving and that for a large proportion of this growth we are dependent on the savings of the rich out of their superfluity. Our argument does not affect the first of these considerations. But it may considerably modify our attitude towards the second. For we have seen that, up to the point where full employment prevails, the growth of capital depends not at all on a low propensity to consume but is, on the contrary, held back by it; and only in conditions of full employment is a low propensity to consume conducive to the growth of capital. Moreover, experience suggests that in existing conditions saving by institutions and through sinking funds is more than adequate, and that measures for the redistribution of incomes in a way likely to raise the propensity to consume may prove positively favourable to the growth of capital.

New York: Harcourt, Brace & World.

The existing confusion of the public mind on the matter is well illustrated by the very common belief that the death duties are responsible for a reduction in the capital wealth of the country. Assuming that the State applies the proceeds of these duties to its ordinary outgoings so that taxes on incomes and consumption are correspondingly reduced or avoided, it is, of course, true that a fiscal policy of heavy death duties has the effect of increasing the community's propensity to consume. But inasmuch as an increase in the habitual propensity to consume will in general (i.e. except in conditions of full employment) serve to increase at the same time the inducement to invest, the inference commonly drawn is the exact opposite of the truth.

Thus our argument leads towards the conclusion that in contemporary conditions the growth of wealth, so far from being dependent on the abstinence of the rich, as is commonly supposed, is more likely to be impeded by it. One of the chief social justifications of great inequality of wealth is, therefore, removed. I am not saying that there are no other reasons, unaffected by our theory, capable of justifying some measure of inequality in some circumstances. But it does dispose of the most important of the reasons why hitherto we have thought it prudent to move carefully. This particularly affects our attitude towards death duties: for there are certain justifications for inequality of incomes which do not apply equally to inequality of inheritances.

For my own part, I believe that there is social and psychological justification for significant inequalities of incomes and wealth, but not for such large disparities as exist today. There are valuable human activities which require the motive of money-making and the environment of private wealth-ownership for their full fruition. Moreover, dangerous human proclivities can be canalised into comparatively harmless channels by the existence of opportunities for money-making and private wealth, which, if they cannot be satisfied in this way, may find their outlet in cruelty, the reckless pursuit of personal power and authority, and other forms of self-aggrandisement. It is better that a man should tyrannise over his bank balance than over his fellow-citizens; and whilst the former is sometimes denounced as being but a means to the latter, sometimes at least it is an alternative. But it is not necessary for the stimulation of these activities and the satisfaction of these proclivities that the game should be played for such high stakes as at present. Much lower stakes will serve the purpose equally well, as soon as the players are accustomed to them. The task of transmuting human nature must not be confused with the task of managing it. Though in the ideal commonwealth men may have been taught or inspired or bred to take no interest in the stakes, it may still be wise and prudent statesmanship to allow the game to be played, subject to rules and limitations, so long as the average man, or even a significant section of the community, is in fact strongly addicted to the money-making passion.

There is, however, a second, much more fundamental inference from our argument which has a bearing on the future of inequalities of wealth; namely, our theory of the rate of interest. The justification for a moderately high rate of interest has been found hitherto in the necessity of providing a sufficient inducement to save. But we have shown that the extent of effective saving is necessarily determined by the scale of investment and that the scale of investment is promoted by a low rate of interest, provided that we do not attempt to stimulate it in this way beyond the point which corresponds to full employment. Thus it is to our best advantage to reduce the rate of interest to that point relatively to the schedule of the marginal efficiency of capital at which there is full employment.

There can be no doubt that this criterion will lead to a much lower rate of interest than has ruled hitherto; and, so far as one can guess at the schedules of the marginal efficiency of capital corresponding to increasing amounts of capital, the rate of interest is likely to fall steadily, if it should be practicable to maintain conditions of more or less continuous full employment unless, indeed, there is an excessive change in the aggregate propensity to consume (including the State).

I feel sure that the demand for capital is strictly limited in the sense that it would not be difficult to increase the stock of capital up to a point where its marginal efficiency had fallen to a very low figure. This would not mean that the use of capital instruments would cost almost nothing, but only that the return from them would have to cover little more than their exhaustion by wastage and obsolescence together with some margin to cover risk and the exercise of skill and judgment. In short, the aggregate return from durable goods in the course of their life would, as in the case of short-lived goods, just cover their labour costs of production *plus* an allowance for risk and the costs of skill and supervision.

Now, though this state of affairs would be quite compatible with some measure of individualism, yet it would mean the euthanasia of the rentier, and, consequently, the euthanasia of the cumulative oppressive power of the capitalist to exploit the scarcity-value of capital. Interest today rewards no genuine sacrifice, any more than does the rent of land. The owner of capital can obtain interest because capital is scarce, just as the owner of land can obtain rent because land is scarce. But whilst there may be intrinsic reasons for the scarcity of land, there are no intrinsic reasons for the scarcity of capital. An intrinsic reason for such scarcity, in the sense of a genuine sacrifice which could only be called forth by the offer of a reward in the shape of interest, would not exist, in the long run, except in the event of the individual propensity to consume proving to be of such a character that net saving in conditions of full employment comes to an end before capital has become sufficiently abundant. But even so, it will still be possible for communal saving through the agency of the State to be maintained at a level which will allow the growth of capital up to the point where it ceases to be scarce.

I see, therefore, the rentier aspect of capitalism as a transitional phase which will disappear when it has done its work. And with the disappearance of its rentier aspect much else in it besides will suffer a sea-change. It will be, moreover, a great advantage of the order of events which I am advocating, that the euthanasia of the rentier, of the functionless investor, will be nothing sudden, merely a gradual but prolonged continuance of what we have seen recently in Great Britain, and will need no revolution.

Thus we might aim in practice (there being nothing in this which is unattainable) at an increase in the volume of capital until it ceases to be scarce, so that the functionless investor will no longer receive a bonus; and at a scheme of direct taxation which allows the intelligence and determination and executive skill of the financier, the entrepreneur *et hoc genus omne* (who are certainly so fond of their craft that their labour could be obtained much cheaper than at present), to be harnessed to the service of the community on reasonable terms of reward.

At the same time we must recognise that only experience can show how far the common will, embodied in the policy of the State, ought to be directed to increasing and supplementing the inducement to invest; and how far it is safe to stimulate the average propensity to consume, without foregoing our aim of depriving capital of its scarcity-value within one or two generations. It may turn out that the propensity to consume will be so easily strengthened by the effects of a falling rate of interest, that full employment can be reached with a rate of accumulation little greater than at present. In this event a scheme for the higher taxation of large incomes and inheritances might be open to the objection that it would lead to full employment with a rate of accumulation which was reduced considerably below the current level. I must not be supposed to deny the possibility, or even the probability, of this outcome. For in such matters it is rash to predict how the average man will react to a changed environment. If, however, it should prove easy to secure an approximation to full employment with a rate of accumulation not much greater than at present, an outstanding problem will at least have been solved. And it would remain for separate decision on what scale and by what means it is right and reasonable to call on the living generation to restrict their consumption, so as to establish in course of time, a state of full investment for their successors.

In some other respects the foregoing theory is moderately conservative in its implications. For whilst it indicates the vital importance of establishing certain central controls in matters which are now left in the main to individual initiative, there are wide fields of activity which are unaffected. The State will have to exercise a guiding influence on the propensity to consume partly through its scheme of taxation, partly by fixing the rate of interest, and partly, perhaps, in other ways. Furthermore, it seems unlikely that the influence of banking policy on the rate of interest will be sufficient by itself to determine an optimum rate of investment. I conceive, therefore, that a somewhat comprehensive socialisation of investment will prove the only means of securing an approximation to full employment; though this need not exclude all manner of compromises and of devices by which public authority will co-operate with private initiative. But beyond this no obvious case is made out for a system of State Socialism which would embrace most of the economic life of the community. It is not the ownership of the instruments of production which it is important for the State to assume. If the State is able to determine the aggregate amount of resources devoted to augmenting the instruments and the basic rate of reward to those who own them, it will have accomplished all that is necessary. Moreover, the necessary measures of socialisation can be introduced gradually and without a break in the general traditions of society.

Our criticism of the accepted classical theory of economics has consisted not so much in finding logical flaws in its analysis as in pointing out that its tacit assumptions are seldom or never satisfied, with the result that it cannot solve the economic problems of the actual world. But if our central controls succeed in establishing an aggregate volume of output corresponding to full employment as nearly as is practicable, the classical theory comes into its own again from this point onwards. If we suppose the volume of output to be given, i.e. to be determined by forces outside the classical scheme of thought, then there is no objection to be raised against the classical analysis of the manner in which private self-interest will determine what in particular is produced, in what proportions the factors of production will be combined to produce it, and how the value of the final product will be distributed between them. Again, if we have dealt otherwise with the problem of thrift, there is no objection to be raised against the modern classical theory as to the degree of consilience between private and public advantage in conditions of perfect and imperfect competition respectively. Thus, apart from the necessity of central controls to bring about an adjustment between the propensity to consume and the inducement to invest, there is no more reason to socialise economic life than there was before.

To put the point concretely, I see no reason to suppose that the existing system seriously misemploys the factors of production which are in use. There are, of course, errors of foresight; but these would not be avoided by centralising decisions. When 9,000,000 men are employed out of 10,000,000 willing and able to work, there is no evidence that the labour of these 9,000,000 men is misdirected. The complaint against the present system is not that these 9,000,000 men ought to be employed on different tasks, but that tasks should be available for the remaining 1,000,000 men. It is in determining the volume, not the direction, of actual employment that the existing system has broken down.

Thus I agree with Gesell that the result of filling in the gaps in the classical theory is not to dispose of the "Manchester System," but to indicate the nature of the environment which the free play of economic forces requires if it is to realise the full potentialities of production. The central controls necessary to ensure full employment will, of course, involve a large extension of the traditional functions of government. Furthermore, the modern classical theory has itself called attention to various conditions in which the free play of economic forces may need to be curbed or guided. But there will still remain a wide field for the exercise of private initiative and responsibility. Within this field the traditional advantages of individualism will still hold good.

Let us stop for a moment to remind ourselves what these advantages are. They are partly advantages of efficiency—the advantages of decentralisation and of the play of self-interest. The advantage to efficiency of the decentralisation of decisions and of individual responsibility is even greater, perhaps, than the nineteenth century supposed; and the reaction against the appeal to self-interest may have gone too far. But, above all, individualism, if it can be purged of its defects and its abuses, is the best safeguard of personal liberty in the sense that, compared with any other system, it greatly widens the field for the exercise of personal choice. It is also the best safeguard of the variety of life, which emerges precisely from this extended field of personal choice, and the loss of which is the greatest of all the losses of the homogeneous or totalitarian state. For this variety preserves the traditions which embody the most secure and successful choices of former generations; it colours the present with the diversification of its fancy; and, being the handmaid of experiment as well as of tradition and of fancy, it is the most powerful instrument to better the future.

Whilst, therefore, the enlargement of the functions of government, involved in the task of adjusting to one another the propensity to consume and the inducement to invest, would seem to a nineteenth-century publicist or to a contemporary American financier to be a terrific encroachment on individualism. I defend it, on the contrary, both as the only practicable means of avoiding the destruction of existing economic forms in their entirety and as the condition of the successful functioning of individual initiative.

For if effective demand is deficient, not only is the public scandal of wasted resources intolerable, but the individual enterpriser who seeks to bring these resources into action is operating with the odds loaded against him. The game of hazard which he plays is furnished with many zeros, so that the players *as a whole* will lose if they have the energy and hope to deal all the cards. Hitherto the increment of the world's wealth has fallen short of the aggregate of positive individual savings; and the difference has been made up by the losses of those whose courage and initiative have not been supplemented by exceptional skill or unusual good fortune. But if effective demand is adequate, average skill and average good fortune will be enough.

The authoritarian state systems of today seem to solve the problem of unemployment at the expense of efficiency and of freedom. It is certain that the world will not much longer tolerate the unemployment which, apart from brief intervals of excitement, is associated and in my opinion, inevitably associated with present-day capitalistic individualism. But it may be possible by a right analysis of the problem to cure the disease whilst preserving efficiency and freedom.

I have mentioned in passing that the new system might be more favourable to peace than the old has been. It is worth while to repeat and emphasise that aspect.

War has several causes. Dictators and others such, to whom war offers, in expectation at least, a pleasurable excitement, find it easy to work on the natural bellicosity of their peoples. But, over and above this, facilitating their task of fanning the popular flame, are the economic causes of war, namely, the pressure of population and the competitive struggle for markets. It is the second factor, which probably played a predominant part in the nineteenth century, and might again, that is germane to this discussion.

I have pointed out in the preceding chapter that, under the system of domestic laissez-faire and an international gold standard such as was orthodox in the latter half of the nineteenth century, there was no means open to a government whereby to mitigate economic distress at home except through the competitive struggle for markets. For all measures helpful to a state of chronic or intermittent under-employment were ruled out, except measures to improve the balance of trade on income account.

Thus, whilst economists were accustomed to applaud the prevailing international system as furnishing the fruits of the international division of labour and harmonising at the same time the interests of different nations, there lay concealed a less benign influence; and those statesmen were moved by common sense and a correct apprehension of the true course of events, who believed that if a rich, old country were to neglect the struggle for markets its prosperity would droop and fail. But if nations can learn to provide themselves with full employment by their domestic policy (and, we must add, if they can also attain equilibrium in the trend of their population), there need be no important economic forces calculated to set the interest of one country against that of its neighbours. There would still be room for the international division of labour and for international lending in appropriate conditions. But there would no longer be a pressing motive why one country need force its wares on another or repulse the offerings of its neighbour, not because this was necessary to enable it to pay for what it wished to purchase, but with the express object of upsetting the equilibrium of payments so as to develop a balance of trade in its own favour. International trade would cease to be what it is, namely, a desperate expedient to maintain employment at home by forcing sales on foreign markets and restricting purchases, which, if successful, will merely shift the problem of unemployment to the neighbour which is worsted in the struggle, but a willing and unimpeded exchange of goods and services in conditions of mutual advantage.

Is the fulfilment of these ideas a visionary hope? Have they insufficient roots in the motives which govern the evolution of political society? Are the interests which they will thwart stronger and more obvious than those which they will serve?

I do not attempt an answer in this place. It would need a volume of a different character from this one to indicate even in outline the practical measures in which they might be gradually clothed. But if the ideas are correct—an hypothesis on which the author himself must necessarily base what he writes—it would be a mistake, I predict, to dispute their potency over a period of time. At the present moment people are unusually expectant of a more fundamental diagnosis; more particularly ready to receive it; eager to try it out, if it should be even plausible. But apart from this contemporary mood, the ideas of economists and political philosophers, both when they are right and when they are wrong, are more powerful than is commonly understood. Indeed the world is ruled by little else. Practical men, who believe themselves to be quite exempt from any intellectual influences, are usually the slaves of some defunct economist. Madmen in authority, who hear voices in the air, are distilling their frenzy from some academic scribbler of a few years back. I am sure that the power of vested interests is vastly exaggerated compared with the gradual encroachment of ideas. Not, indeed, immediately, but after a certain interval; for in the field of economic and political philosophy there are not many who are influenced by new theories after they are twenty-five or thirty years of age, so that the ideas which civil servants and politicians and even agitators apply to current events are not likely to be the newest. But, soon or late, it is ideas, not vested interests, which are dangerous for good or evil.

International Financial and Trade Arrangements

MILTON FRIEDMAN

The problem of international monetary arrangements is the relation among different national currencies: the terms and conditions under which individuals are able to convert U.S. dollars to pounds sterling, Canadian dollars to U.S. dollars, and so on. This problem is closely connected with the control of money. It is connected also with governmental policies about international trade, since control over international trade is one technique for affecting international payments.

THE IMPORTANCE OF INTERNATIONAL MONETARY ARRANGEMENTS FOR ECONOMIC FREEDOM

Despite its technical character and forbidding complexity, the subject of international monetary arrangements is one that a liberal cannot afford to neglect. It is not too much to say that the most serious short-run threat to economic freedom in the United States today—aside, of course, from the outbreak of World War III—is that we shall be led to adopt far-reaching economic controls in order to "solve" balance of payments problems. Interferences with international trade appear innocuous; they can get the support of people who are otherwise apprehensive of interference by government into economic affairs; many a business man even regards them as part of the "American Way of Life"; yet there are few interferences which are capable of spreading so far and ultimately being so destructive of free enterprise. There is much experience to suggest that the most effective way to convert a market economy into an authoritarian economic society is to start by imposing direct controls on foreign exchange. This one step leads inevitably to the rationing of imports, to control over domestic production that uses imported products or that produces substitutes for imports, and so on in a never-ending spiral. Yet even so generally staunch a champion of free enterprise as Senator Barry Goldwater has at times been led, when discussing the so-called "gold flow," to suggest that restrictions on transactions in foreign exchange may be necessary as a "cure." This "cure" would be vastly worse than the disease.

There is seldom anything truly new under the sun in economic policy, where the allegedly new generally turns out to be the discard of a prior century in flimsy disguise. Unless I am mistaken, however, full-fledged exchange controls and so-called "inconvertibility of currencies" are an exception and their origin reveals their authoritarian promise. To the best of my knowledge they were invented by Hjalmar Schacht in the early years of the Nazi regime. On many occasions in the past, of course, currencies have been described as inconvertible. But what the word then meant was that the government of the day was unwilling or unable to convert paper currency into gold or silver, or whatever the monetary commodity was, at the legally stipulated rate. It seldom meant that a country prohibited its citizens or residents from trading pieces of paper promising to pay specified sums in the monetary unit of that country for corresponding pieces of paper expressed in the monetary unit of another country—or for that matter for coin or bullion. During the Civil War in the United States and for a decade and a half thereafter, for example, U.S. currency was inconvertible in the sense that the holder of a greenback could not turn it in to the Treasury and get a fixed amount of gold for it. But throughout the period he was free to buy gold at the market price or to buy and sell British pounds for U.S. greenbacks at any price mutually agreeable to the two parties. In the United States, the dollar has been inconvertible in the older sense ever since 1933. It has been illegal for American citizens to hold gold or to buy and sell gold. The dollar has not been inconvertible in the newer sense. But unfortunately we seem to be adopting policies that are highly likely, sooner or later, to drive us in that direction.

FLOATING EXCHANGE RATES AS THE FREE MARKET SOLUTION

There are only two mechanisms that are consistent with a free market and free trade. One is a fully automatic international gold standard. This, as we saw in the preceding chapter, is neither feasible nor desirable. In any event, we cannot adopt it by ourselves. The other is a system of freely floating exchange rates determined in the market by private transactions without governmental intervention. This is the proper free-market counterpart to the monetary rule advocated in the preceding chapter. If we do not adopt it, we shall inevitably fail to expand the area of free trade and shall sooner or later be induced to impose widespread direct controls over trade. In this area, as in others, conditions can and do change unexpectedly. It may well be that we shall muddle through the difficulties that are facing us as this is written (April, 1962) and indeed that we may find ourselves in a surplus rather than deficit position, accumulating reserves rather than losing them. If so, this will only mean that other countries will be faced with the necessity of imposing controls. When, in 1950, I wrote an article proposing a system of floating exchange rates, it was in the context of European payments difficulties accompanying the then alleged "dollar shortage." Such a turnabout is always possible. Indeed, it is the very difficulty of predicting when and how such changes occur that is the basic argument for a free market. Our problem is not to "solve" a balance of payments problem. It is to solve the balance of payments problem by adopting a mechanism that will enable free market forces to provide a prompt, effective, and automatic response to changes in conditions affecting international trade.

Though freely floating exchange rates seem so clearly to be die appropriate free-market mechanism, they are strongly supported only by a fairly small number of liberals, mostly professional economists, and are opposed by many liberals who reject governmental intervention and governmental price-fixing in almost every other area. Why is this so? One reason is simply the tyranny of the status quo. A second reason is the confusion between a real gold standard and a pseudo gold standard. Under a real gold standard, the prices of different national currencies in terms of one another would be very nearly rigid since the different currencies would simply be different names for different amounts of gold. It is easy to make the mistake of supposing that we can get the substance of the real gold standard by the mere adoption of the form of a nominal obeisance to gold—the adoption of a pseudo gold standard under which the prices of different national currencies in terms of one another are rigid only because they are pegged prices in rigged markets. A third reason is the inevitable tendency for everyone to be in favor of a free market for everyone else, while regarding himself as deserving of special treatment. This particularly affects bankers in respect of exchange rates. They like to have a guaranteed price. Moreover, they are not familiar with the market devices that would arise to cope with fluctuations in exchange rates. The firms that would specialize in speculation and arbitrage in a free market for exchange do not exist. This is one way the tyranny of the status quo is enforced. In Canada, for example, some bankers, after a decade of a free rate which gave them a different status quo, were in the forefront of those favoring its continuation and objecting to either a pegged rate or government manipulation of the rate.

More important than any of these reasons, I believe, is a mistaken interpretation of experience with floating rates, arising out of a statistical fallacy that can be seen easily in a standard example. Arizona is clearly the worst place in the U.S. for a person with tuberculosis to go because the death rate from tuberculosis is higher in Arizona than in any other state. The fallacy is in this case obvious. It is less obvious in connection with exchange rates. When countries have gotten into severe financial difficulties through internal monetary mismanagement or for any other reason, they have had ultimately to resort to flexible exchange rates. No amount of exchange control or direct restrictions on trade enabled them to peg an exchange rate that was far out of line with economic realities. In consequence, it is unquestionably true that floating exchange rates have frequently been associated with financial and economic instability—as, for example, in hyperinflations, or severe but not hyperinflations such as have occurred in many South American countries. It is easy to conclude, as many have, that floating exchange rates produce such instability.

Being in favor of floating exchange rates does not mean being in favor of unstable exchange rates. When we support a free price system at home, this does not imply that we favor a system in which prices fluctuate wildly up and down. What we want is a system in which prices are free to fluctuate but in which the forces determining them are sufficiently stable so that in fact prices move within moderate ranges. This is equally true of a system of floating exchange rates. The ultimate objective is a world in which exchange rates, while free to vary, are, in fact, highly stable because basic economic policies and conditions are stable. Instability of exchange rates is a symptom of instability in the underlying economic structure. Elimination of this symptom by administrative freezing of exchange rates cures none of the underlying difficulties and only makes adjustments to them more painful.

THE POLICY MEASURES NECESSARY FOR A FREE MARKET IN GOLD AND FOREIGN EXCHANGE

It may help bring out in concrete terms the implications of this discussion if I specify in detail the measures that I believe the U.S. should take to promote a truly free market in both gold and foreign exchange.

1. The U.S. should announce that it no longer commits itself to buy or sell gold at any fixed price.
2. Present laws making it illegal for individuals to own gold or to buy and sell gold should be repealed, so that there are no restrictions on the price at which gold can be bought or sold in terms of any other commodity or financial instrument, including national currencies.
3. The present law specifying that the Reserve System must hold gold certificates equal to 25 per cent of its liabilities should be repealed.
4. A major problem in getting rid completely of the gold price-support program, as of the wheat price-support program, is the transitional one of what to do with accumulated government stocks. In both cases, my own view is that the government should immediately restore a free market by instituting steps 1 and 2, and should ultimately dispose of all of its stocks. However, it would probably be desirable for the government to dispose of its stocks only gradually. For wheat, five years has always seemed to me a long enough period, so I have favored the government committing itself to dispose of one-fifth of its stocks in each of five years. This period seems reasonably satisfactory for gold as well. Hence, I propose that the government auction off its gold stocks on the free market over a five-year period. With a free gold market, individuals may well find warehouse certificates for gold more useful than actual gold. But if so, private enterprise can certainly provide the service of storing the gold and issuing certificates. Why should gold storage and the issuance of warehouse certificates be a nationalized industry?
5. The U.S. should announce also that it will not proclaim any official exchange rates between the dollar and other currencies and in addition that it will not engage in any speculative or other activities aimed at influencing exchange rates. These would then be determined in free markets.
6. These measures would conflict with our formal obligation as a member of the International Monetary Fund to specify an official parity for the dollar. However, the Fund found it possible to reconcile Canada's failure to specify a parity with its Articles and to give its approval to a floating rate for Canada. There is no reason why it cannot do the same for the U.S.
7. Other nations might choose to peg their currencies to the dollar. That is their business and there is no reason for us to object so long as we undertake no obligations to buy or sell their currency at a fixed price. They will be able to succeed in pegging their currency to ours only by one or more of the measures listed earlier—drawing on or accumulating reserves, co-ordinating their internal policy with U.S. policy, tightening or loosening direct controls on trade.

ELIMINATING U.S. RESTRICTIONS ON TRADE

A system such as that just outlined would solve the balance of payments problem once and for all. No deficit could possibly arise to require high government officials to plead with foreign countries and central banks for assistance, or to require an American President to behave like a harried country banker trying to restore confidence in his bank, or to force an administration preaching free trade to impose import restrictions, or to sacrifice important national and personal interests to the trivial question of the name of the currency in which payments are made. Payments would always balance because a price—the foreign exchange rate—would be free to produce a balance. No one could sell dollars unless he could find someone to buy them and conversely.

A system of floating exchange rates would therefore enable us to proceed effectively and directly toward complete free trade in goods and services—barring only such deliberate interference as may be justified on strictly political and military grounds; for example, banning the sale of strategic goods to communist countries. So long as we are firmly committed to the strait jacket of fixed exchange rates, we cannot move definitively to free trade. The possibility of tariffs or direct controls must be retained as an escape valve in case of necessity.

A system of floating exchange rates has the side advantage that it makes almost transparently obvious the fallacy in the most popular argument against free trade, the argument that "low" wages elsewhere make tariffs somehow necessary to protect "high" wages here. Is 100 yen an hour to a Japanese worker high or low compared with $4 an hour to an American worker? That all depends on the exchange rate. What determines the exchange rate? The necessity of making payments balance; i.e., of making the amount we can sell to the Japanese roughly equal to the amount they can sell to us.

Suppose for simplicity that Japan and the U.S. are the only two countries involved in trade and that at some exchange rate, say 1,000 yen to the dollar, Japanese could produce every single item capable of entering into foreign trade more cheaply than the U.S. At that exchange rate the Japanese could sell much to us, we, nothing to them. Suppose we pay them in paper dollars. What would the Japanese exporters do with the dollars? They cannot eat them, wear them, or live in them. If they were willing simply to hold them, then die printing industry—printing the dollar bills—would be a magnificent export industry. Its output would enable us all to have the good things of life provided nearly free by the Japanese.

But, of course, Japanese exporters would not want to hold die dollars. They would want to sell them for yen. By assumption, there is nothing they can buy for a dollar that they cannot buy for less than the 1,000 yen that a dollar will by assumption exchange for. This is equally true for other Japanese. Why then would any holder of yen give up 1,000 yen for a dollar that will buy less in goods than the 1,000 yen will? No one would. In order for die Japanese exporter to exchange his dollars for yen, he would have to offer to take fewer yen—the price of the dollar in terms of the yen would have to be less than 1,000, or of the yen in terms of the dollar more than 1 mill. But at 500 yen to the dollar Japanese goods are twice as expensive to Americans as before; American goods half as expensive to the Japanese. The Japanese will no longer be able to undersell American producers on all items.

Where will the price of the yen in terms of dollars settle? At whatever level is necessary to assure that all exporters who desire to do so can sell the dollars they get for the goods they export to America to importers who use them to buy goods in America. To speak loosely, at whatever level is necessary to assure that the value of U.S. exports (in dollars) is equal to the value of U.S. imports (again in dollars). Loosely, because a precise statement would have to take into account capital transactions, gifts, and so on. But these do not alter the central principle.

It will be noted that this discussion says nothing about the level of living of the Japanese worker or the American worker. These are irrelevant. If the Japanese worker has a lower standard of living than the American, it is because he is less productive on the average than the American, given the training he has, the amount of capital and land and so on that he has to work with. If the American worker is, let us say, on the average four times as productive as the Japanese worker, it is wasteful to use him to produce any goods in the production of which he is less than four times as productive. It is better to produce those goods at which he is more productive and trade them for the goods at which he is less productive. Tariffs do not assist the Japanese worker to raise his standard of living or protect the high standard of the American worker. On the contrary, they lower the Japanese standard and keep the American standard from being as high as it could be.

Given that we should move to free trade, how should we do so? The method that we have tried to adopt is reciprocal negotiation of tariff reductions with other countries. This seems to me a wrong procedure. In the first place, it ensures a slow pace. He moves fastest who moves alone. In the second place, it fosters an erroneous view of the basic problem. It makes it appear as if tariffs help the country imposing them but hurt other countries, as if when we reduce a tariff we give up something good and should get something in return in the form of a reduction in the tariffs imposed by other countries. In truth, the situation is quite different. Our tariffs hurt us as well as other countries. We would be benefited by dispensing with our tariffs even if other countries did not.[1] We would of course be benefited even more if they reduced theirs but our benefiting does not require that they reduce theirs. Self interests coincide and do not conflict.

I believe that it would be far better for us to move to free trade unilaterally, as Britain did in the nineteenth century when it repealed the corn laws. We, as they did, would experience an enormous accession of political and economic power. We are a great nation and it ill behooves us to require reciprocal benefits from Luxembourg before we reduce a tariff on Luxembourg products, or to throw thousands of Chinese refugees suddenly out of work by imposing import quotas on textiles from Hong Kong. Let us live up to our destiny and set the pace not be reluctant followers.

I have spoken in terms of tariffs for simplicity but, as already noted, non-tariff restrictions may now be more serious impediments to trade than tariffs. We should remove both. A prompt yet gradual program would be to legislate that all import quotas or other quantitative restrictions, whether imposed by us or "voluntarily" accepted by other countries, be raised 20 per cent a year until they are so high that they become irrelevant and can be abandoned, and that all tariffs be reduced by one-tenth of the present level in each of the next ten years.

There are few measures we could take that would do more to promote the cause of freedom at home and abroad. Instead of making grants to foreign governments in the name of economic aid — and thereby promoting socialism—while at the same time imposing restrictions on the products they succeed in producing—and thereby hindering free enterprise—we could assume a consistent and principled stance. We could say to the rest of the world: We believe in freedom and intend to practice it. No one can force you to be free. That is your business. But we can offer you full co-operation on equal terms to all. Our market is open to you. Sell here what you can and wish to. Use the proceeds to buy what you wish. In this way co-operation among individuals can be world wide yet free.

Beyond the Washington Consensus: A New Bandung?

GIOVANNI ARRIGHI AND LU ZHANG

This chapter analyzes what we may call the "strange death" of the Washington Consensus with special reference to the economic empowerment of China and a fundamental change in relations between the global North and South.[1] What is "strange" about this death is that it occurred at a time of seemingly undisputed sway of the neo-liberal doctrines propagated by the Consensus. For that very reason, the death went largely unnoticed, and to the extent that it did not, its causes and consequences remain shrouded in great confusion.

Part of the confusion arises from the continuing influence on world politics of various aspects of the defunct Consensus. As Walden Bello has noted, "neoliberalism [remains] the default mode for many economists and technocrats that... lost confidence in it, simply out of inertia." Moreover, new doctrines are emerging, mostly in the global North, that attempt to revive aspects of the old Consensus in more palatable and realistic forms. Our analysis rules out neither the residual influence by default of neoliberalism nor the possibility of its rebirth in new forms. It simply points out that the neoliberal counterrevolution of the early 1980s, of which the Washington Consensus was an integral component, has backfired, creating conditions of a reversal of power relations between the global North and South that may well be reshaping world politics as well as the theory and practice of national development.

We begin by sketching the origins and objectives of the neoliberal turn or counterrevolution in US policies and ideology of 1979–82. After highlighting the immediate impact of the neoliberal turn on North-South relations, we focus on the Chinese economic ascent as its most important *unintended* consequence with deep roots in Chinese traditions, including the revolutionary tradition of the Mao era. We conclude by pointing to the impact of the Chinese ascent on North-South relations, with special reference to the possible emergence of a new Southern alliance on more solid foundations than the one established at Bandung in the 1950s, as well as to the challenges and opportunities that the current global economic crisis creates for China and other developing countries.

THE WASHINGTON CONSENSUS AND THE NEOLIBERAL COUNTERREVOLUTION

The neoliberal turn began in the last year of the Carter administration, when a serious crisis of confidence in the US dollar prompted Paul Volker, then Chairman of the US Federal Reserve, to switch from the highly permissive monetary policies of the 1970s to highly restrictive policies. It nonetheless materialized fully only when the Reagan administration, drawing ideological inspiration from Margaret Thatcher's slogan "There Is No Alternative" (TINA), declared all variants of social Keynesianism obsolete and proceeded to liquidate them through a revival of early-twentieth-century beliefs in the "magic" of allegedly self-regulating markets. The liquidation occurred through a drastic contraction in the money supply, an equally drastic increase in interest rates, major reductions in corporate taxation, the elimination of controls on capital, and a sudden switch of US policies towards the Third World from promotion of the "development project" launched in the late 1940s and early 1950s to promotion of the neo-liberal agenda that later came to be known as the Washington Consensus. Directly or through the IMF and the World Bank, the US government withdrew its support from the "statist" and "inward-looking" strategies (such as import-substitution industrialization) that most theories of national development had advocated in the 1950s and 1960s, and began to promote capital-friendly "shock therapies" aimed at transferring assets from public to private hands at bargain prices and at liberalizing foreign trade and capital movements.

The change has been widely characterized as a "counterrevolution" in economic thought and political ideology. The neo-liberal turn was counterrevolutionary vis-à-vis both labor and the Third World. As Thatcher's advisor Alan Budd publicly admitted in retrospect, "What was engineered in Marxist terms was a crisis of capitalism which recreated a reserve army of labor, and has allowed the capitalists to make high profits ever since." In so far as the US government was concerned, however, this dis-empowerment of labor was less an end in itself than a means to the objective of reversing the relative decline in US wealth and power that had gained momentum with the US defeat in Vietnam and culminated at the end of the 1970s in the Iranian Revolution, the Soviet invasion of Afghanistan, and the previously mentioned run on the US dollar.

Although the Washington Consensus was first and foremost a strategy aimed at reestablishing US power, it was presented as a new developmental strategy. Taking this claim at face value, discussions of the impact of the neo-liberal turn have generally focused on trends since 1980 in world income inequality measured by synthetic indicators such as the Gini or the Theil. While a fairly general agreement has emerged that within-country inequality has increased, trends in between-country inequality remain the object of some controversy.

Even in this respect, however, the consensus is that, whatever the trends,

> improvement in world income inequality and poverty [since 1980] was not broadly based, but rather highly dependent, like the overall growth in world income, on the impressive growth performance of China and the substantial growth of India. When China is excluded from the calculations, inequality increases by most measures. When India is excluded along with China, not only is there a more marked deterioration in the distribution of world income, but poverty incidence remains about constant.

In short, sums up Albert Berry, China and India "can be considered to have rescued the world from a dismal overall performance over the [last] two decades." The data that Berry provides also show that the modest decline in the Gini that he detects from 1980 to 2000 did not affect negatively the richest 10% of world population (which has in fact further improved its relative position) but results exclusively from a redistribution of income from middle income to upper and lower income countries.

Table 1 provides more details concerning this redistribution. As the table shows, in so far as the *overall* North-South income divide is concerned, the neoliberal counterrevolution made little difference, resulting at first in a minor decrease and then in a minor increase in the income per capita of the Third World relative to that of the First World. It did nonetheless make a big difference for individual regions both of the North and of the South. For our present purposes, it is sufficient to focus on three main tendencies. First, in the 1990s the United States did succeed in reversing its relative decline of the 1960s and 1970s but the reversal was entirely compensated by a deterioration of the relative position of Western and Southern Europe and Japan. Second, in the 1980s Sub-Saharan Africa and Latin America both experienced a major relative decline, from which they never recovered, followed by an equally significant relative decline of the former Soviet Union in the 1990s. Third, the greatest gains were those of East Asia and Japan up to 1990 and of India and China in the 1980s and 1990s, although China's advance was far more substantial than India's.[2]

These tendencies have been widely interpreted as the result of the closer integration of China, India and the former Soviet Union in the global economy. Richard Freeman, for example, has claimed that this closer integration effectively doubled the labor force producing for the world market without increasing the effective supply of capital. As twice as many workers compete for working with the same capital, not only has the balance of power shifted away from labor toward capital, but the prospects for economic growth of middle-income countries that were already integrated in the global economy have deteriorated.

> Countries that had hoped to grow through exports of low-wage goods must look for new sectors in which to advance–if they are to make it in the global economy . . . Mexico, Colombia or South Africa cannot compete with China in manufacturing, as long as Chinese wages are one-quarter or so of theirs–especially since Chinese labor is roughly as productive as theirs.

If true, this contention would provide a highly parsimonious explanation of the double redistribution of income noted above: from lower to higher income groups within countries and from middle-income to low- and high-income countries. The contention, however, does not stand up to empirical scrutiny primarily because, before and after the US embrace of the TINA doctrine, the predominant feature of the global economy has been a large and expanding supply of surplus capital as much as (if not more than) an unlimited supply of surplus labor. While in the 1970s this expanding supply of surplus capital flowed primarily from high- to low and especially middle-income countries, and squeezed profits rather than wages, the neoliberal turn shifted the downward pressure from profits to wages and, above all, brought about a massive rerouting of capital flows towards the United States. This rerouting turned TINA into a self-fulfilling prophecy: whatever alternative to cut-throat competition for increasingly mobile capital might have existed before 1980, it became moot once the world's largest and wealthiest

Table 1: GNP Per Capita as % of First World's GNP Per Capita

Region	1960	1970	1980	1985	1990	1995	2000	2005
Sub-Saharan Africa (w/ SA)	5.6	4.7	3.9	3.1	2.7	2.5	2.0	2.3
Latin America	19.7	16.4	17.6	14.4	12.3	12.9	13.4	11.2
West Asia and North Africa	8.7	7.8	8.7	7.9	7.4	7.2	7.7	8.4
South Asia (w/o India)	1.9	1.7	1.3	1.4	1.4	1.5	1.6	1.6
East Asia (w/o China and Japan)	6.0	6.1	8.0	8.6	11.0	13.8	11.5	11.8
China	0.9	0.7	0.8	1.2	1.3	2.1	3.2	4.6
India	1.5	1.3	1.1	1.2	1.2	1.4	1.6	1.9
Third World*	**4.5**	**4.0**	**4.3**	**4.1**	**4.1**	**4.7**	**4.9**	**5.2**
Third World (w/o China)*	**6.5**	**5.7**	**6.1**	**5.5**	**5.3**	**5.9**	**5.6**	**5.5**
Third World (w/o China and India)*	**9.3**	**8.1**	**8.8**	**7.7**	**7.5**	**8.2**	**7.7**	**7.3**
North America	123.7	105.0	100.7	101.6	98.2	98.9	116.4	112.5
Western Europe	111.1	104.6	104.6	101.5	100.5	98.5	92.0	99.7
Southern Europe	51.9	58.2	60.0	57.6	58.6	59.2	61.5	70.2
Australia and New Zealand	94.8	83.5	74.7	73.3	66.4	70.6	68.6	84.5
Japan	78.7	126.4	134.4	140.8	149.8	151.9	121.0	103.1
First World**	**100**	**100**	**100**	**100**	**100**	**100**	**100**	**100.0**
Eastern Europe	-	-	-	-	11.1	10.6	13.4	18.6
Former USSR w/ Russian Fed	-	-	-	-	10.7	5.9	4.6	8.2
Russian Federation	-	-	-	-	14.1	8.2	6.0	11.8
Former USSR w/o Russian Fed	-	-	-	-	7.1	3.6	3.1	4.6
Eastern Europe and Former USSR***	**-**	**-**	**-**	**-**	**10.8**	**7.1**	**6.9**	**11.0**

Source: Calculations based on World Bank (WDI - 2001, 2006).
GNP in constant 1995 US$ for 1960–1995, GNP in current US$ Atlas method for 2000 and 2005.
*Countries included in Third World:
Sub-Saharan Africa: Benin, Botswana, Burkina Faso, Burundi, Cameroon, Central African Republic, Chad, Rep. of Congo, Congo Dem. Rep., Cote d'Ivoire, Gabon, Ghana, Kenya, Lesotho, Madagascar, Malawi, Mauritania, Mauritius, Niger, Nigeria, Rwanda, Senegal, South Africa, Tanzania, Togo, Uganda, Zambia, Zimbabwe.
Latin America: Argentina, Bolivia, Brazil, Chile, Colombia, Costa Rica, Dominican Rep, Ecuador, El Salvador, Guatemala, Haiti, Honduras, Jamaica, Mexico, Nicaragua, Panama, Paraguay, Peru, Trinidad & Tobago, Uruguay, Venezuela.
West Asia & North Africa: Algeria, Arab Rep of Egypt, Morocco, Saudi Arabia (1971 for 1970), Sudan, Syrian Arab Rep., Tunisia (1961 for 1960), Turkey.
South Asia: Bangladesh, India, Nepal, Pakistan, Sri Lanka.
East Asia: China, Hong Kong, Indonesia, South Korea, Malaysia, Philippines, Singapore, Taiwan (Taiwan National Statistics), Thailand.
**Countries included in First World:
North America: Canada, United States.
Western Europe: Austria, Belgium, Denmark, Finland, France, Germany, Luxembourg, Netherlands, Norway, Sweden, Switzerland, United Kingdom.
Southern Europe: Greece, Ireland, Israel, Italy, Portugal, Spain.
Australia and New Zealand
Japan
***Countries included in Eastern Europe and the Former USSR:
Eastern Europe: Albania, Bulgaria, Croatia, Czech Republic, Hungary, Poland, Romania, Slovak Republic, Slovenia
Former USSR: Armenia, Azerbaijan, Belarus, Estonia, Georgia, Kazakhstan, Kyrgyz Republic, Latvia, Lithuania, Moldova, Russian Federation, Tajikistan, Turkmenistan, Ukraine, Uzbekistan.

economy led the world down the road of ever more extravagant concessions to capital. This was especially the case for Third and Second World (mostly middle-income) countries which, as a result of the change in US policies, experienced a sharp contraction both in the demand for their natural resources and in the availability of credit and investment at favorable conditions.

The extent of the rerouting of capital flows can be gauged from the change in the current account of the US balance of payments. As Figure 2 shows, in so far as the United States is concerned, the alleged expansion in the global supply of cheap labor has been accompanied by a virtually unlimited supply of capital from the rest of the world. Moreover, as Figure 3 shows, in the 1980s and especially after the East Asian crisis of 1997–98, this unlimited supply of capital has come from the former Third and Second Worlds. Whatever the reason of the shift of the balance of power from labor to capital in the United States-where the shift came earlier and has been more pronounced than in other wealthy countries-it cannot be attributed to an expansion of the global supply of cheap labor *unmatched* by a proportionate expansion of the global supply of capital, as Freeman, among others, maintains.

Low- and middle-income countries have faced an altogether different situation. In these countries, the rerouting of global capital flows toward the United States turned the "flood" of capital that they had experienced in the 1970s into the sudden "drought" of the 1980s. First signaled by the Mexican default of 1982, the drought was probably the single most important factor in promoting both an escalation of interstate competition for capital and the major divergence among Southern regions shown in Table 1. Some regions (most notably East Asia) succeeded in taking advantage of the increase in US demand for cheap industrial products that ensued from US trade liberalization and the escalating US trade deficit. These regions tended to benefit from the redirection of capital flows towards the United States, because the improvement

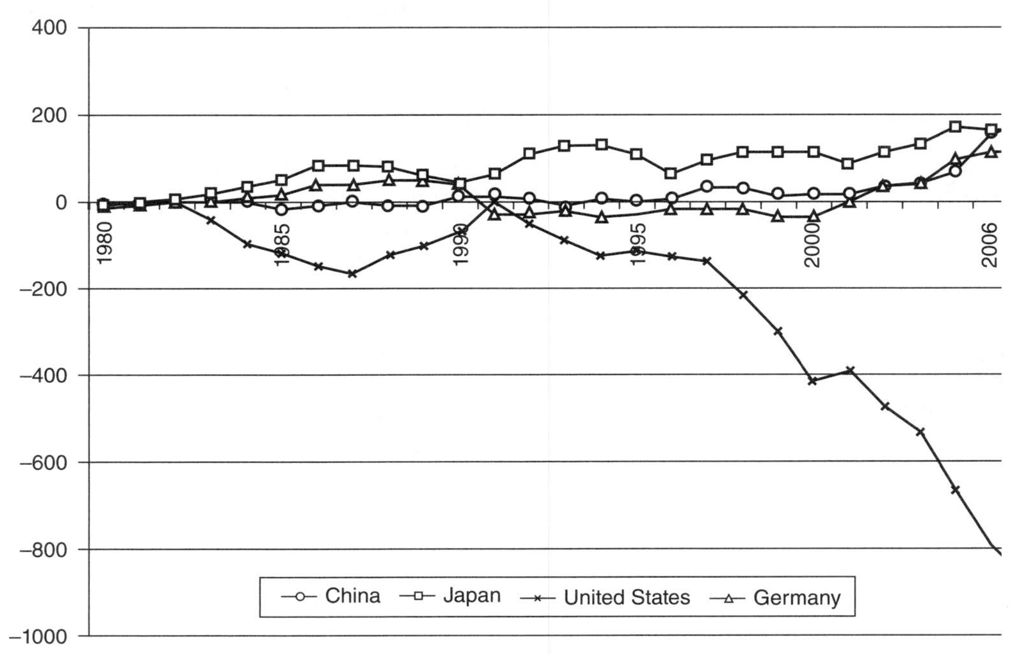

Figure 2. Current Account Balance (1980–2005)
*Figures in billions of current US dollars.
Source: International Monetary Fund, World Economic Outlook Database, September 2006.

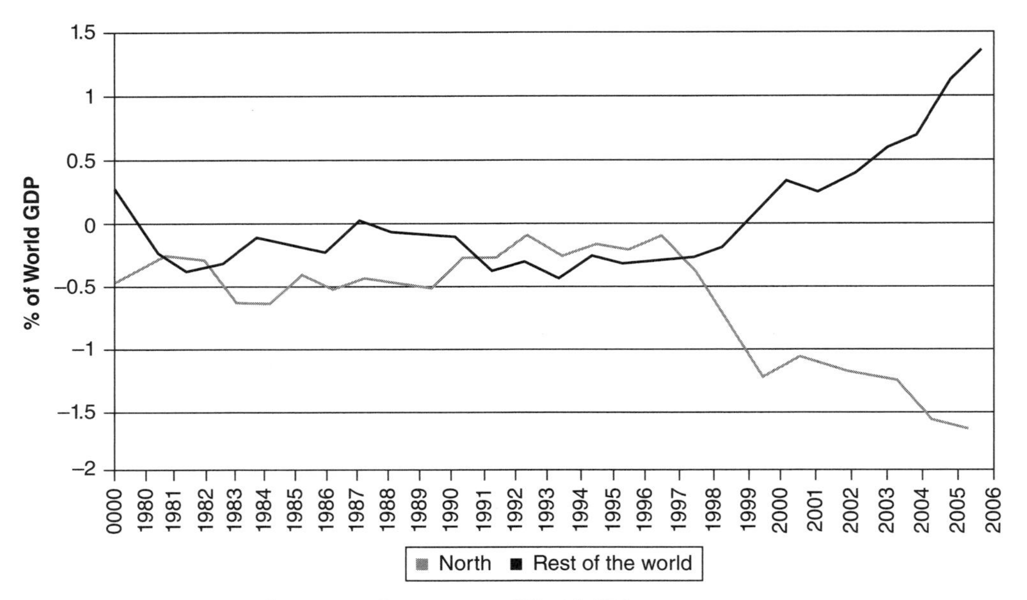

Figure 3. Current Account Balance as a Percentage of World GDP
Source: IMF World Economic Outlook Database; September 2006.

in their balance of payments lessened their need to compete with the United States in world financial markets, and indeed turned some of them into major lenders to the United States. Other regions (most notably, Latin America and Sub-Saharan Africa), in contrast, did not manage to compete successfully for a share of the North American demand. These regions tended to run into balance of payments difficulties that put them into the hopeless position of having to compete directly with the United States in world financial markets. US business and governmental agencies were able to take advantage of both outcomes for the South: they were able to mobilize the cheap commodities and credit that Southern "winners" eagerly supplied, as well as the assets that Southern "losers" willy nilly had to alienate at bargain prices. As Table 1 shows, the overall result was that, while the United States succeeded in reversing its economic decline, the gains and losses of Southern regions relative to the North largely balanced one another.

In short, the prime mover of the intensification of competitive pressures on labor and on Southern countries has not been the integration in world markets of China's and India's allegedly unlimited supplies of labor but the US sponsored neo-liberal counterrevolution. Freeman's emphasis on unlimited supplies of cheap labor does highlight the fact that the Southern regions that have performed best in the competition initiated by the counterrevolution were endowed with large reserves of low-productivity agricultural labor that could be moved into higher-productivity, industrial and service jobs. Indeed, Jeffrey Sachs and Wing Thye Woo have contended that the existence of a huge farm sector is the crucial difference that explains the greater success of economic reforms in China in comparison with Russia.

Arguments of this kind can nonetheless be criticized on two grounds. First, as Thomas Rawski has asked with specific reference to Sachs' and Woo's interpretation of Chinese achievements, "If millions of ill-educated, over-regulated and under-employed farmers represent 'advantages of backwardness,' why do we see no big growth spurts in Egypt, India, Bangladesh, Pakistan, Nigeria and other nations that have long enjoyed such 'advantages'?" Second, a large reservoir of low-productivity agricultural labor is not the only source of exploitable labor. Marxists, for example, have long emphasized that capitalist development tends to create an expanding reserve army of labor that can prevent real wages from growing as fast as labor productivity, while regarding the existence of a large reservoir of agricultural labor with access to the means of producing means of subsistence not as an advantage but as a handicap for economic development. The question then arises of whether a large peasantry only partially separated from the means of producing its subsistence, like the Chinese, constitutes a greater competitive advantage in attracting capital and promoting economic growth than the urban and semi-urban masses of unemployed and underemployed labor of which sub-Saharan Africa and Latin America are better endowed than China. If it does, should we revise or altogether reject Marxist theories of the reserve army of labor and of accumulation by dispossession? And if it does not, what other circumstances can account for China's success, in comparison with sub-Saharan Africa and Latin America, in turning to its advantage the world economic conjuncture created by the neo-liberal counterrevolution?

TOWARD A NEW BANDUNG?

Joshua Cooper Ramo, a member of the Council on Foreign Relations in the US and of the Foreign Policy Center in Britain, has characterized the emerging Chinese challenge as the displacement of the Washington Consensus by a Beijing Consensus–the China-led emergence of "a path for other nations around the world" not simply to develop but also "to fit into the international order in a way that allows them to be truly independent, to protect their way of life and political choices."

> The Washington Consensus . . . left a trail of destroyed economies and bad feelings around the globe. China's new development approach is . . . flexible enough that it is barely classifiable as a doctrine. It does not believe in uniform solutions for every situation. It is defined… by a lively defense of national borders and interests, and by the increasingly thoughtful accumulation of tools of asymmetric power projection. . . . While the US is pursuing unilateral policies designed to protect United States interests, China is assembling the resources to eclipse the US in many essential areas of international affairs and constructing an environment that will make US hegemonic action more difficult. . . . China's path to development and power is, of course, unrepeatable by any other nation. It also remains fraught with contradictions, tensions and pitfalls. Yet many elements of the country's rise have engaged the developing world.

Among these elements, Ramo mentions a development model in which "the massive contradictions of Chinese development" make "sustainability and equality . . . first considerations," and "a theory of self-determination . . . that stresses using leverage to move big, hegemonic powers that may be tempted to tread on your toes." Ramo's notion of a Beijing Consensus has been criticized for presuming the existence of a consensus where none exists, or for establishing a contrast with the Washington Consensus that some observers consider overdrawn. Neither criticism seems to us appropriate, because Ramo himself emphasizes the variety of developmental paths implicit in the Beijing Consensus, in sharp contrast to the one-size-fits-all doctrine of the Washington Consensus. Ramo nonetheless does not tell us whether the Chinese ascent may actually contribute to a collective empowerment of the global South and not just to the empowerment of one or more of its national components. The relevant question in this connection is under which circumstances the Beijing Consensus can lead to the formation of a new and more effective Bandung—i.e., a new version of the Third World alliance of the 1950s and 1960s better suited than the old at countering the economic and political subordination of Southern to Northern states in an age of unprecedented global economic integration.

The temptation for China to settle for cooptation in a US- or Northern-dominated world order and for other Southern countries to seek or accept Northern support for their mutual jealousies should not be underestimated. But neither should we overestimate the power of the United States, even in collusion with Europe, to succeed once again in rolling back Southern advances, as it did for almost 20 years through the neoliberal counterrevolution. For one thing, the Iraqi debacle has confirmed the limits of coercive means in enforcing the Northern will against Southern resistance. More important in a capitalist world, the financial underpinnings of US and Northern dominance rest on increasingly shaky grounds. A crucial turning point in this respect has been the Asian financial crisis of 1997–8. Robert Wade and Frank Veneroso have claimed that this crisis confirmed the validity of the dictum that "in a depression assets return to their rightful owners."

> The combination of massive devaluations, IMF-pushed financial liberalization, and IMF-facilitated recovery may have precipitated the biggest peacetime transfer of assets from domestic to foreign owners in the past fifty years anywhere in the world, dwarfing the transfers from domestic to US owners in Latin America in the 1980s or in Mexico after 1994.

By focusing on the immediate effects of the crisis, this diagnosis nonetheless missed its longer term effects on North-South relations. As Figure 2 shows, the 1997–8 crisis was followed by a huge bifurcation between the Northern deficit and the rest-of-the world's surplus in the current accounts of their respective balances of payments. Much of this surplus still flows to the US financial entrepot, both to finance the escalating US deficit and to be reinvested around the world, including the global South, to the benefit of the United States. But the basic fact underlying the bifurcation is that the North, especially the United States, can produce less and less goods and services at lower prices than the rest of the world. More important, a significant and growing portion of that surplus is bypassing the US entrepot, both to build up currency reserves and to flow directly to other Southern destinations, thereby weakening the hold of the IMF and other Northern-controlled financial institutions on Southern countries.[3] Flush with cash and eager to regain control over their economic policies, Southern countries "have voted with their feet and paid off the IMF, thus avoiding to take its advice."[4] The IMF's annual meetings thus "become lonely affairs. Editorials in the financial press wondered if the fund had a mission left." And as market-oriented central bankers began, in effect, nationalizing banks, "Western championing of free markets came in for a good deal of ridicule from states that had resisted the end-of-government enthusiasm of globalizers. Globalization, far from burying the state, now depended on states for rescue."

Notwithstanding its massive purchases of US treasury bonds, China has played a leading role both in re-routing the Southern surplus to Southern destinations and in providing neighboring and distant Southern countries with attractive alternatives to the trade, investment and assistance of Northern countries and financial institutions. "Here comes a very large new player on the block that has the potential of changing the landscape of overseas development assistance," noted in 2006 the director for the Philippines at the Asian Development Bank (ADB) shortly after China announced an extraordinary package of $2 billion in loans to the Philippines each year for three years, which made the $200 million offered by the World Bank and the ADB look puny; easily outstripped a $1 billion loan under negotiation with Japan; and sheltered the Philippines from Washington's disfavor after President Arroyo pulled the country's troops out of Iraq. This was just one of many similar deals in which China has been out-competing Northern agencies by offering Southern countries more generous terms for access to their natural resources; larger loans with fewer political strings attached and without expensive consultant fees; and big and complicated infrastructure projects in distant areas at as little as half the cost of Northern competitors.

Supplementing and complementing Chinese initiatives, oil-rich countries have also redirected their surpluses to the South. Of great political and symbolic significance has been Venezuela's use of windfall proceeds from high oil prices to assume the role of new "lender of last resort" for Latin American countries, thereby reducing Washington's historically enormous influence over economic policy in the region. Equally important, and potentially more disruptive of Northern financial dominance, has been the interest that West Asian countries have recently shown in re-routing at least part of their surpluses from the United States and Europe to East and South Asia. The reasons are partly the unpopularity of the

Iraqi war and things like the backlash in the US that forced Dubai's port company to sell off American holdings after it bought the British port operator P&O. But the most compelling reason is economic: China and all fast growing Asian economies want West Asian oil, and the West Asian capital and liquidity generated by that oil are searching for investments with higher returns than US Treasury bonds.

When in May 2006 India's prime minister, Manmohan Singh, urged Asian nations at the annual meeting of the ADB to re-direct Asian surpluses toward Asian development projects, one US observer found the speech "stunning"—"the harbinger of the end of the dollar and of American hegemony." In reality, whether Asian and other Southern countries continue to use US dollars is not the most important issue. Just as the pound sterling continued to be used as an international currency three-to-four decades after the end of British hegemony, so may the dollar. What really matters for the future of North-South relations is whether Southern countries will continue to put the surpluses of their balances of payments at the disposal of US-controlled agencies, to be turned into instruments of Northern domination, or will instead use them as instruments of Southern emancipation. From this standpoint, there is nothing stunning about Singh's statement, which merely lends support to a practice that is already in place. What is truly stunning is the lack of awareness—in the South no less than in the North—of the extent to which the neoliberal counterrevolution has backfired, creating highly favorable conditions for the emergence of a new and more powerful Bandung.

The foundations of the old Bandung were strictly political-ideological and, as such, were easily destroyed by the neoliberal counterrevolution. The foundations of the Bandung that may be emerging now, along with a political-ideological component, are primarily economic and, as such, far more solid. As Yashwant Sinha, a former Indian foreign minister put it in a 2003 speech: "In the past, India's engagement with much of Asia . . . was built on an idealistic conception of Asian brotherhood, based on shared experiences of colonialism and of cultural ties." The Asian dynamic today, in contrast, "is determined . . . as much by trade, investment and production as by history and culture." Sinha's contention applies, not just to Asia, but to the global South more generally. Under the old Bandung, ideologically and politically motivated Third World solidarity had no economic foundation. Indeed, it had to run against the current of world market processes over which Third World countries had little or no control. Today, in contrast, a rapidly expanding South-South trade, investment, and cooperation in a growing variety of fields—including regional economic integration, national security, health and the environment—rest primarily on the increasing competitiveness of Southern countries in world production. Although idealistic conceptions of Third World solidarity still play a role, they are seldom the only or even the main determinant of South-South cooperation.

Four countries in particular—China, India, Brazil and South Africa (CIBS)—are leading the way in this direction. Besides accounting for 40 per cent of world population, these countries are jointly emerging as major sources of capital, technology and effective demand for the products of the surrounding regions and the global South at large. Notwithstanding their leading role in shifting the balance of economic and political power in favor of the global South, the CIBS countries have been criticized for establishing relations with other Southern countries similar in motivation and outcome to traditional North-South relations. China in particular has been taken to task for establishing relations with its commercial partners that reproduce their specialization in primary production at the expense of manufacturing and other high-value-added activities.

In so far as they point to national self-interest rather than idealistic Third World solidarity as the foundation of Southern cooperation, these critiques are largely correct but miss the strengths of the new Bandung in comparison with the old. They miss first of all the subversion of the structural foundations of the global hierarchy of wealth and power entailed by the emergence of the CIBS, and especially China, as competitors of the North in world production, trade and finance. Not only do these countries provide other Southern countries with better terms of trade, aid, and investment than Northern countries—including substantial cancellations of debt; by so doing they also intensify competitive pressures on Northern countries to provide Southern countries with better terms than they otherwise would. Closely related to the above, critiques that emphasize the specialization of China's and India's trading partners in primary production miss the ongoing reversal of the terms of trade between manufacturing and primary production brought about by industrial convergence between North and South. Just as "industrialization" has ceased to be a correlate of "development," so specialization in primary production as such may no longer be a correlate of "underdevelopment."

More important, in so far as the critiques in question point to the socially exploitative practices in which the CIBS may engage at home, or indirectly encourage abroad through their foreign trade and investment, they disregard the fact that exclusion from trade and production, rather than exploitation as such, is more often than not the main cause of Southern "underdevelopment." They also disregard the fact that power relations play a crucial role in setting standards of morality in the global political economy. Today these standards are for the most part set by the governments and institutions of the countries that occupy the upper reaches of the global hierarchy of wealth. The emergence of the CIBS, however, may well be creating a situation in which the governments and institutions of countries that occupy the middle and lower reaches might at last have a say. Crucial in this respect is what China and India—which by themselves account for more than one-third of world population—will chose to do. Should they choose to cooperate—as Howard French has envisaged commenting in the *International Herald Tribune* on news of huge investments by China and India in each other's economies—"the day when a cozy club of the rich—the United States, the strongest economies of Western Europe and Japan—sets the pace for the rest of world, passing out instructions and assigning grades, [would] fast [draw] to a close."

The 2008 Wall Street meltdown has sped up the collapse of the Washington Consensus. As neoliberal American-style capitalism-—including limited government, minimal regulation, and the free-market allocation of credit—lost credibility, many commentators wondered whether China's state-led capitalism could be an alternative. As Huang noted,

> In contemplating alternatives to the fallen American model, some looked to China, where markets are tightly regulated and financial institutions controlled by the state. In the aftermath of Wall Street's meltdown, fretted Francis Fukuyama in Newsweek, China's state-led capitalism is "looking more and more attractive." Washington Post columnist David Ignatius hailed the global advent of a Confucian-inspired "new interventionism"; invoking Richard Nixon's backhanded tribute to John Maynard Keynes, Ignatius declared, "We are all Chinese now."

At the same time, the fact that China's economy was not immune from the US-centered global economic crisis—especially its slumping exports and slow-down of economic growth—prompted a reassessment of the export-led growth model that China had adopted in the 1990s.[5] Indeed, Chinese officials have been aware of the constraints imposed on growth by low levels of domestic consumption. The current economic crisis may very well be what was needed to induce them to shift towards a more balanced, domestic consumption-driven, development path. Such a shift would inevitably involve a recession, which nonetheless is probably a necessary step in the direction of long-run sustainable development. As Naughton projected in 2006, "hundreds of firms will go bankrupt, trade tensions will increase further as failing companies seek to dump product on world markets, and sentiment toward China will swing from positive to negative."[6] But, as should be clear from this article, there are also good reasons to anticipate that the 2008 economic crisis might eventually lead a resumption of Chinese growth on more sustainable long-run foundations and to brighter prospects for a new Bandung.

Notes

Forthcoming in Jon Shefner and Patricia Fernández-Kelly (editors), *Globalization and Beyond:*

New Examinations of Global Power and its Alternatives, Penn State University Press, 2011. We would like to thank Astra Bonini, Kevan Harris and Daniel Pasciuti for assistance in producing the figures and Kevan Harris, Jon Shefner, Beverly Silver and the graduate students in the Research in International Development seminar at Johns Hopkins University for comments on earlier drafts of the chapter.

[1]We borrow the expression "strange death" from George Dangerfield's classic account, first published in 1935, of the dramatic upheaval and political change that overwhelmed liberal England at a time of seemingly undisputed economic and political power.

[2]World Bank data are subject to frequent and unexplained revisions that make them particularly unreliable in measuring short-term variations between specific countries. This unreliability, however, has little effect on the long-term trends among regions shown in Table 1.

[3]For most of these countries, "reserves are simply insurance against financial disaster . . . As the dust settled over the ruins of many former 'emerging' economies, a new creed took hold among policy makers in the developing world: Pile up as much foreign exchange as possible." E. Porter, "Are Poor Nations Wasting Their Money on Dollars?" *The New York Times,* April 30, 2006; F. Kempe, "Why Economists Worry About Who Holds Foreign Currency Reserves." *The Wall Street Journal,* May 9, 2006.

[4]As a result, the Fund's loan portfolio has dropped from $150 billion in 2003 to $17 billion in 2007, its lowest level since the 1980s. M. Weisbrot, "IMF Misses Epoch-Making Changes in the Global Economy." *International Herald Tribune,* 19 October, 2007. A shrinking loan portfolio, besides diminishing the IMF's influence over Southern governments, reduces its interest income and cash reserves. "In an irony that has provoked tittering among many [Southern] finance ministers, the agency that has long preached belt-tightening now must practice it itself." M. Moffett and B. Davis, "Booming Economy Leaves the IMF Groping for Mission." *The Wall Street Journal,* April 21, 2006.

[5]According to *Xinhua News* (December 18th, 2008), exports in China fell in November 2008 for the first time in seven years. In Guangdong province where the export-oriented manufacturing push began, more than 7,000 companies closed or moved elsewhere in the first nine months of 2008.

[6]B. Naughton, "Arguing Against the Motion: Without significantly accelerated reforms and major new policy actions, China's rapid growth will unravel before its economy overtakes the U.S.," at Refraining China Policy: The Carnegie Debates Series 2: China's Economy, December 1, 2006. U.S. Capitol, Washington, DC.

The Post-Washington Consensus: Development After the Crisis

NANCY BIRDSALL AND FRANCIS FUKUYAMA

The last time a global depression originated in the United States, the impact was devastating not only for the world economy but for world politics as well. The Great Depression set the stage for a shift away from strict monetarism and laissez-faire policies toward Keynesian demand management. More important, for many it delegitimized the capitalist system itself, paving the way for the rise of radical and antiliberal movements around the world.

This time around, there has been no violent rejection of capitalism, even in the developing world. In early 2009, at the height of the global financial panic, China and Russia, two formerly noncapitalist states, made it clear to their domestic and foreign investors that they had no intention of abandoning the capitalist model. No leader of a major developing country has backed away from his or her commitment to free trade or the global capitalist system. Instead, the established Western democracies are the ones that have highlighted the risks of relying too much on market-led globalization and called for greater regulation of global finance.

Why has the reaction in developing countries been so much less extreme after this crisis than it was after the Great Depression? For one, they blame the United States for it. Many in the developing world agreed with Brazilian President Luiz Inácio Lula da Silva when he said, "This is a crisis caused by people, white with blue eyes." If the global financial crisis put any development model on trial, it was the free-market or neoliberal model, which emphasizes a small state, deregulation, private ownership, and low taxes. Few developing countries consider themselves to have fully adopted that model.

Indeed, for years before the crisis, they had been distancing themselves from it. The financial crises of the late 1990s in East Asia and Latin America discredited many of the ideas associated with the so-called Washington consensus, particularly that of unalloyed reliance on foreign capital. By 2008, most emerging-market countries had reduced their exposure to the foreign financial markets by accumulating large foreign currency reserves and maintaining regulatory control of their banking systems. These policies provided insulation from global economic volatility and were vindicated by the impressive rebounds in the wake of the recent crisis: the emerging markets have posted much better economic growth numbers than their counterparts in the developed world.

Thus, the American version of capitalism is, if not in full disrepute, then at least no longer dominant. In the next decade, emerging-market and low-income countries are likely to modify their approach to economic policy further, trading the flexibility and efficiency associated with the free-market model for domestic policies meant to ensure greater resilience in the face of competitive pressures and global economic trauma. They will become less focused on the free flow of capital, more concerned with minimizing social disruption through social safety net programs, and more active in supporting domestic industries. And they will be even less inclined than before to defer to the supposed expertise of the more developed countries, believing—correctly—that not only economic but also intellectual power are becoming increasingly evenly distributed.

THE FOREIGN FINANCE FETISH

One of the central features of the old, pre-crisis economic consensus was the assumption that developing countries could benefit substantially from greater inflows of foreign capital—what the economist Arvind Subramanian has labeled "the foreign finance fetish." The idea that the unimpeded flow of capital around the globe, like the free flow of goods and services, makes markets more efficient was more or less taken for granted in policy circles. In the 1990s, the United States and international financial institutions such as the International Monetary Fund (IMF) pushed developing-country borrowers to open up their capital markets to foreign banks and dismantle exchange-rate controls.

Although the benefits of free trade have been well documented, the advantages of full capital mobility are much less clear. The reasons for this have to do with the fundamental differences between the financial sector and the "real" economy. Free capital markets can indeed allocate capital efficiently. But large interconnected financial institutions can also take risks that impose huge negative externalities on the rest of the economy in a way that large manufacturing firms cannot.

One of the paradoxical consequences of the 2008–9 financial crisis may thus be that Americans and Britons will finally learn what the East Asians figured out over a decade ago, namely, that open capital markets combined with unregulated financial sectors is a disaster in the waiting. At the conclusion of the Asian financial crisis, many U.S. policymakers and economists walked back their previous stress on quick liberalization and started promoting "sequencing," that is, liberalization only after a strong regulatory system with adequate supervision of banks has been put in place.

But they devoted little thought to whether certain developing countries were capable of enacting such regulation quickly or what an appropriate regulatory regime would look like. And they overlooked the relevance of their new message to their own case, failing to warn against the danger of the huge, unregulated, and overleveraged shadow financial sector that had emerged in the United States.

MOVING TO MULTIPOLARITY

Years from now, historians may well point to the financial crisis as the end of American economic dominance in global affairs. But the trend toward a multipolar world began much earlier, and the implosion of Western financial markets and their weak recoveries have merely accelerated the process. Even before the crisis, the international institutions created after World War II to manage economic and security challenges were under strain and in need of reform. The IMF and the World Bank suffered from governance structures that reflected outdated economic realities. Starting in the 1990s and continuing into the new century, the Bretton Woods institutions have come under increasing pressure to grant more voting power to emerging-market countries such as Brazil and China. Meanwhile, the G-7, the elite group of the six most economically important Western democracies plus Japan, remained the world's informal steering committee when it came to issues of global economic coordination, even as other power centers emerged.

The financial crisis finally led to the demise of the G-7 as the primary locus of global economic policy coordination and its replacement by the G-20. In November 2008, heads of state from the G-20 gathered in Washington, D.C., to coordinate a global stimulus program—a meeting that has since grown into an established international institution. Since the G-20, unlike the G-7, includes emerging countries such as Brazil, China, and India, the expansion of economic coordination represents an overdue recognition of a new group of global economic players.

The crisis also breathed new life and legitimacy into the IMF and the World Bank. Beforehand, the IMF had looked like it was rapidly becoming obsolete. Private capital markets provided countries with financing on favorable terms without the conditions often attached to IMF loans. The organization was having trouble funding its own activities and was in the process of reducing its staff.

But the outlook changed in 2009, when the G-20 leaders agreed to ensure that the Bretton Woods institutions would have as much as $1 trillion in additional resources to help countries better weather future financing shortfalls. Countries such as Brazil and China were among the contributors to the special funds, which have ended up supporting Greece, Hungary, Iceland, Ireland, Latvia, Pakistan, and Ukraine.

By requesting that emerging markets take on a bigger leadership role in global affairs, the Western democracies are implicitly admitting that they are no longer able to manage global economic affairs on their own. But what has been called "the rise of the rest" is not just about economic and political power; it also has to do with the global competition of ideas and models. The West, and in particular the United States, is no longer seen as the only center for innovative thinking about social policy. Conditional cash transfer schemes, for example, were first developed and implemented in Latin America. As for industrial policy, the West has contributed little innovative thinking in that realm in the last 30 years. One has to turn to emerging-market countries, rather than the developed world, to see successful models in practice. And when it comes to international organizations, the voices and ideas of the United States and Europe are becoming less dominant. Those of emerging-market countries—states that have become significant funders of the international financial institutions—are being given greater weight.

All this signals a clear shift in the development agenda. Traditionally, this was an agenda generated in the developed world that was implemented in—and, indeed, often imposed on—the developing world. The United States, Europe, and Japan will continue to be significant sources of economic resources and ideas, but the emerging markets are now entering this arena and will become significant players. Countries such as Brazil, China, India, and South Africa will be both donors and recipients of resources for development and of best practices for how to use them. A large portion of the world's poor live within their borders, yet they have achieved new respect on the global scene in economic, political, and intellectual terms. In fact, development has never been something that the rich bestowed on the poor but rather something the poor achieved for themselves. It appears that the Western powers are finally waking up to this truth in light of a financial crisis that, for them, is by no means over.

VISUAL REVIEW

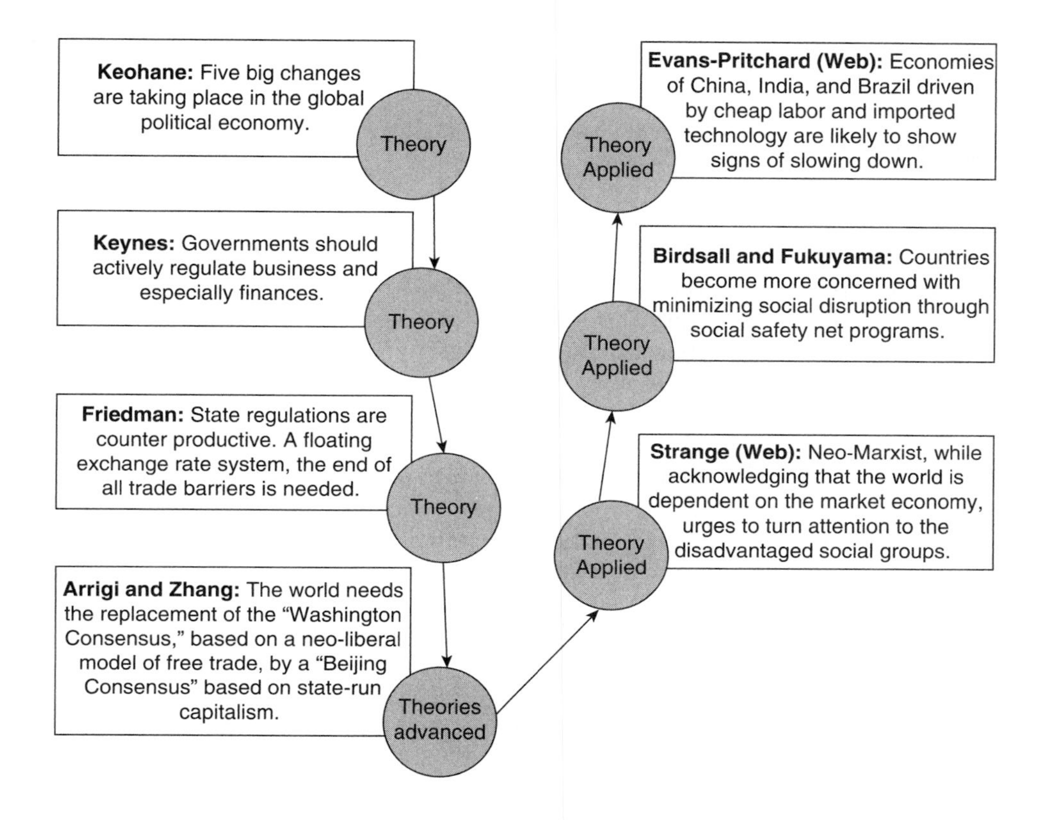

Critical Thinking and Discussion Questions for Part II

SECTION 5

1. **There are twenty-eight arguments used in the piece selected from Von Clausewitz (on the companion website [http://oup.com/us/shiraev]) to describe and explain war. Apply arguments 3–9 to the following:**
    - The U.S.'s military actions in Afghanistan started in 2001
    - The U.S.'s military actions in Iraq started in 2003
    - The conflict in Ukraine in 2014
    - A military conflict of your choice

2. **Explain the "political object of war" according to Von Clausewitz.**
    - Has this objective been achieved in the war in Afghanistan that started in 2001?
    - Has this objective been achieved in the war in Iraq that started in 2003?
    - Has this objective been achieved in the conflict in Ukraine that started in 2014?

3. **Explain the polarity principle offered by Von Clausewitz.**
    - Apply this principle to modern U.S.–China relations.
    - Apply this principle to modern U.S.–Iran relations.
    - Apply this principle to modern U.S.–Russia relations.
    - Apply this principle to modern North Korea–South Korea relations.

4. **McMaster describes the "conditions of uncertainty" in modern warfare. (See this article on the companion website [http://oup.com/us/shiraev].) What are they?**
    - Suggest other uncertainties that, in your view, have not been mentioned in the article.

5. **What were the mistakes of the Israeli military strategists in the 2006 war in Lebanon, according to McMaster? What lessons do you think Israel learned from these mistakes today? (See this article on the companion website [http://oup.com/us/shiraev].)**

6. **What is being commonly called today the "collateral damage" in war?**
    - What is your personal view of the "collateral damage" concept in warfare?
    - If you were President, what would you do to reduce the "collateral damage" in a military conflict?

7. **Recall the key strategies of terrorism identified by Kydd and Walter. Explain them.**

8. **Michel Wieviorka distinguishes between "classical" and contemporary forms of terrorism. Describe both.**
   - Describe the most significant differences between the two forms. Suggest examples.
   - Discuss the similarities between these two forms. Suggest examples.

9. **Could the demands of modern "global" terrorist groups be largely satisfied to avoid global, continuous violence? If yes, which demands? Which demands cannot be addressed? Explain your point of view.**

10. **Terrorist actions can be effective (Kydd and Walter) not simply because they instill fear in target populations, but because they cause governments and individuals to respond in ways that aid the terrorists' cause.**
    - Look for examples (different from those used in the article) or illustrations supporting this statement.
    - Look for examples that disprove the previous statement about the effectiveness of terrorist actions.

11. **Recall the five ultimate goals of terrorism identified by Kydd and Walter. Explain each of them.**

12. **As Max Boot suggests, because mass media in democratic countries report heavily on casualties and destruction caused by insurgency's actions, public opinion in such countries may develop a "war fatigue" faster.**
    - What is "war fatigue" and how does it develop?
    - "War fatigue" can come and go, which means it may increase or diminish. Do you think that today "war fatigue" in the United States is increasing or decreasing? Explain your view.

13. **Imagine the United States becomes energy independent in 2021. However, as Charles Glaser discusses (on the companion website [http://oup.com/us/shiraev]), the United States' forthcoming energy independence does not necessarily guarantee security. What are his arguments?**
    - In your views, will the energy independence significantly improve security of the United States and why?
    - Will the impact of energy independence be significant or insignificant?

14. **Glaser mentions new oil-driven dangers are emerging in Northeast Asia. What are they?**
    - What other resources-driven conflicts may emerge in your view in five years and where?
    - What other resources-driven conflicts may emerge in fifteen years?

15. **Lucas Kello writes that future massive cyberattacks could undermine a country's military capabilities and disturb a regional or global order.**
    - Discuss a scenario (or several scenarios) in which such an attack was launched against the United States and the United Kingdom simultaneously. How would this attack disrupt global order?
    - Which countries could be (a) most and (b) least vulnerable compared to others facing cyberattacks?

16. **Explain five difficulties in conceptualizing cyberattacks, suggested by Kello.**

17. **Kello writes that cyber security studies require "a congress of disciplines that includes not only the engineering sciences but also the political and social sciences." What in your view can be an input from**
    - political science;
    - sociology;
    - history; and
    - political psychology.

18. **Provide examples of "supply chain risks" in cyber security. How would you address these risks if you were a decision maker?**

19. **Apply David Lake's argument (see the article on the companion website [http://oup.com/us/shiraev]) that security policies still depend on the balance of gains and losses to specific policies of the United States:**
    - toward China and Taiwan;
    - toward North and South Korea;
    - toward Russia and its neighbors; and
    - toward Israel, Saudi Arabia, and its neighbors.

20. **Judith Stiehm claims (on the companion website [http://oup.com/us/shiraev]) that there should be "gender-mainstreamed" foreign policy, meaning that more women must be involved in countries' institutional security and defense policies.**
    - Using open sources on the Web, find out how many female defense secretaries there are in the world now.
    - See if the number of women admirals and generals increased in the United States' armed forces over the past ten years. Discuss the findings.

21. **In your opinion, which moral dilemmas would new technologies bring to current and future military conflicts?**
    - How do drones change the nature of a conflict?
    - How do software-based weapons change the nature of war?

SECTION 6

1. **Hugo Grotius in his writings (on the companion website [http://oup.com/us/shiraev]) refers a number of times to God. Underline all these references.**
    - Compare these references. What other topics are discussed or mentioned in these statements?
    - Is there a main theme or an underlying idea that can summarize these references to divine power in the context of law (or references to law in the religious context)?

2. **The Hague Peace Conferences of 1899 and 1907 (see the companion website [http://oup.com/us/shiraev]) were inspired by the desire of a number of the world leaders to establish a set of common rules to reduce the risk of war and diminish its cruelties. However, wars and atrocities did not stop after the Conferences.**
    - Do you think that the Hague agreements were generally useful or useless in the context of history? Explain your view.

3. **Identify and discuss the strengths and weaknesses of the Treaty on the Non-Proliferation of Nuclear Weapons. (See the companion website [http://oup.com/us/shiraev].)**
    - What steps should be taken to make this treaty more effective by 2018?
    - Discuss the argument that if all countries possessed nuclear weapons, the world would be a safer place simply because the governments would start acting very carefully out of fear of provoking nuclear war.

4. **We know that sovereign countries (states) are solely responsible for the decisions they make. In this case, what is your personal view on the necessity to have international law?**

5. **What are main weaknesses of international law?**
    - Use the League of Nations case to illustrate.
    - Use the record of the United Nations' decisions and actions to illustrate.
    - Use other recent examples to illustrate.

6. **According to Neff, what is the role of natural law in international law?**

7. **Using the Neff article, ask your professor to suggest examples from the past of successful applications or functioning of international law. Discuss them.**
    - Find and discuss other, more contemporary examples (from the past or this year) to underline international law's success.

8. **Describe and discuss the conditions (based on the Huth et al. article) when international law becomes a more powerful force for order and peaceful change than military strength.**

9. **Under what conditions do sovereign states prefer a process of legal dispute resolution (i.e., adjudication or arbitration) to bilateral negotiations?**

10. **Discuss several reasons why distribution problems are central to territorial disputes.**
    - Use the dispute in The South China Sea as an example.
    - Use the dispute in Kashmir, involving India and Pakistan, as an example.
    - Use the 2014 conflict in Ukraine and its later developments.

11. **Suggest two or three potential territorial disputes emerging by 2020**
    - What legal measures should be taken now to prevent these conflicts from growing?

12. **Yoffie writes that international law can offer concrete steps toward statehood, but if applied too rapidly or too harshly, it can also undermine international stability. In addition to the Palestinian problem discussed in the article, could you provide other examples supporting this statement?**

13. **What legal steps does a country have to take to obtain U.N. membership?**
    - Why could not Palestinian authorities obtain U.N. membership applying through the "conventional path," such as U.N. institutions?

14. **What is an unconventional path to statehood that was largely unavailable during the twentieth century but may be available these days, according to Yoffie?**

15. **Explain the essence of the "cultural cold war" that broke out between American and Russian museums in 2010–2011 (and the legal authorities that represented them).**

16. **How did Barcia explain the biggest problem (or problems) in international culture property disputes?**

17. **Two parties who are willing to compromise can draft a bilateral agreement (according to Barcia). Give an example of such successful bilateral agreements.**

SECTION 7

1. **Why were most economists in the 1970s ignoring politics? Why were specialists in international relations dismissing political economy, according to Robert Keohane?**
   - What has changed in the international environment since the 1970s to bring attention to international political economy?

2. **How do new communication technologies affect international trade?**
   - How would these technological changes affect international relations in the future?

3. **What is mercantilism's view about the best route to national prosperity? (See the article on mercantilism on the companion website [http://oup.com/us/shiraev].)**
   - Imagine for a minute that every country has turned to mercantilist policies. What impact would this switch have on international relations?

4. **Discuss why China's economic policies may be considered as partly mercantilist.**
   - Do you think that China will soon change some of its mercantilist policies?
   - What are liberal elements in China's economic policies?

5. **Discuss the argument that the global financial and economic crisis that began in 2008 has been overcome because the principles of *Keynesian economics* were successfully applied by the United States and its European allies.**

6. **Milton Friedman argued against the government planning of economy. What were his major objections against such policies?**
   - Discuss the countries that exercise today the most significant state planning over their economies.
   - Suggest arguments in support of state planning under particular circumstances.
   - In your view, is the state planning necessary (and to what extent) when it is applied to international trade and why?

7. **What is the "financial oligarchy" described by Lenin? (See his work on the companion website [http://oup.com/us/shiraev].)**
   - Does the financial oligarchy exist today?
   - If it does, how does it impact international relations?

8. **Apply the arguments of Lenin related to imperialism to today's international relations.**
   - Which one of his arguments would be important debating today?

9. **What was the "neoliberal counter-revolution" according to Arrighi and Zhang? Provide several examples of this "counter-revolution" at work.**

10. **Discuss the "Beijing consensus" proposed by Arrighi and Zhang. Can it be become a rival of Washington Consensus?**

11. **Should or should not the United States or the European Union borrow a few elements from the Chinese model of economic and political development? Discuss your opinion.**

12. **Explain the meaning of "internationalization of production" by Susan Strange (on the companion website [http://oup.com/us/shiraev]).**
    - What consequences to international relations did this phenomenon have so far?

13. **Which groups should receive most attention in contemporary global economic policies, according to Susan Strange?**

14. **Describe the Washington Consensus and its main principles.**
    - Why did Birdsall and Fukuyama criticize these principles?
    - Provide arguments in defense of the Washington Consensus.
    - In which ways should the principles of the Washington Consensus be amended and further developed?

15. **What are the favorable and unfavorable conditions for a post–Washington Consensus?**

16. **Birdsall and Fukuyama write that what has been called "the rise of the rest" is not just about economic and political power. "It also has to do with the global competition of ideas and models."**
    - Which countries' economic models do you think can become attractive tomorrow?
    - How could Western liberal models regain their appeal?

17. **As Ambrose Evans-Pritchard assesses (on the companion website [http://oup.com/us/shiraev]), economies of China, India, and Brazil have been driven so far by (a) cheap labor and (b) imported technology.**
    - What are the potential dangers in relying on cheap labor and imported technology now?
    - What global trends may affect the cost of labor in the near future?
    - What may change in terms of the cost and availability of imported technologies?

PART III

TWENTY-FIRST CENTURY CHALLENGES

Environmental Challenges, Human Rights Protection and Development, Culture and Nationalism, and Forecasting the World of 2025 (Editorial Introduction)

When we compiled this reader, we assumed it would be very important to discuss the developments of the past two decades. Among these developments is the renewed and increased attention of the world community to environmental problems and policies, to human rights and other humanitarian issues, and to factors in world politics such as nationalism. These topics reflect on the challenges that are likely to remain very important tomorrow. Yet do these challenges compel us to rethink the classical approaches to international relations and reconsider their applications? Answers vary.

It is an understatement to say that the world is facing overwhelming environmental challenges. Coal and oil remain key sources of energy contributing to dangerous atmospheric pollution. These dangers are acknowledged not only by scientists but also by the vast majority of governments around the world. The international community launched new programs and initiatives to address environmental problems. A whole new dimension of international relations has emerged. Just several decades ago, it was enough for a group of economically advanced countries to coordinate their policies and address certain environmental issues, such as the depletion of the ozone layer in the atmosphere. Several countries have acted and the problem was for the most part resolved. A different effort is required today. It has to be persistent, and it has to be global. Can the current international system handle the environmental problems of a global magnitude? (See Figure 11.)

International environmental policies can be understood as a continuum. On one side of this continuum is environmentalism, the movement that stands for urgent and

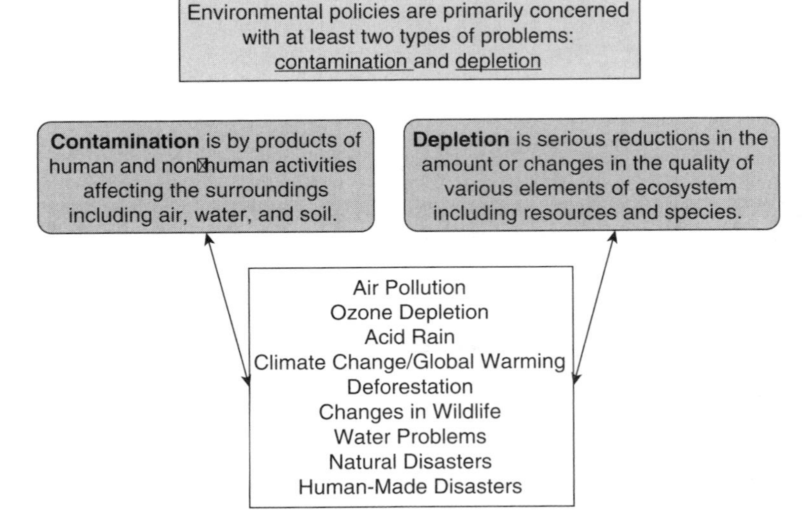

Figure 11. Key Environmental Challenges

comprehensive actions to protect the environment. Environmentalists support conservation of natural resources, push for sustained measures against contamination, and endorse sustainable development: economic growth coupled with environmental protection. They believe that many environmental problems are urgent and that the Earth's natural resources are limited. George Monbiot writes in *The Guardian* that environmentalists do not form a unitary actor; they are a community of actors that agree on many things yet disagree among themselves on methods, tactics, and the scope of environmental policies. Vigorous environmental policies created an opposition, the skeptics, who question the sincerity and scientific foundations of environmentalism. Bjørn Lomborg, one of these skeptics, does not deny the need for global environmental policies. Yet he doubts the efficiency of costly international conservation efforts and questions many strict forms of environmental regulations. Environmentalists argue back and claim that people like Lomborg serve the interests of big business and transnational corporations that seek to avoid policies of conservation and protection of nature.

The disagreements about polices exist, yet environmental activists and nongovernmental organizations provide compelling evidence connecting new and old environmental problems with developing and existing international challenges. Thomas Homer-Dixon wrote almost two decades ago about emerging environmental changes as causes of acute conflict. These environmental changes may shift the balance of power between states, thus creating instability. Warmer temperatures, for example, may increase contention over ice-free zones of accessible resources. In rich countries, environmental problems may widen social inequality. The gap between the global North and the global South may also increase, thus inevitably causing tensions between wealthy and poor countries. Food supplies may become very tight and many jobs may be lost. New waves of environmental refugees will occur and may affect cross-border tensions. Poor countries, however, will be more susceptible to environmental change than rich ones, and tensions are more likely to occur in the developing world due to decreased agricultural production, economic decline, population displacement, and disruption of social order.

Recent developments in the Arctic region can illustrate how some ongoing environmental changes affect international affairs and vice versa. Charles Ebinger and Evie Zambetakis argue that the continuing melting of the Arctic ice should pose economic, military, and environmental challenges to all countries in this region and beyond. The melting of the ice gives countries more opportunities to explore and extract oil, gas, and minerals, and to seek greater access for commercial shipping and fishing. These opportunities create competition and, potentially, international tensions. The authors believe it is crucial for all "Arctic states," including yet not limited to Russia, Canada, the United States, Denmark, and Norway, to agree on the codes of conduct and avoid rivalries that may aggravate detrimental environmental changes. New international agreements will be needed. If the countries bordering this region fail to agree on constraints on commercial development of the Arctic, then serious, more significant environmental and security problems are inevitable.

Some experts believe that energetic environmental policies have already paid off. Fossil fuels—like coal, oil, and natural gas—that contribute to pollution should soon, in this view, become obsolete due to technological innovations and the appearance of reliable substitutes for petroleum. Getting the United States off fossil fuels (by developing the alternative sources of energy) would inevitably affect this country's foreign policy, as Amory Lovins writes. A world where the United States and other developed countries depend less on oil would have fewer oil-sponsored dictatorships and less corruption, terrorism, conflict, and war. Phasing out fossil fuels would stimulate global economic development and reduce the gap between the global South and North, which is also in the United States' interest. How plausible are such expectations? Recent breakthroughs in fracking (hydraulic fracturing) technology and the extraction of large quantities of relatively inexpensive natural gas and oil will certainly affect global politics as well as the optimistic forecasts about the lessening importance of fossil fuels.

However, history shows that a collective effort and mutual compromises have solved several serious environmental problems in the past. Are countries today ready to cooperate and sacrifice for the sake of everyone's future? The debates about global environment and environmental policies will continue to define and divide ideological and political identities in the years to come.

Why do we need to have a separate discussion of humanitarian problems? All in all, the study of international relations is about studying human beings. Moreover, as some argue, this field is not only about studying. It is also about caring for people's rights and their security. These arguments are correct. Nevertheless, nowadays, governments and nongovernmental organizations should pay significantly more attention to the means and ways to alleviate suffering of millions of people, particularly in the developing and economically poor countries. These people too often become victims of political and ethnic violence, natural disasters, acute infectious diseases, abusive policies, and forceful migration. Sometimes consequences of human-made political actions and natural disasters are so significant that they require engagement and assistance of many states and organizations acting together. Often, the whole international community is supposed to be involved in addressing humanitarian crises—incidents or continuing problems threatening the health, safety, security, and well-being of many, usually in a distinct geographic area. (See Figure 12.)

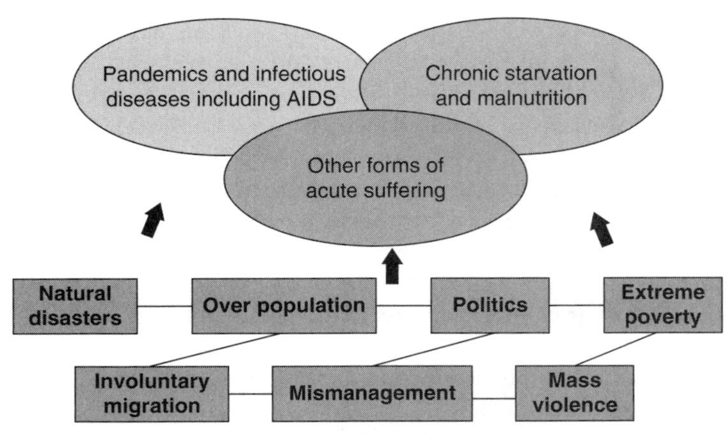

Figure 12. Key Humanitarian Problems and Their Causes

Humanitarian policies are based on three fundamental principles: humanity, impartiality, and independence. Humanity means that policies, first of all, must save lives and alleviate suffering. Impartiality means no preferences for any political leader, country, or group. Independence means that humanitarian policies are conducted independently of political, economic, or military objectives of participating states. One of the means of humanitarian policies is effective communications. As Hafner-Burton writes in *Sticks and Stones: Naming and Shaming the Human Rights Enforcement Problem*, placing certain countries in a spotlight for human rights violations and openly criticizing their governments in the media may prompt some leaders to begin addressing humanitarian problems for which they are criticized. However, the words of shame are frequently not enough to make a difference. Too often governments (especially in failing states) have no means or motivation to address a humanitarian crisis that causes or threatens to cause massive suffering or loss of life. Therefore, there is a need for humanitarian interventions, which are the actions of international community, guided by the United Nations, nongovernmental organizations, or some sovereign countries to prevent or alleviate a humanitarian crisis. Such humanitarian interventions may take place with or without the approval of a legal authority controlling the area.

There is an ongoing debate about the legality and effectiveness of humanitarian interventions. One of the objections against them is that such interventions, in fact, violate sovereignty of countries and often involve the use of the military to enforce humanitarian policies. The critics of humanitarian interventions argue that, according to international law, all governments have the ultimate right (as a feature of their sovereignty) to accept or reject humanitarian interventions on their territories. The advocates of humanitarian interventions disagree and argue that the humanitarian tradition, or humanitarianism, should provide a necessary moral justification for such interventions: people who suffer at the hand of their government or because of this government's neglect have no other sources of help. Applied to international relations, this means that governments have the responsibility to protect their citizens from the consequences of natural disasters, mass violence, starvation, or infectious diseases. If they do not fulfill their responsibility, other countries should.

Both critics and supporters of humanitarian interventions draw on a rich intellectual and legal tradition. The British philosopher John Stuart Mill (1806–1873) argued in the nineteenth century that the British Empire should set limits on when one country should intervene in the internal affairs of another, especially during a civil war in that country. He believed that any foreign intervention, however benign its proclaimed intent, must be judged as an act of violence driven by cynical self-interest. This view remains important today. It is accepted that, unfortunately, any intervention, even if it is planned on sound ethical arguments, may result in the suffering and death of human beings and have other unintended negative consequences. Second, although ethical arguments can be offered as a pretext for the use of violence, intervening countries cannot *know* for sure whether they are doing the right thing when they offer their help to others (think, for example, of the U.S. actions in Afghanistan in the past decade). Despite disagreements, it is generally accepted that governments must work to reduce both long-term and short-term civilian harm in war, atone for lawful as well as unlawful deaths, and cooperate to bring nonstate actors that target civilians to justice (think about and discuss, for instance, the consequences of the downing of the Malaysian Airlines civilian plane over Ukraine in 2014).

The humanitarian tradition claims that countries have the moral right to intervene in affairs of other countries for humanitarian reasons and not just out of strategic or security considerations. The responsibility to protect (often known as R2P or RtoP) is a new legal concept stating that if a sovereign country does not protect its own people from identifiable causes of death and acute suffering, then the international community must act. First appearing in scholarly publications and political discussions in the early 2000s, this concept was embraced at the UN World Summit in 2005.

The events of the past twenty years demonstrate that R2P has gained support in some countries but not in others. Russia and China argue, for instance, that in Yugoslavia in 1999 and in Libya in 2011, the use of NATO forces was not properly justified. R2P supporters argue back that interventions should be used with caution and only if a government is manifestly failing to protect its own people. Only then should international protection be provided in accordance with the United Nations Charter.

As Edward Luck writes, the responsibility to protect is an evolving concept. It is based on politics, values, identity, current contexts, and many other factors. Values often shape diplomatic priorities, and sometimes they affect the political will to use force. On the one hand, studies have shown both that peacekeepers, when properly mandated and equipped, can offer protection from atrocious crimes and that international engagement has already helped to prevent genocidal acts in troubled societies. On the other hand, there is a very delicate balance between a country's sovereignty and international humanitarian activism. In 1999, the United States and other NATO countries started a military campaign against Yugoslavia as a humanitarian intervention to stop the "ethnic cleansing" of ethnic Albanians living in Kosovo. Russia disagreed and protested the war, citing the absence of the UN resolutions to use force in Kosovo. In 2014 and later, Russia portrayed the consequences of the Ukrainian government's actions against separatists in Easter Ukraine as a humanitarian crisis. This time Western courtiers chose to disagree. As you remember from Part II, in international relations, perceptions of other states' actions matter.

Moral principles are often mentioned as the most important justifications for humanitarian actions. In reality, implementation of humanitarian activism runs into many practical dilemmas and difficult impasses. Among the most significant are the evolving contradictions between moral values and legal rules: we may believe that we are right, yet are our actions legal? Another issue is a conflict between the genuine desire to help and the fallacies of self-righteousness. Yet another problem is that some countries, particularly nondemocracies, often claim that humanitarian interventionism is just another excuse for the dominant Western countries to impose their will and shape the international system according to their interests.

Humanitarian actions and the use of force to implement them will be discussed for years to come. Besides the moral aspect of such actions, there is also concern about the effectiveness of some humanitarian policies. Jacob Mchangama and Guglielmo Verdirame turn their attention to the phenomenon that they call "human rights proliferation." Liberal democracies, in their view, should not weaken their effort by overextending. Even the most resourceful governments and organizations cannot do too many things in too many places. Instead, they should pay the most serious attention to the most egregious violations of human rights and focus on the most significant threats before turning to others.

Numerous examples from the history of international relations show that international peace and lasting cooperation cannot be ensured by military and economic domination alone. Peace and cooperation require an informed consent of diverse groups of people, the consent of "hearts and minds." In today's world there are regions where such consent is difficult to reach. We know that some ideas and symbols are shared globally. Look, for instance, at the success of European soccer or American basketball: they are winning the hearts of hundreds of millions of followers globally. At the same time, as in the past, many people today resist foreign political influence and simply reject any ideas and policies that are coming from abroad. Cultural divides contribute to international conflicts. Nationalist sentiments and religious passions can shape and change international politics as profoundly as the issues related to economic inequality and military security. International politics can be complicated and aggravated by clashes of ideas and values.

The very nature of values and ideas in international relations is a disputed issue, with many perspectives competing. One sweeping view has been offered by feminism. J. Ann Tickner emphasizes the urgent importance of "gendering" international relations, arguing that most concepts and doctrines in this field have been drawn from the male perspective. She explains how feminism as a political movement influenced academic feminism and it has, in turn, affected our understanding of international politics.

Another perspective comes from research in social psychology. Holger Mölder introduces an important psychological dimension to the discussion of international politics: he calls it "a culture of fear." Fear, as an emotion, is an individual's response to a threat, as well as to uncertainty and instability. Political leaders can provoke fear in their citizens. They can even cultivate a culture of fear in their countries. Social problems, ethnic tensions, and diplomatic disputes may strengthen the culture of fear. Where such a culture exists, interstate compromises become more difficult and the risk of war significantly increases. Cultural factors also affect the success of military operations, as Mansoor points out in *The Softer Side of War.* Cultural factors become a major aspect in managing relations between international allies. Values, identities, and beliefs are also important to study because they help explain the worldview and motivations of potential adversaries.

Nationalism is one of the most intriguing phenomena in the study of international relations, the arena where interests, identities, and values mesh together. Nationalism is also a powerful political force. Nationalist ideas capture the imagination of individuals and large groups easily and often rapidly. Nationalism is not exclusively rooted in psychological factors. Jerry Muller sees the core of nationalism to be a shared cultural heritage, which usually includes a common language, a common faith, and often (but not always) a common ethnic ancestry. In Europe in the late nineteenth century the growth of nationalism coexisted with the rise of political representation, industrial capitalism, bureaucratic state, modern communications, universal literacy, and urbanization. As railroads and public schools undermined local identities, as the power of the clan, the guild, and the church was diminishing, Europeans developed allegiance to "nation-states." In other countries, this process was different.

The formation of nation-states is most likely not over. The collapse of the Soviet Union in 1991, for instance, gave birth to an independent Ukraine and many other sovereign countries that used to be in the union. Ukraine and Russia historically shared very close cultural and linguistic ties. Igor Torbakov in *History, Memory, and National Identity* shows how the national identities of these two countries have been under attack from nationalist historians and politicians. In 2014 and later the world was a witness of how these debates escalated into open hostilities between Ukraine and Russia. The territorial conflict became aggravated by the clash of historical memories and national identities. Violent forms of nationalism have been fueled by state-sponsored propaganda on both sides, which made any quick dissemination of tension between these two countries very difficult.

If people become increasingly secular (there are almost 1 billion people on Earth who claim no religious identity), will this trend weaken nationalism? Secularization, as some believe, goes hand in hand with modernization, the spread of education, science, technology, prosperity, and tolerance. Scott Thomas disputes this assumption. He writes that the trend toward secularization has also given way to religious resurgence, including the rise of religious fundamentalism. Religion is increasingly often a matter of individual choice, not tradition. Religion spreads among educated urban professionals. Globalization and global migration facilitate the detachment of religion from traditional ethnic and national roots. There are new, virtual, Web-based communities that know no borders and reach out across ethnic and national groups. This new religious revival has already changed the nature of international relations. In the past, for example, especially during the Cold War, the West had a strong political but also faith-based consensus on its foreign actions, especially regarding the atheist Soviet Union. Today, there is no longer consent in Western countries, even among religious believers, on foreign policy.

The concluding section introduces several important ideas about the future of international relations. No single theory has the power to predict the future because there are too many factors out there to influence world politics. Predictions have always been difficult in this field. Experts did not anticipate the quick implosion of Communism in Eastern Europe in 1989 and the collapse of the Soviet Union in 1991. Very few predicted a global financial meltdown in 2008 in the United States and the crisis of Eurozone in 2011. Even fewer could foresee the revolutionary turmoil in the

Arab world in recent years. Almost nobody projected Russia taking over Crimea from Ukraine in 2014. This list can be easily expanded.

Why are there so few good forecasts in international relations? In part, the problem is in what we call *intellectual conformism*: the majority of experts, as well as journalists, tend to have a "pack mentality." This means that they rarely dissent from the majority opinion, even when there are facts and other indicators urging them to abandon the consensus or at least to question it. Therefore, to battle intellectual conformism, we think that it is more important to compare different, sharply diverging views on the future of international relations.

The American scholar Jack Goldstone points to the changing demographics as a vital indicator to watch. He argues that the relative demographic weight of the richest countries will drop; the developed countries' labor forces will substantially age; most of the world's expected population growth will increasingly be concentrated in today's poorest countries; and most people in the world will become urbanized. He shows that, because of low birth rates in the West, economic power will be shifting to the developing nations. There are other consequences of demographic decline for Western countries. As its indigenous population continues to age and decline, the demand for immigrant workers will grow. At the same time, the world's youngest population will be increasingly concentrated in today's poorest countries, which have a dangerous lack of quality education, investments, and jobs. Moreover, most of the world's population will become urbanized, with the largest urban centers being in the world's poorest countries, where decent living conditions are scarce. This could lead to a deepening global polarization, increased political instability, and social unrest.

Will the demographic, social, and economic problems undermine the spread of democracy? Could these problems push the world into new authoritarianism? Almost seven decades ago, George Orwell published *Nineteen Eighty-Four*. This widely acclaimed novel described the world of 1984 in which three empires divide the world and are constantly engaged in mega-wars among themselves. All power belongs to an "inner party," an authoritarian and well-organized clique. The masses are obedient, terrorized, and distracted by propaganda and cheap entertainment. All facts are manipulated, extorted beyond recognition, and simply exchanged for lies. Although the novel has never been considered a scholarly analysis of the future, today's experts from different fields use it as an allegory for pessimistic scenarios of international relations.

Today, however, deeply pessimistic forecasts alluding to a global revival of authoritarianism are rare. In fact, an opposite trend—many forecasts filled with optimism and confidence—has emerged in scholarly analyses of the future of international relations. Alexander Wendt proposes a global state, which in his view is inevitable in one hundred years or so. He predicts a gradual evolution of the international order, which will move from a congregation of states to a society of states, and finally, to a world state, which will be nonauthoritarian and peaceful. He further explains why and how countries will support the gradual reduction of their sovereignty in favor of international institutions and international norms.

Daniel Deudney and G. John Ikenberry provide another example of an optimistic forecast. They see no viable alternative to a global democratic project. Even authoritarian countries have no choice but to play by the rules set by economic and political liberalism. In particular, China, they argue, would not challenge the liberal order because the Chinese leaders want to benefit from its policies, practices, and institutions while being in the center of the global liberal system. As Ikenberry further argues in *The Illusion of Geopolitics*, some "backsliding" from the liberal order has occurred, such as Russia's challenge to the West. However, the more significant trend has been the emergence of a group of democratic countries such as Australia, Brazil, India, Indonesia, Mexico, South Korea, and Turkey. They are acting as participants or "stakeholders" in the international system of the twenty-first century: pursuing multilateral cooperation, assuming greater responsibilities, and exercising influence through peaceful means.

Which countries are likely to play the key economic role in the world of tomorrow? There is an argument that any country that hopes to become an economic superpower must be large, vibrant, and globally integrated. It cannot be isolated. Most experts mention at least three names as potential candidates to lead the world economically in the near future: the United States, the European Union, and China. Other authors sometimes put Brazil and India on this list, but such inclusions are rather infrequent. There is practically no mention of Russia as a candidate for the global leadership: it is argued that the country's economy is too dependent on its gas and oil, and its population is not increasing.

What about the role of the United States in the global world? A body of research is showing that the United States over the past decade was in decline relative to China. Others point out that this decline was the result of globalization and the inability of the United States to respond to global challenges. Michael Beckley argues that both views are wrong. The United States in the second decade of the twenty-first century remains wealthier, more innovative, and more militarily powerful than China. Furthermore, globalization and hegemony reinforce U.S. power, not erode it. The United States continue to set the rules, norms, and values of the international system—all much to its benefit.

History tells us that no great power, including the United States, can retain its leadership in world politics forever. Yet the United States is likely to remain for some time a major economic and military power and a center of technological innovations, education, and science.

GENERAL DISCUSSION QUESTIONS RELATED TO THE READING MATERIALS ON ENVIRONMENTAL CHALLENGES, HUMANITARIAN PROBLEMS, IDENTITY AND CULTURE FACTORS, AND FORECASTS

These general questions are for class discussions as well as individual assignments. The discussion of these questions should help students think critically and better understand the materials in this section. Other, more specific critical-thinking and practice questions related to the reading materials appear at the end of Part III.

- Do any of the global environmental problems directly affect you or people you know personally? If yes, in what way? Suggest an example.
- Using a case of your choice, analyze a *depletion* problem that has led or might lead to an international conflict. Consider water or other resources (and access to them) as an illustration.

- Contemporary environmental discussions resemble the longtime debate between cornucopians (a reference to the "cornucopia," or horn of plenty), who believed that natural resources are practically limitless, and neo-Malthusians, the followers of the nineteenth-century British scholar Thomas Robert Malthus, who predicted that the inevitable depletion of natural resources would generate conflicts. Would you consider yourself a "cornucopian," a "neo-Malthusian," somewhere in between, or neither of these two choices? Discuss your position.
- Despite their differences, environmentalists and skeptics may agree on a few issues. Which ones, and why?
- Imagine that affordable alternative energy sources have finally emerged tomorrow and fossil fuel such as oil and coil have become too expensive and thus obsolete.
  - How would this new energy situation affect international relations?
  - If oil no longer is a top commodity on the global market, will this new development affect (1) Washington's policies toward Saudi Arabia and (2) European Union's policies toward Russia?
- Will it be possible, in your opinion, to eradicate global poverty during your lifetime? What should be done in terms of international policies to eradicate global poverty?
- Investigate and suggest the conditions when a restrictive migration (immigration) policy—within one country as well as between two or more countries—becomes a humanitarian problem.
- In most countries these days, children's education is mandatory and paid for by the government. A child's access to education is considered a basic right. Do you think that every person by 2025 should have guaranteed access to health care and employment regardless of where this person lives? Should the right to receive health care be a universal human right? Will it be achievable in 10 years? Explain you view.
- Why are values and identities important in international relations? How might a leader's cultural identity affect his or her decisions in foreign policy? Give one example.
- We know about negative consequences of religious intolerance and fundamentalism. Suggest examples when religious values can positively affect international relations by promoting peace, tolerance, and care.
- We all know that perceptions matter in politics. What factors (such as specific policies), in your view, should diminish anti-American stereotypes among some people in the non-Western world?
- Global fertility rates are declining, which means that today, on average, women tend to have fewer children than they had twenty years ago. In many countries (including Latin America, Turkey, and Iran) the fertility rate is at a record low, which is around two children per woman. Discuss how the falling fertility rates may affect cultural values involving the family, traditions, and interpersonal communications. Discuss how the ongoing demographic changes would affect countries' polices and, ultimately, international relations by 2015.
- Does China have economic incentives to challenge the global liberal order? Will China, in your opinion, challenge this order for any other reasons? Explain your view.

Environmental Challenges and Policies

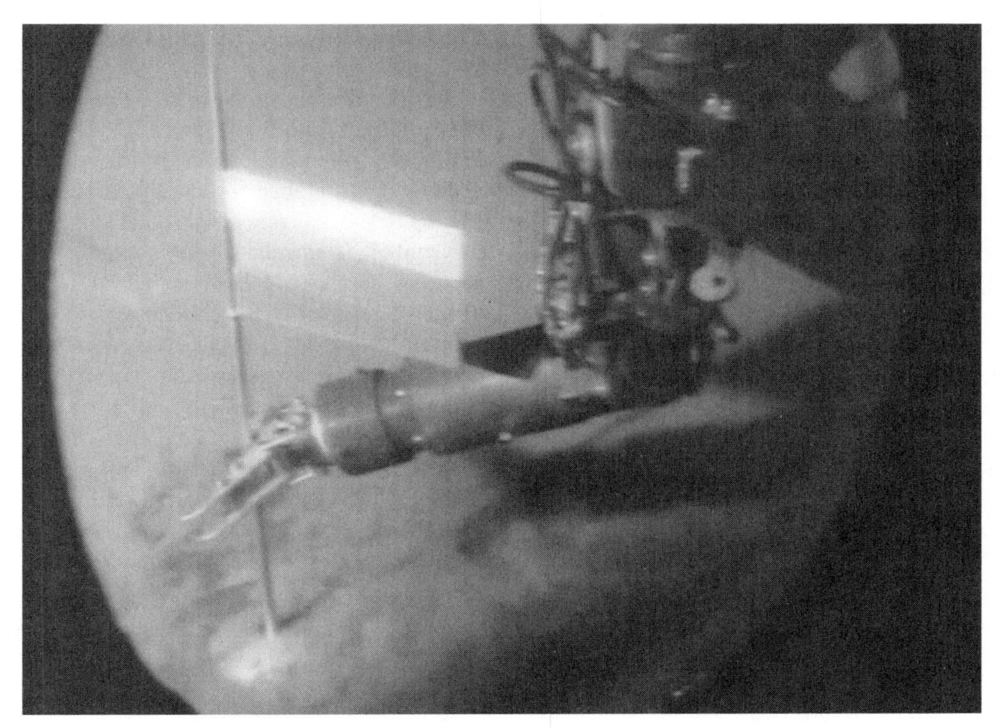

An operator of a Russian mini-submarine plants a titanium capsule with the Russian flag during a record dive in the Arctic Ocean under the ice at the North Pole in 2007. For years now, Russia has claimed much of the Arctic's oil-and-mineral wealth. If the Arctic ice continues melting, the world might plunge into a dangerous conflict, as Charles Ebinger and Evie Zambetakis warn in their article. However, as Amory Lovins suggests, with the diminished value of fossil fuels, the probability of such conflicts should diminish. Which view seems more plausible to you?
Source: TV/Associated Press

On the Threshold: Environmental Changes as Causes of Acute Conflict

THOMAS F. HOMER-DIXON

This article proposes a research agenda to guide the study of environmental change and acute conflict. Before we can formulate plausible hypotheses, however, we need a clear analytical framework, such as suggested by Figure 13. This and subsequent figures in this article provide the basis for a detailed causal-path analysis of the links between environmental change and conflict. Such an analysis can help bring some order into the profusion of predictions concerning these issues, and it can also help researchers address several of the impediments to research.

Figure 13 suggests that the total effect of human activity on the environment in a particular ecological region is mainly a function of two variables: first, the product of total population in the region and physical activity per capita, and second, the vulnerability of the ecosystem in that region to those particular activities. Activity per capita, in turn, is a function of available physical resources (which include nonrenewable resources such as minerals, and renewable resources such as water, forests, and agricultural land) and ideational factors, including institutions, social relations, preferences, and beliefs. The figure also shows that environmental effects may cause social effects that in turn could lead to conflict. For example, the degradation of agricultural land might produce large-scale migration, which could create ethnic conflicts as migratory groups clash with indigenous populations. There are important feedback loops from social effects and conflict to the ideational factors and thence back to activity per capita and population. Thus, ethnic clashes arising from migration could alter the operation of a society's markets and thereby its economic activity.

To clarify the research agenda, we can divide the "how" question (how will environmental change lead to conflict?) into two independent questions. First, what are the important social effects of environmental change? Second, what types of acute conflict, if any, are most likely to result from these social effects? The first question asks about the nature of the arrow in Figure 13 between "environmental effects" and "social effects," while the second asks about the arrow between "social effects" and "conflict."

My focus on these two causal linkages does not deny the importance of the other variables and linkages in the figure. We must be aware of the role of population growth, demographic structure, and patterns of population distribution. And we must understand the effect of the ideational factors at the top of the diagram. This social and psychological context is immensely broad and complex. It includes patterns of land distribution (as in the Soccer War); family and community structure; the economic and legal incentives to consume and produce goods, including the system of property rights and markets; perceptions of the probability of long-run political and economic stability; historically rooted patterns of trade and interaction with other societies (as with debt and export relations between the Philippines and the North); the distribution of coercive power within and among nations; the form and effectiveness of institutions of governance; and metaphysical beliefs about the relationship between humans and nature (as in medieval Castile).

Without a full understanding of these intervening factors we cannot begin to grasp the true nature of the relationships between human activity, environmental change, social disruption, and conflict. These factors largely determine the vulnerability and adaptability of a society when faced with environmental stresses. There is historical evidence that certain societies have technological,

Thomas Homer-Dixon, 'On the Threshold: Environmental Changes as Causes of Acute Conflict.', International Security, Vol. 16, No. 2 (Autumn, 1991), pp. 76–116.

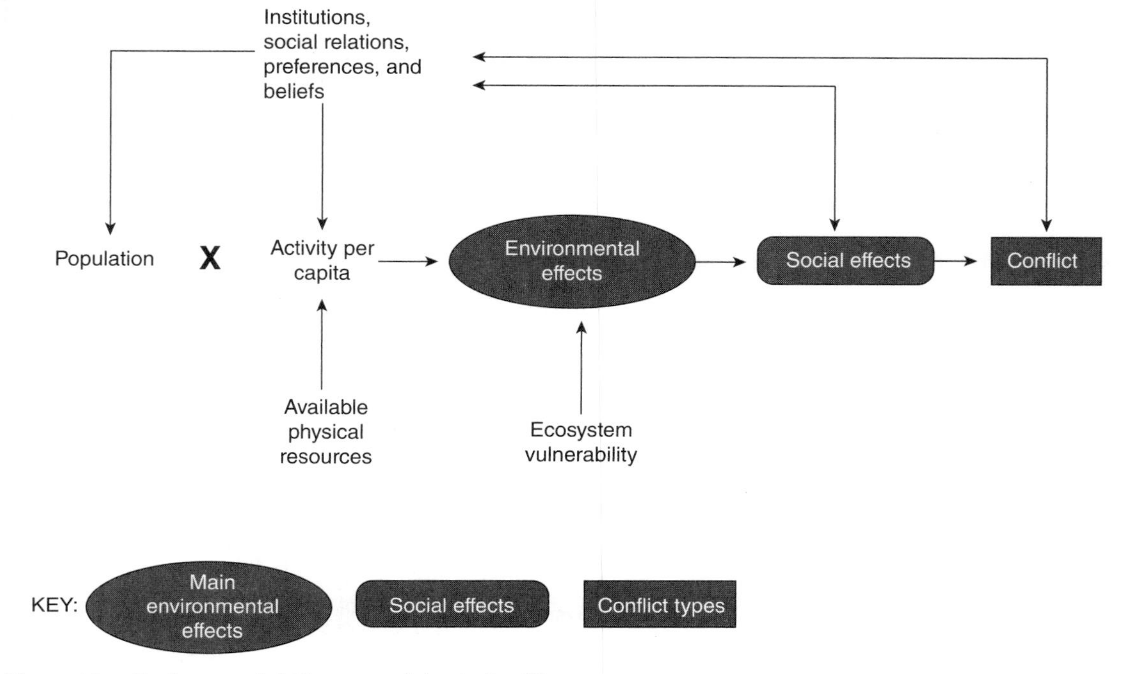

Figure 13. Environmental Change and Acute Conflict

institutional, or cultural characteristics that make them very resilient to such pressures. Not only do we need to identify the thresholds beyond which given societies cannot effectively respond, we need to determine why some societies respond better than others.

Figure 13 clarifies these aspects of our research agenda. If we wish to understand a society's capacity to prevent severe social disruption (where the preventive action could be either mitigation of, or adaptation to, the environmental stress), we need to understand the arrows between the ideational factors at the top of the figure and "population," "activity per capita," and "social effects" along the main spine of the figure. If we wish to understand a society's propensity toward conflict (given certain social effects due to the environmental stress), we need to understand the arrow between the ideational factors and "conflict." When sufficiently advanced, this research should help identify key intervention points where policymakers might be able to alter the causal processes linking human activity, environmental degradation, and conflict. These interventions will fall into two general categories: those that seek to prevent negative social effects and those that seek to prevent the conflict that could result from these social effects. In the following pages I refer to these as "first-stage" and "second-stage" interventions.

THE RANGE OF ENVIRONMENTAL PROBLEMS

Developing countries are likely to be affected sooner and more severely by environmental change than rich countries. By definition, they do not have the financial, material, or intellectual resources of the developed world; furthermore, their social and political institutions tend to be fragile and riven with discord. It is probable, therefore, that developing societies will be less able to apprehend or respond to environmental disruption.

Seven major environmental problems (the "environmental effects" in Figure 13) might plausibly contribute to conflict within and among developing countries: greenhouse warming, stratospheric ozone depletion, acid deposition, deforestation, degradation of agricultural land, overuse and pollution of water supplies, and depletion of fish stocks. These problems can all be crudely characterized as large-scale human-induced problems, with long-term and often irreversible consequences, which is why they are often grouped together under the rubric "global change." However, they vary greatly in spatial scale: the first two involve genuinely global physical processes, while the last five involve regional physical processes, although they may appear in locales all over the planet. These seven problems also vary in time scale: for example, while a region can be deforested in only a few years, and severe ecological and social effects may be noticeable almost immediately, human-induced greenhouse warming will probably develop over many decades and may not have truly serious implications for humankind for half a century or more after the signal is first detected. In addition, some of these problems (for instance, deforestation and degradation of water supplies) are much more advanced than others (such as greenhouse warming and ozone depletion) and are already producing serious social disruption. This variance in tangible evidence for these problems contributes to great differences in our certainty about their ultimate severity. The uncertainties surrounding greenhouse warming, for example, are thus far greater than those concerning deforestation.

Many of these problems are causally interrelated. For instance, acid deposition damages agricultural land, fisheries, and forests. Greenhouse warming may contribute to deforestation by moving northward the optimal temperature and precipitation zones for many tree species, by increasing the severity of windstorms and wildfires, and by expanding the range of pests and diseases. The release of carbon from these dying forests would reinforce the greenhouse effect. The increased incidence of ultraviolet radiation due to the depletion of the ozone layer will probably damage trees and crops, and it may also damage the phytoplankton at the bottom of the ocean food chain.

Finally, when we consider the social effects of environmental change, especially of climate change, we should be especially aware of changes in the incidence of "extreme" environmental events. Social impacts result "not so much from slow fluctuations in the mean, but from the tails of the distribution, from extreme events." While a two-to-three degree celsius mean global warming might not seem too significant for agricultural production, it may produce a large increase in crop-devastating droughts, floods, heat waves, and storms.

Four Principal Social Effects

Environmental degradation may cause countless often subtle changes in developing societies. These range from increased communal cooking as fuelwood becomes scarce around African villages, to worsened poverty of Filipino coastal fishermen whose once-abundant grounds have been destroyed by trawlers and industrial pollution. Which of the many types of social effect might be crucial links between environmental change and acute conflict? This is the first part of the "how" question. To address it, we must use both the best knowledge about the social effects of environmental change and the best knowledge about the nature and causes of social conflict.

In thus working from both ends towards the middle of the causal chain, I hypothesize that four principal social effects may, either singly or in combination, substantially increase the probability of acute conflict in developing countries: decreased agricultural production, economic decline, population displacement, and disruption of legitimized and authoritative institutions and social relations. These effects will often be causally interlinked, sometimes with reinforcing relationships. For example, the population displacement resulting from a decrease in agricultural production may further disrupt agricultural production. Or economic decline may lead to the flight of people with wealth and education, which in turn could eviscerate universities, courts, and institutions of economic management, all of which are crucial to a healthy economy.

Agricultural Production

Decreased agricultural production is often mentioned as potentially the most worrisome consequence of environmental change, and Figure 14

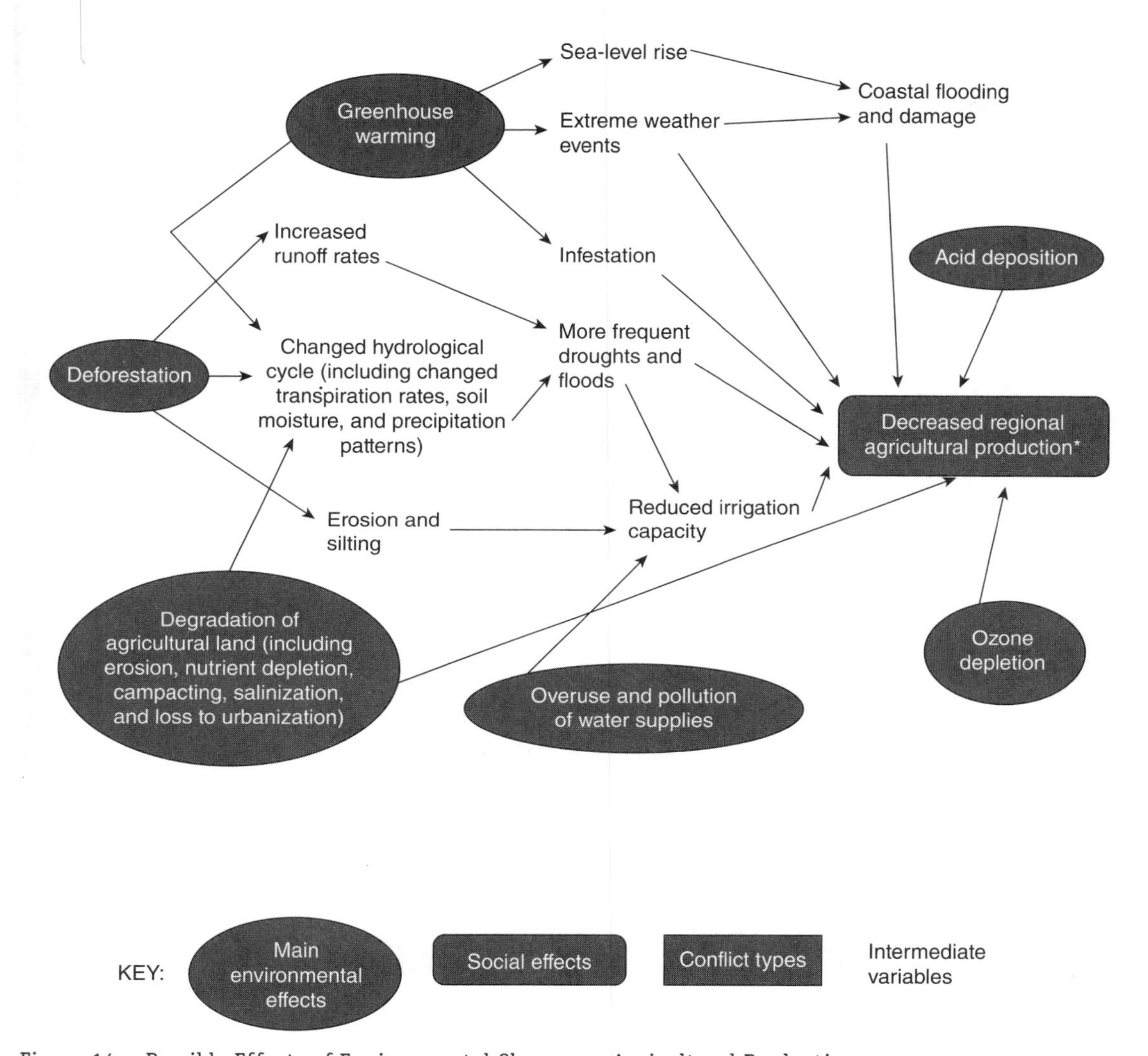

Figure 14. Possible Effects of Environmental Change on Agricultural Production

presents some of the causal scenarios frequently proposed by researchers.

Economic Decline

If we are interested in environment-conflict linkages, perhaps the most important potential social effect of environmental degradation is the further impoverishment it may produce in developing societies. In Figure 15, I suggest some key causal processes. The figure shows that economic productivity may be influenced directly by environmental disruption, or indirectly via other social effects such as decreased agricultural production. While few developing countries will exhibit all causal links indicated in Figure 15, most will exhibit some.

Population Displacement

Some commentators have suggested that environmental degradation may produce vast numbers of "environmental refugees." Sea-level rise may drive people back from coastal and delta areas in Egypt; spreading desert may empty Sahelian countries as their populations move south; Filipino fishermen may leave their depleted fishing grounds for the

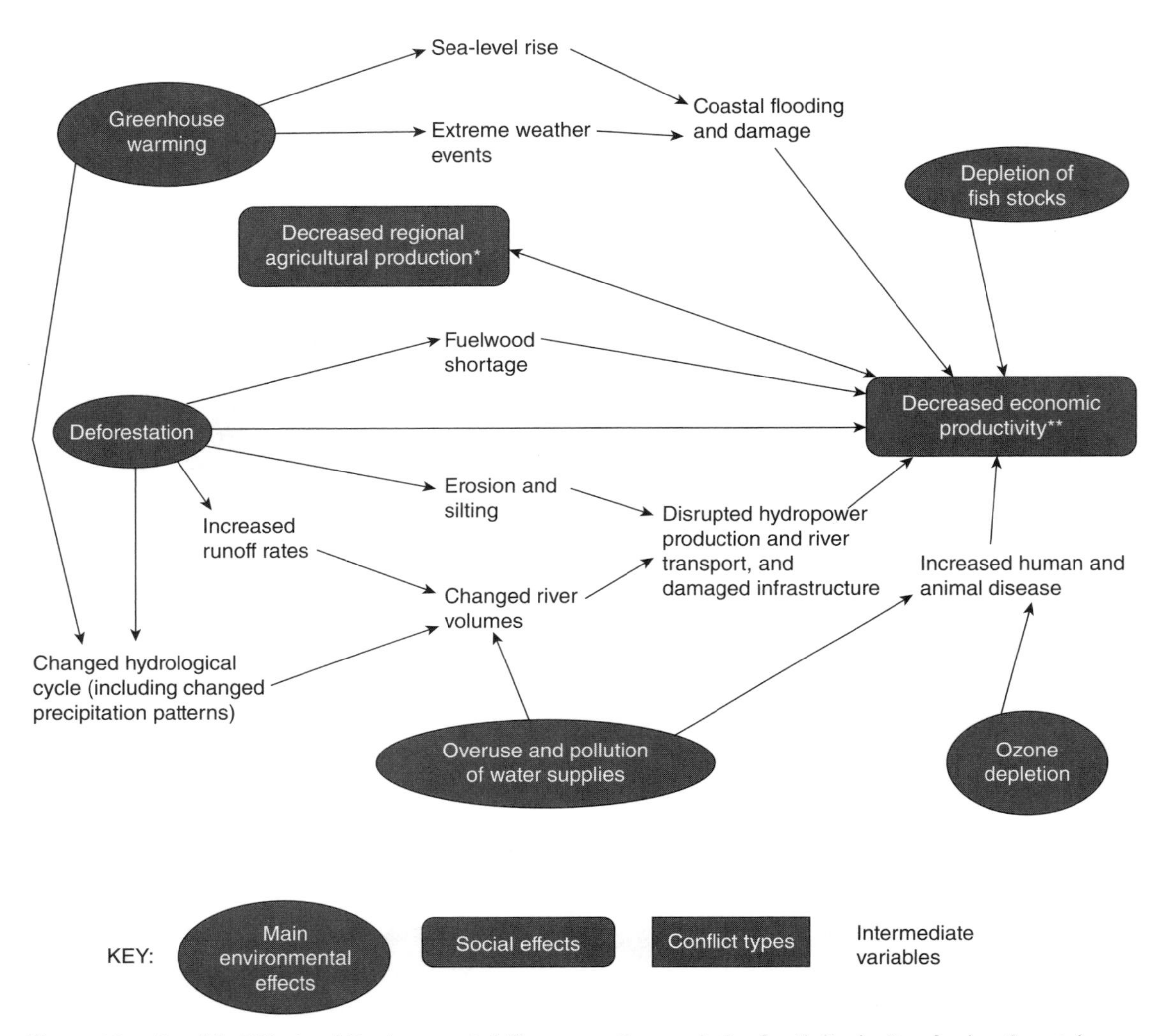

Figure 15. Possible Effects of Environmental Change on Economic Productivity in Developing Countries

cities. The term "environmental refugee" is somewhat misleading, however, because it implies that environmental disruption could be a clear, proximate cause of refugee flows. Usually, though, environmental disruption will be only one of many interacting physical and social variables, including agricultural and economic decline, that ultimately force people from their homelands.

Disrupted Institutions and Social Relations

The fourth social effect especially relevant to the connection between environment change and acute conflict is the disruption of institutions and of legitimized, accepted, and authoritative social relations. In many developing societies, the three social effects described above are likely to tear this fabric of custom and habitual behavior. A drop in agricultural output may weaken rural communities by causing malnutrition and disease, and by encouraging people to leave; economic decline may corrode confidence in the national purpose, weaken the tax base, and undermine financial, legal, and political institutions; and mass migrations of people into a region may disrupt labor markets, shift class relations, and upset the traditional balance of economic and political authority between ethnic groups.

TYPES OF CONFLICT

It seems likely that first-stage policy interventions will not be fully successful in preventing the four principal social effects posited above. We therefore turn to the second part of the "how" question: if agricultural production drops, if developing societies slide further into poverty, if large numbers of people are forced from their homelands, and if institutions and social relations are disrupted, what kinds of conflict are likely to develop? At present, we can bring only limited empirical evidence to bear on this question. This may be partly because environmental and population pressures have not yet passed a critical threshold of severity in many developing countries; also, there has been little case-study research on environment-conflict linkages. In what follows, therefore, I propose some further hypotheses for testing.

Three Theoretical Perspectives on Conflict

Drawing on these theories, I hypothesize that severe environmental degradation will produce three principal types of conflict. These should be considered ideal types: they will rarely, if ever, be found in pure form in the real world.

Simple Scarcity Conflicts

Simple scarcity conflicts are explained and predicted by general structural theories. They are the conflicts we would expect when state actors rationally calculate their interests in a zero-sum or negative-sum situation such as might arise from resource scarcity. We have seen such conflicts often in the past; they are easily understood within the realist paradigm of international relations theory, and they therefore are likely to receive undue attention from current security scholars.

Group-Identity Conflicts

Group-identity conflicts are explained and predicted by group-identity theories. Such conflicts are likely to arise from the large-scale movements of populations brought about by environmental change. As different ethnic and cultural groups are propelled together under circumstances of deprivation and stress, we should expect intergroup hostility, in which a group would emphasize its own identity while denigrating, discriminating against, and attacking outsiders. The situation in the Bangladesh-Assam region may be a good example of this process; Assam's ethnic strife over the last decade has apparently been provoked by migration from Bangladesh.

As population and environmental stresses grow in developing countries, migration to the developed world is likely to surge. "The image of islands of affluence amidst a sea of poverty is not inaccurate." People will seek to move from Latin America to the United States and Canada, from North Africa and the Middle East to Europe, and from South and Southeast Asia to Australia. This migration has already shifted the ethnic balance in many cities and regions of developed countries, and governments are struggling to contain a xenophobic backlash. Such racial strife will undoubtedly become much worse.

Relative-Deprivation Conflicts

Relative-deprivation theories indicate that as developing societies produce less wealth because of environmental problems, their citizens will probably become increasingly discontented by the widening gap between their actual level of economic achievement and the level they feel they deserve. The rate of change is key: the faster the economic deterioration, it is hypothesized, the greater the discontent. Lower-status groups will be more frustrated than others because elites will use their power to maintain, as best they can, access to a constant standard of living despite a shrinking economic pie. At some point, the discontent and frustration of some groups may cross a critical threshold, and they will act violently against other groups perceived to be the agents of their economic misery or thought to be benefiting from a grossly unfair distribution of economic goods in the society.

CONFLICT OBJECTIVES AND SCOPE

Table 2 compares some attributes of the principal types of acute conflict that I hypothesize may result

Table 2: Comparison of Conflict Types

Conflict Type	Objective Sought	Conflict Scope
Simple scarcity	Relief from scarcity	International
Group identity	Protection and reinforcement of group identity	International or domestic
Relative deprivation	Distributive justice	Domestic (with international repercussions)

from environmental change. The table lists the objectives sought by actors involved in these conflicts (which are, once again, ideal types). There is strong normative content to the motives of challenger groups involved in relative-deprivation conflicts: these groups believe the distribution of rewards is unfair. But such an "ought" does not necessarily drive simple-scarcity conflicts: one state may decide that it needs something another state has, and then try to seize it, without being motivated by a strong sense of unfairness or injustice.

Table 2 also shows that the scope of conflict can be expected to differ. Although relative-deprivation conflicts will tend to be domestic, we should not underestimate their potentially severe international repercussions. The correlation between civil strife and external conflict behavior is a function of the nature of the regime and of the kind of internal conflict it faces. For example, highly centralized dictatorships threatened by revolutionary actions, purges, and strikes are especially prone to engage in external war and belligerence. In comparison, less centralized dictatorships are prone to such behavior when threatened by guerrilla action and assassinations. External aggression may also result after a new regime comes to power through civil strife: regimes borne of revolution, for example, are particularly good at mobilizing their citizens and resources for military preparation and war.

While environmental stresses and the conflicts they induce may encourage the rise of revolutionary regimes, other results are also plausible: these pressures might overwhelm the management capacity of institutions in developing countries, inducing praetorianism or widespread social disintegration. They may also weaken the control of governments over their territories, especially over the hinterland (as in the Philippines). The regimes that do gain power in the face of such disruption are likely to be extremist, authoritarian, and abusive of human rights. Moreover, the already short time horizons of policymakers in developing countries will be further shortened. These political factors could seriously undermine efforts to mitigate and adapt to environmental change. Soon to be the biggest contributors to global environmental problems, developing countries could become more belligerent, less willing to compromise with other states, and less capable of controlling their territories in order to implement measures to reduce environmental damage.

If many developing countries evolve in the direction of extremism, the interests of the North may be directly threatened. Of special concern here is the growing disparity between rich and poor nations that may be induced by environmental change. Robert Heilbroner notes that revolutionary regimes "are not likely to view the vast difference between first class and cattle class with the forgiving eyes of their predecessors." Furthermore, these nations may be heavily armed, as the proliferation of nuclear and chemical weapons and ballistic missiles continues. Such regimes, he asserts, could be tempted to use nuclear blackmail as a "means of inducing the developed world to transfer its wealth on an unprecedented scale to the underdeveloped world." Richard Ullman, however, argues that this concern is overstated. Third world nations are unlikely to confront the North violently in the face of the "superior destructive capabilities of the rich." In light of the discussion in this article, we might conclude that environmental stress and its attendant social disruption will so debilitate the economies of developing countries that they will be unable to amass sizeable armed forces, conventional or otherwise. But the North would surely be unwise to rely on impoverishment and disorder in the South for its security.

CONCLUSIONS

This article sets out a research agenda for studying the links between environmental change and acute conflict. Given current theories and data, we probably cannot go much further than the preliminary analysis offered here. Case studies of specific societies focused on the "where" question—where are the different kinds of environmentally derived conflict most likely to occur?—will help us test our hypotheses about *how* environmental change might contribute to conflict.

Such research will also reveal important things about real societies in the real world. We must in particular look for intervening variables—including institutions, technologies, and market mechanisms—that humankind might influence in order to change the course of environmental-social systems. We may learn that there are real opportunities for intervention; hardship and strife are not preordained. But it seems likely that, as environmental degradation proceeds, the size of the potential social disruption will increase, while our capacity to intervene to prevent this disruption decreases. It is therefore not a reasonable policy response to assume we can intervene at a late stage, when the crisis is upon us. Developing countries, in concert with the North, should act now to address the forces behind environmental degradation.

The Geopolitics of Arctic Melt

CHARLES K. EBINGER AND EVIE ZAMBETAKIS

Global climate change has catapulted the Arctic into the centre of geopolitics, as melting Arctic ice transforms the region from one of primarily scientific interest into a maelstrom of competing commercial, national security and environmental concerns, with profound implications for the international legal and political system.

The significance of an Arctic rendered increasingly accessible by the melting of ice as a result of rising global temperatures should not be underestimated. As the region opens to increased human activity such as traffic from commercial shipping, tourism, and oil and gas exploration, soot emitted by maritime vessels and operations will land on the ice. Greying of the icecap, as black carbon from incomplete hydrocarbon combustion lodges itself in snow and ice, causes what was once a reflective surface to absorb more sunlight, melt, and warm the water. The resulting dangerous feedback loop is part of an alarming phenomenon that is pushing the current drive for policies to slow down climate change.

Increasing water temperatures are changing the distribution of sea ice and having grave impacts on ice-dependent flora and fauna. In September 2009 nearly 3,500 walruses congregated on Alaska's north-west coast off the Chukchi Sea because of reduced sea ice; the same happened in 2007 with over 6,000 walruses. Polar bears are likely to face extinction in less than 70 years as they lose their traditional breeding and hunting grounds to melting ice. Red foxes are migrating ever northwards and displacing smaller Arctic foxes. The list goes on.

The loss of permafrost, animals and fish could have a devastating effect on the native peoples of the region, whose cultures continue to be linked intimately with them. The Inuit hunting culture is directly threatened by changes not only in the physical geography of the environment but in the composition of the animal population. Villages along the Bering and Chukchi coasts have been relocated because of melting permafrost and

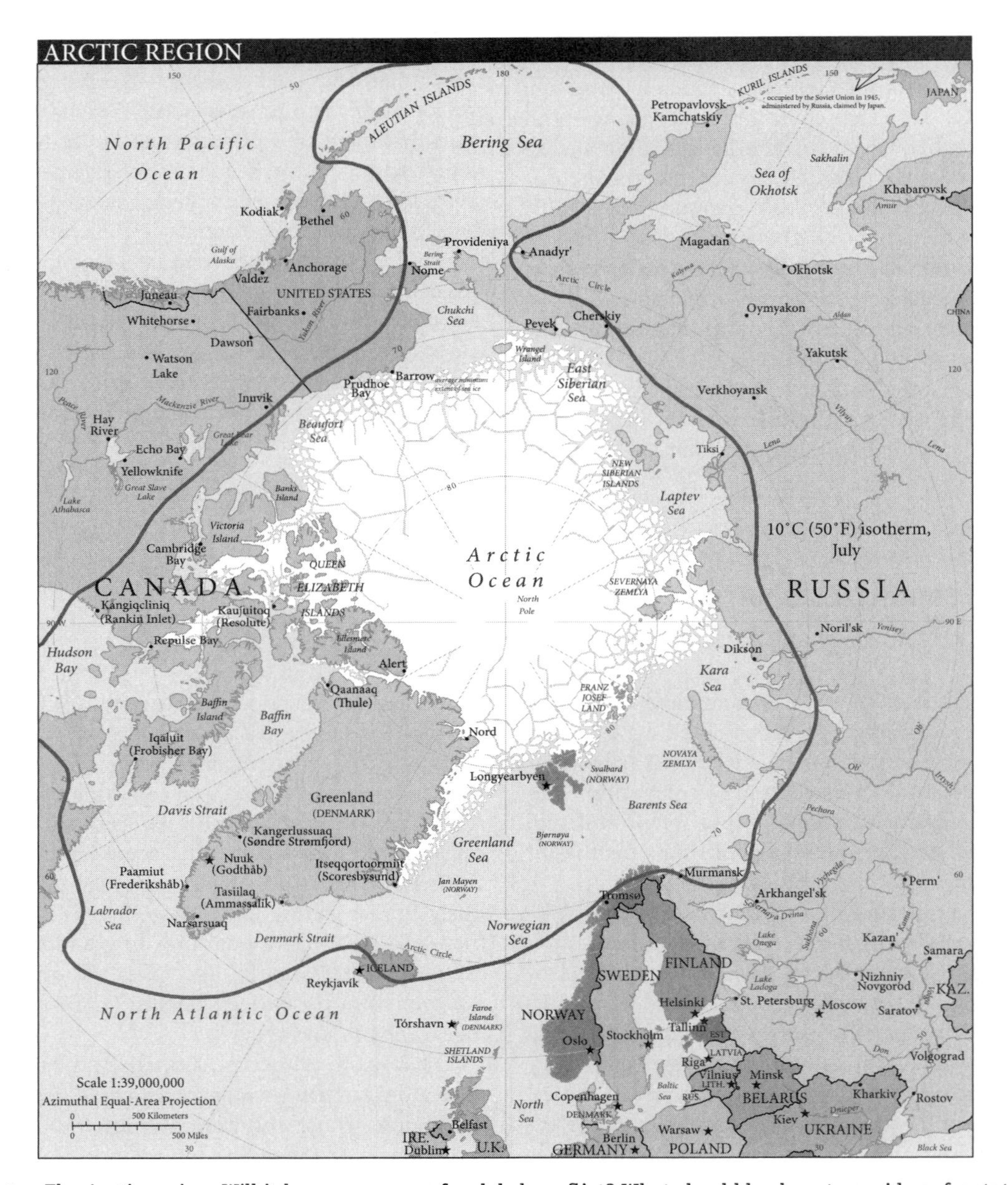

Map 1. The Arctic region: Will it become a zone of a global conflict? What should be done to avoid confrontation?

consequent coastal erosion. And while the impact on marine life is not yet known, signs of change can already be observed in the migration of certain fish species off the coast of Greenland, and in fish growth and size. Any changes in marine life will also affect the nature of fisheries in the region, and will require policies to facilitate sustainable operations and address potential conflict as fishing grounds and national boundaries overlap.

These events are not limited to the North American Arctic. For the last few years, the Northern Sea Route along Russia's north coast has seen similar ice changes, providing Russia with greater access to its vast Siberian resources and leading to bold assertions of its sovereignty over vast swathes of the polar sea. Indeed, the region has already opened to global commerce with the announcement on 21 August 2009 that, for the first time, two German commercial ships unaccompanied by icebreakers were traversing the Northern Sea Route on a voyage from Vladivostok to the Netherlands.

The prospect of longer ice-free periods in the Arctic has momentous implications for the region's commercial development, which risks further melting of the Arctic ice. In a 2009 report the United States Geological Survey (USGS) postulated that over 90 billion barrels of oil, 1,669 trillion cubic feet of natural gas and 44 billion barrels of natural gas liquids are located in the Arctic (84 per cent of which could potentially be found in offshore areas). With longer ice-free periods now available to explore for hydrocarbons, a new scramble for oil and gas could occur, especially if oil prices recover to levels above $100 a barrel. In addition, new technological developments in marine surface and undersea logistics, as well as deep-water drilling technology, have increased the salience of issues relating to the extension of coastal states' respective continental shelves under the United Nations Convention on the Law of the Sea (UNCLOS) and the Commission on the Limits of the Continental Shelf (CLCS).

It is the thesis of the authors that Arctic melt does and will continue to pose economic, military and environmental challenges to governance of the region, and that technological factors will most likely be a barrier to access in the short term and an enabler in the longer term. Decreased sea ice gives countries more opportunities to plant infrastructure to enable the exploitation of hydrocarbons and minerals, and to gain greater access for commercial shipping and fishing. While the military has a longstanding presence in the Arctic, greater access means the nature of this presence will have to adjust to take on new roles and capabilities, such as increased capacity for search-and-rescue operations and border patrolling, and submarine adaptation to reduced opaque ice cover and potentially increased monitoring of the waters by the Arctic states. Working within existing institutions and building capacity is preferable to the proliferation of new institutions, although the full structure and scope of the legal and regulatory frameworks that may be needed are at present unclear. What is clear is that the genie of increased Arctic access cannot be put back into the proverbial bottle.

ENVIRONMENT

The Arctic is a complex environment. While sea passages may be "ice-free" for a portion of the year, that term can be misleading. Multi-year ice is receding, but freely floating, younger, uncharted ice is more dangerous to navigate.

In addition to releasing harmful greenhouse gases, the warming of the Arctic tundra is leading to the proliferation of rapid large plant growth, which—like black carbon—darkens the landscape and further warms the icecaps. Melting tundra also raises vexing problems about the construction of land-based energy infrastructure in projects such as the Alaska Natural Gas Transportation System, which would bring Alaskan and Canadian natural gas to the lower 48 states and to southern Canada, since the unstable ground may not be able to support the overland pipeline infrastructure required for the project. If these developments continue as forecast, they may focus attention increasingly on the possibilities for seaborne transportation of liquefied natural gas (LNG), with significant implications for the geopolitics of the far north.

As ice melts and waters warm, fish are moving ever further northwards. Fish do not recognize national boundaries, which makes management of fisheries potentially contentious as stocks cross maritime frontiers. Moreover, as some species of fish move north, animals such as the walrus which live south of the far polar north are seeing their traditional sources of protein disappear, and are at grave risk as a result. Inuit tribes report massive drops in the walrus and seal populations, two vital commodities for their own livelihoods. The polar bear, already adversely affected by changes in fish and other marine populations, has access to ever less of the floating ice that is vital to its habitat.

INDIGENOUS PEOPLES

As noted above, the indigenous peoples of the Arctic are intimately tied to the environment. The effects of climate change on the region are a double-edged sword for these communities who at present lack access to some of the basic amenities of modernity by virtue of geographic location, geophysical terrain and neglect by central governments. On the one hand, melting ice will be to their disadvantage in respect of their traditional way of life, based on hunting and fishing. On the other hand, an Arctic region that is more accessible to lucrative activities such as the exploitation of hydrocarbons, fish and minerals will necessarily attract increased governmental attention, and this could benefit the citizens of the region.

While these communities have gained limited measures of political power, they have yet to exploit their economic potential. Oil and mining companies will increasingly have to consider the interests of the indigenous communities when evaluating potential projects in the Arctic. The Sami of northern Norway already have legal rights to certain local resources and are pushing for compensation from the companies that exploit them. The Inuit Circumpolar Council, which represents the Inuit of Denmark, Canada, the US and Russia, launched its Circumpolar Inuit Declaration on Arctic Sovereignty on 28 April 2009, stating: "It is our right to freely determine our political status, freely pursue our economic, social, cultural and linguistic development, and freely dispose of our natural wealth and resources." Denmark is scaling back its massive subsidies to Greenland's Inuit population, in line with the latter's moves towards greater independence and potential for wealth generation from the exploitation of hydrocarbons and minerals.

The presence of these populations in the region extends the national interest of Arctic states such as Canada, the US, Denmark, Sweden, Norway and Russia far north, but these communities must be treated as more than "flag holders" at their countries' respective northernmost borders.

RESOURCES AND SHIPPING ROUTES

The potential hydrocarbon bonanza of the Arctic holds much potential economic benefit for indigenous communities and the Arctic states they call home. Although detailed information on Arctic petroleum resources remains limited, according to the USGS report it appears that the ratio of natural gas to oil in the region's hydrocarbon resources is approximately three to one. While the Arctic may have tremendous potential in the long run its contribution to energy resources in the short term should not be overestimated, as other areas are cheaper, less contentious and less technologically challenging to exploit.

The technology required to recover Arctic resources year-round is not readily available, and will not become so in the short term. Transport difficulties add to the problems to be overcome. Natural gas requires pipelines or expensive and complex liquefaction infrastructure. The former is the less likely option, because pipelines would have to cover very large distances. With technological breakthroughs in the development of shale oil resources in the lower 48 states over the last several years, meanwhile, US natural gas reserves have nearly quadrupled.

Technology is a key barrier to Arctic access in other ways. Icebreakers, many nuclear powered, are necessary for presence and power projection in the region year-round. The various Arctic nations have widely divergent capabilities. For example, Russia has 20 icebreakers; Canada has 12, and is working on budgeting for 8 more; the US has, to all intents and purposes, just one functional icebreaker. These ships take eight to ten years to build, and cost approximately $1 billion each. The global economic crisis has, however, put a strain on budgets, and icebreaker fleets are unlikely to expand rapidly in the short term. Nonetheless, even if the US started building tomorrow it would long remain far behind other Arctic states such as Russia and Canada, taking decades and at least $20 billion to catch up.

Much of the geology supporting the presence of hydrocarbons in the Arctic is already located within the exclusive economic zones (EEZs) of the Arctic littoral states. Therefore, an extension of a state's continental shelf beyond its EEZ may not necessarily yield that much more oil and gas. The perception of strategic finds, however, can be enough to motivate territorial claims, and fuels the use of hyperbole like "scramble for the Arctic" with reference to what is otherwise an orderly process following international laws and norms.

In addition to hydrocarbon resources, new shipping routes opened up as the Arctic ice vanishes will reduce substantially the maritime distances between Europe and Asia, while also providing strategic alternatives to other countries such as Japan, which would have an interest in Arctic access owing to its current dependence on shipping through the Strait of Malacca for most of its energy supplies.

Use of the North-West Passage over North America could shorten shipping routes between Asia and the US east coast by 5,000 miles. However, even though Canada is a strong ally of the US, there are disputes between the two countries over the waters of the Canadian archipelago, which Canada claims are internal waters not subject to the conventions of "innocent passage," while the US regards them as a strait for international navigation, through which ships should be allowed to pass without interference by Canadian authorities. While neither country wishes to see the issue loom larger in their bilateral relations and both prefer at the moment to agree to disagree, under the current position all US Coast Guard vessels are designated as research vessels, which are therefore required to request transit permission from the Canadian government. This is not a long-term solution, however. If the waterway does indeed become ever more ice-free in the future, Canada will be forced formally to resolve its dispute with the United States over the status of the North West Passage.

The Northern Sea Route over Eurasia is also important since it shortens shipping routes between northern Europe and north-east Asia by 40 per cent compared with the existing routes through the Suez or Panama canals, and takes thousands of miles off maritime routes round Africa or Latin America. While experts have diverse views over which new maritime passage will become more important, there is a fledgling consensus that the Northern Sea Route will open sooner than the North-West Passage—a contention bolstered by the passage of the German ships this year.

As well as shorter shipping times, the potential benefits of an ice-free Arctic throughway include the ability to avoid dangerous chokepoints beset by piracy, and lower transportation costs. However, despite optimistic public perceptions often shaped by the mainstream media, the potential risks may actually counter and delay perceived benefits. These routes will not necessarily be more efficient. Ice-capable ships, required for the transit of Arctic waters, are more expensive to build and procure, and burn much more fuel, than those currently used for long-distance transport. Likewise, while Arctic ice melt may be accelerating, year-to-year variations can still occur, meaning that passages open one year may be closed the next. The uncertainty of when and whether passages are open increases the risk of commercial cargoes incurring large demurrage charges if they are late in arriving at final destinations, thereby offsetting some of the cost advantages of shorter routes. Finally, the potential for dangerous weather patterns to emerge in warming waters, combined with difficult-to-navigate broken ice and the lack of adequate maritime traffic management, make Arctic transit a treacherous undertaking even under the best of conditions.

Hydrocarbon prices and concerns about energy security are key drivers in accelerating interest in the Arctic, since high energy prices will generate new technological developments that are difficult to justify with prices even at current levels. New technology, especially that which allows drilling in deep water, also potentially opens vast areas of the Arctic to oil and gas exploration. New technology that can withstand ice flows will be of special benefit to Russia, since most of the waters along the Northern Sea Route are relatively shallow with huge sedimentary basins extending up to 200 or 300 miles offshore. Conducting business in the Arctic requires specialized ice-capable equipment, ranging from drilling and transportation infrastructure to established refuelling depots. To the extent that high energy prices support these costly projects, they will accelerate commercial interest in the region. Domestic and global economic conditions will also affect the progress, scale and feasibility of major Arctic projects and efforts. Canada, for example, has already cut back on its proposed Arctic expenditures.

BILATERAL ISSUES

Because the Arctic is a semi-enclosed sea encircled by littoral states, extensions of continental shelves and delimitations of maritime boundaries will lead invariably to overlapping sovereignty claims.

Norway has been a major source of energy security for Europe with new discoveries of Arctic gas, especially in the light of recent Russian curtailments of gas to Europe through Ukraine. With additional gas pipelines planned by Russia from its own Arctic and other gas resources, Norwegian gas will remain a critical component of European energy supply. This importance of Norway for European energy security means, however, that Norway must explore ever further northwards, creating tensions with Russia in terms of territorial claims over the disputed boundary of the Barents Sea. Norway claims the Gakkel Ridge as an extension of its continental shelf via the Svalbard Islands. Naval manoeuvres by Russia have disrupted Norwegian air traffic in offshore areas, and there are often aerial harrassment between Russian fighter jets and Norwegian jets trying to intercept them at the border. Norway—a NATO state bordering Russia—has moved its centre of military operations from its southern location in Jåttå, outside Stavenger, to Reiter, outside Bodø, in the north, reinforcing the strategic importance of the high north to both Norwegian and NATO foreign policy.

The Spitsbergen Treaty of 9 February 1920 grants Norway territorial sovereignty over what is now known as the Svalbard archipelago. At the time the treaty was negotiated, states had the exclusive legal right to resources in their territorial waters up to a distance of 3 miles from the coastline. However, the treaty also provides for equal access to Spitsbergen's resources for all signatory powers. On this basis, Russia has operated a coaling station there for many years. With changes under international law brought about by UNCLOS and other legal regimes over the years, Russia argues that, as a signatory to the treaty, it has the right to look for resources further offshore, though clearly under a resource extraction regime that would remain under Norway's legal jurisdiction. The significance of these claims should not be underestimated, especially given Norway's membership of NATO. During the Cold War, the region between Svalbard and northern Norway was the centre of a dangerous cat-and-mouse game between NATO and the Soviet Union. At that time, Soviet strategic doctrine was based on the necessity either before the outbreak of a conflict with the West or in its earliest hours to move its northern fleet out of Murmansk and into the North Atlantic through the Svalbard/Norwegian gap; the same is true of Russian strategic doctrine today. This action was deemed vital for Russia's force projection in the Atlantic, or, in the worst case, for a strategic nuclear strike against the American east coast. Clearly Moscow's worst fear is that NATO could bottle its fleet up, severely affecting the balance of forces in a major conflict.

Even since the end of the Cold War and its attendant fears of nuclear annihilation, Russia has remained nervous that offshore listening platforms might be installed on offshore oil and gas platforms, providing NATO with important capabilities for monitoring Russian commercial and strategic activities in the region.

Two of the most sensitive issues involving claims for additional offshore territorial extensions under UNCLOS centre on conflicting claims by Russia, Denmark and Canada over the Lomonosov and Mendeleev Ridges. Each country claims that the ridges are natural geological extensions of its territory, and each is collecting geological data to support its claims. In August 2007 Russian explorers planted a titanium flag on the Lomonosov seabed, mainly for domestic political consumption but also to send a message about their perceptions of sovereignty to the other Arctic states. In March 2009 Russia announced plans to establish a military force to protect its Arctic interests, as the region is expected to be an extremely important supplier of energy resources within the next 10–15 years.

Among the other Arctic littoral states, Canada is setting up a deep-water docking port on Baffin Island at Nanisivik and opening an Arctic military training centre in Resolute Bay in an attempt to bolster its territorial claims in its high north. The US and Canada have unresolved overlapping claims, not only over the international boundary between the two countries through the Beaufort Sea, but also on the sea floor. Resolution of this matter is especially important, since there is believed to be tremendous oil potential off the shore of Alaska, which is often referred to in the petroleum industry as the "next Gulf of Mexico."

Greenland obtained self-government from the Danish parliament in 1979. It then voted for increased self-rule in November 2008. The issue of Denmark's sovereignty over Greenland, which is based on historical exploration and settlement, became more complex on 20 June 2009, when Greenland obtained a new self-government agreement, under which it is recognized by the international community as a separate entity from Denmark with control of its internal affairs and of any international agreements pertaining specifically to Greenland. Denmark will retain control over foreign affairs, defence and finances, but will gradually decrease its substantial annual subsidy (currently comprising nearly 60 per cent of Greenland's total government revenues), and cede some control of Greenland's natural resources. Greenland's new status will move it towards independence. This development was anticipated by many analysts, given the possibility of massive oil, gas and diamond reserves beneath and around Greenland.

Following Greenland's most recent move towards greater autonomy, Danish members of parliament approved a plan to set up an Arctic military command and task force for 2010–2014, which will focus on Greenland and the Faroe Islands. Danish armed forces will have a greater role as melting ice increases the geopolitical significance of the region: plans include the establishment of a joint-service Arctic Command and an Arctic Response Force that may include combat aircraft, and the expansion of the military base at Thule, Greenland.

As noted above, the question of access to the Arctic is relevant not only to the states in the region, but also to those further south. Arctic shipping routes are an attractive prospect, in theory, to China, Japan, South Korea and Taiwan. South Korea is one of the major builders of ice-capable vessels. China carried out Arctic research in 1999 and 2003, and in 2004 built an Arctic satellite observation centre at New Olson, Spitsbergen Island, in Norway. The construction of such centres has been permitted by the Norwegian government to the original signatories to the 1920 Spitsbergen Treaty, and China, Japan, Germany, Italy, France and South Korea, among others, have taken advantage of the opportunity. China's application to the Arctic Council for permanent observer status, however, was turned down in 2009, and the full ministerial meeting of the Council will not convene again to consider applications until 2011. Also turned down were applications by the EU, South Korea and Italy. Other contentious issues centre on whaling and sealing, Canada, Denmark and Norway disagreeing with the EU ban on seal products.

CHALLENGES TO GOVERNANCE

While the Arctic Council and Arctic Five want more effective implementation of existing regimes, the EU advocates establishing a new regime: an international treaty for the protection of the Arctic. The European Parliament sees Arctic policy as vital to European security, and in March 2008 stated that conventions need to be altered to reflect the potential new energy balance stemming from the discovery of Arctic resources while reducing the size of Norwegian claims in the Arctic. While the EU remains committed to UNCLOS and recognizes the work of the Arctic Council, the European Parliament has called for specific EU Arctic policies to increase the role that the EU can play in the region to enhance current multilateral agreements or make up for the shortcomings of what it considers to be a fragmented legal framework.

Given the USGS assessment of the potential for substantial oil and gas reserves in the region—including within national EEZs—it is possible that a serious diplomatic row may at some point break out among those nations that border the region, including those that want their territorial claims extended, those that argue that some of the Arctic belongs to no one and that they therefore should have unfettered access, and those that believe that, given its fragile and unique nature, the region (or at least large areas of it) is the common heritage of humankind and should come under international jurisdiction.

CONCLUSION

The Arctic is governed by international customary maritime law in the form of UNCLOS, and cooperation is fostered by the Arctic Council, in addition to bilateral agreements or understandings between states with competing claims. The EU, while not having an official position on the matter, also supports a multilateral approach. This has been and continues to be the context in which the Arctic states operate, and there is reason to believe that this spirit of cooperation will continue. The uncertainty here lies in the timeline, as the horizon for an easily accessible Arctic Ocean lies far in the future. The point at which climate conditions, ice-capable technology, high energy prices, delineation of maritime and continental shelf boundaries, and legal and regulatory frameworks for management of maritime traffic will converge sufficiently to render the region a practical prospect for investment and utilization is a long way off, thereby rendering talk of any potential "heating up" or "Arctic scramble" inappropriate. However, while terminology connoting speed may not accurately characterize the Arctic region, this does not mean that action must not be taken now to ensure preparedness and the development of a comprehensive economic, environmental, legal and political approach to Arctic governance.

Arctic access and exploration are not matters for the future. The Arctic's time has already come; however, it will gain in geopolitical importance only when there is a confluence of factors that focus attention on the region:

1. Oil prices will have to rise and be expected to remain high enough to justify the costly technological and infrastructure projects that will take many years to amortize.
2. Ice-capable technology will have to be available to ensure that access to the region can be sustained over time, despite seasonal and year-to-year ice fluctuations.
3. The geopolitical community must be convinced that the opportunities for commercial development will not exacerbate greenhouse gas emissions and the degradation of the Arctic environment to an unacceptable degree.
4. Interest in new maritime shipping routes, already high, will continue to increase in direct proportion to geopolitical tensions in traditional shipping chokepoints and channels—especially where potential military conflicts are brewing.
5. Heightened commercial and other interests in the Arctic will rise when boundaries are clearly delineated and legal frameworks in place to create a favourable investment environment, and when all Arctic states agree to abide by internationally recognized legally binding agreements and codes of conduct.

Speaking as Americans, the authors note that the US has over 1,000 miles of Arctic coastline. If the US wishes to play a leading role in creating an effective regime for the region, as well as protecting its own national interests, Washington must focus funds and policy attention on the Arctic. The actions it should take include signing UNCLOS; putting innovation to work on ice-capable technologies and military training; cooperating with Canada and other Arctic states on improved management of maritime traffic, research efforts, and search-and-rescue and accident clean-up capacities; and building a sizeable ice-capable commercial, scientific and naval fleet, including investment of at least $10 billion in building ten new icebreakers, with another $1 billion for maintenance of existing ships until the new ones are ready for use. The time for action is now. Let's get on with the job!

The Climate-Policy Trap

BJORN LOMBORG

ROME—Today's policies to combat climate change cost much more than the benefits they produce. Unfortunately, bad political choices often make these policies even less cost-effective.

Consider the European Union's 20-20 policy, which targets a 20% reduction in CO_2 emissions below 1990 levels by 2020. It is important to examine this approach, not only because the EU is pursuing the world's largest and most ambitious climate policy, but also because other climate policies suffer from similar shortcomings.

The most cost-efficient way to achieve the 20% target would be to operate a single, EU-wide carbon-market, which would cost the EU about $96 billion annually by 2020. But the benefits to the entire world would be much lower. Indeed, the only peer-reviewed overview of EU climate policy estimates that it can avoid climate-related damage of about $10 billion per year. So, for every dollar spent, the EU stands to avoid about ten cents of damage.

This does not mean that climate change is not important; it means only that the EU's climate policy is not smart. Over the course of this century, the ideal EU policy would cost more than $7 trillion, yet it would reduce the temperature rise by just 0.05°C and lower sea levels by a trivial nine millimeters. After spending all that money, we would not even be able to tell the difference.

Advocates of the EU's policy often argue that we should pursue such policies nonetheless, because there is a risk that global warming will be much more severe than currently expected. But, though this argument is valid in principle, economic models show that this risk has only a moderate effect on the best policy. Moreover, the absence of any temperature rise over the past 10–17 years has made such worse-than-expected outcomes extremely unlikely.

The real risk concerns the potential for bad political choices to make climate policies worse than necessary. The EU did not just implement a single carbon market in order to meet its target for CO_2 emissions. Instead, the EU made a bad deal a lot costlier through a host of partly contradictory policies.

For example, the EU demanded that renewables like wind and solar account for 20% of energy supplies by 2020, though this is by no means the cheapest way to cut emissions.

In fact, putting up a wind turbine cuts *no* extra CO_2, because total emissions are already capped under the EU-wide carbon-trading scheme. It simply means that when Great Britain installs a wind turbine, it becomes cheaper to burn coal in Portugal or Poland.

Taking into account such poor policies and averaging all macroeconomic models, the EU is more likely to pay around $280 billion per year to avert $10 billion in damage. In other words, the poor design of EU climate policies triples the cost and prevents only three cents of climate damage per dollar spent.

But it gets worse, because these models still assume that the EU picks the cheapest renewables to fulfill its requirements. Instead, most EU countries give higher subsidies to the most costly renewables.

For example, cutting a ton of CO_2 with onshore wind turbines in Germany probably costs about $35, avoiding about 14 cents of climate damage per dollar. But offshore wind turbines cost about $150 per ton of CO_2, avoiding just three cents of climate damage per dollar.

Biofuels are even less efficient, costing more than $300 per ton of CO_2 avoided, while doing just over one cent of good per dollar. And solar takes the absolute prize, costing more than $800 per ton of CO_2 to do less than a cent of good per dollar spent.

These prices are not unique to Europe. China pays $38 per ton of CO_2 avoided with wind power, for example, while the US pays around $600 for cutting a ton of CO_2 with biofuels.

Moreover, when the EU decides to cut its domestic emissions, part of the reduction simply migrates elsewhere. If making a product in the EU costs more because of higher energy costs, the product will likely be made somewhere else, where energy is cheaper, and then imported into the EU.

In fact, new studies show that 38% of the EU carbon cuts leak elsewhere, meaning that European climate policy avoids not three cents of climate damage per dollar spent, but less than two. From 1990 to 2008, the EU cut its emissions by about 270 million metric tons of CO_2. But it turns out that the increase in imports from China alone implied an almost equal volume of extra emissions outside the EU. Essentially, the EU had simply shipped part of its emissions offshore.

Finally, the negative effects of poor climate policies are not just financial. Biofuels, for which the EU alone is now paying more than $10 billion annually to do less than one cent of good for every dollar spent, also take up fields that otherwise would have produced food.

That means that food production moves elsewhere, often to farmland created by cutting down forests, which releases more CO_2 and damages biodiversity. It also drives up food prices, which so far has pushed at least 30 million poor people into starvation, with another 40–130 million expected to be starving by 2020.

We need a smarter approach to tackling climate change. Rather than relying on cutting a few tons of incredibly overpriced CO_2 now, we need to invest in research and development aimed at innovating down the cost of green energy in the long run, so that everyone will switch.

For now, our current climate policies are poor—and our politicians consistently find ways to make them even poorer. They may please farmers and other interest groups, but overall they simply drive up costs and reduce already-minimal benefits.

Let's Face It: None of Our Environmental Fixes Break the Planet-Wrecking Project

GEORGE MONBIOT

You think you're discussing technologies, and you quickly discover that you're discussing belief systems. The battle among environmentalists over how or whether our future energy is supplied is a cipher for something much bigger: who we are, who we want to be, how we want society to evolve. Beside these concerns, technical matters—parts per million, costs per megawatt hour, cancers per sievert—carry little weight. We choose our technology—or absence of technology—according to a set of deep beliefs: beliefs that in some cases remain unexamined.

The case against abandoning nuclear power, for example, is a simple one: it will be replaced either by fossil fuels or by renewables that would otherwise have replaced fossil fuels. In either circumstance, greenhouse gases, other forms of destruction and human deaths and injuries all rise.

The case against reducing electricity supplies is just as clear. For example, the *Zero Carbon Britain report* published by the Centre for Alternative Technology urges a 55% cut in overall energy demand by 2030—a goal I strongly support. It also envisages a near-doubling of electricity production. The reason is that the most viable means of decarbonising both transport and heating is to replace the fuels they use with low-carbon electricity. Cut the electricity supply and we're stuck with oil and gas. If we close down nuclear plants, we must accept an even greater expansion of renewables than currently proposed. Given the tremendous public resistance to even a modest increase in windfarms and new power lines, that's going to be tough.

What the nuclear question does is to concentrate the mind about the electricity question. Decarbonising the economy involves an increase in infrastructure. Infrastructure is ugly, destructive and controlled by remote governments and corporations. These questions are so divisive because the same worldview tells us that we must reduce emissions, defend our landscapes and resist both the state and big business. The four objectives are at odds.

But even if we can accept an expansion of infrastructure, the technocentric, carbon-counting vision I've favoured runs into trouble. The problem is that it seeks to accommodate a system that cannot be accommodated: a system that demands perpetual economic growth. We could, as Zero Carbon Britain envisages, become carbon-free by 2030. Growth then ensures that we have to address the problem all over again by 2050, 2070 and thereon after.

Accommodation makes sense only if the economy is reaching a steady state. But the clearer the vision becomes, the further away it seems. A steady state economy will be politically possible only if we can be persuaded to stop grabbing. This in turn will be feasible only if we feel more secure. But the global race to the bottom and its destruction of pensions, welfare, public services and stable employment make people less secure, encouraging us to grasp as much for ourselves as we can.

Reprinted by permission of The Guardian. May 2.

If this vision looks implausible, consider the alternatives. In the latest edition of his excellent magazine *The Land*, Simon Fairlie responds furiously to my suggestion that we should take industry into account when choosing our energy sources. His article exposes a remarkable but seldom noticed problem: that most of those who advocate an off-grid, land-based economy have made no provision for manufactures. I'm not talking about the pointless rubbish in the *FT's How To Spend It* supplement. I'm talking about the energy required to make bricks, glass, metal tools and utensils, textiles (except the hand-loomed tweed Fairlie suggests we wear), ceramics and soap: commodities that almost everyone sees as the barest possible requirements.

Are people like Fairlie really proposing that we do without them altogether? If not, what energy sources do they suggest we use? Charcoal would once again throw industry into direct competition with agriculture, spreading starvation and ensuring that manufactured products became the preserve of the very rich. (Remember, as *EA Wrigley* points out, that half the land surface of Britain could produce enough charcoal to make 1.25m tonnes of bar iron—a fraction of current demand—and nothing else.) An honest environmentalism needs to explain which products should continue to be manufactured and which should not, and what the energy sources for these manufactures should be.

There's a still bigger problem here: even if we make provision for some manufacturing but, like Fairlie, envisage a massive downsizing and a return to a land-based economy, how do we take people with us? Where is the public appetite for this transition?

A third group tries to avoid such conflicts by predicting that the problem will be solved by collapse: doom is our salvation. Economic collapse, these people argue, is imminent and expiatory. I believe this is wrong on both counts.

Last week something astonishing happened: Fatih Birol, the chief economist of the International Energy Agency, revealed that peak oil has already happened. *"We think that the crude oil production has already peaked, in 2006."* If this is true, we should be extremely angry with the IEA. In 2005 its executive director mocked those who predicted peak oil as "doomsayers." Until 2008 (two years after the IEA now says it happened) the agency continued to dismiss the possibility that peak oil would occur.

But this also raises an awkward question for us greens: why hasn't the global economy collapsed as we predicted? Yes, it wobbled, though largely for other reasons. Now *global growth is back with a vengeance: it reached 4.6% last year*, and the IMF predicts roughly the same for 2011 and 2012. The reason, as Birol went on to explain, is that natural gas liquids and tar sands are already filling the gap. Not only does the economy appear to be more resistant to resource shocks than we assumed, but the result of those shocks is an increase, not a decline, in environmental destruction.

The problem we face is not that we have too little fossil fuel, but too much. As oil declines, economies will switch to tar sands, shale gas and coal; as accessible coal declines, they'll switch to ultra-deep reserves (using *underground gasification* to exploit them) and *methane clathrates*. The same probably applies to almost all minerals: we will find them, but exploiting them will mean trashing an ever greater proportion of the world's surface. We have enough non-renewable resources of all kinds to complete our wreckage of renewable resources: forests, soil, fish, freshwater, benign weather. Collapse will come one day, but not before we have pulled everything down with us.

And even if there were an immediate economic cataclysm, it's not clear that the result would be a decline in our capacity for destruction. In east Africa, for example, I've seen how, when supplies of paraffin or kerosene are disrupted, people don't give up cooking; they cut down more trees. History shows us that wherever large-scale collapse has occurred, psychopaths take over. This is hardly conducive to the rational use of natural assets.

All of us in the environment movement, in other words—whether we propose accommodation, radical downsizing or collapse—are lost. None of us yet has a convincing account of how humanity can get out of this mess. None of our chosen solutions break the atomising, planet-wrecking project. I hope that by laying out the problem I can encourage us to address it more logically, to abandon magical thinking and to recognise the contradictions we confront. But even that could be a tall order.

VISUAL REVIEW

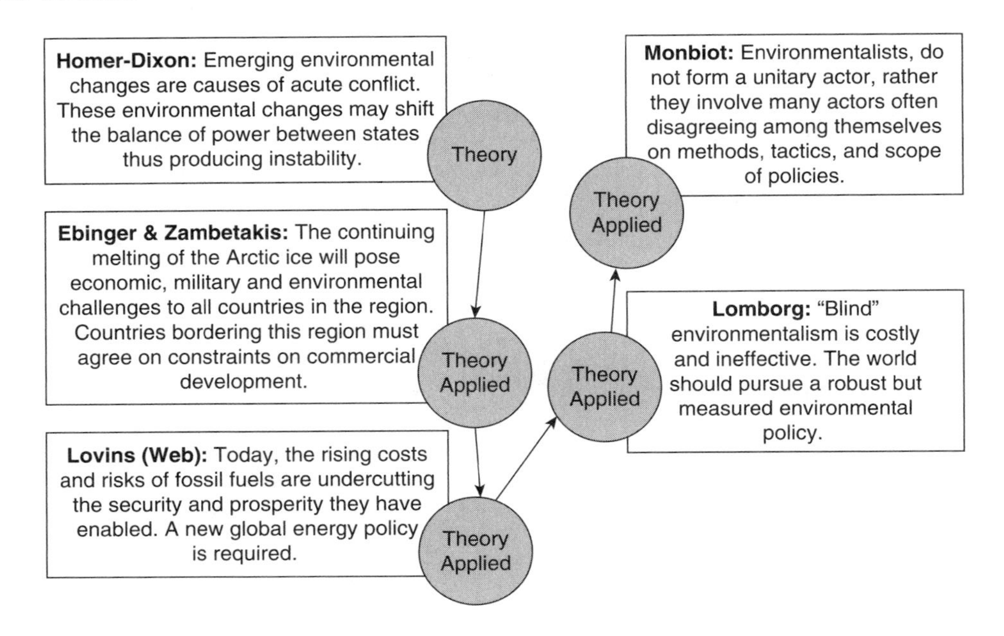

Section 9

Human Rights in the World: Their Protection and Development

Afghan women wait in line to receive their donated sacks of wheat distributed by the World Food Program in Kabul, Afghanistan, 2013. The World Food Program distributed food and firewood mostly to widows, refugees, the disabled, and poor families. Ethnic and political conflicts continue to devastate many countries. Who has the responsibility to protect the defenseless and alleviate the suffering of civilians victimized by politics?
Source: Rahmat Gul/Associated Press

Ethical Dimensions of an Interventionist Foreign Policy

A fine essay by John Stuart Mill, first published in 1859, offers keen insight into the thinking behind today's policies

JASON COWLEY

In October 1967, the American poet Robert Lowell, who was jailed for his pacifism during the Second World War, marched on the Pentagon in Washington as part of an anti-Vietnam war demonstration. Before a crowd of as many as 100,000 people and alongside Norman Mailer, he read the final stanza from one of his finest poems of public address, "Waking Early Sunday Morning":

Pity the planet, all joy gone
from this sweet volcanic cone;
peace to our children when they fall
in small war on the heels of small
war - until the end of time
to police the earth, a ghost
orbiting forever lost
in our monotonous sublime.

Lowell understood the burden, loneliness and corruption of America's chosen role as world policeman. He had a premonition of what the future held for a nation that was, because of its imperial ambition and sense of its own higher moral purpose, destined repeatedly to be ensnared in conflicts in distant lands.

COMPETING OBJECTIVES

For too long, the debate about liberal interventionism has been conducted in absolutist terms. On the one hand, you have the neoconservatives, or ultra-interventionists, with their Manichaean worldview, and their beliefs that rogue states can be bombed into submission and democracy imposed through violence and external agencies, rather than through internal pressures of the kind which led to the fall of tyrants in Egypt and Tunisia. On the other hand, you have those who would oppose all intervention as a form of neo-imperialism.

The art of successful foreign policy is the art of measuring competing objectives; of knowing when to intervene (as in Kosovo in 1999 and Sierra Leone in 2000) and when not to (Iraq in 2003). Under Tony Blair, liberal interventionism itself became a kind of absolutist dogma. For Blair, there was a "moral obligation" to intervene "to make the world better." Emboldened by the success of his action in Sierra Leone to defeat the militias that had laid waste to an entire nation, and the Nato-led assault on Serbia during the Kosovo war, Blair wrongfully supported the Americans in their illegal war in Iraq. The inconsistencies of his positions abounded. Why intervene in Iraq and not in, say, Iran or Darfur? Similarly, why now should we intervene in Libya and not in Yemen, where civilians are being murdered by an autocrat every bit as repugnant as Gaddafi?

Perhaps we should turn to the great liberal philosopher J S Mill for help. In 1859, writing against the backdrop of the Crimean war, the Indian mutiny and the construction of the Suez Canal, Mill published an essay titled "A Few Words on Non-intervention," still one of the best I have read on the subject. Mill was not opposed to all foreign adventurism. As a servant of imperialism, he believed in the "civilising" mission of the British empire, but he set limits on when a state should intervene in the internal affairs of another, especially during a civil war or revolt. Mill was conscious that any foreign intervention would be viewed from the outside as an act not of humanitarianism, but of cynical self-interest. It's all about the oil! He believed that if a people did not have "a sufficient love of liberty to be able to wrest it from merely domestic oppressors, the liberty which is bestowed on them by other hands rather

Ethical dimensions of an interventionist foreign policy A fine essay by John Stuart Mill, first published in 1859, offers keen insight" by Jason Cowley published 24 MARCH, 2011, first published in The New Statesman.

than their own, will have nothing real, nothing permanent."

SELF-DETERMINATION

Mill continued: "When the contest is only with native rulers, and with such native strength as those rulers can enlist in their defence, the answer I should give to the question of the legitimacy of intervention is, as a general rule, No."

No people, Mill thought, "ever was or remained free, but because it was determined to be so . . . If a people—especially one whose freedom has not yet become prescriptive—does not value it sufficiently to fight for it, and maintain it against any force which can be mustered within the country, even by those who have the command of the public revenue, it is only a question of how few years or months that people will be enslaved."

Unlike in Sierra Leone, where militias were supported by an outside agent—the Liberian warlord Charles Taylor—or Kosovo, where ethnic Albanians were struggling against the aggression of a Greater Serbia, the struggle of the Libyan rebels is against a native ruler. How long would they have been prepared to continue the freedom fight? We shall never know, because of the haste with which the western powers have rushed to intervene as they seek to police the earth, ghosts orbiting forever lost.

Sticks and Stones: Naming and Shaming the Human Rights Enforcement Problem

EMILIE M. HAFNER-BURTON

On 2 October 2007, the United Nations Human Rights Council adopted a resolution deploring the violent repression of peaceful demonstrations in Myanmar and urging the government to stop beating and killing protestors. Later that month, Amnesty International issued a press release condemning Angolan police for unlawful arrests, torture, and killings, and denouncing the government's near-total impunity for these crimes. Later that month *The Economist* printed an article shaming the dictators of Sudan and Zimbabwe for human rights abuses and discouraging Western governments from negotiating with tyrants. These efforts are commonplace—governments, nongovernmental organizations (NGOs), and the news media often "name and shame" perpetrators of human rights abuses. Are these global publicity efforts followed by better government protections for human rights?

Some regard global publicity tactics as cheap talk that perpetrators of human rights abuses ignore. A few worry about unintended consequences—that naming and shaming could aggravate rather than subdue perpetrators. Others believe that shining a spotlight on bad behavior can help sway perpetrators to reform, especially when actors with upright intentions and practices denounce countries for abuses. Anecdotes support each position.

This article offers the first global statistical analysis of the issue. The focus here is whether international publicity by NGOs, the news media, and the UN is followed by government reductions of murder, torture, indiscriminate killing, forced disappearance, and other forms of political terror, as well as abuses of the electoral process and other violations of political rights.

The evidence shows that naming and shaming is not all cheap talk. On the one hand, governments named and shamed as human rights violators often improve protections for political rights after being publicly criticized—they hold elections or pass legislation to increase political pluralism or participation. On the other hand, naming and shaming

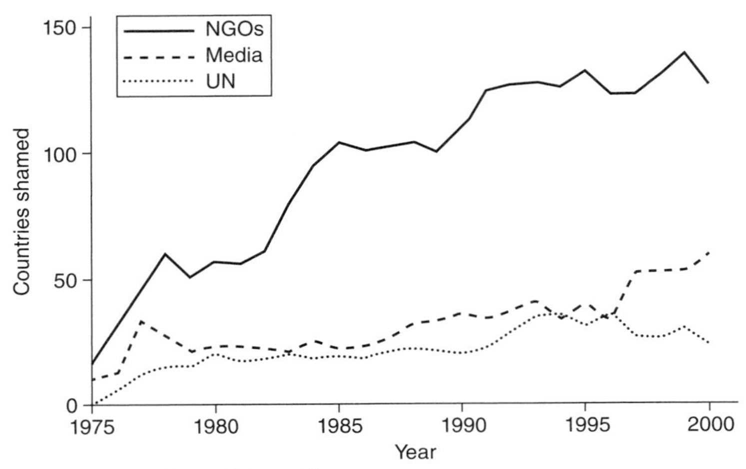

Figure 16. Number of Countries Shamed Over Time

rarely is followed by the cessation of political terror and, paradoxically, sometimes is followed by more. Different reasons explain the paradox. One reason is that some governments' capacities for reform vary by types of human rights violations—it may be easier for some governments to reform their legal or political structures, at least on paper, by holding elections or passing legislation to better protect some political rights, than to stop agents of terror that are out of their direct control. Another reason is that some governments abuse human rights strategically—when faced with global pressures for reform, some despots use terror, such as killings or beatings, to counteract the effectiveness of political reforms they make in response to international pressures, such as holding elections.

THE POLITICS OF SHAMING

Whether and how naming and shaming works might also depend on when and where the spotlight is shone. Organizations—whether NGOs, news media, or the UN—shine the spotlight selectively. Some countries guilty of horrible abuses never draw much publicity, while others responsible for lesser abuses draw much attention. For instance, political terror has been widespread in Uganda and North Korea for decades, yet these countries receive far less publicity from the international community than do Cuba, China, South Africa, or Turkey, which are more often put in the spotlight for less severe abuses. Figure 17 plots the level of political rights abuses and terror taking place inside countries put in the spotlight by NGOs, the Western news media, and the UN. These organizations widely publicized human rights abuses in countries repressing political rights and using acts of political terror (shown in the upper right quadrant of each graph), including Colombia, Indonesia, and Iran. In some instances, the same organizations also widely publicized violations in rights-abiding countries (shown in the lower left quadrant of each graph), such as Cyprus, the United Kingdom, and the United States. In other instances, they chose not to publicize abuses in especially repressive countries, such as Angola.

Fortunately, scholars have done research on the politics of shaming using large samples. Ron, Ramos, and Rodgers examine the factors that shape Amnesty International's publicity tactics on 148 countries from 1986 to 2000. Their statistical analyses show that Amnesty reports more on powerful countries and countries where there is Western government complicity, such as military assistance. Ramos, Ron, and Thorns study the factors that shape *The Economist* and *Newsweek*'s reporting on human rights violations for the same countries and years. Their statistical analyses show that these organizations more frequently shame countries with higher levels of human rights abuses, economic development, and population, as well as with more political

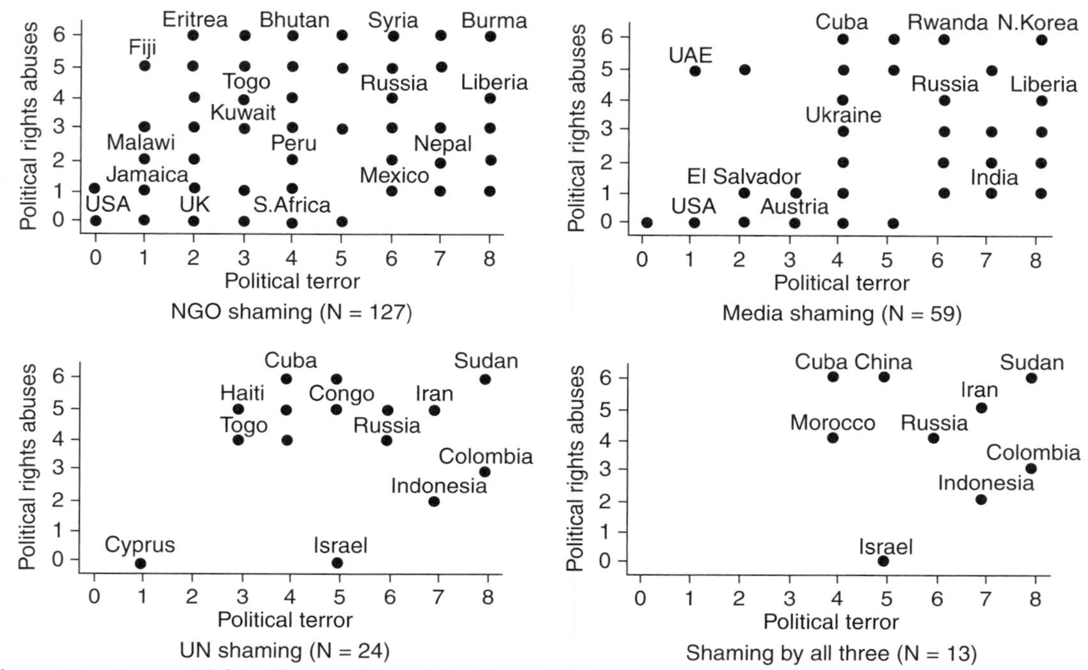

Figure 17. Human Rights Abuses of Countries Shamed in 2000

Note: To economize, only some countries are labeled. Several observations represent multiple countries.

openness, battle deaths, and stronger civil societies, although these latter effects were less robust. Hafner-Burton and Ron show that this coverage also varies by region, with some areas of the world receiving more Western media attention than others, notably, Latin America. Likewise, Lebovic and Voeten analyze the actions of the UNCHR from 1977 to 2001.

Their statistical findings show that after the Cold War, the UN's shaming was less based on power politics and partisan ties and more on countries' treaty commitments, military capabilities, and active participation in cooperative endeavors such as peacekeeping operations. Below, the findings of these four studies inform the selection of instrumental variables to model the effects of naming and shaming on repression.

EXPLANATION AND EXAMPLE

Naming and shaming is not just cheap talk. But neither is it a remedy for all abuses. Governments put in the global spotlight for violations often adopt better protections for political rights afterward, but they rarely stop or appear to lessen acts of terror. Worse, terror sometimes increases after publicity.

There are several reasons. One is that, in the face of international pressures to reform, some leaders want improvements but have more capacity to pass and implement legislation protecting political rights than to stop terror. This is because some agents of terror are decentralized outside the leader's control, while the rule of law, at least on paper, is more under state control: many terrorist groups operate independently of government efforts and policies to stop them, and many police officers and prison guards operate without strong oversight by central government authorities. In these cases, shaming is often followed by, but does not necessarily cause, government terror. Publicity may nonetheless provoke acts of violence by nonstate actors that governments respond to with more violence.

Another reason is that some abusive leaders adjust their methods of abuse in economical ways in reply to the spotlight, aiming to boost their legitimacy at home or abroad in the least costly way to themselves. Some dampen down only those abuses that help them to dodge blame for other violations they intend to continue. Others ramp up abuses that allow them to counteract reforms they make to take the edge off international pressure—they make small upgrades to political rights, improving practices or legislation, such as holding an election, to signal conformity with global norms and laws but persist with, or even increase, acts of terror that may help offset the other improvements. A common example is when leaders hold elections but terrorize voters and opposition to reduce their influence. In these cases, shaming is followed by, but could also provoke, government terror.

Recent events in Nigeria illustrate both types of political processes, capacity and strategic behavior, that may explain the statistical trends presented here. In June 1993, Chief Moshood Abiola, a Yoruba Muslim from southwestern Nigeria, won the presidential election. In July, Nigeria ratified the UN Covenant on Civil and Political Rights—it had signed the Convention Against Torture several years earlier. In November, General Sani Abacha annulled the election, threw Abiola in prison for treason (where he later died), and seized power. During the next five years Abacha jailed his critics, gunned down protesters, and suspended the Constitution. Dissidents were tortured, beaten, and starved. Political prisoners were held without trial, or tried and sentenced before secret martial courts. Criminals were shot without the right to appeal. In 1995, despite pressure from America and Europe, Abacha hanged the novelist Ken Saro-Wiwa and eight others who had campaigned for the rights of the Ogoni people against the devastation of the Niger Delta by oil companies. He jailed and killed many others during his reign. For Abacha, human rights abuses brought him to power and kept him in charge.

The world shone a spotlight on Nigeria for these abuses. Amnesty International and Human Rights Watch published dozens of press releases and background reports on the atrocities, asking Nigeria to uphold international law and hold elections, Western governments to punish the regime for these abuses, and consumers to pressure oil companies to stop drilling in Nigeria. The Western news media printed report after report naming these atrocities and shaming the government of Nigeria for committing them. *Newsweek* called Abacha "Africa's No. 1 outlaw dictator," while *The Economist* called him a "despot" that is "repressive, visionless and so corrupt that the parasite of corruption has almost eaten the host." Transparency International named Nigeria the most corrupt country on the planet. Meanwhile, the UN passed resolutions expressing deep concern about the human rights situation in Nigeria. The General Assembly repeatedly asked Abacha to restore habeas corpus, release all political prisoners and ensure full respect for the rights of all individuals. The UNCHR shamed the regime for using acts of terror against political opposition: it asked Abacha to respect the right to life, release political prisoners, among them, Chief Abiola, human rights advocates, and journalists, to hold fair trials, and restore democracy.

Despite the publicity, terror worsened, as Abacha's security forces continued to commit numerous serious human rights abuses, including imprisonment and torture of critics. While crowds of Nigerians packed bars to watch the fall of Indonesia's President Suharto facing mass demonstrations, Nigerian security forces shot demonstrators—*The Economist* chalks this up to the "CNN factor," where global publicity of democracy movements elsewhere gave Nigerian's momentum to protest at home, which led to a government crackdown. Meanwhile, Abacha became concerned about the global spotlight on him. In reaction to the bad publicity, he issued a video and book, entitled "Not in Our Character," reassuring listeners that Nigeria's bad image is fabricated by people who "have become instruments or tools of foreign propaganda, a foreign machine to undermine the survival, the stability and subvert the unity of the nation." His government organized "spur-of-the-moment" rallies to show the world that Nigerians support their regime. They also held local government elections and made a few other marginal improvements to political rights legislation, all the while terrorizing citizens to keep them from the polls. And then, in the middle of the night, Abacha died of a heart attack.

General Abubakar, head of Nigeria's military, took over the government for eleven months in 1998. He came to power promising to return the country to civilian rule. He released several political prisoners, including Olusegun Obasanjo, who won the presidency in 1998. NGOs, the Western press, and the UN all reacted. Press releases were issued, articles written, and resolutions passed on Nigeria's new democratically elected president—the global spotlight was shone again, this time urging the new president to respect human rights and restore rule of law. Obasanjo made political improvements. He opened public investigations into Nigeria's past human rights abuses. He fired some of the top military and customs officials and took actions to reduce government corruption. He began to restructure the police system. Freedom House reports dramatic improvements in the protection of political rights after Obasanjo took office. Terror, meanwhile, flared up. The new spate of terror was mainly the consequence of ethnic and local fighting, especially in the Niger Delta, where angry groups took up arms against each other. Within a few months of the transition, almost 1,000 people were killed. In the South, many died in clashes between Ibo communities. In the North, fights between Yorubas and Hausas left people dead or homeless.

The statistical analyses here cannot distinguish which political rationale, capacity or strategic behavior, drives this syndrome in which place. Case studies show each has occurred in different countries at different times. In Nigeria, both played a role. Abacha used terror to maintain his power, making a few meager adjustments to political rights, holding local elections, partly in response to outside pressures. He also instructed government agents to crack down hard on Nigerians to keep them from uprising, sometimes in reaction to the spotlight on him and also other governments, such as Indonesia. While he cracked down on citizens, Abacha ran a public relations campaign in response to global criticism. A similar dynamic is playing out in Zimbabwe, where President Mugabe, responding to international pressures, holds elections but then sends his agents to beat and torture his political opponents and voters who support them. Obasanjo's problem, by contrast, was partly one of capacity. He came to office with some intentions to reform human rights—pressured by the international community and some Nigerians. He was able to pass new laws and partly reform the political system but not to disarm citizens or diffuse the ethnic or religious tensions fueling terror. Terror continues despite the global spotlight. Chile also showed a similar pattern of behavior, when the Pinochet government made a variety of human rights improvements in response to naming and shaming by the international community, while continuing, or even worsening, others. This paradox has played out in Haiti, El Salvador, Brazil, Bulgaria, Ukraine, Niger, Algeria, Sudan, Turkey, Saudi Arabia, Thailand, Indonesia, and other countries too.

The findings in this study thus provide some evidence of success but also warn of hazards and cheap talk. In a few places, global publicity is followed by more repression in the short term, exacerbating leaders' insecurity and prompting them to use terror, especially when armed opposition groups or elections threaten their monopoly on power. This was likely the case for Abacha in Nigeria and Mugabe in Zimbabwe, where more terror followed the spotlight. Causality is hard to determine with statistical confidence. A variety of data reporting problems could also explain the statistical findings, including problems of scale and conservative reporting practices that present troubles for quantitative analyses of terror generally. Counterfactual scenarios that are hard to observe could also explain them. Countries subjected to the human rights spotlight may use more terror afterward but less terror than they would have if they were never named and shamed. One example is the Israeli military's restraint in responding to the Palestinian Intifada. What is apparent from studies of countries such as Chile and Zimbabwe, though, is that many governments, some driven by strategic behavior and some by capacity problems, act erratically after they are shamed widely by the global community. They make human rights reforms in some areas, holding elections or passing legislation to enhance some features of political participation, but do nothing or even exacerbate the problem in others, allowing or using acts of terror. At least some are making these choices strategically, using terror to offset improvements they make to political rights in response to international pressures.

CONCLUSION

As human rights idioms become mainstream, global shaming efforts grow. Placing countries in a spotlight for human rights violations, though, is followed by complex politics of human rights abuse and enforcement. This study is a beginning. It shows that governments subjected to global publicity efforts often behave in contradictory ways, reducing some violations of political rights afterward—sometimes because these violations are easier or less costly to temper yet some governments continue or expand their use of political terror—sometimes because terror is less in governments' control or can be used to cancel out other improvements governments make but do not want to work.

The Responsibility to Protect After Libya and Syria

HON GARETH EVANS

Of all the human rights issues that shock our conscience at home and abroad, I think we would agree that the ones that most offend, and challenge, every precept of our common humanity are the mass atrocity crimes: genocide, ethnic cleansing, crimes against humanity and large-scale war crimes—those catastrophic human rights violations where men, women and children are murdered, tortured, raped, starved or forcibly expelled for no other reason than their race, ethnicity, religion, nationality, caste, class or ideology.

The extraordinary thing is how long it has taken for any kind of genuine international consensus to develop as to how to respond to these catastrophic crimes. Even after the horrors of the Holocaust and all the many developments in international human rights law and international humanitarian law that followed World War II, when it came to reacting to reacting to cases like Cambodia, East Pakistan, and Uganda in the 1970s and '80s, and Rwanda, Bosnia and Kosovo in the '90s, the world was in almost total disarray.

There was at least real debate about these issues in the '90s, but it was only about "humanitarian intervention": the so-called "right to intervene" militarily. Hardly anyone talked about prevention or less extreme forms of engagement and intervention. The options were "Send in the Marines" or do nothing. The global North often rallied to the "right to intervene" cry, but the global South was understandably deeply reluctant—after all its unhappy historical experience—to accept the idea that big guys had the right to throw their weight around in this way. So we had all the division and inaction and despair that most of us here will remember all too vividly: saying each time "never again," but then having to look back over again, and again, with a mixture of anger, incomprehension and shame, asking ourselves how it could possibly have happened again.

It was to find a way through this agonizing lack of consensus—this consensus-free zone—that the concept of the responsibility to protect ("R2P") was born: initiated in the 2001 report of the International Commission on Intervention and State Sovereignty (ICISS), sponsored by the Canadian government which I co-chaired with the African diplomat Mohammed Sahnoun, and then, after a long, complicated and often cantankerous diplomatic process, endorsed unanimously by the UN General Assembly sitting at head of state and government level at the 2005 World Summit, in what has been described by the British political and Holocaust historian Martin Gilbert as "the most significant adjustment to national sovereignty in 360 years."

There were, and remain, crucial differences between R2P and the "right of humanitarian intervention," and it is a fundamental mistake to maintain, as some still do, that R2P is no more than old humanitarian intervention wine in a new bottle. In the first place, R2P is primarily about prevention, whereas humanitarian intervention is only about reaction. Secondly, R2P is about a whole continuum of reactive responses—from diplomatic persuasion, to pressure, to non-military measures like sanctions and International Criminal Court process, and only in extreme, exceptional and last resort cases military action, whereas humanitarian intervention is only about military reaction. And thirdly, R2P is about a wide range of actors, whereas humanitarian intervention focuses only on the role of those capable of applying coercive military force.

More specifically, R2P involves three distinct levels of responsibility. The primary responsibility is that of the sovereign state itself to its own people—one that is absolute, unconditional, and continuing—not to perpetrate or allow atrocity crimes on its territory (the so-called "Pillar I"). The second responsibility is that of others in the international community—including other states and intergovernmental organizations—to assist states to discharge that primary responsibility, if they are willing to be so assisted ("Pillar II"). The third responsibility is that of others—if prevention fails, and a state is manifestly failing to protect its own people—to then provide that protection by every means prescribed, and circumscribed, by the United Nations Charter ("Pillar III").

Since 2005, there has been a long period of international discussion and argument about the meaning, scope and limits of R2P, in a variety of contexts. But what we can now say, following the major debates in the UN General Assembly in 2009, 2010 and 2011 is that—even after the controversy about Libya which I will come to in a moment—it has won a remarkable degree of acceptance in principle. Secretary General Ban Ki-Moon was not exaggerating when he said in September last year, "Our debates are about how, not whether to implement the Responsibility to Protect. No government questions the principle."

But, and it's a very big "but" indeed, we have to acknowledge that a good deal of the debate about how to implement R2P in practice, at least at the sharp end—when prevention has manifestly failed and violence is actually occurring—is still very fierce and very divisive. From the high point we reached in the Security Council in February and March last year—when there *was* real consensus both about the steps that had to be taken to stop atrocity crimes that were happening in Libya and feared likely to happen on an even bigger scale—we have now, in relation to the even worse human rights situation in Syria, reached the low point of paralysis in the Council, even on adopting non-military measures like targeted sanctions, an arms embargo, or reference to the International Criminal Court (ICC).

So why did consensus fell away, and what can be done to re-establish it?

Sixteen months ago, in March 2011, the United Nations Security Council, with no dissenting voices, and expressly invoking the principle of the responsibility to protect, authorized the use of "all necessary measures" to protect civilians at imminent risk of massacre in Benghazi and elsewhere in Gaddafi's Libya. A NATO-led airborne military operation immediately followed, and those thousands of lives at imminent risk were unquestionably saved.

The March resolution followed a unanimous one three weeks earlier, also invoking R2P, which condemned Gaddafi's violence against unarmed citizens, demanded that it stop, and sought to concentrate his mind by applying targeted sanctions, an arms embargo and the threat of ICC prosecution. Only when that was ignored was the military intervention authorized.

I and many others hailed these resolutions as the coming of age of R2P, a textbook example of the doctrine working as it was supposed to, saving lives imminently at risk, and at last decisively cutting across centuries of state practice treating sovereignty almost as a license to kill. If the Council had acted as decisively and robustly in the 1990s as it did in Libya, the lives of 8,000 others would have been saved in Srbrenica and 800,000 in Rwanda.

But now, over Syria, despite a rapidly climbing death toll of as many as 17,000 or more, the Security Council remains, as it has been for over a year, almost completely paralysed, barely able to agree on condemnation of the violence and a diplomatic mission to address it, let alone more robust measures.

Part of the reason for hesitation—and certainly the unwillingness to even *begin* to think about coercive military intervention—is that the geopolitics of the Syrian crisis are very different: complex internal sectarian divisions with potentially explosive regional implications, anxiety about the democratic credentials of many of those in opposition, no Arab League unanimity in favour of tough action, a long Russian commitment to the Assad regime, and a strong Syrian army meaning that any conceivable intervention would be difficult and bloody.

But there's more to it than that. We have to explain why it is that it took until February this year for the Security Council to even formally condemn the violence, and why there has been no consensus whatever even about non-military coercive measures like targeted sanctions of the kind that which were unanimously agreed for Libya at a stage when the Gaddafi regime's violence was much less than Assad's. Consensus *has* simply evaporated in a welter of recrimination about how the NATO-led implementation of the Council's Libya mandate "to protect civilians and civilian populated areas under threat of attack" was actually carried out. We have to frankly recognize that there has been some infection of the whole R2P concept by the perception, accurate or otherwise, that the civilian protection mandate granted by the Council was manifestly exceeded by that military operation.

Leading the critical charge have been the "BRICS" (Brazil, Russia, India, China and South Africa), all of whom were sitting on the Security Council last year—in an interesting foretaste of the kind of Security Council membership more representative of current world power balances that many of us have been arguing for. Their complaints have been not about the initial military response—destroying Libyan air force infrastructure, and air attacks on the ground forces advancing on Benghazi—but what came after, when it became rapidly apparent that the three permanent member states driving the intervention (the US, UK and France, or "P3") would settle for nothing less than regime change, and do whatever it took to achieve that.

Particular concerns are that the interveners rejected ceasefire offers that may have been serious, struck fleeing personnel that posed no immediate risk to civilians and locations that had no obvious military significance (like the compound in which Gaddafi relatives were killed) and, more generally, comprehensively supported the rebel side in what rapidly became a civil war, ignoring the very explicit arms embargo in the process.

The P3 is not without some answers. If civilians were to be protected house-to-house in areas like Tripoli under Gaddafi's direct control, they say, that could only be by overturning his whole regime. If one side was taken in a civil war, it was because one-sided regime killing sometimes leads (as now in Syria) to civilians acquiring arms to fight back and recruiting army defectors. Military operations cannot micromanaged with a "1,000 mile screwdriver." And a more limited "monitor and swoop" concept of operations would have led to longer and messier conflict, politically impossible to sustain in the US and Europe, and likely to have produced many more civilian casualties.

And yet. These arguments all have force, but the P3 resisted debate on them at any stage in the Security Council itself, and other Council members were never given sufficient information to enable them to be evaluated. Maybe not all the BRICS are to be believed when they say that, had better process been followed, more common ground could have been achieved. But they can be when they say they feel bruised by the P3's dismissiveness during the Libyan campaign—and that those bruises will have to heal before any consensus can be expected on tough responses to such situations in the future.

The better news is that a way forward has opened up. Brazil has been arguing for some months that the R2P concept, as it has evolved so far, needs not overthrowing but rather *supplementing* by a complementary set of principles and procedures which it has labeled "responsibility while protecting" ("RWP"). Its two key proposals are for a set of criteria to be fully debated and taken into account before the Security Council mandates any use of military force, and for some kind of enhanced monitoring and review processes which would enable such mandates to be seriously debated by all Council members during their implementation phase.

One way of approaching the criteria issue—which I certainly favour, and about which I will be speaking to the Brazilian Foreign Minister in Rio next month—would be return directly to the so far unimplemented recommendations of my ICISS Commission (and reports which followed it, including from Secretary-General Kofi Annan himself) that the Security Council apply specific prudential guidelines whenever considering any authorization of coercive military action under Chapter VII of the Charter.

Five such guidelines have been proposed. First, seriousness of risk: is the threatened harm of such a kind and scale as to justify prima facie the use of force? Second, primary purpose: is the use of force primarily to halt or avert the threat in question, whatever secondary motives might be in play for different states? Third, last resort: has every non-military option been fully explored and the judgment reasonably made that nothing less than military force could halt or avert the harm in question? Fourth, proportionality: are the scale, duration, and intensity of the proposed military action the minimum necessary to meet the threat? And fifth, what will often be the hardest legitimacy test to satisfy, balance of consequences: will those at risk ultimately be better or worse off, and the scale of suffering greater or less?

The completely effective implementation of R2P is going to be work in progress for some time yet. Renewed consensus on how to implement it in the hardest of cases in future is going to be hard to achieve, and will take time to achieve: it will certainly come too late to be very helpful in solving the present crisis in Syria, for which the only alternative to a strongly Russian-supported diplomatic solution—still some distance away, and maybe completely unachievable—appears to be, unhappily, a full scale civil war bloodbath.

But I don't think there is any policymaker in the world who fails to understand that if the Security Council does *not* find a way of genuinely cooperating to resolve these cases, working within the nuanced and multidimensional framework of the R2P principle, the alternative is a return to the bad old days of Rwanda, Srebrenica and Kosovo.

The Responsibility to Protect: Growing Pains or Early Promise?

EDWARD C. LUCK

The ever-expanding literature on the responsibility to protect (RtoP) could now fill a small library. The number of graduate theses alone devoted to the topic has been nothing less than staggering. RtoP's contribution to both conceptual thought and policy planning concerning how to prevent genocide and

Reprinted by permission of FOREIGN AFFAIRS, Online, July 24, 2013. Copyright 2013 by the Council on Foreign Relations, Inc. www.ForeignAffairs.com

other mass atrocities, therefore, is beyond question. But RtoP was not envisioned as an academic or planning exercise. Nine years after the principle was first articulated by the independent International Commission on Intervention and State Sovereignty (ICISS) and five years after it was refined and adopted by the 2005 World Summit,[1] some are beginning to ask whether, where, and how the concept has made a difference in terms of international and state policy and, more important, in terms of preventing such horrific crimes in the first place. Understandably, many of these early assessments are skeptical. As the official charged with developing the conceptual, political, and institutional elements of RtoP for United Nations Secretary-General Ban Ki-moon, I have followed this growing assessment literature with keen attention. One of the more thoughtful and constructive contributions to this genre appeared in a recent volume of this journal. In "The Responsibility to Protect—Five Years On," Alex J. Bellamy provides a balanced, cogent, and—as the following suggests—provocative analysis of the strengths and weaknesses of RtoP as a policy tool.

Professor Bellamy, the author of one of the better books on RtoP, comments on a series of humanitarian crises since 2005 in which he believes RtoP was either used too little (Somalia), used ineffectively (Darfur), or employed effectively (Kenya). He draws useful lessons from each. Such comparative studies remind us that the ability of RtoP to deliver has been (and will continue to be) mixed. There is no dispute about that. They also demonstrate, however, that it is a bit early in RtoP's young life to judge what it will be when it grows up as a mature policy tool. There is reason to question, as well, whether Somalia and Darfur are the best tests of RtoP's potential.

None of these situations can be understood only through an RtoP lens. In Somalia, establishing viable governance and reestablishing state control over the country's territory have both been first-order goals of the international community. Without functioning governance, no one can be held fully responsible or accountable for the assaults on civilians. In cases of extreme state fragility and long-running armed conflict, the resolution of the underlying conflict may be a prerequisite for fully achieving RtoP goals. Integrating RtoP and genocide prevention perspectives into policy-making in such situations—whether in terms of peacemaking, peacekeeping, or post-conflict peacebuilding—may be critical to furthering human protection goals. But, as Professor Bellamy recognizes, these perspectives cannot offer magical solutions to stubborn and deeply entrenched political, economic, and security problems. Nor will they, or should they, be the sole basis for policy choices.

The prevention and resolution of armed conflict poses one set of policy challenges, the prevention and curbing of atrocity crimes a distinct but related one. Though these goals are often mutually reinforcing, that is not always the case. Both their distinct and overlapping dimensions should be borne in mind by scholars and practitioners concerned with better policy choices and outcomes. In the months leading to the Rwanda genocide in 1994, for instance, the premium was placed on conflict resolution, as policy-makers in capitals and at the UN ignored the inconvenient warnings of looming genocide. Recent research by Lisa Hultman has found that, historically, the deployment of peacekeepers to situations of ongoing armed conflict has been associated with increasing levels of violence by rebel groups against civilians. More encouragingly, however, when such operations have had an explicit mandate to protect civilians, the incidence of such violence by rebel groups against civilians has actually decreased—that is, the mandates have made a positive difference. Much seems to depend, she suggests, on how each side of the conflict calculates how the arrival of international peacekeepers will affect its power position in the end game and whether attacks on civilians will boost its bargaining position. It should be recognized, as well, that sometimes RtoP crimes are directly associated with armed conflict, but sometimes they are not, as in Kyrgyzstan, Cambodia, and the Holocaust.

In none of Bellamy's cases are the governments the only parties of concern, though international inquiries and the International Criminal Court have found the government in Khartoum to have been responsible for the worst atrocities in Darfur. As the secretary-general's RtoP strategy recognizes—and earlier state-centric versions of RtoP did not—states are not the only actors that commit such mass crimes. If armed groups control territory, as in parts of the Democratic Republic of the Congo (DRC), then they should also be expected to bear a parallel responsibility to protect populations within that territory. As the secretary-general has pointed out, in Sierra Leone international military assistance to the government was required to defeat rebel groups that were committing crimes against humanity. And, as he reminded the Security Council in August of this year, the mass rapes in eastern DRC—surely another crime against humanity—pose a brutal challenge to "our collective responsibility" to protect civilians in conflict zones.

Only one of the situations addressed by Bellamy—Kenya—erupted after the 2005 World Summit adopted RtoP. The worst violence occurred in Darfur before either the World Summit embraced RtoP or the Security Council made protection of civilians a key element of the peacekeeping mandate there. It is a stretch to expect a principle to address successfully violence that raged long before it was accepted by member state governments, much less embodied in international policies and processes. Even in the case of post-election violence in Kenya, the United Nations decided in early 2008 to try to apply RtoP principles to the situation, even though it had not yet developed dedicated machinery for addressing such situations properly. As Professor Bellamy underscores, the ongoing effort to create a joint office on genocide prevention and the promotion of the responsibility to protect at the United Nations offers some promise of an earlier, more coherent, and more consistent effort across the UN system to address such crimes and violations in the future. But so far there is more promise than practice. Moreover, of these cases, only Kenya, as Professor Bellamy readily acknowledges, was chiefly a matter of prevention, the centerpiece of both the 2005 Summit and Secretary-General Ban's RtoP strategy. The latter calls for an early and flexible response tailored to the circumstances of each situation, but its clear preference is for preventive action—both structural and operational—so that a response to "the manifest failure to protect," to use the words of paragraph 139 of the 2005 Outcome Document, is not necessary.

NORMS, EXPECTATIONS, AND COMPLIANCE PULL

Though he does not put it in quite such bald terms, Professor Bellamy, like any number of other scholars and analysts, at heart appears to object to RtoP as a "speech act" out of an understandable concern that member states and international officials will, when push comes to shove, give little more than lip service to the principle. This is a recurrent worry for practitioners as well. As he phrases it, "this persistent gap between what is needed and what is delivered cannot be primarily ascribed to the situation's complexity, but instead reflects the limited extent to which RtoP has the capacity to generate 'compliance pull' in international society" (pp. 153–54). However, surely it is not a question of whether the invocation of RtoP exerts no pull, as the very political opposition (as well as enthusiasm) the concept generates speaks to the widespread perception of its potency as a political rallying cry. Nor could one credibly assert that it exerts sufficient compliance pull as to ensure either consistent compliance with RtoP principles around the world or effective response to breaches when they do occur. The road to full implementation remains both long and steep. So how full or empty is the RtoP glass? More to the point, is the level rising or falling when it comes to RtoP's compliance pull?

This author, naturally, tends to see the glass, though less than half full at this point, filling slowly and unevenly. As Professor Bellamy's assessment implies, the secretary-general's strategy and the initial steps he is taking to operationalize RtoP are meant, in part, to provide further sustenance and sustainability to this larger enterprise. The annual reports and dialogues in the General Assembly, discussed above, are one means of trying to keep the issue on the minds of policymakers in capitals and of diplomats in New York. The lively academic discourse and the dedicated efforts of NGOs, such as the Global Centre for the Responsibility to Protect, the International Coalition for the Responsibility to Protect, and the Asia-Pacific Centre for the Responsibility to Protect, both reflect and encourage the continuing interest in civil society to move RtoP from words to deeds. What is most needed, of course, are more cases where RtoP and the UN's new tools are both invoked and make a demonstrable, positive difference on the ground and in people's lives. Political will is not a given or static quantity. It can be built or destroyed by actions over time.

Here, expectations matter. RtoP is particularly susceptible to the best-being-the-enemy-of-the-good syndrome. If we expected norms, standards, and principles to be respected and implemented at all places, all of the time, then we would not have any. The bar would be too high. Generally, if pursued with some vigor and consistency, compliance tends to expand and deepen over time, as has been the case with human rights and humanitarian norms. Moreover, the most consequential standards and norms have important aspirational qualities, as goals of behavior to be emulated and attained over time. If they simply described current behavior, they would add little of consequence.

In terms of expectations, Professor Bellamy's lucid discussion of "RtoP as a norm" (pp. 160–62) does not travel well from the realm of political science to the realm of politics, though he usually manages to straddle this fault line better than most. Drawing from Martha Finnemore and Kathryn Sikkink, he posits that norms "are shared expectations of appropriate behavior for actors with a given identity" (p. 160). By that definition, RtoP would surely qualify as a norm. In intergovernmental discourse, however, norms are to have a binding legal quality that RtoP lacks, though some of its component parts, like genocide prevention, do not. Definition aside, Professor Bellamy raises two more consequential questions related to the normative character of RtoP. One, he asks whether the second and third pillars of the secretary-general's strategy, on international assistance to the state and on an international response to the manifest failure to protect, respectively, should be "properly called norms" (p. 161). Two, in casting doubt on such a claim, he contends that they exert insufficient compliance pull because "they are weakened by the problem of indeterminacy" (p. 161). Each of these assertions bears closer scrutiny.

To this author, at least, to test whether the second and third pillars are norms—even in political science terms—is to raise something of a straw man. The secretary-general's strategy aims to be just that, a hopefully integrated and coherent set of ideas for implementing the RtoP norms, principles, or standards adopted by the heads of state and government in 2005. It does not seek to add new norms or standards to the ambitious ones that had been agreed at that point. The strategy draws faithfully and diligently from the 2005 consensus text. The most unequivocal RtoP statement of that document comes in paragraph 138, where the world leaders, referring to the responsibility of "each individual state" to protect populations by preventing the four crimes or their incitement, assert that "we accept that responsibility and will act in accordance with it." This is unambiguous and unconditional. On the other hand, the international community "should, as appropriate, encourage and help States to exercise their responsibility" (paragraph 138) and "also has the responsibility" to use appropriate means under Chapters VI and VIII of the UN Charter "to help protect populations" from these crimes (paragraph 139). They are "prepared to take collective action, in a timely and decisive manner, through the Security Council" under the conditions noted earlier (paragraph 139). The international commitment is to help and, in certain circumstances, to act collectively.

Even if that collective action is to be "timely and decisive," it is to be decided through a political process in the Security Council (or, less frequently, the General Assembly). Pacific measures may be taken by the secretary-general under Chapter VI, or regional arrangements may act under Chapter VIII of the Charter. There is no pre-commitment to take coercive enforcement action, no automaticity or rigid template demanding a particular course of action on this or any other nonprocedural matter before the Security Council. That conception of the Council's role was rejected at the UN's founding conference in San Francisco in

1945, as well as through more than six decades of practice since.

The wording of paragraph 139 imposes an obligation on the international community to consider a range of possible actions to help protect populations and to respond to cases of manifest failure to protect. However, it does not, and cannot, require a successful outcome. For one thing, there is no certain way of knowing beforehand which course of action will make the most positive difference. This is not a science. Outcomes are not pre-ordained. And these dilemmas are hardly new. States parties have long had obligations under the 1948 Convention on the Prevention and Punishment of Genocide. Interestingly, the International Court of Justice (ICJ), in its 2007 judgment in the case of *Bosnia and Herzegovina v. Serbia and Montenegro,* found that states parties have a duty "to employ all measures reasonably available to them so as to prevent genocide as far as possible." According to the ICJ, "the obligation in question is one of conduct and not one of result, in the sense that a State cannot be under an obligation to succeed, whatever the circumstances, in preventing the commission of genocide." This obligation to try falls most heavily on the fifteen members of the Security Council and on others with a capacity to make a positive difference. The ICJ asked whether Serbian authorities had exercised "due diligence" in terms of the massacre at Srebrenica, and determined that they had not.

At times, UN-authorized force maybe justified as part of a "timely and decisive" response. At times, it may be the only way to prevent further bloodletting. But it hardly qualifies as the cure-all some would want it to be. Like other policy tools, military interventions for humanitarian purposes do not always succeed in saving lives or in sticking to their humanitarian purposes. Their costs and risks tend to be high, while assessments of their effectiveness over time vary. Moreover, there have been relatively few instances of intervention for primarily humanitarian purposes, whether undertaken unilaterally or collectively. Though some critics fret that RtoP could prove to be a humanitarian veneer by which powerful states could justify military intervention in the developing world, more often the problem has been the opposite: that the capable have stood by as the slaughter of civilians unfolded before the world's—and sometimes even UN peacekeepers'—eyes. They have looked for excuses not to act, rather than for reasons to intervene. Indeed, the Security Council's selectivity and seeming indifference to such suffering have been criticized more often in the General Assembly debates on RtoP than has its supposed eagerness to intervene. The core purpose of the ICISS exercise and of its invention of the responsibility to protect concept in the first place, it should be recalled, was to get beyond the then already stale debate on humanitarian intervention by military means.

In an intriguing but ultimately unpersuasive line of reasoning, Professor Bellamy contends that the very flexibility of RtoP as a policy instrument is a weakness in terms of its compliance pull. In his words, "The more precisely a norm indicates the behavior it expects in a given situation, the stronger its compliance-pull" (p. 161). Because RtoP does not specify precisely what is expected of external actors "once states agree that *something* ought to be done" (p. 162), "the extent to which actors are satisfying shared expectations of appropriate behavior" (ibid.) would be unclear, thus reducing compliance pull. But could not the same thing be said for almost all norms, which tend to be specific about what kind of behavior is prohibited but vague about how others should respond to gross violations? Which human rights or humanitarian norm also stipulates detailed enforcement or compliance mechanisms? What RtoP brings to existing norms on genocide prevention, war crimes, ethnic cleansing, and crimes against humanity, in fact, is the nucleus of a multilateral compliance mechanism.

Agreeing that something ought to be done when an important international standard has been breached in unacceptable ways is the critical first step. That is why norms and standards matter. Their task is not to determine with any precision what the most appropriate policy response should be in each case. Here, as with his discussion of pillars two and three as norms, there is some confusion between norms and the policy agenda for encouraging their implementation.

Whatever one thinks about compliance pull, there is strong reason to believe that the RtoP provisions of the 2005 Outcome Document would never have been agreed upon if they were any more specific on the course of action that would have to be followed in cases of manifest failure to protect. Paragraph 139 takes care to specify who should decide on collective measures—the Security Council—and what should be the guiding framework—the UN Charter. Legal authority would be critical, but then it would be up to the political processes laid out in the Charter to decide an appropriate response. As this author has noted elsewhere, decision-making sovereignty was every bit as important in 2005 to powerful states as territorial sovereignty was to less powerful ones. Member states—big and small ones alike—just do not like to be told that there is a particular course of action that they are obligated to take in certain circumstances. Under Article 25, all member states "agree to accept and carry out the decisions of the Security Council in accordance with the present Charter." But the binding quality of its decisions makes the Council unique. It is not about to be bound by others or to be told how it must act in these or other circumstances.

POLITICAL WILL AND THE FUTURE

Ultimately, of course, it is all about political will. This is true for those considering inciting or committing such atrocities, for those within the society who could help curb those impulses, for neighboring countries and for regional and subregional bodies, for international NGOs and secretariats, and for the members of the United Nations and its Security Council. That is why the responsibility to protect is a political rather than a legal concept, why the work of RtoP-focused NGOs and of independent scholars, such as Professor Bellamy, matter so much; why it is essential that RtoP assessments and perspectives become better integrated in country-specific decision-making processes in the UN, regional institutions, and national governments; and why the moral imperative that RtoP represents should not be neglected even in our most hardheaded analyses of the choices ahead. Values shape priorities, and sometimes even political will.

At this point, the responsibility to protect could expect no mark other than an incomplete. It has yet to prove that it can make a deep and sustained difference in terms of either preventing genocide and other atrocity crimes and their incitement or offering or spurring a modicum of protection to vulnerable populations. But studies have shown both that peacekeepers, when properly mandated and equipped, can offer protection from atrocity crimes and that international engagement and expressions of concern have helped to prevent genocidal acts in troubled societies. The secretary-general's efforts to reach out to all 192 member states have demonstrated the possibility of building wider, deeper, and more diverse constituencies for the operationalization of RtoP. The upside potential is clearly there. What would we have said in 1953 about the chances that the Universal Declaration on Human Rights or the Genocide Convention, when they were just five years old, would come to play a transformative role in international policy and in the relations between the state and its people? Who would have been prescient enough to foresee in those dire days either how much the world would change or how much these conventions would change the world? We live in much more fluid and dynamic times, not least in the realm of ideas, values, and institutions. For all of RtoP's faults and frailties, time may well be on its side.

Note

[1]At the 2005 World Summit, the heads of state and government unanimously pledged to protect their populations by preventing genocide, war crimes, ethnic cleansing, and crimes against humanity, as well as by preventing the incitement of such acts. They agreed, also, that the international community should assist and support states in that regard, including "those which are under stress before crimes and conflicts break out." They pledged to "support the United Nations in establishing an early warning capability." They noted the international community's responsibility to use peaceful means under Chapters VI and VIII of the UN Charter to offer protection. When such "means [are] inadequate," they underscored that they "are prepared to take collective action, in a timely and decisive manner, through

the Security Council." In January 2009, UN Secretary-General Ban Ki-moon offered a three-part strategy for turning these fine words into deeds. The first pillar is the prevention and protection responsibility of the state, something for which international institutions can rarely substitute. The second pillar is the responsibility of the international community to help states meet those core responsibilities.

The Danger of Human Rights Proliferation: When Defending Liberty, Less Is More

JACOB MCHANGAMA AND GUGLIELMO VERDIRAME

If human rights were a currency, its value would be in free fall, thanks to a gross inflation in the number of human rights treaties and nonbinding international instruments adopted by international organizations over the last several decades. These days, this currency is sometimes more likely to buy cover for dictatorships than protection for citizens. Human rights once enshrined the most basic principles of human freedom and dignity; today, they can include anything from the right to international solidarity to the right to peace.

Consider just how enormous the body of binding human rights law has become. The Freedom Rights Project, a research group that we co-founded, counts a full 64 human-rights-related agreements under the auspices of the United Nations and the Council of Europe. A member state of both of these organizations that has ratified all these agreements would have to comply with 1,377 human rights provisions (although some of these may be technical rather than substantive). Add to this the hundreds of non-treaty instruments, such as the resolutions of the UN General Assembly and Human Rights Council (HRC). The aggregate body of human rights law now has all the accessibility of a tax code.

Supporters of human rights should worry about this explosion of regulation. If people are to demand human rights, then they must first be able to understand them—a tall order given the current bureaucratic tangle of administrative regulation.

What explains the proliferation of human rights? The process has been driven partly by well-meaning lobbies for special interest groups that are looking for the trump card of having their cause recognized as a human rights issue. International human rights advocates, some national governments, and technocrats in international organizations seeking larger bureaucratic domains have also played a role.

But there is also a darker agenda behind the expansion of human rights law. Put simply, illiberal states have sought to stretch human rights law to give themselves room to hide behind it. They have even used it to mount political attacks against liberal states. A critical look at the UN's often dysfunctional HRC is illustrative. Although it cannot adopt treaties or pass binding resolutions, the HRC is an important forum for developing new human rights standards and shaping the international human rights discourse. Judged by respect for human rights, its membership covers a wide spectrum, from democracies to tyrannies.

States ranked "free" in *Freedom House's index* tend to take a robust approach to human rights centered on what are called first-generation rights,

Reprinted by permission of FOREIGN AFFAIRS. Foreign Affairs, July 24. Online Version.

such as free speech and freedom from torture. Although these countries are not necessarily opposed to what are called second-generation rights, which include quality of life issues such as housing and health, they are frequently skeptical about what are referred to as third-generation rights. This latter category encompasses ill-defined rights that protect collective rather than individual interests and includes the right to development, the right to international solidarity, and the right to peace.

In contrast, "partly free" and "not free" states have become the main proponents of third-generation rights. For most of them, of course, these commitments in practice mean very little, since countries that do not adhere to the rule of law at home rarely take international legal obligations seriously. But by presenting themselves as the champions of these new human rights, they seek to knock liberal states off the moral high ground and shore up their own political legitimacy.

A similar process plays out at the Universal Periodic Review, a human rights exam that all member states at the UN have to undergo every four and a half years. In 2009, no less a human rights abuser than North Korea received praise from Cuba, Iran, Russia, and Syria for working "to consolidate a socialist and just society, which guarantees equality and social justice." In May 2013 North Korea, and Sudan in turn encouraged Cuba to "work through the UN mechanism in progressive development of the third generation of human rights, particularly the value of international solidarity."

The expanded and diluted notion of human rights allows illiberal states to change the focus from core freedoms to vague and conceptually unclear rights that place no concrete obligations on states. Enabled by such rhetoric, no human rights violation can stand scrutiny on its own merits. Instead, human rights violations are relativized—intellectually dismembered and discarded when it is politically expedient. In this world, cuts in development aid can be labeled human rights violations just like torture in North Korea. Crucially, this unprincipled politics of human rights helps authoritarian states deflect criticism. In 2007, Cuba, which has one of the worst human rights records in the Western Hemisphere, succeeded in persuading a majority of HRC members to axe the specific mandate for monitoring its own human rights record. The praise authoritarian states shower on one another for supposedly upholding new, vague and abstract rights are therefore not just empty rhetoric but can produce real political gains.

Unfortunately, much of the human rights community has not only shied away from expressing qualms about rights proliferation, it has often led the process. But this approach has not helped advance the core freedoms that make the difference between liberal and non-liberal states: According to Freedom House, global respect for basic civil and political rights is in decline *for the seventh consecutive year.* Of course, it is exactly those basic rights that non-free states want to neuter. When everything can be defined as a human right, the premium on violating such rights is cheap. To raise the stock and ensure the effectiveness of human rights, their defenders need to acknowledge that less is often more.

Respect for human rights around the world would likely be stronger if human rights law had stuck to a narrower and more clearly defined group of rights. The efforts and resources of human rights advocates and international institutions could have been much more targeted. Greater focus might have also resulted in better monitoring and more robust enforcement. Illiberal states would not have been able to lay any claim to human rights—let alone invoke them to delegitimize liberal states. Liberal states might have also concentrated their efforts on human rights institutions that, unlike the HRC, actually offer prospects of improvement through reform. The Strasbourg-based European Court of Human Rights, for example, partly through its own interpretive overreach, which has seen it expand existing rights and invent new ones, is losing credibility in some important member states such as the United Kingdom. European states have not done enough to address the crisis of Europe's oldest human rights institution.

Instead of rushing to respond to the human rights flavor of the month—be it protecting the elderly or defending the peasants—liberal democracies should support institutions and treaties that embody the ideals that inspired the human rights movement in the first place.

VISUAL REVIEW

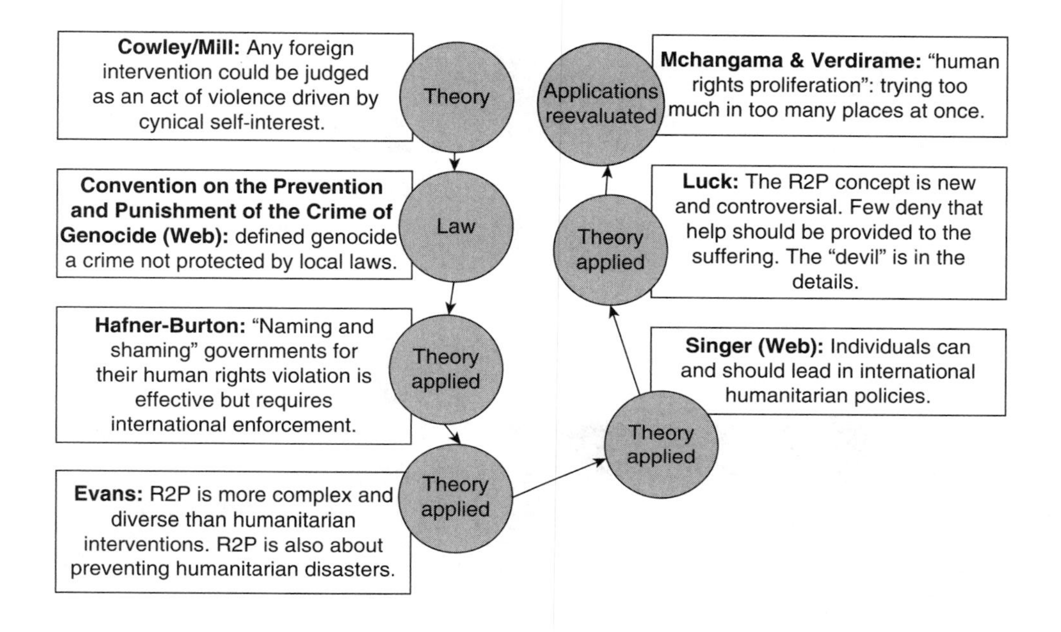

Section 10

Hearts and Minds: Culture and Nationalism

A "YES" supporter and a "NO" supporter have a chat outside a polling station in Hillhead, Glasgow, at the Scottish Independence Referendum, Glasgow, United Kingdom, September 18, 2014. The majority voted against independence. Which countries today may potentially face a breakup based on ethnic divisions? Why does the United States, in your opinion, support the plight for independence of some countries but not others?
Source: Jane Stockdale/REX/Associated Press

A Feminist Voyage Through International Relations

J. ANN TICKNER

No academic discipline would be complete without its origins stories. Since the beginning of feminist international relations is so recent—dating back about twenty-five years—it has been documented frequently. Putting together some of my writings over these years has given me an opportunity to look back at my part in this collective effort and reflect on how far we have come, thanks to the dedication and creative work of so many committed feminist scholars. It is a pleasure to have the opportunity to revisit some of my earlier work and reflect on how my thinking has evolved over the past twenty-five years. Before presenting this work, I will offer a few reflections about my own personal journey and how remarkable it has been to find so many others in different parts of the world and in different disciplines embarking on similar journeys. Creating feminist knowledge has always been a collective effort, and the first twenty-five years of feminist international relations (IR) has been no exception.

It is always easier to look back and detect a coherent pattern in the development of one's intellectual interests than to see it while living it. Nevertheless, I do see a number of connecting themes that eventually led me to my feminist journey through international relations. I was born in London in 1937 shortly before the beginning of World War II. Though I was too young to understand its causes and consequences, my wartime childhood gave me some firsthand experience of the effects of war on ordinary people's lives, a concern that has been central to feminists when they study war and conflict. Nightly bombing raids that forced us into shelters seemed "normal" to me. However, for adults, war was not a normal reality; they coped with bans on driving, putting up blackout curtains every night, lighting fires each morning to keep us warm with small amounts of rationed coal, making sure our gas masks operated correctly, and staying awake at night waiting for the sirens that warned of impending bombing raids.

Postwar Britain was slow to recover. It must have come as a relief to my parents when, in 1951, my father was invited to join the staff of the United Nations Secretariat. These were times when the United States was optimistic about the United Nations' future success; Americans welcomed UN families enthusiastically. Assuming that my family would go back to Britain, I continued my education at a British boarding school and later at the University of London, becoming a transatlantic commuter, mostly by sea, in days when air travel was still a luxury.

This transatlantic lifestyle unsettled my sense of national identity; chastised by my severe English boarding school teachers for losing my British accent but always appearing quite British to Americans, I could never decide where I belonged, a question that frequently arises, albeit in a different context, for those of us who have chosen a feminist path through international relations. Although relatively few young people went to university in England at that time and in spite of my choice of an all-women's college, most of my fellow graduates expected to go into secondary school teaching. This was the best option for women in Britain with a university degree at that time and one that was often regarded as a temporary stage on the way to full-time motherhood. Having studied history as an undergraduate I decided to pursue a master's degree in international relations at Yale. The realities of war and the promise of peace, enshrined in the UN Charter, were foundational for my interest in international relations, especially my evolving interest in peace studies. Yet even after I received a master's degree, it was hard to imagine a career in what was then not a very hospitable environment for women academics in IR—a very male-dominated field. I left academia, somewhat gratefully, and devoted the next ten

Reprinted courtesy of Oxford University Press. Oxford Studies in Gender and International Relations. Introduction.

years to full-time motherhood—"not working," as it was always described to me. Although the irony of this label escaped me at the time, I always try to remind my students that indeed their mothers do "work," even if it is not remunerated work.

Ten years later, I went back to graduate school to pursue a Ph.D. in political science at Brandeis University. I had spent the previous year in Geneva, Switzerland, where I participated in a course at The Graduate Institute taught by Norwegian peace researcher Johan Galtung. His particular interest at that time was small-scale self-reliant development as a strategy for newly emerging economies. My decision to pursue this theme for my Ph.D. thesis was not particularly feminist—indeed, I had not yet been exposed to feminist thinking at that time—but the topic was still unconventional for IR. *Self-Reliance versus Power Politics: American and Indian Experiences in Building Nation-States* (1987), the title under which my dissertation was published, compared strategies of building national-power favored by both the United States during its early development and post-independence India, with small-scale agrarian strategies, favored in the early writings of Thomas Jefferson and by Mohandas Gandhi as his vision for India's development. In retrospect, one could project a gendered analysis onto these two very different strategies—one dedicated to building national power, the other toward the development of basic needs; in both cases, the national power strategy won out.

Entering the job market to teach international relations with a somewhat unconventional dissertation, I was fortunate to be offered a position at the College of the Holy Cross, in Worcester, Massachusetts, a small liberal arts college where the quality of one's research was more valued than whether one was working in an "acceptable" IR paradigm. When I started teaching in the 1980s, nuclear strategy and the Cold War rivalry between the United States and the Soviet Union were central issues in introductory courses in international relations. Well before I was exposed to any feminist literature, I became aware of how many of my women students were quite uncomfortable with, or unmotivated by, my introductory IR course, often seeming quite alienated from the material. Besides the problem that there was nothing to assign by women authors, much of the subject matter—a great deal of it on war and nuclear strategy—seemed to leave them feeling fundamentally disempowered and disinterested. I myself had been trained in conventional IR in graduate school, and I had never thought to question the absence of women either as creators of, or as subject matter in, the discipline of international relations. It was not until a few years into teaching and going to professional conferences where women seldom appeared on panels that I began to develop a feminist consciousness or even ask the basic question, where are the women?[1]

Trying to figure out why extremely capable students felt so alienated from the material, with its emphasis on national security and conflict, motivated me to start thinking about IR as gendered masculine. A defining moment for me was reading Evelyn Fox Keller's *Reflections on Gender and Science* (1985) and attending her class on gender and science at MIT in 1986. Keller, a physicist by training, claimed in her book that the natural sciences are gendered, and gendered masculine, in both the questions they ask and the ways they go about answering them. This is a claim that I thought might equally be applied to IR. My first article began to develop this idea, applying it to Hans Morgenthau's principles of political realism.

My first encounter with feminism and international relations was when I was invited to attend a conference on Women and International Relations at the London School of Economics (LSE) in 1988. It is safe to say that before that the presence of women and gender issues had been completely ignored by the IR discipline.[2] As Fred Halliday noted in his introduction to the *Millennium* special issue that published the conference papers, there had been some recognition of women and gender in the social sciences, mainly in history and sociology. However, as he claimed, women remained hidden from international relations. The following year Halliday introduced the first course on women and international relations into the MA program at LSE. I was fortunate to be able to participate. There was little material that we would call IR in the disciplinary sense that we could assign to the students. Guest speakers were mostly development specialists from international agencies who were responding to calls from the international women's movement of the 1970s to consider women's needs (for the first time) in development planning.

Bringing feminist perspectives into the discipline of international relations began through conferences and collaboration—a feminist way of doing things. Shortly after the conference at the London School of Economics in 1988, Jane Jaquette and Spike Peterson, professors at Occidental College and the University of Arizona, respectively, organized a second one at the University of Southern California (USC) in 1989 entitled "Women, the State and War: What Difference Does Gender Make?" Close to seventy participants attended from a variety of social science disciplines, including feminist scholars and a number of senior international relations scholars who had had little previous exposure to feminist analysis. In the following year a third conference, which I organized, together with Peggy McIntosh of the Wellesley Center for Research on Women, was held at Wellesley College and funded by the Ford Foundation. Collective efforts, such as these, and the sharing of ideas have been important aspects of building this new discipline, which has since evolved into a thriving academic community. Since academic feminism was born out of the women's movement of the 1960s and 1970s, an important aspect of these collective efforts has been an attempt to broaden conversations to include policy-makers and activists. To this end, ten years after the initial Wellesley conference, the Ford Foundation funded two additional conferences entitled "Gender in International Relations: From Seeing Women and Recognizing Gender to Transforming Policy Research," held at Wellesley College and USC in 2001. Participants included policy-makers, activists, and academics; many IR feminist scholars are explicit in their normative commitments to effecting social change and identify themselves as scholar-activists, an identity that appears somewhat unconventional in a discipline committed to "objective scientific" research but one that is extremely important in feminist research. By 2001, I had moved to take up a position in the School of International Relations at USC, an institution that supported non-conventional approaches to IR. This position gave me an opportunity to train graduate students who, together with many other young scholars from all over the world, are continuing to push boundaries and produce innovative work beyond what those of us could have imagined at the beginning.

When these efforts at introducing feminist perspectives were first launched, at the end of the 1980s, it seemed like a promising time for new thinking in the international relations discipline. The Cold War was ending and, not coincidentally, I believe, IR was both broadening its subject matter and opening up to critical approaches in terms of methodological perspectives, described at the time as "a post-positivist era." There was the optimistic sense that feminism was one of a number of new and exciting critical approaches that would enrich and expand a field that had been so caught up with explaining the national security behavior of the great powers and with using neo-positivist methodologies to do so.

With the exception of some subfields of sociology, most of the social sciences were late in adopting a gender perspective—particularly in matters related to global affairs. Nevertheless, when this did happen, it was remarkable the extent to which scholars in different parts of the world, and in different disciplines, began to think along similar lines at about the same time. In 1993 Jan Jindy Pettman published an article in Australia's leading international affairs journal entitled "Gendering International Relations".[3] Two years earlier, Hilary Charlesworth and her coauthors' article in the *American Journal of International Law* had already drawn attention to the gendered foundations of International Law. That same year, Marianne Ferber and Julie Nelson edited *Beyond Economic Man*, which made similar claims about the masculine foundations of the discipline of economics.

What were we doing in those early days? Some of us were trying to find women. Cynthia Enloe suggested that international relations was so thoroughly gendered that no one had noticed that women were missing. Besides finding women in places not normally considered within the boundaries of IR, feminists were also attempting to redefine some of the core concepts of the field—concepts such as security, anarchy, and sovereignty. In the words of Spike Peterson, these initial feminist endeavors were engaged in three knowledge projects—first, exposing the extent and effect of masculinist bias; second, attempting to rectify the systematic exclusion of women by adding women to existing frameworks; and third, and by far the most radical and least understood, reconstructing theory by recognizing gender as an analytical and structural category. It continues to be the case that the third goal, recognizing international relations as gendered (both in the disciplinary and "real-world" sense), is the most radical move and remains the least understood by the wider discipline.

This research presents some of my interventions into a field that, in the last twenty-five years, has produced a rich array of scholarship that has developed from these initial goals. Happily it has now extended beyond its Anglo-American/Australian foundations to include scholars in all parts of the world; like feminism more generally, it is paying increasing attention to the issue of the intersectionality of race, class, and gender. While feminist research has been successful in making women visible, it has gone much deeper. Getting beyond women *and* IR, and even beyond gender *and* IR, it has successfully demonstrated—though maybe not as much as we would like to the discipline as a whole—that IR theory is thoroughly gendered, both in the questions it chooses to ask, as well as how it goes about answering them.

One of the most creative moves feminism has made is to challenge disciplinary boundaries and to bring in new issues and voices. Rich empirical case studies—using methodologies not normally employed by IR scholars—have shed light on those on the margins (both women and men) whose lives are deeply impacted by global politics and economics. Feminists have successfully demonstrated how the lives of sex workers, domestic servants, home-based workers, and those who work at unremunerated caring and reproductive labor are intertwined with global politics and the global economy. They have also suggested that the security of states is sometimes dependent on rendering insecure the lives of certain, often marginalized, people and that the global capitalist economy could not function without unremunerated labor, the majority of which is performed by women. IR feminists have also pointed to the inadequacies of social scientific methodologies for answering many of the questions they want to ask. There is now an emerging literature on feminist methodologies—much needed for our research students who have often gone outside the discipline to seek the kind of methodological training necessary to do empirical feminist research. Two books, one edited by Brooke Ackerly, Maria Stern, and Jacqui True and the other authored by Ackerly and True, provide important guides for the many different methods and methodologies that IR feminists are using to do their empirical work.[4]

This rich array of interdisciplinary scholarship is evident in an increasing flow of books, book series, and journal articles. Much of this has been supported by workshops at the International Studies Association (ISA) and by its Feminist Theory and Gender Studies Section (FTGS). As I mentioned earlier, in the 1980s large professional organizations such as the ISA were inhospitable territory for women scholars and feminist research. Happily, this is no longer the case, and a rich array of feminist scholarship is presented at annual meetings of the ISA and other professional organizations.[5] Thanks to Jindy Pettman and many other capable and innovative editors who have followed in her footsteps, feminist IR now has its own journal, *The International Feminist Journal of Politics (IFJP)*, which was launched at the Australian National University (ANU) in 1999. In her introduction to the tenth anniversary issue of the *IFJP*, Pettman pointed to the 1990s, when the journal was launched, as optimistic times for feminist IR. A transnationalist feminist movement was being built and was having some impact on the international stage; this created an interest in feminist publications across the fields of development studies, international political economy, international law, and cultural studies. In the same issue, Meghana Nayak praised the *IFJP* for providing a sense of community for feminist scholars, one that they often lack in lonely spaces within academic departments. Since its launch in Australia, *IFJP*'s editorial home has moved to the United Kingdom and Canada. In 2013 it moved under the coeditorship of three scholars in the United States, South Africa, and the United Kingdom, making it a truly international journal that attracts articles from a wide array of disciplines and many parts of the world.

When I tried to explain to Peggy McIntosh, the co-organizer of the 1990 Wellesley conference (not herself an IR scholar) what IR was about, her reaction was that IR seemed to be neither international nor about relations. I think that, in the last twenty-five years, feminists have demonstrated that IR can be truly international and that it can be about relations. IR feminists have engaged in collaborative work and research ventures across various disciplinary and international boundaries. But, in spite of this sense of optimism, feminism has never sat easily in the IR discipline. IR feminists have devoted quite a bit of time trying to converse with the wider discipline on these issues. Peterson's radical goal—reconstructing theory by recognizing gender as an analytical and structural category—has never been acknowledged by non-feminists. Feminist work is not regularly cited either by mainstream or critical scholars, and gender is rarely recognized as a legitimate category of analysis by non-feminists.[6] Whereas the subject matter that feminists address is frequently deemed important and interesting, nevertheless it is often thought to be outside the subject matter of disciplinary IR. The methods that feminists use to answer the questions they ask are often dismissed as not being "scientific." These misunderstandings and lack of recognition have led some IR feminists to leave the IR discipline and migrate to women's studies programs. Many who do choose to stay find more hospitable homes outside the United States where tolerance for a broader range of issues and methodologies is more evident.

Looking back at my own writings and teachings, I am aware of both the successes and frustrations. On the positive side, some of the articles reproduced in this book are regularly used in IR classes, and some have been reprinted in IR readers. However, the biggest frustration for me has been over issues of methodology—a series of my articles address the continuing challenge issued to IR feminists, that they are not doing legitimate "scientific" research unless they use conventional methodologies. This has been a continuing hurdle for those trying to publish in mainstream US journals.[7]

Thanks to the ideas of so many creative feminist scholars, one of the greatest rewards for me in my journey through feminism has been not only to look for women but also for other marginalized people who have also been "hidden from international relations." My recent articles, on religion and retelling IR's foundational stories mark the beginnings of my efforts to look at religion, imperialism, and race, issues hitherto neglected by IR. While I realize that there has been more attention recently to religion, very little of it comes out of a feminist perspective. Apart from the work of postcolonial scholars and feminists, IR has almost completely ignored race.

However, as I look back at my work, I realize that I too have been guilty of ethnocentrism and what many have suggested is an excessive focus on the US mainstream. I have learned so much from scholars in other parts of the world: at the University of Uppsala, where I was introduced to Swedish peace research, an important formative framework for my definition of comprehensive security; multiple visits to Australia and New Zealand, which, besides introducing me to the lively feminist IR communities there, exposed me to feminist international law and, in New Zealand, to Maori scholarship. I have appreciated my many visits to the United Kingdom to celebrate the success of the rich array of feminist scholarship there. Time and space, the theme of the 2006 Russian International Studies Association meeting, afforded me my first opportunity to try out ideas about postcolonialism. I intend to explore these very diverse multidisciplinary literatures that feminist scholars have been producing over the past twenty years more fully in my future work. But when I first started on my feminist journey, my intention was to attempt to speak to the US mainstream of IR, my first intellectual home. While such a strategy has placed constraints on my writings, I hope that, in some small measure, it has allowed me to speak to IR students who might not otherwise have encountered feminist perspectives in their traditional IR classes.

As I reflect on the writings included in this book, I see my intellectual development as a feminist scholar in terms of three phases—not necessarily time sequential: first, putting women and gender into the theoretical concepts of, and approaches to, IR; second, methodological interventions and attempts at "conversations" with the IR mainstream (mainly in the US) on the scientific validity of feminist research; third, investigations into areas, such as race, imperialism, and religion, that have traditionally been under-recognized in IR. For me, the third phase signals new beginnings—one that starts to look at IR from the perspective of those whose voices have never been heard in the field. As I have taken this feminist journey, I, like all feminists, have become increasingly aware of the issues of knowledge and power—whose knowledge gets validated and whose is forgotten or never heard. Thanks to all the innovative paths that IR feminists are now taking, many of these hidden voices are now coming to light.

Notes

[1]The person with whom this question is associated in IR is Cynthia Enloe. I remember Enloe visiting my classes, picking up the students' textbooks, and searching, usually in vain, for the words "women" or "gender" in the index.

[2]This is not to say that feminists were not writing about global issues before this date. Significant work was being done on women and war and women in the military. See, for example, Elshtain (1985), Enloe (1983), and Stiehm (1983).

[3]Pettman's subsequent 1996 book *Worlding Women* was an important early statement, introducing feminist perspectives into IR.

[4]Ackerly and True first worked together as postdoctoral fellows at the Center for International Studies at USC in 2000–2001 when I directed the Center. They have continued to collaborate and bring young scholars together around methodological issues concerned with doing feminist research.

[5]At the 2012 annual meeting of the ISA, FTGS sponsored or cosponsored fifty-five panels.

[6]This is changing somewhat with respect to critical scholars. Today many introductory IR textbooks include a chapter on feminist international relations.

[7]There is a large body of gender work that does use positivist, often quantitative, methodologies. See, for example, Caprioli (2000), Caprioli and Boyer (2001), Carpenter (2006), and Hudson et al. (2008/2009).

The Culture of Fear in International Politics—A Western-Dominated International System and Its Extremist Challenges

HOLGER MÖLDER

THE CULTURE OF INTERNATIONAL SYSTEMS

Hedley Bull stated that an international system comes into force "when two or more states have sufficient contact between them, and have sufficient impact on one another's decisions to cause them to behave as parts of a whole."[1] Although since the 1990s the role and importance of other actors (e.g. international institutions, transnational networks, etc.) has notably grown, states have still maintained a status of principal international actors within the international system.

An international system is a governing body that has an ability to arrange relations between different political, social, and cultural entities and operates by using various international regimes for this purpose. It is a self-regulative structure, not a

ENDC Proceedings, Volume 14, 2011, pp. 241–263.

cultural entity, but various political cultures can influence the development of a system. In its turn, the system has an ability to shape its cultural environment. Modern and post-modern international systems have been predominantly influenced by the Western political cultures, and therefore can be identified as Hobbesian, Lockean and Kantian systems depending on which political culture prevails within the system.[2] The international actors will normally accept mutually recognized norms, which support interactions within the system.

Various social forces may intervene for the transformation of anxious emotions into fear.[3] The extremist actors and ideologies may force the culture of fear facilitating their political gains. The culture of fear is also influenced by the concept of security dilemma, which refers to a situation in which actors provoke an increase of mutual tensions in order to improve their own security.[4] There will emerge a *'moral panic'*—that occurs when a "condition, episode, person or group of persons emerges to become defined as a threat to societal values and interests."[5] If the culture of fear is empowered by populist politicians from both sides, it may lead to the non-solvable security dilemma transferred into the sphere of emotions and irrational narratives powered by fear. Such dilemmas are most complicated to manage.

The culture of fear, practiced by powerful international actors, can destabilize international systems. Which is important, certain ideologies, particularly Nationalism and Marxism in their extreme representations, tend to play an important role in producing system-related security dilemmas. Eric Hobsbawm called the 20th century the age of extremes with two global wars and the rise and fall of the messianic faith of Communism.[6] The ideological societies, which emerged rapidly after the World War I, promoted the culture of fear not regionally as it happened in the 19th century but already in global terms. The Marxist revolution in Russia set up an ideological alternative to the world society and positioned Russia as a deviant actor, similarly to North Korea or Iran within the current international system, having only a limited access to mainstream international politics. Systemic confrontations between the international system and deviant actors continued through the activities of Fascist Italy from 1922, Nazi Germany from 1933 or Shōwa Nationalist Japan from 1920s-1930s. These three ideologies founded common paradigms in uniting nationalism, socialism and militarism together for creating an alternative subsystem to the post-World War I Versailles system.[7]

The Westphalian concept of national sovereignty is based on two general principles: recognition of territorial integrity of states and recognition of the rule that external actors have no right to interfere into the domestic matters of states.[8] These principles have prevailed throughout modern society, until the last modern international system, the Cold War's bipolarity, ended. The end of the Cold War marks another breakthrough from the overwhelmingly Hobbesian/Lockean modern international systems to the Kantian post-modern one. The transition was accompanied by a cultural clash, which stems from different cultural practices and narratives used by modern and postmodern actors within the system.

Since the 1990s, a liberal democracy has been the main incentive for stimulating cooperative international regimes in the Euro-Atlantic security environment, which is shifting towards a global community of democratic states. The majority of European states started to follow the principles of the Kantian political culture, which helped to end the emergence of violent international conflicts in most parts of Europe. However, the introduction of the Kantian international system did not exclude the co-existence of the Hobbesian actors and environments with the Kantian trend of the system. The cultural differences between the Hobbesian/Lockean actors and the Kantian actors reflect the ideological clash between the Western liberal democracy and the rest of the world, where the modern ideologies like Nationalism or Marxism retained their influential positions in many countries and regions.

The logic of postmodern society recognizes supranational principles (e.g. human rights, liberal democracy), which do not entirely fit with the concept of national sovereignty prevailing in the modern society. The conflict between the logic of modern society and the logic of post-modern society may produce cultural security dilemmas between actors and environments representing different cultures and values. Several powerful countries, first of all China and Russia, prefer to keep alive modern principles of the international system, which complicates the involvement of international society in stabilizing the whole system by emphasizing peace, stability, and human rights.

International systems existentially depend on two dependant paradigms: polarity and stability. Polarity implies that there are competing antagonistic subsystems within a system. The Hobbesian and Lockean systems are polarized international systems, while the Kantian system intends to avoid the polarization and if any actor will find itself in opposition with the Kantian system, it may be identified as a deviant actor, outside of the system. The stability within the system may be changed by actions usually taken by major powers. In the long-run, the Soviet invasion to Afghanistan in 1979 caused the crash of the Cold War system. The invasion of the US-led coalition to Iraq in 2003 destabilized the post-modern Kantian system.

Societies stemming from the Hobbesian and Lockean political cultures tend to treat polarity as a natural behavior of the international system. This would indeed describe the 19th century society wherein the ideological differences had a minor influence on the international society and the motives of actors manifested quite similar characteristics. A century later, major powers under the auspices of the Western democracy were forced to find consolidating factors and curb their national interests in standing against the competing extremist ideologies from German National Socialism to Soviet Communism. Lebow explains that, contrary to the realist assumptions, within a non-polar system powerful actors attempt to conform to the rules of the system as the system would help them to use their power capabilities in the most efficient and effective manner.[9] In return, they should limit their national goals to those which others consider as legitimate and the interests of the community as a whole.

EXTREMISM IN INTERNATIONAL POLITICS

The culture of fear polarizes and destabilizes international systems as it is able to force emotional motives, which are able to avoid rational calculations and lead to a political extremism. In their extreme manifestations,[10] Nationalism, Marxism and certain religion-affiliated ideologies may produce ideological states and ideological societies. Lebow explains fear as one of the general motives shaping international relations, which settles security as a primary goal for fear-based societies and uses power as an instrument to achieve more security in eternal competition for increasing security-related capabilities.[11]

Organic ideologies may attribute a certain status of ideal to the community—*we are going the right way, and all those who behave differently, are trying to hinder the achievement of the desired ideal.* Consequently, it would be necessary to provide for all those who as renegade deviate from these ideals. In extreme cases, it may lead to the use of violence in order to bring the renegades back to the "right track." The ideological societies, which are based on a strong sense of identity with Us and Others contrasted and polarized, would impact their positioning towards the system related to some other cultural environment. "As a general rule, individuals, groups, organizations and political units attempt to create, sustain and affirm identities in their interactions with other actors."[12]

In interstate relations, a fear is an emotion, which demands that security is guaranteed through the direct acquisition of military power and economic well-being is a tool for establishing such a power requirement. Brian Frederking includes interactions that produce mistrust and hostilities between actors (traditional nation-state warfare, Israeli-Palestinian relations, imperialism, and Global War on Terrorism) as manifestations of the Hobbesian security culture,[13] which is traditionally characterized by producing uncertainty and misperceptions between actors. The Lockean culture in its turn intends to create some collective actions in balancing security-related fears (i.e. doctrines increasing state security under the circumstances of international anarchy like power balancing, bandwagoning or neutrality).

The Kantian culture of the post-Cold War international society looked for opportunities to produce a more stable non-polarized environment.

In Europe, Kantian principles progressed significantly through the European Union and the transforming of NATO. The post-Communist societies of Eastern Europe could fall under the influence of extremist ideologies, if they did not succeed in the transition to consolidated liberal democracies. State extremism can more easily emerge in illiberal democracies and non-democracies than in consolidated democracies.[14] The experience of the former Yugoslavia and the Soviet Union, which in many cases were not able to avoid violent post-dissolution conflicts, confirms this assessment. Therefore, the immediate objective of the European institutions after the Cold War required the engagement of the Central European countries with the rest of Europe.

The Gulf War, the Yugoslavian conflicts, the Afghanistan operation and many others manifest violent interactions between the Kantian and the Hobbesian environments in the post-modern international system. Some environments in the European neighborhood and beyond are mistrustful of the Kantian security culture and hold cultural security dilemmas to be actual. The Greater Middle East, which includes vast areas from Morocco and Mauritania in West Africa to Afghanistan and Pakistan in Central Asia, represents a foremost security concern for the Kantian international system in the near future, as the region is marked by recurrent violence and instability. Despite some progress in the peace processes, the Middle-East remains to be an unstable and polarized region. Besides the Middle-East, Africa poses another serious concern for Europe, as it is still an unstable continent with huge amounts of potential global and regional security risks, including civil wars, ethnic clashes, political, economic and social instability, poverty and famine among others.

The Self-Other binary draws support from Foucault's assertion[15] that order and identity are created and maintained through discourses of deviance (Lebow 2008, 476).[16] If the self-identification of a particular actor contrasts with the culture used by the international system, it may cause the appearance of extremist behavior in the actor-system relationship. There are countries on the world map, which submit challenges to the valid Kantian international system, while practicing the Hobbesian culture towards the system—i.e. North Korea, Iran, Sudan, and Venezuela among others. The extremist stance in international politics may directly or indirectly force deviant countries to support illegitimate actions, international terrorism among others. The Global War on Terrorism has been regarded as a manifestation of the culture of fear in the post-Cold War society,[17] which was able to evoke challenges to the prevailing Kantian political culture and thus destabilize the whole international system.

Lebow notes that deviant actors "attempt to gain attention and recognition by violating norms of the system."[18] Countries like North Korea, Cuba, Libya, Sudan, Iran, Syria, Iraq of Saddam Hussein, Yugoslavia of Milosevic, or Afghanistan of the Taliban have taken actions that did not fit with the general principles of the international society.

ASYMMETRIC AXIS

The post-Cold War arrangement in international relations favors globalization and an enhanced interdependence between nations. Collective punitive actions against Iraq in 1991 and against Serbia in Bosnia and Kosovo some years later symbolize the cooperative goals of the international society, which corresponded to the principles fixed within the UN Charter, chapters VI and VII. Even while the states have remained as main actors in the international arena, the role and importance of non-governmental entities has rapidly grown. These trends have been accompanied by the increasing importance of asymmetric risks and threats. These are risks and threats with possible international influence, which can emerge at some other level than states, from global risks to domestic risks as well. Asymmetric actors may include international interest groups, non-governmental organizations, transnational companies, individuals—which all may go beyond a particular citizenship.

After 2001, the international societal environment fostered the emergence of a culture of fear, while terrorism, which has never been a "mainstream political tool," has been promoted to the next level by a small and relatively little-known Islamic fundamentalist group Al-Qaeda. Al-Qaeda succeeded in increasing the amount of uncertainty, which produced instability within the whole international system and caused political risks to be taken by actors.[19] As follows, the international society was confronted "with an increased awareness of risks because more decisions are taken in an atmosphere of uncertainty."[20] International terrorism has often been mentioned among the most important manifestations of a new asymmetric axis, which involves transnational networks and therefore comes into conflict with the traditional approaches to international systems based on national interests performed by states. Jessica Stern, while analyzing the effectiveness of Al-Qaeda, notes its capability for change, which makes Al-Qaeda more attractive for new recruits and allies.[21] Colin Wight notes that Al-Qaeda followed a structural form without clear lines of hierarchy and channels of control over the cells, which makes it harder to detect and destroy it.[22]

A global transnational network corresponds to the timely principles of the post-modern society. It is somehow symbolic as NATO for the first time throughout its history used its article V against the asymmetric threat, terrorism, and on behalf of its major military power, the United States. The attacks organized against international terrorism are justified in that they are not against states but terrorist organizations, the United States fought in Afghanistan against the Taliban and Al-Qaeda, and in 2006 Israel fought against a Lebanese Shia extremist militant group Hezbollah, not Lebanon, which moves asymmetric groups to the level comparable with states.[23] Notably, the United Nations performed sanctions against Al-Qaeda and the Taliban in 1998 and against Hezbollah in 2006.[24]

In 1990s Samuel Huntington invented a descriptive theory that prescribes general trends in international politics while emphasizing a possible cultural conflict between opposing civilizations.[25] The attack of September 11, 2001 led to the Global War on Terrorism with the world divided between "good" and "evil" once again and polarity-based policies started gradually to return. The offensive strategy characterizing the counterterrorist policies carried through the western world during the GWoT, which frequently demonized the Muslim faith and the Islamic civilization, fitted more with the Hobbesian security culture practicing enmities between different entities and has evidently promoted the direction towards the clash of civilizations, once predicted by Huntington and damaged hopes for the end of history as described ten years ago by Francis Fukuyama.[26]

Although the defensive actions against international terrorism, including military operations in Afghanistan, have been widely approved by the international society, the Kantian world favoring democratic peace, multiculturalism and international cooperation did not satisfy apologists of power policies. Extremist movements were successful in splitting a still fragile Western unity. The emerging culture of fear could be observed as a counterideology to the rising Islamic fundamentalism especially in the United States, where the neo-conservative ideological movement strengthened with Bush's presidency of the United States.

During the Cold War, the Islamists were often treated as natural allies of the Western bloc because of their fighting against the spread of Communist ideologies. Their opposition to Atheism practiced by the Communist regimes made Islamism a powerful competing ideology especially in the Third World countries. Huntington mentioned that "at one time or another during the Cold War many governments, including those of Algeria, Turkey, Jordan, Egypt, and Israel, encouraged and supported Islamists as a counter to communist and hostile nationalist movements."[27] Pro-Western countries provided massive funding to the Islamists groups in various parts of the world. The United States often saw Islamists as an opposition to the Soviet influence under the circumstances of the bipolar competition of the Cold War.

At the same time, secular movements in Islamic countries, contrariwise, often flirted with Marxism and thus gained support from the Soviet Union. The Pan-Arabist leaders of Egypt, Syria, Iraq and Algeria shared the anti-American and anti-Imperialist views of the Soviet ideological establishment. From 1979, the situation gradually started to change with the Islamic revolution in Iran and the Soviet occupation of Afghanistan, which strengthened Islamic solidarity instead of socialist and nationalist sentiments. Whilst pan-Arabism followed the structure of Western ideologies and settled it into the specific Nationalist environment with Socialist influences, the contemporary Islamic Fundamentalism is a direct challenge to the Western model of the state and politics, and constitutes a form of political resistance.[28]

In 1980s, the Western governments supported the Sunni resistance in the Afghanistan conflict and only a smaller Shia community of Islam was mostly involved in the anti-Western confrontation. The revolution in Iran established a new regime that was simultaneously anti-Western and anti-Soviet and did not suit with the Cold War's bipolarity. Sunnis remained silent and used Western support in Afghanistan and other conflict areas, whereby they fought for their values and identities. Paradoxically, in the course of the Iraqi-Iran war 1980–1988, the East and the West both supported the leftist Arab nationalist regime of Saddam Hussein against Iran.

The post-Cold War era produced some regrouping between international powers and groups of interests. The Islamic militants started to stand against the spread of western liberal democracy, which did not fit with their ideological goals. In the 1990s, the clash between western liberal democracy and Islamic fundamentalism developed rapidly. The Sunni fundamentalist Taliban movement established their control over Afghanistan in 1996. More serious signs of ideological clash emerged in 1998, when Al-Qaeda terrorists attacked the US embassies in East-Africa. With the GWoT, cultural conflicts became indeed more visible. The confrontation between Western liberal democracy and Islamic fundamentalism verified that Huntington was right in predicting a clash of civilizations.

The transnational character of asymmetric actors allows them to introduce non-traditional methods effectively (e.g. international terrorism) as they have no territoriality or sovereignty to defend, which makes it more efficient in balancing the possible sanctions from the valid international system. Legally, there is a difference between asymmetric transnational terrorism and symmetric state terrorism—terrorist organizations have no legitimate right to kill, contrariwise to political communities, though they may apply to some form of revolutionary vanguard the term, "good people" who destroy "bad people."[29] The promotion of a culture of fear would be one of the most important challenges caused by international terrorism. Strategies of terrorist groups aim to produce chaos and political, economic, social and military damage, hoping that the destabilization of existing societies following the terrorist attack may help them to validate their ideological goals.

CONCLUSIONS

A culture of fear most effectively supports the logic of the Hobbesian culture, which emphasizes a state of war between international actors. It may provoke extremist challenges against peace and stability and conflicting ideologies compose a powerful agenda for initiating fear-based polarizations. Fear in the hands of ideologies has an enormous capability to provoke irrational decisions and security dilemmas. At first glance, the rise of Islamic fundamentalism and the culture of fear seem to be depending on each other. The Hollywood-like scenario of September 11, 2001, by which the charismatic leader of Al-Qaeda Osama Bin Laden recorded himself in the history of the world, caused the worldwide diffusion of fear, which in its turn opened the door for the extremist neo-conservative reaction in the United States. Recent news about the liquidation of the protean enemy hardly makes the world safer.

The post-modern Kantian international system continually includes multiple Hobbesian security environments. The variety of cultural environments makes the whole international system conflict-prone and it is able to produce a culture of fear involving different civilizations, identities or ideologies. Deviant actors often find themselves manipulating the culture of fear in justifying their legitimacy within the international system. The axis-building policies between good and evil can destabilize the international system by introducing new polarizations. Various factors reproducing a culture of fear (e.g. social problems, ethnic tensions with strengthening national sentiments, nuclear dilemmas) may inflict the emergence of most problematic security dilemmas into the Kantian international system. The successful alternative to fear-based political incentives largely depends on maintaining a non-polarized cooperative framework within the valid international system. A less ideologized world tends to be a safer world.

Notes

[1]Hedley Bull. The Anarchical Society: A Study of Order in World Politics. New York: Columbia University Press, 1977, pp. 9–13.
[2]See also Holger Mölder. Cooperative Security Dilemma—practicing the Hobbesian security culture in the Kantian security environment. Tartu: Tartu University Press, 2010, pp. 94–100.
[3]See also Frank Furedi. The Politics of Fear. Beyond Left and Right. Continuum International Publishing Group, 2005.
[4]Ken Booth and Nicholas J. Wheeler. The Security Dilemma. Fear, Cooperation and Trust in World Politics. New York: Palgrave MacMillan, 2008, p. 9.
[5]Stanley Cohen. Folk Devils and Moral Panics. St Albans: Paladin, 1973, p. 9.
[6]Eric Hobsbawm. The Age of Extremes. A History of World, 1914–1991. London: Michael Joseph and Pelham Books, 1994.
[7]The Versailles system may be identified as the first Kantian international system, see Mölder 2010, pp. 94–100.
[8]See also Stephen D. Krasner. Sovereignty: organized hypocrisy. Princeton: Princeton University Press, 1999.
[9]Lebow 2008, p. 497.
[10]If ideologies are capable of forcing conflict within societies, their behavior can be identified as extremist. For example, Chauvinism is an extreme manifestation of Nationalism and Communism respectively refers to Marxist extremism.
[11]Lebow 2008, p. 90.
[12]Lebow 2008, p. 497.
[13]Brian Frederking. Constructing Post-cold War Collective Security. – American Political Science Review, 3/2003, p. 368.
[14]This does not refer to other formations of extremism.
[15]Reference is made to Michel Foucault's book: The Archaelogy of Knowledge and the Discourse on Language. New York: Pantheon Books, 1972.
[16]Richard Ned Lebow. Identity and International Relations. – International Relations, 4/2008 (a), p. 476.
[17]Lebow 2008, p. 544.
[18]Lebow 2008, p. 488.
[19]See Mary Douglas; Aaron Wildavsky. Risk and Culture: An essay on the selection of technical and environmental dangers. Berkeley: University of California Press, 1982.
[20]Frank Furedi. Culture of Fear: Risk Taking and the Morality of Low Expectation. Continuum International Publishing Group, 2002, p. 8.
[21]Jessica Stern. A1 Qaeda: the Protean Enemy. – Foreign Affairs, 4/2003.
[22]Colin Wight. Theorising terrorism: The State, Structure, and History. – International Relations 1/2009, p. 105.
[23]Daren Bowyer. The moral dimension of asymmetrical warfare: accountability, culpability and military effectiveness. – Baarda, Th. A. van; Verweij, D. E. M. (eds.). The moral dimension of asymmetrical warfare: counter-terrorism, democratic values and military ethics. Leiden: Martinus Njihoff, 2009, p. 139.
[24]UN Security Council Sanctions Committees. Available online at: <http://www.un.org/sc/committees/>, (accessed 06.05.2011).
[25]Samuel P. Huntington. The Clash of Civilizations. Remaking World Order. New York: Touchstone Book, 1997.
[26]In his book: Francis Fukuyama. The End of History and the Last Man. New York: Free Press, 1992.
[27]Huntington 1997, p. 115.
[28]Wight 2009, p. 104.
[29]Carl Ceulemans. Asymmetric warfare and morality: from moral asymmetry to amoral symmetry?— Baarda, Th. A. van; Verweij, D. E. M. (eds.). The moral dimension of asymmetrical warfare: counterterrorism, democratic values and military ethics. Leiden: Martinus Njihoff, 2009.

Us and Them: The Enduring Power of Ethnic Nationalism

JERRY Z. MULLER

Projecting their own experience onto the rest of the world, Americans generally belittle the role of ethnic nationalism in politics. After all, in the United States people of varying ethnic origins live cheek by jowl in relative peace. Within two or three generations of immigration, their ethnic identities are attenuated by cultural assimilation and intermarriage. Surely, things cannot be so different elsewhere.

Americans also find ethnonationalism discomfiting both intellectually and morally. Social scientists go to great lengths to demonstrate that it is a product not of nature but of culture, often deliberately constructed. And ethicists scorn value systems based on narrow group identities rather than cosmopolitanism.

But none of this will make ethnonationalism go away. Immigrants to the United States usually arrive with a willingness to fit into their new country and reshape their identities accordingly. But for those who remain behind in lands where their ancestors have lived for generations, if not centuries, political identities often take ethnic form, producing competing communal claims to political power. The creation of a peaceful regional order of nation-states has usually been the product of a violent process of ethnic separation. In areas where that separation has not yet occurred, politics is apt to remain ugly.

A familiar and influential narrative of twentieth-century European history argues that nationalism twice led to war, in 1914 and then again in 1939. Thereafter, the story goes, Europeans concluded that nationalism was a danger and gradually abandoned it. In the postwar decades, western Europeans enmeshed themselves in a web of transnational institutions, culminating in the European Union (EU). After the fall of the Soviet empire, that transnational framework spread eastward to encompass most of the continent. Europeans entered a postnational era, which was not only a good thing in itself but also a model for other regions. Nationalism, in this view, had been a tragic detour on the road to a peaceful liberal democratic order.

This story is widely believed by educated Europeans and even more so, perhaps, by educated Americans. Recently, for example, in the course of arguing that Israel ought to give up its claim to be a Jewish state and dissolve itself into some sort of binational entity with the Palestinians, the prominent historian Tony Judt informed the readers of The New York Review of Books that "the problem with Israel . . . [is that] it has imported a characteristically late-nineteenth-century separatist project into a world that has moved on, a world of individual rights, open frontiers, and international law. The very idea of a 'Jewish state' . . . is an anachronism."

Yet the experience of the hundreds of Africans and Asians who perish each year trying to get into Europe by landing on the coast of Spain or Italy reveals that Europe's frontiers are not so open. And a survey would show that whereas in 1900 there were many states in Europe without a single overwhelmingly dominant nationality, by 2007 there were only two, and one of those, Belgium, was close to breaking up. Aside from Switzerland, in other words—where the domestic ethnic balance of power is protected by strict citizenship laws—in Europe the "separatist project" has not so much vanished as triumphed.

Far from having been superannuated in 1945, in many respects ethnonationalism was at its apogee in the years immediately after World War II. European stability during the Cold War era was in fact due partly to the widespread fulfillment of the ethnonationalist project. And since the end of the Cold War, ethnonationalism has continued to reshape European borders.

In short, ethnonationalism has played a more profound and lasting role in modern history than is commonly understood, and the processes that led to the dominance of the ethnonational state and the separation of ethnic groups in Europe are likely to reoccur elsewhere. Increased urbanization, literacy, and political mobilization; differences in the fertility rates and economic performance of various ethnic groups; and immigration will challenge the internal structure of states as well as their borders. Whether politically correct or not, ethnonationalism will continue to shape the world in the twenty-first century.

THE RISE OF ETHNONATIONALISM

Today, people tend to take the nation-state for granted as the natural form of political association and regard empires as anomalies. But over the broad sweep of recorded history, the opposite is closer to the truth. Most people at most times have lived in empires, with the nation-state the exception rather than the rule. So what triggered the change?

The rise of ethnonationalism, as the sociologist Ernest Gellner has explained, was not some strange historical mistake; rather, it was propelled by some of the deepest currents of modernity. Military competition between states created a demand for expanded state resources and hence continual economic growth. Economic growth, in turn, depended on mass literacy and easy communication, spurring policies to promote education and a common language—which led directly to conflicts over language and communal opportunities.

Modern societies are premised on the egalitarian notion that in theory, at least, anyone can aspire to any economic position. But in practice, everyone does not have an equal likelihood of upward economic mobility, and not simply because individuals have different innate capabilities. For such advances depend in part on what economists call "cultural capital," the skills and behavioral patterns that help individuals and groups succeed. Groups with traditions of literacy and engagement in commerce tend to excel, for example, whereas those without such traditions tend to lag behind.

As they moved into cities and got more education during the nineteenth and early twentieth centuries, ethnic groups with largely peasant backgrounds, such as the Czechs, the Poles, the Slovaks, and the Ukrainians found that key positions in the government and the economy were already occupied—often by ethnic Armenians, Germans, Greeks, or Jews. Speakers of the same language came to share a sense that they belonged together and to define themselves in contrast to other communities. And eventually they came to demand a nation state of their own, in which they would be the masters, dominating politics, staffing the civil service, and controlling commerce.

Ethnonationalism had a psychological basis as well as an economic one. By creating a new and direct relationship between individuals and the government, the rise of the modern state weakened individuals' traditional bonds to intermediate social units, such as the family, the clan, the guild, and the church. And by spurring social and geographic mobility and a self-help mentality, the rise of market-based economies did the same. The result was an emotional vacuum that was often filled by new forms of identification, often along ethnic lines.

Ethnonationalist ideology called for a congruence between the state and the ethnically defined nation, with explosive results. As Lord Acton recognized in 1862, "By making the state and the nation commensurate with each other in theory, [nationalism] reduces practically to a subject condition all other nationalities that may be within the boundary. . . . According, therefore, to the degree of humanity and civilization in that dominant body which claims all the rights of the community, the inferior races are exterminated, or reduced to servitude, or outlawed, or put in a condition of dependence." And that is just what happened.

THE GREAT TRANSFORMATION

Nineteenth century liberals, like many proponents of globalization today, believed that the spread of international commerce would lead people to recognize the mutual benefits that could come from peace and trade, both within polities and between them. Socialists agreed, although they believed that harmony would come only after the arrival of socialism. Yet that was not the course that twentieth-century history was destined to follow. The process of "making the state and the nation commensurate" took a variety of forms, from voluntary emigration (often motivated by governmental discrimination against minority ethnicities) to forced deportation (also known as "population transfer") to genocide. Although the term "ethnic cleansing" has come into English usage only recently, its verbal correlates in Czech, French, German, and Polish go back much further. Much of the history of twentieth-century Europe, in fact, has been a painful, drawn-out process of ethnic disaggregation.

Massive ethnic disaggregation began on Europe's frontiers. In the ethnically mixed Balkans, wars to expand the nation-states of Bulgaria, Greece, and Serbia at the expense of the ailing Ottoman Empire were accompanied by ferocious interethnic violence. During the Balkan Wars of 1912–13, almost half a million people left their traditional homelands, either voluntarily or by force. Muslims left regions under the control of Bulgarians, Greeks, and Serbs; Bulgarians abandoned Greek-controlled areas of Macedonia; Greeks fled from regions of Macedonia ceded to Bulgaria and Serbia.

World War I led to the demise of the three great turn-of-the-century empires, unleashing an explosion of ethnonationalism in the process. In the Ottoman Empire, mass deportations and murder during the war took the lives of a million members of the local Armenian minority in an early attempt at ethnic cleansing, if not genocide. In 1919, the Greek government invaded the area that would become Turkey, seeking to carve out a "greater Greece" stretching all the way to Constantinople. Meeting with initial success, the Greek forces looted and burned villages in an effort to drive out the region's ethnic Turks. But Turkish forces eventually regrouped and pushed the Greek army back, engaging in their own ethnic cleansing against local Greeks along the way. Then the process of population transfers was formalized in the 1923 Treaty of Lausanne: all ethnic Greeks were to go to Greece, all Greek Muslims to Turkey. In the end, Turkey expelled almost 1.5 million people, and Greece expelled almost 400,000.

Out of the breakup of the Hapsburg and Romanov empires emerged a multitude of new countries. Many conceived of themselves as ethnonational polities, in which the state existed to protect and promote the dominant ethnic group. Yet of central and eastern Europe's roughly 60 million people, 25 million continued to be part of ethnic minorities in the countries in which they lived. In most cases, the ethnic majority did not believe in trying to help minorities assimilate, nor were the minorities always eager to do so themselves. Nationalist governments openly discriminated in favor of the dominant community. Government activities were conducted solely in the language of the majority, and the civil service was reserved for those who spoke it.

In much of central and eastern Europe, Jews had long played an important role in trade and commerce. When they were given civil rights in the late nineteenth century, they tended to excel in professions requiring higher education, such as medicine and law, and soon Jews or people of Jewish descent made up almost half the doctors and lawyers in cities such as Budapest, Vienna, and Warsaw. By the 1930s, many governments adopted policies to try to check and reverse these advances, denying Jews credit and limiting their access to higher education. In other words, the National Socialists who came to power in Germany in 1933 and based their movement around a "Germanness" they defined in contrast to "Jewishness" were an extreme version of a more common ethnonationalist trend.

The politics of ethnonationalism took an even deadlier turn during World War II. The Nazi regime tried to reorder the ethnic map of the continent by force. Its most radical act was an attempt to rid Europe of Jews by killing them all—an attempt that largely succeeded. The Nazis also used ethnic German minorities in Czechoslovakia, Poland, and elsewhere to enforce Nazi domination, and many of the regimes allied with Germany engaged in their own campaigns against internal ethnic enemies. The Romanian regime, for example, murdered hundreds of thousands of Jews on its own, without orders from Germany, and the government of Croatia murdered not only its Jews but hundreds of thousands of Serbs and Romany as well.

POSTWAR BUT NOT POSTNATIONAL

One might have expected that the Nazi regime's deadly policies and crushing defeat would mark the end of the ethnonationalist era. But in fact they set the stage for another massive round of ethnonational transformation. The political settlement in central Europe after World War I had been achieved primarily by moving borders to align them with populations. After World War II, it was the populations that moved instead. Millions of people were expelled from their homes and countries, with at least the tacit support of the victorious Allies.

Winston Churchill, Franklin Roosevelt, and Joseph Stalin all concluded that the expulsion of ethnic Germans from non-German countries was a prerequisite to a stable postwar order. As Churchill put it in a speech to the British parliament in December 1944, "Expulsion is the method which, so far as we have been able to see, will be the most satisfactory and lasting. There will be no mixture of populations to cause endless trouble. . . . A clean sweep will be made. I am not alarmed at the prospect of the disentanglement of population, nor am I alarmed by these large transferences." He cited the Treaty of Lausanne as a precedent, showing how even the leaders of liberal democracies had concluded that only radically illiberal measures would eliminate the causes of ethnonational aspirations and aggression.

Between 1944 and 1945, five million ethnic Germans from the eastern parts of the German Reich fled westward to escape the conquering Red Army, which was energetically raping and massacring its way to Berlin. Then, between 1945 and 1947, the new postliberation regimes in Czechoslovakia, Hungary, Poland, and Yugoslavia expelled another seven million Germans in response to their collaboration with the Nazis. Together, these measures constituted the largest forced population movement in European history, with hundreds of thousands of people dying along the way.

The handful of Jews who survived the war and returned to their homes in eastern Europe met with so much anti-Semitism that most chose to leave for good. About 220,000 of them made their way into the American-occupied zone of Germany, from which most eventually went to Israel or the United States. Jews thus essentially vanished from central and eastern Europe, which had been the center of Jewish life since the sixteenth century.

Millions of refugees from other ethnic groups were also evicted from their homes and resettled after the war. This was due partly to the fact that the borders of the Soviet Union had moved westward, into what had once been Poland, while the borders of Poland also moved westward, into what had once been Germany. To make populations correspond to the new borders, 1.5 million Poles living in areas that were now part of the Soviet Union were deported to Poland, and 500,000 ethnic Ukrainians who had been living in Poland were sent to the Ukrainian Soviet Socialist Republic. Yet another exchange of populations took place between Czechoslovakia and Hungary, with Slovaks transferred out of Hungary and Magyars sent away from Czechoslovakia. A smaller number of Magyars also moved to Hungary from Yugoslavia, with Serbs and Croats moving in the opposite direction.

As a result of this massive process of ethnic unmixing, the ethnonationalist ideal was largely realized: for the most part, each nation in Europe had its own state, and each state was made up almost exclusively of a single ethnic nationality. During the Cold War, the few exceptions to this rule included Czechoslovakia, the Soviet Union, and Yugoslavia. But these countries' subsequent fate only demonstrated the ongoing vitality of ethnonationalism. After the fall of communism, East and West Germany were unified with remarkable rapidity, Czechoslovakia split peacefully into Czech and Slovak republics, and the Soviet Union broke apart into a variety of different national units. Since then, ethnic Russian minorities in many of the post-Soviet states have gradually immigrated to Russia, Magyars in Romania have moved to Hungary, and the few remaining ethnic Germans in Russia have largely gone to Germany.

A million people of Jewish origin from the former Soviet Union have made their way to Israel. Yugoslavia saw the secession of Croatia and Slovenia and then descended into ethnonational wars over Bosnia and Kosovo.

The breakup of Yugoslavia was simply the last act of a long play. But the plot of that play—the disaggregation of peoples and the triumph of ethnonationalism in modern Europe—is rarely recognized, and so a story whose significance is comparable to the spread of democracy or capitalism remains largely unknown and unappreciated.

DECOLONIZATION AND AFTER

The effects of ethnonationalism, of course, have hardly been confined to Europe. For much of the developing world, decolonization has meant ethnic disaggregation through the exchange or expulsion of local minorities.

The end of the British Raj in 1947 brought about the partition of the subcontinent into India and Pakistan, along with an orgy of violence that took hundreds of thousands of lives. Fifteen million people became refugees, including Muslims who went to Pakistan and Hindus who went to India. Then, in 1971, Pakistan itself, originally unified on the basis of religion, dissolved into Urdu-speaking Pakistan and Bengali-speaking Bangladesh.

In the former British mandate of Palestine, a Jewish state was established in 1948 and was promptly greeted by the revolt of the indigenous Arab community and an invasion from the surrounding Arab states. In the war that resulted, regions that fell under Arab control were cleansed of their Jewish populations, and Arabs fled or were forced out of areas that came under Jewish control. Some 750,000 Arabs left, primarily for the surrounding Arab countries, and the remaining 150,000 constituted only about a sixth of the population of the new Jewish state. In the years afterward, nationalist-inspired violence against Jews in Arab countries propelled almost all of the more than 500,000 Jews there to leave their lands of origin and immigrate to Israel. Likewise, in 1962 the end of French control in Algeria led to the forced emigration of Algerians of European origin (the so-called pieds-noirs), most of whom immigrated to France. Shortly thereafter, ethnic minorities of Asian origin were forced out of postcolonial Uganda. The legacy of the colonial era, moreover, is hardly finished. When the European overseas empires dissolved, they left behind a patchwork of states whose boundaries often cut across ethnic patterns of settlement and whose internal populations were ethnically mixed. It is wishful thinking to suppose that these boundaries will be permanent. As societies in the former colonial world modernize, becoming more urban, literate, and politically mobilized, the forces that gave rise to ethnonationalism and ethnic disaggregation in Europe are apt to drive events there, too.

THE BALANCE SHEET

Analysts of ethnic disaggregation typically focus on its destructive effects, which is understandable given the direct human suffering it has often entailed. But such attitudes can yield a distorted perspective by overlooking the less obvious costs and also the important benefits that ethnic separation has brought.

Economists from Adam Smith onward, for example, have argued that the efficiencies of competitive markets tend to increase with the markets' size. The dissolution of the Austro-Hungarian Empire into smaller nation-states, each with its own barriers to trade, was thus economically irrational and contributed to the region's travails in the interwar period. Much of subsequent European history has involved attempts to overcome this and other economic fragmentation, culminating in the EU.

Ethnic disaggregation also seems to have deleterious effects on cultural vitality. Precisely because most of their citizens share a common cultural and linguistic heritage, the homogenized states of postwar Europe have tended to be more culturally insular than their demographically diverse predecessors. With few Jews in Europe and few Germans in Prague, that is, there are fewer Franz Kafkas.

Forced migrations generally penalize the expelling countries and reward the receiving ones. Expulsion is often driven by a majority group's resentment of a minority group's success, on the mistaken assumption that achievement is a zero-sum game. But countries that got rid of their Armenians, Germans, Greeks, Jews, and other successful minorities deprived themselves of some of their most talented citizens, who simply took their skills and knowledge elsewhere. And in many places, the triumph of ethnonational politics has meant the victory of traditionally rural groups over more urbanized ones, which possess just those skills desirable in an advanced industrial economy.

But if ethnonationalism has frequently led to tension and conflict, it has also proved to be a source of cohesion and stability. When French textbooks began with "Our ancestors the Gauls" or when Churchill spoke to wartime audiences of "this island race," they appealed to ethnonationalist sensibilities as a source of mutual trust and sacrifice. Liberal democracy and ethnic homogeneity are not only compatible; they can be complementary.

One could argue that Europe has been so harmonious since World War II not because of the failure of ethnic nationalism but because of its success, which removed some of the greatest sources of conflict both within and between countries. The fact that ethnic and state boundaries now largely coincide has meant that there are fewer disputes over borders or expatriate communities, leading to the most stable territorial configuration in European history.

These ethnically homogeneous polities have displayed a great deal of internal solidarity, moreover, facilitating government programs, including domestic transfer payments, of various kinds. When the Swedish Social Democrats were developing plans for Europe's most extensive welfare state during the interwar period, the political scientist Sheri Berman has noted, they conceived of and sold them as the construction of a folkhemmet, or "people's home."

Several decades of life in consolidated, ethnically homogeneous states may even have worked to sap ethnonationalism's own emotional power. Many Europeans are now prepared, and even eager, to participate in transnational frameworks such as the EU, in part because their perceived need for collective self-determination has largely been satisfied.

NEW ETHNIC MIXING

Along with the process of forced ethnic disaggregation over the last two centuries, there has also been a process of ethnic mixing brought about by voluntary emigration. The general pattern has been one of emigration from poor, stagnant areas to richer and more dynamic ones.

In Europe, this has meant primarily movement west and north, leading above all to France and the United Kingdom. This pattern has continued into the present: as a result of recent migration, for example, there are now half a million Poles in Great Britain and 200,000 in Ireland. Immigrants from one part of Europe who have moved to another and ended up staying there have tended to assimilate and, despite some grumbling about a supposed invasion of "Polish plumbers," have created few significant problems.

The most dramatic transformation of European ethnic balances in recent decades has come from the immigration of people of Asian, African, and Middle Eastern origin, and here the results have been mixed. Some of these groups have achieved remarkable success, such as the Indian Hindus who have come to the United Kingdom. But in Belgium, France, Germany, the Netherlands, Sweden, the United Kingdom, and elsewhere, on balance the educational and economic progress of Muslim immigrants has been more limited and their cultural alienation greater.

How much of the problem can be traced to discrimination, how much to the cultural patterns of the immigrants themselves, and how much to the policies of European governments is difficult to determine. But a number of factors, from official multiculturalism to generous welfare states to the ease of contact with ethnic homelands, seem to have made it possible to create ethnic islands where assimilation into the larger culture and economy is limited.

As a result, some of the traditional contours of European politics have been upended. The left, for example, has tended to embrace immigration in the name of egalitarianism and multiculturalism. But if there is indeed a link between ethnic homogeneity and a population's willingness to support generous income-redistribution programs, the encouragement of a more heterogeneous society may end up undermining the left's broader political agenda. And some of Europe's libertarian cultural propensities have already clashed with the cultural illiberalism of some of the new immigrant communities.

Should Muslim immigrants not assimilate and instead develop a strong communal identification along religious lines, one consequence might be a resurgence of traditional ethnonational identities in some states—or the development of a new European identity defined partly in contradistinction to Islam (with the widespread resistance to the extension of full EU membership to Turkey being a possible harbinger of such a shift).

FUTURE IMPLICATIONS

Since ethnonationalism is a direct consequence of key elements of modernization, it is likely to gain ground in societies undergoing such a process. It is hardly surprising, therefore, that it remains among the most vital—and most disruptive—forces in many parts of the contemporary world.

More or less subtle forms of ethnonationalism, for example, are ubiquitous in immigration policy around the globe. Many countries—including Armenia, Bulgaria, Croatia, Finland, Germany, Hungary, Ireland, Israel, Serbia, and Turkey—provide automatic or rapid citizenship to the members of diasporas of their own dominant ethnic group, if desired. Chinese immigration law gives priority and benefits to overseas Chinese. Portugal and Spain have immigration policies that favor applicants from their former colonies in the New World. Still other states, such as Japan and Slovakia, provide official forms of identification to members of the dominant national ethnic group who are noncitizens that permit them to live and work in the country. Americans, accustomed by the U.S. government's official practices to regard differential treatment on the basis of ethnicity to be a violation of universalist norms, often consider such policies exceptional, if not abhorrent. Yet in a global context, it is the insistence on universalist criteria that seems provincial.

Increasing communal consciousness and shifting ethnic balances are bound to have a variety of consequences, both within and between states, in the years to come. As economic globalization brings more states into the global economy, for example, the first fruits of that process will often fall to those ethnic groups best positioned by history or culture to take advantage of the new opportunities for enrichment, deepening social cleavages rather than filling them in. Wealthier and higher-achieving regions might try to separate themselves from poorer and lower-achieving ones, and distinctive homogeneous areas might try to acquire sovereignty—courses of action that might provoke violent responses from defenders of the status quo.

Of course, there are multiethnic societies in which ethnic consciousness remains weak, and even a more strongly developed sense of ethnicity may lead to political claims short of sovereignty. Sometimes, demands for ethnic autonomy or self-determination can be met within an existing state. The claims of the Catalans in Spain, the Flemish in Belgium, and the Scots in the United Kingdom have been met in this manner, at least for now. But such arrangements remain precarious and are subject to recurrent renegotiation. In the developing world, accordingly, where states are more recent creations and where the borders often cut across ethnic boundaries, there is likely to be further ethnic disaggregation and communal conflict. And as scholars such as Chaim Kaufmann have noted, once ethnic antagonism has crossed a certain threshold of violence, maintaining the rival groups within a single polity becomes far more difficult.

This unfortunate reality creates dilemmas for advocates of humanitarian intervention in such conflicts, because making and keeping peace between groups that have come to hate and fear one another is likely to require costly ongoing military missions rather than relatively cheap temporary ones. When communal violence escalates to ethnic cleansing, moreover, the return of large numbers of refugees to their place of origin after a ceasefire has been reached is often impractical and even undesirable, for it merely sets the stage for a further round of conflict down the road.

Partition may thus be the most humane lasting solution to such intense communal conflicts. It inevitably creates new flows of refugees, but at least it deals with the problem at issue. The challenge for the international community in such cases is to separate communities in the most humane manner possible: by aiding in transport, assuring citizenship rights in the new homeland, and providing financial aid for resettlement and economic absorption. The bill for all of this will be huge, but it will rarely be greater than the material costs of interjecting and maintaining a foreign military presence large enough to pacify the rival ethnic combatants or the moral cost of doing nothing.

Contemporary social scientists who write about nationalism tend to stress the contingent elements of group identity—the extent to which national consciousness is culturally and politically manufactured by ideologists and politicians. They regularly invoke Benedict Anderson's concept of "imagined communities," as if demonstrating that nationalism is constructed will rob the concept of its power. It is true, of course, that ethnonational identity is never as natural or ineluctable as nationalists claim. Yet it would be a mistake to think that because nationalism is partly constructed it is therefore fragile or infinitely malleable. Ethnonationalism was not a chance detour in European history: it corresponds to some enduring propensities of the human spirit that are heightened by the process of modern state creation, it is a crucial source of both solidarity and enmity, and in one form or another, it will remain for many generations to come. One can only profit from facing it directly.

History, Memory and National Identity: Understanding the Politics of History and Memory Wars in Post-Soviet Lands

IGOR TORBAKOV

> Tell me what you remember and I'll diagnose your condition
>
> —ALEKSANDR KUSTARYOV

At the end of June 2010, a remarkable text appeared on the website of the Russian liberal radio station *Ekho Moskvy*. Its author, the prominent Russian lawmaker Konstantin Kosachev, suggested that it was time for Russia to elaborate upon what he called a comprehensive "set of principles, an 'historical doctrine' of sorts" that would help Moscow to disclaim, once and for all, any political, financial, legal or moral responsibility for the policies and actions of the Soviet authorities on the territories of the former USSR and the states of Eastern Europe. Kosachev's proposal is simple, blunt and seemingly effective. In a nutshell, it boils down to the two key points: (1) Russia fulfills all international obligations of the USSR as its successor state; however, Russia does not recognize any moral responsibility or any legal obligations for the actions and crimes committed by the Soviet authorities; and (2) Russia does not accept any political, legal or financial claims against it for violations by the Soviet authorities of international or domestic laws enforced during the Soviet period.

To be sure, Kosachev's proposal didn't emerge out of the thin air. His idea should be placed into the broader context of Russia's attempts at crafting and pursuing the robust "politics of history." Like other members of the country's ruling elite, Kosachev appears to perceive memory and history as an important ideological and political battleground: Russia's detractors—both foreign and domestic—allegedly seek to spread interpretations of past events that are detrimental to Russia's interests, and there is an

"History, Memory and National Identity: Understanding the Politics of History and Memory Wars in Post-Soviet Lands." Igor Torbakov, first published in Demokratizatsiya, 2011, reprinted with permission of the publisher.

urgent need to resolutely counter these unfriendly moves. Several elements of such politics of history have already been introduced in Russia: a set of officially sponsored and centrally approved textbooks with the highly pronounced statist interpretation of 20th-century Russian history; the attempts to establish the "regime of truth" using legislative means; and the creation of a bureaucratic institution to fight the "falsification of history."

There appears to be a consensus among professional historians and political analysts that over the past several decades, the "politics of history" has become a significant aspect of domestic politics and international relations, both within Europe and in the world at large. One could thus suggest that Russia's latest moves should be seen in perspective and perceived as a manifestation of a Europe-wide trend, their clumsiness and cartoonish character notwithstanding. This trend toward politicizing and instrumentalizing of history might take on various shapes and forms in different countries, but there are basically two main objectives that are usually pursued. First is the construction of a maximally cohesive national identity and rallying the society around the powers that be. Second is eschewing the problem of guilt. The two are clearly interlinked: having liberated oneself of the sense of historical, political, or moral responsibility, it is arguably much easier to take pride in one's newly minted "unblemished" identity based on the celebratory interpretation of one's country's "glorious past," which is habitually regarded as "more a source of comfort than a source of truth." I would thus argue that it is extremely important to investigate the vital links between history, memory and national identity. The main objective of this article, then, is to explore how the memories of some momentous developments in the tumultuous 20th century (above all, the experience of totalitarian dictatorships, World War II, the "division" and "reunification" of Europe, the collapse of the Soviet Union) and their historical interpretations relate to concepts of national identity in the post-Soviet lands. Identities are understood here not as something immutable; by contrast, I proceed from the premise that identities are constantly being constructed and reconstructed in the course of historical process. "As communities and individuals interpret and reinterpret their [historical] experiences . . . they create their own constantly shifting national identities in the process."

I will begin with the analysis of the reasons underlying the intensification of "history wars" between Russia and its neighbors. I will then discuss the prominent role that the reinterpretation of the history of World War II plays in the politics and geopolitics of identity in post-Soviet Eurasia. The analysis of Russia's symbolic politics will come next. I will conclude with exploring possible ways of reconciling national memories and historical narratives.

WHY ESCALATION?

The past two decades following the collapse of the Soviet Union have witnessed an escalation of memory wars in which Russia has largely found itself on the defensive, its official historical narrative being vigorously assaulted by the number of the newly independent ex-Soviet states. Suffice it to recall just the most important episodes of this monumental "battle over history." Following the Soviet collapse, Museums of Occupation were set up in Latvia and Estonia; one of the museums' main objectives is to highlight the political symmetry between the two totalitarian regimes that occupied the Baltics in the 20th century—German national socialism and Soviet Communism. In May 2006, a Museum of Soviet Occupation opened in Tbilisi, Georgia, following the Baltic States' example. That same month, the Institute of National Memory was established in Ukraine, inspired by the Polish model. That same year also saw the adoption of two international documents that couldn't fail to rile official Moscow—a resolution of the European Parliament entitled "On European Conscience and Totalitarianism" and a resolution passed by the Parliamentary Assembly of the Organization for Security and Cooperation in Europe entitled "Divided Europe Reunited: Promoting Human Rights and Civil Liberties in the OSCE Region in the 21st Century." Both resolutions branded Nazism and Stalinism as similar totalitarian regimes, bearing equal responsibility for the outbreak of World War II and the crimes against humanity committed during that period. The resolutions strongly called for the unconditional international condemnation of European totalitarianism. Moscow's reaction to all of this was unambiguously negative; in particular, Russian lawmakers, incensed at Stalinism and Nazism being lumped together, called the OSCE resolution an "offensive anti-Russian provocation" and "violence over history."

There appear to be two sets of reasons behind the increasingly acrimonious disputes over history in which Russia is pitted against the former imperial borderlands. First is what might be called the "classical" politics of identity following the collapse of a multinational empire. Second, there is a specific geopolitical conjuncture primarily connected with the expansion of the European Union and the growing rivalry between the EU and Russia over their overlapping neighborhoods. An important subplot linked with both the Soviet Union's unravelling and the EU's eastward thrust is the struggle over the contested issue of Russia's own shifting identity.

Students of anthropology, political science and postcolonialism have long explored history writing (and mythmaking) as part of an overarching problem of nationalism, national identity and nation-building. Their key premise has been that (re) writing history and (re)making myths is what nation-states generally do, history being a principal tool to construct national identity. It has also been argued (particularly forcefully within the field of postcolonial studies) that any regime change inevitably entails a confrontation with the past: "a new future requires a new past." In cases when regime change, state-creation and nation-building coincide, the confrontation with the past becomes particularly acute. This is precisely the situation in which the countries that emerged from under the rubble of the Soviet Union found themselves.

The key problem here is this: new states have emerged from the debris of the Soviet Union, but in many cases they exist without clear-cut identities or links to logically conceived "nations." Yet, identity, as some scholars argue, is decisively a question of empowerment. As Jonathan Friedman has perceptively noted, "The people without history . . . are the people who have been prevented from identifying themselves for others." So what were, realistically, the available strategies that the newly independent ex-Soviet countries could resort to?

Under Communism, studies of nationalism or national identities were not a terribly popular topic. "National question" in the Soviet Union was routinely explored as an aspect of class paradigm. As it has famously been postulated, liquidation of class distinctions (creation of classless society) would automatically lead toward the solution of national problem—through the creation of the "new historical entity" (the "Soviet people") in which national/ethnic differences would be preserved in their harmless (i.e., non-political) ethnographic form. National histories of the Soviet Union's multifarious peoples were secondary (and highly controlled) narratives—the component parts of the Soviet grand narrative.

Following the demise of Communism and the Soviet Union's unraveling, the incipient nation-states either returned to national historiographic tradition (where it existed) or hastily set about creating one. One common feature has been the "nationalization of history" whereby the history of a newly born post-Soviet state is conceptualized as the history of a titular nation, the latter being associated with the titular ethic group.

Yet this strategy of nationalizing history inevitably leads to strains, both internally and externally. As Clifford Geertz noted, defining the national particularism may be fraught with inherent difficulties because "new states tend to be bundles of competing traditions gathered accidentally into concocted political frameworks rather than organically evolving civilizations." Thus, "nationalization" of history centered on a titular nation cannot help but produce what can be called "mutually exclusive" histories, whereby national minorities are excluded and/or designated as *Others.* In the situation when all post-Soviet states are multiethnic and multicultural, the exclusivist narrative is counterproductive at best and outright dangerous at worst.

Following the demise of Communism and the Soviet Union's unraveling, the incipient nation-states either returned to national historiographic tradition . . . or hastily set about creating one.

A recent Russian study based on the examination of nearly 200 school history textbooks and teacher guides from Russia's 12 post-Soviet neighbors demonstrated that the trends toward nationalizing history and "othering" are gaining momentum in most new independent states. The report, released in Moscow in the end of 2009 and entitled "The Treatment of the Common History of Russia and the Peoples of the Post-Soviet Countries in the History Textbooks of the New Independent States," argues that Russia's neighbors are now using textbooks that present Russia in all its historical incarnations as the enemy of the peoples of these countries.

Some Russian historians appear to have been unpleasantly surprised, even hurt, by what they called the blatantly nationalistic and viciously anti-Russian interpretations of Russian imperial and Soviet history by non-Russian scholars from neighboring states. "It is a revisiting, at a new level, of the theory of 'absolute evil' which used to be popular during the early Soviet period," contends Moscow University Professor Aleksandr Vdovin. "Back then, this nefarious role in Soviet historiography was played by the [Russian] Tsarism that 'oppressed the peoples of the empire.' Now it is Russia that is painted as the 'absolute evil.'" But more perceptive Russian and international commentators seem to agree that a certain degree of anti-Russian bias in the new independent countries' historiographies was all but inevitable. It should not be treated as an "unexpected phenomenon," argues one Russian analyst; rather, it should be understood as a "norm." In their efforts to assert their still shaky and fragile national identities and root them in the (re)invented national traditions, the new countries were bound to "push against" Russia's official historical narrative. "The shaping of an image of the ethnic or cultural Other has become an inalienable part of the cultural and political mobilization as well as of the politics of memory pursued by the newly independent states," writes the prominent Ukrainian historian Georgiy Kasyanov. It should come as no surprise, adds Kasyanov, that in the post-Soviet space it was "Russia and the Russians" who ended up being the "absolute champions" as far as the forming of negative ethnic stereotypes and "othering" are concerned. Thus the ground for "history wars" was in fact inherent in the post-imperial situation. These conflicts could have been somewhat attenuated had Russia—a former imperial overlord—had at least a modest success in what Germans call *Vergangenheitsbewältigung*, meaning coming to terms with the past. But it hadn't. I will address Russia's stance in greater detail below.

GEOPOLITICS OF IDENTITY

Why this sudden spike in the politicization of history? It would appear that the EU enlargement has undermined a historical consensus that used to exist within and among the Western European countries with regard to World War II and postwar experiences. As some scholars have pointed out recently, three main narratives of war and dictatorship exist in regard to Europe: a Western European story, a Soviet/Russian story, and an Eastern European story. Interestingly, the first two are somewhat similar in that both tend to highlight the glorious victory over Nazi Germany, successful postwar reconstruction, and the long period of postwar peace and economic development. By contrast, Eastern Europeans were largely focusing not so much on "liberation" as on the dark years of Soviet occupation and dreaming of their eventual "return to Europe."

The leading Western historians of Eastern Europe, such as Norman Davies and Timothy Snyder, long argued that the West badly misunderstood the East European experience. "What seems to have happened is that western opinion was only gradually informed about the war in Eastern Europe over forty to fifty years and that the drip-feeding was insufficient to inspire radical adjustments to the overall conceptual framework," Davies argued several years ago. But it is precisely Eastern Europe's devastating war experience that needs to be "recovered" and reintegrated into a European historical narrative. One has to remember that arguably the most awful acts of carnage and violence in Europe in the 20th century occurred in what Snyder calls the "bloodlands": the territories of Poland, Lithuania, Belarus and Ukraine. The sad irony, though, is that because after the war's end these countries found themselves behind the

Iron Curtain and under Stalinist rule, their histories were marginalized or expelled altogether from a general European account. This "postwar exorcism," to use Michael Geyer's term, was carried out through a particular organization of knowledge about Europe. The latter, neatly following the postwar division of Europe, was split into *national histories* of Western Europe and *area studies* for Eastern Europe. Thus, "historiographic elision" was firmly institutionalized. Curiously, it appears to linger on, even more than twenty years after the Wall fell. As Snyder contends, "[E]ven as East Europeans gained the freedom to write and speak of their own histories as they chose after 1989 or 1991, and even as many East European countries acceded to the European Union in 2004 and 2007, their national histories have somehow failed to become accepted as European. Their histories have failed to flow into a larger European history that all, in East and West, can recognize as such."

But now the enlargement has made the accommodation of the Eastern European perspective inevitable—as a necessary precondition for the solidarity of the extended EU. Pushing aside "the other half" of European history runs the risk of undermining the project of Europeanizing national histories. Furthermore, "it thwarts an assessment of Europe as a whole."

But as Eastern Europeans are pushing for the reintegration of their disastrous war experience into a (pan-)European narrative, they rarely manage to resist the temptation to turn the reinterpretation of World War II into the key element of their countries' politics of history. The reason behind this is simple. Most Eastern European nations now view the wartime and postwar period as a "useable past"—crucial for strengthening separate identity, giving a boost to populist nationalism, externalizing the Communist past, and casting their particular nation as a hapless victim of two bloodthirsty totalitarian dictatorships. The German historian Wilfried Jilge specifically points to the tendency of Eastern European intellectuals to construct what he terms the "national Holocausts" and thus confer on their nations a status of victim—and the perceived moral high ground that goes along with it. "From this position of moral superiority, the crimes of one's own nation are justified as defensive actions," writes Jilge in an article tellingly titled "The Competition of Victims"—the phrase he borrowed from the former Polish Foreign Minister Wladyslaw Bartoszewski. "In this context," Jilge goes on, "national stereotypes serve to distance 'one's own' national history from 'false' Soviet history and thus to 'cleanse' 'one's own' nation of everything that is Soviet."

This is yet another example of how Russia's Eastern European neighbors, while reinterpreting their most dramatic 20th-century experiences, are also reshaping their identities. They craft their historical narratives in such a way as to reposition themselves in Europe, seeking to strengthen their own sense of Europeanness and distinguish themselves from Russia, which is often cast as a non-European, Eurasian power—in a word, as Europe's constitutive *Other*. This is, of course, a problematic historiographical strategy. A number of Eastern European intellectuals note that almost everywhere in Eastern Europe, the new ruling elites chose to base—in varying degrees and shapes—their ideological legitimization on the conservative counterrevolutionary tradition that was dominant in the region during the interwar period, as well as on the mythology of the "national resistance" whose multifarious forms also included the collaboration with Nazi Germany, perceived as a suitable ally in the struggle against "Russian Communism." For this purpose, the Eastern European elites seek to (re)construct their countries' wartime histories as a story of the "national liberation struggle." In these new historical narratives, says Tamas Krausz, one of the leading Hungarian specialists in Eastern European history, "Russia is made a scapegoat." Another negative consequence of this historical reinterpretation, Krausz and other like-minded Eastern European intellectuals argue, is that it is being accompanied by the rehabilitation of the ethnic nationalist thinking.

I would argue that the Eastern Europeans' lingering wariness of Russia is directly linked to the present-day Russia's ambiguous international identity. On the one hand, Russia claims legitimacy in Europe as a post-Soviet *European* state; on the other, it presents itself as the legal continuation of the

Soviet Union. The latter stance entails two important implications: Russia's claim to a status of great power with a sphere of "privileged interests," and its reluctance to fully recognize Soviet/Stalinist crimes.

RUSSIA'S PREDICAMENT: FACING UP TO THE DIFFICULT PAST WHILE COMING TO TERMS WITH THE GREAT LOSS

There is no question that Russia is seriously affected by this new historiographic situation stemming from the confluence of the post-imperial controversies and the history debates born of the recent geopolitical changes in Europe. It should not then come as a surprise that Moscow responds, sometimes very harshly, to what it perceives as a challenge to its national interests. The latter are believed to be particularly gravely threatened by the "hostile interpretations" of World War II (or what is better known in Russia as the "Great Patriotic War"). My key point here is that, similar to its Eastern European neighbors, Moscow's conduct, too, can only be properly understood within the context of Russian identity politics. After all, what is at stake—as it is perceived by the Russian elites—in the ongoing history wars with the former Eastern Bloc satellites and ex-Soviet republics is no less than Russia's status as a "European nation."

So long as the erstwhile historical consensus remained intact, Russia's victory over Nazism legitimized its "great power" status in Europe and its sphere of influence in the eastern part of the continent. The new historical controversies over the nature of the Soviet "liberation" of Eastern Europe effectively undermine Russia's status as the "liberator of Europe" and erode whatever symbolic capital it might claim to prop up its "Europeanness." What we are witnessing is basically a "clash" of two very different notions of "liberation." In today's Europe (and, for that matter, the United States), the liberation of Europe in World War II is inseparably welded with the idea of democracy—the restoration of democratic order in that part Europe which was cleansed by the Western Allies of the "brown plague." Such interpretation presupposes that whatever the Soviet Union did in the eastern half of Europe that fell under Stalin's control could be called anything but "liberation."

Nowhere was the Russian official narrative—and the identity based upon it—challenged so vigorously of late as at the 2009 Vilnius Conference on "European Histories." Addressing the gathering, Valdas Adamkus, the outgoing president of Lithuania, reminded his audience that for Eastern Europeans, it is not just the defeat of Nazi Germany that comes to mind on May 8, 1945. "For Lithuania, like many other eastern European nations, May 8 of 1945 did not bring victory over violence, but simply change of oppressor," Adamkus has forcefully stated. "Once again, history was turned into the handmaiden of politics and ideology and thrust upon Lithuania and its people to cover up injustice and crime, distort facts, slander independence and freedom fighters." Yale historian Timothy Snyder would completely concur. Attacking in a 2005 article what he called a "common European narrative"—which is largely shared by Moscow—Snyder asserted that 1945 "means something entirely different in most of Eastern Europe—for most citizens of the states admitted to the Union in May 2004. For them, 1945 means a transition from one occupation to another; from Nazi rule to Soviet rule." Now, participating in the Vilnius gathering, Snyder offered his reinterpretation of Europe's tragic 20th-century experience that, according to one observer, "in key respects threw into question the established historical consensus."

Such treatment of the wartime and postwar developments is regarded in Moscow as a direct attack on Russia's image as a great *European* power—a status that the Kremlin leadership values highly. To get a better sense of the true extent of Moscow's wrath, one has to understand that 1945 represents the absolute pinnacle of Russia's geopolitical might: some scholars have argued that following its defeat in the Crimean war in 1856 and until the Soviet victory in WWII Russian power has been in a relative decline. "Don't forget," Tony Judt reminded us,

> that as seen from a historian's perspective, a historian of contemporary Europe, Stalin was in many ways the natural successor to Catherine the Great, and the tsars of the 19th century, expanding into the Russian near west, and to the Russian southwest in particular—territories that Catherine

began her expansion into, which have always been regarded as crucial by Russian strategists, both because of access to resources, access to warm water ports, and because it gives Russia a role in Europe, as well as in Asia.

Just consider two plain historical facts: Russia was among the biggest losers in World War I, and saw its statehood crumbling and the borderlands seceding, while World War II results confirmed at Yalta and Potsdam turned Russia (in the form of the Soviet Union) into the world's second superpower—a status that included Moscow's immense geopolitical clout in Europe. However, Russia's four-decades-long dominance over Eastern Europe was brought down in a series of "velvet revolutions" in 1989. As one pithy comment put it, "Russia was the main victor in WWII and the main loser in 1989."

But what is particularly important for my discussion here is that, unlike most of its Eastern European neighbors, the post-Soviet Russia has refused to view the EU as a norm-maker and is reluctant to accept its standards and values. At the same time, Russian leadership adamantly insists that its country is inherently European—as European as any other major European state. One cannot find a better expression of this attitude than a defiant passage in Vladimir Putin's 2005 Annual Address to the Federal Assembly. As if reiterating Catherine the Great's famous dictum, Putin forcefully asserted that "Above all else Russia was, is and will, of course, be a major European power":

> Achieved through much suffering by European culture, the ideals of freedom, human rights, justice and democracy have for many centuries been our society's determining values. For three centuries, we—together with the other European nations—passed hand in hand through reforms of Enlightenment, the difficulties of emerging parliamentarianism, municipal and judiciary branches, and the establishment of similar legal systems . . . I repeat we did this together, sometimes behind and sometimes ahead of European standards.

Such a stance, naturally, implies that Europe should be held to *Russian* standards of Europeanness, too. So when Moscow castigates the "rehabilitation of fascism" in certain parts of Europe or lashes out at the "glorification of Nazi collaborators" in some Baltic states or in Ukraine, it claims it protects *European* values—the ones that the EU itself allegedly chose to ignore. Thus Russian leadership's jeremiads against the "inadmissible revision of WWII results" should be read as an element of its strategic ideological ambition to advance an alternative interpretation of what *Europe* means.

There is also a very important domestic dimension of Russian leadership's struggle against the "revision of World War II history." Here, a myth of the "Great Patriotic War" or, more precisely, a myth of the "great Victory" plays a pivotal role. Created in the 1960s, this myth—in which the memory of *war*, with all its unbearable everyday hardships, untold number of victims, millions of POWs, chaos of evacuation, etc., had been replaced by the memory of *victory*—was successfully exploited by the Soviet Communist rulers. First, it provided an effective means of legitimization for the political power. Second, it was a powerful instrument of identity politics as it told an uplifting story of a "birth of the Soviet people in the crucible of the total war."

The official commemoration of the "Great Patriotic War" also appears to be the sole ideological mechanism that can be employed to foster Russia's social cohesion. According to Carnegie Moscow Center analyst Nikolai Petrov, "There is absolutely nothing else in the whole of Russian history that can be used to unite the nation." Petrov's remark is significant in that it reveals what arguably constitutes Russia's most formidable "historiographical" problem—namely, the lack of even a minimal consensus within the Russian society as to the interpretation of the country's turbulent past, following the century of violent political upheavals. To achieve a healthy degree of cohesion, within any society there should be a certain public agreement as to the basic values system upon which rests the whole edifice of historical memory of the given society. After all, any "memorial construct" is a system of values; the "memory as such" simply does not exist. As the Russians fail to agree on how to treat the most significant episodes of their country's past, the "victory myth" is being used by the ruling elites as a kind of "social glue."

Treating the "Great Patriotic War" as a "usable past" also fits into a broader strategy of "normalizing" Soviet history which has been vigorously pursued under Putin. "Normalization" of the Soviet past as a "part of our glorious thousand year old history" contributes to the revived ideology of statism as a perennial source of Russian identity.

Integrating the Stalin period into a greater Russian story is not just an elite project—the polls demonstrate that it is generally supported by the masses. For the West in general and Russia's Eastern European neighbors in particular, the process appears both puzzling and menacing; increasingly, there is talk about Moscow's backlash and imperial comeback. There is, however, a compelling psychological reason for the rise of such public attitudes, and some more astute commentators contended that a backlash in one form or another was inevitable. One has to understand, notes Judt, that for the majority of Russians, the demise of the Soviet Union involved the loss of not just territory and status but also of a *history* that they could live with. "Everything has been unraveled before their eyes," says he, adding that any other nation would have been morally devastated by such an experience.

> If this had happened to Americans, or Brits, it would have been culturally catastrophic; to lose the equivalent of, say Texas and California, to be told that all the founding fathers right down to FDR were a bunch of criminals, to discover that you are regarded as on the par with Hitler, in terms of the accepted description of 20th-century evils that we have since overcome.

No wonder, then, that the "trope of loss," as Serguei Oushakine demonstrates so well in his *The Patriotism of Despair*, has become the most effective and widely used symbolic device which Russians employ to make sense of their Soviet experience in the post-Soviet context.

There is, of course, a vexed question about the interrelation between the glory of the "Great Patriotic War" and the horrors of Stalinist terror. Some liberal Russian scholars have skillfully demonstrated how the memory of the war is being (ab) used to construct a kind of "blocking myth" in order to suppress the memories of the totalitarian regime's terror, of the Gulag and other crimes of the period. If the atrocities perpetrated by the Soviet regime do occasionally pop up in the official narrative, they are presented as some insignificant episode in the otherwise heroic and glorious Soviet history. But one also must bear in mind the existence of significant differences in the ways the trauma of the Soviet collapse affected public perceptions and memories of Russians and those of their neighbors in Eastern Europe: "In Russia itself, the disintegration of the USSR was linked much more closely with the painful immediacy of everyday survival than with archived horrors of the Great Terror . . . The need to equate the Soviet Union with the Stalinist regime, which was so crucial for many Western [and East European] commentators, was less obvious in the midst of [Russia's] post-Soviet changes."

And yet, the ambiguity of a Russian official position, rooted in the inability of making a comprehensive and honest assessment of the nature of the Soviet regime, makes it extremely difficult for Moscow to approach the crucial issue of responsibility that appears to be at the heart of history wars in the post-Soviet space.

CONCLUSION

Is it realistic to believe that post-Soviet states will ever do without politics of history and that the memory wars between them will eventually end? I would begin discussion of this question by suggesting that while national images of the past will never fully coincide, it appears feasible to reach some reconciliation between them and thus avoid creating negative identities. Such reconciliation can be achieved in the course of a broad and mutually respectful dialogue between national memories and historical narratives. All the participants of this dialogue would agree that while national memories are not congruent and historical narratives might diverge, one's image of the past could only be enriched through the knowledge of alternative interpretations.

Such dialogue, however, will only be possible if three formidable obstacles are overcome.

The most important obstacle is authoritarian political culture. As Karl Schlögel argues, "Authoritarian conditions are hostile to memory. A mature historical culture and a civil culture belong together." Indeed, scholars have noted the close correlation between regime type and the degree of regime's reliance on historical myths. True, all regimes resort to and rely on myth-making. But in liberal democracies, political legitimacy is much less dependent on the unifying historical narrative that would foster compliance with government policies than it is in authoritarian regimes. Genuine democracies are thus much more tolerant of dissent, controversy, competing ideas and can afford the luxury of treating history that challenges habitual assumptions with relative equanimity. This trait, in the words of the eminent British historian Michael Howard, is a mark of maturity. By contrast, authoritarian leaders prefer to feed their subjects with what Howard calls "nursery history." In his view, "[A] good definition of the difference between a Western liberal society and a totalitarian one—whether it is Communist, Fascist, or Catholic authoritarian—is that in the former the government treats its citizens as responsible adults and in the latter it cannot."

The second problem is the widespread perceptions that mass publics hold about what history actually is. Sociological surveys demonstrate that in most post-Soviet states, people are largely unaware of one fundamental thing—that studying history is a complex and continuous process in the course of which what used to be perceived as "historical truth" can (and should) be refuted as new evidence emerge or new interpretations are advanced. According to the recent data provided by VTsIOM, a Russian pollster, 60 percent of the respondents hold that history should not be revised, that past events should be studied in such a way which would exclude "repeat research" leading to new approaches and interpretations. Only 31 percent of those polled believe that the study of history is a continuous and open-ended process. Furthermore, 79 percent spoke in favor of using one single textbook when teaching history course in schools—lest the young minds get confused by alternative interpretations. Symptomatically, 78 percent supported the creation of the presidential commission charged with fighting "falsification of history," and 60 percent said the passing of a "memory law" criminalizing the "revision of WWII results" would be a good thing. Ironically, when 61 percent of Russians say that "national interpretations" of the past are inadmissible, they appear to be oblivious of the fact that their own interpretation is no less "national."

This picture of public attitudes should correct an oversimplified perception of symbolic politics in the post-Soviet lands as basically a one-way street whereby the discourse that serves the interests of ruling elites is being imposed upon society. In more ways than one, the prevalent attitudes toward history and memory demonstrate the meeting of the minds between the rulers and the ruled in Eurasia.

It would appear that these attitudes can be changed only slowly through the changes in the way national histories are written in Russia and other ex-Soviet republics. And this is the third big problem that needs to be tackled. It would be naive to believe that national governments (or die-hard nationalists, for that matter) will one day stop regarding (and exploiting) historical narrative as a useful means of nationalist mobilization. After all, common history is what holds the imagined community together. So an ethnic-centric, "nationalized" history is likely to persist. But what is needed, assert some leading historians, is to supplement a traditional national narrative by *multiethnic* or, better still, *transnational* approach. "Transnational" or "transcultural" history, argues Andreas Kappeler, would be based on "multiperspectivity and comparison, investigate interactions, communications and overlapping phenomena and entanglements between states, nations, societies, economies, regions, and cultures."

These new approaches would probably still not help overcome the divide between memories in the post-Soviet world. But as I have stated above, there is no need to try bridging the gap between national memories. This goal is unattainable. The objective to be pursued is much more modest: to promote understanding of other perspectives and interpretations.

VISUAL REVIEW

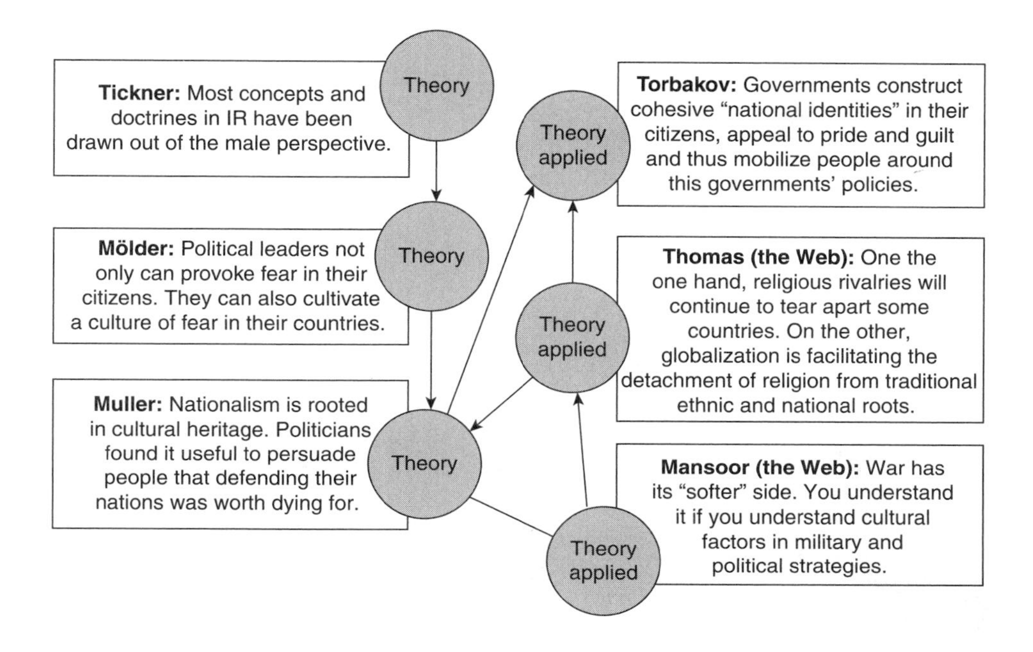

Section 11

Global Forecasting: The World of 2025

Presidential candidate Marina Silva of the Brazilian Socialist Party campaigning in Brazil back in 2014. Could we predict the impact of these elections on Brazil's foreign policy a few years later? Check how elections have affected Brazil's position in the world today.
Source: Tiago Mazza Chiaravalloti/Associated Press

Why a World State Is Inevitable

ALEXANDER WENDT

In this article I propose a teleological theory of the "logic of anarchy" which suggests that a world state is inevitable. Like any structural tendency, the speed with which this one will be realized is historically contingent. At the micro-level the process is neither deterministic nor linear, and forward movement may be blocked for periods of time. There are many pathways by which a world state may be achieved, and human agency matters along every one. In that sense "anarchy is [still] what states make of it". However, I am not concerned here with historical contingencies or timing. My own guess is that a world state will emerge within 100–200(?) years, but nothing below turns on that prediction. Instead, I am concerned with the macro-structure of all pathways, which channel the international system's development toward an inevitable end-state. In that respect the theory is progressivist, although in an explanatory rather than normative sense.

Resistance to progressivist, much less teleological, thinking runs deep within contemporary IR scholarship. Realists are skeptical, arguing that the logic of anarchy is one of endless conflict and war. Liberals are more optimistic, arguing that international institutions, interdependence and/or democratic states can lead to cooperation and peace within anarchy. However, liberal progressivism is contingent, not teleological. If institutions are upheld, if interdependence deepens and/or if democracy spreads, then progress is possible. The forecast is based on extrapolating lawlike regularities from the past into the future, assuming certain conditions continue to hold. Since there is no guarantee they will, we cannot say that any given future is inevitable.

Indeed, if there is one thing almost all social scientists today agree on, from the most hardened positivists to the most radical postmodernists, it is that teleological explanations are illegitimate. To call a theory "teleological" is considered a decisive criticism, with no need even to explain why. This may be due to the fact that teleology has been considered unscientific since the triumph of the mechanistic worldview in the 17th century, and is also sometimes thought to deny human agency in the social world. In my view both objections are unfounded, and with them a priori resistance to teleological thinking about world politics.

To show this, in the first section I synthesize recent attempts to rehabilitate teleological explanation. These efforts span many disciplines and indicate that, although the scientific status of teleology remains controversial, it is being taken increasingly seriously. One reason is that much of this literature builds on self-organization theory, which is emerging as an important challenge to the neo-Darwinian theory of evolution. Self-organization theory hypothesizes that order in nature emerges not only through the mechanism of mutation-selection-retention, but also "spontaneously" from the channeling of system dynamics by structural boundary conditions toward particular end-states. With a few exceptions this theory has been little noticed by IR scholars, who are just beginning to engage neo-Darwinism. But in the social sciences more generally the idea of self-organization has been around since the "spontaneous order" tradition of the Scottish empiricists, and is getting considerable attention today. Much of this work is not teleological, and many self-organization theorists might vigorously reject any such reading of their approach. On the other hand, many others do see a connection, arguing that self-organization theory provides a scientific basis for teleological explanation.

Assuming that is possible, toward what end-state does the international system move, and by what mechanism does it get there? Three end-states suggest themselves—a pacific federation of republican states, a realist world of nation-states in which war remains legitimate, and a world state.

European Journal of International Relations Vol. 9(4): 491–542.

The first is associated with Kant and the second with Hegel, both of whom based their projections on explicitly teleological arguments. In rejecting the possibility of a world state, therefore, they agreed that, strictly speaking, anarchy would remain the organizing principle of the system, albeit different kinds of anarchy. As to the mechanism of progress, in different ways Kant and Hegel also both emphasized the role of conflict—Kant in man's "unsociable sociability," and Hegel in the "struggle for recognition."

I am in no position here to engage in an exegesis and critique of Kant and Hegel's arguments. However, since I share their emphasis on conflict as a mechanism of development but reach a different conclusion, it may be useful to introduce my argument by highlighting two ways in which it departs from theirs. The first concerns the effects of conflict on state identity. While envisioning a tendency for conflict to create republican states, Kant did not expect them to develop a collective identity. His states remain egoists who retain their sovereignty. Hegel provides the basis for a different conclusion, since the effect of the struggle for recognition is precisely to transform egoistic identity into collective identity, and eventually a state. But Hegel expects this outcome only in the struggle between individuals. States too seek recognition, but in his view they remain self-sufficient totalities. Their struggle for recognition does not produce supranational solidarity, leaving us at the "end of history" with a world of multiple states. Some critics have suggested that Hegel's reasoning here is inconsistent, and that he should have argued for a world state. Be that as it may, I argue that the struggle for recognition between states will have the same outcome as that between individuals, collective identity formation and eventually a state. One reason for this concerns the second difference in my approach, which concerns the role of technology. Kant rejected the possibility of a world state in part because the technology of his day precluded it, and in positing an end-state in which war remained legitimate Hegel did not think its costs would become intolerable. Neither anticipated the dramatic technological changes of the past century, which are in part caused by the security dilemma and thus endogenous to anarchy. As Daniel Deudney convincingly argues, these changes have greatly increased the costs of war and also the scale on which it is possible to organize a state. With these material changes the struggle for recognition among states undermines their self-sufficiency and makes a world state inevitable. Via the struggle for recognition, in short, the logic of anarchy leads to its own demise.

THE LOGIC OF ANARCHY

The struggle for recognition is the bottom-up aspect of the argument. I now turn to its top-down aspect. I argue that the process of world state formation progresses through five stages of recognition, the first four constituting distinct cultures of anarchy. Each culture imposes boundary conditions that increasingly constrain the interactions of the system's parts, but in so doing enable growing subjectivity and freedom at the global level. What drives the system forward is the logic of anarchy, which through downward causation conditions struggles for recognition in two ways—by making it possible to seek recognition through violence, and by generating improved military technology that makes such violence increasingly intolerable.

What follows is a conceptual rather than historical argument, in the sense that the proposed stages refer less to a necessary temporal sequence than to logical problems of recognition that must be solved for a world state to emerge. I have ordered these problems chronologically because solutions to the "earlier" problems seem to have fewer preconditions than the later ones, and as such are likely to be discovered by the system first, but that does not preclude the possibility of skipping stages or solving several problems at once. Moreover, the proposed progression of stages is compatible with backsliding in a given historical moment. The argument is not linear; it claims only that any step backwards will eventually be balanced by two steps forward. With those qualifications in mind I take up each stage in turn.

Stage One: The System of States

This is the stage of complete non-recognition, what Hobbes called the "warre of all against all" and

Bull a "system" of states. This system is constituted by three boundary conditions—the fact of multiple interacting states (individuals are not actors at all here), or simple difference; the absence of any mechanism to enforce cooperation among these states (anarchy); and a mutual belief that they are "enemies", with no rights and thus social constraints on what they may do. Because there is no recognition there is no perceived collective identity in the system, and by implication states do not even have genuine subjectivity. Insofar as states share an awareness that they are in a Hobbesian system it will constitute a culture, but this culture and its implicit collective identity will be "repressed".

The Hobbesian stage is unstable in the long run because it does not begin to meet needs for recognition. Taking the dyadic case first, we can see this instability and its developmental consequences by considering the two possible outcomes of a struggle for recognition in such a system. One, which we would expect if one state is significantly stronger than the other, is the conquest of the weaker state. The dyad becomes a single unit, and the locus of self-organization then shifts to the interaction of this enlarged state with other states. If success begets success and conquests continue, eventually only one state will be left, and the system will no longer be anarchic. Such an outcome might even come to be seen as legitimate by its subjects and thus be stable for some time. However, if the conqueror does not recognize its victims then they will eventually try to break away, thereby recreating an anarchic system. In other words, a Weberian world state that is not also a Hegelian one—an "empire"—will be unstable in the long run. On the other hand, if the world conqueror does turn around and recognize its victims as full subjects, then a stable world state will have been achieved without the intermediate stages of development.

The second possible outcome would occur if the two states are equal in power. In that case neither can conquer the other, and they will continue to struggle for recognition. This need not involve constant warfare, but will require constant preparations for war that drain societal resources, and war will remain a significant probability. This dynamic too is not stable. Either one side will eventually get the upper hand and conquer the other, or they will "wear each other out" to the point that they realize that continued struggle is pointless, and agree to mutual recognition. The effect of anarchy on military technology is important here, since over time it will increase the cost of war, and with it negative feedback on a policy of non-recognition. Conversely, mutual recognition would create positive feedback, since it would allow competitors to devote more resources to other purposes, including struggles with third parties. This may be seen as a stylized account of the process that led to the Peace of Westphalia, and one might expect a similar outcome in, for example, the Israeli–Palestinian conflict today.

Whichever outcome transpires, therefore, a Hobbesian anarchy is unstable in the long run, and will eventually move toward a non-Hobbesian attractor. In principle that could be any of the remaining developmental stages mentioned later, including a world state. However, so that I can detail the entire logic let's assume that the system can only solve one developmental problem at a time.

Stage Two: The Society of States

The instabilities of the Hobbesian culture can be resolved by moving to a "society of states" or Lockean culture of anarchy. In this culture states recognize each other's legal sovereignty as independent subjects, but not that of each other's citizens. Thus, while states no longer constitute each other as "enemies," they still do so as "rivals". This generates two sources of instability.

First, even though positional wars do not threaten states' "lives," they can still be costly, and these costs will rise over time with secular improvements in military technology. Today, even conventional wars between equal states can be enormously destructive, and will be only more so in the future, a fact which may help explain their contemporary rarity.

Second, even if states don't get "killed" in positional wars, people do. As such, as in the Hobbesian culture, here too individuals are not recognized outside their own state, and thus as subjects in the world system. Individuals do not like dying in war, especially when their group identity is already at least minimally recognized by other states. Given the importance of group identity to individuals, sacrifice in war makes sense in a Hobbesian culture, since people are fighting for individual recognition as well. But in a Lockean culture states have gained some recognition, and so it is less clear how sacrifice for the state would meet individuals' needs. Over time we can expect individuals to make those needs apparent to their leaders, inducing the latter toward growing caution in the use of force as a tool of diplomacy, particularly as the costs of war rise. Eventually, through this pressure from below states in a Lockean culture will learn to desist from war altogether, and to find non-violent means to solve foreign policy problems (at least among states that are similarly reluctant to go to war). What we see here is the emergence of individuals' struggle for recognition alongside that of states as a force at the system level. The problem of war means that individual recognition must be external as well as internal, which requires breaking down its mediation by state boundaries.

This narrative of instability is similar to the logic of the "democratic peace," in which the reluctance of individuals to die for their country helps pacify relations among democratic states. However, it is not clear that my story depends on democracy at the unit-level. Such states may be sufficient for translating individuals' desires for recognition into inter-state peace, but we do not know if they are necessary. Since what matters to the argument is only that individuals' desire for recognition by outsiders be somehow realized, it seems wise at this point to leave open exactly how this would be accomplished at the domestic level.

Stage Three: World Society

The immediate problem of war is solved by creating a universal pluralistic security community, which adds the requirement of non-violent dispute resolution to the boundary conditions of the system. Mutual recognition at the system level now begins to extend to individuals as well as states, making it analogous to the recognition found in fully formed territorial states. As such this stage might be called a cosmopolitan or world society. The system has now constrained the liberty of its parts even more (they are no longer free to make war), but in so doing has developed a thicker form of solidarity than a society of states, which expands positive freedom for both individuals and states.

Yet, this developmental stage too is not a stable end-state, because of the absence of collective protection against aggression. Even if everyone today is committed to peaceful dispute resolution, there is always the possibility in the future of rogue or "criminal" states emerging through domestic revolution, which reject non-violence and attack other members of the system. In principle there are two ways to deal with this problem, neither of which is available in this culture. One is by centralized coercion. That is unavailable because in a world society states retain sovereignty. The other is decentralized enforcement by a collective security system. That is unavailable as well, because a security community is compatible with states being indifferent to each other's fate; it imposes no requirement of mutual aid. A state threatened by a rogue could therefore not be certain others would defend it against aggression. To sustain a world society actors need a more demanding form of recognition, one that imposes not only negative duties (non-violence) but also positive ones (mutual aid).

Where does the system go from here? There is always the possibility of degeneration back to Stage Two or even One, but as we saw earlier those outcomes are not stable in the long run, and so will only bring us back to Stage Three again. Conversely, there are good reasons to move forward toward a commitment of mutual aid. Consider a system of three states, A, B and C. If A and B form a security community they will both experience positive feedback—no fear of war, at least on one flank; less need for costly arms; and recognition of both group and individual subjectivities. A and B will be reluctant to give these benefits up, and so once peace has been achieved they will have an interest in its being perpetual. Now let C become an existential threat to B (only). This would create the possibility for A that a previously peaceful border would be occupied by a hostile state, plunging the border back to a state of war. That gives A an interest in helping B, even though A is not directly threatened. In effect, the anticipated negative feedback of its neighbor's demise sustains the positive feedback provided by their peaceful relationship. Since these incentives are mutual, both have reason to care about each other's fate, and form a permanent alliance. This does not mean that states will always recognize these benefits, but those that do deepen their solidarity will have a better chance of survival than those that do not, suggesting that in the long run they will colonize the system. Once the system reaches the stage of world society, therefore, the desire to reproduce it will induce it to develop even farther.

Stage Four: Collective Security

At this stage the system acquires an additional boundary condition: not only must its members—now both individuals and states—recognize each other's sovereignty and practice non-violent dispute resolution, but they are expected to defend each other against threats on the principle of "all for one, one for all." The system has now reached a "Kantian culture" of collective security or "friendship". Actors have a well-developed sense of collective identity with respect to security, such that each sustains its difference by identifying with the fate of the whole. Although today we are far having from such an identity on a global scale, its benefits have already been demonstrated at the regional level. The ease with which the US was able to put together coalitions to fight the first Gulf War and the War on Terrorism, the persistence of NATO after the end of the Cold War, and even the Concert of Europe are all best explained by perceived common fate. In all these cases mutual recognition had positive rather than just negative behavioral requirements.

However, a universal collective security system is not a world state. Territorial states retain their sovereignty, and as such its functioning depends on their consent. A collective security system cannot require its elements to continue recognizing each other, in the sense of commanding a legitimate monopoly of force to enforce it. The system is voluntary in a way that a state is not. Strictly speaking, it remains anarchic. On the other hand, given that collective security seems to meet both individual and group needs for recognition, and has some ability to enforce that recognition, it is not immediately clear why anything more is needed.

An argument for the inevitability of one more stage must begin with the instability of collective security as a solution to the struggle for recognition. Perhaps the most commonly adduced instability, usually emphasized by Realists, is that collective action problems make collective security inadequate as a deterrent to aggression; when it is most needed it is most likely to fail. While this problem has some force, it points not toward a world state but to the degeneration of anarchy back to a Lockean culture, if not to the war of all against all. Moreover, the Realist argument presupposes that states remain self-interested egoists, which is undercut by the kind of collective identity formation that I have argued would accompany the development of a collective security system. However, two other sources of instability are not so easily handled.

First, because collective security is a consensus-based system in which states retain their sovereignty, it would have no right to prevent a state from seceding and then arming itself for aggressive purposes. Kant tried to deal with this problem by calling for voluntary disarmament, but even if that were successful it does not solve the problem of possible rearmament in the future. Second, and more importantly, collective security does not fully satisfy desires for recognition. For what, in the end, is the retention of sovereignty if not retention of the right to decide, unilaterally, to revoke an actor's recognized status and possibly kill them? A state might promise not to exercise this right, and even keep that promise for a long time. But as long as the right to kill is not permanently surrendered to an authority with the capability to enforce recognition, Others will remain vulnerable to a change of policy by the Self. These problems suggest that a collective security system would not be a stable end-state. But we still need an argument for why this would lead to a world state rather than back to more primitive forms of anarchy. Three considerations suggest themselves.

One is a collective memory of what anarchy was like before collective security, which with the experience of World Wars I and II has been an important source of European integration. True, collective memories imply a "collective," and today collective identities are much thicker at the regional than global level. But rising interdependence is deepening collective identity at the system level, and when coupled with the rapid growth of transnational publicity, truly global memories, such as 9/11, are becoming possible for the first time. Further painful global memories in the future—a regional nuclear war?—could therefore be a source of universal integration. Much like Hobbes' retrospective argument for the state, these memories would constrain the system's degeneration, making a move back toward anarchy less attractive than a move forward to a world state.

A second factor is that if states have formed a deep enough collective identity to defend each other even when they are not themselves threatened, then de facto they do recognize obligations to each other and their citizens, and the de jure issue is moot. The only reason not to make recognition binding—to constitutionalize it—is to leave open the possibility of changing their minds, but that seems hard to square with a genuine commitment to universal recognition. Here Hegel's argument that unreciprocated recognition is ultimately unsatisfying may come into play. The kinds of actors most likely to be vulnerable to such dissatisfaction are precisely those found at this stage of history—ones whose self-conception is that of civilized, law-abiding actors who believe that all individuals and groups should be recognized. More than most, such actors would be susceptible to the "civilizing force of hypocrisy", and so find it hard in the long run to justify not constitutionalizing their recognition of outsiders.

However, while removing constraints on world state formation, these first two considerations are still in a sense negative, since they amount to reasons not to resist the attraction of a world state, not to embrace it. A third factor is therefore crucial—the struggle for recognition itself. Recognition that is not enforceable is in the end not really recognition at all, since it depends on the goodwill and choice of the recognizer. Genuine recognition means that the recognized has a right to recognition, and the Self therefore has a duty to the Other. Genuine recognition is about obligation, not charity. Only when acting on behalf of the Other has become an enforceable obligation is recognition secure.

Stage Five: The World State

This brings us to the world state. With the transfer of state sovereignty to the global level individual recognition will no longer be mediated by state boundaries, even though as recognized subjects themselves states would retain some individuality (particularism within universalism). Individuals and states alike will have lost the negative freedom to engage in unilateral violence, but gained the positive freedom of fully recognized subjectivity. The system will have become itself an "individual".

The question remains, however, whether a world state would be a stable end-state, or be itself subject to instabilities that ultimately undo it. In other words, even if we assume that the logic of anarchy is teleological, how do we know that it involves a fixed-point attractor rather than, for example, a periodic attractor that would induce cycles of anarchy and world states?

A partial answer is that a world state would have the capability to prevent secession, giving it a stronger homeostatic logic than any culture of anarchy. However, coercion alone does not seem enough, since individuals and groups will continue to evolve, and might decide that what satisfied their desires for recognition in the past no longer does so. Efforts to crush such aspirations by force have not prevented some existing states from breaking up, and imposing recognition by force is in any case at odds with the basic principle that recognition that is not freely given is not really "recognition" at all. At most, therefore, the ability to prevent secession would ensure temporary security, not recognition.

In thinking about whether the logic of anarchy has a fixed-point attractor, it is important to emphasize this need not imply that a world state must survive for ever. Equilibria are always vulnerable to exogenous shocks. Since even a world state would remain an at least partially open system, such shocks could cause it to fall apart. Instead, for the logic of anarchy to have an end-state other than a fixed-point attractor, there must be something internal to the system itself that would necessarily induce an eventual collapse, sending it along another developmental path. Addressing this question permits consideration of three objections to my argument, each of which highlights a potential endogenous source of instability in a world state.

The first is Kant's worry about despotism. Could a world state be despotic? If a world state met only the thin Weberian criterion of a legitimate monopoly of force, then in principle it could be despotic, an "empire." But in that case it would not be a stable end-state, since it would not satisfy the thicker Hegelian criterion of mutual recognition of equality. In such a state the struggle for recognition would go on. Since my argument is that we will get a Weberian world state by creating a Hegelian one, the real question is whether the latter could be despotic, which seems unlikely. The most obvious threat is a "democratic deficit". The sheer scale of a world state and the corresponding dilution of voice for its members would create a huge distance between them and the state. Although today's worries about the democratic deficit stem primarily from the absence of virtually any formal means by which transnational power structures can be held accountable, they are already a source of resistance to political integration and might intensify as the latter deepens.

On the other hand, large democracies today already face this problem, yet are not for that reason considered unstable. Modern communications technology and institutional compromises like representative democracy and subsidiarity can mitigate democratic worries to a substantial degree. But the real lesson of modern states is that democracy is not the only basis of political legitimacy. The enforcement of mutual recognition of equality, economic well-being and efficiency may be equally important, and could be even more so in a world state. Moreover, consider the alternative to a world state, an anarchic world in which territorial states retain their sovereignty. It is of the essence of sovereignty that power and violence can be exercised against non-members without any accountability. Is not *that* "despotism"? Whether justified or not, to whom is the United States accountable for its recent killing of thousands of civilians in Kosovo, Afghanistan and Iraq? Whatever the accountability problems in a world state might be, they seem far less than those in anarchy.

A second potential threat is nationalism, which in the last century has substantially increased the number of states in the system through decolonization, thus at least temporarily reversing the historical pattern of global political consolidation. However, the rise of nationalism can actually be seen as evidence for my argument, because it is about the struggle for recognition. In 1945 a majority of the world's population lived in empires that did not recognize them as full subjects. As a result they struggled for self-determination and eventually won it. In that sense nationalism has made it possible for previously unrecognized actors to participate in the system, and even contemplate binding themselves to supranational institutions. Any such constraints they accept will be consensual and correspondingly stable. Nationalist struggles for recognition are not over, and more new states—"more anarchy"—may be created. But while further fragmentation is in one sense a step back, it is also a precondition for moving forward, since it is only when difference is recognized that a larger identity can be stable. "The greater the diversity between individuals or particulars, the higher the identity or universal in which the differences meet." Far from suppressing nationalism, a world state will only be possible if it embraces it.

A last potential source of instability in a world state involves what might seem like a contradiction at the heart of my analysis. On the one hand, like today's states I am arguing that a world state would be a subject—a corporate persons or Self. On the other hand, my explanation for the inevitability of a world state assumes that a stable Self depends on mutual recognition of equality with an Other. By assimilating all subjects into one collective identity, a world state would seem to lack such an Other and thus be unstable.

Do politics and history come to an end? If by "politics" and "history" we mean what they do in anarchy, namely struggles for recognition mediated by war, then yes, in one sense they would be over. I say "in one sense" because a world state would still need to reproduce itself and thus be for ever in process, and since even a world state would not be a closed system it will always be vulnerable to temporary disruptions. However, a world state would differ from anarchy in that it would constitute such disruptions as crime, not as politics or history. The possibility of crime may always be with us, but it does not constitute a stable alternative to a world state. Moreover, politics or history in a different, non-anarchic sense would clearly not be over. A world state would not be a utopia in which there was nothing left to struggle over. Think of what goes on inside states today. They are full of problems—crime, poverty, pollution—which are the stuff of politics. Indeed, even struggles for recognition, in the thick sense, would continue. There are always new ways to constitute thick recognition, and in that sense the struggle for it is part of the human condition. But once a world state has emerged those struggles will be domesticated by enforceable law, and so for purposes of state formation will be no longer important. Rather than a complete end of history, therefore, it might be better to say that a world state would be the end of just one kind of history. Even if one telos is over, another would be just beginning.

CONCLUSION

Against the perpetual war of Realism and the contingent perpetual peace of modern liberalism, I have argued that a world state is inevitable. Its cause is the teleological logic of anarchy, which channels struggles for recognition toward an end-state that transcends that logic. As such, the argument reverses social scientists' traditional "rearview mirror" perspective on time and causation, since it suggests that "the ultimate organizing principle [of the system] is in the outcome of the process and not its genetic origin." One might even say that the logic at work here is that of recognition, not anarchy, since only a world state can realize or complete the mutual recognition of sovereignty first laid down in the society of states.

It is natural at this point to ask whether a world state would be desirable. Although this question is not directly relevant to my argument and cannot be addressed here, on my view the answer is clearly yes. Other things being equal, it seems hard to argue that a world in which recognition is unequal and the right to engage in organized violence is privatized would be normatively superior to one in which recognition is equal and violence is collectivized. That does not mean that a world state would satisfy all the demands of justice, but it would be a minimum condition for a just world order.

I have argued that a world state will emerge whether or not anyone intends to bring it about. Since this might be criticized for leaving out human agency, by way of conclusion I want to show that this is not the case, at either the micro- or macro-level.

At the micro-level agency matters just as much here as it does in non-teleological theories. Struggles for recognition are intentional, and there is nothing in the logic of anarchy that forces them to go in one direction or another at any given moment. Anarchy is (still) what states (and other actors) make of it, and so they are still responsible for the quality of life in world politics. Moreover, in addition to the intentionality of actors struggling for their own recognition, there is also the possibility for a more globally oriented intentionality in the form of actors who believe in the inevitability of a world state, and try to speed it up. To be sure, this kind of agency is a double-edged sword. On the one hand, belief in an inevitable world state would give people reasons to intentionally redefine their interests in terms consistent with it, thereby facilitating the process. On the other hand, such a belief could also be used to justify forcing history along, and even for war against those who refuse to see the light. Some of the worst historical excesses of human agency—Nazism, Bolshevism, and so on—have been committed in the name of just such a teleological faith. But such is the human condition—the fact that the pathway to a world state is open to such possibilities is an argument for more "good" agency, not less.

Moreover, my argument has an interesting policy implication for grand strategy. Grand strategies should be based on a correct theory of where the world system is going. If Realists are right that anarchy is programmed for war, then it makes sense to define one's sovereignty and interests in egoistic terms and act on that basis. International law is irrelevant or an impediment to the national interest, and one should pursue a unilateralist policy whenever possible. On the other hand, if a world state is inevitable (and, importantly, not so far off to be meaningless for policy), then a different grand strategy emerges. Rather than go down with the ship of national sovereignty, states should try to "get the best deal" they can in the emerging global constitution, which counsels acceptance of international law and participation in multilateral institutions. Ironically, if a world state is inevitable, states that pursue such policies will do better for themselves in the long run than those that take a Realist view. In short, better to "get with the program" than wait till it gets to you.

Finally, there is an intriguing but more controversial possibility for agency at the macro-level, in the form of the world system being an agent in its own development. I have not argued that here, limiting my treatment of the macro-level process to its non-intentional aspect. Yet, like states today, a completed world state would be an intentional actor. Such an actor could not intend its own creation (that would be backward causation), but it seems counter-intuitive to think that prior to its emergence there would be no intentionality at all at the system level, until it suddenly appears fully formed in a world state. Instead, it seems more plausible to suggest that the process of world state formation involves a progressive "amplification" of intentionality from individuals and groups to the global level. Early on the degree of systemic intentionality is quite low, but as the system matures it acquires more and more, enabling it increasingly to participate as an agent in its own development. While necessarily imposing boundaries on the agency of its members, it only in this way that they can fully realize their own subjectivity.

The Illusion of Geopolitics: The Enduring Power of the Liberal Order

G. JOHN IKENBERRY

Walter Russell Mead paints a disturbing portrait of the United States' geopolitical predicament. As he sees it, an increasingly formidable coalition of illiberal powers—China, Iran, and Russia—is determined to undo the post–Cold War settlement and the U.S.-led global order that stands behind it. Across Eurasia, he argues, these aggrieved states are bent on building spheres of influence to threaten the foundations of U.S. leadership and the global order. So the United States must rethink its optimism, including its post–Cold War belief that rising non-Western states can be persuaded to join the West and play by its rules. For Mead, the time has come to confront the threats from these increasingly dangerous geopolitical foes.

But Mead's alarmism is based on a colossal misreading of modern power realities. It is a misreading of the logic and character of the existing world order, which is more stable and expansive than Mead depicts, leading him to overestimate the ability of the "axis of weevils" to undermine it.

And it is a misreading of China and Russia, which are not full-scale revisionist powers but part-time spoilers at best, as suspicious of each other as they are of the outside world. True, they look for opportunities to resist the United States' global leadership, and recently, as in the past, they have pushed back against it, particularly when confronted in their own neighborhoods. But even these conflicts are fueled more by weakness—their leaders' and regimes'—than by strength. They have no appealing brand. And when it comes to their overriding interests, Russia and, especially, China are deeply integrated into the world economy and its governing institutions.

Mead also mischaracterizes the thrust of U.S. foreign policy. Since the end of the Cold War, he argues, the United States has ignored geopolitical issues involving territory and spheres of influence and instead adopted a Pollyannaish emphasis on building the global order. But this is a false dichotomy. The United States does not focus on issues of global order, such as arms control and trade, because it assumes that geopolitical conflict is gone forever; it undertakes such efforts precisely because it wants to manage great-power competition. Order building is not premised on the end of geopolitics; it is about how to answer the big questions of geopolitics.

Indeed, the construction of a U.S.-led global order did not begin with the end of the Cold War; it won the Cold War. In the nearly 70 years since World War II, Washington has undertaken sustained efforts to build a far-flung system of multilateral institutions, alliances, trade agreements, and political partnerships. This project has helped draw countries into the United States' orbit. It has helped strengthen global norms and rules that undercut the legitimacy of nineteenth-century-style spheres of influence, bids for regional domination, and territorial grabs. And it has given the United States the capacities, partnerships, and principles to confront today's great-power spoilers and revisionists, such as they are. Alliances, partnerships, multilateralism, democracy—these are the tools of U.S. leadership, and they are winning, not losing, the twenty-first-century struggles over geopolitics and the world order.

THE GENTLE GIANT

In 1904, the English geographer Halford Mackinder wrote that the great power that controlled the heartland of Eurasia would command "the World-Island" and thus the world itself. For Mead, Eurasia has returned as the great prize of geopolitics. Across the far reaches of this supercontinent, he argues, China, Iran, and Russia are seeking to establish their spheres of influence and challenge U.S. interests, slowly but relentlessly attempting to dominate Eurasia and thereby threaten the United States and the rest of the world.

This vision misses a deeper reality. In matters of geopolitics (not to mention demographics, politics, and ideas), the United States has a decisive advantage over China, Iran, and Russia. Although the United States will no doubt come down from the peak of hegemony that it occupied during the unipolar era, its power is still unrivaled. Its wealth and technological advantages remain far out of the reach of China and Russia, to say nothing of Iran. Its recovering economy, now bolstered by massive new natural gas resources, allows it to maintain a global military presence and credible security commitments.

Indeed, Washington enjoys a unique ability to win friends and influence states. According to a study led by the political scientist Brett Ashley Leeds, the United States boasts military partnerships with more than 60 countries, whereas Russia counts eight formal allies and China has just one (North Korea). As one British diplomat told me several years ago, "China doesn't seem to do alliances." But the United States does, and they pay a double dividend: not only do alliances provide a global platform for the projection of U.S. power, but they also distribute the burden of providing security. The military capabilities aggregated in this U.S.-led alliance system outweigh anything China or Russia might generate for decades to come.

Then there are the nuclear weapons. These arms, which the United States, China, and Russia all possess (and Iran is seeking), help the United States in two ways. First, thanks to the logic of mutual assured destruction, they radically reduce the likelihood of great-power war. Such upheavals have provided opportunities for past great powers, including the United States in World War II, to entrench their own international orders. The atomic age has robbed China and Russia of this opportunity. Second, nuclear weapons also make China and Russia more secure, giving them assurance that the United States will never invade. That's a good thing, because it reduces the likelihood that they will resort to desperate moves, born of insecurity, that risk war and undermine the liberal order.

Geography reinforces the United States' other advantages. As the only great power not surrounded by other great powers, the country has appeared less threatening to other states and was able to rise dramatically over the course of the last century without triggering a war. After the Cold War, when the United States was the world's sole superpower, other global powers, oceans away, did not even attempt to balance against it. In fact, the United States' geographic position has led other countries to worry more about abandonment than domination. Allies in Europe, Asia, and the Middle East have sought to draw the United States into playing a greater role in their regions. The result is what the historian Geir Lundestad has called an "empire by invitation."

The United States' geographic advantage is on full display in Asia. Most countries there see China as a greater potential danger—due to its proximity, if nothing else—than the United States. Except for the United States, every major power in the world lives in a crowded geopolitical neighborhood where shifts in power routinely provoke counterbalancing—including by one another. China is discovering this dynamic today as surrounding states react to its rise by modernizing their militaries and reinforcing their alliances. Russia has known it for decades, and has faced it most recently in Ukraine, which in recent years has increased its military spending and sought closer ties to the EU.

Geographic isolation has also given the United States reason to champion universal principles that allow it to access various regions of the world. The country has long promoted the open-door policy and the principle of self-determination and opposed colonialism—less out of a sense of idealism than due to the practical realities of keeping Europe, Asia, and the Middle East open for trade and diplomacy. In the late 1930s, the main question facing the United States was how large a geopolitical space, or "grand area," it would need to exist as a great power in a world of empires, regional blocs, and spheres of influence. World War II made the answer clear: the country's prosperity and security depended on access to every region. And in the ensuing decades, with some important and damaging exceptions, such as Vietnam, the United States has embraced postimperial principles.

It was during these postwar years that geopolitics and order building converged. A liberal international framework was the answer that statesmen such as Dean Acheson, George Kennan, and George Marshall offered to the challenge of Soviet expansionism. The system they built strengthened and enriched the United States and its allies, to the detriment of its illiberal opponents. It also stabilized the world economy and established mechanisms for tackling global problems. The end of the Cold War has not changed the logic behind this project.

Fortunately, the liberal principles that Washington has pushed enjoy near-universal appeal, because they have tended to be a good fit with the modernizing forces of economic growth and social advancement. As the historian Charles Maier has put it, the United States surfed the wave of twentieth-century modernization. But some have argued that this congruence between the American project and the forces of modernity has weakened in recent years. The 2008 financial crisis, the thinking goes, marked a world-historical turning point, at which the United States lost its vanguard role in facilitating economic advancement.

Yet even if that were true, it hardly follows that China and Russia have replaced the United States as the standard-bearers of the global economy. Even Mead does not argue that China, Iran, or Russia offers the world a new model of modernity. If these illiberal powers really do threaten Washington and the rest of the liberal capitalist world, then they will need to find and ride the next great wave of modernization. They are unlikely to do that.

THE RISE OF DEMOCRACY

Mead's vision of a contest over Eurasia between the United States and China, Iran, and Russia misses the more profound power transition under way: the increasing ascendancy of liberal capitalist democracy. To be sure, many liberal democracies are struggling at the moment with slow economic growth, social inequality, and political instability. But the spread of liberal democracy throughout the world, beginning in the late 1970s and accelerating after the Cold War, has dramatically strengthened the United States' position and tightened the geopolitical circle around China and Russia.

It's easy to forget how rare liberal democracy once was. Until the twentieth century, it was confined to the West and parts of Latin America. After World War II, however, it began to reach beyond those realms, as newly independent states established self-rule. During the 1950s, 1960s, and early 1970s, military coups and new dictators put the brakes on democratic transitions. But in the late 1970s, what the political scientist Samuel Huntington termed "the third wave" of democratization washed over southern Europe, Latin America, and East Asia. Then the Cold War ended, and a cohort of former communist states in eastern Europe were brought into the democratic fold. By the late 1990s, 60 percent of all countries had become democracies.

Although some backsliding has occurred, the more significant trend has been the emergence of a group of democratic middle powers, including Australia, Brazil, India, Indonesia, Mexico, South Korea, and Turkey. These rising democracies are acting as stakeholders in the international system: pushing for multilateral cooperation, seeking greater rights and responsibilities, and exercising influence through peaceful means.

Such countries lend the liberal world order new geopolitical heft. As the political scientist Larry Diamond has noted, if Argentina, Brazil, India, Indonesia, South Africa, and Turkey regain their economic footing and strengthen their democratic rule, the G-20, which also includes the United States and European countries, "will have become a strong 'club of democracies,' with only Russia, China, and Saudi Arabia holding out." The rise of a global middle class of democratic states has turned China and Russia into outliers—not, as Mead fears, legitimate contestants for global leadership.

In fact, the democratic upsurge has been deeply problematic for both countries. In eastern Europe, former Soviet states and satellites have gone democratic and joined the West. As worrisome as Russian President Vladimir Putin's moves in Crimea have been, they reflect Russia's geopolitical vulnerability, not its strength. Over the last two decades, the West has crept closer to Russia's borders. In 1999, the Czech Republic, Hungary, and Poland entered NATO. They were joined in 2004 by seven more former members of the Soviet bloc, and in 2009, by Albania and Croatia. In the meantime, six former Soviet republics have headed down the path to membership by joining NATO's Partnership for Peace program. Mead makes much of Putin's achievements in Georgia, Armenia, and Crimea. Yet even though Putin is winning some small battles, he is losing the war. Russia is not on the rise; to the contrary, it is experiencing one of the greatest geopolitical contractions of any major power in the modern era.

Democracy is encircling China, too. In the mid-1980s, India and Japan were the only Asian democracies, but since then, Indonesia, Mongolia, the Philippines, South Korea, Taiwan, and Thailand have joined the club. Myanmar (also called Burma) has made cautious steps toward multiparty rule—steps that have come, as China has not failed to notice, in conjunction with warming relations with the United States. China now lives in a decidedly democratic neighborhood.

These political transformations have put China and Russia on the defensive. Consider the recent developments in Ukraine. The economic and political currents in most of the country are inexorably flowing westward, a trend that terrifies Putin. His only recourse has been to strong-arm Ukraine into resisting the EU and remaining in Russia's orbit. Although he may be able to keep Crimea under Russian control, his grip on the rest of the country is slipping. As the EU diplomat Robert Cooper has noted, Putin can try to delay the moment when Ukraine "affiliates with the EU, but he can't stop it." Indeed, Putin might not even be able to accomplish that, since his provocative moves may serve only to speed Ukraine's move toward Europe.

China faces a similar predicament in Taiwan. Chinese leaders sincerely believe that Taiwan is part of China, but the Taiwanese do not. The democratic transition on the island has made its inhabitants' claims to nationhood more deeply felt and legitimate. A 2011 survey found that if the Taiwanese could be assured that China would not attack Taiwan, 80 percent of them would support declaring independence. Like Russia, China wants geopolitical control over its neighborhood. But the spread of democracy to all corners of Asia has made old-fashioned domination the only way to achieve that, and that option is costly and self-defeating.

While the rise of democratic states makes life more difficult for China and Russia, it makes the world safer for the United States. Those two powers may count as U.S. rivals, but the rivalry takes place on a very uneven playing field: the United States has the most friends, and the most capable ones, too. Washington and its allies account for 75 percent of global military spending. Democratization has put China and Russia in a geopolitical box.

Iran is not surrounded by democracies, but it is threatened by a restive pro-democracy movement at home. More important, Iran is the weakest member of Mead's axis, with a much smaller economy and military than the United States and the other great powers. It is also the target of the strongest international sanctions regime ever assembled, with help from China and Russia. The Obama administration's diplomacy with Iran may or may not succeed, but it is not clear what Mead would do differently to prevent the country from acquiring nuclear weapons. U.S. President Barack Obama's approach has the virtue of offering Tehran a path by which it can move from being a hostile regional power to becoming a more constructive, nonnuclear member of the international community—a potential geopolitical game changer that Mead fails to appreciate.

REVISIONISM REVISITED

Not only does Mead underestimate the strength of the United States and the order it built; he also overstates the degree to which China and Russia are seeking to resist both. (Apart from its nuclear ambitions, Iran looks like a state engaged more in futile protest than actual resistance, so it shouldn't be considered anything close to a revisionist power.) Without a doubt, China and Russia desire greater regional influence. China has made aggressive claims over maritime rights and nearby contested islands, and it has embarked on an arms buildup. Putin has visions of reclaiming Russia's dominance in its "near abroad." Both great powers bristle at U.S. leadership and resist it when they can.

But China and Russia are not true revisionists. As former Israeli Foreign Minister Shlomo Ben-Ami has said, Putin's foreign policy is "more a reflection of his resentment of Russia's geopolitical marginalization than a battle cry from a rising empire." China, of course, is an actual rising power, and this does invite dangerous competition with U.S. allies in Asia. But China is not currently trying to break those alliances or overthrow the wider system of regional security governance embodied in the Association of Southeast Asian Nations and the East Asia Summit. And even if China harbors ambitions of eventually doing so, U.S. security partnerships in the region are, if anything, getting stronger, not weaker. At most, China and Russia are spoilers. They do not have the interests—let alone the ideas, capacities, or allies—to lead them to upend existing global rules and institutions.

In fact, although they resent that the United States stands at the top of the current geopolitical system, they embrace the underlying logic of that framework, and with good reason. Openness gives them access to trade, investment, and technology from other societies. Rules give them tools to protect their sovereignty and interests. Despite controversies over the new idea of "the responsibility to protect" (which has been applied only selectively), the current world order enshrines the age-old norms of state sovereignty and nonintervention. Those Westphalian principles remain the bedrock of world politics—and China and Russia have tied their national interests to them (despite Putin's disturbing irredentism).

It should come as no surprise, then, that China and Russia have become deeply integrated into the existing international order. They are both permanent members of the UN Security Council, with veto rights, and they both participate actively in the World Trade Organization, the International Monetary Fund, the World Bank, and the G-20. They are geopolitical insiders, sitting at all the high tables of global governance.

China, despite its rapid ascent, has no ambitious global agenda; it remains fixated inward, on preserving party rule. Some Chinese intellectuals and political figures, such as Yan Xuetong and Zhu Chenghu, do have a wish list of revisionist goals. They see the Western system as a threat and are waiting for the day when China can reorganize the international order. But these voices do not reach very far into the political elite. Indeed, Chinese leaders have moved away from their earlier calls for sweeping change. In 2007, at its Central Committee meeting, the Chinese Communist Party replaced previous proposals for a "new international economic order" with calls for more modest reforms centering on fairness and justice. The Chinese scholar Wang Jisi has argued that this move is "subtle but important," shifting China's orientation toward that of a global reformer. China now wants a larger role in the International Monetary Fund and the World Bank, greater voice in such forums as the G-20, and wider global use of its currency. That is not the agenda of a country trying to revise the economic order.

China and Russia are also members in good standing of the nuclear club. The centerpiece of the Cold War settlement between the United States and the Soviet Union (and then Russia) was a shared effort to limit atomic weapons. Although U.S.-Russian relations have since soured, the nuclear component of their arrangement has held. In 2010, Moscow and Washington signed the New START treaty, which requires mutual reductions in long-range nuclear weapons.

Before the 1990s, China was a nuclear outsider. Although it had a modest arsenal, it saw itself as a voice of the nonnuclear developing world and criticized arms control agreements and test bans. But in a remarkable shift, China has since come to support the array of nuclear accords, including the Nuclear Nonproliferation Treaty and the Comprehensive Nuclear Test Ban Treaty. It has affirmed a "no first use" doctrine, kept its arsenal small, and taken its entire nuclear force off alert. China has also played an active role in the Nuclear Security Summit, an initiative proposed by Obama in 2009, and it has joined the "P5 process," a collaborate effort to safeguard nuclear weapons.

Across a wide range of issues, China and Russia are acting more like established great powers than revisionist ones. They often choose to shun multilateralism, but so, too, on occasion do the United States and other powerful democracies. (Beijing has ratified the UN Convention on the Law of the Sea; Washington has not.) And China and Russia are using global rules and institutions to advance their own interests. Their struggles with the United States revolve around gaining voice within the existing order and manipulating it to suit their needs. They wish to enhance their positions within the system, but they are not trying to replace it.

HERE TO STAY

Ultimately, even if China and Russia do attempt to contest the basic terms of the current global order, the adventure will be daunting and self-defeating. These powers aren't just up against the United States; they would also have to contend with the most globally organized and deeply entrenched order the world has ever seen, one that is dominated by states that are liberal, capitalist, and democratic. This order is backed by a U.S.-led network of alliances, institutions, geopolitical bargains, client states, and democratic partnerships. It has proved dynamic and expansive, easily integrating rising states, beginning with Japan and Germany after World War II. It has shown a capacity for shared leadership, as exemplified by such forums as the G-8 and the G-20. It has allowed rising non-Western countries to trade and grow, sharing the dividends of modernization. It has accommodated a surprisingly wide variety of political and economic models—social democratic (western Europe), neoliberal (the United Kingdom and the United States), and state capitalist (East Asia). The prosperity of nearly every country—and the stability of its government—fundamentally depends on this order.

In the age of liberal order, revisionist struggles are a fool's errand. Indeed, China and Russia know this. They do not have grand visions of an alternative order. For them, international relations are mainly about the search for commerce and resources, the protection of their sovereignty, and, where possible, regional domination. They have shown no interest in building their own orders or even taking full responsibility for the current one and have offered no alternative visions of global economic or political progress. That's a critical shortcoming, since international orders rise and fall not simply with the power of the leading state; their success also hinges on whether they are seen as legitimate and whether their actual operation solves problems that both weak and powerful states care about. In the struggle for world order, China and Russia (and certainly Iran) are simply not in the game.

Under these circumstances, the United States should not give up its efforts to strengthen the liberal order. The world that Washington inhabits today is one it should welcome. And the grand strategy it should pursue is the one it has followed for decades: deep global engagement. It is a strategy in which the United States ties itself to the regions of the world through trade, alliances, multilateral institutions, and diplomacy. It is a strategy in which the United States establishes leadership not simply through the exercise of power but also through sustained efforts at global problem solving and rule making. It created a world that is friendly to American interests, and it is made friendly because, as President John F. Kennedy once said, it is a world "where the weak are safe and the strong are just."

The New Population Bomb: The Four Megatrends That Will Change the World

JACK A. GOLDSTONE

Forty-two years ago, the biologist Paul Ehrlich warned in *The Population Bomb* that mass starvation would strike in the 1970s and 1980s, with the world's population growth outpacing the production of food and other critical resources. Thanks to innovations and efforts such as the "green revolution" in farming and the widespread adoption of family planning, Ehrlich's worst fears did not come to pass. In fact, since the 1970s, global economic output has increased and fertility has fallen dramatically, especially in developing countries.

The United Nations Population Division now projects that global population growth will nearly halt by 2050. By that date, the world's population will have stabilized at 9.15 billion people, according to the "medium growth" variant of the UN's authoritative population database World Population Prospects: The 2008 Revision. (Today's global population is 6.83 billion.) Barring a cataclysmic climate crisis or a complete failure to recover from the current economic malaise, global economic output is expected to increase by two to three percent per year, meaning that global income will increase far more than population over the next four decades.

But twenty-first-century international security will depend less on how many people inhabit the world than on how the global population is composed and distributed: where populations are declining and where they are growing, which countries are relatively older and which are more youthful, and how demographics will influence population movements across regions.

These elements are not well recognized or widely understood. A recent article in *The Economist*, for example, cheered the decline in global fertility without noting other vital demographic developments. Indeed, the same UN data cited by *The Economist* reveal four historic shifts that will fundamentally alter the world's population over the next four decades: the relative demographic weight of the world's developed countries will drop by nearly 25 percent, shifting economic power to the developing nations; the developed countries' labor forces will substantially age and decline, constraining economic growth in the developed world and raising the demand for immigrant workers; most of the world's expected population growth will increasingly be concentrated in today's poorest, youngest, and most heavily Muslim countries, which have a dangerous lack of quality education, capital, and employment opportunities; and, for the first time in history, most of the world's population will become urbanized, with the largest urban centers being in the world's poorest countries, where policing, sanitation, and health care are often scarce.

Taken together, these trends will pose challenges every bit as alarming as those noted by Ehrlich. Coping with them will require nothing less than a major reconsideration of the world's basic global governance structures.

EUROPE'S REVERSAL OF FORTUNES

At the beginning of the eighteenth century, approximately 20 percent of the world's inhabitants lived in Europe (including Russia). Then, with the Industrial Revolution, Europe's population boomed, and streams of European emigrants set off for the Americas. By the eve of World War I, Europe's population had more than quadrupled. In 1913, Europe had more people than China, and the proportion of the world's population living in Europe and the former European colonies of North America had risen to over 33 percent.

But this trend reversed after World War I, as basic health care and sanitation began to spread to poorer countries. In Asia, Africa, and Latin America, people began to live longer, and birthrates remained high or fell only slowly. By 2003, the combined populations of Europe, the United States, and Canada accounted for just 17 percent of the global population. In 2050, this figure is expected to be just 12 percent—far less than it was in 1700. (These projections, moreover, might even understate the reality because they reflect the "medium growth" projection of the UN forecasts, which assumes that the fertility rates of developing countries will decline while those of developed countries will increase. In fact, many developed countries show no evidence of increasing fertility rates.)

The West's relative decline is even more dramatic if one also considers changes in income. The Industrial Revolution made Europeans not only more numerous than they had been but also considerably richer per capita than others worldwide. According to the economic historian Angus Maddison, Europe, the United States, and Canada together produced about 32 percent of the world's GDP at the beginning of the nineteenth century. By 1950, that proportion had increased to a remarkable 68 percent of the world's total output (adjusted to reflect purchasing power parity).

This trend, too, is headed for a sharp reversal. The proportion of global GDP produced by Europe, the United States, and Canada fell from 68 percent in 1950 to 47 percent in 2003 and will decline even more steeply in the future. If the growth rate of per capita income (again, adjusted for purchasing power parity) between 2003 and 2050 remains as it was between 1973 and 2003—averaging 1.68 percent annually in Europe, the United States, and Canada and 2.47 percent annually in the rest of the world—then the combined GDP of Europe, the United States, and Canada will roughly double by 2050, whereas the GDP of the rest of the world will grow by a factor of five. The portion of global GDP produced by Europe, the United States, and Canada in 2050 will then be less than 30 percent—smaller than it was in 1820.

These figures also imply that an overwhelming proportion of the world's GDP growth between 2003 and 2050—nearly 80 percent—will occur outside of Europe, the United States, and Canada. By the middle of this century, the global middle class—those capable of purchasing durable consumer products, such as cars, appliances, and electronics—will increasingly be found in what is now considered the developing world. The World Bank has predicted that by 2030 the number of middle-class people in the developing world will be 1.2 billion—a rise of 200 percent since 2005. This means that the developing world's middle class alone will be larger than the total populations of Europe, Japan, and the United States combined. From now on, therefore, the main driver of global economic expansion will be the economic growth of newly industrialized countries, such as Brazil, China, India, Indonesia, Mexico, and Turkey.

AGING PAINS

Part of the reason developed countries will be less economically dynamic in the coming decades is that their populations will become substantially older. The European countries, Canada, the United States, Japan, South Korea, and even China are aging at unprecedented rates. Today, the proportion of people aged 60 or older in China and South Korea is 12–15 percent. It is 15–22 percent in the European Union, Canada, and the United States and 30 percent in Japan. With baby boomers aging and life expectancy increasing, these numbers will increase dramatically. In 2050, approximately 30 percent of Americans, Canadians, Chinese, and Europeans will be over 60, as will more than 40 percent of Japanese and South Koreans.

Over the next decades, therefore, these countries will have increasingly large proportions of retirees and increasingly small proportions of workers. As workers born during the baby boom of 1945–65 are retiring, they are not being replaced by a new cohort of citizens of prime working age (15–59 years old). Industrialized countries are experiencing a drop in their working-age populations that is even more severe than the overall slowdown in their population growth. South Korea represents the most extreme example. Even as its total population is projected to decline by almost 9 percent by 2050 (from 48.3 million to 44.1 million), the population of working-age South Koreans is expected to drop by 36 percent (from 32.9 million to 21.1 million), and the number of South Koreans aged 60 and older will increase by almost 150 percent (from 7.3 million to 18 million). By 2050, in other words, the entire working-age population will barely exceed the 60-and-older population. Although South Korea's case is extreme, it represents an increasingly common fate for developed countries. Europe is expected to lose 24 percent of its prime working-age population (about 120 million workers) by 2050, and its 60-and-older population is expected to increase by 47 percent. In the United States, where higher fertility and more immigration are expected than in Europe, the working-age population will grow by 15 percent over the next four decades—a steep decline from its growth of 62 percent between 1950 and 2010. And by 2050, the United States' 60-and-older population is expected to double.

All this will have a dramatic impact on economic growth, health care, and military strength in the developed world. The forces that fueled economic growth in industrialized countries during the second half of the twentieth century—increased productivity due to better education, the movement of women into the labor force, and innovations in technology—will all likely weaken in the coming decades. College enrollment boomed after World War II, a trend that is not likely to recur in the twenty-first century; the extensive movement of women into the labor force also was a one-time social change; and the technological change of the time resulted from innovators who created new products and leading-edge consumers who were willing to try them out—two groups that are thinning out as the industrialized world's population ages.

Overall economic growth will also be hampered by a decline in the number of new consumers and new households. When developed countries' labor forces were growing by 0.5–1.0 percent per year, as they did until 2005, even annual increases in real output per worker of just 1.7 percent meant that annual economic growth totaled 2.2–2.7 percent per year. But with the labor forces of many developed countries (such as Germany, Hungary, Japan, Russia, and the Baltic states) now shrinking by 0.2 percent per year and those of other countries (including Austria, the Czech Republic, Denmark, Greece, and Italy) growing by less than 0.2 percent per year, the same 1.7 percent increase in real output per worker yields only 1.5–1.9 percent annual overall growth. Moreover, developed countries will be lucky to keep productivity growth at even that level; in many developed countries, productivity is more likely to decline as the population ages.

A further strain on industrialized economies will be rising medical costs: as populations age, they will demand more health care for longer periods of time. Public pension schemes for aging populations are already being reformed in various industrialized countries—often prompting heated debate. In theory, at least, pensions might be kept solvent by increasing the retirement age, raising taxes modestly, and phasing out benefits for the wealthy. Regardless, the number of 80- and 90-year-olds—who are unlikely to work and highly likely to require nursing-home and other expensive care—will rise dramatically. And even if 60- and 70-year-olds remain active and employed, they will require procedures and medications—hip replacements, kidney transplants, blood-pressure treatments—to sustain their health in old age.

All this means that just as aging developed countries will have proportionally fewer workers, innovators, and consumerist young households, a large portion of those countries' remaining economic growth will have to be diverted to pay for the medical bills and pensions of their growing elderly populations. Basic services, meanwhile, will be increasingly costly because fewer young workers will be available for strenuous and labor-intensive jobs. Unfortunately, policymakers seldom reckon with these potentially disruptive effects of otherwise welcome developments, such as higher life expectancy.

YOUTH AND ISLAM IN THE DEVELOPING WORLD

Even as the industrialized countries of Europe, North America, and Northeast Asia will experience unprecedented aging this century, fast-growing countries in Africa, Latin America, the Middle East, and Southeast Asia will have exceptionally youthful populations. Today, roughly nine out of ten children under the age of 15 live in developing countries. And these are the countries that will continue to have the world's highest birthrates. Indeed, over 70 percent of the world's population growth between now and 2050 will occur in 24 countries, all of which are classified by the World Bank as low income or lower-middle income, with an average per capita income of under $3,855 in 2008.

Many developing countries have few ways of providing employment to their young, fast-growing populations. Would-be laborers, therefore, will be increasingly attracted to the labor markets of the aging developed countries of Europe, North America, and Northeast Asia. Youthful immigrants from nearby regions with high unemployment—Central America, North Africa, and Southeast Asia, for example—will be drawn to those vital entry-level and manual-labor jobs that sustain advanced economies: janitors, nursing-home aides, bus drivers, plumbers, security guards, farm workers, and the like. Current levels of immigration from developing to developed countries are paltry compared to those that the forces of supply and demand might soon create across the world.

These forces will act strongly on the Muslim world, where many economically weak countries will continue to experience dramatic population growth in the decades ahead. In 1950, Bangladesh, Egypt, Indonesia, Nigeria, Pakistan, and Turkey had a combined population of 242 million. By 2009, those six countries were the world's most populous Muslim-majority countries and had a combined population of 886 million. Their populations are continuing to grow and indeed are expected to increase by 475 million between now and 2050—during which time, by comparison, the six most populous developed countries are projected to gain only 44 million inhabitants. Worldwide, of the 48 fastest-growing countries today—those with annual population growth of two percent or more—28 are majority Muslim or have Muslim minorities of 33 percent or more.

It is therefore imperative to improve relations between Muslim and Western societies. This will be difficult given that many Muslims live in poor communities vulnerable to radical appeals and many see the West as antagonistic and militaristic. In the 2009 Pew Global Attitudes Project survey, for example, whereas 69 percent of those Indonesians and Nigerians surveyed reported viewing the United States favorably, just 18 percent of those polled in Egypt, Jordan, Pakistan, and Turkey (all U.S. allies) did. And in 2006, when the Pew survey last asked detailed questions about Muslim-Western relations, more than half of the respondents in Muslim countries characterized those relations as bad and blamed the West for this state of affairs.

But improving relations is all the more important because of the growing demographic weight of poor Muslim countries and the attendant increase in Muslim immigration, especially to Europe from North Africa and the Middle East. (To be sure, forecasts that Muslims will soon dominate Europe are outlandish: Muslims compose just three to ten percent of the population in the major European countries today, and this proportion will at most double by midcentury.) Strategists worldwide must consider that the world's young are becoming concentrated in those countries least prepared to educate and employ them, including some Muslim states. Any resulting poverty, social tension, or ideological radicalization could have disruptive effects in many corners of the world. But this need not be the case; the healthy immigration of workers to the developed world and the movement of capital to the developing world, among other things, could lead to better results.

URBAN SPRAWL

Exacerbating twenty-first-century risks will be the fact that the world is urbanizing to an unprecedented degree. The year 2010 will likely be the first time in history that a majority of the world's people live in cities rather than in the countryside. Whereas less than 30 percent of the world's population was urban in 1950, according to UN projections, more than 70 percent will be by 2050.

Lower-income countries in Asia and Africa are urbanizing especially rapidly, as agriculture becomes less labor intensive and as employment opportunities shift to the industrial and service sectors. Already, most of the world's urban agglomerations—Mumbai (population 20.1 million), Mexico City (19.5 million), New Delhi (17 million), Shanghai (15.8 million), Calcutta (15.6 million), Karachi (13.1 million), Cairo (12.5 million), Manila (11.7 million), Lagos (10.6 million), Jakarta (9.7 million)—are found in low-income countries. Many of these countries have multiple cities with over one million residents each: Pakistan has eight, Mexico 12, and China more than 100. The UN projects that the urbanized proportion of sub-Saharan Africa will nearly double between 2005 and 2050, from 35 percent (300 million people) to over 67 percent (1 billion). China, which is roughly 40 percent urbanized today, is expected to be 73 percent urbanized by 2050; India, which is less than 30 percent urbanized today, is expected to be 55 percent urbanized by 2050. Overall, the world's urban population is expected to grow by 3 billion people by 2050.

This urbanization may prove destabilizing. Developing countries that urbanize in the twenty-first century will have far lower per capita incomes than did many industrial countries when they first urbanized. The United States, for example, did not reach 65 percent urbanization until 1950, when per capita income was nearly $13,000 (in 2005 dollars). By contrast, Nigeria, Pakistan, and the Philippines, which are approaching similar levels of urbanization, currently have per capita incomes of just $1,800-$4,000 (in 2005 dollars).

According to the research of Richard Cincotta and other political demographers, countries with younger populations are especially prone to civil unrest and are less able to create or sustain democratic institutions. And the more heavily urbanized, the more such countries are likely to experience Dickensian poverty and anarchic violence. In good times, a thriving economy might keep urban residents employed and governments flush with sufficient resources to meet their needs. More often, however, sprawling and impoverished cities are vulnerable to crime lords, gangs, and petty rebellions. Thus, the rapid urbanization of the developing world in the decades ahead might bring, in exaggerated form, problems similar to those that urbanization brought to nineteenth-century Europe. Back then, cyclical employment, inadequate policing, and limited sanitation and education often spawned widespread labor strife, periodic violence, and sometimes—as in the 1820s, the 1830s, and 1848—even revolutions.

International terrorism might also originate in fast-urbanizing developing countries (even more than it already does). With their neighborhood networks, access to the Internet and digital communications technology, and concentration of valuable targets, sprawling cities offer excellent opportunities for recruiting, maintaining, and hiding terrorist networks.

DEFUSING THE BOMB

Averting this century's potential dangers will require sweeping measures. Three major global efforts defused the population bomb of Ehrlich's day: a commitment by governments and nongovernmental organizations to control reproduction rates; agricultural advances, such as the green revolution and the spread of new technology; and a vast increase in international trade, which globalized markets and thus allowed developing countries to export foodstuffs in exchange for seeds, fertilizers, and machinery, which in turn helped them boost production. But today's population bomb is the product less of absolute growth in the world's population than of changes in its age and distribution. Policymakers must therefore adapt today's global governance institutions to the new realities of the aging of the industrialized world, the concentration of the world's economic and population growth in developing countries, and the increase in international immigration.

During the Cold War, Western strategists divided the world into a "First World," of democratic industrialized countries; a "Second World," of communist industrialized countries; and a "Third World," of developing countries. These strategists focused chiefly on deterring or managing conflict between the First and the Second Worlds and on launching proxy wars and diplomatic initiatives to attract Third World countries into the First World's camp.

CREATIVE REFORMS AT HOME

The aging industrialized countries can also take various steps at home to promote stability in light of the coming demographic trends. First, they should encourage families to have more children. France and Sweden have had success providing child care, generous leave time, and financial allowances to families with young children. Yet there is no consensus among policymakers—and certainly not among demographers—about what policies best encourage fertility.

George Friedman's "The Next 100 Years; A Forecast for the 21st Century"

"Europe is extinct." "China cannot survive a billion pissed off peasants." "Turkey is a power."

"The U.S. will dominate the 21st century."

These are a few of the audacious and often controversial predictions of George Friedman, author of *The Next 100 Years, A Forecast for the 21st century,* which has recently been issued in paperback with a new preface.

Friedman, founder and editor of Stratfor, a respected subscription global intelligence service, was recently in Washington DC, and sat down with Joëlle Attinger and Bill Marmon of the European Institute to talk about his book.

Although Friedman concedes that details of his predictions are likely to be off, he thinks he will succeed if he identifies "what will really matter" when looking back at the 21st century.

And what will matter?

First, the U.S. will dominate the century because of its military and economic power and its favorable geography with Atlantic and Pacific coasts. No power will rise to challenge successful U.S. dominance.

Second, the population explosion of the past century will end and populations will begin to shrink, creating profound changes, including the positive importance of attracting immigrants.

Third, advanced countries will develop technologies to deal with shrinking populations, including harnessing solar power and new computer and robotic technologies.

What will NOT matter?

Neither Europe nor China will be major players in the 21st century. Wow. That is a mouthful.

Friedman takes pleasure in building a powerful case against what passes for conventional wisdom.

"Europe has been in decline since 1917 and the destruction of Germany," says Friedman. "It emerged from World War II as an occupied continent that had lost its empire." But since the collapse of the Soviet Union in 1991, "Europe has re-entered history, and started building structures (such as the European Union)." But problems are not solved and "Europe is in reality just staggering into the 21st Century."

"Europe is too busy congratulating itself," says Friedman. He adds, "It is like the U.S. announcing victory in 1810. There is a way to go. Big problems remain."

And Friedman does not think Europe will solve its problems or bridge its internal differences. He discounts the creation of the European Union and the euro zone as no more than a "customs union or trade bloc."

"As long as Europe cannot speak with one voice on foreign policy it is hard to see how it can influence geopolitics," says Friedman. And because European countries have not given up sovereignty and because individual countries have different interests, it seems unlikely to Friedman that integration will coalesce enough to give Europe a meaningful role on the world stage.

And what about the recently adopted Treaty of Lisbon and the appointment of a president and high commissioner for foreign affairs.

"What do they do. What are their powers?" asks Friedman. "These officials could have been given powers, but Europe chose not to do that. The president has no army, no police force. The bureaucracy in Brussels does not have to be obeyed. Europe will say this is a work in process. But I see no process under way."

"As long as the decision to go to war is not in Brussels but rests with nation states, there is no integration," says Friedman. He sees no easy or speedy end to the tension between France and Germany on one hand and other parts of Europe, like the UK, Eastern Europe and the Iberian Peninsula on the other hand.

What he does see is the increasing rise of Eastern Europe in an evolution not unlike the power shift that moved from Spain in the 16th century, to France and England and later to Germany.

"Every couple of centuries there is a changing of the guard in Europe," says Friedman. He sees Poland as the "heart of dynamism" in Europe today.

Another problem with Europe, says Friedman is the "profound divergence" between the elite perception of Europe and the popular (man-on-the-street) perception. A good example of this disconnect, says Friedman, was the strong vote in Switzerland to prohibit the construction of Islamic mosque minarets. The importance of the event, says Friedman, was not that 57 percent of the population voted against minarets, but that the elite was so surprised at the result. "That showed how far out of touch the elite has become." The broad masses in Europe, says Friedman, "are very uneasy about what is happening to Europe."

The recent economic crisis demonstrated many of the weaknesses of Europe, thinks Friedman. The crisis was not tackled in Brussels but in the individual capitals, and Germany and France declined to assist Eastern Europe, which had to depend on the International Monetary Fund (IMF). And problems continue in the weaker economies like Greece, Portugal, Italy and Spain.

"Greece will probably be ok in the end," says Friedman. "But Spain is too big to save."

"Europe is tired, worldly, decadent," says Friedman. "They are exhausted, and they call it a virtue."

Turkey on the other hand is growing and dynamic. But Europe is missing the point and almost surely will not allow Turkey in the EU, says Friedman. "The European image of Turkey is fixed at around 1960 as a vision of impoverished, semi-literates coming to do construction work."

In reality, says Friedman, Turkey has the largest and most competent army in Europe. It has influence in the Baltics, in the Caucasus and in Central Asia. "I know of no European country that is acting as confidently and as unilaterally as Turkey," says Friedman.

"Turkey is not a future power," says Friedman. "Turkey is a power." Accession to the EU—which is unlikely to happen—is important to the secularists in Turkey who want "to nail down secularism." But much of the country, including Prime Minister Tayyip Erdogen, can "take it [the EU] or leave it." Friedman says Turkey was lucky NOT to be in the EU during the financial crisis, since it has recovered much more quickly and robustly than Europe.

Friedman thinks that Russia will present a near term issue as it attempts to regain the sphere of influence of the old Soviet Union. Russia is making progress already in reasserting its sphere of influence in the "Stans," in the Ukraine, in Belarus and even in Georgia.

But, Friedman says, the same forces that destroyed the Soviet Union, including demographic diversity, will rise again and around 2020 the Russian resurgence will fail. "It is hard to see how Russia, which has abandoned its industrial base in favor of exporting commodities, will be able to sustain itself against a dynamic Poland backed up by the U.S."

Perhaps Friedman's most audacious prediction concerns China, which he feels will not become an important player in the 21st century.

"China is an incredibly poor country with a small segment that is essentially an extension of the United States," he says. Friedman notes that one of seven export containers out of China go to Wal-Mart. "This shows the vulnerability of the country," says Friedman. "All of the prosperity of China is built on the willingness of the U.S. and Europe to buy its products."

Friedman does not think that the Chinese "miracle" can be extended to the almost one billion persons still living in poverty. Even moving its manufacturing plants to the interior to address unemployment will be a problem, says Friedman, because that will drive up Chinese costs and the margin on Chinese products is too thin to sustain the increase.

"China is in crisis," he says. "It will take three years before the crisis becomes apparent." He thinks the signs will be an increasingly nationalistic and oppressive society. "If you are a Chinese leader you don't have an economic solution to your problems," says Friedman, "but you do have a political solution."

And what should the U.S. do to ensure the dominance that Friedman predicts for it?

"America is in the position of Great Britain in the 19th century. Its national interests are served by maintaining a policy that balances powers off against each other. U.S. interest is not to have a global peer power. As long as that does not happen, the U.S. can make as many mistakes as it wants. If a global peer power does emerge, the world gets much more dangerous."

BILL MARMON
Is Assistant Managing Editor of European Affairs Magazine.

VISUAL REVIEW

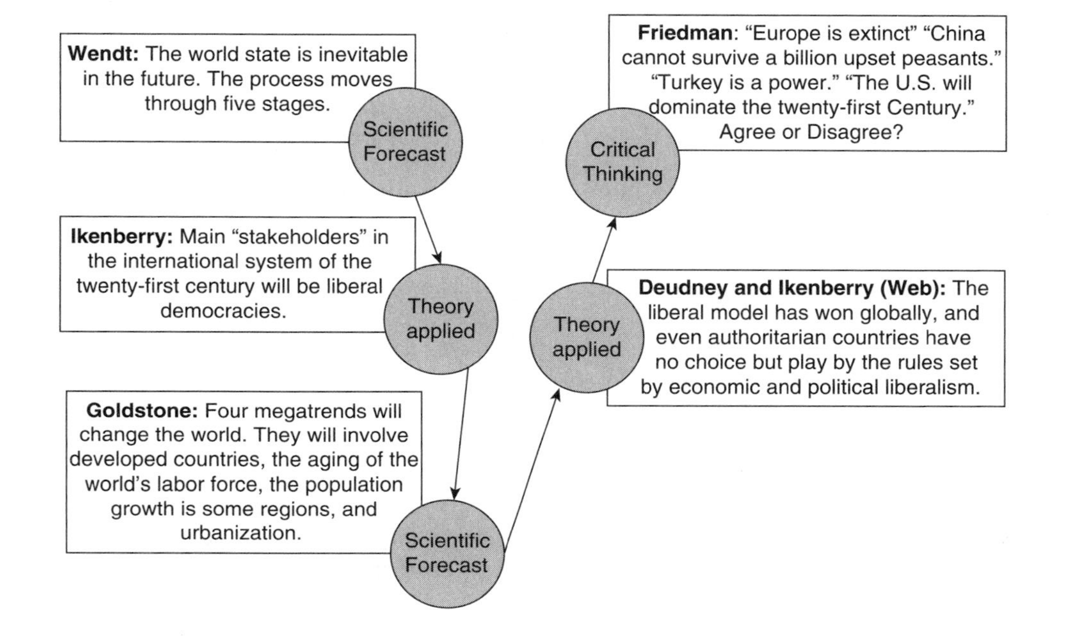

Critical Thinking and Discussion Questions for Part III

SECTION 8

1. Thomas Homer-Dixon wrote more than two decades ago about emerging environmental changes as causes of acute conflict.
- What were they?
- Which of his warnings were correct and which were not?

2. Pick three of Homer-Dixon's warnings and discuss if they are still applicable to today's global environmental situation.
- Which environmental threats described by Homer-Dixon have been addressed, at least to some degree, today?
- Which environmental threats have become worse than those twenty years ago?

3. Ebinger and Zambetakis warn about the Arctic melt and the threats for international relations it may pose in the near future. What specific threats do they envision?
- Imagine you have political power and resources. How would you specifically address these threats to avoid conflict?
- Should an increase in the global use of alternative sources of energy reduce the threats of a major conflict in the Arctic region?

4. Do you support the idea of environmental and natural resources equality?
- Do you think that the world should have an agreement guaranteeing all countries "fair access" to natural resources? How would you define fairness in this case?
- Specifically, do you believe that other countries, like China or India, that have no access to the Arctic Sea should have an international mandate to establish such access? Explain your opinion.

5. How does oil, according to Amory Lovins (on the companion website [http://oup.com/us/shiraev]), "contribute" to dictatorships, corruption, terrorism, conflict, and war?
- Do you believe that the scope of corruption and incidences of war may diminish if the world turns to nuclear energy instead of oil? Explain.
- Would corruption and violence significantly diminish if most fossil fuel resources were under international control? Explain.

6. Should a moratorium on commercial whaling be lifted since the number of whales is increasing again globally?

7. **What is the *Climate Policy Trap,* according to Lomborg?**
   - Search the Web to find criticisms of Lomborg's views. Which ideas (Lomborg's or his critics) do you find most plausible?
   - Lomborg offers a "smarter" approach to tackling climate change. What does he suggest, and do you agree with his general plans?

8. **Imagine environmentalism and environmental skepticism are on the opposite ends of an imaginable spectrum. Where do you place your views of global environment and environmental policies? Explain your choice.**

9. **How important are renewable energy strategies for international relations?**
   - India has a central ministry in charge of the renewables. Should all governments have similar government ministries and why?
   - What will be the major economic and political obstacles to global renewable energy policies?

10. **Do you believe that countries should continue having total environmental sovereignty over their territories?**
    - Could you suggest scenarios under which such sovereignty should be lifted, at least temporarily?
    - Could such sovereignty be lifted without the use of force? How?

SECTION 9

1. **John Stuart Mill in the nineteenth century argued that any foreign intervention, however benign its proclaimed intent was, could be judged by others as an act of violence driven by cynical self-interest.**
   - Discuss contemporary examples that prove this assertion.
   - Discuss contemporary examples that disprove this assertion.
   - Which international factors can affect one country's perceptions of other countries' actions?

2. **What specific political steps should be implemented by the United States and its allies to make sure that the key provisions of the Convention on the Prevention and Punishment of the Crime of Genocide are working? (See the companion website [http://oup.com/us/shiraev].)**
   - If some of the provisions are violated, do you think that the United States has a right to impose those provisions for moral reasons?

3. **Discuss legal arguments surrounding the implementation of the R2P (RtoP) concept.**

4. **In your view, under what circumstances (if any) may the R2P concept be applied unilaterally, that is, by one country, without a broad international consensus?**

5. **The responsibility to protect (R2P) is an evolving concept. Its definitions may change. However, R2P proponents maintain that its evolving definitions should clearly state that R2P leads to humanitarian actions and not aggressive wars.**
   - Discuss the differences between humanitarian actions and aggression.
   - Is it necessary for any country to have the approval of the United Nations to carry out a humanitarian intervention with the use of armed forces?

6. **Imagine that an authoritarian country, acting without international approval, uses the R2P arguments to violate the sovereignty of another country. How would you react as President of the United States?**
   - Consider Russia's military interference in Ukraine in 2014 and later. Ask your professor, if necessary, to provide the details. Compare Russia's actions with the war in Kosovo, where NATO carried out a humanitarian intervention against Yugoslavia.
   - Think (hypothetically) of and discuss the situation in and around the United States or Canada that would allow other countries like China to apply the R2P concept toward North America?

7. **What is the "naming and shaming" strategy about? Provide examples.**

8. **Has the "naming and shaming" strategy been successful?**
   - Suggest positive, successful examples.
   - Discuss difficulties that these strategy faces or may face.

9. **Peter Singer (see the companion website [http://oup.com/us/shiraev]) uses a metaphor of a drowning child to justify the necessity of humanitarian interventions. Discuss this analogy in the context of international relations.**
   - Why does this analogy appear strong under some circumstances, and why is it weak in other contexts?
   - What other behavioral analogy would you personally suggest to defend R2P?

10. **Peter Singer (see the companion website [http://oup.com/us/shiraev]) writes that "it is wrong to spend anything at all on any luxury as long as there are people starving in the world." Do you personally agree with this statement?**
    - How would the "spending less" strategy help the starving people? Suggest several ways for this strategy's implementation.
    - Critics disagree with this strategy and maintain that even if all of us stop buying luxuries, the world won't change for the better. What is your view on this?
    - Do you think this will be a great idea to introduce a global luxury tax and to use the funds for humanitarian assistance? Which products would you tax and how much?

11. How would, according to Singer, lower fertility rates help the extremely poor globally?

12. Dan Bulley (see the companion website [http://oup.com/us/shiraev]) writes about moral factors in foreign policy. Describe these factors.
- What should an "ethical" foreign policy be in your view?
- Is this policy practically achievable?
- Should the United States or the United Kingdom adhere to strict ethical rules in their foreign policy even when many other countries break them?

13. Why was the 2003 intervention in Iraq unethical, from Bulley's standpoint?

14. Could you provide two or three examples of ethical interventions?

15. What is human rights proliferation? Do you agree or disagree with the argument about the diminishing capacity of the human rights movement?
- Provide examples of human rights proliferation.
- Suggest your own examples that are not mentioned in the text.

16. Which human right, from your view, is in the most danger today?
- In which parts of the world or in which countries are such rights most threatened today?

SECTION 10

1. What is the "male perspective" in international relations?

2. How does Tickner understand the process of "gendering" international relations?
- How do you think this process of "gendering," if it is implemented, could change international politics?

3. Why does culture matter in international relations?
- In which ways are cultural and political factors connected?
- How do cultural factors affect foreign policy, in your view, and vice versa?

4. Describe a "culture of fear," according to Holger Mölder.
- How does this culture result in specific foreign policy actions?
- What can be done to change the "culture of fear"?

5. The *culture of fear,* practiced by powerful international actors, can affect international relations and destabilize international systems.
- Discuss two or three examples of such *cultures of fear* in history. Ask your professor for help. How did these cultures of fear affect policies?

6. **How does Jerry Muller understand nationalism?**
   - How did European nationalism, according to Muller, differ from non-European forms of nationalism?
   - What are some examples of different ethnic groups living peacefully together within a nation state?
   - What conditions are necessary to avoid ethnic tension and violence?

7. **Explain what a strategic culture is (according to Adamsky in the article by Mansoor; see the companion website).**
   - What is in your view the current strategic culture of the United States?
   - What is in your view the current strategic culture of another country of your choice?

8. **What are the impacts of a "softer side" of war on a military campaign execution? (See the companion website.)**

9. **Describe (referring to Luft and Mansoor) five instances in which Western armies operated in close alliance with non-Western allies. (See the companion website.)**

10. **How would you describe a memory wars in the post-Soviet space discussed by Torbakov?**
    - What role do security fears and economic interests play in the disputes about historical narratives and history textbooks?
    - Why and how can "memory wars" aggravate regional crises and inter-state conflicts, such as Russian-Ukrainian conflict that started in 2014?
    - Can similar "memory wars" be observed in other parts of the world? Search for examples.

11. **How would religion, according to Scott Thomas (on the companion website [http://oup.com/us/shiraev]), change global politics?**
    - What is your view on the role of religion in international relations today: is it mostly positive, mostly negative, or mixed?
    - Will religious tensions increase, decrease, or remain the same in ten years?

12. **Do you see the forthcoming clash of civilizations and religions (see Huntington, Section 1) or do you see the detachment of religion from particular territories, as Thomas claims?**

SECTION 11

1. **Explain the reasons why Wendt believes that a global government is inevitable in the future.**
   - Recall and describe the stages of the countries' transition to the global state.

2. **Do you personally support or oppose the idea of a global government? Explain your arguments.**

3. **What role should the United States play in such a government if it is established in ten or twenty years or so?**

4. **How would demographic factors change world politics according to Goldstone?**
    - What is the most significant demographic change, in your opinion, that would impact international relations in five to ten years? In twenty years?
    - How, in which ways, would this change impact international relations?

5. **Do you see particular tendencies of global authoritarian revival today that resemble George Orwell's descriptions in *Nineteen Eighty-Four?* (See the companion website [http://oup.com/us/shiraev].)**
    - Investigate (use, for example, the Freedom House criteria) how many countries were considered authoritarian in 2000.
    - How many countries are authoritarian today? Several think-tanks use several "democracy indexes" to rank countries. Discuss your findings.
    - Can modern authoritarian countries manipulate information in the same way as Orwell described in his novel?

6. **Do you agree or disagree with Ikenberry's thesis that the age of geopolitics may be over and soon? Explain why.**

7. **Why do Deudney and Ikenberry (on the companion website [http://oup.com/us/shiraev]) believe that the liberal model of international relations should prevail in the future?**
    - Do you personally agree or disagree with this prediction and why?
    - Do you see the signs that the liberal model is winning today?

8. **Discuss Fred Bergsten's claims that any country that needs to be an economic superpower must be large, vibrant, and globally integrated, not isolated. (See the companion website [http://oup.com/us/shiraev].)**
    - Which country or countries fit this profile now?
    - Which country or countries may fit this profile in ten years?

9. **Consider and discuss the situation in which Russia and China challenge the existing liberal order.**
    - Which actions would you qualify as a "challenge" to the existing liberal order?
    - What will be the response of the United States and NATO to the challenge?
    - Would you call Russia's behavior today as a challenge to the liberal order? Why?
    - Would you call China's behavior today as a challenge to the liberal order? Why?
    - What will be the consequences of a strategic partnership between Russia and China in support for the liberal order?

10. **Which practices, policies, or traditions could China offer to other countries so that they follow China's global lead and eventually accept it?**

11. **Have these predictions and discussions strengthened (we hope) your interest in international relations?**

Index